Fodor's 2014

NEW YORK CITY

WELCOME TO NEW YORK CITY

From Wall Street's skyscrapers to the neon of Times Square to Central Park's leafy paths, New York City pulses with an irrepressible energy. History meets hipness in this global center of entertainment, fashion, media, and finance. World-class museums like MoMA and unforgettable icons like the Statue of Liberty beckon, but discovering the subtler strains of New York's vast ambition is equally rewarding: ethnic enclaves and shops, historic streets of dignified brownstones, and trendy bars and eateries all add to the urban buzz.

TOP REASONS TO GO

★ **Landmarks:** With towering edifices and awe-inspiring bridges, the skyline says it all.

★ **Shopping:** Whether you're in the market for top designers or inexpensive souvenirs.

★ **Food:** Dim sum to pizza and everything in between, NYC has what you're craving.

★ **Museums:** Art is it, with museums like the Guggenheim and galleries all over town.

★ **The Dazzle:** From the lights of Broadway to celebrity sightings, NYC is full of stars.

★ **Brooklyn and Elsewhere:** Cool neighborhoods and restaurants are a subway ride away.

Fodor's NEW YORK CITY 2014

Publisher: Amanda D'Acierno, *Senior Vice President*

Editorial: Arabella Bowen, *Executive Editorial Director*; Linda Cabasin, *Editorial Director*

Design: Fabrizio La Rocca, *Vice President, Creative Director*; Tina Malaney, *Associate Art Director*; Chie Ushio, *Senior Designer*; Ann McBride, *Production Designer*

Photography: Melanie Marin, *Associate Director of Photography*; Jessica Parkhill and Jennifer Romains, *Researchers*

Maps: Rebecca Baer, *Map Editor*; Mark Stroud, Moon Street Cartography, and David Lindroth, *Cartographers*

Production: Linda Schmidt, *Managing Editor*; Evangelos Vasilakis, *Associate Managing Editor*; Angela L. McLean, *Senior Production Manager*

Sales: Jacqueline Lebow, *Sales Director*

Marketing & Publicity: Heather Dalton, *Marketing Director*; Katherine Fleming, *Senior Publicist*

Business & Operations: Susan Livingston, *Vice President, Strategic Business Planning*; Sue Daulton, *Vice President, Operations*

Fodors.com: Megan Bell, *Executive Director, Revenue & Business Development*; Yasmin Marinaro, *Senior Director, Marketing & Partnerships*

Writers: Sarah Amandolare, Jessica Colley, David Farley, Anuja Madar, Megan Eileen McDonough, Jess Moss, Jacinta O'Halloran, John Rambow, Christina Valhouli

Editor: Caroline Trefler

Production Editor: Jennifer DePrima, *Senior Production Editor*

ISBN 978-0-7704-3212-6

ISSN 0736-9395

SPECIAL SALES

This book is available at special discounts for bulk purchases for sales promotions or premiums. For more information, e-mail specialmarkets@randomhouse.com

PRINTED IN COLOMBIA

10 9 8 7 6 5 4 3 2 1

CONTENTS

Fodor's Features

MAPS

ABOUT THIS GUIDE

Fodor's Recommendations

Everything in this guide is worth doing—we don't cover what isn't—but exceptional sights, hotels, and restaurants are recognized with additional accolades. **Fodor's Choice** ★ indicates our top recommendations; and **Best Bets** call attention to notable hotels and restaurants in various categories. Care to nominate a new place? Visit Fodors.com/contact-us.

Trip Costs

We list prices wherever possible to help you budget well. Hotel and restaurant price categories from **$** to **$$$$** are noted alongside each recommendation. For hotels, we include the lowest cost of a standard double room in high season. For restaurants, we cite the average price of a main course at dinner or, if dinner isn't served, at lunch. For attractions, we always list adult admission fees; discounts are usually available for children, students, and senior citizens.

Hotels

Our local writers vet every hotel to recommend the best overnights in each price category, from budget to expensive. Unless otherwise specified, you can expect private bath, phone, and TV in your room. For expanded hotel reviews, facilities, and deals visit Fodors.com.

Top Picks
- ★ Fodor's Choice

Listings
- Address
- Branch address
- Telephone
- Fax
- Website
- E-mail
- Admission fee
- Open/closed times
- Subway
- Directions or Map coordinates

Hotels & Restaurants
- Hotel
- Number of rooms
- Meal plans
- Restaurant
- Reservations
- Dress code
- No credit cards
- Price

Other
- See also
- Take note
- Golf facilities

Restaurants

Unless we state otherwise, restaurants are open for lunch and dinner daily. We mention dress code only when there's a specific requirement and reservations only when they're essential or not accepted. To make restaurant reservations, visit Fodors.com.

Credit Cards

The hotels and restaurants in this guide typically accept credit cards. If not, we'll say so.

EXPERIENCE NEW YORK CITY

NEW YORK CITY TODAY

The phrase "in a New York minute" is clichéd for a reason: in this wonderful, frenetic, and overwhelming city, things really do change in a flash. Even for those of us who live here, keeping up with the latest in news, art, music, food, sports, and politics can be exhausting. But it is never dull. In 2012, New York elected its first openly gay official as speaker of the City Council (go Christine Quinn!) and locals and tourists lined up for hours to try and grab a seat at culinary hot spots Mission Chinese Food and Pok Pok Ny. "Artisanal" was another buzzword from 2012 that continues to be bandied about in 2013, arguably most prevalent in Brooklyn—sure, it may be home to the gigantic, new Barclays Center, but it is also a creative and culinary hotbed of talent. Where else can you find such a high concentration of artisans dedicated to producing small batches of handcrafted beer, jams, chocolate, pickles, granola, and saltwater taffy? One of our favorites is Mast Brothers chocolate—the brothers send their own vintage schooner to South America to source cacao beans that are brought back to their Williamsburg factory and turned into handcrafted chocolate bars. Only in New York, folks.

In 2012 the city braced itself against Hurricane Sandy, and experienced unprecedented—and devastating—flooding and blackouts. The damage is still being repaired but as history has shown us, the city—and its people—will bounce back better than ever.

With 2013 under way as we go to press, here's what's on our radar for 2014:

Politics

No doubt there will be the usual "sex, lies, and videotape" political antics to challenge the headline writers of the local media, but there's also no doubt that the main story in New York City politics will be the new mayor.

Economy

We're optimistic about the economy and opportunity in New York. A few quick positive indicators: the hotel sector is growing at a record-setting pace. Sixty-eight hotels are slated to open in 2014 (after 50 new places were added in 2013). Tourists keep on coming too; 2012 had a record number of visitors—around 52 million, up from the previous year's 50.9 million. The Manhattan real estate market is strong, especially the luxury real

WHAT'S NEW?

New York City is looking to become the new Paris or Copenhagen with a public bike-sharing system that will provide on-demand bikes to locals and visitors. This may be the year that New Yorkers embrace this cheap and easy transportation option and get off their cynical butts and onto bikes.

With its final phase due to open in early 2014, the High Line Park is still the subject of much New York chatter and attention. That said, some New Yorkers are turning their attentions to the next big thing—a proposal to develop an abandoned trolley station below Delancey Street on the Lower East Side. Known as the Low Line, this underground park will require cutting-edge

estate market; a penthouse apartment on Central Park West recently sold for a record $88 million, so things can't be that bad, right?

Sports

If there's something the quintessential New Yorker can't get enough of, it's sports, so if you're looking to make small talk with a local, just pick a team. But which one? This is where it gets complicated. Fans can now see the Brooklyn Nets (Jay Z is a part owner) in their brand-new digs in Brooklyn at the Barclays Center. The NY Giants won the Super Bowl in 2012 (their fourth), so fans will be hoping for a repeat soon. Non–New Yorkers love to hate the Yankees because, well, they're so good (they've won the World Series 27 times as of press time). And don't forget about New York's other teams—we also root for the Jets (football), the Mets (baseball), and the New York Liberty, the women's basketball team. Soccer fans also have a team to support: the New York Red Bulls. Need more? Don't forget the Rangers and Islanders (hockey) and, of course, the Knicks (basketball). Then there's the US Open, which attracts the best in tennis every year.

The Arts

Before the Whitney decamps to its larger space in the Meatpacking District, its blockbuster exhibit of 2014 will be a retrospective of Jeff Koons's work. It will be the first time a single artist has ever taken over almost the entire museum. The Met will exhibit several hundred pieces of jewelry from New York–born jewelry designer Joel A. Rosenthal in the first retrospective of his work, and there will also be an exhibit of works by French sculptor Jean-Baptiste Carpeaux. In 2014, the MoMA (The Museum of Modern Art) will showcase the works of Isa Genzken, arguably one of the most important and influential female artists of the past 30 years. Many of the nearly 200 works in the exhibition are on view in the United States for the first time.

On Broadway in 2014, there will be revivals of Cole Porter's *Can-Can* and *Pippin*. Disney will bring *Aladdin* to the stage.

design and technology (like fiber optics to pump the underground with natural sunlight), which has locals anticipating the next big thing after that—green and sunny subway stations!

Escaping the city in summer is something locals think about way in advance of the season, making plans early in the year for housing shares in the Hamptons or Fire Island. But for those without the means, the summertime hot spot of late is Governors Island. The short ferry ride, free concerts, easy biking, and cool history make it popular with out-of-towners and locals alike.

PLANNER

When to Go

New York City weather, like its people, is a study in extremes. Much of winter brings bone-chilling winds and an occasional traffic-snarling snowfall, but you're just as likely to experience mild afternoons sandwiched by cool temperatures.

In late spring and early summer, streets fill with parades and street fairs, and Central Park has free performances. Late-August temperatures sometimes claw skyward, bringing subway station temperatures over 100°F (no wonder the Hamptons are so crowded). This is why September brings palpable excitement, with stunning yellow-and-bronze foliage complementing the dawn of a new cultural season. Between October and May, museums mount major exhibitions, most Broadway shows open, and formal opera, ballet, and concert seasons begin.

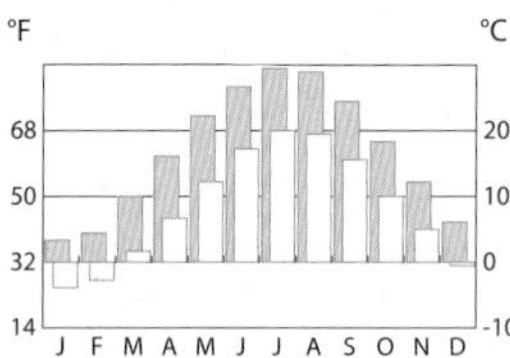

Getting Around

Without a doubt, the best way to explore New York is on foot. No matter what neighborhood you're headed to, you'll get a better sense of it by wandering around; you can check out the architecture, pop into cool-looking shops and cafés, and observe the walk-and-talk of the locals. And if you get lost, you'll find that New Yorkers are surprisingly helpful with directions.

After walking, New York's subway system is by far the most efficient and cost-effective way to get around, and it runs 24 hours a day. It can be a little intimidating at first, but other riders are generally more than happy to help you figure out your best route; they'll also help you decode loudspeaker announcements that can be difficult to understand on all but the newest trains. The subway is safe, but be smart; try to avoid riding alone—especially late at night, and avoid riding in empty cars. Speaking of empty cars, they're nonexistent during rush hours, when you'll likely find that all the subway seats are taken, and you'll have to join in the particular New York sport of "strap-hanging." Train floors are sticky, stations are sweltering in summer, and platforms are grimy year-round, but this all just adds to the "charm" of riding on a system that is more than 100 years old.

If you've got a long way to go and would rather be comfy than thrifty, hail one of the ubiquitous yellow cabs that troll New York's streets around the clock. You'll be out $2.50 just for getting in, but you can use a credit card—all taxis are now required to accept plastic. Be sure to give your destination's address like a local, by using cross streets: ask to be taken to "55th and Madison" rather than "545 Madison." Avoid trying to hail a cab between 4 and 4:30 pm, when drivers change shifts.

A Guide to the Grid

The map of Manhattan is, for the most part, easy to follow: north of 14th Street, streets are laid out in a numbered grid pattern. Numbered streets run east and west (crosstown), and broad avenues, most of them also numbered, run north (uptown) and south (downtown). The main exception is Broadway, which runs the entire length of Manhattan on a diagonal. Below 14th Street, street patterns get chaotic. In the West Village, West 4th Street intersects West 11th Street, Greenwich Street runs roughly parallel to Greenwich Avenue, and Leroy Street turns into St. Luke's Place for one block and then becomes Leroy again. There's an East Broadway and a West Broadway, both of which run north–south, and neither of which is an extension of Broadway, leaving even locals scratching their heads.

Street Smarts

Avoid deserted blocks in unfamiliar neighborhoods. A brisk, purposeful pace helps deter trouble wherever you go. New York City is a safe city, but it's still a city, so keep jewelry out of sight on the street; better yet, leave valuables in your hotel safe.

Of course, you want to capture every "New York minute," but instead of parading your camera—and your tourist status—consider securing it (especially if it's a pricey and bulky DSLR) in a nondescript cross-body bag.

When in bars or restaurants, never hang your purse or bag on the back of a chair or put it underneath the table. Travel light if possible so that you can wear your bag or put it on the table in front of you.

Never leave your bags unattended; they might get swiped, or worse—swooped upon by well-meaning citizens, prompted to report orphan bags thanks to the heavily promoted public-service campaign, "If you see something, say something."

Expect to have yourself and your possessions inspected thoroughly in such places as airports, sports stadiums, museums, and city buildings. Police officers stationed by subway-token booths also reserve the right to check your bags before you pass through the turnstile to enter the platform.

Politely ignore panhandlers on the streets and subways, people who offer to hail you a cab, and limousine and gypsy-cab drivers who (illegally) offer rides.

Opening Hours

Subways and buses run around the clock, as do plenty of restaurants, pharmacies, and fitness clubs. Some shops and services have more extensive hours than you'll find elsewhere in the United States, so you can get groceries, or get your hair and nails done, at 11 pm. In general, though, you can safely assume that most shops are open seven days a week, from about 10 to 7 Monday–Saturday and from noon to 6 on Sunday. Bars generally close at 4 am, though some after-hours clubs are open later.

Money-Saving Tips

Consider buying a CityPass, a group of tickets to six top-notch attractions in New York: the Empire State Building, the Guggenheim Museum or Top of the Rock, the American Museum of Natural History, the Museum of Modern Art, the Metropolitan Museum of Art (including the Cloisters), and Circle Line Cruises or admission to Liberty and Ellis islands. The $89 pass, which saves you half the cost of each individual ticket, is good for nine days from first use.

Sign up for social discount shopping sites like Groupon, Gilt, Bloomspot, and LivingSocial a month before your visit to New York to score discounts on everything from trendy restaurants and clubs to beauty treatments and attractions.

WHAT'S WHERE

Numbers refer to chapters

2 Lower Manhattan. The Financial District, NY Harbor, and TriBeCa. Heavy-duty landmarks anchor the southern tip of Manhattan, including Wall Street and the waterfront parks of Battery Park City. The ferry terminals dispatch boats to Ellis Island and the Statue of Liberty. The evolving construction site at Ground Zero is also down here.

3 SoHo, NoLIta, Little Italy, and Chinatown. Luxe shops dominate in SoHo these days, while NoLIta, to the east, has lots of boutiques and restaurants. Little Italy is a shrinking zone of touristy red-sauce eateries. Farther south, Chinatown teems with street vendors selling knockoff handbags and side streets with Chinese herb shops and noodle joints.

4 The East Village and the Lower East Side. Once an edgy neighborhood of artists and punks, the East Village is now a melting pot of students, artists, and professionals. The once seedy, now trendy Lower East Side has live-music clubs, independent clothing shops, and wine bars.

5 Greenwich Village and the West Village. Artists with rent-controlled apartments, out-and-proud gays, and university students still live in the Village but because those town houses have become so expensive, residents also include wealthy media moguls, celebrities, and socialites. From 14th Street south to Houston and from the Hudson River east to 5th Avenue, the blocks are a jumble of jazz clubs, restaurants, former speakeasies, and rainbow flags.

6 Chelsea and the Meatpacking District. Chelsea, like its namesake London district, has a small-town personality with big-city prices. It has also supplanted the Village as the center of gay life in the city. To the south, the Meatpacking District has evolved into a swanky clubbing and restaurant scene by night and—with the High Line and high-end boutiques—a shopping and strolling destination by day.

7 Union Square, the Flatiron District, and Gramercy Park. Bustling Union Square Park hosts the city's best greenmarket. On the 14th Street edge are broad steps where break dancers and other performers busk for onlookers. Nearby, private Gramercy Park is surrounded by storied mansions and town houses.

MIDTOWN EAST
MURRAY HILL
CHELSEA
GRAMERCY
KIPS BAY
FLATIRON
STUYVESANT TOWN
MEATPACKING DISTRICT
UNION SQUARE
EAST VILLAGE
WEST VILLAGE
GREENWICH VILLAGE
NOLITA
LOWER EAST SIDE
SOHO
LITTLE ITALY
TRIBECA
CHINATOWN
FINANCIAL DISTRICT
LOWER MANHATTAN
NEW YORK HARBOR
BROOKLYN
East River
Hudson River
Ground Zero
South Street Seaport
TO LIBERTY AND ELLIS ISLANDS
TO STATEN ISLAND
TO GOVERNOR'S ISLAND
Battery Park
Brooklyn-Battery Tunnel
Holland Tunnel
Williamsburg Bridge
Manhattan Bridge
Brooklyn Bridge
FDR Drive
Madison Sq.
Gramercy Park
Stuyvesant Sq.
Washington Sq.
Abingdon Sq.
High Line Park
0 1/4 miles
0 400 meters
1
2
3
4
5
6
7

WHAT'S WHERE

8 Midtown East and Murray Hill. Midtown from 5th Avenue to the East River is the refined big sister of flashy Midtown West, with grand hotels, grand shopping, the Chrysler Building, and Grand Central Terminal. Murray Hill is a mix of quiet tree-and-townhouse–lined streets and attractions like the Empire State Building and the Morgan Library.

9 Midtown West. Head to 42nd Street to see Times Square in all its neon and massive-TV-screen glory. Towering office buildings line Broadway up to Columbus Circle at the edge of Central Park. At Rockefeller Center are the famous ice rink and tree (in season), and nearby are swank shops like Saks and Bergdorf Goodman.

10 The Upper East Side. The Upper East Side is home to more millionaires than any other part of the city. Tucked into this stretch of 5th Ave. are the Museum Mile and Madison Avenue's haute boutiques.

11 Central Park. Fredrick Law Olmstead's ode to the pastoral in the heart of New York, Central Park is the place to escape the bustle of the city. There's a small zoo, a boathouse, and activities as diverse as rock climbing, softball, and Frisbee.

12 The Upper West Side with the Cloisters. Wide sidewalks and ornate prewar buildings set the tone, and the American Museum of Natural History and Lincoln Center are big draws. Farther north is the Cloisters, a branch of the Metropolitan Museum of Art housing medieval works in a reconstructed monastery.

13 Harlem. A hotbed of African American and Hispanic American culture for almost a century, Harlem still sizzles. The brownstone-lined blocks are being refurbished, boutiques and restaurants are popping up, and music venues from the 1920s and '30s are still in full swing.

14 Brooklyn. Manhattan's largest borough counts among its stars Coney Island, Prospect Park, and the Brooklyn Botanic Gardens. Its distinct neighborhoods include Williamsburg, Fort Greene, and Brighton Beach.

15 Queens, the Bronx, and Staten Island. Queens is known for its ethnic communities and Citi Field. The Bronx may be best known for Yankee Stadium, but the New York Botanical Garden and the Bronx Zoo also score home runs. Staten Island's most compelling feature might be the ferry, but there are also reasons to stick around.

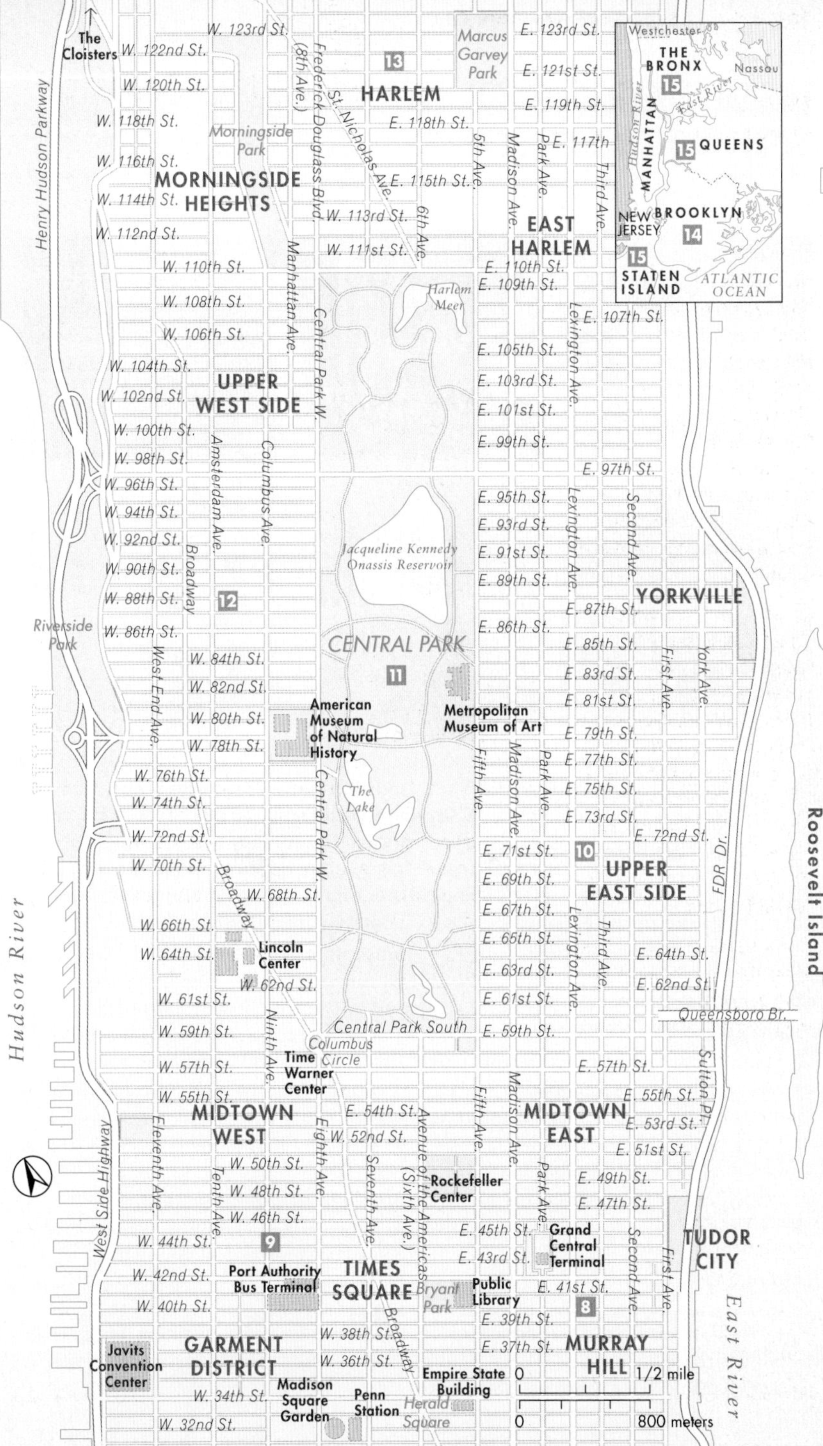

The Cloisters
Henry Hudson Parkway
W. 123rd St.
W. 122nd St.
W. 120th St.
W. 118th St.
W. 116th St.
W. 114th St.
W. 112nd St.
W. 110th St.
W. 108th St.
W. 106th St.
W. 104th St.
W. 102nd St.
W. 100th St.
W. 98th St.
W. 96th St.
W. 94th St.
W. 92nd St.
W. 90th St.
W. 88th St.
W. 86th St.
W. 84th St.
W. 82nd St.
W. 80th St.
W. 78th St.
W. 76th St.
W. 74th St.
W. 72nd St.
W. 70th St.
W. 68th St.
W. 66th St.
W. 64th St.
W. 62nd St.
W. 61st St.
W. 59th St.
W. 57th St.
W. 55th St.
W. 54th St.
W. 52nd St.
W. 50th St.
W. 48th St.
W. 46th St.
W. 44th St.
W. 42nd St.
W. 40th St.
W. 38th St.
W. 36th St.
W. 34th St.
W. 32nd St.
Marcus Garvey Park
E. 123rd St.
E. 121st St.
E. 119th St.
E. 118th St.
E. 117th
E. 115th St.
E. 110th St.
E. 109th St.
E. 107th St.
E. 105th St.
E. 103rd St.
E. 101st St.
E. 99th St.
E. 97th St.
E. 95th St.
E. 93rd St.
E. 91st St.
E. 89th St.
E. 87th St.
E. 86th St.
E. 85th St.
E. 83rd St.
E. 81st St.
E. 79th St.
E. 77th St.
E. 75th St.
E. 73rd St.
E. 72nd St.
E. 71st St.
E. 69th St.
E. 67th St.
E. 65th St.
E. 64th St.
E. 63rd St.
E. 62nd St.
E. 61st St.
E. 59th St.
E. 57th St.
E. 55th St.
E. 54th St.
E. 53rd St.
E. 51st St.
E. 49th St.
E. 47th St.
E. 45th St.
E. 43rd St.
E. 41st St.
E. 39th St.
E. 37th St.
13
HARLEM
Frederick Douglass Blvd (8th Ave.)
St. Nicholas Ave.
6th Ave.
5th Ave.
Madison Ave.
Park Ave.
Third Ave.
Morningside Park
MORNINGSIDE HEIGHTS
EAST HARLEM
W. 113rd St.
W. 111st St.
Manhattan Ave.
Central Park W.
Lexington Ave.
Harlem Meer
UPPER WEST SIDE
Amsterdam Ave.
Columbus Ave.
Broadway
Second Ave.
Jacqueline Kennedy Onassis Reservoir
12
YORKVILLE
Riverside Park
West End Ave.
CENTRAL PARK
11
American Museum of Natural History
Metropolitan Museum of Art
First Ave.
York Ave.
Fifth Ave.
The Lake
10
UPPER EAST SIDE
FDR Dr.
Roosevelt Island
Hudson River
Lincoln Center
Ninth Ave.
Central Park South
Columbus Circle
Queensboro Br.
Sutton Pl.
Time Warner Center
MIDTOWN WEST
MIDTOWN EAST
West Side Highway
Eleventh Ave.
Tenth Ave.
Eighth Ave.
Seventh Ave.
Avenue of the Americas (Sixth Ave.)
Rockefeller Center
9
Grand Central Terminal
TUDOR CITY
Port Authority Bus Terminal
TIMES SQUARE
Bryant Park
Public Library
8
East River
GARMENT DISTRICT
MURRAY HILL
Javits Convention Center
Madison Square Garden
Penn Station
Empire State Building
Herald Square
0
1/2 mile
800 meters
Westchester
THE BRONX
Nassau
15
East River
Hudson River
MANHATTAN
QUEENS
NEW JERSEY
BROOKLYN
14
STATEN ISLAND
ATLANTIC OCEAN

NEW YORK CITY TOP ATTRACTIONS

Metropolitan Museum of Art

(A) The largest art museum in the Western Hemisphere, the Met is a mecca for art lovers of all stripes. Treasures from all over the world and every era of human creativity make up its expansive collection. If you need a breather, you can always retire to the Temple of Dendur or the rooftop café.

Times Square

(B) Times Square is the most frenetic part of New York City: a cacophony of languages and flashing lights, outré street performers, shoulder-to-shoulder crowds, and back-to-back billboards. These days it's also a pedestrian-friendly zone, so you won't have to take your eyes off the excitement to watch for traffic.

Empire State Building

(C) It may not be the tallest building in New York anymore (the Freedom Tower reclaimed the title for the World Trade Center in May 2012), but its status as most iconic will never change. Take in the panoramic views of the city from its observatories, or just enjoy it from afar—after dark it's illuminated by colored lights that correspond to different holidays and events.

Museum of Modern Art

(D) Airy and spacious, with soaring-ceiling galleries suffused with natural light and masterpieces that include Monet's *Water Lilies* and Van Gogh's *Starry Night,* this one-of-a-kind museum designed by Japanese architect Yoshio Taniguchi is as famous for its architecture as for its collections.

Brooklyn Bridge

(E) New York City's most famous bridge connects the island of Manhattan to the borough of Brooklyn, and serves thousands of pedestrians, vehicles, skaters, and bicyclists a day. Walking across is an essential New York experience.

Statue of Liberty

(F) Presented to the United States in 1886 as a gift from France, Lady Liberty is a near-universal symbol of freedom and democracy, standing 152 feet high atop an 89-foot pedestal on Liberty Island.

American Museum of Natural History

(G) The towering, spectacularly reassembled dinosaur skeletons that greet you when you enter this museum might stop you in your tracks, but there's much more to see here, including exhibits of ancient civilizations, the live Butterfly Conservatory (October–May), a hall of oceanic creatures overlooked by a 94-foot model of a blue whale, and space shows at the adjoining Rose Center for Earth and Space.

Central Park

The literal and spiritual center of Manhattan, Central Park has 843 acres of meandering paths, tranquil lakes, ponds, and open meadows. For equestrians, softball and soccer players, strollers, skaters, birdwatchers, boaters, picnickers, and outdoor performers, it's an oasis of fresh air and greenery amid the hustle of the city.

Ground Zero

The memorial at the World Trade Center site is a moving tribute to the lives lost on 9/11. After a decade of clean-up and construction, the memorial opened to the public on the 10th anniversary of the terrorist attacks; construction of a museum and work on other parts of the site continues.

NEW YORK CITY LIKE A LOCAL

New Yorkers love their city—and with good reason as there's no place like it on earth. But living here can also be challenging, from the high rents to battling crowds and lines at Sunday brunch. But there are plenty of tricks to navigating the city and getting the most out of your trip. And at the risk of compromising our New York credibility (after all, we consider ourselves members of an exclusive club and guard our secrets accordingly), we've decided to share those tricks here. Just don't tell anyone we told you.

Getting Around Like a Local

Hit the Ground Walking

Spend a day in a New Yorker's shoes and you'll understand why we have the reputation for being skinny: New Yorkers walk. Pounding the pavement can often be the fastest way to get around but remember—move quickly. We're in a hurry. Unless you're holding the hand of a small child, single file is the rule. If you need to check your smart phone, pull over and get out of the way.

Take the Subway

If you have to travel a long distance, the subway is usually cheaper than a cab and often faster, too. The subway runs 24 hours a day, 7 days a week (with reduced frequency late at night and on weekends). If you're planning to make extensive use of the subway while you're in town, buy a MetroCard, a magnetically encoded card that debits the fare with every swipe at the turnstile (it's cheaper than paying single fares).

The most common mistake for a subway novice is to hop on a train going in the wrong direction. We've all done it. First, determine if you are going uptown or downtown. Then, figure out which train—designated by numbers or letters—stops near where you're going. Note: the signs outside some stations indicate "Uptown Only" or "Downtown Only," so pay attention on your way in. Even seasoned New Yorkers ask for or confirm directions, so don't be shy. If you're traveling with a Smartphone, the website HopStop will help you figure out the best route.

Trains can run "local" (stopping at all stops on the line) or "express," so if you're uncertain just stick with a local train; better to delay your journey by a few stops than to miss your stop altogether!

All Hail the Taxi Cab

There is no shortage of yellow cabs in Manhattan; there's just a shortage of *available* cabs—especially when it's raining or you're in a hurry. You can tell whether a taxi is available by checking its rooftop light. If the center panel is lighted and the side panels are dark, the driver is looking for passengers (so stick out your arm!); taxis whose roof lights are lighted only at the edges—not the center—are off-duty.

Once you're in a cab, know your passenger rights. Although your driver will likely careen at high speeds while simultaneously cursing, leaning on his horn, and chattering into his cell-phone headset, you're entitled to ask him to slow down. You're also allowed to ask him to turn off his phone or blaring car radio, and if he doesn't comply, refrain from tipping him. Cabbies make almost nothing aside from tips, so tack 15% to 20% onto your fare after a satisfactory ride; all cabs are now required to take credit cards, too.

Speaking of fares, you'll be charged $2.50 just for getting into the cab. After that,

the cost is 40 cents for every ⅕ mile (or every 60 seconds in stalled or slow traffic). You'll have to cover any bridge or tunnel tolls, and while you're at it, a surcharge of $1 between 4 and 8 pm.

Finally, know where you're going before you get into a cab. A quick map check or call to your destination will give you the cross streets and ensure a direct route.

Dining Like a Local

Breakfast

Forget the heavy breakfast—at least on weekdays. Although weekend brunch is a New York institution, if you want your day to start quickly, do what New Yorkers do. Grab a coffee and bagel (or a fried egg sandwich) from a café or a deli. Sure, you can eat it on the run but we also recommend enjoying it on a park bench to take in the sights and people watch.

Lunch

New York offers dining experiences at every single level, from budget to blowout, and trendy to classic, with nearly all global cuisine represented here (craving Sri Lankan food? No problem). New Yorkers are passionate about food and will travel to try out new restaurants—and so should you. Explore as many of the city's restaurants as you can and remember that as long as you avoid the heavily touristed areas such as Times Square, you're pretty much guaranteed a decent meal. Don't miss the various food-trucks parked around the city. Finding them has become a competitive sport with Twitter feeds and blogs tracking their whereabouts (try 🌐 *EdibleCity.com*). And don't forget to stop by the city's various greenmarkets, too, to sample the fruit, produce, and artisanal treats.

Dinner

Don't skip lunch whatever you do, because if you want to experience the real New York dinner scene, you'll need to dine late. Most New York restaurants are empty around 6 pm and don't fill up until at least 7:30 or 8, so if you eat early, you'll have your pick of tables but little company. Prime-time dinner reservations—between 8 and 10 pm—are the hardest to score, but will ensure that you're surrounded by dining companions.

Of course, if you can't get a good reservation, pull up a seat at the bar or communal table. You'll get the same great food and people-watching, plus you'll get to feel like an insider while other folks are still waiting for a table.

Coffee

It's the city that never sleeps so you know the coffee's good and plentiful. Skip the generic coffee chains posted on every other corner and caffeinate like a discerning local with a cup from an artisanal roaster, served by an enthusiastic barista, often with free Wi-Fi on the side. Some local faves include: Joe in the West Village; 9th Street Espresso in Alphabet City, Chelsea Market, and Tompkins Square; Abraco in the East Village; Kaffe 1668 in TriBeCa; and Gimme! Coffee in NoLIta. Portland's Stumptown Coffee Roasters and San Francisco's Blue Bottle Coffee also have locations in Manhattan. Find your fuel by name, neighborhood, or location at 🌐 *NYCMugged.com*.

SITTING IN A TV AUDIENCE

Tickets to tapings of TV shows are free, but can be hard to get on short notice. Most shows accept advance requests by email, phone, or online—but for the most popular shows the backlog is so deep, you might have to wait a few months. Same-day standby tickets are often available, but be prepared to wait in line for several hours, sometimes starting at 5 or 6 am, depending on how hot the show is, or the wattage of that day's celebrity guests. And we hate to tell you this, but standby tickets do not guarantee a seat in the audience. You can also follow your favorite shows on Twitter for updates on last-minute tickets.

The Shows

The Colbert Report. Stephen Colbert leads his "nation" through shows Monday through Thursday. Check the website for dates with open tickets. Sign-up for standby tickets happens in front of the studio at 4 pm the day of the show. ✉ *513 W. 54th St., between 10th and 11th Aves., Midtown West* 🌐 *www.colbertnation.com* Ⓜ *C, E to 50th St.*

The Daily Show with Jon Stewart. The amiable, and incisive Jon Stewart pokes fun at news headlines on this half-hour cable show. The program tapes from Monday through Thursday; you can request advance tickets by checking the calendar on the website. For standby tickets, show up well before the 5:45 pm doors-open time. Audience members must be 18 or older. ✉ *733 11th Ave., between W. 51st and W. 52nd Sts., Midtown West* 🌐 *www.thedailyshow.com* Ⓜ *C, E to 50th St.*.

Good Morning America. Robin Roberts and George Stephanopoulos host this early-morning news and entertainment standby. *GMA* airs live, weekdays from 7 to 9 am, and ticket requests (online only) should be sent four to six months in advance. ✉ *7 Times Sq., at W. 44th St. and Broadway, Midtown West* 🌐 *www.abcnews.go.com* Ⓜ *1, 2, 3, 7, N, Q, R, S to 42nd St./Times Sq.*

Late Night with Jimmy Fallon. Musician, singer, actor, and comedian Jimmy Fallon has solidified his place in late night TV, thanks to his house band The Roots and a steady rotation of hot musicians, singers, actors, and comedians. For tickets, call the Ticket Information Line for a maximum of four tickets, about a month in advance. Single standby tickets are available on taping days—Monday through Friday—at the West 49th Street side of 30 Rockefeller Plaza; arrive before 9 am. You must be 17 years or older. ✉ *30 Rockefeller Plaza, Midtown West* ☎ *212/664–3056 ticket information line* 🌐 *www.latenightwithjimmyfallon.com* Ⓜ *B, D, F, M to 47th–50th Rockefeller Center.*

The Late Show with David Letterman. Letterman's famously offbeat humor and wacky Top 10 Lists have had fans giggling for more than two decades. For advance tickets (two maximum), you can submit a request online or fill out an application in person at the theater. For stand-by tickets, call 212/247–6497 starting at 11 am on tape days—Monday through Thursday. Be prepared: you may be asked to answer Letterman-related trivia to secure your ticket. You must be 18 or older to sit in the audience. ✉ *Ed Sullivan Theater, 1697 Broadway, between W. 53rd and W. 54th Sts., Midtown West* ☎ *212/975–5853* 🌐 *www.lateshowaudience.com* Ⓜ *1, C, E to 50th St.; B, D, E to 7th Ave.*

Live! with Kelly and Michael. The sparks fly on this morning program, which books an eclectic roster of cohosts and guests. Tickets are available online about a month

in advance, or by mail up to a year in advance. Standby tickets become available weekdays at 7 am at the **ABC Studios** (✉ *7 Lincoln Sq., corner of W. 67th St. and Columbus Ave., Upper West Side*). Children under 10 aren't allowed in the audience. ☎ *212/456–3054* 🌐 *www.dadt.com/live* Ⓜ *1 to 66th St./Lincoln Center.*

Rachael Ray Show. This bubbly chef helms a daytime talk show that covers everything from cooking and fashion tips to celebrity interviews. Her set looks like a cozy kitchen, and the show tapes on Monday, Tuesday, and Thursday at 11:30 am and 3:30 pm. Guests must be 16 or older to be in the audience. Advance tickets are only available on Rachael Ray's website. Be sure to read the guidelines—there is a suggested dress code. No crazy prints; go for solid colors and smart business casual. ✉ *Chelsea Television Studios, 221 W. 26th St., between 7th and 8th Aves., Chelsea* 🌐 *www.rachaelrayshow.com/show-info/audience-tickets/* Ⓜ *1 to 28th St.*

Saturday Night Live. *SNL* continues to captivate audiences. Standby tickets—only one per person—are distributed at 7 am on the day of the show at the West 49th Street entrance to 30 Rockefeller Plaza. You may ask for a ticket for either the dress rehearsal (8 pm) or the live show (11:30 pm). Requests for advance tickets (two per applicant) must be submitted by email only in August to snltickets@nbcuni.com; recipients are determined by lottery. You must be 16 or older to sit in the audience. ✉ *NBC Studios, Saturday Night Live, 30 Rockefeller Plaza, between W. 49th and W. 50th Sts., Midtown West* ☎ *212/664–3056* 🌐 *www.nbc.com/saturday-night-live* Ⓜ *B, D, F, M to 47th–50th Sts./Rockefeller Center.*

TIPS

■ Prepare to have your pockets and bags checked before you enter, and leave the camera at home, as snapping a shot during a show—even with a camera phone—isn't allowed.

■ Wear layers: TV studios blast the air-conditioning.

■ Sitting in a TV audience can be more boring than watching the show at home. You'll have to wait intermittently while sets are changed and stars' makeup is refreshed; if your seats are in back, you may feel far from the action.

■ Audience laughter is carefully orchestrated. There will be "Applause" signs signaling when to clap and staffers gesturing for you to laugh louder.

Today. The *Today* show doesn't have a studio audience but if you get yourself to the corner of Rockefeller Center and 49th Street before dawn, with posterboard and markers (fun signs always get camera time), comfortable shoes (you'll be on your feet for hours), and a smiley, fun attitude you might get on camera. America's first morning talk–news show airs weekdays from 7 to 10 am in the glass-enclosed, ground-level NBC studio across from its original home at 30 Rockefeller Plaza. You may well be spotted on TV by friends back home while you're standing behind anchors Matt Lauer, Al Roker, and Savannah Guthrie. ✉ *Rockefeller Plaza at W. 49th St., Midtown West* 🌐 *www.today.msnbc.msn.com* Ⓜ *B, D, F, M to 47th–50th Sts./Rockefeller Center.*

NEW YORK CITY FOR FREE

If you think everything in New York costs too much, well, you're right—almost. In fact, the city has tons of free attractions and activities; you just need to know where to look for them.

Outdoor Fun

Walk across the Brooklyn Bridge for spectacular views of the Financial District, Brooklyn, the seaport, and Manhattan.

Ride the Staten Island Ferry to see the Statue of Liberty, Ellis Island, and the southern tip of Manhattan from the water. A one-way trip takes 30 minutes and offers magnificent views—and inexpensive beer and snacks. Note that you have to disembark at St. George Terminal. Ⓜ *1 to South Ferry; 4, 5 to Bowling Green.*

Catch a free movie screening in Bryant Park in summertime. A tradition since 1992, watching films alfresco surrounded by tall Midtown buildings is a summertime rite of passage for New Yorkers. Bring a blanket and a picnic basket, and be prepared to stake out a good spot on the lawn well in advance. Movie schedules are posted at 🌐 *www.bryantpark.org.* Ⓜ *B, D, F, M to 42nd St.*

Wander Battery Park City's waterfront promenade. The breeze and passing boats will make you forget you're in the gritty city, though the view of the Statue of Liberty will remind you that you couldn't be anywhere but New York. Ⓜ *4, 5 to Bowling Green; 1 to South Ferry.*

Let botany grow on you with free visits to the New York Botanical Garden (free all day Wed. and Sat. 10–11 am), Brooklyn Botanic Garden (free all day Tues. and Sat. 10 am–noon), and Queens Botanical Garden (free Wed. 3–6 pm and Sun. 4–6 pm). 🌐 *www.nybg.org* 🌐 *www.bbg.org* 🌐 *www.queensbotanical.org.*

Head to Governor's Island, a 172-acre island oasis in the heart of New York Harbor, just a seven-minute ferry ride from Lower Manhattan. You can visit the former military base turned sculpture park and public playground late May to late September to bike, picnic, wander forts, and enjoy a variety of cultural offerings and festivals. 🌐 *www.govisland.com for a schedule of events and ferry information* Ⓜ *1 to South Ferry; 4, 5 to Bowling Green; R to Whitehall.*

Taste the goods at the Union Square greenmarket (Mon., Wed., Fri., and Sat.), where farmers offer samples of their organically grown produce, artisanal cheeses, and fresh bread. Ⓜ *4, 5, 6 to Union Sq.*

Stroll the Coney Island boardwalk for some old-school kitsch (before it's redeveloped into swanky condos). There are also plenty of free annual events, including the outrageous Mermaid Parade and the Fourth of July hot dog–eating contest. Ⓜ *B, F, N, Q to Stillwell Ave.*

Discover Central Park with a free, volunteer-led guided tour from the Central Park Conservancy. Explore the park's history, design, and ecology with one- to two-hour tours that focus on different areas of the park: its woodlands, romantic vistas, Conservatory garden, Seneca Village, and secret corners and off-the-beaten path walks. Tours meet at different points in the park so check the website for details. 🌐 *www.centralparknyc.org.*

Head to the High Line for a stroll through this park built on top of elevated, abandoned railroad tracks. Take in the aerial views of the city, stop to people-watch, or check out the various art installations along the way. The park runs from Gansevoort Street up to 30th Street; see the

website for entry point details. 🌐 *www.thehighline.org.*

Music, Theater, and Dance

Watch tango dancers and jazz musicians *outside* Lincoln Center at the annual month-long Out of Doors festival, held in August. It includes more than 100 performances of spoken word, beatboxing, and bigwigs like Dave Brubeck and Arlo Guthrie. Ⓜ *1 to 66th St./Lincoln Center.*

Hit Central Park Summerstage for big-name performers like Afrobeat bandleader Seun Kuti and Columbia University's own Vampire Weekend. There's also a second series of concerts in Brooklyn.

Catch rising stars in music, drama, and dance at the Juilliard School's free student concerts (check 🌐 *www.juilliard.edu* for a calendar of events). Free tickets are available at the Juilliard box office for theater performances; standby tickets are available an hour before the show. ✉ *144 W. 65th St. 1 to 66th St./Lincoln Center.*

Get thee entertained at Shakespeare in the Park, one of New York City's most beloved events. Shows usually feature celebrities earning their olde English acting chops. Get in line early at the Public Theater for a shot at tickets, or head to the Delacorte Theater in Central Park. ✉ *425 Lafayette St.* 🌐 *www.shakespeareinthepark.org* Ⓜ *6 to Astor Pl.*

Get gratis giggles at the Upright Citizens Brigade Theatre's comedy shows. Professional comedians, including UCB cofounder and *Saturday Night Live* alumna Amy Poehler, are sprinkled in with amateurs during the performances. Check the schedule for free shows. ✉ *307 W. 26th St.* 🌐 *www.ucbtheatre.com* Ⓜ *A, C, E to 23rd St.*

Art and Literature

Visit the Metropolitan Museum of Art. The $25 entry fee is actually a suggested donation. Smaller donations may get some eye-rolling from the cashier, but it's a small price to pay for access to world-famous works. ✉ *1000 5th Ave. at 80th St.* 🌐 *www.metmuseum.org* Ⓜ *6 to 86th St.*

Browse the galleries scattered throughout the city. Chelsea's full of expensive galleries with free access to superstar artists, though things get edgier the closer you get to the West Side Highway; you'll also find a trendy art scene in Williamsburg, Brooklyn.

Attend a reading at one of the city's bookstores—big (Barnes & Noble) and small (Housing Works Bookstore Café). Or you can get your fix of free words at KGB in the East Village, where authors have been reading since 1993. In Williamsburg, Pete's Candy Store has a reading series on alternate Thursday nights.

MoMA is free on Friday between 4 and 8 pm, when the $25 entry fee is waived. Arrive as close to 4 as you can, and once you get your ticket (the line is long but fast), avoid the crowds by working your way down from the fifth floor. ✉ *11 W. 53rd St., between 5th and 6th Aves.* 🌐 *www.moma.org* Ⓜ *E, M to 5th Ave./53rd St.; B, D, F to 47–50th St./Rockefeller Center.*

Learn about the American Indian at Smithsonian's National Museum of the American Indian, located in the grand Alexander Hamilton U.S. Customs House in Bowling Green. Admission is free every day to the museum's collections, public programs, music and dance performances, and films. 🌐 *www.nmai.si.edu/visit/newyork* Ⓜ *4, 5 to Bowling Green; R to Whitehall St.*

MIDTOWN ARCHITECTURE: LOOK UP!

Midtown is the heart of the city during the workday. From every direction, people pour into the city to give it a jolt of energy. That vibrancy is intense, but is also an unmissable aspect of city life worth exploring for the average visitor. Midtown is home to many beautiful architectural sights, so don't be embarrassed to look at them.

The East Side: From the United Nations to Grand Central

Start near the river, at New York City's first glass-curtain skyscraper, the UN Building (⊠ *760 United Nations Plaza*), completed in 1949 and designed by Le Corbusier. (Technically, it's not on New York's land, but we still count it.) The iconic structure is a monument to diplomacy, though being the city's first skyscraper isn't all glory: the air-conditioning is famously persnickety in the summer months. Continuing west, you'll pass the murals of the Daily News Building (⊠ *220 E. 42nd St.*) on the south side of the street. The lobby is home to a giant globe (from the era when the *News* had international correspondents) and murals are in the WPA-style, as the art-deco building was finished in 1929. Also a can't-miss: the Chrysler Building (⊠ *405 Lexington Ave.*), which out–art decos any other structure in New York. (Dig the wheels with wings in place of gargoyles on the exterior.) Continue walking and you'll see Grand Central Terminal (⊠ *1 E. 42nd St.*), the largest train station in the world. This Beaux-Arts structure was saved from the wrecking ball by concerned citizens in the '70s, a fate that similarly styled Penn Station didn't escape. Step inside for a look at the constellations painted on the soaring ceiling, for a nibble at the Grand Central Oyster Bar, or a cocktail at the swanky Campbell Apartment.

Midtown: Bryant Park and the New York Public Library

By the time you hit 5th Avenue, you'll be staring at the lions that guard the New York Public Library (⊠ *455 5th Ave.*). Built in 1911, the structure is a hub of learning and hosts many lecture series throughout the year. It's abutted by Bryant Park, which offers free Wi-Fi, ice skating in the winter, and films in the summer. The library, too, was brought back from the dead during New York's darkest days. There's also the renovated Nat Sherman store (⊠ *12 E. 42nd St.*), which even has a room for smokers to sample their wares.

The West Side: The Heart of Times Square

Keep walking west and you'll hit the razzle and dazzle of Times Square. It's better than it's ever been. No, not from Guiliani's cleanup—those seedy days are long since past, and Disney predominates—but thanks to a series of pedestrian-friendly improvements, including the closure of some lanes to traffic and the addition of lawn chairs, making it easier to navigate. Be sure to note the futuristic-looking 4 Times Square, where Anna Wintour of Vogue dictates the world of style from on high, and the kid-friendly confines of Madame Tussaud's (⊠ *234 W. 42nd St.*). Finish off by seeing the lights of Broadway from the many theaters on this stretch between 8th and 9th avenues.

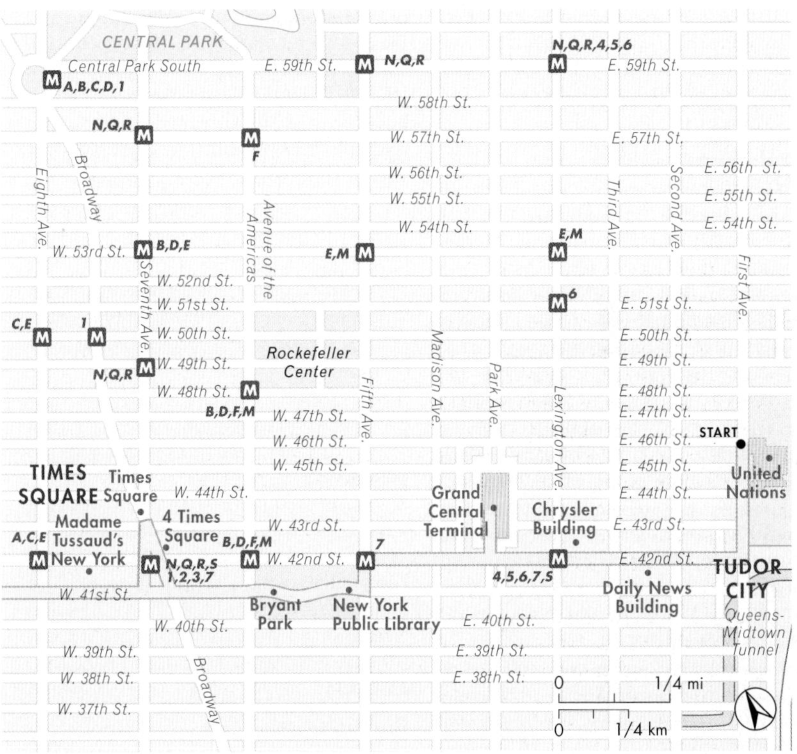

Where to Start:	United Nations, especially for those who are architecturally inclined
Length:	1½ miles (two hours)
Where to Stop:	Grand Central, Bryant Park
Best Time to Go:	Early afternoons; weekends
Worst Time to Go:	Weekday evenings, when the after-work crush is at its peak
Highlights:	Grand Central, Chrysler Building, New York Public Library

NYC'S WATERFRONT PARKS

If Central Park makes you think, "been there, done that," head to one of the several waterfront parks. Many New Yorkers are just discovering some of these green getaways, too.

The Hudson River Park

This 5-mile greenway park hugs the Hudson River from 59th Street to Battery Park. Although the park has a unified design, it's divided into seven distinct sections that reflect the different neighborhoods just across the West Side Highway. Along with refurbished piers with grass and trees, there are also attractions like the *Intrepid* Sea, Air, and Space Museum at Pier 86 across from 46th Street. A few blocks south, the Circle Line and World Yacht offer boat tours of the Hudson. At Piers 96 and 40, the Downtown Boat House (🌐 *www.downtownboathouse.org*) offers free kayaking. There's a mammoth sports center, Chelsea Piers, between Piers 59 and 61, and a mini-golf course and beach volleyball court at Pier 25. The park also sponsors free tours and classes, including free fishing. For a calendar of events and activities, go to 🌐 *www.hudsonriverpark.org*. North of Hudson River Park is one of Manhattan's more well-known parks, **Riverside Park.** ⇨ *For more information see Chapter 12: Upper West Side.*

Getting Here

Hudson River Park is on the far west side of the city, adjacent to the West Side Highway. Crosstown buses at 14th, 23rd, and 42nd streets will get you close, but you'll still have to walk a bit. It's worth it.

Governors Island

A recent addition to the city's parks scene, this little island feels like a small town just 800 yards from the tip of Manhattan. Tourists love the unparalleled views of the harbor and Lower Manhattan, and locals love the out-of-the-city experience. The 172-acre park, built in part from landfill from subway excavations, was a base for the U.S. Army and Coast Guard for almost two centuries. Until 2003, it was off-limits to the public, which could be why the 19th-century homes here are so well preserved. The island is open to the public from May to October, with weekend programs, including art showings, concerts, and family programs. Bikers can take a bike over on the ferry or rent one on the island. For more information, including updated ferry schedules and a calendar of activities, go to 🌐 *www.govisland.org*.

Getting Here

A free seven-minute ferry ride takes passengers to Governors Island from a dock at 10 South St., next to the Staten Island Ferry. Get to the ferry by subway: 1 to South Ferry Station; 4, 5 to Bowling Green; or R, W to Whitehall St. Station. By bus: M1 (weekdays only), M6, M9, and M15.

The High Line

Once an elevated railroad track that serviced the long-ago factories along the lower west side, the High Line was converted into a park (really more of a promenade) that integrates landscaping with rail-inspired design and provides a fresh perspective on the city. Vegetation here includes 210 species of plants, trees, and shrubs intended to reflect the wild plants that flourished for decades after the tracks were abandoned in 1980. The park—30 feet above street level—is open between Gansevoort Street in the Meatpacking District to 30th Street. Sweeping views of the Hudson River and an extended sight line of the Meatpacking District are the

highlights. For information on tours, public programs, and a calendar of events, go to *www.thehighline.org* or call 212/500–6035.

Getting Here

The High Line is accessible at Gansevoort and every two blocks between 14th and 30th streets with elevator access at 14th, 16th, 23rd, and 30th streets (no bikes allowed). It's two blocks west of the subway station at 14th Street and 8th Avenue, served by the L, A, C, E. You can also take the C, E to 23rd Street and walk two blocks west. The 1, 2, 3 stops at 14th Street and 7th Avenue, three blocks away. By bus: M11 to Washington Street, M11 to 9th Avenue, M14 to 9th Avenue, M23 to 10th Avenue, M34 to 10th Avenue.

Battery Park City

Built on landfill jutting out into the Hudson River, Battery Park City is a high-rise residential neighborhood split in two by the World Financial Center and its marina. The Hudson River Park promenade borders BPC along the West Side Highway. In South Battery Park City, you'll pass by the Museum of Jewish Heritage, at 36 Battery Place. Nearby are several reasonably priced outdoor restaurants with stunning views of the Statue of Liberty. There is some interesting public art scattered throughout BPS, too. If you have kids, don't miss the excellent Teardop Park, with its huge slide.

Getting Here

By subway: South Battery Park: 1, R to Rector Place; 4, 5 to Wall Street. North Battery Park: 1, 2, 3, A, C to Chambers Street; E to World Trade Center. By bus: M9, M20, M22.

The East River State Park

Stretching along the East River in the Williamsburg neighborhood of Brooklyn, this seven-acre park has stunning views of the Manhattan skyline. Locals come here to fly kites, picnic, take in the expansive waterfront views, shop the Brooklyn Flea next door, eat at Smorgasburg (Brooklyn's food market), and attend free and ticketed concerts. Skip the subway and arrive via the East River Ferry to really make a day of it. Check *www.nywaterway.com* for schedule and stop information.

Getting Here

By subway: L to Bedford Ave. and walk toward the water to Kent Avenue. East River Ferry to North Williamsburg stop.

The East River Park

This recently landscaped waterfront park, stretching from Montgomery Street to 12th Street along the East River, is one of the Lower East Side's best-kept secrets, with ball fields, bike paths, tennis courts, playgrounds, gardens, and picnic areas—along with impressive views of the Brooklyn skyline and Williamsburg Bridge. Either way, it's a cool spot to chill by the river. You have to cross a footbridge over the FDR Drive to get to the park.

Getting Here

By subway: J, M, Z to Essex St.; F to 2nd Ave.

NEW YORK CITY WITH KIDS

Though much of New York revolves around the adult pursuits of making and spending money, it's also a great city for kids. Our top activities include the following:

American Museum of Natural History. This favorite could entertain most children for a week. The dinosaurs alone are worth the trip, as is the live Butterfly Conservatory (October through May). You'll also find an IMAX theater, ancient-culture displays, and wildlife dioramas with taxidermied creatures that hit the right mix of fascinating and creepy. The space shows at the Hayden Planetarium (tickets sold separately) are a big bang with kids.

Bronx Zoo. The country's largest metropolitan wildlife park is home to more than 4,000 animals, including endangered and threatened species. Plan to spend a whole day here, so your kids don't have to choose between Congo Gorilla Forest and the Siberian cats at Tiger Mountain. The World of Darkness has a black-lighted indoor exhibit of nocturnal creatures. Special tours with a docent for children can be arranged.

Central Park Zoo. Three climatic regions—Rain Forest, Temperate Territory, and Polar Circle—are represented at this small zoo. The rain-forest frogs, red pandas, and performing sea lions are all nifty—but the winner is the underwater viewing window into the polar bear pool.

Chelsea Piers. With a climbing wall, batting cages, ice-skating rinks, basketball and volleyball courts, indoor soccer fields, bowling, sailing, golf, gymnastics, and an Explorer Center with a ball pit and slides, this ginormous athletic and entertainment complex between 18th and 23rd streets along Manhattan's Hudson River is a five-block energy outlet for local and visiting kids of all ages. Book ahead to take advantage of classes or drop in for spontaneous play. 🌐 *www.chelseapiers.com.*

Children's Museum of Manhattan. Interactive exhibits in this five-floor museum change frequently—but they're always fun. As well as visiting with TV friends like Dora the Explorer, little ones can build castles in the sand laboratory, and—in warm weather—race boats on a zigzagging outdoor watercourse.

Coney Island and the New York Aquarium. The whole family can enjoy a walk along Coney Island's famous boardwalk to take in the beach, Luna Park's amusement rides, the landmark Cyclone wooden roller coaster (54-inch height requirement), and Nathan's hot dogs. The New York Aquarium is set to reopen in late spring 2013, after sustaining damage from Hurricane Sandy, so check before you plan a trip.

The DiMenna Children's History Museum. This interactive museum-within-a-museum at the recently renovated New-York Historical Society invites kids (8 and up) to be "history detectives," finding clues, exploring different time periods in the history of New York and America, and connecting to history through the lives of real New York children from the past. Hands-on activities include video games, cross-stitching, and interactive maps.

DUMBO. Short for Down Under the Manhattan Bridge Overpass, this former industrial neighborhood is now a cool and cultural hot spot and home to family-friendly attractions like Brooklyn Bridge Park (a picnic-perfect waterfront park with several inventive playgrounds), Jane's Carousel, Brooklyn Ice Cream Factory, a newly opened public swimming

pool, and a variety of kid-centric music, arts, and kite-flying festivals.

East River Ferry. When you need the journey to be as much fun as the destination, take the East River Ferry. Operated by NY Waterway, and with seven stops along the Manhattan, Brooklyn, and Queens waterfront, a day-pass allows you to hop on and off all day to sample the city's many neighborhoods. Family-friendly attractions just off the boat include Brooklyn Bridge Park's carousel, playgrounds, and ice-cream factory; Williamsburg's markets and festivals; and Governor's Island's mini golf, bike paths, and festivals. It's especially fun in summer when you can take full advantage of the sea breeze and summer festivals. 🌐 *nywaterway.com.*

Just Kidding at Symphony Space. Designed for kids ages 3–9 and their adults, the Just Kidding series at performing arts center Symphony Space (Broadway and 95th St.), inspires and entertains with established and emerging family-friendly artists. Performances include music, dance, comedy, storytelling, and dancing. Interacting is encouraged. 🌐 *symphonyspace.org.*

MoMA's Tours for Fours. A visit to MoMA fits almost every traveler profile but MoMA's free Tours for Fours weekend programs are tailored very specifically to—you guessed it—four-year-olds and their adult guardians. Unlike most look-and-listen type museum programs, Tours for Fours encourages kids to move, create, and interact with art. Themes change monthly so the fun never gets old. Programs begin at 10 am and tickets are on a first-come basis so get there by 9:30 at the latest. MoMa also offers family gallery talks, art labs, and workshops for families with wider age ranges.

Museum of Mathematics. What's the common denominator between hands-on exhibits, didactic sculptures, and interactive displays designed to illustrate math and physics principals? Fun! This two-story museum gets kids excited about math in a physical way; from the tricycles with square wheels to the two-story calculator, almost every exhibit can be touched, climbed-upon, or interacted-with in some way. 🌐 *www.momath.org.*

New York Botanical Garden. Fifty gardens and plant collections fill this gorgeous 250-acre space; there are flowering rose and water-lily gardens in the warm months, and hothouses full of tropical flowers in winter. Don't miss the Children's Adventure Garden and its boulder maze.

Sony Wonder Technology Lab. The line to get into this futuristic fantasy world might be long (entry is free) but don't worry—a slightly freaky talking robot will keep kids entertained while you wait. Inside, kids can program their own robots, record their own digital music, movies, and games, and perform open-heart surgery using Haptic technology.

South Street Seaport Museum. The fleet of historic square-riggers with looming masts might be the first thing to catch your children's eyes—but there's much more going on here, including weekend concerts, 16 new galleries with exhibits that include intricate replicas of ships in bottles, and special guided tours for families.

SIGHTSEEING NEW YORK CITY

Sometimes a guided tour is a great idea, even if you usually prefer flying solo. They can be a great way to investigate out-of-the-way areas, or learn about interesting aspects of the city's history, inhabitants, or architecture. In addition to the listings below, these are some other highly recommended tours to keep in mind: Foraging with Steve Brill ☎ *914/835–2153* 🌐 *www.wildmanstevebrill.com*. A Slice of Brooklyn Pizza Tour ☎ *212/209–3370* 🌐 *www.asliceofbrooklyn.com*.

Boat Tours

Circle Line Sightseeing Cruise. In good weather a Circle Line Sightseeing Cruise around Manhattan Island is one of the best ways to get oriented in the city. Three-hour, $38 cruises run at least once daily; a shorter, two-hour "semi-Circle" option is $34. ✉ *Pier 83 at W. 42nd St., Midtown West* ☎ *212/563–3200* 🌐 *www.circleline42.com* 🎫 *$38*.

Manhattan By Sail. Looking for a more historical experience? Manhattan By Sail has an 82-foot yacht dating from the 1920s that makes daily 90-minute public sails and Sunday brunch sails from mid-April through mid-October. They also offer two-hour sunset sails in June, July, and August. Reservations are advised. Fares start at $45. ✉ *North Cove Marina at World Financial Center, Lower Manhattan* ☎ *212/619–0907* 🌐 *www.manhattanbysail.com*.

Bus Tours

Gray Line New York Sightseeing. Gray Line runs various "hop-on, hop-off" double-decker bus tours, including a downtown Manhattan loop, an upper Manhattan loop, and a Brooklyn loop. Packages include entrance fees to attractions. ✉ *777 8th Ave., between 46th and 47th Sts., Midtown West* ☎ *800/669–0051* 🌐 *www.graylinenewyork.com*.

Walking Tours

Big Onion Walking Tours. The wisecracking PhD candidates of Big Onion Walking Tours lead themed tours such as "Irish New York" and "Satan's Seat: New York During Prohibition," as well as multiethnic eating tours and guided walks through every neighborhood from Harlem to the Financial District and Brooklyn. Tours run daily and cost $20; there's an additional $5 tacked on for tours that include making various stops to eat. ☎ *888/606–9255* 🌐 *www.bigonion.com*.

The Municipal Art Society of New York. MAS conducts walking tours that emphasize the architecture and history of particular neighborhoods. The cost is $20 per person. They also have a tour of Grand Central Terminal every Wednesday from 12:30–2, with a $10 suggested donation. Call or reserve tours online. ✉ *111 W. 57th St.* ☎ *212/935–3960, 212/935–3960 recorded information* 🌐 *www.mas.org*.

New York City Cultural Walking Tours. Alfred Pommer's walking tours cover such topics as buildings' gargoyles and the Millionaire's Mile of 5th Avenue. Two-hour tours run on some Sundays from March to December, and are $15 per person (no reservations needed); private tours can be scheduled throughout the week at $60 per hour with a minimum of two hours. ☎ *212/979–2388* 🌐 *www.nycwalk.com*.

New York Food Tours. Options from the New York Food walking tours include "The Freakiest and Funniest Food" and a "Tastes of Chinatown" tour. Prices start at $49 for 2½ hours' worth of walking and noshing. ☎ *347/559–0111* 🌐 *www.foodtoursofny.com*.

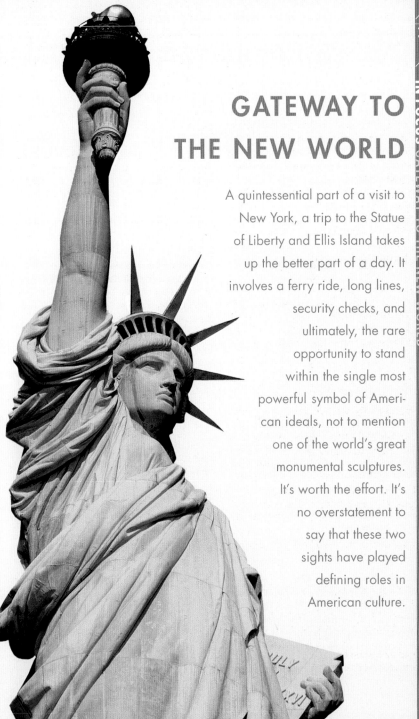

GATEWAY TO THE NEW WORLD

A quintessential part of a visit to New York, a trip to the Statue of Liberty and Ellis Island takes up the better part of a day. It involves a ferry ride, long lines, security checks, and ultimately, the rare opportunity to stand within the single most powerful symbol of American ideals, not to mention one of the world's great monumental sculptures. It's worth the effort. It's no overstatement to say that these two sights have played defining roles in American culture.

THE STATUE OF LIBERTY

Impressive from the shore, the Statue of Liberty is even more majestic up close. For millions of immigrants, the first glimpse of America was Lady Liberty, growing from a vaguely defined figure on the horizon into a towering, stately colossus. Visitors approaching Liberty Island on the ferry from Battery Park may experience a similar sense of wonder as they approach. At press time, the Statue of Liberty is set to reopen on July 4, 2013. Ellis Island is still closed indefinitely due to damage from Hurricane Sandy. Check www.nps.gov/stli for updates.

What's Here

The statue itself stands atop an 89-foot pedestal designed by American Richard Morris Hunt, with Emma Lazarus's sonnet "The New Colossus" ("Give me your tired, your poor, your huddled masses yearning to breathe free . . .").

Inside the pedestal is an informative and entertaining museum. Highlights include the torch's original glass flame that was replaced because of water damage (the current flame is 24-karat gold and lit at night by floodlights), full-scale copper replicas of Lady Liberty's face and one of her feet, Bartholdi's alternative designs for the statue, and a model of Eiffel's intricate framework.

The observatory platform is a great place for a photo op; you're 16 stories high with all of Lower Manhattan spread out in front of you. If you're one of the lucky few with a ticket to visit the crown (they must be reserved in advance), you'll head from here up the 354 stairs—about a 20-minute journey—to the statue's highest accessible point. If not, you'll descend to the promenade at the bottom of the base, where you're still four stories high.

Liberty Island has a pleasant outdoor café.

Know Before You Go

You're allowed access to the museum only as part of one of the free tours of the promenade (which surrounds the base of the pedestal) or the observatory (at the pedestal's top). The tours are limited to 3,000 participants a day. **To guarantee a spot on one of the tours, you must order tickets ahead of time—they can be reserved up to one year in advance, by phone or over the Internet.** There are a limited amount of same-day standby tickets available at the Castle Clinton and Liberty State Park ticket offices, where you catch the ferry.

Thanks to renovations completed in 2012, the pedestal is now accessible via elevator. To reach the crown (accessible via stairs only), advance tickets ($3) are essential and limited to 320 visitors a day. Public access to the torch has been banned since 1916.

Once you reach the island, there are no tickets available. And without a ticket, there is absolutely no admittance into the museum or observatory. You can get a good look at the statue's inner structure on the observatory tour through glass viewing windows that look straight into the statue. Be sure to try the view from several different viewing spots to get the whole interior.

Liberty Highlights

- The surreal chance to stand next to, and be dwarfed by, the original glass torch and the copper cast of Lady Liberty's foot.
- The vistas of New York from the observatory platform.
- The rare opportunity to look up the skirt of a national monument.

Statue Basics

- ☎ 212/363–3200; 877/523–9849 ticket reservations
- www.nps.gov/stli
- Free; ferry $17 round-trip (includes Ellis Island); crown tickets $3
- Daily 9:30 –5:00; extended hours in summer.

Liberty helicopters

ALTERNATIVE VIEWS

- The free Staten Island Ferry offers a great view of New York Harbor and of the Statue of Liberty from a distance (see Chapter 2).
- Webcams placed around the statue's torch allow you to see what Lady Liberty sees—wide views of the New York City skyline, the Hudson River, and ships in the harbor—from your computer or phone.
- Liberty Helicopters has sightseeing tours that fly over the crown and torch (see Chapter 1).

FAST FACT: To move the Statue of Liberty from its initial home on a Paris rooftop to its final home in the New York Harbor, the statue was broken down into 350 individual pieces and packed in 214 crates. It took four months to reassemble it.

FAST FACT: The face of Lady Liberty is actually a likeness of sculptor Frederic-Auguste Bartholdi's mother—quite a tribute.

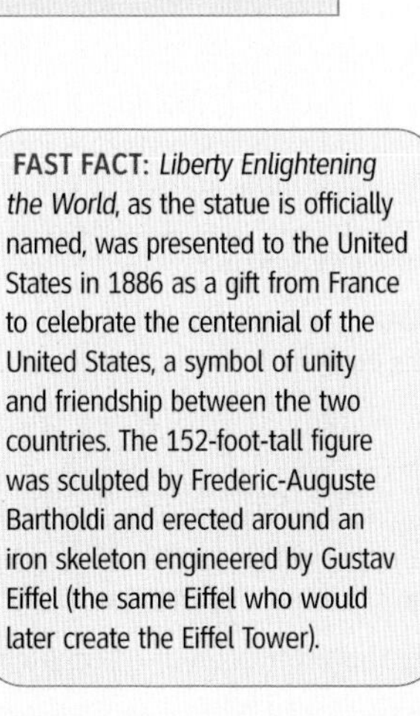

FAST FACT: *Liberty Enlightening the World*, as the statue is officially named, was presented to the United States in 1886 as a gift from France to celebrate the centennial of the United States, a symbol of unity and friendship between the two countries. The 152-foot-tall figure was sculpted by Frederic-Auguste Bartholdi and erected around an iron skeleton engineered by Gustav Eiffel (the same Eiffel who would later create the Eiffel Tower).

ELLIS ISLAND

Chances are you'll be with a crowd of international tourists as you disembark at Ellis Island. Close your eyes for a moment and imagine the jostling crowd 100 times larger. Now imagine that your journey has lasted weeks at sea and that your daypack contains all your worldly possessions, including all your money. You're hungry, tired, jobless, and homeless. This scenario just begins to set the stage for the story of the millions of poor immigrants who passed through Ellis Island at the turn of the 20th century. Between 1892 and 1924, approximately 12 million men, women, and children first set foot on U.S. soil at the Ellis Island federal immigration facility. By the time the facility closed in 1954, it had processed the ancestors of more than 40% of Americans living today.

WHAT'S HERE

The island's main building, now a national monument, reopened in 1990 as the Ellis Island Immigration Museum, with more than 30 galleries of artifacts, photographs, and taped oral histories. The centerpiece of the museum is the Registry Room (also known as the Great Hall). It feels dignified and cavernous today, but photographs show that it took on many configurations over the years, always packed with humanity. While you're there, look out the Registry Room's tall, arched windows and try to imagine what passed through immigrants' minds as they viewed lower Manhattan's skyline to one side and the Statue of Liberty to the other.

Along with the Registry Room, the museum includes the ground-level **Peopling of America Center,** a major expansion that explores immigration to the United States before and after Ellis Island was a portal for immigrants. Graphics and poignant audio stories give firsthand accounts of the immigrants' journeys—from making the trip and arriving in the United States to their struggle and survival here. There is also the **American Family Immigration Center,** where you can search Ellis Island's records for your own ancestors; the **American Flag of Faces,** an interactive display filled with images of immigrants submitted online (submit yours at *FlagofFaces.org*). Outside, the **American Immigrant Wall of Honor,** which has the names of more than 600,000 immigrant Americans against the Manhattan skyline.

MAKING THE MOST OF YOUR VISIT

Because there's so much to take in, it's a good idea to make use of the museum's interpretive tools. **Check at the visitor desk for free film tickets, ranger tour times, and special programs.**

Consider starting your visit with a viewing of the free film *Island of Hope, Island of Tears.* A park ranger starts off with a short introduction, then the 25-minute film takes you through an immigrant's journey from the troubled conditions of European life (especially true for ethnic and religious minorities), to their nervous arrival at Ellis Island, and their introduction into American cities. The film is a primer into all the exhibits and will deeply enhance your experience.

The audio tour, which is included in the ticket price, is also worthwhile: it takes you through the exhibits, providing thorough, engaging commentary interspersed with recordings of immigrants themselves recalling their experiences.

ELLIS ISLAND HIGHLIGHTS

- Surveying the Great Hall.
- The moving film *Island of Hope, Island of Tears.*
- Exploring the Peopling of America Center to gain a deeper understanding of the history of immigration in America.
- Reading the names on the American Immigrant Wall of Honor.
- Researching your own family's history.

Ellis Island Basics

☎ 212/363–3200 Ellis Island; 212/561–4500 Wall of Honor information
🌐 www.nps.gov/stli
🎫 Free; ferry $17 round-trip (includes Liberty Island)
🕒 Daily 9:30–5:00; extended in summer.

IMMIGRANT HISTORY TIMELINE

Starting in the 1880s, troubled conditions throughout Europe persuaded both the poor and the persecuted to leave their family and homes to embark on what were often gruesome journeys to come to the golden shores of America.

1880s 5.7 million immigrants arrive in U.S.

1892 Federal immigration station opens on Ellis Island in January.

1901–1910 8.8 million immigrants arrive in U.S.; 6 million processed at Ellis Island.

1907 Highest number of immigrants (860,000) arrives in one year, including a record 11,747 on April 17.

1910 75% of the residents of New York, Chicago, Detroit, Cleveland, and Boston are now immigrants or children of immigrants.

1920s Federal laws set immigration quotas based on national origin.

1954 Ellis Island immigration station is closed.

New arrivals line up to have their eyes inspected.

FAST FACT: Some immigrants who passed through Ellis Island later became household names. A few include Charles Atlas (1903, Italy); Irving Berlin (1893, Russia); Frank Capra (1903, Italy); Bob Hope (1908, England); Knute Rockne (1893, Norway); and Baron Von Trapp and his family (1938, Germany).

FAST FACT: In 1897, a fire destroyed the original pine immigration structure on Ellis Island, including all immigration records dating back to 1855.

FAST FACT: The first test that immigrants had to pass was known as the "six-second medical exam." As they entered the Great Hall, they were watched by doctors; if anyone seemed disabed, their clothing was marked with chalk and they were sent for a full exam.

Four immigrants and their belongings, on a dock, look out over the water; view from behind.

PLANNING

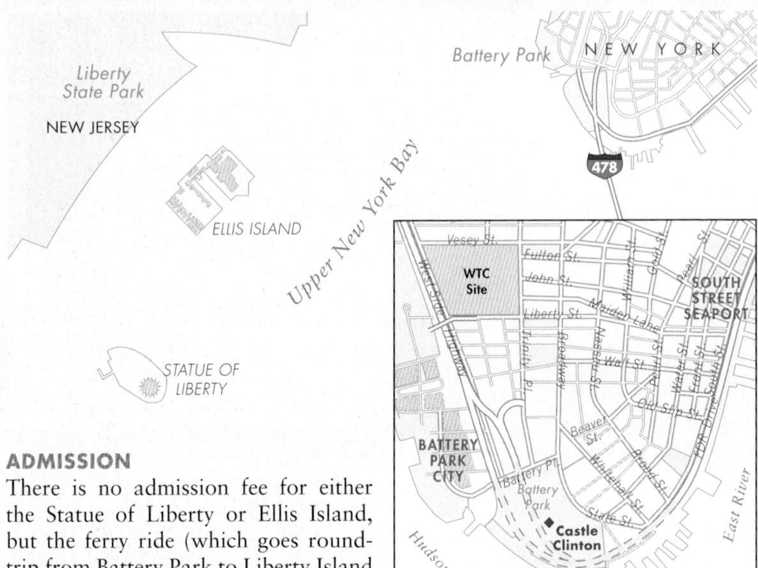

ADMISSION

There is no admission fee for either the Statue of Liberty or Ellis Island, but the ferry ride (which goes round-trip from Battery Park to Liberty Island to Ellis Island) costs $17. Ferries leave from Battery Park (see Ch. 2) every 30 to 40 minutes, depending on the time of year. There are often long lines, so arrive early, especially if you have a reserved-time ticket. (Oversize bags and backpacks aren't permitted on board.) Reserve tickets online—you'll still have to wait in line, both to pick up the tickets and to board the ferry, but you'll be able to pick up a Monument Pass for access to the pedestal, the museum, and the statue's interior. There is no fee for the Monument Pass, but you cannot enter the statue without it.

WHERE TO CATCH THE FERRY

Broadway and Battery Pl., Lower Manhattan Ⓜ Subway: 4, 5 to Bowling Green.

PLANNING TIPS

Buy tickets in advance. This is the only way to assure that you'll have tickets to actually enter the Statue of Liberty museum and observatory platform.

Be prepared for intense security. At the ferry security check, you will need to remove your coat; at the statue, you will need to remove your coat as well as your belt, watch, and any metal accessories. At this writing, no strollers, large umbrellas, or backpacks are allowed in the statue.

Check ferry schedules in advance. Before you go, check www.statuecruises.com.

Keep in mind that even though the last entry time for the monument is at 4:30 PM, **the last ferry to the Statue of Liberty and Ellis Island is at 3:30 PM.** You need to arrive by at least 3 PM (to allow for security checks and lines) if you want to make the last ferry of the day.

2

LOWER MANHATTAN

with the Financial District, New York Harbor, and TriBeCa

GETTING ORIENTED

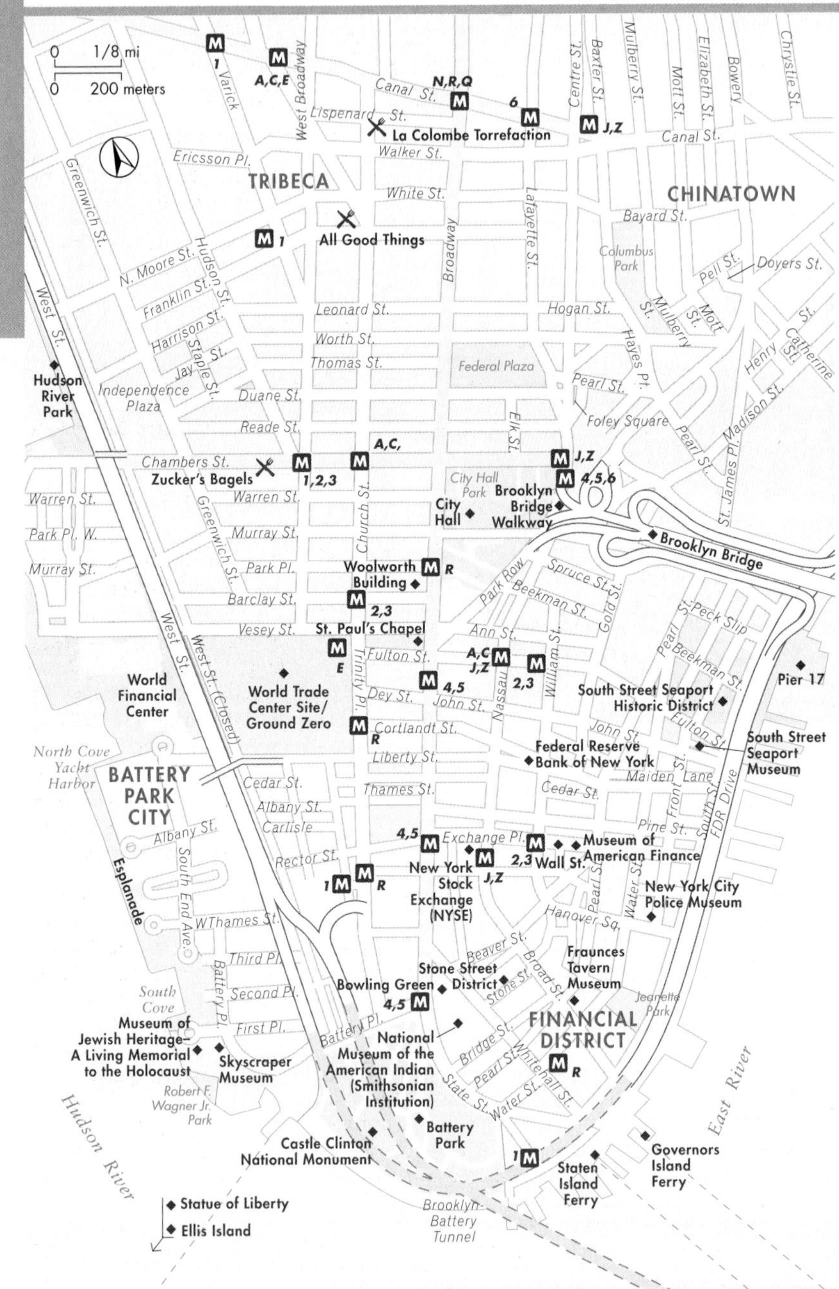

MAKING THE MOST OF YOUR TIME

Visit the Financial District during the weekend and you might feel like a lone explorer in a canyon of buildings; even on weeknights the decibel level of the neighborhood reduces significantly after about 6. Weekdays, however, the sidewalks bustle so much that you can expect to be jostled if you stand still too long. End your visit by watching the sunset over the Hudson River.

The sights of the New York Harbor are some of the most quintessential of New York, but be prepared for long lines for Ellis Island and the Statue of Liberty, especially on weekends. TriBeCa is one of the quieter neighborhoods in Manhattan, being mostly residential. There are pleasant shops, restaurants, and local bars but the neighborhood tends not to be a tourist attraction, unless the film festival is going on.

COFFEE AND QUICK BITES

All Good Things. Rub elbows with locals shopping for bread, cheese, and treats at this upscale food hall. Grab a quick bite for any meal of the day or gather ingredients for a picnic in nearby Hudson River Park. ✉ *102 Franklin St., TriBeCa* ☎ *212/966–3663.*

La Colombe Torrefaction. In this loft-like space just below Canal Street, expect excellent espresso drinks and impressive latte art. This relaxed spot harks back to a time when the café was a place for conversation and people watching. ✉ *319 Church St., at Lispenard St., TriBeCa* ☎ *212/343–1515* 🌐 *www.lacolombe.com.*

Zucker's Bagels. This is one of the few stores left in the city that serves hand-rolled, kettle-boiled New York bagels. Baked throughout the day, the bagels can be eaten with a shmear of scallion cream cheese or filled with Nova Scotia salmon. ✉ *146 Chambers St., Financial District* ☎ *212/608–5844* 🌐 *www.zuckersbagels.com.*

TOP EXPERIENCES

Visiting the National 9/11 Memorial.

Riding the Staten Island Ferry.

Touring Ellis Island and the Statue of Liberty.

Snapping a photo in front of Wall Street's bull.

Strolling through Hudson River Park.

BEST FOR KIDS

Castle Clinton and Battery Park

South Street Seaport Museum

GETTING HERE

Many subway lines connect to the Financial District. The Fulton Street station is serviced by eight different subway lines (A, C, J, Z, 2, 3, 4, 5) and puts you within walking distance of City Hall, South Street Seaport, and the World Trade Center site (⇨ *Ground Zero feature in this chapter*). To get to the Brooklyn Bridge, take the 4, 5, or 6 to Brooklyn Bridge–City Hall.

For sights around New York Harbor, take the R to Whitehall, or the 4 or 5 to Bowling Green. (Note that you can also reach the Harbor area via the 1 train to South Ferry. The 1 subway line stops in the heart of TriBeCa (Franklin Street).

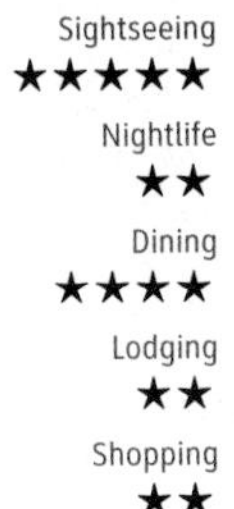

Sightseeing ★★★★★
Nightlife ★★
Dining ★★★★
Lodging ★★
Shopping ★★

Lower Manhattan, or in the parlance of New Yorkers emphatically giving directions to tourists, "all the way downtown," has long been where the action—and transaction—is. Originally the Dutch trading post called New Amsterdam (1626–47), this neighborhood is home to historic, cobbled streets next to soaring skyscrapers. This mix of old and new, the bustle of Wall Street, and a concentration of city landmarks all lure visitors to the tip of Manhattan.

FINANCIAL DISTRICT AND SOUTH STREET SEAPORT

Updated by Jessica Colley

Little from Manhattan's colonial era is left in lower Manhattan (apart from a precious few structures built in the 1700s) but you can still feel a sense of history in the South Street Seaport's 19th-century brick facades and pedestrianized Stone Street lined with picnic tables. There's life to be found within the skyscraper-lined canyons of Wall Street and lower Broadway, as locals move into the neighborhood and fill the barstools in candlelit watering holes. Bounded by the East and Hudson rivers to the east and west, respectively, and by Chambers Street and Battery Park to the north and south, the Financial District is best appreciated by getting lost in its streets.

You'll want to see what's here, but above all you'll want to see what's not, most notably in that empty gulf among skyscrapers: the World Trade Center site where two 1-acre pools represent the footprints of the fallen Twin Towers.

TOP ATTRACTIONS

FAMILY **Battery Park.** Jutting out at the southernmost point of Manhattan, tree-filled Battery Park is a respite from the narrow, winding, and (on weekdays) jam-packed streets of the Financial District. Even if you don't plan to stay for long, carve out a few minutes of sightseeing time to sit on a bench and take in the view, which includes the Statue of Liberty and Ellis Island. On clear days you can see all the way to Port Elizabeth's cranes, which seem to mimic Lady Liberty's stance; to Governors Island, a former Coast Guard installation now managed by the National Park Service; a hilly Staten Island in the distance; and the old railway terminal in Liberty State Park, on the mainland in Jersey City, New Jersey. Looking away from the water and toward Lower Manhattan's skyscrapers, there's a feeling that you're at the beginning of the city, and a sense of all the possibility it possesses just a few blocks in.

BROOKLYN BRIDGE FACTS

- Overall length: 6,016 feet
- Span of twin Gothic-arch towers: 1,595½ feet
- Distance from top of towers to East River: 272 feet
- Distance from roadway to the water: 133 feet
- Number of times the line "If you believe that, I've got a bridge to sell you" is used referring to the Brooklyn Bridge: Infinite

The park's main structure is **Castle Clinton National Monument,** the ticket office site and takeoff point for ferries to the Statue of Liberty and Ellis Island. This monument was once 200 feet off the southern tip of the island located in what was called the Southwest Battery, and was erected during the War of 1812 to defend the city. (The East Battery sits across the harbor on Governors Island.) As dirt and debris from construction were dumped into the harbor, the island expanded, eventually engulfing the landmark. Later, from 1855 to 1890, it served as America's first official immigration center (Ellis Island opened in 1892).

Inside Battery Park are several monuments and statues, including *The Sphere,* which for three decades stood on the plaza at the World Trade Center as a symbol of peace. Damaged but still intact after the collapse of the towers, it serves as a temporary memorial to those who lost their lives.

The southern link in a chain of parks connecting Battery Park north to Chambers Street, Robert F. Wagner Jr. Park has a flat, tidy lawn and wide benches from which to view the harbor or the stream of runners and in-line skaters on the promenade. A brick structure at the southeast section of Battery Park has public bathrooms and a restaurant with additional views from its flat roof. ✉ *Battery Park* ☎ *212/417–2000* 🌐 *www.nycgovparks.org/parks/batterypark* Ⓜ *4, 5 to Bowling Green.*

Fodor's Choice ★ **Brooklyn Bridge.** "A drive-through cathedral" is how the journalist James Wolcott described the Brooklyn Bridge, one of New York's noblest and most recognized landmarks, perhaps outdoing Walt Whitman's comment that it was "The best, most effective medicine my soul has yet partaken." The bridge stretches over the East River, connecting Manhattan and Brooklyn. A walk across its promenade—a boardwalk elevated above the roadway, shared by pedestrians, in-line skaters, and cyclists—takes about 40 minutes and delivers exhilarating views. If you start from downtown Manhattan, you'll end up in the heart of Brooklyn

Heights. It's worth noting that on weekends when the weather is nice, the path can get pretty congested; it's most magical, and quietest, early in the morning or during sunset when the city lights come to life. ✉ *E. River Dr., Lower Manhattan* Ⓜ *4, 5, 6 to Brooklyn Bridge/City Hall; J, Z to Chambers St.; A, C to High St.–Brooklyn Bridge.*

Ground Zero. *See highlighted feature in this chapter.*

New York Stock Exchange (NYSE). Unfortunately you can't tour it, but it's certainly worth ogling. At the intersection of Wall and Broad streets, the exchange is impossible to miss. The neoclassical building, designed by architect George B. Post, opened on April 22, 1903. It has six Corinthian columns supporting a pediment with a sculpture titled *Integrity Protecting the Works of Man,* featuring a tribute to the then-sources of American prosperity: Agriculture and Mining to the left of Integrity; Science, Industry, and Invention to the right. The Exchange was one of the world's first air-conditioned buildings. ✉ *11 Wall St., Financial District* ☎ *866/368–3375* 🌐 *www.nyse.com* Ⓜ *1, 4, 5, N, R to Rector St.; 2, 3 to Wall St.; J, Z to Broad St.*

South Street Seaport Historic District. Had this charming cobblestone corner of the city not been declared a historic district in 1977, the city's largest concentration of early-19th-century commercial buildings would have been destroyed. Today, the area is largely mobbed with tourists, and if you've been to Boston's Quincy Market or Baltimore's Harborplace, you may feel a flash of déjà vu—the same company leased, restored, and adapted the existing buildings, with the result being the blend of a quasi-authentic historic district with a slightly homogenous shopping mall.

At the intersection of Fulton and Water streets, the gateway to the seaport, is the ***Titanic* Memorial,** a small white lighthouse commemorating the sinking of the RMS *Titanic* in 1912. Beyond the lighthouse, Fulton Street turns into a busy pedestrian mall. On the south side of Fulton is the seaport's architectural centerpiece, **Schermerhorn Row,** a redbrick terrace of Georgian- and Federal-style warehouses and counting houses built from 1811 to 1812. Some upper floors house gallery space, and the ground floors are occupied by shops, bars, and restaurants. Cross South Street, once known as the Street of Ships, under an elevated stretch of FDR Drive to **Pier 16,** where historic ships are docked, including the *Pioneer,* a 102-foot schooner built in 1885; the *Peking,* the second-largest sailing bark in existence; the iron-hulled *Wavertree*; and the lightship *Ambrose.* The Pier 16 ticket booth provides information and sells tickets to the museum, ships, tours, and exhibits. Pier 16 is the departure point for various seasonal cruises.

To the north is **Pier 17,** a dockside shopping mall filled mostly with chain retailers. The weathered-wood decks at the rear of the pier are a choice spot from which to catch sight of the river. Pier 17 used to be the home of the Fulton Fish Market, which first opened in South Manhattan in 1807; starting in 1939 it was housed in the New Market Building, just north of the Seaport, but that closed in 2005 when operations were moved to a new facility in the Bronx. ✉ *South Street Seaport* ☎ *212/732–8257 events and shopping information* 🌐 *www.southstreetseaport.com* Ⓜ *2, 3, 4, 5, A, C, J, Z to Fulton St./Broadway–Nassau.*

South Street Seaport Museum. Enter the main lobby of the South Street Seaport Museum at 12 Fulton Street for exhibits, walking tours, a fleet of eight historic vessels, and fantastic educational programs for children—all with a nautical theme. Recent shows in the museum's three floors of galleries included *Timescapes,* a 22-minute history of New York, a photo exhibit of street life called *Street Shots/NYC,* and an exhibit of watercolors entitled *Romancing New York.* ✉ *12 Fulton St., between Water and South Sts., South Street Seaport* ☎ *212/748–8600* 🌐 *www.southstreetseaportmuseum.org* 🎫 *$10* 🕒 *Daily 10–6.*

Stone Street Historic District. Nestled amid skyscrapers and the towering New York Stock Exchange, the low-rise, two-block oasis of bars and restaurants along historic Stone Street feels more like a village than the center of the financial universe. In the summer, tables spill out into the cobblestone street and the mood is convivial—especially on Thursday and Friday nights. This was Manhattan's first paved street and today the cluster of buildings along here, with South William and Pearl streets, and Coenties Alley, make up the Stone Street Historic District. ✉ *Financial District.*

WORTH NOTING

Bowling Green. Perhaps most recognized as the home of Arturo Di Modica's 7,000-pound, bronze *Charging Bull* statue (1989), Bowling Green, at the foot of Broadway, became New York's first public park in 1733. Legend has it that before that, this was the sight where Peter Minuit purchased the island of Manhattan from the Native Americans, in 1626, supposedly for what amounted to 24 U.S. dollars. On July 9, 1776, a few hours after citizens learned about the signing of the Declaration of Independence, rioters toppled a statue of British King George III that had occupied the spot for 11 years; much of the statue's lead was melted down into bullets. In 1783, when the occupying British forces fled the city, they defiantly hoisted a Union Jack on a greased, uncleated flagpole so it couldn't be lowered; patriot John Van Arsdale drove his own cleats into the pole to replace the flag with the Stars and Stripes. The copper-top subway entrance here is the original one, built in 1904–05. ✉ *Broadway at Whitehall St., Financial District* Ⓜ *4, 5 to Bowling Green.*

City Hall. What once marked the northernmost point of Manhattan today houses the office of the mayor and serves as a gathering place for demonstrators voicing concerns and the news crews that cover their stories. This is the oldest City Hall in the country, a striking (but surprisingly small) building dating back to 1803. If the history of local politics and architecture is your thing, free tours are available (sign up in advance online). Tours begin outside. Indoors, highlights include the Victorian-style **City Council Chamber,** the Rotunda where President Lincoln lay in state in 1865 under a soaring dome supported by 10 Corinthian columns, and the **Governor's Room,** an elegantly preserved space with intricate portraits of historic figures and a writing table that George Washington used in 1789 when New York was the U.S. capital. If nothing else, take a moment to snap a photo of the columned exterior and see the small but lovely City Hall Park, bound by Broadway to the west and Chambers Street to the north. This park is an underrated place

Continued on page 54

A GLIMPSE OF THE FUTURE WORLD TRADE CENTER

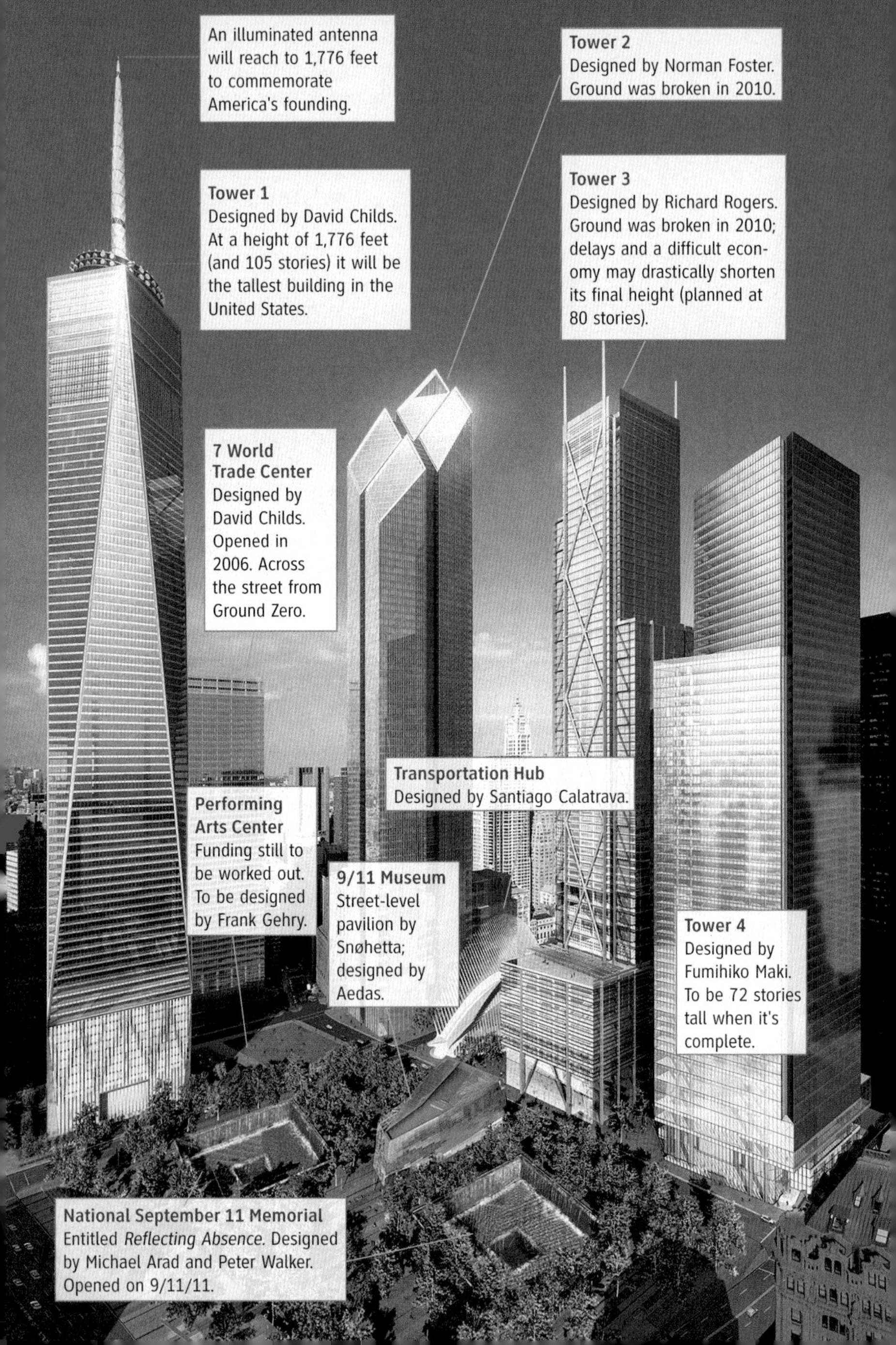

An illuminated antenna will reach to 1,776 feet to commemorate America's founding.

Tower 2
Designed by Norman Foster. Ground was broken in 2010.

Tower 1
Designed by David Childs. At a height of 1,776 feet (and 105 stories) it will be the tallest building in the United States.

Tower 3
Designed by Richard Rogers. Ground was broken in 2010; delays and a difficult economy may drastically shorten its final height (planned at 80 stories).

7 World Trade Center
Designed by David Childs. Opened in 2006. Across the street from Ground Zero.

Transportation Hub
Designed by Santiago Calatrava.

Performing Arts Center
Funding still to be worked out. To be designed by Frank Gehry.

9/11 Museum
Street-level pavilion by Snøhetta; designed by Aedas.

Tower 4
Designed by Fumihiko Maki. To be 72 stories tall when it's complete.

National September 11 Memorial
Entitled *Reflecting Absence.* Designed by Michael Arad and Peter Walker. Opened on 9/11/11.

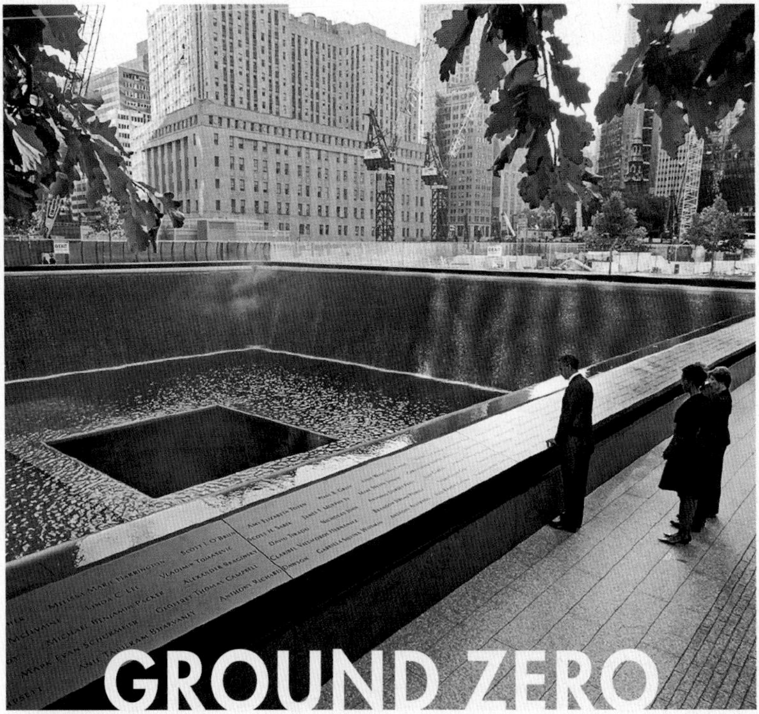

GROUND ZERO

THE WORLD TRADE CENTER SITE

A decade after September 11, 2001, the 9/11 Memorial opened, giving Ground Zero's thousands of annual visitors a solemn place to reflect and think about that brutal day. Its accompanying underground museum has experienced construction delays, but will open on the same bedrock once used by the Twin Towers' foundation. It will be a fitting place to display artifacts from 9/11 and its aftermath. As you plan your visit, set aside time to visit other key parts of the story, such as St. Paul's Chapel and the "Ten House" firehouse on Liberty Street.

(above) President Obama, Michelle Obama, former President George W. Bush, and Laura Bush at the National 9/11 Memorial. (below) Names on the 9/11 Memorial; (opposite) Rendition of the future WTC site.

LOOKING BACK AT THE TOWERS AND 9/11

THE TOWERS

The World Trade Towers, each 110 stories tall, were an impressive feat of engineering. Construction began in 1968, and the Twin Towers officially opened in 1973. Avoiding the typical construction used at the time, the architects gave each building an exterior skeleton made up of 244 slim steel columns and an inner "core" tube that supported the weight of the tower.

Approximately 50,000 people worked in the north tower (1 World Trade Center) and south tower (2 World Trade Center), and another 40,000 people visited the 16-acre complex every day. Beneath the towers was a multi-level mall with nearly 100 stores and restaurants.

The Twin Towers prior to 9/11

EVENTS OF THE DAY On September 11, 2001, terrorist hijackers steered two jets into the World Trade Center's Twin Towers, demolishing them and five outlying buildings.

- The first hijacked jet, American Airlines Flight 11, crashed into the north tower, 1 World Trade Center, at 8:46 AM, cutting through floors 93 to 99. The tower collapsed at 10:28 AM. Cantor Fitzgerald, a brokerage firm headquartered between the 101st and 105th floors, lost 658 of its 1,050 employees. At the Windows on the World restaurant (floors 106 and 107), 100 patrons and 72 staff members died.
- The second hijacked jet, United Airlines Flight 175, hit the south tower, 2 World Trade Center, at 9:03 AM, crashing through the 77th to 85th floors. The plane banked as it hit, so portions of the building remained undamaged on impact floors. Consequently, one stairwell initially remained passable from at least the 91st floor down. The tower collapsed at 9:58 AM.
- The attack killed 2,753 people. (Deaths are still being counted; recent casualties include Jerry J. Borg who died in late 2010 from pulmonary sarcoidosis, a lung disease caused by inhaling toxins from the dust cloud that formed when the towers collapsed.) The fenced-in 16-acre work site that emerged from the rubble, almost immediately dubbed Ground Zero, came to symbolize the personal, political, and historical impact of September 11.

(above) Towers burning after attack.

THE DAMAGE

Why *did* the towers fall? A three-year federal study revealed several reasons. The two airplanes used in the attack, both Boeing 767s, hit their respective towers at roughly 500 mph. They both damaged the exterior columns, destroying core supports for at least three of the north tower's floors and up to six of the south tower's floors. Ensuing fires, fed by tens of thousands of gallons of jet fuel, further weakened the buildings. The collapse of the most heavily damaged floors then triggered a domino effect, causing the towers to crumple at an estimated speed of about 125 mph.

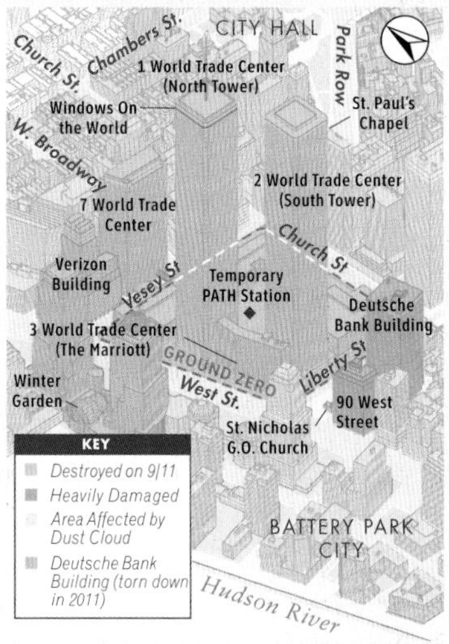

Many other area buildings suffered collateral damage. The World Financial Center office complex, to the west of Ground Zero, has as its centerpiece the 10-story glass-domed Winter Garden. After having nearly all its glass blown out in the attacks, the atrium reopened in September 2002 after repairs that included the installation of 2,000 windows and 1.2 million pounds of stone.

The 47-story 7 World Trade Center, to the north of Ground Zero, was struck by large chunks of falling debris from the north and south towers. The building remained standing at first, but subsequent fires caused it to collapse later that afternoon. A new 52-story 7 World Trade Center opened in May 2006 with a much smaller footprint than its predecessor.

St. Paul's Chapel, across the street from Ground Zero, sustained no major damage; staff there credit a huge sycamore that toppled over during the attack. Its gigantic root system, now above ground, helped to shield the building and the headstones in its attached cemetery from falling debris.

Although the New York Stock Exchange's building wasn't physically harmed during the attacks, the market remained closed for six days (including 9/11). When trading resumed on September 17, the Dow Jones industrial average dropped 684.81 points, or 7.13 percent. The American Stock Exchange (Amex), however, sustained some damage on 9/11, and for two weeks Amex stocks and exchange-traded funds were traded on the NYSE floor.

(above) A New York City fire fighter looks up at what remains of the World Trade Center after its collapse; a 9/11 memorial wreath; the "Tribute in Light" memorial on the fifth anniversary of 9/11.

A LOOK TO THE FUTURE

A vision of the future Manhattan skyline

It may have taken longer than most observers could have imagined, but a new World Trade Center is now a reality, at least partially. Following the master plan laid down by the architect Daniel Libeskind, the footprints of the original towers have been made into pools, their rushing waterfalls part of a powerful memorial. When all the work is finished—and there's still a great deal to do—the World Trade Center will include office buildings, a transit hub, and a performing arts center.

Future downtown skyline at dusk

NATIONAL SEPTEMBER 11 MEMORIAL

The architect Michael Arad, working in partnership with the landscape architect Peter Walker, won the international contest to design the memorial. It is entitled "Reflecting Absence," and it takes up about half of the 16-acre complex. It opened on the tenth anniversary of 9/11.

No buildings are in the space where the Twin Towers once stood. In their place are recessed waterfalls cascading thirty feet down into two subterranean reflecting pools that limn the Twin Towers' original footprints (each roughly an acre in size). The water then tumbles down into smaller square holes at the center of each pool. The effect manages to be both moving and solemn but not sentimental. In the words of Paul Goldberger, the *New Yorker's* architecture critic, "Arad figured out how to express the idea that what were once the largest solids in Manhattan are now a void, and he made the shape of this void into something monumental."

Surrounding each waterfall on the plaza level is a low bronze wall with the names of the 2,887 victims of the 9/11 attacks (including those at the Pentagon and on flights 11, 77, 93, and 175), and the six people who died in the first World Trade Center bombing, in 1993. The names are sorted by affiliation, so that names lie etched near those of people they worked with or otherwise knew. Kiosks on the edge of the site help with finding out which panel holds a particular name or group (the information can also be found online, at *www.911memorial.org*, and through a smartphone app). Surrounding the waterfalls is a stark plaza punctuated with hundreds of swamp white-oak saplings, which some day will be 70 feet tall. Joining them is the so-called "survivor tree," a Callery pear tree that was plucked from the rubble, nursed back to health elsewhere, and replanted on the site as a symbol of resilience.

Construction as of December 2011.

Fumihiko Maki, Larry Silverstein, and Norman Foster

Standing at an angle to the memorial's pools is the small center that will serve as the entrance to the memorial's accompanying museum, an ambitious project that has experienced some construction delays. From here, visitors will walk down a ramp to the bedrock the towers were built on, 71 feet below. One exhibit will be the "last column," the last piece of steel to be removed from the site, which was covered with slogans and memorials from rescue crews and others.

ONE WORLD TRADE CENTER

Known for a time as the Freedom Tower, this 105-story skyscraper will have a roof that's 1,368 feet tall—identical to that of the taller of the Twin Towers. An illuminated antenna will further increase the building's height to 1,776 feet to commemorate America's founding (and make it the country's tallest building). Designed by David Childs of Skidmore, Owings & Merrill, the new 1 WTC is expected to be finished by late 2013. The three other office buildings on the site (all at various stages of construction) are each by a different prominent architect: Fumihiko Maki, Richard Rogers, and Norman Foster.

TRANSPORTATION HUB

Intended to connect New Jersey's PATH subway with 13 of New York's subway lines, this transportation hub was designed by the Spanish architect Santiago Calatrava. Inspired by the image of a child releasing a dove, the massive glass-roofed building is likely to be awe-inspiring once it's finished, but soaring costs and a complicated design mean that the tentative completion date of 2014 may be delayed.

For more information on the new structures, visit www.lowermanhattan.info and www.911memorial.org.

A GROUND ZERO WALK

Names on the 9/11 Memorial Wall.

This tour starts near the WTC Tribute Center, which runs its own well-regarded walking tours that include the memorial and other sites important to the history of 9/11. If you're just doing this walking tour, you can do it in any order.

1 One place to start your walk is at the corner of Liberty and Greenwich streets, just a short distance from where the World Trade Center's South Tower once stood. This is Ten House, a firehouse named for the number of its engine and ladder companies. On 9/11, the station was nearly destroyed, and six of its members lost their lives after responding to the disaster. The station's restored exterior is now covered with a 56-foot bronze bas-relief "dedicated to those who fell and to those who carry on." The Tribute WTC Visitor Center, a project of the September 11th Families' Association, is next-door. Its exhibits give a heartbreaking picture of the many lives lost on that day.

Inspired by the giant sycamore that fell under the rubble and helped protect old headstones in St. Paul's graveyard, the *Trinity Root* sculpture, a 9/11 memorial pictured here, can be seen at Trinity Church

2 Head around the corner to the National 9/11 Memorial, which incorporates the footprints of the Twin Towers into two pools of water. If the 9/11 Museum has opened (funding and construction issues delayed the projected 2012 opening), then proceed there. Its 110,000 square feet, nearly all of them underground, take up the seven stories of space that were once occupied by the stores and parking garage under the original Twin Towers.

3 After you've finished paying your respects, head south to exit the memorial (the current exit, as of early 2013, leaves you near the corner of Albany and West streets), making a quick stop at the nearby 9/11 Memorial Visitor Center, at 90 West Street. From here, take the next left (onto Albany Street) and walk over to Trinity Place (which

The firefighters' memorial.

turns into Church Street), turn left (north) and continue until you reach the churchyard behind St. Paul's, the Episcopal chapel that became a dormitory, mess hall, and medical center in the months after 9/11. Even George Washington's pew was called back into service for the exhausted rescue workers. Across the street, at 20 Vesey Street, is the 9/11 Memorial Preview Site, which has models of what the entire World Trade Center will look like once it's completed. It also has a good selection of books and other items about 9/11 and its aftermath.

The Tribute WTC Visitor Center

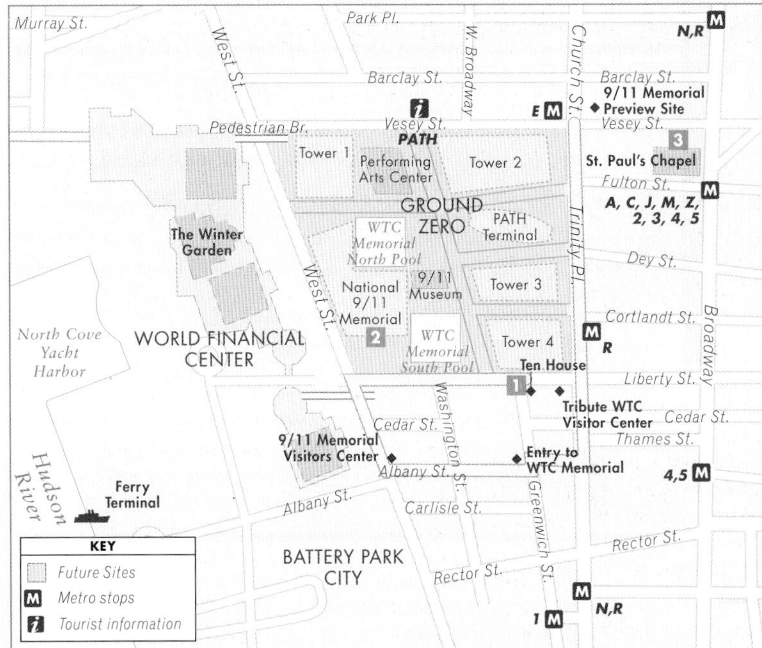

VISITING THE MEMORIAL

There is airport-like security at the memorial, and no large bags are allowed, there's no bag storage, and there are no bathrooms. Entry is via free, timed tickets, available online; book ahead. Standby tickets are sometimes available at the site itself. Allow at least an hour to visit the memorial and museum, more at a busy times of the year.

VISITOR CENTERS

An **information booth** on Vesey Street, near the temporary PATH station, has maps of the area. The 9/11 Memorial Visitor Center (90 West St., 212/225-1009, www.national911memorial.org,) is open daily, 10–8:30, early Mar.–early Oct. and around Thanksgiving and Christmas; it's open 10–7 the rest of the year. The 9/11 Memorial Preview Site (20 Vesey St., 212/267-2047, free) is open daily, 10–7:30 early Mar.–early Oct. and around Thanksgiving and Christmas, and 9–7 other times. The **Tribute WTC Center** (120 Liberty St., 866/737-1184, www.tributewtc.org, $15) is open 10–6, Mon.–Sat., 10–5 on Sun.

TOURS

The Tribute WTC Center leads hour-long walking tours that include the National September 11 Memorial and nearby sites. The $20 cost ($5 if you've already paid to see the exhibits; keep your receipt) includes admission to the Tribute WTC Center exhibits. You don't need to book in advance. Booking a tour with the Tribute WTC Visitor Center saves you having to get your own timed ticket for the 9/11 memorial.

GETTING THERE

Subway: 1, N, R to Rector St.; 2, 3, 4, 5, A, C, J, Z to Fulton St./Broadway-Nassau; E to World Trade Center/Church St.

PATH: Any line to World Trade Center.

CLOSE UP

The Gangs of Five Points

In the mid-19th century the Five Points area was perhaps the city's most notorious and dangerous neighborhood. The confluence of five streets—Mulberry, Anthony (now Worth), Cross (now Park), Orange (now Baxter), and Little Water (no longer in existence)—had been built over a drainage pond that had been filled in the 1820s. When the buildings began to sink into the mosquito-filled muck, middle-class residents abandoned their homes. Buildings were chopped into tiny apartments that were rented to the poorest of the poor, who at this point were newly emancipated slaves and Irish immigrants fleeing famine. Newspaper accounts at the time tell of daily robberies and other violent crimes. And with corrupt political leaders like William Marcy "Boss" Tweed more concerned with lining their pockets than patrolling the streets, keeping order was left to the club-wielding hooligans portrayed in *Gangs of New York*. The neighborhood, finally razed in the 1880s to make way for Columbus Park, has left a lasting legacy: In the music halls where different ethnic groups grudgingly came together, the Irish jig and the African-American shuffle combined to form a new type of fancy footwork called tap dancing.

to stop and take a breath away from the typical congestion of Lower Manhattan. ✉ *City Hall Park, Financial District* ☎ *212/788–2656 for tour reservations* 🌐 *www.nyc.gov/html/artcom/html/tours/city_hall.shtml* 🎟 *Free* 🕓 *Tours available some weekdays; reserve online or by phone* Ⓜ *2, 3 to Park Pl.; R to City Hall; 4, 5, 6 to Brooklyn Bridge/City Hall; J, Z, A, C to Chambers St.*

Federal Reserve Bank of New York. With its imposing mix of sandstone, limestone, and ironwork, the Federal Reserve looks the way a bank ought to: strong and impregnable. The gold ingots in the subterranean vaults here are worth roughly $350 billion—reputedly a third of the world's gold reserves. Forty-five-minute-long tours (conducted six times a day and requiring reservations made at least five days in advance) include a visit to the gold vault, the trading desk, and "FedWorks," a multimedia exhibit center where you can track hypothetical trades. Visitors must show an officially issued photo ID, such as a driver's license or passport, and pass through scanning equipment to enter the building. The Fed advises arriving 20 minutes before your tour to accommodate security screening. Photography is not permitted. ✉ *33 Liberty St., between William and Nassau Sts., Financial District* ☎ *212/720–6130* 🌐 *www.newyorkfed.org* 🎟 *Free* 🕓 *Tour by advance reservation, weekdays 11:15–4* Ⓜ *A, C to Nassau; J, Z, 2, 3, 4, 5 to Fulton St.*

Fraunces Tavern Museum. This former tavern, where General George Washington celebrated the end of the Revolutionary War in 1783, is now a museum covering two floors above a restaurant and bar. Here, in his pre-presidential days, Washington bid an emotional farewell to his officers upon the British evacuation of New York. Today this historic landmark has two fully furnished period rooms—including the Long Room, site of Washington's address—and other modest displays of

18th- and 19th-century American history. You'll find more tourists and Wall Street types than revolutionaries in the recently reopened tavern and restaurant on the ground floor these days, but a cozy colonial atmosphere and a decent hearty meal is also on offer. ✉ *54 Pearl St., at Broad St., Financial District* ☎ *212/425–1778* 🌐 *www.frauncestavernmuseum.org* 🎟 *$7* ⏲ *Daily noon–5* Ⓜ *R to Whitehall St.; 4, 5 to Bowling Green; 1 to South Ferry; J, Z to Broad St.*

Museum of American Finance. Pre-9/11, a visit to the New York Stock Exchange was the ultimate high; the energy of the floor and the proximity to so much power couldn't be beat. Post-9/11 security prohibits tours of the Exchange but you can still get a feel—albeit a less exhilarating feel—for what makes the financial world go 'round (and down) by visiting this museum. Located in the grandiose former banking hall of the Bank of New York, this Smithsonian Institution affiliate is home to artifacts of the financial market's history; interactive exhibits on the financial markets, banking, entrepreneurship, and Alexander Hamilton; and well-executed temporary exhibits. ✉ *48 Wall St., at William St., Financial District* ☎ *212/908–4110* 🌐 *www.moaf.org* 🎟 *$8* ⏲ *Tues.–Sat. 10–4* Ⓜ *2, 3 to Wall St.*

Museum of Jewish Heritage—A Living Memorial to the Holocaust. In a granite 85-foot hexagon at the southern end of Battery Park City, this museum pays tribute to the 6 million Jews who perished in the Holocaust. Architects Kevin Roche and John Dinkeloo built the museum in the shape of a Star of David, with three floors of exhibits demonstrating the dynamism of 20th-century Jewish culture. Visitors enter through a gallery that provides a context for the early-20th-century artifacts on the first floor: an elaborate screen hand-painted for the fall harvest festival of Sukkoth, wedding invitations, and tools used by Jewish tradesmen. Original documentary films play throughout the museum. The second floor details the rise of Nazism and anti-Semitism, and the ravages of the Holocaust. A gallery covers the doomed voyage of the SS *St. Louis,* a ship of German Jewish refugees that crossed the Atlantic twice in 1939 in search of a safe haven. Signs of hope are also on display, including a trumpet that Louis Bannet (the "Dutch Louis Armstrong") played for three years in the Auschwitz-Birkenau inmate orchestra. The third floor covers postwar Jewish life. New exhibits added in early 2013 explore American Jews who tried to rescue European Jews leading up to and during the Holocaust, as well as the rich Jewish history of Oswiecim, the town the Germans called Auschwitz. The museum's east wing has a theater, a memorial garden, a library, more galleries, and a café. An audio guide, with narration by Meryl Streep and Itzhak Perlman, is available at the admissions desk for $5. ✉ *36 Battery Pl., Battery Park City, Financial District* ☎ *646/437–4202* 🌐 *www.mjhnyc.org* 🎟 *$12, free Wed. 4–8* ⏲ *Thurs. and Sun.–Tues. 10–5:45, Wed. 10–8, Fri. and eve of Jewish holidays 10–3* Ⓜ *4, 5 to Bowling Green.*

National Museum of the American Indian (Smithsonian Institution). Massive granite columns rise to a pediment topped by a double row of statues at the impressive Beaux-Arts Alexander Hamilton U.S. Custom House building (1907), which houses the New York branch of this Smithsonian museum (the other branch is in Washington DC). Inside,

DID YOU KNOW?

Liberty Enlightening the World, as the Statue of Liberty is officially named, was given by France to the United States in 1886 to mark the U.S. centennial.

the egg-shape stairwell and rotunda embellished with shipping-theme murals (completed in the 1930s) are also worth a pause. The permanent exhibit, "Infinity of Nations," is an encyclopedic survey of Native cultures from throughout the Americas, including 700 objects from ancient times to present day. The venue also presents changing exhibits, videos and films, dance, music, and storytelling programs. ✉ *1 Bowling Green, between State and Whitehall Sts., Financial District* ☎ *212/514–3700* 🌐 *www.nmai.si.edu* 🎟 *Free* ⏲ *Mon.–Wed. and Fri.–Sun. 10–5, Thurs. 10–8* Ⓜ *4, 5 to Bowling Green.*

FAMILY **New York City Police Museum.** Why are police called cops? Why does a police badge have eight points? When was fingerprinting first used to solve a crime? The answers to these questions and much more can be found at this museum dedicated to New York's Finest. The force's history from colonial times to the present is covered through the permanent "9/11 Remembered" installation—which includes a video featuring interviews with first responders to the attack—as well as rotating exhibits. The Hall of Heroes honors police officers who have fallen in the line of duty. The Junior Officers Discovery Zone, an interactive children's exhibit, includes a model of a mobile crime lab, a police car, fingerprint labs, and other tools used for investigations. Special events include a vintage police-car show the first weekend every June. At press time, the museum remained closed due to damage caused by Hurricane Sandy. Call ahead for re-opening dates and times. ✉ *100 Old Slip, near South St., Financial District* ☎ *212/480–3100* 🌐 *www.nycpolicemuseum.org* 🎟 *$8* ⏲ *Mon.–Sat. 10–5, Sun. noon–5* Ⓜ *2, 3 to Wall St.*

Skyscraper Museum. Why get a crick in your neck—or worse, risk looking like a tourist—while appreciating New York City's famous skyline, when you can visit the Skyscraper Museum instead? At this small museum that shares a building with the Ritz Carlton in Battery Park City, you can appreciate highly detailed hand-carved miniature wood models of midtown and downtown Manhattan; explore the past, present, and future of the skyscraper—from New York City's Empire State Building to Dubai's Burj Khalifa (taller than the Empire State Building and Chicago's Sears Tower combined); and examine both the history of the Twin Towers at the World Trade Center and the ongoing rebuilding at Ground Zero. Expect models of current or future buildings, videos, drawings, floor plans, talks, and exhibits that reveal the influence of history, real estate, and individuals on shaping city skylines. ✉ *39 Battery Pl., across from Museum of Jewish Heritage, Financial District* ☎ *212/968–1961* 🌐 *www.skyscraper.org* 🎟 *$5* ⏲ *Wed.–Sun. noon–6* Ⓜ *4, 5 to Bowling Green.*

St. Paul's Chapel. For more than a year after the World Trade Center attacks, the chapel's fence served as a shrine for visitors seeking solace. People from around the world left tokens of grief and support, or signed one of the large drop cloths that hung from the fence. After serving as a 24-hour refuge where rescue and recovery workers could eat, pray, rest, and receive counseling, the chapel, which amazingly suffered no damage, reopened to the public in fall 2002. The powerful ongoing exhibit, titled Unwavering Spirit: Hope & Healing at Ground Zero, honors the efforts of rescue workers in the months after September 11 with

On a typical weekday, five ferries make roughly 110 trips back and forth between Staten Island and Manhattan, transporting about 60,000 passengers.

photos, drawings, banners, and other items sent to them as memorials. Open since 1766, St. Paul's is the oldest public building in continuous use in Manhattan. ✉ *209 Broadway, at Fulton St., Financial District* ☎ *212/233–4164* 🌐 *www.saintpaulschapel.org* 🕓 *Weekdays 10–6, Sat. 10–4, Sun. 7 am–9 pm* Ⓜ *2, 3, 4, 5, A, C, J, Z to Fulton St.; E to Chambers St.; 6 to Brooklyn Bridge–City Hall.*

NEW YORK HARBOR

The southern tip of Manhattan has often served as a microcosm for a city that offers as many first shots as it does second chances, so it's appropriate that the key point of departure for the Statue of Liberty and Ellis Island is here. This experience should never be dismissed as too touristy. Like nothing else, the excursion will remind you that New York is a city of immigrants and survivors.

TOP ATTRACTIONS

Fodor's Choice ★ **Ellis Island.** *See highlighted feature at the end of Chapter 1.*

FAMILY Fodor's Choice ★ **Governors Island.** Governors Island is open to the public from May to October: get there via a short, free ferry ride. It's essentially a big, charming park that looks like a small New England town—it's popular with locals for biking and running trails, festivals, art shows, concerts, and family programs. Wouter Van Twiller, a representative for Holland, supposedly purchased the island for his private use, in 1637, from Native Americans for two ax heads, a string of beads, and a handful of nails. It was confiscated by the Dutch a year later, and for the next decade its ownership switched back and forth between the Dutch and British until the Brits gained firm control in the 1670s. The island was officially named in 1784 for His Majesty's Governors, and was used by the American military until the 1960s, when the Coast Guard took it over. After their facilities were abandoned in 1995, the island was purchased by the public in 2002 and started welcoming visitors in 2003. The ferry to the island departs from the Battery Maritime Building. ✉ *Battery Maritime Building, 10 South St., for ferry, New York Harbor* 🌐 *govisland.com* 🎫 *Free* 🕓 *June–Oct., Fri. 10–5; weekends 10–7* Ⓜ *1 to South Ferry; 4, 5 to Bowling Green; R to Whitehall St.*

Fodor's Choice ★ **Staten Island Ferry.** Every day, some 60,000 people ride the free ferry to Staten Island, one of the city's outer boroughs, and you should be one of them. Without paying a cent, you get phenomenal views of the Lower Manhattan skyline, the Statue of Liberty, and Ellis Island during the 25-minute boat ride across New York Harbor. You'll also pass tugboats, freighters, and cruise ships—a reminder that this is very much still a working harbor. The boat embarks every 15 to 30 minutes from the Whitehall Terminal at Whitehall and South streets, near the east end of Battery Park. You must disembark once you reach the opposite terminal, but you can just get back in line to board again if you don't plan to stay. ✉ *Battery Park* ☎ *212/639–9675* 🌐 *www.siferry.com* 🎫 *Free* Ⓜ *1 to South Ferry; R to Whitehall St.; 4, 5 to Bowling Green.*

Fodor's Choice ★ **Statue of Liberty.** *See highlighted feature at the end of Chapter 1.*

TRIBECA

Tucked on the west side, south of Canal Street, residential TriBeCa (the triangle below Canal Street) has a quieter vibe than most other Manhattan neighborhoods. Walk the photogenic streets, especially the stretch of Federal row houses on Harrison Street, and you'll understand why so many celebrities own apartments here. The two-block-long Staple Street, with its connecting overhead walkway, is a favorite of urban cinematographers. Although TriBeCa's money is often hidden behind grand cast-iron facades, you can get a taste of it at posh neighborhood restaurants and cocktail bars, or at the star-studded TriBeCa Film Festival in spring.

WORTH NOTING

FAMILY **Hudson River Park.** The quiet places of New York City are treasured by locals, and one of the best options is Hudson River Park, a 5-mile path from Battery Place to 59th Street. This riverside stretch has been renovated into a landscaped park, incorporating the piers that jut out into the Hudson, with walking and cycling paths, a seasonal mini golf course, dog runs, and skate parks. The TriBeCa portion consists of Piers 25 and 26 and offers picnic spaces, playgrounds, and a sand volleyball court. The area adjacent to the West Village (Piers 45 and 46) and near Chelsea (Piers 63 and 64) are equally attractive, with lots of green spaces. ✉ *TriBeCa* ☎ *212/627–2020* 🌐 *www.hudsonriverpark.org* Ⓜ *1 to Franklin St.*

SOHO, NOLITA, LITTLE ITALY, AND CHINATOWN

GETTING ORIENTED

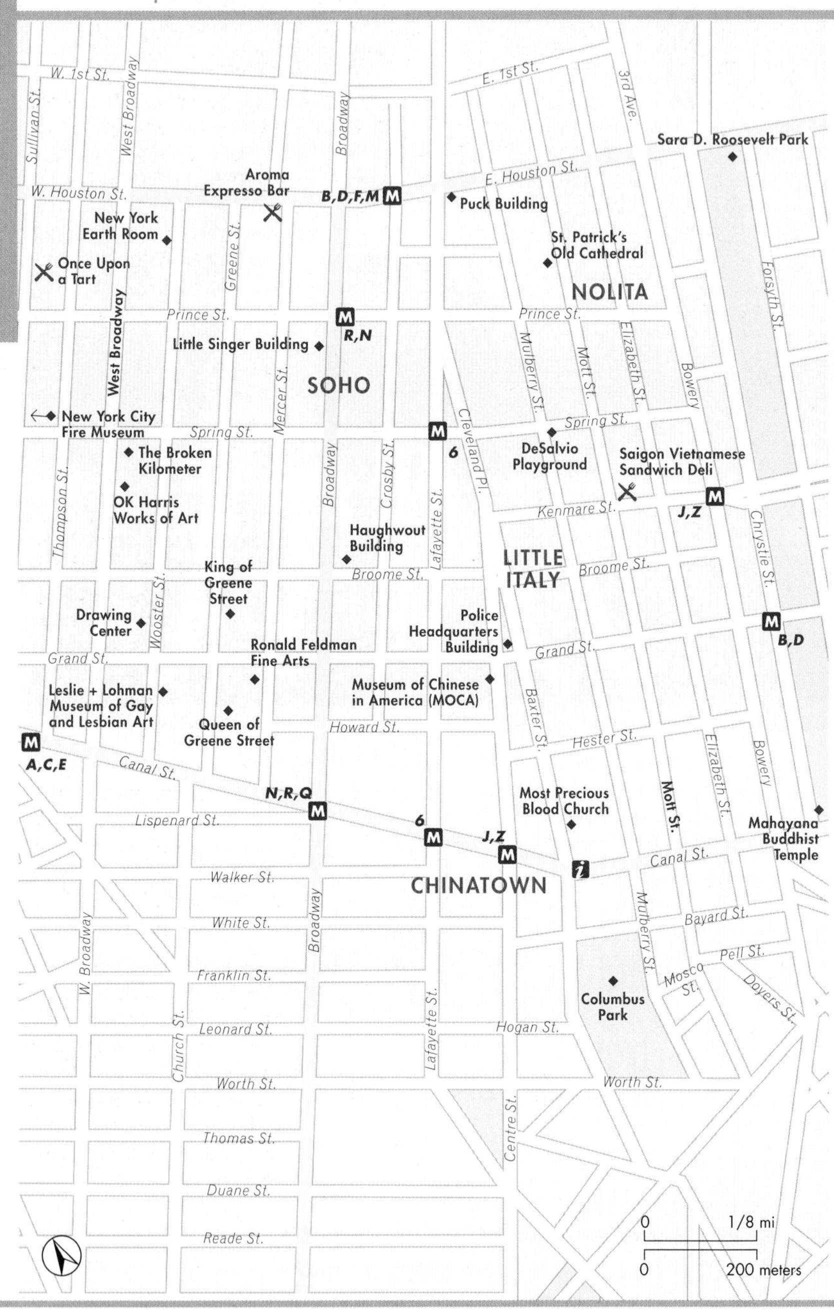
W. 1st St.
Sullivan St.
West Broadway
Broadway
E. 1st St.
3rd Ave.
Sara D. Roosevelt Park
W. Houston St.
Aroma Expresso Bar
B,D,F,M
E. Houston St.
Puck Building
New York Earth Room
Greene St.
St. Patrick's Old Cathedral
Once Upon a Tart
NOLITA
Forsyth St.
Prince St.
R,N
Little Singer Building
Mulberry St.
Mott St.
Elizabeth St.
Bowery
SOHO
Mercer St.
New York City Fire Museum
Spring St.
Cleveland Pl.
6
The Broken Kilometer
DeSalvio Playground
Saigon Vietnamese Sandwich Deli
Thompson St.
Crosby St.
Lafayette St.
OK Harris Works of Art
Kenmare St.
J,Z
Chrystie St.
Haughwout Building
LITTLE ITALY
King of Greene Street
Broome St.
Wooster St.
Drawing Center
Police Headquarters Building
B,D
Ronald Feldman Fine Arts
Grand St.
Leslie + Lohman Museum of Gay and Lesbian Art
Museum of Chinese in America (MOCA)
Baxter St.
Queen of Greene Street
Howard St.
Hester St.
A,C,E
Canal St.
N,R,Q
Most Precious Blood Church
Lispenard St.
Mahayana Buddhist Temple
Walker St.
CHINATOWN
White St.
Bayard St.
Pell St.
W. Broadway
Franklin St.
Mosco St.
Doyers St.
Columbus Park
Church St.
Leonard St.
Hogan St.
Worth St.
Thomas St.
Centre St.
Duane St.
Reade St.
0 1/8 mi
0 200 meters

MAKING THE MOST OF YOUR TIME

If you're coming to shop in SoHo and NoLIta, there's no need to rush out the door, because most shops don't open until 10 or 11 am; many stay open until early evening. If art is your thing, avoid Sunday, because most galleries are closed. SoHo, with national chains lining its section of Broadway, is almost always a madhouse (unless it's raining), but weekdays are somewhat less frenetic. NoLIta, with less traffic, fewer chains, and more boutiques, is calmer and less crowded.

Little Italy is a small area nowadays, having lost ground to a growing Chinatown. Note that food-wise, most of the checkered-tablecloth spots in Little Italy itself are touristy, with mediocre food.

If you're visiting New York in mid-September, you'll time it right for the San Gennaro festival—a huge street fair in honor of the patron saint of Naples—and you, along with thousands of others, can easily spend an entire day and night exploring the many food and souvenir booths and playing games of chance. Given that few Italian-Americans live in the area anymore, it's not exactly like visiting old Napoli, but it is a fun way to spend an hour or two.

Chinatown bustles with local shoppers pretty much any time of day, but there are more tourists on the weekends, when it gets so busy there isn't much room on the sidewalk.

TOP EXPERIENCES

Browsing boutiques and people-watching in SoHo and NoLIta.

Ogling the out-of-the-ordinary produce and seafood in Chinatown.

Gallery hopping in SoHo.

Eating dim sum in Chinatown.

A cocktail in NoLIta.

GETTING HERE AND AROUND

SoHo (South of Houston) is bounded by Houston Street, Canal Street, 6th Avenue, and Lafayette Street. To the east, NoLIta (North of Little Italy) is contained within Houston, the Bowery, Kenmare, and Lafayette. Plenty of subways service the area: take the 6, C, or E to Spring St.; the N or R to Prince St.; or the B, D, F, or M to Broadway–Lafayette St. For Chinatown, farther south, take the J, N, Q, R, Z, or 6 to Canal St. or the B or D to Grand St.

COFFEE AND QUICK BITES

Aroma Espresso Bar. Large corner windows make this spot perfect for people-watching. Sandwiches, salads, and excellent coffee are on the menu. ✉ *145 Greene St., at West Houston St., SoHo* ☎ *212/533–1094* 🌐 *www.aroma.us.*

Once Upon a Tart. A great name, with the goods to back it up, both sweet and savory. ✉ *135 Sullivan St., between West Houston and Prince Sts., SoHo* ☎ *212/387–8869* 🌐 *www.onceuponatart.com.*

Saigon Vietnamese Sandwich Deli. This storefront keeps the hungry gallery-hoppers, shoppers, and locals happy with its complicated and delicious sandwiches. ✉ *369 Broome St., between Mott and Elizabeth Sts., SoHo* ☎ *212/219–8341* 🌐 *www.vietnamese-sandwich.com.*

3

Sightseeing ★★★
Nightlife ★★★
Dining ★★★★
Lodging ★★★
Shopping ★★★★★

SoHo, NoLIta, Little Italy, and Chinatown all tend to be jam-packed with humanity, all the more perfect for people-watching as you shop and wander. Parts of SoHo and NoLIta are the destinations for super-trendy shopping as well as popular chains and department stores: the boutiques are often overpriced but it's undeniably glamorous. Little Italy and Chinatown are more about local shopping.

SOHO

Updated by John Rambow

SoHo was the epicenter of New York's art scene in the late 1970s, and has since evolved into a shopping destination of mostly chain retailers. (Where are the galleries? They've scattered, with Chelsea taking the lion's share of the more established names, and the East Village, Lower East Side, and several Brooklyn neighborhoods incubating many up-and-comers.) Compared with other neighborhoods, SoHo takes more work to find a local vibe, but a bit of bohemia still exists. It can be found on the cobblestone side streets where there are still a few galleries, as well as sidewalks jammed with tables full of handmade beaded jewelry, tooled leather belts, and hats and purses. There are also unique clothing boutiques, gourmet food shops, and even a few divey bars thrown into the mix.

WORTH NOTING

Drawing Center. At this nonprofit organization the focus is only on drawings—contemporary and historical. Works shown in the three galleries often push the envelope on what's considered drawing; many projects are commissioned especially by the center. ✉ *35 Wooster St., between Broome and Grand Sts., SoHo* ☎ *212/219–2166* 🌐 *www.drawingcenter.org* 🎫 *$5* 🕑 *Wed. and Fri.–Sun. noon–6, Thurs. noon–8* Ⓜ *N, Q, R, J, Z, 6, A, C, E to Canal St.*

Leslie + Lohman Museum of Gay and Lesbian Art. Founded in the late 1980s, this museum has roots in the collection of its founders, Charles

Leslie and Fritz Lohman. The well-curated exhibits are usually photographic, with much of it sexually charged or at least homoerotic. ✉ *26 Wooster St., between Grand and Canal Sts., SoHo* ☎ *212/431–2609* 🌐 *www.leslielohman.org* ⏲ *Tues.–Sun. noon–6* Ⓜ *A, C, E to Canal St.*

KIDS IN SOHO AND LITTLE ITALY

This is primarily a grown-up section of town, unless you're raising dedicated shoppers, but there are things for the kids to do here. Check out the Scholastic bookstore (✉ 557 Broadway). Steam can be blown off at Little Italy's DeSalvio Playground at the corner of Spring and Mulberry streets—it's nothing fancy, but the kids may enjoy clambering on the red, white, and green equipment.

New York City Fire Museum. In the former headquarters of Engine Company No. 30—a handsome Beaux-Arts building dating from 1904—retired firefighters volunteer their time in the morning and early afternoon to answer visitors' questions. The collection of firefighting tools from the 18th century to the present includes hand-pulled and horse-drawn engines, speaking trumpets, pumps, and uniforms. A memorial exhibit with photos, paintings, children's artwork, and found objects relating to the September 11 attacks is also on view—a poignant reminder and tribute to the 343 firefighters who died on 9/11. The museum is two subway stops (via the E train) north of the Ground Zero site. ✉ *278 Spring St., between Hudson and Varick Sts., SoHo* ☎ *212/691–1303* 🌐 *www.nycfiremuseum.org* 🎫 *$8* ⏲ *Daily 10–5* Ⓜ *C, E to Spring St.*

New York Earth Room. Noted "earthworks" artist Walter De Maria's 1977 avant-garde installation consists of 140 tons of gently sculpted soil (22 inches deep). It fills 3,600 square feet of a second-floor gallery maintained by the Dia Art Foundation since 1980. As *The New York Times* put it in 1999, "a loamy smell definitely permeates the space." You can't touch or walk on the dirt, nor can you take its photo. If you like this installation, check out De Maria's equally odd and impressive work called *The Broken Kilometer,* an 18.75-ton installation that consists of five columns of a total of 1,000 meter-long brass rods, which cover the wood floors of an open loft space. It's a few blocks away at 393 West Broadway, and has the same hours as the Earth Room. ✉ *141 Wooster St., 2nd fl., between W. Houston and Prince Sts., SoHo* ☎ *212/989–5566* 🌐 *www.earthroom.org* 🎫 *Free* ⏲ *Wed.–Sun. noon–6 (closed 3–3:30 and mid-June–mid-Sept.)* Ⓜ *R to Prince St.; B, D, F, M to Broadway–Lafayette St.*

SOHO WAS HELL

SoHo once had the less trendy moniker "Hell's Hundred Acres," so named because the crowded slums were repeatedly beset by frequent fires, but it boomed after the Civil War, when the neighborhood came to be known simply as the Eighth Ward and filled up with manufacturing and dry-goods stores.

OK Harris Works of Art. Since 1969, this contemporary fine-arts gallery has showed a wide range of painting, photography, and sculptures. The gallery is closed from mid-July

D&G
DOLCE & GABBANA
NYC

DID YOU KNOW?

Artists with their wares line West Broadway, south of Houston, most weekends.

CLOSE UP

SoHo and NoLIta Architecture

There are plenty of beautiful people in SoHo and NoLIta, but tilt your eyes up, beyond the turn-of-the-20th-century lampposts adorned with cast-iron curlicues, and you'll also find some of New York's most impressive architecture. SoHo has one of the world's greatest concentrations of cast-iron buildings, created in response to fires that wiped out much of Lower Manhattan in the mid-18th century. Look down and you'll see Belgian brick cobblestones lining some of the streets. Along Broadway and the neighboring streets of SoHo, you'll see lights in the sidewalk: starting in the 1850s, these vault lights were set into sidewalks to permit daylight to reach basements.

The **King of Greene Street,** at 72–76 Greene, between Grand and Canal, is a five-story Renaissance-style 1873 building with a magnificent projecting porch of Corinthian columns and pilasters. These days it's unmistakably painted in high-gloss ivory. Over at 28–30 Greene Street is the **Queen of Greene Street,** a graceful 1873 cast-iron beauty that exemplifies the Second Empire style with its dormers, columns, window arches, projecting central bays, and roof.

The **Haughwout Building,** at 488–492 Broadway, north of Broome, is best known for what's no longer inside—the world's first commercial passenger elevator, invented by Elisha Graves Otis. The building's exterior is worth a look, though: nicknamed the Parthenon of Cast Iron, the five-story, Venetian palazzo–style structure was built in 1857 to house department-store merchant E. V. Haughwout's china, silver, and glassware store. Each window is framed by Corinthian columns and rounded arches.

Built in 1904, the **Little Singer Building,** at 561 Broadway, is a masterpiece of cast-iron styling, its delicate facade covered with curlicues of wrought iron. The L-shape building's second facade is around the corner on Prince Street.

Charlton Street, not technically in SoHo but across 6th Avenue in the West Village, is Manhattan's longest stretch of Federal-style redbrick row houses from the 1820s and '30s. The high stoops, paneled front doors, leaded-glass windows, and narrow dormer windows are all intact. King and Vandam streets also have historic houses. Much of this was the site of a mansion called Richmond Hill, and, in the late 18th century the surrounding area was a beautiful wild meadow from where you could see the nearby "hamlet" of Greenwich Village.

Over in Little Italy/NoLIta, the magnificent old **Police Headquarters** building at 240 Centre Street, between Broome and Grand, might be familiar from Martin Scorsese's *Gangs of New York*. The 1909 Edwardian baroque structure with its striking copper dome was the headquarters of the New York City Police Department until 1973. Designed to "impress both the officer and the prisoner with the majesty of the law," it was converted into luxury condos in 1988 and is known today as the Police Building Apartments.

The 1885 Romanesque Revival **Puck Building,** at 295 Lafayette Street, on the southeast corner of Houston, is a former magazine headquarters and now a busy event space—look for the statue of Puck just over the door.

The stark, simple interior of OK Harris Works of Art illustrates the typical gallery space in SoHo.

through Labor Day. Its building was built in the 1860s for drying and storing tobacco. ✉ *383 W. Broadway, between Spring and Broome Sts., SoHo* ☎ *212/431–3600* 🌐 *www.okharris.com* ⏲ *Mid-Sept.–June, Tues.–Sat. 10–6; early to mid-July, Tues.–Fri. noon–5* Ⓜ *C, E to Spring St.*

Ronald Feldman Fine Arts. Founded in 1971 and in SoHo since the 1980s, this gallery represents more than 30 international contemporary artists; exhibits contemporary painting, sculpture, installations, drawings, and prints; and hosts performances. It has a large selection of Andy Warhol prints, paintings, and drawings. ✉ *31 Mercer St., between Grand and Canal Sts., SoHo* ☎ *212/226–3232* 🌐 *www.feldmangallery.com* ⏲ *Winter, Tues.–Sat. 10–6; summer, Mon.–Thurs. 10–6, Fri. 10–3* Ⓜ *N, Q, R, J, A, C, E, 6 to Canal St.*

NOLITA

NoLIta is a lot less frantic and crowded than either SoHo or Chinatown, and the upscale boutiques, indie shops, quirky cafés, small eateries, and other gentrifying influences here evoke, in some ways, the spirit of old SoHo. A great place to stop for a break or picnic is DeSalvio Playground at the corner of Spring and Mulberry streets, where kids play on red, white, and green equipment (in honor of the Italian flag) and people play chess on stone game tables.

WORTH NOTING

St. Patrick's Old Cathedral. If you've watched *The Godfather,* you've peeked inside New York's first Roman Catholic cathedral—the interior shots of the infamous baptism scene were filmed here. Dedicated in 1815, this church lost its designation as the seat of New York's bishop when the current St. Patrick's opened uptown, in 1879. The unadorned exterior of the cathedral gives no hint of the splendors within, which include an 1868 Henry Erben pipe organ. The interior dates from the 1860s, after a large fire gutted most of the original design. The enormous marble altar surrounded by hand-carved niches (reredos) houses an extraordinary collection of sacred statuary and other Gothic exuberance. There's a maze of mortuary vaults underneath the cathedral (older residents of Little Italy recall playing hide-and-seek in the vaults). Sunday Mass in English at 9:15 and 11:45. ✉ *263 Mulberry St., corner of Mott and Prince Sts., NoLIta* ☎ *212/226–8075* 🌐 *www.oldcathedral.org* 🕓 *Hrs vary, usually open daily 8–5* Ⓜ *R to Prince St.; 6 to Bleecker St.*

LITTLE ITALY

Just east of Broadway, you'll find the remains of what once was a thriving, lively community of Italian Americans: the tangle of streets that make up Little Italy. The few nostalgic blocks surrounding Mulberry Street between NoLIta and bustling Canal Street are still a cheerful salute to all things Italian, with red-green-and-white street decorations on permanent display and specialty grocers and cannelloni makers dishing up delights. It is all a bit touristy these days, and you should look elsewhere if you're looking for a great Italian restaurant meal. Still, Little Italy is fun to walk around, and several of the food stores on Grand Street are worth a stop if you're after an edible souvenir.

Every September, Mulberry Street becomes the giant Feast of San Gennaro, a crowded 11-day festival that sizzles with the smell of sausages and onions (don't miss John Fasullo's braciole, an iconic sandwich filled with fillet of pork roasted over a coal pit and topped with peppers and onions). This is by far the city's most extensive annual street fair.

If you're looking for a bigger and more bustling Little Italy, head up to Arthur Avenue in the Bronx (⇨ *Chapter 15*) and you'll find several good restaurants and a cornucopia of authentic Italian goods, all of them marketed to New Yorkers and tourists alike.

WORTH NOTING

Most Precious Blood Church. The National Shrine of San Gennaro, a replica of the grotto at Lourdes, is the high point of Most Precious Blood Church's richly painted interior. The church becomes a focal point during the annual San Gennaro festival. Sunday Mass is in English at 9 and noon ✉ *113 Baxter St., between Canal and Hester Sts., Little Italy* ☎ *212/226–6427* Ⓜ *N, Q, R, 6 to Canal St.; J, Z to Canal St.*

CHINATOWN

Chinatown is a living, breathing, anything-but-quiet ethnic enclave: a quarter of the city's nearly 700,000 Chinese residents live here. The neighborhood started as a seven-block area, but now covers some 40-plus blocks above and below Canal Street (encroaching on what was once a thriving Little Italy), with 200-plus restaurants serving every

Some of the storefronts and signage in Chinatown are bilingual—but some are just in Chinese.

imaginable regional Chinese cuisine crammed into about 2 square miles. Head to **Mott Street,** south of Canal, Chinatown's main thoroughfare, where the first Chinese immigrants (mostly men) settled in tenements in the late 1880s. Today, the street is dense with restaurants, hair salons and barbershops, massage parlors, bakeries, tea parlors, and souvenir shops, as well as Buddhist temples, herbalists, and acupuncturists. The few blocks above Canal overflow with food shops selling vegetables and fish (some still alive and squirming). Walk carefully, as the sidewalks can be slick from the ice underneath the eels, blue crabs, snapper, and shrimp that seem to look back at you as you pass by. If you plan it right, you can create a movable feast, starting with soup dumplings, a specialty from Shanghai, and continuing with Peking duck, a yellow custard cake, and a jasmine bubble tea, each at a different place. A city tourist-information kiosk on a traffic island where Canal, Baxter, and Walker streets meet can help you with tours, and also has a map that's very useful for unraveling the tangled streets in the area.

WORTH NOTING

Columbus Park. People-watching is the thing in this park. If you swing by in the morning, you'll see men and women practicing tai chi; the afternoons bring intense games of mah-jongg. In the mid-19th century the park was known as the Five Points—the point where Mulberry Street, Anthony (now Worth) Street, Cross (now Park) Street, Orange (now Baxter) Street, and Little Water Street (no longer in existence) intersected—and was notoriously ruled by dangerous Irish gangs. In the 1880s a neighborhood-improvement campaign brought about the park's creation. ✉ *Chinatown* 🌐 *www.nycgovparks.org/parks/M015* Ⓜ *4, 6 J, N, Q, Z to Canal St.*

Kimlau Square. Ten streets converge at this labyrinthine intersection criss-crossed at odd angles by pedestrian walkways. Standing on an island in this busy area is the **Kimlau Arch,** named for Ralph Kimlau, a bomber pilot who died in World War II; the arch is dedicated to all Chinese-Americans who "lost their Lives in Defense of Freedom and Democracy." A statue on the square's eastern edge pays tribute to a Qing Dynasty official named Lin Ze Xu, the Fujianese minister who sparked the Opium War by banning the drug. ✉ *Chatham Square, Bowery and E. Broadway, Chinatown* 🌐 *www.nycgovparks.org/parks/kimlausquare* Ⓜ *4, 5, 6 to Brooklyn Bridge–City Hall; J, Z to Chambers St.*

Mahayana Buddhist Temple. This pleasant and bright Buddhist temple is at a very busy corner, at the foot of the Manhattan Bridge Arch on the Bowery. There's an excellent gift shop on the second floor. Before its reincarnation as a place of worship in 1997, this was the Rosemary, a theater showing a mix of kung fu and porn movies. ✉ *133 Canal St., at the Bowery, Chinatown* ☎ *212/925–8787* 🌐 *en.mahayana.us* 🎫 *Donations accepted* 🕒 *Daily 8–6* Ⓜ *B, D to Grand St.*

Museum of Chinese in America (MOCA). Founded in 1980, this museum is dedicated to preserving and presenting the history of the Chinese people and their descendants in the United States. Its current building, which opened in 2009 near the boundary between Chinatown and Little Italy (technically, many would say, it's in Little Italy), was designed by Maya Lin, architect of the Vietnam Veterans Memorial in Washington, DC. MOCA's permanent exhibit on Chinese-American history, titled With a Single Step: Stories in the Making of America, includes artwork, personal and domestic artifacts, historical documentation, and films. Chinese laundry tools, a traditional general store, and antique business signs are some of the unique objects on display. Rotating shows, some of which examine the sometimes turbulent relations between Asian Americans and the rest of the country, are on display in the second gallery. MOCA sponsors workshops, walking tours, lectures, and family events. ✉ *215 Centre St., between Grand and Howard Sts., Chinatown* ☎ *212/619–4785* 🌐 *www.mocanyc.org* 🎫 *$10* 🕒 *Tues., Wed., and Fri.–Sun., 11–6; Thurs. 11–9* Ⓜ *6, J, M, N, Q, R, Z to Canal St.*

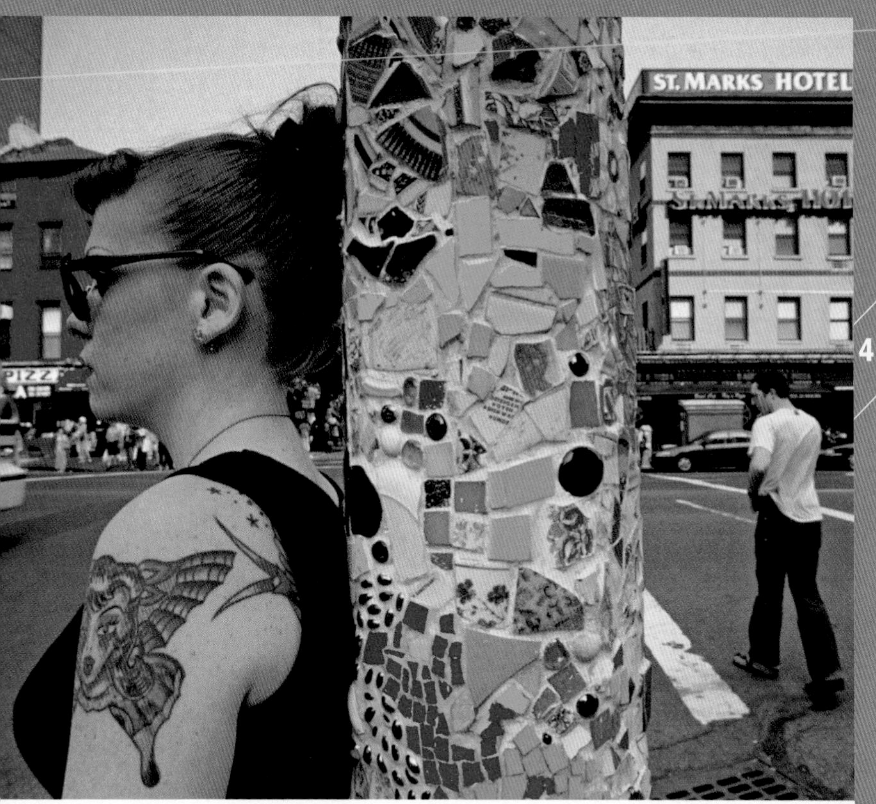

4

THE EAST VILLAGE AND THE LOWER EAST SIDE

GETTING ORIENTED

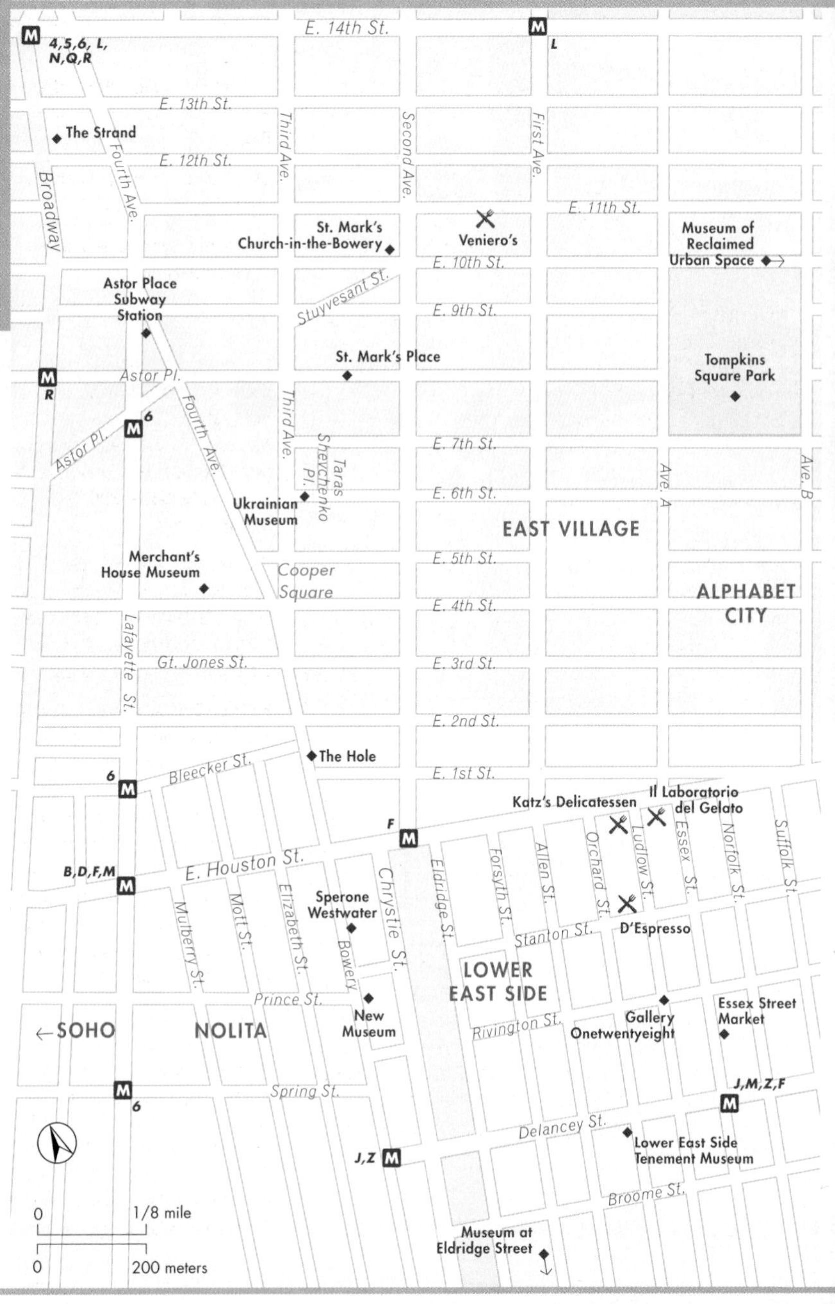
E. 14th St.
4,5,6, L, N,Q,R
L
E. 13th St.
The Strand
Fourth Ave.
E. 12th St.
Third Ave.
Second Ave.
First Ave.
Broadway
E. 11th St.
St. Mark's Church-in-the-Bowery
Veniero's
Museum of Reclaimed Urban Space
E. 10th St.
Astor Place Subway Station
Stuyvesant St.
E. 9th St.
St. Mark's Place
Tompkins Square Park
R
Astor Pl.
6
Fourth Ave.
Third Ave.
Astor Pl.
Taras Shevchenko Pl.
E. 7th St.
Ave. A
Ave. B
E. 6th St.
Ukrainian Museum
EAST VILLAGE
Merchant's House Museum
E. 5th St.
Cooper Square
E. 4th St.
ALPHABET CITY
Lafayette St.
Gt. Jones St.
E. 3rd St.
E. 2nd St.
The Hole
Bleecker St.
6
E. 1st St.
Katz's Delicatessen
Il Laboratorio del Gelato
F
E. Houston St.
B,D,F,M
Sperone Westwater
Chrystie St.
Eldridge St.
Forsyth St.
Allen St.
Orchard St.
Ludlow St.
Essex St.
Norfolk St.
Suffolk St.
Mulberry St.
Mott St.
Elizabeth St.
Bowery
Stanton St.
D'Espresso
LOWER EAST SIDE
Prince St.
New Museum
Rivington St.
Gallery Onetwentyeight
Essex Street Market
←SOHO
NOLITA
Spring St.
J,M,Z,F
6
Delancey St.
Lower East Side Tenement Museum
J,Z
Broome St.
0
1/8 mile
0
200 meters
Museum at Eldridge Street

MAKING THE MOST OF YOUR TIME

Houston Street runs east–west and neatly divides the East Village (north of Houston) and the Lower East Side (south of Houston). The eastern boundary of the East Village and Lower East Side is the East River; the western boundary is 4th Avenue and the Bowery. So many communities converge in these neighborhoods that each block seems like a new neighborhood unto itself.

The East Village lets loose on weekend nights, when nightlife seekers converge on the area, filling up the bars and spilling out onto the sidewalks. Weekday evenings are less frenetic, with more of a local vibe—although the term "local" around here always means a large number of students from New York University. Daytime is great for shopping in the local boutiques, and brunch on weekends around here generally can mean lines for hot spots like Prune and Back Forty, which fill with patrons lingering over coffee.

The Lower East Side does not tend to be an early-riser destination any day of the week. Although there's plenty to see during the day, nightfall offers a different vision: blocks that were previously empty rows of pulled-down gratings transform into clusters of throbbing bars. On the trendy streets around Rivington and Stanton, stores, bars, and cafés buzz all week.

GETTING HERE AND AROUND

For the East Village, take the N/R subway line to 8th Street, the 6 to Astor Place, or the L to 3rd Avenue. To reach Alphabet City, take the L to 1st Avenue or the F to 2nd Avenue. For the Lower East Side, head southeast from the 2nd Avenue stop on the F, or take the F/M/J/Z to the Delancey Street–Essex Street stop.

TOP EXPERIENCES

People-watching on St. Marks Place or at Tompkins Square Park.

Shopping at boutiques and vintage clothing stores.

Visiting the Lower East Side Tenement Museum.

COFFEE AND QUICK BITES

D'espresso. Italian coffee, sandwiches, and sweets are the draw at this tiny spot. ✉ *100 Stanton St., between Ludlow and Orchard Sts., Lower East Side* ☎ *212/982–7300* 🌐 *www.despresso.com.*

Il Laboratorio del Gelato. Seasonal flavors make this gelato la crème de la crème. ✉ *188 Ludlow St., at E. Houston St., Lower East Side* ☎ *212/343–9922.*

Katz's Delicatessen. Given Katz's location and its equally lost-in-time vibe, this deli goes as well with visits to the Tenement Museum as a Cel-Ray soda goes with pastrami (ask for a sample). Just don't lose your ticket. ✉ *205 E. Houston St., at Ludlow St., Lower East Side* ☎ *212/254–2246* 🌐 *www.katzsdelicatessen.com.*

Veniero's Pastry. This Italian bakery has been turning out cookies, coffee, and elaborate cakes and tarts since 1894—and the late hours it keeps only sweetens the deal. ✉ *342 E. 11th St., between 1st and 2nd Aves., East Village* ☎ *212/674–7070* 🌐 *www.venierospastry.com.*

Sightseeing ★★
Nightlife ★★★★★
Dining ★★★★★
Lodging ★★
Shopping ★★★★

American punk was born in the East Village, at the now-defunct CBGB, and the punk-rock and indie scene is kept alive at the many small music venues here and on the Lower East Side, as well as in Brooklyn. Both neighborhoods are tamer than they once were—as the arrival of Whole Foods and several glass-and-chrome condos attests—but there's definitely still a gritty edge. Spend some time wandering these bohemian side streets, and you'll be struck by the funky pastiche of ethnicities whose imprints are visible in the neighborhood's restaurants, shops, and, of course, people.

EAST VILLAGE

Updated by John Rambow

The concept of "La Bohème meets hipsters in vintage clothing," better known as the musical *Rent*, pegged the East Village as a community of artists, activists, and other social dissenters—and this is still the essential vibe here, although the neighborhood has become more upscale in recent years. These days, for example, St. Marks Place evokes less of the gritty, counterculture scene it once had in favor of a pastiche of students, well-earning postgrads, and Japanese expats.

East of 1st Avenue is Alphabet City, once the city's seedy drug haunt but now an ever more gentrified neighborhood. There is still a young, artistic vibe in and around Tompkins Square Park.

TOP ATTRACTIONS

Alphabet City. The north–south avenues east of 1st Avenue, from Houston Street to 14th Street, are all labeled with letters, not numbers, which gives this area its nickname. Avenues A, B, and C are full of restaurants, cafés, stores, and bars that run from the low-rent and scruffy to the rarified and genteel—the streets are more mixed than in other neighborhoods downtown. Parts of Avenues A and B run along Tompkins

CLOSE UP

Keep Your Eyes Peeled

The East Village's reputation for quirkiness is evidenced not only by its residents and sites but also in the many incongruous structures that somehow coexist so easily that they can go almost unnoticed. Keep your eyes open as you explore the streets. You never know what might turn up: the Hells Angels' Headquarters tucked into a residential block of 3rd Street between 1st and 2nd avenues, surrounded by a bevy of show-stopping bikes. The architectural "joke" on New York City atop the Red Square building on Houston Street at Norfolk, where a statue of Lenin points to the sky and a clock has lost its notion of time. The shingled Cape Cod–style house perched on the apartment building at the northwest corner of Houston and 1st Avenue, one of the city's many unique rooftop retreats. It's best viewed from the east. Two privately owned, nearly hidden but airy "marble" cemeteries (New York Marble Cemetery and the New York City Marble Cemetery) established in the 1830s on 2nd Avenue between 2nd and 3rd streets hold the remains of thousands in underground, marble-lined vaults thought to prevent the spread of disease in a time marked by cholera epidemics. The gardens are surrounded by 12-foot walls made of Tuckahoe marble, and are entered through wrought-iron gates. Although rarely open to the public they can be visited by appointment.

Square park. A close-knit Puerto Rican community makes its home around Avenue C, also called Loisaida Avenue (a Spanglish creation meaning "Lower East Side"). Although it's still filled with many Latino shops and bodegas, it's also now home to some trendy restaurants and bars. Avenue D remains rough around the edges—in part because of the uninterrupted row of projects that are on its east side. The East River Park, farther east, provides some nice views of Williamsburg and other parts of Brooklyn. To reach the park, cross Avenue D and take one of the pedestrian bridges that crosses the FDR Drive at East 10th or East 5th streets, or cross the road at East Houston Street. ✉ *East Village* Ⓜ 6 *to Astor Pl.; L to 1st Ave.; F to 2nd Ave.*

St. Marks Place. The longtime hub of the edgy East Village, St. Marks Place is the name given to idiosyncratic East 8th Street between 3rd Avenue and Avenue A. During the 1950s, beatniks Allen Ginsberg and Jack Kerouac lived and wrote in the area. The 1960s brought Bill Graham's Fillmore East (nearby, at 105 2nd Ave.), and Andy Warhol's Dom and the Electric Circus nightclub (both at Nos. 19–25 St. Marks), where the Velvet Underground performed. The studded, pink-haired, and shaved-head punk scene followed, and there's a good chance you'll still see some pierced rockers and teenage Goths on the block. Trash & Vaudeville, the punk store at No. 4, is the real deal—it's been open since 1971. Farther down, at No. 33, is where the punk store Manic Panic first foisted its lurid hair dyes and make-up on the world. And at No. 57 stood the short-lived Club 57, a church basement that attracted such 80s stalwarts as Keith Haring, Ann Magnuson, Klaus Nomi, Kenny Scharf, and Fab Five Freddy.

These days, there's not much cutting edge left. Some of the grungy facades lead to luxury condos, and the area has become a Little Japan, with several ramen and dumpling shops, some sake bars, and lots of young Japanese students. The blocks between 2nd and 3rd avenues can feel like a shopping arcade, crammed with body-piercing and tattoo salons, and shops selling cheap jewelry, sunglasses, incense, and out-there sloganed T-shirts. The cafés and bars along here and over to Avenue A attract customers late into the night. ✉ *8th St. between 3rd Ave. and Ave. A, East Village* Ⓜ *6 to Astor Pl.*

FAMILY **Tompkins Square Park.** This leafy park fills up with locals year-round, partaking in picnics and drum circles, and making use of the playground and the dog run. Free Wi-Fi (strongest on the north side of the park) joins the shade, benches, and an elegant 1891 water fountain (donated by a teetotaling benefactor) as some of the best amenities here. There are movie screenings and music gatherings throughout the summer, a year-round farmers market on Sunday, and an annual Halloween dog-costume event. But it wasn't always so rosy in the park: in 1988 police followed then-mayor David Dinkins's orders to clear the many homeless who had set up makeshift homes here, and homeless rights and anti-gentrification activists fought back with sticks and bottles. The park was reclaimed and reopened in 1992 with a midnight curfew, still in effect today. ✉ *Bordered by Aves. A and B and E. 7th and E. 10th Sts., East Village* 🌐 *www.nycgovparks.org/parks/tompkinssquarepark* Ⓜ *6 to Astor Pl.; L to 1st Ave.*

WORTH NOTING

Astor Place Subway Station. At the beginning of the 20th century almost all of the city's Interborough Rapid Transit (IRT) subway entrances resembled the one here—an ornate cast-iron replica of a Beaux-Arts kiosk marking the subway entrance for the uptown No. 6 train. This traffic-island entrance, which was—and still is—the stop to get to the venerable Cooper Union college, is now on the National Register of Historic Places. Inside, plaques of beaver emblems line the tiled station walls, a reference to the fur trade that contributed to John Jacob Astor's fortune. Milton Glaser, the Cooper Union graduate who originated the "I [heart] NY" logo, designed the station's murals. ✉ *On traffic island at E. 8th St. and 4th Ave., East Village* Ⓜ *6 to Astor Pl.*

The Hole. Run by Kathy Grayson, the former director of the highly influential Deitch Projects, this contemporary-arts gallery generally hosts two simultaneous shows a month. Its artists lean more toward the up-and-coming rather than the establishment. The on-site Hole Shop carries lots of weird zines, posters, books, and art objects. ✉ *312 Bowery, between Bleecker and E. Houston Sts., East Village* ☎ *212/466–1100* 🌐 *www.theholenyc.com* 🕒 *Tues.–Sat. noon–7.*

Merchant's House Museum. Built in 1832, this redbrick house, combining Federal and Greek Revival styles, provides a glimpse into the domestic life of the period 30 years before the Civil War. Retired merchant Seabury Tredwell and his descendants lived here from 1835 until 1933. The home became a museum in 1936, with the original furnishings and architectural features preserved; family memorabilia are also on display. The fourth-floor servants' bedroom, where the Tredwell family's Irish servants slept and did some of their work, offers a rare and intimate look at the lives of Irish domestics in the mid-1800s. A guided tour is offered at 2pm. ✉ *29 E. 4th St., between Bowery and Lafayette St., East Village* ☎ *212/777–1089* 🌐 *www.merchantshouse.org* 🎟 *$10* 🕐 *Thurs.–Mon. noon–5; guided tours Thurs.–Mon. at 2* Ⓜ *6 to Astor Pl. or Bleecker St.; B, D, F, M to Broadway–Lafayette St.; R to 8th St.*

Museum of Reclaimed Urban Space. Opened in late 2012, this self-described "living archive of urban activism" covers the vexatious postwar period in New York, during which the city's public housing was often woefully mismanaged and hundreds of apartments lay abandoned and crumbling. Zines, photographs, and videos fill the small exhibit space inside a tenement's storefront and its basement. Squatters, community gardens, the Tompkins Square riots, and the renaissance of bicycling in the city are all given their due, as is Occupy Wall Street. Tours of community gardens, activist landmarks, and other squats, both legal and otherwise, are also run by the museum. ✉ *C-Squat, 155 Ave. C, between E. 9th and E. 10th Sts., East Village* ☎ *973/818–8495* 🌐 *www.morusnyc.org* 🎟 *$5 suggested donation; tours $20* 🕐 *Thurs.–Sun. and Tues. 11–7.*

4

St. Mark's Church in-the-Bowery. This charming 1799 fieldstone country church, which is Episcopalian, stands on what was once Governor Peter Stuyvesant's *bouwerie,* or farm. It's Manhattan's second-oldest church, and both Stuyvesant and Commodore Perry are buried in vaults here. Check out the gorgeous modern stained-glass windows on the balcony, which replaced the more traditional windows (like those on the ground level) after a fire in the late '70s. Over the years St. Mark's has hosted many avant-garde arts events, including readings by poet Carl Sandburg and dance performances by Martha Graham and Merce Cunningham. The tradition has continued with Danspace, the Poetry Project, and the Incubator Arts Project, which give performances throughout the year. Services are held Sunday at 11. ✉ *131 E. 10th St., at 2nd Ave., East Village* ☎ *212/674–6377* 🌐 *www.stmarksbowery.org* Ⓜ *6 to Astor Pl.; L to 3rd Ave.*

Stuyvesant Street. This diagonal slicing through the block bounded by 2nd and 3rd avenues and East 9th and 10th streets is unique in Manhattan: it's the oldest street laid out precisely along an east–west axis. Among the handsome 19th-century redbrick row houses are the Federal-style **Stuyvesant-Fish House** at No. 21, built as a wedding gift for a great-great-granddaughter of the Dutch governor Peter Stuyvesant, and **Renwick Triangle,** an attractive group of Anglo-Italianate brick and brownstone residences, that face Stuyvesant and East 10th streets. Ⓜ *6 to Astor Pl.*

Ukrainian Museum. From the late nineteenth century through the end of World War II, tens of thousands of Ukrainians made their way to New York City—and particulaly to "Little Ukraine," as much of the East Village was known. This museum, which opened in 2005, examines Ukrainian Americans' dual heritage, with a permanent collection made up of folk art, fine art, and documentary materials about the immigrants' lives. Ceramics, jewelry, hundreds of brilliantly colored

Easter eggs, and an extensive collection of Ukrainian costumes and textiles are the highlights. If you're feeling like a little Ukrainian food to continue the experience, the nearby Veselka diner awaits. ✉ *222 E. 6th St., between 2nd and 3rd Aves., East Village* ☎ *212/228–0110* 🌐 *www.ukrainianmuseum.org* 🎟 *$8* 🕓 *Wed.–Sun. 11:30–5* Ⓜ *6 to Astor Pl.*

LOWER EAST SIDE

Often referred to simply as LES, the Lower East Side was the historic "Gateway to America," after waves of Irish, German, Jewish, Hispanic, and Chinese immigrants pulled up stakes and moved to New York in search of a better life. Today, a cool arts and nightlife scene, several distinctively modern high-rises, and the ultracontemporary New Museum exist alongside buildings and cultural centers staunchly rooted in the past.

On Saturday night, the scene can be as raucous as in a college town, especially on Rivington and Orchard streets, but Ludlow Street, one block east of Orchard, has become the main drag for twentysomethings with attitude, its boutiques wedged in between bars and low-key restaurants.

The best time to experience the neighborhood's past is by day. The excellent Lower East Side Tenement Museum movingly captures the immigrant legacy of tough times and survival instincts. You might not find many pickles being sold from barrels anymore, but this remains a good place to nosh on typical Jewish food from Katz's Delicatessen or Russ & Daughters.

TOP ATTRACTIONS

Gallery Onetwentyeight. Inside this narrow space, artist Kazuko Miyamoto directs crisp and provocative group shows. The art space celebrated its 25th anniversary in 2012. ✉ *128 Rivington St., between Essex and Norfolk Sts., Lower East Side* ☎ *212/674–0244* 🌐 *www.galleryonetwentyeight.org* Ⓜ *F to Delancey St.; J, M, Z to Essex St.*

FAMILY Fodor's Choice ★ **Lower East Side Tenement Museum.** Step back in time and into the partially restored 1863 tenement building at 97 Orchard Street, where you can squeeze through the preserved apartments of immigrants, learn about the struggles of past generations, and gain historical perspective on the still contentious topic of immigration. This is America's first urban living-history museum dedicated to the life of immigrants. The museum itself is only accessible by guided tour, each offered at various times each day and limited to 15 people, so it's a good idea to buy tickets in advance. The building tour called "Hard Times" visits the homes of Natalie Gumpertz, a German-Jewish dressmaker (dating from 1878), and Adolph and Rosaria Baldizzi, Catholic immigrants from Sicily (1935). "Sweatshop Workers" visits the Levines' garment shop–apartment and the home of the Rogarshevsky family from Eastern Europe (1918). "Irish Outsiders" explores the life of the Moores, an Irish American family living in the building in 1869, and shows a re-created tenement backyard. "Shop Life," which opened in 2012, looks at the various businesses run on the street level here, including a

German-style bar, a kosher butcher, an auctioneer, and, in the 1970s, a discount underwear store. A two-hour extended experience tour with a chance for in-depth discussion is offered every day. Walking tours of the neighborhood are also held daily. Note that most tours don't allow kids under 5. ✉ *103 Orchard St., at Delancey St., Lower East Side* ☎ *212/982–8420* 🌐 *www.tenement.org* *$22–$25 for a building tour* ⏲ *Daily 10–6, last tour leaves at 5* Ⓜ *B, D to Grand St.; F to Delancey St.; J, M, Z to Essex St.*

WORTH NOTING

Essex Street Market. Started in 1940 as an attempt by Mayor Fiorello LaGuardia to establish a place for street pushcarts and vendors (and thereby get them off the streets), the Essex Street Market was defined early on by the Jewish and Italian immigrants of the Lower East Side. After being run cooperatively by the merchants for years, the market was taken over by a private developer in 1992. Then in 1995, the New York City Economic Development Corporation assumed control and began a $1.5 million renovation and consolidation of the space. These days the market is reinvigorated and filled with small grocery stores, coffee shops, sellers of meat, fish, and gourmet cheeses, and even a barber and a botanica. Standouts include Saxelby Cheesemongers and local favorite Shopsins, an eccentric and strangely appealing restaurant that moved in here in 2007 after decades in the West Village. ✉ *120 Essex St., between Rivington and Delancey Sts., Lower East Side* ☎ *212/388–0449* 🌐 *www.essexstreetmarket.com* ⏲ *Mon.–Sat. 8–7, Sun. 10–6; vendors' hrs vary* Ⓜ *F, V to Delancey St.; J, M, Z to Essex St.*

Museum at Eldridge Street. The exterior of this Orthodox synagogue, the first to be built by the many Eastern European Jews who settled in the Lower East Side in the late 19th century, is a striking mix of Romanesque, Gothic, and Moorish motifs. Inside is an exceptional hand-carved ark of mahogany and walnut, a sculptured wooden balcony, jewel-tone stained-glass windows, vibrantly painted and stenciled walls, and an enormous brass chandelier. The synagogue can be viewed as part of an hour-long tour, which begins at the small museum downstairs where interactive "touch tables" teach all ages about Eldridge Street and the Lower East Side. The crowning piece of the synagogue's decades-long restoration is a stained-glass window by artist Kiki Smith and architect Deborah Gans. Installed in 2010 to replace 1940s glass brick, the window weighs 6,000 pounds and has more than 1,200 pieces of glass. ✉ *12 Eldridge St., between Canal and Division Sts., Lower East Side* ☎ *212/219–0302* 🌐 *www.eldridgestreet.org* *$10* ⏲ *Sun.–Thurs. 10–5; Fri. 10–3; tours on the hr* Ⓜ *F to E. Broadway; B, D to Grand St.; N, R to Canal St.*

New Museum. This seven-story, 60,000-square-foot structure—a glimmering metal mesh-clad assemblage of off-centered squares—caused some neighborhood uproar when it was built in 2007, with some residents slow to accept the nontraditional building. Not surprisingly, given the museum's name and the building, shows are all about contemporary art: previous exhibitions have included the popular Carsten Höller: Experience, with a slide connecting the fourth and second floors, and a sensory deprivation tank, among other things. Studio 231, the museum's adjacent, ground-floor space at 231 Bowery, gives emerging artists the opportunity to create work outside the confines of the main museum building in a studiolike space. If you're visiting on the weekend, check out the seventh-floor "sky room" and its panoramic view of Lower Manhattan. From 10 to noon on the first Saturday of every month, the museum runs free family-oriented programs and events. And Thursday's free night always brings a fun-loving, hipster-heavy crowd out of the woodwork. ✉ *235 Bowery, at Prince St., Lower East Side* ☎ *212/219–1222* 🌐 *www.newmuseum.org* 🎫 *$14; free Thurs. 7–9* 🕓 *Wed. and Fri.–Sun. 11–6, Thurs. 11–9* Ⓜ *6 to Spring St.; F, M to 2nd Ave.*

Sperone Westwater. Founded in 1975 in SoHo, and after spending nearly a decade in Chelsea, Sperone Westwater now finds itself a major part of the artification of the Lower East Side. In 2010, the gallery moved into this nine-story building, which it commisioned for itself, a vote of confidence in both its Bowery surroundings and the continued importance of its artists, which have included Bruce Nauman, William Wegman, Gerhard Richter, and a host of blue-chip minimalists. The narrow building, designed by Norman Foster, rivals the New Museum (a few doors down) for crisp poise: in 2011 New York's Municipal Art Society deemed it the best new building of the year. Its Big Red Box, essentially a huge room-like freight elevator, is a major contributor to the building's good looks. ✉ *257 Bowery, between E. Houston and Stanton Sts., Lower East Side* ☎ *212/999–7337* 🌐 *www.speronewestwater.com.*

5

GREENWICH VILLAGE AND THE WEST VILLAGE

GETTING ORIENTED

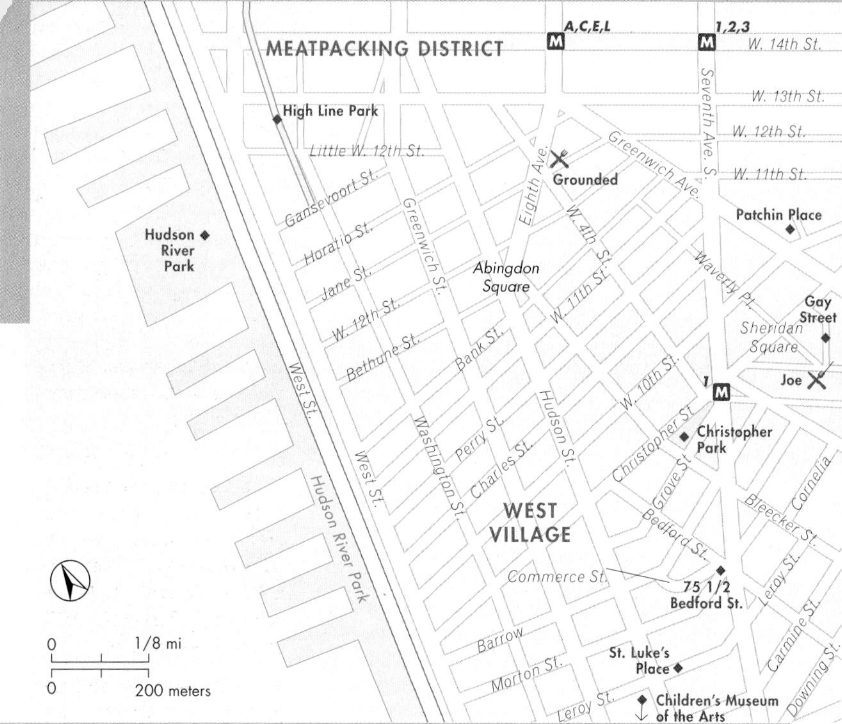

TOP EXPERIENCES	MAKING THE MOST OF YOUR TIME
People-watching in Washington Square Park. Strolling and window-shopping along the pretty streets of the West Village. Relaxing in one of the many cafés. Walking along Hudson River Park by the water. Eating your way along Bleecker Street.	Greenwich Village proper—around New York University and Washington Square Park—is busy any time of day with locals (especially students) and visitors. A visit to Washington Square Park is a must for people-watching and relaxing on a bench. There are lots of restaurants and shops in the neighborhood, though they do tend to be touristy. The West Village—basically from 7th Avenue to the Hudson River—is more residential, and tends to be pretty quiet, which makes it pleasant for strolling the carefully tended and tree-lined streets. Upscale boutiques line Bleecker Street and Greenwich Avenue (note that there is also a Greenwich Street in this neighborhood, to confuse things). The windy streets of the West Village often seem mazelike, even to locals, because most of the streets here are named rather than numbered and they're not organized on a grid system. Assume that you're going to get a little bit lost, but don't hesitate to ask for directions.

GETTING HERE AND AROUND

The West 4th Street subway stop—serviced by the A, B, C, D, E, F, and M—puts you in the center of Greenwich Village. Farther west, the 1 train has stops at West Houston Street and at Christopher Street–Sheridan Square. The A, C, E, and L trains stop at 14th Street, which is the northern boundary of the West Village.

BEST FOR KIDS

Hudson River Park

Washington Square Park

Taking time out for pizza or dessert

COFFEE AND QUICK BITES

Coffee options abound in this part of town; these are some of our favorites.

Caffe Reggio. Usually packed, this gently lit café dates back to the 1920s, making it one of the oldest coffeehouses in the city. ✉ *119 MacDougal St., between W. 3rd and Carmine Sts., Greenwich Village* ☎ *212/475-9557* 🌐 *www.cafereggio.com.*

Grounded. At this welcoming café, the usual lattes are joined by equally strong (and free) Wi-Fi. The pastries and the people-watching are a cut above. ✉ *28 Jane St., between 8th and Greenwich Aves., West Village* ☎ *212/647-0943* 🌐 *www.groundedcoffee.com.*

Joe. The coffee is exquisitely sourced and prepared at this small café, the first of what is now a small chain. The *caffè macchiato* has a buzz that will last for hours. ✉ *141 Waverly Pl., at Gay St., Greenwich Village* 🌐 *www.joenewyork.com.*

Sightseeing
★★★
Nightlife
★★★★
Dining
★★★★★
Lodging
★★★
Shopping
★★★★

Long the home of writers, artists, bohemians, and bon vivants, the Village—subdivided here into Greenwich Village proper, surrounding Washington Square Park; and the West Village, between 7th Avenue and the Hudson River—is a magical section of the city. Greenwich Village, set as it is in prime New York University territory, has lots of young people, while the West Village is primarily residential, with lots of well-to-do couples and families and a large (though slowly dwindling) community of older gay men and some lesbians. Both areas also have many restaurants, cafés, and boutiques with a warm and charming neighborhood vibe.

GREENWICH VILLAGE

Updated by John Rambow

Fertile doesn't even begin to describe Greenwich Village's yield of creative genius. In the late 1940s and early 1950s, abstract expressionist painters Franz Kline, Jackson Pollock, Mark Rothko, and Willem de Kooning congregated here, as did Beat writers Jack Kerouac, Allen Ginsberg, and Lawrence Ferlinghetti. The 1960s brought folk musicians and poets, notably Bob Dylan and Joan Baez. Its bohemian days may be long gone, but there is still a romantic allure lingering along tree-lined streets and at the back of the cafés, behind the frenetic clamor of NYU students and the professional veneer of multimillion-dollar town houses.

One of the neighborhood's top sites is Washington Square Park, where you can find just about every sort of person imaginable lounging on a summer day, from skateboarders and students to local moms and nannies to people who look like they've lived in the park for years, playing chess and checkers at the stone tables. The grand Washington Memorial

DID YOU KNOW?

Greenwich Village has a long bohemian history: for years it was an enclave of counterculture, from beatniks to the antiwar movement to gay rights. Today this neighborhood is better known for its celebrity residents and sky-high housing costs.

CLOSE UP

Halloween in the Village

All things weird and wonderful, all creatures great and small, all things witty and fantastical, New York City has them all—and on All Hallows' Eve they freak through the streets in New York's Halloween parade. White-sheeted ghouls feel dull compared with fishnets and leather, sequins and feathers posing and prancing along 6th Avenue in this vibrant display of vanity and insanity.

In 1973 mask-maker and puppeteer Ralph Lee paraded his puppets from house to house visiting friends and family along the winding streets of his Greenwich Village neighborhood. His merry march quickly outgrew its original, intimate route and now, decades later, it parades up 6th Avenue, from Spring Street to 21st Street, attracting 90,000 creatively costumed exhibitionists, artists, dancers, and musicians, hundreds of enormous puppets, scores of bands, and more than 2 million spectators. Anyone with a costume can join in, no advance registration required, although the enthusiastic interaction between participants and spectators makes it just as much fun simply to watch. It's a safe "street event" for families and singles alike, and a joyful night unlike any other.

The parade lines up on 6th Avenue between Canal and Spring streets from 6:30 to 8:30 pm. The walk actually starts at 7, but it takes about two hours to leave the staging area. It's best to arrive from the south to avoid the crush of strollers and participants. Get there a few hours early if possible. Costumes are usually handmade, clever, and outrageous, and revelers are happy to strike a pose. The streets are crowded along the route, with the most congestion below 14th Street. Of course, the best way to truly experience the parade is to march, but if you're not feeling the face paint, it's possible to volunteer to help carry the puppets. For information visit 🌐 *www.halloween-nyc.com.*

—Jacinta O'Halloran

Arch looks north to two blocks of lovingly preserved Greek Revival and Federal-style town houses known as the Row.

TOP ATTRACTIONS

Bleecker Street. Walking the stretch of Bleecker Street between 5th and 7th avenues provides a smattering of just about everything synonymous with Greenwich Village these days: NYU buildings, used-record stores, Italian cafés and food shops, pizza and takeout joints, some nightclubs, and funky boutiques. Grab an espresso and sample some of the city's best pizza. Notable along the Greenwich Village length of the street is Our Lady of Pompeii Church, at Bleecker and Carmine, where Mother Cabrini, a naturalized Italian immigrant who became the first American citizen to be a saint, often prayed. Foodies love the blocks between 6th and 7th avenues for the specialty purveyors like Murray's Cheese (⊠ 254 Bleecker Street). West of 7th Avenue, where Bleecker crosses the border into the West Village, things get more upscale, with fashion and home-furnishings boutiques featuring antiques, eyeglasses, shoes, and designer clothing. ⊠ *Bleecker St., Greenwich Village.*

FAMILY Fodor'sChoice ★ **Washington Square Park.** NYU students, street musicians, skateboarders, jugglers, chess players, and those just watching the grand opera of it all generate a maelstrom of activity in this physical and spiritual heart of Greenwich Village. The 9¾-acre park had inauspicious beginnings as a cemetery, principally for yellow-fever victims—an estimated 10,000–22,000 bodies lie below (a headstone was actually unearthed in 2009). At one time, plans to renovate the park called for the removal of the bodies; however, local resistance prevented this from happening. In the early 1800s the park was a parade ground and the site of public executions; bodies dangled from a conspicuous Hanging Elm that still stands at the northwest corner of the square. Today that gruesome past is all but forgotten, as playgrounds attract parents with tots in tow, dogs go leash-free inside the popular dog runs, and everyone else seems drawn toward the large central fountain.

The triumphal European-style **Washington Memorial Arch** stands at the square's north end, marking the start of 5th Avenue. The original wood-and-papier-mâché arch, originally situated a half block north, was erected in 1889 to commemorate the 100th anniversary of George Washington's presidential inauguration. The arch was reproduced in Tuckahoe marble in 1892, and the statues—*Washington as General Accompanied by Fame and Valor* on the left, and *Washington as Statesman Accompanied by Wisdom and Justice* on the right—were added in 1916 and 1918, respectively. ⊠ *5th Ave. between Waverly Pl. and 4th St., Greenwich Village* Ⓜ *A, B, C, D, E, F, M to W. 4th St.*

5

WORTH NOTING

Gay Street. A curved, one-block lane lined with small row houses, Gay Street was probably named after an early landowner and definitely had nothing to do with gay rights. In the 1930s this tiny thoroughfare and nearby Christopher Street became famous nationwide after Ruth McKenney began to publish somewhat zany autobiographical stories based on what happened when she and her sister moved to No. 14 Gay Street from Ohio. The stories, first published in *The New Yorker* birthed many adaptations, including the 1953 Broadway musical *Wonderful Town* (revived in 2004) and the 1942 and 1955 movies *My Sister Eileen.* ⊠ *Gay St. between Christopher St. and Waverly Pl., Greenwich Village* Ⓜ *1 to Christopher St.–Sheridan Sq.; A, B, C, D, E, F, M to W. 4th St.*

Patchin Place. This little cul-de-sac off West 10th Street between Greenwich and 6th avenues has 10 diminutive 1848 row houses. Around the corner on 6th Avenue is a similar dead-end street, **Milligan Place,** with five small houses completed in 1852. The houses in both quiet enclaves were originally built for waiters who worked at 5th Avenue's high-society Brevoort Hotel, long since demolished. Later Patchin Place residents included writers Theodore Dreiser, e. e. cummings, Jane Bowles, and Djuna Barnes. Milligan Place became popular among playwrights, including Eugene O'Neill. Ⓜ *A, B, C, D, E, F, M to W. 4th St.*

The Row. Built from 1833 through 1837, this series of Greek Revival and Federal row houses along Washington Square North, between University Place and MacDougal Street, once belonged to merchants and bankers, then to writers and artists such as John Dos Passos and Edward

Out and On Display: George Segal's sculptures of two gay couples in Christopher Park illustrate gay pride in Greenwich Village.

Hopper. Many are now owned by New York University and used for housing and offices. Although the houses' facades remain beautifully preserved, the interiors have been drastically altered over the years. ✉ *1–13 and 19–26 Washington Sq. N, between University Pl. and MacDougal St., Greenwich Village* Ⓜ *A, B, C, D, E, F, M to W. 4th St.*

Washington Mews. A rarity in Manhattan, this pretty, brick-covered street—really a glorified alley—is lined on one side with the former stables of the houses on "the Row," as it's known, on Washington Square North. Although the street is private and owned by New York University, which uses many of the stables for offices, it's open to pedestrian traffic from 7 am through 11 pm. ✉ *Between 8th St. and Washington Sq. N, between 5th Ave. and University Pl., Greenwich Village* Ⓜ *A, B, C, D, E, F, M to W. 4th St.*

WEST VILLAGE

High-rises and office towers have little business among the labyrinth of small curving streets, peculiar alleys, and historic town houses here, although a new boom in distinctive apartment living by designer architects has emerged around the western edges near the Hudson River. It's easy to see why the tree-lined streets of the West Village, which are primarily residential, are in such demand—think charming cafés, carefully disheveled celebrities out and about, and well-dressed children playing in parks.

It's easy to feel like a local while shopping here. Unlike 5th Avenue or SoHo, the pace is slower, the streets are relatively quiet, and the

CLOSE UP

Bleecker Street's Little Italy

Little Italy can be besieged by slow-moving crowds, touristy shops, and restaurant hosts hollering invitations to dine inside. Bleecker Street between 6th and 7th avenues, on the other hand, with its crowded cafés, bakeries, pizza parlors, and old-world merchants, offers a more pleasurable, equally vital alternative to the traditional tourist trap.

For an authentic Italian bakery experience, step into **Pasticceria Rocco** (No. 243) for wonderful cannoli, cream puffs, and cookies packed up, or order an espresso and linger over the treats.

Step into the past at the old-style (and now high-end) butcher shops, such as **Ottomanelli & Sons** (No. 285) and **Faicco's Pork Store** (No. 260), where locals have bought their sausage and custom-cut pork since 1900.

The sweet (or stinky) smell of success is nowhere more evident than at **Murray's Cheese** (No. 254), at Cornelia Street. The original shop, opened in 1940 by Murray Greenberg (not Italian), was not much larger than the display case that stocked the stuff. Now it's a fromage-fiend's emporium, with everything from imported crackers and bamboo cutting boards to a full-service sandwich counter. Samples of cheese, salami, gelato, and other goodies are frequently offered.

In a town that's fierce about its pizza, some New Yorkers swear by **John's Pizzeria** (No. 278), where a coal oven has been baking (and often slightly charring) pies since 1929. But be forewarned: they do whole thin-crust pies only—no individual slices. Luckily, one of the city's best slice joints is right around the corner, **Joe's Pizza** (7 Carmine Street). To complicate the Bleecker Street pizza situation further, **Kesté Pizza & Vino** (271 Bleecker Street) serves Neapolitan pies that some would argue give even Da Michele in Naples a run for its money. It is also the official location in the United States for the Associazione Pizzaiuoli Napoletani, whose mission is to promote pizzas made in the Neapolitan tradition, using Neapolitan products.

5

scale is small. This is the place to come for unusual finds as well as global-brand goods. The West Village section of Bleecker Street is a particularly good place to indulge all sorts of shopping appetites; high-fashion foragers prowl the stretch between West 10th Street and 8th Avenue. Hudson Street and Greenwich Avenue are also prime boutique-browsing territory.

Christopher Street has long been the symbolic heart of New York's gay and lesbian community, though places like Chelsea, Hell's Kitchen, and parts of Brooklyn attract more gay and lesbians these days. On Christopher, among cafés, lifestyle boutiques, and clothing shops, is one of the city's most acclaimed off-Broadway theaters, the Lucille Lortel, where major playwrights like David Mamet, Eugene Ionesco, and Edward Albee have their own markers in the sidewalk. Nearby, at 51–53 Christopher Street, is the site of the Stonewall Inn and the historic Stonewall riots, one of the signal events in the gay rights movement. Across the street is a green triangle named Christopher Park, where there are commemorative statues of two gay and lesbian couples.

TOP ATTRACTIONS

Hudson River Park. *See the listing in the TriBeCa section of Chapter 2: Lower Manhattan.*

WORTH NOTING

75½ Bedford Street. Rising real-estate rates inspired the construction of New York City's narrowest house—just 9½ feet wide and 32 feet deep—in 1873. Built on a lot that was originally a carriage entrance of the Isaacs-Hendricks House next door, this sliver of a building was home to actor John Barrymore and poet Edna St. Vincent Millay. ✉ *75½ Bedford St., between Commerce and Morton Sts., West Village* Ⓜ *A, B, C, D, E, F, M to W. 4th St.*

FAMILY **Children's Museum of the Arts.** The CMA seeks to give children ages 1 to 15 room to get really creative through a variety of mediums. Along with the requisite children's museum offerings like pencils, chalk, and paint, you'll find a clay bar; a media lab with mounted cameras and a recording studio; a small slide and colorful ball pond that kids can play in; an airy exhibition space with rotating exhibits (and workshops inspired by exhibits); a permanent collection of children's art from more than 50 countries; and classes in ceramics, origami, animation, filmmaking, and more. Check the website for a busy calendar of events. ✉ *103 Charlton St., between Hudson and Greenwich Sts., West Village* ☎ *212/274–0986* 🌐 *www.cmany.org* 🎟 *$10* 🕒 *Mon.–Wed. noon–5, Thurs. and Fri. noon–6, weekends 10–6* Ⓜ *6 to Spring St.*

Christopher Park. You might have to share a bench in this tiny park with George Segal's life-size sculptures of a lesbian couple. The painted bronzes, cast in 1980 and titled *Gay Liberation,* also include a gay male couple, captured in mid-chat nearby. ✉ *Bordered by W. 4th, Grove, and Christopher Sts., West Village* Ⓜ *1 to Christopher St.–Sheridan Sq.*

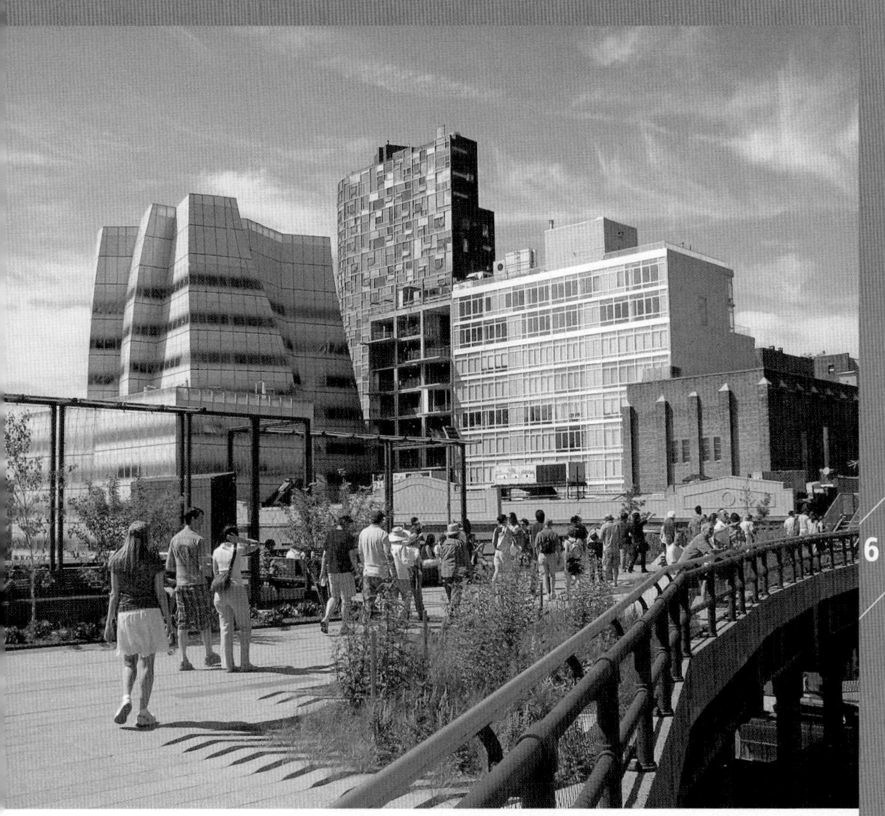

6

CHELSEA AND THE MEATPACKING DISTRICT

GETTING ORIENTED

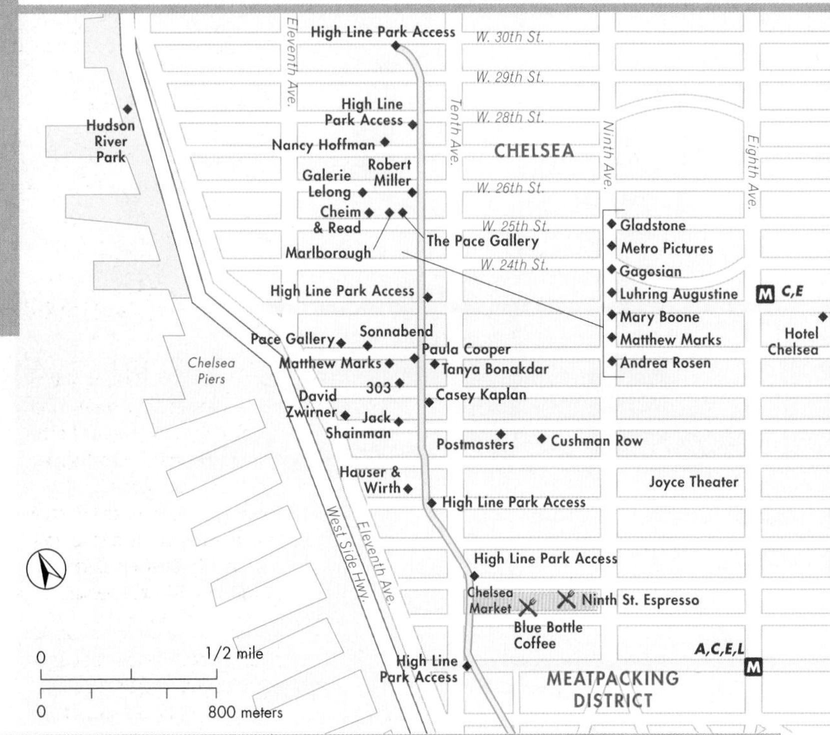

GETTING HERE AND AROUND	MAKING THE MOST OF YOUR TIME
The A, C, E, 1, 2, 3, and L trains stop at 14th Street for both the Meatpacking District and Chelsea. The latter is further served by the C, E, 1, F, and M lines at the 23rd Street stop and the 1 stop at 28th Street. 14th Street and 23rd Street are both also served by the PATH trains.	Chelsea has a dual life: Typical gallery hours are Tuesday–Saturday 10–6, but at night the neighborhood changes into a party town, with bars (gay and straight) and high-profile nightclubs that don't rev up until after 11. To truly appreciate the Meatpacking District, make a 9 pm or later dinner reservation at a hot restaurant, then hit the bars to see where the glitterati are this week. If shopping is your pleasure, weekdays are great; come after noon, though, or you'll find most spots shuttered.

TOP EXPERIENCES

Gallery hopping in Chelsea.

Walking along the High Line.

Checking out the Meatpacking District's nightlife.

Eating your way through Chelsea Market.

Shopping at the classy shops in the Meatpacking District.

BEST FOR KIDS

Chelsea Piers

The High Line

Hudson River Park

COFFEE AND QUICK BITES

Blue Bottle Coffee. If you're serious about your coffee and equally serious about fresh-baked pastries, eco-friendly practices, and good-old-fashioned service, you need to stop in at this trendy multi-level coffee shop in Chelsea. Seriously. ✉ *450 W. 15th St., Chelsea.*

Donut Pub. Care for an apple fritter or old-fashioned doughnut with your coffee? Pull up a stool. ✉ *203 W. 14th St., at 7th Ave., Chelsea* ☎ *212/929–0126.*

Ninth Street Espresso. The outlet of Ninth Street Espresso in Chelsea Market is popular all day, though the lines in the morning are longest. The lattes here are sublime. ✉ *Chelsea Market, 9th Ave. between 15th and 16th Sts., Chelsea* ☎ *212/228–2930.*

Sightseeing ★★★
Nightlife ★★★★★
Dining ★★★★★
Lodging ★★★
Shopping ★★★★

Chelsea long ago usurped SoHo as the epicenter of New York contemporary art galleries, but the opening of the High Line above 10th Avenue created a new artery of life in this part of the city. More foot traffic means more gentrification and more restaurants. Not surprisingly, this also means more real-estate development and rising rents, which means less of the smaller galleries that transformed Chelsea from a dead area to an art hub in the first place.

MEATPACKING DISTRICT

Concentrated in a few blocks of what is essentially the West Village, between the Hudson River and 9th Avenue, from Little West 12th Street to about West 17th Street, the Meatpacking District used to be the center of the wholesale meat industry for New York City. Other than beloved meat purveyor Pat LaFrieda, though, there are few meat markets left in this now rather quaint, cobblestoned area—but it's definitely a metaphorical meat market at night, when the city's trendiest frequent the equally trendy restaurants and bars here. The area is also home to some of the city's trendiest retailers, with boutiques of fashion designers like Alexander McQueen and Stella McCartney.

CHELSEA

Updated by Jacinta O'Halloran

Most of Chelsea's art galleries are found from about 20th to 27th streets, primarily between 10th and 11th avenues. The range of contemporary art on display includes almost every imaginable medium and style; if it's going on in the art world, it'll be in one of the 300 or so galleries here. While some of the small and midsize galleries have been squeezed uptown due to high rents, the big players in the art world are getting bigger. Giant standouts include the new five-story David Zwirner Gallery on West 20th Street; Hauser & Wirth's cavernous industrial space on West 18th Street; the Robert Miller Gallery on West 26th Street, whose proprietor is a titan in the New York art world and represents the likes of Ai Weiwei, among others; and the galleries of Gagosian, Matthew Marks, and Pace (which has extended its presence to four galleries in this neighborhood).

TOP ATTRACTIONS

FAMILY **Chelsea Market.** This former Nabisco plant—where the first Oreos were baked in 1912—now houses more than two dozen gourmet food, wine, and flower shops, as well as an Anthropologie store, and one of NYC's last independent book stores (Posman Books). Reknowned specialty purveyors including L'Arte del Gelato, Fat Witch Bakery, Amy's Bread, Jacques Torres Chocolate, and Ninth Street Espresso flank the interior walkway that stretches from 9th to 10th avenues. The market's funky industrial design—a tangle of glass and metal for an awning, a factory pipe converted into an indoor waterfall—complements the eclectic assortment of shops. There is some seating inside but if the weather's nice, take your goodies to go and eat outside on the High Line. ✉ *75 9th Ave., between W. 15th and W. 16th Sts., Chelsea* ☎ *212/652–2117* 🌐 *www.chelseamarket.com* 🕐 *Mon.–Sat. 7–9, Sun. 8–8* Ⓜ *A, C, E, L to 14th St.*

6

David Zwirner. Zwirner further solidifies his commitment to contemporary art with this new, purpose-built, five-story exhibition and project space to compliment the programming of the gallery's three existing West 19th Street locations a block away. His galleries show works in all mediums by artists like Dan Flavin, Donald Judd, Palermo, Richard Serra, Gordon Matta-Clark, Diana Thater, and Yutaka Sone. ✉ *537 W. 20th St., between 10th and 11th Aves., Chelsea* ☎ *212/517–8677* 🌐 *www.davidzwirner.com* 🕐 *Tues.–Sat. 10–6* Ⓜ *C, E to 23rd St.*

Gagosian Gallery. This enterprising modern gallery has two large Chelsea branches (the other is at 522 West 21st Street, between 10th and 11th avenues) and a third on the Upper East Side, as well as nine more outposts in cities around the world. All show works by heavy hitters such as Pablo Picasso, Jean-Michel Basquiat, sculptor Richard Serra, and the late pop-art icon Roy Lichtenstein. ✉ *555 W. 24th St., at 11th Ave., Chelsea* ☎ *212/741–1111* 🌐 *www.gagosian.com* 🕐 *Tues.–Sat. 10–6* Ⓜ *C, E to 23rd St.*

Hauser & Wirth. On the site of the former Roxy nightclub and roller rink on West 18th Street, this Hauser & Wirth gallery is the opposite of its narrow townhouse location on the Upper East Side. The space is huge (23,000 square feet) and cavernous, and begs for sprawling exhibits and large-scale works. Emerging and established contemporary artists in the powerful Hauser & Wirth fold that show here include Dieter Roth, Paul McCarthy, Eva Hesse, and Jason Rhoades. ✉ *511 W. 18th St., Chelsea* ☎ *212/790–3900* 🌐 *www.hauserwirth.com.*

The High Line. Once a railroad track carrying freight trains, this elevated space has been transformed into a green retreat in the spirit of Paris's Promenade Plantée and is one of the most visited public parks in the city. A long "walking park" with benches, public art installations, and views of the Hudson River and the Manhattan skyline, the High Line

DID YOU KNOW?

Once teeming with more than 200 slaughterhouses, the Meatpacking District has done an abrupt 180° in the last two decades to become the epicenter of all things hot.

ITS BEER REMIXED.
NO PARKING

is set above 10th Avenue in West Chelsea. Reclining chaise longues and strategically situated benches are perfect for a picnic lunch (Chelsea Market is a convenient place to pick up sandwiches). The first section of the High Line, between Gansevoort and West 20th streets, opened in 2009 and was immediately the talk of the town. The second section of the park, up to West 30th Street, opened in 2011, doubling the length of the walkway. The final section of the park, currently under construction, will run between West 30th and West 34th streets and wrap around the Hudson Yards Redevelopment Project. Plans include a performance space, a kids' playspace, picnic areas, and panoramic views of the cityscape and Hudson River. Construction will be completed in three phases, with the final phase opening in 2014. ✉ *10th Ave. from Gansevoort St. to 30th St., Chelsea* ☎ *212/206–9922* 🌐 *www.thehighline.org* Ⓜ *L to 8th Ave.; 1 to 14th St., 23rd St., or 28th St.; 2 and 3 to 14th St.; A, C, E to 14th St.*

Hudson River Park. *See the listing in the TriBeCa section of Chapter 2.*

Marlborough Chelsea. With galleries in London, Monaco, and Madrid, the Marlborough empire also operates two of the largest and most influential galleries in New York City. The Chelsea location (the other is on 57th Street) shows the latest work of modern artists, with a focus on sculptural forms, such as the boldly colorful paintings of Andrew Kuo. Red Grooms, Richard Estes, and Fernando Botero are just a few of the 20th-century luminaries represented. ✉ *545 W. 25th St., between 10th and 11th Aves., Chelsea* ☎ *212/463–8634* 🌐 *www.marlboroughgallery.com* ⏲ *Tues.–Sat. 10–5:30* Ⓜ *C, E to 23rd St.*

Matthew Marks Gallery. A hot venue for both the New York and international art crowd, openings at any of the four Matthew Marks galleries are always an interesting scene—there are three other locations along 22nd Street, between 10th and 11th avenues. Swiss artist Ugo Rondinone made his U.S. debut here, as did Andreas Gursky. Luigi Ghirri, Darren Almond, Nan Goldin, Ellsworth Kelly, and a cast of illustrious others also show here. ✉ *523 W. 24th St., between 10th and 11th Aves., Chelsea* ☎ *212/243–0200* 🌐 *www.matthewmarks.com* ⏲ *Tues.–Sat. 10–6* Ⓜ *C, E to 23rd St.*

The Pace Gallery. The impressive roster of artists represented by the Pace Gallery includes a variety of upper-echelon artists, sculptors, and photographers, including Elizabeth Murray, Chuck Close, Sol LeWitt, and Robert Rauschenberg. There are four spaces in Chelsea, along West 25th Street, as well as a Midtown location. ✉ *534 W. 25th St., between 10th and 11th Aves., Chelsea* ☎ *212/929–7000* 🌐 *www.thepacegallery.com* ⏲ *Tues.–Sat. 10–6* Ⓜ *C, E to 23rd St.*

Paula Cooper Gallery. SoHo pioneer Paula Cooper moved to Chelsea in 1996, and enlisted architect Richard Gluckman to transform a warehouse into a dramatic space with tall ceilings and handsome skylights. There are now two galleries (the other is at 521 West 21st Street) that showcase the minimalist sculptures of Carl André, among other works. ✉ *534 W. 21st St., between 10th and 11th Aves., Chelsea* ☎ *212/255–1105* 🌐 *www.paulacoopergallery.com* ⏲ *Tues.–Sat. 10–6* Ⓜ *C, E to 23rd St.*

WORTH NOTING

FAMILY **Chelsea Piers.** This sports-and-entertainment complex along the Hudson River between 17th and 23rd streets, a phenomenal example of adaptive reuse, is the size of four 80-story buildings if they were laid out flat. There's pretty much every kind of sports activity going on inside and out, from golf (check out the multitiered, all-weather, out-door driving range) to ice-skating, rock climbing, soccer, bowling, gymnastics, and basketball. Plus there's a spa, elite sport-specific training, film studios, and a brewery with a restaurant. Chelsea Piers is also the jumping-off point for some of the city's varied water tours and dinner cruises. ✉ *Piers 59–62 on Hudson River from 17th to 23rd Sts.; entrance at 23rd St., Chelsea* ☎ *212/336–6666* 🌐 *www.chelseapiers.com* Ⓜ *C, E to 23rd St.*

DID YOU KNOW?

The *Titanic* was scheduled to arrive at Chelsea Piers on April 16, 1912. Fate intervened and the "unsinkable" ship struck an iceberg on April 14 and went down. Of the 2,200 passengers aboard, 675 were rescued by the Cunard liner *Carpathia*, which arrived at Chelsea Piers eight days later. Check out Chelsea Piers' historical photos on the wall between Piers 60 and 61.

6

Cushman Row. Built in 1840, this string of homes between 9th and 10th avenues represents some of the country's most perfect examples of Greek Revival row houses. Original details include small wreath-encircled attic windows, deeply recessed doorways with brownstone frames, and striking iron balustrades and fences. Note the pineapples, a traditional symbol of welcome, on top of the black iron newels in front of No. 416. ✉ *406–418 W. 20th St., between 9th and 10th Aves., Chelsea* Ⓜ *C, E to 23rd St.*

Hotel Chelsea. This 12-story Queen Anne–style neighborhood landmark (1884) became a hotel in 1905, although it catered to long-term tenants with a tradition of broad-mindedness and creativity. The literary roll call of live-ins is legendary: Mark Twain, Eugene O'Neill, O. Henry, Thomas Wolfe, Tennessee Williams, Vladimir Nabokov, Mary McCarthy, Arthur Miller, Dylan Thomas, William S. Burroughs, Patti Smith, and Robert Mapplethorpe. In 1966 Andy Warhol filmed a group of fellow artists in eight rooms; the footage was included in *The Chelsea Girls* (1967). The Chelsea Hotel, as it's popularly called, stopped accepting guest reservations in 2011 and is currently closed for renovations. ✉ *222 W. 23rd St., between 7th and 8th Aves., Chelsea* 🌐 *www.hotelchelsea.com* Ⓜ *1, 2, C, E to 23rd St.*

Rubin Museum of Art. This sleek and serene museum spread over six floors is the largest in the Western Hemisphere dedicated to the art of the Himalayas and the pieces shown here include paintings on cloth, metal sculptures, and textiles dating from the 2nd century onward. Many of the works from areas such as Tibet, Nepal, southwest China, and India are related to Buddhism, Hinduism, Bon, and other eastern religions. You'll find a pleasant café and gift shop on the ground floor. The museum marks its tenth anniversary in 2014 so check the website for a schedule of celebratory events. ✉ *150 W. 17th St., near 7th*

Ave., Chelsea ☎ 212/620–5000 🌐 www.rmanyc.org 🎟 $10 ⏲ Mon. and Thurs. 11–5, Wed. 11–7, Fri. 11–10, weekends 11–6 Ⓜ 1 to 18th St.

GALLERIES

303 Gallery. International cutting-edge artists shown here include up-and-coming New York artist Jacob Kassay, photographer Doug Aitken, and installation artists Karen Kilimnik and Jane and Louise Wilson. The 303 Gallery will be moving to 507 West 24th Street but at press time it was unclear when the move would happen so check before you visit. ✉ *547 W. 21st St., between 10th and 11th Aves., Chelsea* ☎ *212/255–1121* 🌐 *www.303gallery.com* ⏲ *Tues.–Sat. 10–6; closed Aug.; closed Sun. July–Sept.* Ⓜ *C, E to 23rd St.*

Andrea Rosen Gallery. Artists on the cutting edge, such as Felix Gonzalez-Torres, video-artists Ryan Trecartin and Lizzie Fitch, sculptor Andrea Zittel, and painter and installation artist Matthew Ritchie, are on view here. In late 2012, Rosen opened a second space, Gallery 2, just down the road and across the street (at 544 West 24th Street) from the gallery headquarters, with shows that place less emphasis on commercial appeal or success. ✉ *525 W. 24th St., between 10th and 11th Aves., Chelsea* ☎ *212/627–6000, 212/627–6100 Gallery 2* 🌐 *www.andrearosengallery.com* ⏲ *Tues.–Sat. 10–6* Ⓜ *C, E to 23rd St.*

Casey Kaplan. Founded in 1995, the Casey Kaplan gallery represents contemporary artists from Europe and the Americas. Sophisticated and ambitious exhibitions have included works by such artists as Henning Bohl, Giorgio Griffa, Matthew Brannon, Johannes Wohnseifer, and Julia Schmidt. ✉ *525 W. 21st St., between 10th and 11th Aves., Chelsea* ☎ *212/645–7335* 🌐 *www.caseykaplangallery.com* ⏲ *Tues.–Sat. 10–6* Ⓜ *C, E to 23rd St.*

Cheim & Read. This prestigious gallery represents artists such as Louise Bourgeois, William Eggleston, Joan Mitchell, Jenny Holzer, Donald Baechler, and Jack Pierson. ✉ *547 W. 25th St., between 10th and 11th Aves., Chelsea* ☎ *212/242–7727* 🌐 *www.cheimread.com* ⏲ *Tues.–Sat. 10–6* Ⓜ *C, E to 23rd St.*

Galerie Lelong. This large gallery presents challenging installations and art, as well as many Latin American artists. Look for work by Yoko Ono, Alfredo Jaar, Andy Goldsworthy, Cildo Meireles, Ana Mendieta, Hélio Oiticica, Sean Scully, and Petah Coyne. ✉ *528 W. 26th St., between 10th and 11th Aves., Chelsea* ☎ *212/315–0470* 🌐 *www.galerielelong.com* ⏲ *Tues.–Sat. 10–6* Ⓜ *C, E to 23rd St.*

Gladstone Gallery. The international roster of artists at this gallery's two Chelsea locations includes sculptor Anish Kapoor, photographer Sharon Lockhart, and multimedia artists Matthew Barney and Cecilia Edefalk. The other location is 530 West 21st Street, between 10th and 11th avenues. ✉ *515 W. 24th St., between 10th and 11th Aves., Chelsea* ☎ *212/206–9300* 🌐 *www.gladstonegallery.com* ⏲ *Tues.–Sat. 10–6* Ⓜ *C, E to 23rd St.*

Jack Shainman Gallery. Emerging and established artists such as L. N. Tallur, a young sculptor from India, and Kerry James Marshall, who deals with African-American issues, are shown here. You might find portrait

You never know what you might see in Chelsea's galleries: works by well-known artists like Alexander Calder, or pieces by up-and-coming artists.

paintings by Barkley L. Hendricks and photography from South African photojournalist Zwelethu Mthethwa. ✉ *513 W. 20th St., between 10th and 11th Aves., Chelsea* ☎ *212/645–1701* 🌐 *www.jackshainman.com* ⏲ *Tues.–Sat. 10–6* Ⓜ *C, E to 23rd St.*

Luhring Augustine Gallery. Owners Lawrence Luhring and Roland Augustine have been working with established and emerging artists from Europe, Japan, and America, since 1985. ✉ *531 W. 24th St., between 10th and 11th Aves., Chelsea* ☎ *212/206–9100* 🌐 *www.luhringaugustine.com* ⏲ *Tues.–Sat. 10–6* Ⓜ *C, E to 23rd St.*

Mary Boone Gallery. Based in SoHo in the late seventies, when it was a hot showcase for younger artists, the Mary Boone Gallery relocated to Midtown in 1996 and then opened this branch in a former garage in Chelsea in 2000. The space here allows for large-scale works and dramatic installations. Boone continues to show established artists such as Barbara Kruger and Eric Fischl, as well as newcomers such as Pierre Bismuth and Jacob Hashimoto. ✉ *541 W. 24th St., between 10th and 11th Aves., Chelsea* ☎ *212/752–2929* 🌐 *www.maryboonegallery.com* ⏲ *Tues.–Sat. 10–6* Ⓜ *C, E to 23rd St.*

Metro Pictures. The hottest talents in contemporary art shown here include Cindy Sherman, whose provocative photographs have brought her international prominence. ✉ *519 W. 24th St., between 10th and 11th Aves., Chelsea* ☎ *212/206–7100* 🌐 *www.metropicturesgallery.com* ⏲ *Tues.–Sat. 10–6* Ⓜ *C, E to 23rd St.*

Nancy Hoffman Gallery. Contemporary painting, sculpture, drawing, photography, and video works by an impressive array of international artists are on display in this light-filled space that has high ceilings

CLOSE UP

Chelsea Galleries 101

Good art, bad art, edgy art, downright disturbing art—it's all here waiting to please and provoke in the contemporary art capital of the world. For the uninitiated, the concentration of nearly 300 galleries within a seven-block radius can be overwhelming, and the sometimes cool receptions on entering and deafening silence, intimidating. Art galleries are not exactly famous for their customer-service skills, but they're free, and you don't need a degree in art appreciation to stare at a canvas or an installation.

There's no required code of conduct, although most galleries are library-quiet and cell phones are seriously frowned upon. Don't worry, you won't be pressured to buy anything; staff will probably be doing their best to ignore you.

Galleries are generally open Tuesday through Saturday from 10 to 6. Gallery hop on a Saturday afternoon—the highest-traffic day—if you want company. You can usually find a binder with the artist's résumé, examples of previous work, and exhibit details (usually including prices) at the front desk. If not, ask. Also ask whether there's information you can take with you.

You can't see everything in one afternoon, so if you have specific interests, plan ahead. Find gallery information and current exhibit details by checking the listings in *The New Yorker* or the weekend section of *The New York Times*. Learn more about the galleries and the genres and artists they represent at *www.artincontext.org*.

—Jacinta O'Halloran

and a sculpture garden. Artists range from Viola Frey, known for her heroic-scale ceramic male and female figures, to other well-established artists such as Don Eddy and Joseph Raffael, to a strong group of young artists embarking with their first solo shows. *520 W. 27th St., between 10th and 11th Aves., Chelsea 212/966–6676 www.nancyhoffmangallery.com Tues.–Sat. 10–6 M C, E to 23rd St.*

Robert Miller Gallery. Miller, a titan of the New York art world, represents some of the biggest names in modern painting and photography, including Ai Weiwei, Diane Arbus, and the estates of Lee Krasner and Alice Neel. *524 W. 26th St., between 10th and 11th Aves., Chelsea 212/366–4774 www.robertmillergallery.com Aug.–June, Tues.–Sat 10–6; July, Mon.–Fri. 10–6 M C, E to 23rd St.*

Sonnabend. This pioneer of the SoHo art scene continues to show important contemporary artists in its Chelsea space, including Jeff Koons, Rona Pondick, Elger Esser, and Clifford Ross. *536 W. 22nd St., between 10th and 11th Aves., Chelsea 212/627–1018 www.sonnabendgallery.com Tues.–Sat. 10–6 M C, E to 23rd St.*

Tanya Bonakdar Gallery. Contemporary artists such as Uta Barth, whose blurry photos challenge ideas about perception, and Ernesto Neto, a Brazilian artist who has made stunning room-size installations of large nylon sacks filled with spices, are shown here. *521 W. 21st St., between 10th and 11th Aves., Chelsea 212/414–4144 www.tanyabonakdargallery.com Tues.–Sat. 10–6 M C, E to 23rd St.*

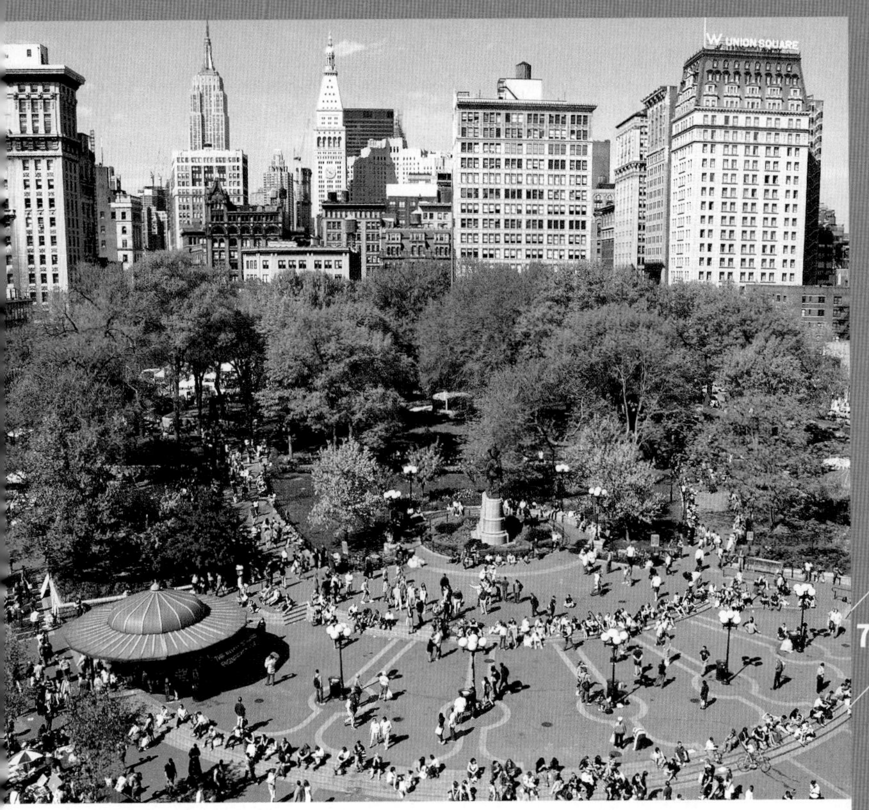

7

UNION SQUARE, THE FLATIRON DISTRICT, AND GRAMERCY PARK

GETTING ORIENTED

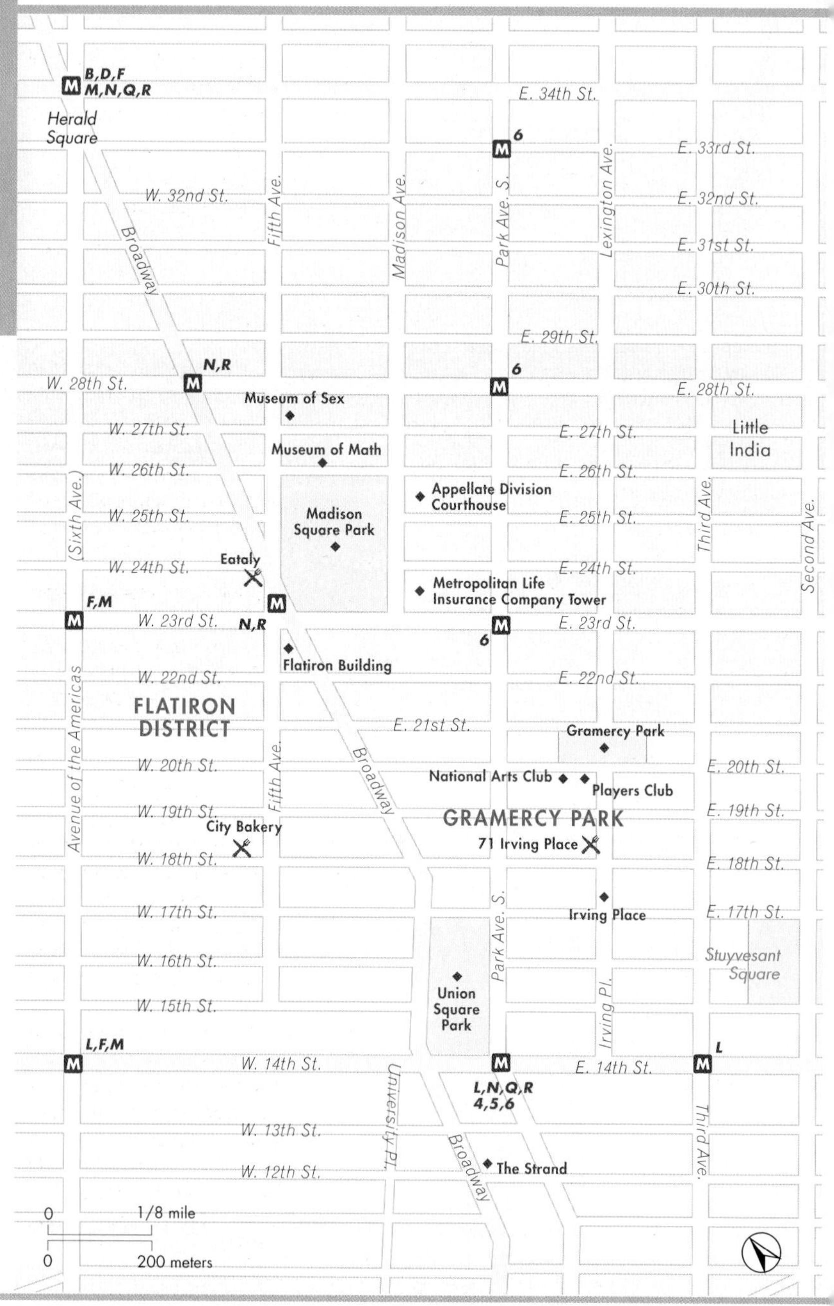

MAKING THE MOST OF YOUR TIME

Union Square seems like it's busy at just about every time of day and night, with commuters and people hanging out on the steps to eat lunch or just hang out, but market days—Monday, Wednesday, Friday, and Saturday—are even busier. Early weekday mornings are quietest, before the market is set up, though without all the people, the area loses its allure.

This is definitely an area for strolling, shopping, and eating, so plan your visit around a meal—or several.

If you're planning to eat at the Shake Shack in Madison Square Park, come at noon if you can; the lines here can get pretty long.

GETTING HERE AND AROUND

Union Square/14th Street is a major subway hub, with the L, N, Q, R, 4, 5, and 6 lines all converging here. For Madison Square Park, take the local R train to 23rd Street. The 6 also stops at 23rd and 28th streets.

TOP EXPERIENCES

Strolling in Union Square Park and checking out the produce and other goodies at the greenmarket.

Browsing the miles of books in the Strand bookstore.

Picnicking in Madison Square Park.

COFFEE AND QUICK BITES

71 Irving Place. Steps from Union Square, this cozy little café roasts their own beans—always a good sign—and serves up good people-watching along with sandwiches, muffins, and snacks. ✉ *71 Irving Pl., Flatiron District* ☎ *212/995–5252.*

City Bakery. "Pretzel croissants," chocolate-chip cookies, and super-thick hot chocolate are just some of the signature snacks here. ✉ *3 W. 18th St., Flatiron District* ☎ *212/366–1414.*

Eataly. Ignore the overpriced produce market by the front entrance of Mario Batali's Italian food emporium and make a beeline for La Piazza for sandwiches made with meticulously sourced ingredients (you can eat them at the standup tables nearby); a full-service pizza and pasta restaurant; a raw bar and fish eatery; and a spot for quaffing wines by the glass and beers on tap. There's also a corridor that's a gourmand's dream, with Italian chocolates, coffees, gelati, and pastries. ✉ *200 5th Ave., at 23rd St., Flatiron District* ☎ *212/229–2560* 🌐 *www.eataly.com.*

Sightseeing ★★★★
Nightlife ★
Dining ★★★
Lodging ★★★
Shopping ★★★★

Union Square is a hub of seemingly never-ending activity and people-watching that anchors the quieter neighborhoods of Gramercy and the Flatiron District. When that certain brand of New Yorker say they don't like to travel above 14th Street, they're usually thinking about Union Square as the cut-off.

UNION SQUARE

Updated by Jacinta O'Halloran

The energy of Union Square reaches its peak during its greenmarket days (Monday, Wednesday, Friday, and Saturday), when more than 140 regional farmers and food purveyors set up shop on the square's north and west sides to peddle everything from produce to meat and fresh fish to baked goods. The market is a great place to rub elbows with—and get elbowed by—local shoppers and chefs and a great source for tasty souvenirs (locally produced honeys, jams, pickles, and cheeses) as well as lunch. Find a bench in the park to savor your goodies and take in the scene. Sometimes political rallies happen here, too.

Even on a nonmarket day, Union Square regularly has vendors of all kinds, selling everything from art to jewelry to T-shirts. New York University students, nannies with their charges, visitors, and locals alike all gather in this open space that can at times feel more like an outdoor version of Grand Central Terminal than a park. Just south of Union Square, on Broadway at 12th Street, is the Strand, the giant bookstore that attracts book lovers like a magnet.

It was in this square, on September 5, 1882, that Labor Day was born, when more than 10,000 New York City unionized workers took an unpaid day off to march from City Hall to Union Square.

TOP ATTRACTIONS

Union Square Park and Greenmarket. A park, farmers' market, meeting place, and site of rallies and demonstrations, this pocket of green space sits in the center of a bustling residential and commercial neighborhood. The name Union originally signified that two main roads—Broadway

DID YOU KNOW?

In 1976 the Union Square Greenmarket began as a handful of farmers selling their goods. Now, in peak season, more than 70 vendors sell everything from wine to wool.

and 4th Avenue—crossed here, but it took on a different meaning in the late 19th and early 20th centuries, when the square became a rallying spot for labor protests; many unions, as well as fringe political parties, moved their headquarters nearby.

TIME OUT!

Union Square's most love-it-or-hate-it feature is the *Metronome* sculpture with its bank of cascading numbers. Half art installation, half timepiece, it sits above Nordstrom Rack, and is actually a clock that counts both time elapsed and time remaining in the day. At noon and midnight huge bursts of steam emerge.

Union Square is at its best on Monday, Wednesday, Friday, and Saturday (8–6), when the largest of the city's greenmarkets brings farmers and food purveyors from the tri-state area. Browse the stands of fruit and vegetables, flowers, plants, fresh-baked pies and breads, cheeses, cider, New York State wines, fish, and meat. Between Thanksgiving and Christmas, there is a popular gift market where artisans sell gift items and food in candy-cane-stripe booths at the square's southwest end.

New York University dormitories, theaters, and cavernous commercial spaces occupy the handsomely restored 19th-century commercial buildings that surround the park, along with chain coffee shops and restaurants. The run of diverse architectural styles on the building at 33 Union Square West, the Decker Building, is as imaginative as its former contents: this was once home to Andy Warhol's studio. The building at 17th Street and Union Square East, now housing the New York Film Academy and the Union Square Theater, was the final home of Tammany Hall, an organization famous in its day as a corrupt and powerful political machine. Statues in the park include those of George Washington, Abraham Lincoln, Mahatma Gandhi (often wreathed in flowers), and the Marquis de Lafayette sculpted by Frederic Auguste Bartholdi, creator of the Statue of Liberty. Plaques in the sidewalk on the southeast and southwest sides chronicle the park's history from the 1600s to 1800s. ✉ *E. 14th to E. 17th Sts., between Broadway and Park Ave. S, Flatiron District* Ⓜ *L, N, Q, R, 4, 5, 6 to Union Sq./14th St.*

FLATIRON DISTRICT

The Flatiron District—anchored by Madison Square Park on the north and Union Square to the south—is one of the city's busiest neighborhoods, particularly along 5th Avenue and Park Avenue South. Once known as Ladies' Mile because of the fashionable row of department stores where women routinely shopped, the area is still a favorite for spotting ladies because of the number of modeling agencies and photography studios here. Lovely Madison Square Park, a pleasant green space hemmed in by the neighborhood's notable architecture—from the triangular Flatiron to the dazzling, gold-pyramid-topped New York Life Building and the Metropolitan Life Tower with its elegant clock face—is the best place to savor the view. Sit and admire the scene with a burger and shake from the park's always-busy Shake Shack or takeout

The wedge-shaped Flatiron Building got its nickname because of its resemblance to the shape of a clothes iron; its original name is the Fuller Building.

from the mother of all Italian markets, Eataly, across the street from the west side of the park.

TOP ATTRACTIONS

Flatiron Building. When completed in 1902, the Fuller Building, as it was originally known, caused a sensation. Architect Daniel Burnham made ingenious use of the triangular wedge of land at 23rd Street, 5th Avenue, and Broadway, employing a revolutionary steel frame that allowed for the building's 22-story, 286-foot height. Covered with a limestone and white terra-cotta facade in the Italian Renaissance style, the building's shape resembled a clothing iron, hence its nickname. When it became apparent that the building generated strong winds, gawkers would loiter at 23rd Street hoping to catch sight of ladies' billowing skirts. Local traffic cops had to shoo away the male peepers—one purported origin of the phrase "23 skidoo." There is a small display of historic building and area photos in the lobby, but otherwise you will have to settle for appreciating this building from the outside . . . at least for now; the building may be converted to a luxury hotel when current occupant leases expire in 2018. ✉ *175 5th Ave., bordered by E. 22nd and E. 23rd Sts., and Broadway, Flatiron District* Ⓜ *R to 23rd St.*

Madison Square Park. The benches of this elegant tree-filled park afford great views of some of the city's oldest and most charming skyscrapers (the Flatiron Building, the Metropolitan Life Insurance Tower, the gold-crowned New York Life Insurance Building, and the Empire State Building) and serve as a perfect vantage point for people-, pigeon-, dog-, or squirrel-watching. Add free Wi-Fi, the Shake Shack, temporary art exhibits, and a summer music series, and you'll realize that a bench here

Lounging on the grass in Madison Square Park.

is definitely the place to be. New York City's first baseball games were played in this 7-acre park in 1845 (though New Jerseyans are quick to point out that the game was actually invented across the Hudson in Hoboken, New Jersey). On the north end of the park, an imposing 1881 statue by Augustus Saint-Gaudens memorializes Civil War naval hero Admiral David Farragut. An 1876 statue of Secretary of State William Henry Seward (the Seward of the term "Seward's Folly," coined when the United States purchased Alaska from the Russian Empire in 1867) sits in the park's southwest corner, though it's rumored that the sculptor placed a reproduction of the statesman's head on a statue of Abraham Lincoln's body. ✉ *E. 23rd to E. 26th Sts., between 5th and Madison Aves., Flatiron District* ☎ *212/538–1884* 🌐 *www.madisonsquarepark.org/* Ⓜ *R to 23rd St.*

WORTH NOTING

Appellate Division Courthouse. Sculpted by Frederick Ruckstuhl, figures representing Wisdom and Force flank the main portal of this imposing Beaux-Arts courthouse, built in 1899. Melding the structure's purpose with artistic symbolism, statues of great lawmakers line the roof balustrade, including Moses, Justinian, and Confucius. In total, sculptures by 16 artists adorn the ornate building, a showcase of themes relating to the law. This is one of the most important appellate courts in the country: it hears more than 3,000 appeals and 6,000 motions a year, and also admits approximately 3,000 new attorneys to the bar each year. Inside the courtroom is a stunning stained-glass dome set into a gilt ceiling. The main hall and the courtroom are open to visitors from 9 to 5, Monday through Friday. All sessions, which are generally held Tuesday to Thursday at 2, are open to the public. (Visitors can call the main number ahead of time to be sure court is in session.) ✉ *27 Madison Ave., entrance on E. 25th St., Flatiron District* ☎ *212/340–0400* 🌐 *www.courts.state.ny.us/courts/ad1* 🕒 *Weekdays 9–5* Ⓜ *N, R, 6 to 23rd St.*

Metropolitan Life Insurance Company Tower. When it was added to the original building on this site, in 1909, the 700-foot tower resembling the campanile of St. Mark's in Venice made this 1893 building the world's tallest; it was surpassed in height a few years later by the Woolworth Building. It was stripped of much of its classical details during renovations in the early 1960s but remains a prominent feature of the Midtown skyline today. The clock's four faces are each three stories high, and their minute hands weigh half a ton each. In 2015, Marriott International and Ian Schrager will open a 355 luxury-room hotel—Edition Hotel—in the long-vacant clock tower portion of the building. ✉ *1 Madison Ave., between E. 23rd and E. 24th Sts., Flatiron District* Ⓜ *R, 6 to 23rd St.*

FAMILY **Museum of Mathematics.** There's no exact formula to get kids excited about math, but the sleek, new two-floor Museum of Mathematics (MoMath)—the only cultural institution devoted to math in all of North America—comes close to finding the perfect ratio of fun-to-math. Kids can ride square-wheeled trikes, create human fractal trees, build virtual 3-D geometric shapes (which can be printed out on a 3-D printer), use lasers to explore cross-sections of objects, solve dozens of puzzles, and just generally bend their minds while they unknowingly multiply brain cells (sshh!). Exhibits are best suited to kids ages 6 and up but preschoolers will still enjoy many of the interactive exhibits, like the Math Square—a light-up floor programmed with math games, simulations, and patterns. ✉ *11 E. 26th St., between 5th and Madison, Flatiron District* ☎ *212/542–0566* 🌐 *www.momath.org* 🎟 *$15* 🕒 *Daily 10–5* Ⓜ *R to 28th St.*

Museum of Sex. Ponder the profound history and cultural significance of sex at this 14,000-square-foot museum while staring at vintage pornographic photos, S&M paraphernalia, anti-masturbation devices from the 1800s, explicit film clips, vintage condom tins, and a collection of artwork. Exhibits probe topics such as desire on the Internet, the sex lives of animals, and classic American pin-up art. The subject matter is given serious curatorial treatment, though the gift shop is full of fun sexual kitsch. Only patrons over 18 are admitted. After visiting the museum's exhibitions, enjoy cocktails in the new Play Bar. ✉ *233 5th Ave., entrance on 27th St., Flatiron District* ☎ *212/689–6337* 🌐 *www.museumofsex.com* 🎟 *$17.50* 🕒 *Sun.–Thurs. 10–8, Fri. and Sat. 10–9* Ⓜ *R to 28th St.*

GRAMERCY PARK

The haste and hullabaloo of the city calms considerably in the more residential neighborhood of Gramercy Park to the east. Dignified Gramercy Park, named for its 1831 gated garden square ringed by historic buildings and private clubs, is an early example of the city's best creative

7

urban planning. Even though you can't unpack your picnic in the exclusive residents-only park, pick a spot on the sidewalk in front of the cast-iron gate and gaze upward to take in the beautiful Greek Revival, Italianate, Gothic Revival, and Victorian Gothic buildings—including the Players Club and the National Arts Club, both established to indulge and encourage a passion for the arts—that flank the sides of the park.

Just north of the park is Ian Schrager's cooler-than-cool reincarnation of the Gramercy Park Hotel on Lexington Avenue, with one of the city's best rooftop bars. Indeed, as gorgeous as Gramercy views may be during the day, its nighttime skyline is doubly spectacular. And south of the park, running north–south from 14th Street is **Irving Place,** a short street honoring Washington Irving, that feels calm, green, and exclusive, and has a combination of old and new eateries, stores, and architecture. Pete's Tavern (⇨ *Nightlife*), on Irving Place since 1864, maintains its claim as the oldest original bar in the city. Two famous writers, O. Henry (*Gift of the Magi*) and Ludwig Bemelmans (*Madeline*), were "inspired" here, probably from the amazing eggnog or Pete's House Ale.

TOP ATTRACTIONS

Gramercy Park. You may not be able to enter this private park, but a look through the bars in the wrought-iron fence that encloses it is well worth your time, as is a stroll around its perimeter. The beautifully planted 2-acre park, designed by developer Samuel B. Ruggles, dates from 1831, and is flanked by grand examples of early-19th-century architecture and permeated with the character of its many celebrated occupants.

When Ruggles bought the property, it was known as Krom Moerasje ("little crooked swamp"), named by the Dutch settlers. He drained the swamp and set aside 42 lots for a park to be accessible exclusively to those who bought the surrounding lots in his planned London-style residential square. The park is still owned by residents of buildings in the surrounding square, although neighbors from the area can now buy visiting privileges. **TIP→ Guests of the Gramercy Park Hotel can enjoy coveted access to this private park.** In 1966 the New York City Landmarks Preservation Commission designated Gramercy Park a historic district. Notable buildings: No. 15 was once home to Samuel Tilden, governor of New York. It was designed by Calvert Vaux in Gothic Revival brownstone with black granite trim and included a secret passageway to 19th Street so Tilden could escape his political enemies. It is now home to the 100-year-old National Arts Club. Next door at No. 16 Gramercy Park South lived the actor Edwin Booth, perhaps most famous for being the brother of Lincoln's assassin. In 1888 he turned his Gothic-trim home into the Players Club, a clubhouse for actors and theatrical types who were not welcome in regular society. A bronze statue of Edwin Booth as Hamlet has pride of place inside the park. ✉ *Lexington Ave. and E. 21st St., Gramercy Park* Ⓜ *L, N, Q, R, 4, 5, 6 to Union Sq./14th St.*

8

MIDTOWN EAST

with Murray Hill

GETTING ORIENTED

N,Q,R
N,Q,R,4,5,6
E. 59th St.
Spanierman Gallery
Edwynn Houk Gallery
E. 58th St.
E. 57th St.
The Pace Gallery
E. 56th St.
Trump Tower
Sony Wonder Technology Lab
E. 55th St.
Third Ave.
Second Ave.
E. 54th St.
Seagram Building
E,M
E,M
TURTLE BAY
First Ave.
6
E. 51st St.
St. Patrick's Cathedral
E. 50th St.
Beekman Place
Waldorf–Astoria
E. 49th St.
Park Ave.
Madison Ave.
E. 48th St.
Japan Society
Fifth Ave.
Lexington Ave.
E. 47th St.
Helmsley Building
E. 46th St.
FDR Drive
Uncle Paul's Pizza
E. 45th St.
United Nations Headquarters
Grand Central Terminal
E. 44th St.
Grand Central Market
Chrysler Building
E. 43rd St.
Tudor City
7
E. 42nd St.
4,5,6,7,S
Daily News Building
Bryant Park
E. 40th St.
Queens-Midtown Tunnel
E. 39th St.
MURRAY HILL
E. 38th St.
Lucid Cafe
Morgan Library and Museum
E. 37th St.
E. 36th St.
B. Altman Building/ New York Public Library— Science, Industry, and Business Library (SIBL)
E. 35th St.
E. 34th St.
Empire State Building
E. 33rd St.
0
1/4 mi
E. 32nd St.
0
1/4 km
Koreatown

MAKING THE MOST OF YOUR TIME

The east side of Midtown is somewhat more laid back than the west side, but there's still lots to keep you busy. Wherever you're headed, try to make sure you at least pass through Grand Central, which celebrated its 100th birthday in 2013—it'll be a madhouse on weekday mornings or right after work, and extremely quiet on the weekends, so you might want to visit on a weekday afternoon.

If you're planning to visit the Empire State Building, try to do so either early or late in the day—morning is the least crowded time, and late at night the city lights are dazzling. Allow at least two hours for your visit if you plan to visit the observation deck.

It's also worth making time for a quick trip out of the United States to visit the "international zone" of the United Nations; take a tour or just wander the grounds and promenade.

TOP EXPERIENCES

Standing in the center of Grand Central Terminal's main concourse.

Strolling down 5th Avenue.

Viewing the rare manuscripts at the Morgan Library.

Dining with locals in Koreatown.

GETTING HERE

To get to the east side of Midtown, take the 4, 5, 6, or the 7 to Grand Central. The S or Shuttle travels back and forth between Grand Central and Times Square.

You can reach the Empire State Building via the B, D, F, N, Q, R, or M line to 34th Street or the 6 to 33rd Street. The 6 also stops at 23rd and 28th streets.

COFFEE AND QUICK BITES

Grand Central Market. The concourse on the lower level of Grand Central Terminal is a cornucopia of gourmet snack options, including Eli Zabar's, Ciao Bella Gelateria, Murray's Cheese, Joe Coffee, and even an outpost of Junior's, the famed Brooklyn restaurant known for their classic cheesecake. ✉ *Grand Central Terminal, main entrance, E. 42nd St., at Park Ave., Midtown East.*

Lucid Cafe. A cozy (okay, tiny) coffee spot in Murray Hill with excellent coffee, espresso, Belgian hot chocolates, and tasty pastries, too. ✉ *311 Lexington Ave., at 38th St., Midtown East* ☎ *212/867-3490.*

Uncle Paul's Pizza. With toppings like caramelized figs, caviar, and lobster, there's a slice for every appetite. The plain slice is decent, too. ✉ *70 Vanderbilt Ave., at 45th St., Midtown East* ☎ *212/922-1200* 🌐 *www.uppny.com.*

Sightseeing
★★★★★
Nightlife
★★
Dining
★★★★
Lodging
★★★★★
Shopping
★★★★★

Fifth Avenue is Manhattan's dividing line, marking the divergence of east side and west side, but the avenue itself seems to connote so much of what the city's East Side is all about. This is where some of the city's most iconic buildings are found, including the Empire State Building, which is technically in the Murray Hill neighborhood.

MIDTOWN EAST

Updated by Jacinta O'Halloran

In terms of architecture, Midtown East has some of the city's most notable gems, including the stately Chrysler Building, considered an art-deco triumph, and the bustling Beaux-Arts masterpiece Grand Central Terminal. At night the streets around here are relatively quiet, but the restaurants are filled with expense-account diners celebrating their successes. Some of the most formal dining rooms and most expensive meals in town can be found here. The lower section of 5th Avenue is also a shopper's paradise, home to megabrand flagships such as Louis Vuitton, Yves Saint Laurent, and Chanel, and some of the world's most famous jewelry stores, including Tiffany, Van Cleef & Arpels, and Harry Winston. Upscale department stores like Bloomingdales and Saks Fifth Avenue are also around here.

TOP ATTRACTIONS

Chrysler Building. A monument to modern times and the mighty automotive industry, the former Chrysler headquarters wins many a New Yorker's vote for the city's most iconic and beloved skyscraper (the world's tallest for 40 days until the Empire State Building stole the honor). Architect William Van Alen, who designed this 1930 Art Deco masterpiece, incorporated car details into its form: American eagle gargoyles made of chromium nickel sprout from the 61st floor, resembling hood ornaments used on 1920s Chryslers; winged urns festooning the 31st floor reference the car's radiator caps. Most breathtaking is the pinnacle, with tiered crescents and spiked windows that radiate out like a magnificent steel sunburst. View it at sunset to catch the light gleaming off the tip. Even better, observe it at night, when its peak illuminates the sky. The inside is sadly off-limits apart from the amazing time-capsule lobby replete with chrome "grillwork," intricately patterned wood elevator doors, marble walls and floors, and an enormous ceiling mural saluting transportation and the human endeavor. ✉ *405 Lexington Ave., at E. 42nd St., Midtown East* Ⓜ *4, 5, 6, 7, S to Grand Central–42nd St.*

Fodor's Choice ★ **Grand Central Terminal.** Grand Central is not only the world's largest (76 acres) and the nation's busiest (nearly 700,000 commuters and subway riders use it daily) railway station, but also one of the world's most magnificent, majestic public spaces. Past the glimmering chandeliers of the waiting room is the jaw-dropping **main concourse,** 200 feet long, 120 feet wide, and 120 feet (roughly 12 stories) high, modeled after an ancient Roman public bath. In spite of it being completely cavernous, Grand Central manages to evoke a certain sense of warmth rarely found in buildings its size. Overhead, a twinkling fiber-optic map of the constellations covers the robin's-egg-blue ceiling. To admire it all with some sense of peace, avoid visiting at rush hour, or brave the chaos at peak travel times and be swept into the tides and eddies of human traffic swirling around the central information kiosk, the room's crown jewel with its polished marble counter and backlit, multifaced clock beaming the time in four directions.

To escape the crowds, head up one of the sweeping staircases at either end, where three upscale restaurants occupy the balcony space. Any would make an enjoyable perch from which to survey the concourse, but for a real taste of the station's early years, head beyond the western staircase to the **Campbell Apartment,** a clubby cocktail lounge housed in the restored private offices and salon of 1920s tycoon John W. Campbell. Located around and below the main concourse are fantastic shops and eateries (this is, of course, home to the eponymous Grand Central Oyster Bar), making this one of the best—if somewhat labyrinthine—"malls" in the city.

8

To best admire Grand Central's exquisite Beaux-Arts architecture, start from its ornate south face on East 42nd Street, modeled after a Roman triumphal arch. Crowning the facade's Corinthian columns and 75-foot-high arched windows, a graceful clock keeps time for hurried commuters. In the central window stands an 1869 bronze statue of Cornelius Vanderbilt, who built the station to house his railroad empire. Also noteworthy is the 1½-ton, cast-iron bald eagle displaying its 13-foot wingspan atop a ball near the corner of 42nd Street and Vanderbilt Avenue.

Grand Central still functions primarily as a railroad station, and might resemble its artless cross-town counterpart, Penn Station, were it not for Jacqueline Kennedy Onassis's 1975 public information campaign to save it as a landmark. Underground, more than 60 ingeniously integrated railroad tracks carry trains upstate and to Connecticut via Metro-North Commuter Rail. The subway connects here as well. A massive four-year renovation completed in October 1998 restored the 1913 landmark to its original splendor—and then some. The **Municipal**

Irish pride takes to the streets and sweeps up 5th Avenue in the annual St. Patrick's Day Parade.

Art Society (☎ *212/935–3960* 🌐 *www.mas.org/tours*) leads an official daily walking tour to explore the 100-year-old terminal's architecture, history, and hidden secrets. Tours begin in the main concourse at 12:30 and last for 75 minutes. Tickets ($20) can be purchased in advance online or from the ticket booth in the main concourse. ✉ *Main entrance, E. 42nd St. at Park Ave., Midtown East* ☎ *212/935–3960* 🌐 *www.grandcentralterminal.com* Ⓜ *4, 5, 6, 7, S to Grand Central–42nd St.*

St. Patrick's Cathedral. This Gothic edifice—the largest Catholic cathedral in the United States, seating approximately 2,400 people—is among Manhattan's most striking churches, with its double spires topping out at 330 feet. St. Pat's, as locals call it, holds a special place in the hearts of many New Yorkers and offers a calm and quiet refuge in the heart of buzzy midtown . . . despite the throngs of tourists (the cathedral receives more than 5.5 million visitors annually) and ongoing renovations.

The church dates back to 1858–79 and has begun to show its age. Hence, the cocoon of scaffolding, inside and out, as it undergoes an extensive $177 million two-year rehabilitation project. The cathedral is open during renovations, but it doesn't look like itself; interior scaffolding obscures its organ loft and the famous rose window (considered stained-glass artist Charles Connick's greatest work), and exterior scaffolding reaches all the way to the top of the spires of the 5th Avenue facade. You can still check out the statues in the alcoves around the nave, including a modern depiction of the first American-born saint, Mother Elizabeth Ann Seton. The church's Pieta sculpture is three times larger than the Pieta in St. Peter's Rome. Construction does not interfere with daily masses or the free guided tours held at 10 am most days (call ahead to confirm). ✉ *5th Ave., between E. 50th and E. 51st Sts., Midtown East* ☎ *212/753–2261 rectory* 🌐 *www.saintpatrickscathedral.org* ⏲ *Daily 6:30 am–8:45 pm* Ⓜ *E, M to 5th Ave./53rd St.*

FAMILY **Sony Wonder Technology Lab.** Have kids in tow? The free Sony Wonder Technology Lab in the Sony Building lets them program robots, create their own animated characters, perform virtual heart surgery, and put their own spin on Alicia Keys' New York anthem, "Empire State of Mind." The lab also shows classic and contemporary films for both young and adult audiences in its HD theater on Thursdays and Saturdays. 2014 marks SWTL's 20th anniversary so visitors can expect a variety of fun and high-tech events to celebrate the milestone. Admission is free but reservations are strongly recommended; they can be made a minimum of 7 days and up to 3 months from the time of visit. A limited number of same-day tickets are available on a first-come basis. ✉ *550 Madison Ave., at E. 56th St., Midtown East* ☎ *212/833–8100* 🌐 *wondertechlab.sony.com* ⏲ *Tues.–Sat. 9:30–5:30* Ⓜ *N, Q, R to 5th Ave./59th St.*

United Nations Headquarters. Officially an "international zone" and not part of the United States, the U.N. Headquarters is a working symbol of global cooperation. Built between 1947 and 1961, the headquarters sits on a lushly landscaped, 18-acre tract on the East River, fronted by flags of member nations. The main reason to visit is the 45-minute guided tour (given in 20 languages; reservations can be made through the website or tickets are available on the day of your visit), which includes the **General Assembly** and major council chambers, though some rooms may be closed on any given day. The newly renovated Conference Building which includes the original chambers of the Security Council, the Trusteeship Council, and the Economic and Social Council, as well as gifts from U.N. Member States like the mosaic representation of Norman Rockwell's "The Golden Rule" are all back on public display. The tour also includes displays on war, peacekeeping, nuclear nonproliferation, human rights, and refugees, and passes corridors overflowing with imaginatively diverse artwork. Free tickets to assemblies are sometimes available on a first-come, first-served basis before sessions begin; pick them up in the General Assembly lobby. If you just want to wander around, the grounds include a beautiful riverside promenade, a rose garden with 1,400 specimens, and sculptures donated by member nations. The complex's buildings (the slim, 505-foot-tall green-glass **Secretariat Building**; the much smaller, domed **General Assembly Building**; and the **Dag Hammarskjöld Library**) evoke the influential French modernist Le Corbusier (who was on the team of architects that designed the complex), and the surrounding park and plaza remain visionary. The public concourse, beneath the visitor entrance, has a coffee shop, gift shops, a bookstore, and a post office where you can mail letters with U.N. stamps. Make sure you take proper ID as you'll have to go through a security check to enter the grounds. ✉ *Visitor entrance, 1st Ave. at E. 46th St., Midtown East* ☎ *212/963–8687* 🌐 *www.un.org* 🎟 *Tour $16 (plus $4 service charge for online ticketing)* ⏲ *Tours weekdays 9:45–4:45; tours in English leave Visitors Lobby every 30 mins; for* *other languages, call 212/963–7539 on the day of your visit* Ⓜ *4, 5, 6, 7, S to Grand Central–42nd St.* ☞ *Children under 5 not admitted.*

WORTH NOTING

Daily News Building. The landmark lobby of this art deco tower contains an illuminated 12-foot globe that revolves beneath a black glass dome. Around it, spreading across the floor like a giant compass and literally positioning New York at the center of the world, bronze lines indicate mileage to various international destinations. Movie fans may recognize the building from its role as the offices of the fictional newspaper the Daily Planet in the original *Superman* movie. The Daily News hasn't called this building home since the mid-1990s. Only the lobby is open to the public (but that's enough). ✉ *220 E. 42nd St., between 2nd and 3rd Aves., Midtown East* ☎ *212/210–2100* Ⓜ *4, 5, 6, 7, S to Grand Central–42nd St.*

Edwynn Houk Gallery. The impressive stable of 20th-century photographers shown here includes Sally Mann, Robert Polidori, Man Ray, and Elliott Erwitt. The gallery also has prints by masters Edward Weston and Alfred Stieglitz. ✉ *745 5th Ave., between E. 57th and E. 58th Sts., 4th fl., Midtown East* ☎ *212/750–7070* 🌐 *www.houkgallery.com* 🕓 *Tues.–Sat. 11–6* Ⓜ *N, R to 5th Ave.*

Helmsley Building. This Warren & Wetmore–designed 1929 landmark was intended to match neighboring Grand Central Terminal in bearing, and it succeeded, with a gold-and-copper roof topped with an enormous lantern (originally housing a 6,000-watt light) and distinctive dual archways for traffic on Park Avenue. The building's history gets quirky, however: When the millionaire real estate investor Harry Helmsley purchased the building in 1977, he changed its name from the New York Central Building to the New York General Building in order to save money by replacing only two letters in the facade (only later did he rename it after himself). During a renovation the following year, however, he actually gilded the building, applying gold paint even to limestone and bronze—it was removed by a succeeding owner. In 2010, after a $100 million renovation, the Helmsley Building became the first prewar office tower to receive LEED Gold certification for energy efficiency. Despite being blocked from view from the south by the MetLife Building (originally, the Pan Am Building), the Helmsley Building remains a defining—and now "green" as opposed to "gold"—feature of one of the world's most lavish avenues. ✉ *230 Park Ave., between 45th and 46th Sts., Midtown East* Ⓜ *4, 5, 6, 7, S to Grand Central–42nd St.*

Japan Society. The stylish, serene lobby of the Japan Society has interior bamboo gardens linked by a second-floor waterfall. Works by well-known Japanese artists are exhibited in the second-floor gallery—past shows have included the first American retrospective of Sakai Hōitsu, a samurai aristocrat turned Buddhist monk who dedicated his life to art and poetry, a display of artwork created by children from Tohoku after Japan's 2011 earthquake, and *Deco Japan: Shaping Art and Culture, 1920–1945*. In July, the museum hosts an annual film festival, Japan Cuts, showcasing contemporary Japanese cinema. ✉ *333 E. 47th St.,*

The restoration and cleaning of Grand Central in the late 1990s uncovered the elaborate astronomical design on the ceiling of the main concourse.

between 1st and 2nd Aves., Midtown East ☎ *212/832–1155* 🌐 *www.japansociety.org* 🎟 *Gallery $15* ⏲ *Building weekdays 9:30–5:30; gallery Tues.–Thurs. 11–6, Fri. 11–9, weekends 11–5* Ⓜ *6 to 51st St.; E, M to Lexington Ave./53rd St.*

8

The Pace Gallery. This leading contemporary art gallery—now with several outposts in Chelsea as well as two in London and a gallery in Beijing—focuses on such modern and contemporary artists as Julian Schnabel, Mark Rothko, James Turrell, and New York School painter Ad Reinhardt. ✉ *32 E. 57th St., between Park and Madison Aves., 2nd fl., Midtown East* ☎ *212/421–3292* 🌐 *www.thepacegallery.com* ⏲ *Tues.–Fri. 9:30–6; Sat. 10–6* Ⓜ *N, R to 5th Ave.*

Seagram Building. Ludwig Mies van der Rohe, a pioneer of modern architecture, built this boxlike bronze-and-glass tower in 1958. The austere facade belies its wit: I-beams, used to hold buildings up, here are merely attached to the surface, representing the *idea* of support. The Seagram Building's innovative ground-level plaza, extending out to the sidewalk, has since become a common element in urban skyscraper design. With its two giant fountains and welcoming steps, it's also a popular lunch spot with midtown workers. Visit late in the afternoon to avoid crowds. ✉ *375 Park Ave., between E. 52nd and E. 53rd Sts., Midtown East* Ⓜ *6 to 51st St.; E, M to Lexington Ave./53rd St.*

Spanierman Gallery. This venerable gallery deals in 19th- and early-20th-century American painting and sculpture. Their inventory list and scholarship is amazing, and they frequently sell to museums looking to broaden their own collections. Just down the block at 53 East 58th Street, Spanierman Modern (🌐 *www.spaniermanmodern.com*)

The view from Midtown over the East River and into Queens.

represents contemporary artists such as Judith Godwin and Frank Bowling. ✉ *45 E. 58th St., between Park and Madison Aves., Midtown East* ☎ *212/832–0208* 🌐 *www.spanierman.com* 🕑 *Mon.–Sat. 9:30–5:30* Ⓜ *N, R to 5th Ave.*

Trump Tower. The tallest all-glass building in Manhattan when it was completed in 1983, this skyscraper's ostentatious atrium flaunts that decade's unbridled luxury, with expensive boutiques and gaudy brass everywhere. You'll half expect the pleasant-sounding waterfall streaming down to the lower-level food court to flow with champagne. These days, the building is best known for its appearances on TV show "Celebrity Apprentice," where Donald Trump hires and fires celebrities. ✉ *725 5th Ave., at E. 56th St., Midtown East* ☎ *212/832–2000* 🌐 *www.trump.com* Ⓜ *N, R to 5th Ave./59th St.*

Tudor City. Before Donald Trump, there was Fred F. French. In 1925 the prominent real-estate developer became one of the first to buy up a large number of buildings—more than 100, in fact, most of them tenements—and join their properties into a single new development. He designed a collection of nine apartment buildings and two parks in the "garden city" mode, which placed a building's green space not in an enclosed courtyard but in the foreground. French also elevated the entire development 70 feet (40 stone steps) above the river and built a 39-by-50-foot "Tudor City" sign atop one of the 22-story buildings. The development's residential towers opened between 1927 and 1930, borrowing a marketable air of sophistication from Tudor-style stonework, stained-glass windows, and lobby design flourishes. An official city landmark, Tudor City has been featured in numerous films, and its gardens remain a popular lunch spot among office workers. The neighborhood was designated an historic district in 1988. ✉ *Between East 40th and East 43rd Sts and 1st and 2nd Aves., Midtown East* Ⓜ *4, 5, 6, 7, S to Grand Central–42nd St.*

MURRAY HILL

Murray Hill stretches roughly from about 30th to 40th streets between 5th and 3rd avenues and is a mix of high-rises, restaurants, and bars filled mostly with a postcollege crowd. The small but solid enclave of Little India (also known as Curry Hill), primarily around Lexington and 28th Street, is a good area to sample authentic cuisine and shop for traditional clothing and other goods in a handful of boutiques. Farther north a few side streets are tree-lined and town house–filled with some high-profile haunts, including the Morgan Library and Museum with its vast book stacks and rare manuscripts. But perhaps the biggest reason to visit this neighborhood is to see New York's biggest icon, the Empire State Building.

TOP ATTRACTIONS

FAMILY
Fodor's Choice ★

Empire State Building. With a pencil-slim silhouette, recognizable virtually worldwide, the Empire State Building is an art deco monument to progress, a symbol for New York City, and a star in some great romantic scenes, on- and off-screen. Its cinematic résumé—the building has appeared in more than 250 movies—means that it remains a fixture of popular imagination, and many visitors come to relive favorite movie scenes. You might just find yourself at the top of the building with *Elf* look-alikes or even the building's own *King Kong* impersonator.

Built in 1931 at the peak of the skyscraper craze, this 103-story limestone giant opened after a mere 13 months of construction. The framework rose at an astonishing rate of 4½ stories per week, making the Empire State Building the fastest-rising skyscraper ever built.

Unfortunately, your rise to the observation deck might not be quite so record breaking. There are three lines to get to the top of the Empire State Building; a line for tickets, a line for security, and a line for the elevators. **TIP→** Save time by purchasing your tickets in advance (🌐 esbnyc.com). You can't skip the security line, but you can skip to the front of both the ticket line and the line for elevators by purchasing an Express ticket ($47.50). If you don't want to pony up for express service, do yourself a favor and skip that last elevator line at the 80th floor by taking the stairs. If this is your first visit, keep yourself entertained during your ascent by renting a headset with an audio tour by Tony, a fictional but "authentic" native New Yorker, available in eight languages.

The 86th-floor observatory (1,050 feet high) has both a glass-enclosed area (heated in winter and cooled in summer) and an outdoor deck spanning the building's circumference. Don't be shy about going outside into the wind (even in winter) or you'll miss half the experience. Also, don't be deterred by crowds; there's an unspoken etiquette when it comes to sharing the views and backdrop, and there's plenty of city to go around. Bring quarters for the high-powered binoculars—on clear days you can see up to 80 miles—or bring binoculars of your own so you can get a good look at some of the city's rooftop gardens. If it rains, the deck will be less crowded and you can view the city between the clouds or watch the rain travel sideways around the building from the shelter of the enclosed walkway.

The views of the city from the 86th-floor deck are spectacular, but the views from 16 stories up on the 102nd-floor observatory are even more so—and yet, fewer visitors make it this far. Instead of rushing back to elevator lines, ask yourself when you'll be back again and then head up to the enclosed 102nd floor. The ticket for both the 86th-floor and 102nd-floor decks costs $42, but you will be rewarded with peaceful, bird's-eye views of the entire city. Also, there are fewer visitors angling for photo ops, so you can linger a while and really soak in the city and experience. **TIP→ Even if you skip the view from up top, be sure to step into the lobby and take in the ceiling, beautifully restored in 2009. The gilded gears and sweeping art deco lines, long hidden under a drop ceiling and decades of paint, are a romantic tribute to the machine age and part of the original vision for the building.** ✉ *350 5th Ave., between E. 33rd and E. 34th Sts., Murray Hill* ☎ *212/736–3100, 877/692–8439* 🌐 *www.esbnyc.com* 🎫 *$25; $42 for 86th fl. and 102nd fl. decks* 🕑 *Daily 8 am–2 am; last elevator up leaves at 1:15 am*

NY SKYRIDE. Although some parents blanch when they discover both how much it costs and how it lurches, the second-floor NY SKYRIDE, New York's only aerial virtual tour simulator, is a favorite of the 7- and 8-year-old set, and it's cheaper than an actual aerial tour of New York. Narrated by actor Kevin Bacon, the ride takes the viewer on a 30 minute virtual tour of New York, soaring by the Brooklyn Bridge, the Statue of Liberty, Central Park, Times Square, Yankee Stadium, and other top attractions along the way. There's also a brief but poignant trip back in time to visit the World Trade Center's Twin Towers—a sight sure to drive you straight into the arms of the first I [Heart] NY T-shirt vendor you see when you leave the building. It's a fun way to get a sense of the city's highlights, though teenagers may find the technology a little dated, and baseball buffs may gripe that the footage has not been updated to reflect the new Yankee Stadium. **TIP→ When you purchase a Skyride–Empire State Building combo ticket, you'll visit the Skyride first and then join the line for the observation deck at the elevators, skipping up to half the wait.** ✉ *Empire State Building, entrance on 33rd St.* ☎ *212/279–9777, 888/759–7433* 🌐 *www.skyride.com* 🎫 *$42; $57 combo Skyride and observatory (significant discounts are available on the website)* 🕑 *Daily 8 am–10 pm* Ⓜ *B, D, F, N, Q, R, M to 34th St.–Herald Sq.; 6 to 33rd St.*

Morgan Library and Museum. The treasures inside this museum, gathered by John Pierpont Morgan (1837–1913), one of New York's wealthiest financiers, are exceptional: medieval and Renaissance illuminated manuscripts, old master drawings and prints, rare books, and autographed literary and musical manuscripts. Crowning achievements produced on paper, from the Middle Ages to the 20th century, are on view here: letters penned by John Keats and Thomas Jefferson; a summary of the theory of relativity in Einstein's own elegant handwriting; three Gutenberg

CLOSE UP

The Lights of the Empire State Building

At night the Empire State Building lights up the Manhattan skyline with a colorful view as awe-inspiring from a distance as the view from the top. The colors at the top of the building are changed regularly to reflect seasons, events, and holidays, so New Yorkers and visitors from around the world always have a reason to look at this icon in a new light.

The building's first light show was in November 1932, when a simple searchlight was used to spread the news that New York–born Franklin Delano Roosevelt had been elected president of the United States. Douglas Leigh, sign designer and mastermind of Times Square's kinetic billboard ads, tried to brighten up prospects at the "Empty State Building" after the Depression by negotiating with the Coca-Cola Company to occupy the top floors. He proposed that Coca-Cola could change the lights of the building to serve as a weather forecast and then publish a small guide on its bottles to decipher the colors. Coca-Cola loved this idea, but the deal fell through because of the bombing at Pearl Harbor, when the US government needed office space in the building.

In 1956 the revolving "freedom lights" were installed to welcome people to America; then in 1964 the top 30 floors of the building were illuminated to mark the New York World's Fair. Douglas Leigh revisited the lights of the ESB in 1976, when he was made chairman of City Decor to welcome the Democratic Convention. He introduced the idea of color lighting, and so the building's tower was ablaze in red, white, and blue to welcome the convention and to mark the celebration of the American Bicentennial. The

color lights were a huge success, and they remained red, white, and blue for the rest of the year.

Leigh's next suggestion of tying the lights to different holidays, a variation on his weather theme for Coca-Cola, is the basic scheme still used today. In 1977 the lighting system was updated to comply with energy conservation programs and to allow for a wider range of colors. Leigh further improved this new system in 1984 by designing an automated color-changing system so vertical fluorescents in the mast could be changed.

In November 2012, the Empire State Building debuted its new LED light system, synchronizing its undulating lights to Alicia Keys' "Girl on Fire" and Jay Z's "Empire State of Mind." For the building's first major exterior lighting renovation in many years, Philips Color Kinetic created a system that can produce both intensely saturated full-color light and dimmable cool white light, allowing for an astonishing and flexible range of dramatic or subtle lighting effects.

For a full lighting schedule, visit *www.esbnyc.com.*

—Jacinta O'Halloran

Bibles; drawings by Dürer, Leonardo da Vinci, Rubens, Blake, and Rembrandt; the only known manuscript fragment of Milton's *Paradise Lost*; Thoreau's journals; and original manuscripts and letters by Charlotte Brontë, Jane Austen, Thomas Pynchon, and many others.

The library shop is within an 1852 Italianate brownstone, once the home of Morgan's son, J. P. Morgan Jr. Outside on East 36th Street, the sphinx in the right-hand sculptured panel of the original library's facade was rumored to wear the face of architect Charles McKim. ✉ *225 Madison Ave., at 36th St., Murray Hill* ☎ *212/685–0008* 🌐 *www.themorgan.org* 🎟 *$15; free Fri. 7–9* 🕒 *Tues.–Thurs. 10:30–5, Fri. 10:30–9, Sat. 10–6, Sun. 11–6* Ⓜ *B, D, F, N, Q, R, V to 34th St.–Herald Sq.; 6 to 33rd St.*

WORTH NOTING

FAMILY **B. Altman Building/New York Public Library–Science, Industry, and Business Library (SIBL).** In 1906 department-store magnate Benjamin Altman gambled that his fashionable patrons would follow him uptown from his popular store in the area now known as the Ladies' Mile Historic District. His new store, one of the first of the grand department stores on 5th Avenue, was designed to blend with the mansions nearby. Note in particular the beautiful entrance on 5th Avenue. In 1996 the New York Public Library set up a high-tech library here. A 33-foot-high atrium unites the building's two floors, the lending library off the lobby and the research collections below. Downstairs a wall of electronic ticker tapes and TVs tuned to business-news stations beams information and instructions to patrons. A free one-hour tour is offered Thursday at 2; meet at the reception desk. ✉ *188 Madison Ave., between E. 34th and E. 35th Sts., Murray Hill* ☎ *917/275–6975* 🌐 *www.nypl.org* 🕒 *Mon., Fri., and Sat. 11–6, Tues.–Thurs. 10–8* Ⓜ *6 to 33rd St.*

Koreatown. Despite sitting in the shade of the Empire State Building, and within steps of Herald Square, Koreatown—or K-Town as it's locally known—is not a tourist destination. In fact, it feels decidedly off-the-beaten-track and insulated, as though locals wryly planted their own place to eat, drink, be merry, and get a massage, right under the noses of millions of tourists. Technically, Koreatown runs from 31st to 36th streets and between Fifth and Sixth avenues, though the main drag is 32nd Street between Fifth and Broadway. Known as Korea Way, this strip is home to 24-7 Korean barbecue joints, karaoke bars, and spas, all piled on top of each other. Fill up on kimchi (spicy pickled cabbage), kimbap (seaweed rice), and red bean doughnuts (delicious), try some authentic Asian karaoke, and then top off your Koreatown experience by stepping into a jade igloo sauna (at Juvenex Spa, 25 West 32nd St.). Expect bang for your buck, to rub elbows with locals, and bragging rights over visitors who followed the crowds to Chinatown. ✉ *Bordered by 31st and 36th Sts., 5th and 6th Aves., Murray Hill* Ⓜ *B, D, F, N, Q, R, M to 34th St.–Herald Sq.; 6 to 33rd St.*

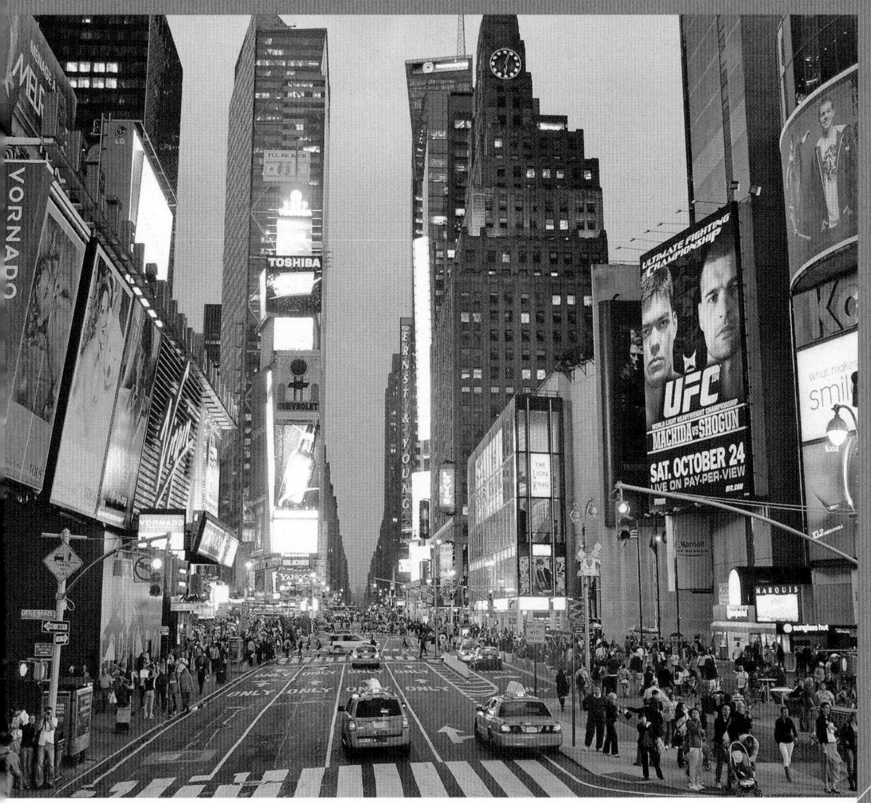

9

MIDTOWN WEST

with Times Square and Rockefeller Center

GETTING ORIENTED

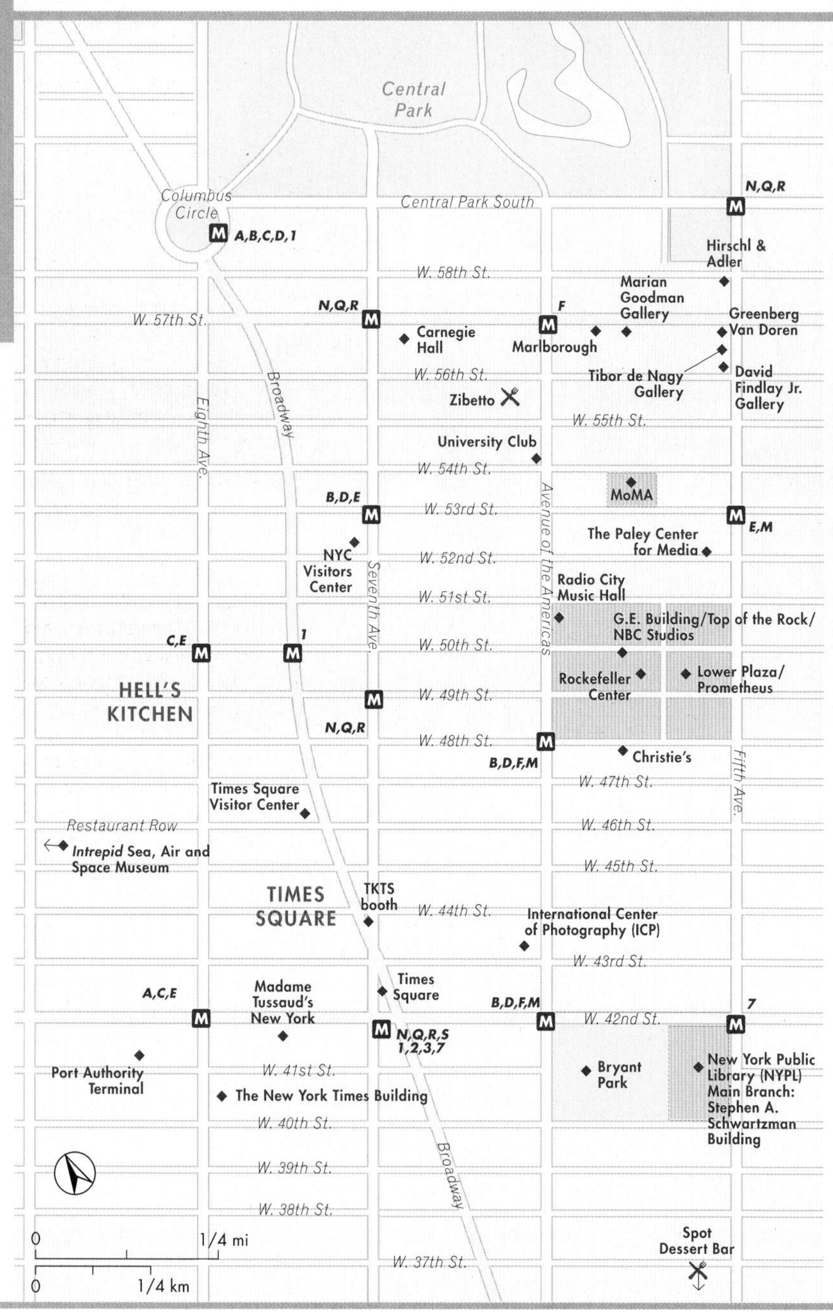

MAKING THE MOST OF YOUR TIME

Most people think of Times Square when they think of Midtown but there's a lot more going on here. The Museum of Modern Art (MoMA) is one of this neighborhood's top attractions, and definitely worth a visit, as is Bryant Park—a cool oasis for Midtown's workers and locals. If you have enough time, hop in a cab and head over to 12th Avenue to visit the space shuttle Enterprise at the *Intrepid* Sea, Air & Space Museum.

Times Square is almost always a frenetic mass of people, staring up at the lights and the giant televisions. If you're in a hurry to get somewhere, try to avoid walking—or cabbing—through here. If you want to experience the thrill of thousands of racing workaday suits, though, visit Rockefeller Center at rush hour on a weekday. If you're staying in Midtown, you can take advantage of the prime location and rise early to be first in line at landmarks, museums, or the TKTS booth for discount day-of theater tickets (⇨ *Chapter 16: Performing Arts*).

COFFEE AND QUICK BITES

Spot Dessert Bar. You'll find the K-town outpost of this uber-popular East Village Asian dessert shop on the second floor of Food Gallery 32. You'll want to save a large spot in your appetite for all the delicious desserts here; if you must choose, try the yuzu eskimo, the chocolate green tea lava cake, or the Vietnamese coffee ice cream. ✉ *11 West 32nd St., 2nd Fl., Midtown West* ☎ *212/967–1678.*

Zibetto Espresso Bar. You won't find any seats but you will find arguably the best espresso drinks in New York, served in ceramic cups (with a glass of water). You'll also find tasty mini pastries. ✉ *1385 6th Ave., at 56th St., Midtown West* ✎ *info@zibetto.com.*

TOP EXPERIENCES

Elbowing your way through Times Square.

Summer film screenings at dusk in Bryant Park.

Skating at Rockefeller Center.

Checking out the views from the Top of the Rock; opinions vary on whether the better views are from here or from the Empire State Building. Either way, if you go at night, the city spreads out below in a mesmerizing blanket of lights.

Soaking in the art and serenity of MoMA's sculpture garden.

GETTING HERE

You can get to Midtown via (almost) all the subways; many make numerous stops throughout the area. For Midtown West, the 1, 2, 3, 7, A, C, E, N, Q, and R serve Times Square and West 42nd Street. The S or Shuttle travels back and forth between Times Square and Grand Central (if you're going to the east side). The B, D, F, and M trains serve Rockefeller Center.

Sightseeing ★★★★★ Nightlife ★★★ Dining ★★★★★ Lodging ★★★★★ Shopping ★★★★★

Big is the buzz in Times Square where giant TV screens, towering skyscrapers, and Broadway theaters play starring roles alongside megastores like Hershey's and Toys "R" Us. Love it or hate it, Times Square is the flashy and flashing heart of Midtown. A visit to New York demands a photo op in Times Square. Just don't forget that there's also a lot more to see and experience on this side of Midtown.

Updated by Jacinta O'Halloran

Luckily, you needn't go far from Times Square to get away from the crowds. Head over to 9th Avenue—also known as Hell's Kitchen (though the food here is heavenly)—and the calmer side streets, home to a mixed bag of locals, many who work in the theater industry. There are lots of eclectic restaurants, pretheater dining options, and cute boutiques for shopping.

You can score good seats to some of the hottest Broadway and Off Broadway shows for half the going rate at the TKTS booth in Duffy Square at 47th Street and Broadway (⇨ *Chapter 20, Performing Arts*). Although people think of Broadway as the heart of the theater scene, few theaters actually line the thoroughfare. For some of the grandes dames, head west on 45th Street. There are several Broadway beauties here, including the **Booth,** the **Schoenfeld,** the **Jacobs,** the **Music Box,** and the **Imperial.** On the southern side of 45th Street there's the pedestrians-only **Shubert Alley,** distinguished by colorful posters advertising the latest hit plays and musicals, and the **Shubert Theatre,** one of Broadway's most lustrous gems. Head west along 44th Street to see the **Helen Hayes,** the **Broadhurst,** the **Majestic,** and the **St. James.**

TOP ATTRACTIONS

FAMILY **Bryant Park.** This lovely green space nestled among landmarks and skyscrapers is one of Manhattan's most popular parks. Tall London plane trees line the perimeter of the sunny central lawn, overlooking stone terraces, formal flower beds, gravel pathways, and a smattering of kiosks selling everything from sandwiches to egg creams (in season). The garden tables scattered about fill with lunching office workers and folks enjoying the park's free Wi-Fi. In summer you can check out free live jazz and "Broadway in Bryant Park" musical theater performances, as well as author readings. Most popular of all is the Summer Film Festival: locals leave work early to snag a spot on the lawn for the outdoor screenings each Monday at dusk. At the east side of the park, near a squatting bronze cast of Gertrude Stein, is the stylish Bryant Park Grill and the adjacent open-air Bryant Park Café, open seasonally. On the south side of the park is an old-fashioned **carousel** ($2) where kids can ride fanciful rabbits and frogs instead of horses, and attend storytellings and magic shows. Big kids can play with the park's selection of lawn and tabletop games, which includes everything from Quoits and Scrabble to Chinese Checkers and Scandinavian Kubb. Come late October the park rolls out the artificial frozen **"pond"** (*Nov.–Feb., Sun–Wed. 8 am–10 pm, Fri. and Sat. 8 am–midnight; skate rental $14*) for ice-skating. Surrounding the ice rink are the Christmas market–like stalls of the **Holiday Shops**, selling handcrafted goods and local foods. ✉ *6th Ave. between W. 40th and W. 42nd Sts., Midtown West* ☎ *212/768–4242* 🌐 *www.bryantpark.org* 🕑 *Hrs vary by month. See website for exact times.* Ⓜ *B, D, F, M to 42nd St.–Bryant Park; 7 to 5th Ave.*

FAMILY ***Intrepid* Sea, Air & Space Museum.** The centerpiece of the *Intrepid* Sea, Air & Space Museum complex is the 900-foot *Intrepid* aircraft carrier, Manhattan's only floating museum. The carrier's most trying moment of service, the day it was attacked in World War II by kamikaze pilots, is recounted in a multimedia presentation. The museum itself was forced to close for several months after 2012's Hurricane Sandy. Fortunately, its unparalleled collection of aircraft was not damaged in the storm. The museum reopened in late December 2012 with a renovated welcome center and a reinforced home for the space shuttle *Enterprise*, NASA's first prototype orbiter which joined the Intrepid in July 2012. *Enterprise* is temporarily housed in a climate-controlled bubble tent on the flight deck of the *Intrepid,* but visitors can check out plans for what will eventually be its permanent home, on the interactive wall outside the Space Shuttle Pavilion. While *Enterprise* never flew in space, it is presented in a dramatic darkened display with blue lighting to evoke the atmosphere of flight. Images and displays share the shuttle's history and that of NASA's 30-year space shuttle program.

9

Docked alongside the *Intrepid,* and also part of the museum, is the *Growler,* a strategic-missile submarine. The interactive Exploreum contains 18 hands-on exhibits. You can experience a flight simulator, transmit messages in Morse code, and see what it was like to live aboard the massive carrier. **TIP→** There are frequent ticket discounts if you purchase through the museum website. ✉ *Pier 86, W 46th St. and 12th Ave., Midtown West* ☎ *212/245–0072, 877/957–7447* 🌐 *www.intrepidmuseum.org* 🎫 *$24* 🕑 *Apr.–Oct., weekdays 10–5, weekends 10–6; Nov.–Mar., Tues.–Sun. 10–5; last admission 1 hr before closing* Ⓜ *A, C, E to 42nd St.–Port Authority; M42 bus to pier.*

Radio City Music Hall. *See the listing in Chapter 20: Performing Arts.*

Rockefeller Center. If Times Square is New York's crossroads, Rockefeller Center is its communal gathering place, where the entire world

CLOSE UP

Keeping It Real in Times Square

How to act like a local in Times Square? Look as if you want to leave. The local art of walking in Times Square involves zigzagging around the slow crowds that gather like obstacles. Avoid looking overtly at the billboards, and whatever you do, don't snap pictures. Display an ironic detachment: you're just passing through.

Why the snide comments? Consider the noise and billboards from a New Yorker's perspective. The chains that dominate here from Applebee's to M&M's World to Toys "R" Us with its Ferris wheel make some locals mourn the old "naughty, bawdy, gaudy" Times Square portrayed in the musical *42nd Street.*

In truth, a visit to Times Square can be great fun when the lights stand out at nighttime, especially if you're with kids (whose hands you must *never* release because of the undertow-like crowds)—just try to focus on the flashing walls of neon colors and not the overwhelming corporate advertising.

Although nobody's really nostalgic (no matter what they may say) for the derelict Times Square of the '70s and '80s, at least that Times Square reflected (however grotesquely) the challenges all the city's residents were facing. New Yorkers pride themselves on their survivor's ability to tough out the harshness of city living. For decades Times Square embodied that toughness ("if I can make it here, I can make it anywhere"). Out in the open, underneath the bright-lighted billboards, it was clear as day what New York City had to offer newcomers, take it or leave it.

The Times Square of today—in which each building is required to give off a minimum amount of light between the ground and 65 feet up—is a family-friendly, open-air promenade of familiar brand names in theme park–like settings, including the world's largest McDonald's. But not all change is bad: there's the stadium seating behind TKTS, and, along Broadway, pedestrian-friendly spaces closed to traffic, including tables and chairs. And, of course, we never lost the rich theater scene itself, which locals frequent along with visitors.

converges to snap pictures, skate on the ice rink, peek in on a taping of the *Today* show, shop, eat, and take in the monumental art-deco structures and public sculptures from the past century. Totaling more than 75 shops and 45 eateries (including Thomas Keller's Bouchon Bakery), the complex runs from 47th to 52nd streets between 5th and 7th avenues. Special events and huge pieces of art dominate the central plazas in spring and summer. In December an enormous twinkling tree towers above the ice-skating rink, causing huge crowds of visitors from across the country and the globe to shuffle through with necks craned and cameras flashing. The first official tree-lighting ceremony was held in 1933.

The world's most famous **ice-skating rink** occupies Rockefeller Center's sunken lower plaza October through April (it's a café in summer). Skaters swoop or stumble across the ice while crowds gather at street level to

The iconic marquee at Radio City Music Hall

watch the spins and spills. The gold-leaf statue of the fire-stealing Greek hero **Prometheus**—Rockefeller Center's most famous sculpture—hovers above, forming the backdrop to zillions of photos. Carved into the wall behind it, a quotation from Aeschylus reads "Prometheus, teacher in every art, brought the fire that hath proved to mortals a means to mighty ends." **TIP→ The lower plaza also provides access to the marble-lined corridors underneath Rockefeller Center, which house restaurants, a post office, and clean public restrooms—a rarity in Midtown.**

Rising up on the Lower Plaza's west side is the 70-story (850-foot-tall) art-deco **GE Building**, a testament to modern urban development. Here Rockefeller commissioned and then destroyed a mural by Diego Rivera upon learning that it featured Vladimir Lenin. He replaced it with the monumental *American Progress* by José María Sert, still on view in the lobby, flanked by additional murals by Sert and English artist Frank Brangwyn. While in the lobby, pick up a free "Rockefeller Center Visitor's Guide" at the **information desk**. Up on the 65th floor sits the now-shuttered city icon and Landmark Rainbow Room, a glittering big-band ballroom from 1934 through 2009. Higher up, Top of the Rock (⇨ *Top of the Rock*) offers what many consider the finest panoramic views of the city. ✉ *30 Rockefeller Plaza* 🌐 *www.rockefellercenter.com* Ⓜ *B, D, F, M 47–50th Sts./Rockefeller Center.*

Times Square. Hands down, this is the most frenetic part of New York City, a cacophony of flashing lights and shoulder-to-shoulder crowds that many New Yorkers studiously avoid. Originally named after *The New York Times* (whose headquarters have relocated nearby), the area has seen many changes since the first subway line, which included a

Ice-skating under the sculpture of Prometheus, at Rockefeller Center, is a winter ritual for many local and visiting families.

42nd street Station, opened in 1904. You won't find speakeasies and unsavory clubs around here nowadays, it's more of a vibrant, family-friendly destination, with a pedestrianized stretch of Broadway and stadium seating behind discount theater ticket seller TKTS, all under the glare of brand names like MTV and M&Ms. If you like sensory overload, the chaotic mix of huge underwear billboards, flashing digital displays, on-location television broadcasts, naked cowboys, and Elmo clones will give you your fix. The focus of the entertainment may have shifted over the years, but showtime is still the heart of New York's theater scene and there are forty Broadway theaters nearby. ✉ *Broadway between 42nd and 44th Sts., Midtown West* ☎ *212/768–1560* 🌐 *www.timessquarenyc.org* Ⓜ *1, 2, 3, 7, N, Q, R, S to Times Sq.–42 St.*

Times Square Visitor Center. After its $1.8 million renovation, this visitor center is the place to take shelter when the crowds start to overwhelm you. On display are a past New Year's Eve ball and a New Year's Eve "Wishing Wall," where you can write on confetti that will become one of the actual pieces to flutter down at midnight on January 1. You can also watch a video on Times Square's unsavory past in a mock–peep booth. Stop by for multilingual kiosks, MetroCards, a peek in the gift shop, sightseeing and theater tickets, and (most important!) free restrooms. Since 2012, the center has partnered with Manhattan Walking Tours to offer two 90-minute walking tours of the area—the Times Square History Tour and the Broadway Walking Tour. ✉ *1560 Broadway, entrance on 7th Ave., between 46th and 47 Sts., Midtown West* ☎ *212/768–1560* 🌐 *www.timessquarenyc.org* 🎫 *Walking tours $25* 🕒 *Daily 8–8. Tours leave daily at 9:45, 11, 12:30, 1:45, 3, and 4:45* Ⓜ *1, 2, 3, 7, N, Q, R, S to Times Sq.–42nd St.*

CLOSE UP

Art in Rockefeller Center

The mosaics, murals, and sculptures that grace Rockefeller Center—many of them considered art-deco masterpieces—were all part of John D. Rockefeller Jr.'s plans. In 1932, as the steel girders on the first of the buildings were heading heavenward, Rockefeller put together a team of advisers to find artists who could make the project "as beautiful as possible." More than 50 artists were commissioned for 200 individual works.

Some artists scoffed at the idea of decorating an office building: Picasso declined to meet with Rockefeller, and Matisse replied that busy businessmen wouldn't be in the "quiet and reflective state of mind" needed to appreciate his art. Those who agreed to contribute, including muralists Diego Rivera and José María Sert, were relatively unknown, though a group of American artists protested Rockefeller's decision to hire "alien" artists.

As Rockefeller Center neared completion in 1932, Rockefeller still needed a mural for the lobby of the main building and he wanted the subject of the 63-by-17-foot mural to be grandiose: "human intelligence in control of the forces of nature." He hired Rivera.

With its depiction of massive machinery moving mankind forward, Rivera's *Man at the Crossroads* seemed exactly what Rockefeller wanted—until it was realized that a portrait of Soviet Premier Vladimir Lenin surrounded by red-kerchiefed workers occupied a space in the center. Rockefeller, who was building what was essentially a monument to capitalism, was less than thrilled. When Rivera was accused of propagandizing, he famously replied, "All art is propaganda."

Rivera refused to remove the offending portrait and, in early 1934, as Rivera was working, representatives for Rockefeller informed him that his services were no longer required. Within a half hour, tar paper had been hung over the mural. Despite negotiations to move it to the Museum of Modern Art, Rockefeller was determined to get rid of the mural once and for all. Not content to have it painted over, he ordered ax-wielding workers to chip away the entire wall.

Rockefeller ordered the mural replaced by a less offensive one by Sert. Rivera did have the last word: he re-created the mural in the Palacio de Bellas Artes in Mexico City, adding a portrait of Rockefeller among the champagne-swilling swells ignoring the plight of the workers.

The largest of the original artworks that remained is Lee Lawrie's two-ton sculpture, *Atlas.* Its building also stirred controversy, as it was said to resemble Italy's fascist dictator, Benito Mussolini. The sculpture, depicting a muscle-bound man holding up the world, drew protests in 1936. Some even derided Paul Manship's golden *Prometheus,* which soars over the ice-skating rink, when it was unveiled the same year. Both are now considered to be among the best public artworks of the 20th century.

Lawrie's sculpture *Wisdom,* perched over the main entrance of 20 Rockefeller Plaza, is another gem. Also look for Isamu Noguchi's stainless-steel plaque *News* over the entrance of the Bank of America Building at 50 Rockefeller Plaza and Attilio Piccirilli's 2-ton glass-block panel called *Youth Leading Industry* over the entrance of the International Building.

Fodor's Choice ★ **Top of the Rock.** Rockefeller Center's multifloor observation deck, the Top of the Rock, on the 69th–70th floors of the building provides views that rival those from the Empire State Building—some would say they're even better because the views include the Empire State Building. Arriving just before sunset affords a view of the city that morphs before your eyes into a dazzling wash of colors, with a bird's-eye view of the tops of the Empire State Building, the Citicorp Building, and the Chrysler Building, and sweeping views northward to Central Park and south to the Statue of Liberty. Reserved-time ticketing eliminates long lines. Indoor exhibits include films of Rockefeller Center's history and a model of the building. Especially interesting is a Plexiglas screen on the floor with footage showing Rock Center construction workers dangling on beams high above the streets; the brave can even "walk" across a beam to get a sense of what it might have been like to erect this skyscraper. A Sun & Stars ticket ($38) allows you to see the city as it rises and sets in the same day. ✉ *Entrance on 50th St., between 5th and 6th Aves., 30 Rockefeller Plaza, Midtown West* ☎ *212/698–2000, 212/698–2000* 🌐 *www.topoftherocknyc.com* 🎫 *$25 adult; children under 6 not admitted* ⏲ *Daily 8–midnight; last elevator at 11* Ⓜ *B, D, F, M to 47th–50th Sts./Rockefeller Center.*

WORTH NOTING

Christie's. One of the first items to be auctioned at the New York outpost of this infamous auction house, when it opened in 2000, was the "Happy Birthday" dress worn by Marilyn Monroe when she sang to President Kennedy (it sold for more than $1.2 million, in case you were wondering). Yes, the auction house has come a long way since James Christie launched his business in England by selling two chamber pots, among other household goods, in 1766. The lobby's specially commissioned abstract Sol Lewitt mural alone makes it worth visiting the 310,000-square-foot space, but you can also participate in Christie's auctions via streaming video. ✉ *20 Rockefeller Plaza, 49th St. between 5th and 6th Aves., Midtown West* ☎ *212/492–5485* 🌐 *www.christies.com* ⏲ *Daily; hrs vary* Ⓜ *B, D, F, M to 47th–50th Sts./Rockefeller Center.*

David Findlay Jr. Gallery. This well-established gallery concentrates on contemporary and 20th-century American artists from Whistler to Herman Cherry, Byron Brown, and David Aronson, and specializes in the New York School. ✉ *724 Fifth Ave., 8th fl., Midtown West* ☎ *212/486–7660* 🌐 *www.davidfindlayjr.com* ⏲ *Mon.–Sat. 10–5:30* Ⓜ *N, R to 5th Ave.*

Hirschl & Adler Gallery. Although this gallery has a selection of European works, it's best known for American paintings, prints, and decorative arts. The celebrated 19th- and 20th-century artists whose works are featured include Stuart Davis, Childe Hassam, Camille Pissarro, and John Singleton Copley. ✉ *730 5th Ave., at W. 57th St., 4th fl., Midtown West* ☎ *212/535–8810* 🌐 *www.hirschlandadler.com* ⏲ *Tues.–Fri. 9:30–5:15, Sat. 9:30–4:45* Ⓜ *N, R to 5th Ave.; F to 57th St.*

International Center of Photography. Founded in 1974 by photojournalist Cornell Capa (photographer Robert Capa's brother), this top-notch photography museum and school has a collection of over 150,000 original prints spanning the history of photography from daguerreotypes to large-scale pigment prints. Changing exhibits display work by famous and should-be-famous photographers, while themed group shows focus on topics such as ecology, health, religion, science, war, and candid street shots. The gift shop has amazing imagery on postcards, posters, and prints, and outstanding photography books. ✉ *1133 Ave. of the Americas, at 43rd St., Midtown West* ☎ *212/857–0000* 🌐 *www.icp.org* 🎫 *$14* 🕒 *Tues.–Wed. and weekends 10–6, Thurs.–Fri. 10–8* Ⓜ *B, D, F, M to 42nd St.–Bryant Park.*

Madame Tussaud's New York. Sit in the Oval Office with President Obama, sing along with Lady Gaga, pose with your favorite heartthrob—be it Justin Bieber or Justin Timberlake, or enjoy a royal chat with the Duke and Duchess of Cambridge, William and Kate. Much of the fun here comes from the photo opportunities—you're encouraged to pose with and touch the nearly 200 realistic replicas of the famous, the infamous, and the downright super. The new Marvel 4D Experience includes wax likenesses of heroes like The Hulk, Captain America, Ironman, and Thor, as well as a short animated movie shown on a 360-degree screen that surrounds the viewer. Other interactive options at the museum include a karaoke café, a celebrity walk down the red carpet, and a haunted town populated with both wax figures and real people. ✉ *234 W. 42nd St., between 7th and 8th Aves., Midtown West* ☎ *866/841–3505* 🌐 *www.madame-tussauds.com* 🎫 *$36* 🕒 *Sun.–Thurs. 10–8; Fri. and Sat. 10–10* Ⓜ *1, 2, 3, 7, A, C, E, N, Q, R, S to Times Sq.–42nd St.*

Marian Goodman Gallery. Perhaps the most respected contemporary art dealer in town, the Marian Goodman Gallery has been introducing top European artists to American audiences for over thirty years. The stable of excellent contemporary artists here includes Gerhard Richter, Jeff Wall, William Kentridge, Thomas Schutte, and Steve McQueen. ✉ *24 W. 57th St., between 5th and 6th Aves., Midtown West* ☎ *212/977–7160* 🌐 *www.mariangoodman.com* 🕒 *Mon.–Sat. 10–6* Ⓜ *F to 57th St.*

9

Marlborough Gallery. The Marlborough gallery has an international reputation, representing modern artists such as Magdalena Abakanowicz, Zao Wou-Ki, Red Grooms, and photorealist Richard Estes. Look for sculptures by Tom Otterness—his whimsical bronzes are found in several subway stations. There is also a branch in Chelsea. ✉ *40 W. 57th St., between 5th and 6th Aves., Midtown West* ☎ *212/541–4900* 🌐 *www.marlboroughgallery.com* 🕒 *Tues.–Sat. 10–5:30* Ⓜ *F to 57th St.*

NBC Studios. The GE Building also houses NBC Studios, whose news tapings, visible at street level, attract gawking crowds. Studio tours (every fifteen minutes daily) delve into the history of television and take you behind the scenes on the network's top shows; you can reserve tickets online. Tours start at the NBC Experience Store (49th Street between 5th and 6th avenues). ✉ *30 Rockefeller Plaza, W. 49th St. between 5th and 6th Aves. Midtown West* ☎ *212/664–3700* 🌐 *www.nbcstudiotour.com* 🎫 *NBC Studio Tour $24* 🕒 *Tours depart every 15 mins Mon.–Thurs. 8:30–5:30, Fri. and Sat. 8:30–6:30, Sun. 9:15–4:30* Ⓜ *B, D, F, M to 47th–50th Sts./Rockefeller Center* ☞ *Children under 6 not permitted.*

New York Public Library (NYPL) Main Branch: Stephen A. Schwarzman Building. In 2011 the "Library with the Lions" celebrated its centennial as a masterpiece of beaux-arts design and one of the great research institutions in the world, with more than 6 million books, 12 million manuscripts, and 3 million pictures. In 2012, this National Historic Landmark was the center of much discussion as the library's board approved a controversial $300 million plan to convert the 5th Avenue flagship into the world's largest combined research and circulating library—a plan that will create two floors of storage space under adjacent **Bryant Park**, create additional public space and computer terminals, and eventually fold two other Manhattan branches under its roof. Construction is expected to begin in late 2013, at which point the library will close for two years—check the website for details.

DID YOU KNOW?

Watching the Macy's Thanksgiving Day Parade is as iconic to the Thanksgiving holiday as turkey and stuffing, but most New Yorkers prefer to watch it on TV. If you're looking for locals, you'll find them the day before Thanksgiving, getting into the holiday spirit at the preparade balloon inflation known as "Inflation Eve." Get in on the ritual by heading to the designated path around the American Museum of Natural History from 3 to 10 pm. Dress warmly!

The library's bronze front doors open into **Astor Hall,** which leads to several special exhibit galleries and, to the left, a stunning periodicals room with wall paintings of New York publishing houses. Ascend the sweeping double staircase to a second-floor balconied corridor overlooking the hall, with panels highlighting the library's development. Continue up to the magisterial **Rose Main Reading Room**—297 feet long (almost two full north–south city blocks); walk through to best appreciate the rows of oak tables and the extraordinary ceiling. Several additional third-floor galleries show rotating exhibits on print and photography (past exhibits have included old New York restaurant menus and a 1455 Gutenberg Bible). Free one-hour tours leave Monday–Saturday at 11 and 2, and Sunday at 2 from Astor Hall. Women's bathrooms are on the ground floor and third floor, and there's a men's bathroom on the third floor. ✉ *5th Ave., between E. 40th and E. 42nd Sts., Midtown West* ☎ *212/930–0800 for exhibit information* 🌐 *www.nypl.org* 🕒 *Mon. and Thurs.–Sat. 10–6, Sun. 1–5, Tues. and Wed. 10–8; exhibitions until 6* Ⓜ *B, D, F, M to 42nd St.–Bryant Park; 7 to 5th Ave.*

The New York Times Building. This 52-story building with its distinctive, ladderlike ceramic rods is a testament to clean-lined modernism. The architect, Renzo Piano, extended the ceramic rods beyond the top of the building so that it would give the impression of dissolving into the sky. One of the skyscraper's best features—and the one that's open to the public—is the building's lobby atrium, which includes an open-air moss garden with 50-foot paper birch trees and a wooden footbridge, a 560-screen media art installation titled *Moveable Type* streaming a mix of the newspaper's near–real time and archival content, and a flagship store by minimalist home goods designer MUJI. Unfortunately, tours

THE MUSEUM OF MODERN ART (MOMA)

✉ 11 W. 53rd St., between 5th and 6th Aves., Midtown West ☎ 212/708-9400 🌐 www.moma.org 🎟 $25 ⏲ Sat.–Mon., Wed., and Thurs. 10:30–5:30, Fri. 10:30–8. Ⓜ E, M to 5th Ave./53rd St.; B, D, F, M to 47th–50th Sts./Rockefeller Center.

TIPS

- Tickets are available online at a reduced price. Entrance between 4 and 8 pm on Friday is free, but expect long lines.
- Free Wi-Fi within the museum allows you to listen to audio tours as you wander through the museum (log on to www.moma.org/wifi with your smartphone).
- MoMA has three movie theaters; film passes to the day's screenings are included with the price of admission.
- Tickets to MoMA also include admission to its affiliated PS1 in Queens. Save your ticket and you can go in for free any time within 30 days of your original purchase.
- Grab a bite at one of MoMA's two cafes—Cafe 2 and Terrace 5—or dine leisurely at the upscale Modern. In summer there is gelato in the Sculpture Garden.

Art enthusiasts and novices alike are often awestruck by the masterpieces before them here, including Monet's *Water Lilies*, Picasso's *Les Demoiselles d'Avignon*, and Van Gogh's *Starry Night*. In 2004, the museum's $425 million facelift by Yoshio Taniguchi increased exhibition space by nearly 50%, including space to accommodate large-scale contemporary installations. The museum continues to collect: most recently it obtained important works by Willem de Kooning, Valie Export, Christian Marclay, David Wojnarowicz, and Kara Walker. One of the top research facilities in modern and contemporary art is housed inside the museum's eight-story Education and Research building.

Highlights

In addition to the artwork, one of the main draws of MoMA is the building itself. A maze of glass walkways permits art viewing from many angles.

The 110-foot atrium entrance (accessed from the museum's lobby on either 53rd or 54th Street) leads to the movie theaters and the main-floor restaurant, Modern, with Alsatian-inspired cuisine.

A favorite resting spot is the Abby Aldrich Rockefeller Sculpture Garden. Designed by Philip Johnson, it features Barnett Newman's *Broken Obelisk* (1962–69). The glass wall lets visitors look directly into the surrounding galleries from the garden, where there's also a reflecting pool and trees.

Contemporary art (1970 to the present) from the museum's seven curatorial departments shares the second floor of the six-story building, and the skylighted top floor showcases an impressive lineup of changing exhibits.

are not offered. ✉ *620 8th Ave., between 40th and 41st Sts., Midtown West* ☎ *212/984–8128* 🌐 *www.newyorktimesbuilding.com* Ⓜ *A, C, E to 42nd St.–Port Authority; 1, 2, 3, 7, N, Q, R, S to Times Sq.–42nd St.*

The Paley Center for Media. With three galleries of photographs and artifacts that document the history of broadcasting, a computerized catalog of more than 150,000 television and radio programs, and public seminars, lectures, and programs, the Paley Center for Media examines the past and constantly evolving present states of media. The past is the main draw here. If you want to see a performance of "Turkey Lurkey Time" from the 1969 Tony Awards, for example, type the name of the song, show, or performer into a computer terminal, then proceed to one of the semiprivate screening areas to watch your selection. People nearby might be watching classic comedies from the '50s, miniseries from the '70s, or news broadcasts from the '90s. Possibly the most entertaining part of these TV shows from yesteryear is the fact that the original commercials are still embedded in many of the programs; if ads are your thing you can also skip the programming altogether and watch compilations of classic commercials. ✉ *25 W. 52nd St., between 5th and 6th Aves., Midtown West* ☎ *212/621–6800* 🌐 *www.paleycenter.org* 💵 *$10* ⏲ *Wed., Fri., and weekends noon–6, Thurs. noon–8* Ⓜ *E, M to 5th Ave./53rd St.; B, D, F, V to 47th–50th Sts./Rockefeller Center.*

Tibor de Nagy Gallery. Founded in 1950, this gallery shows works by 20th-century artists such as Biala, Nell Blaine, Jane Freilicher, and Shirley Jaffe. Instrumental in bringing many of America's finest abstract expressionist artists to public attention in the mid-20th century, the gallery now shows abstract and realistic work. ✉ *724 5th Ave., 12th fl., between W. 56th and W. 57th Sts., Midtown West* ☎ *212/262–5050* 🌐 *www.tibordenagy.com* ⏲ *Tues.–Sat. 10–5:30* Ⓜ *N, R to 5th Ave.*

University Club. Among the best surviving works of McKim, Mead & White, New York's leading turn-of-the-20th-century architects (and members of the club), this 1899 pink Milford granite palace was built for an exclusive club of degree-holding men. Note the crests of various prestigious universities are engraved into the facade above its windows. The club's popularity declined as individual universities built their own clubs and as gentlemen's clubs became less important to the New York social scene. Still, the nine-story Italian High Renaissance Revival building (the facade looks as though it's three stories) is still known for its exclusive membership (male and female), declaring itself "New York's premier social club." The building's interior is a bounty of marble, gilded columns, and murals . . . but the club is private so you'll have to make do with its grand exterior. ✉ *1 W. 54th St., at 5th Ave., Midtown West* ☎ *212/247–2100* 🌐 *www.universityclubny.org* Ⓜ *E, M to 5th Ave./53rd St.*

THE UPPER EAST SIDE

GETTING ORIENTED

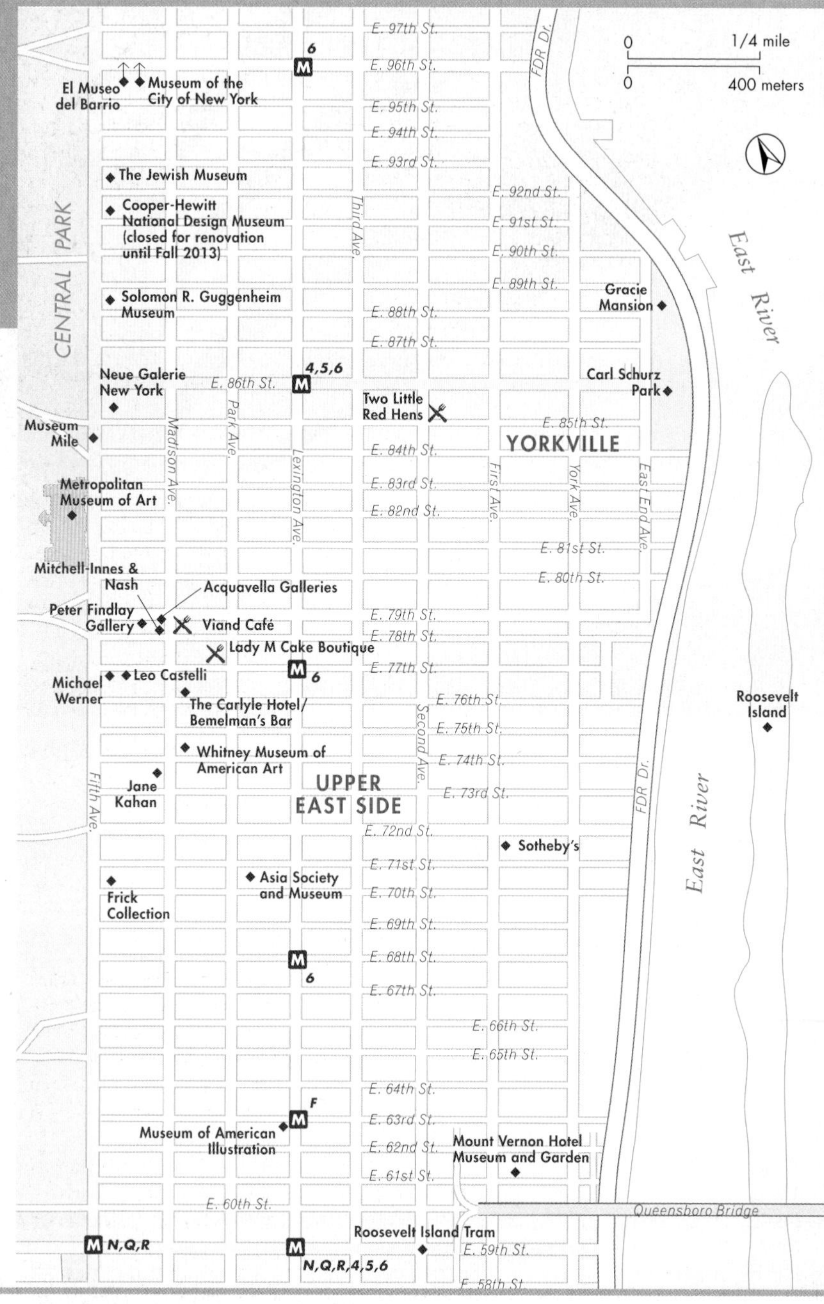

MAKING THE MOST OF YOUR TIME

The Upper East Side lends itself to a surprising variety of simple but distinct itineraries: exploring the landmarks on Museum Mile; languorous gallery grazing; window shopping on Madison Avenue; or bar hopping for just-out-of-college kids on 2nd Avenue. If it's the museums you're after, make sure to plan at least a few hours per museum—with some snack/coffee breaks. There's a lot to see, so we'd advise not more than one museum a day.

The Upper East Side's town houses, boutiques, consignment stores, and hidden gardens are easy to miss unless you take some time to wander. If all that walking wears you out, you can always hit one of the nail salons and indulge in a neighborhood stereotype of the pampered Upper East Sider. A well-deserved post–Museum Mile foot rub and mani/pedi are surprisingly reasonably priced.

GETTING HERE

Take the Lexington Avenue 4 or 5 express trains to 59th or 86th streets. The 6 local train also stops at 59th, 68th, 77th, 86th, and 96th streets. If you're coming from Midtown, the F train will let you out at Lexington Avenue at 63rd Street, where you can transfer to the 4, 5, or 6 after a short walk (and without paying subway fare again). From the Upper West Side, take one of the crosstown buses, the M66, M72, M79, M86, or M96. You can also take the N or R train to 59th Street and Lexington Avenue.

TOP EXPERIENCES

Exploring any of the world-class museums up here—permanent exhibits or temporary shows may guide your interest; make sure to plan a relaxing, restorative lunch, too.

Window-shopping on Madison Avenue.

Strolling in Central Park (⇨ *see Chapter 11*).

Appreciating the views from the recently opened Four Freedoms Park on Roosevelt Island.

COFFEE AND QUICK BITES

Lady M Cake Boutique. You don't know it yet but you're here for the signature Mille Crepes cake. Twenty crepes stacked together with a delicious cream filling. Don't fight it! ✉ *41 East 78th St., Upper East Side* ☎ *212/452-2222.*

Two Little Red Hens. With first-rate joe and delicious cupcakes, cheesecake, and cookies to match, it's no wonder this busy little bakery is a legend with locals. ✉ *1652 2nd Ave., at 86th St., Upper East Side* ☎ *212/452-0476.*

Viand Cafe. This classic New York diner is known as much for its notable clientele (former Mayor Michael Bloomberg is a regular) as for its fresh-baked muffins, turkey sandwiches, and friendly staff. ✉ *1011 Madison Ave., at 78th St., Upper East Side* ☎ *212/249-8250* 🌐 *viandcafenyc.com.*

Sightseeing ★★★
Nightlife ★
Dining ★★
Lodging ★★
Shopping ★★★★

To many New Yorkers the Upper East Side connotes old money and high society—alongside Central Park, between 5th and Lexington avenues, up to East 96th Street, the trappings of wealth are everywhere apparent: posh buildings, Madison Avenue's flagship boutiques, and doormen in braided livery. It's also a key destination for visitors because some of the most fantastic museums in the country are here.

Updated by Jacinta O'Halloran

Although a glance up and down the manicured grass meridian of Park Avenue may conjure scenes from *Bonfire of the Vanities* or *Gossip Girl*, there's more than palatial apartments, elite private schools, and highfalutin clubs up here—starting with fantastic museums. The **Metropolitan Museum of Art,** the **Solomon R. Guggenheim Museum,** the **Whitney Museum,** and many others lie on and around "Museum Mile," as do a number of worthy art galleries. For a local taste of the luxe life, hit up Madison Avenue for its lavish boutiques; strolling this platinum-card corridor between East 60th and East 82nd streets is like stepping into the pages of a glossy magazine. Many fashion houses have their flagships here and showcase their lush threads in equally exquisite settings. Compared with the megastores of Midtown, Madison Avenue feels quieter; it's significantly less crowded and more conducive to leisurely shopping (window or otherwise). Beyond clothing, the boutiques here carry baubles to satisfy anyone's champagne wishes, whether it's a box of truffles at **La Maison du Chocolat** or an intriguing read at **Crawford Doyle Booksellers.**

Venture east of Lexington Avenue and you encounter a less wealthy—and more diverse—Upper East Side, one inhabited by couples seeking some of the last (relatively) affordable places to raise a family south of 100th Street, and recent college grads getting a foothold in the city (on weekend nights 2nd Avenue resembles a miles-long fraternity and sorority reunion). One neighborhood particularly worth exploring is northeast-lying Yorkville, especially between 78th and 86th streets east of 2nd Avenue. Once a remote hamlet with a large German population, its several remaining ethnic food shops, 19th-century row houses, and—one of the city's best-kept secrets—**Carl Schurz Park,** make for a good half-day's exploration, as does touring the most striking residence there, **Gracie Mansion.**

If art galleries are your thing, there are some elegant places to visit on the Upper East Side. In keeping with the tony surroundings, the emphasis here is on works by established masters rather than up-and-coming (or even still-living) artists. Their locations are eminent as well: large town houses and upper stories in and around Madison and 5th avenues. Note that galleries often have limited hours, so make sure to check times in advance.

TOP ATTRACTIONS

Asia Society and Museum. The Asian art collection of Mr. and Mrs. John D. Rockefeller III forms the core of this museum's holdings, which include South Asian stone and bronze sculptures; art from India, Nepal, Pakistan, and Afghanistan; bronze vessels, ceramics, sculpture, and paintings from China; Korean ceramics; and paintings, wooden sculptures, and ceramics from Japan. Founded in 1956, the society has a regular program of lectures, films, and performances, in addition to changing exhibitions of traditional and contemporary art. Trees grow in the glass-enclosed Garden Court Café, which serves an eclectic Asian menu for lunch and dinner. **TIP→ Admission is free on Fridays from 6 to 9 (September to July).** ⊠ *725 Park Ave., at 70th St., Upper East Side* ☎ *212/288–6400* 🌐 *www.asiasociety.org* 🎫 *$10* 🕓 *Tues.–Sun. 11–6, open until 9 on Fri. from the day after Labor Day to July 1* Ⓜ *6 to 68th St.–Hunter College.*

Cooper-Hewitt, National Design Museum, Smithsonian Institution. The Cooper-Hewitt National Design Museum is closed while undergoing renovations that will increase its exhibition space by 60% (from approximately 10,000 square feet to 16,000 square feet). It is scheduled to reopen in 2014. In the meantime the museum is staging exhibitions around the city; check the website for more information. Hours and admission prices are yet to be determined at this writing. ⊠ *2 E. 91st St., at 5th Ave., Upper East Side* ☎ *212/849–1549* 🌐 *www.cooperhewitt.org* Ⓜ *4, 5, 6 to 86th St.*

10

El Museo del Barrio. *El barrio* is Spanish for "the neighborhood" and the nickname for East Harlem, a largely Spanish-speaking Puerto Rican and Dominican community. El Museo del Barrio, on the edge of this neighborhood, focuses on Latin American and Caribbean art, with some ten percent of its collection concentrated on works by self-taught artists from New York, Puerto Rico, the Caribbean, and Latin America. The more than 6,500-object permanent collection includes over 400 pre-Columbian artifacts, sculpture, photography, film and video, and traditional art from all over Latin America. The collection of 360 *santos,* carved wooden folk-art figures from Puerto Rico, is popular. El Museo hosts performances, lectures, films, and cultural events, including a month-long Dia de los Muertos celebration. ⊠ *1230 5th Ave., between E. 104th and E. 105th Sts., Upper East Side* ☎ *212/831–7272* 🌐 *www.elmuseo.org* 🎫 *$9* 🕓 *Tues.–Sat. 11–6, Sun. 1–5* Ⓜ *6 to 103rd St.*

Fodor's Choice ★ **Frick Collection.** Henry Clay Frick made his fortune amid the soot and smoke of Pittsburgh, where he was a coke (a coal fuel derivative) and steel baron, but this lovely museum, once Frick's private New York residence, is decidedly removed from soot. With an exceptional collection of works from the Renaissance through the late 19th century that includes Édouard Manet's *The Bullfight* (1864), a Chinard portrait bust (1809), three Vermeers, three Rembrandts, works by El Greco, Goya, van Dyck, Hogarth, Degas, and Turner, as well as sculpture, decorative arts, and 18th century French furniture, everything here is a highlight. The Portico Gallery, an enclosed portico along the building's 5th Avenue garden, houses the museum's growing collection of sculpture. An audio guide, available in several languages, is included with admission, as are the year-round temporary exhibits. The tranquil indoor garden court is a magical spot for a rest. Children under 10 are not admitted, and those age 10–16 with adult only. ✉ *1 E. 70th St., at 5th Ave., Upper East Side* ☎ *212/288–0700* 🌐 *www.frick.org* 🎫 *$18* ⏲ *Tues.–Sat. 10–6, Sun. 11–5* Ⓜ *6 to 68th St.–Hunter College.*

Gracie Mansion. The official mayor's residence, Gracie Mansion was built in 1799 by shipping merchant Archibald Gracie, and enlarged in 1966. Tours of the impressive interior—which must be scheduled in advance and take place under limited hours—take you through the building's history and its colorful rooms furnished over centuries and packed with American objets d'art. Nine mayors have lived here since it became the official residence in 1942, though Michael Bloomberg broke with tradition and chose to stay in his own 79th Street town house during his three terms as mayor. In 2012, the mansion's kitchen closed for a $1.4 million renovation to eliminate the mazelike layout, install energy-efficient equipment, and improve plumbing and electrical systems. ✉ *Carl Schurz Park, East End Ave. at 88th St., Upper East Side* ☎ *212/570–4778* 🎫 *$7* ⏲ *45-min guided tours Wed. 10–2* Ⓜ *4, 5, 6 to 86th St.*

The Jewish Museum. In a Gothic-style 1908 mansion, the Jewish Museum draws on a large collection of art and ceremonial objects to explore Jewish identity and culture spanning more than 4,000 years. The two-floor permanent exhibition *Culture and Continuity: The Jewish Journey* displays nearly 800 objects complemented by interactive media. The wide-ranging collection includes a 3rd-century Roman burial plaque, 20th-century sculpture by Elie Nadelman, and contemporary art from artists such as Marc Chagall and Man Ray. **TIP→ Admission to the museum is free on Saturday.** ✉ *1109 5th Ave., at E. 92nd St., Upper East Side* ☎ *212/423–3200* 🌐 *www.jewishmuseum.org* 🎫 *$12* ⏲ *Fri.–Tues. 11–5:45, Thurs. 11–8; closed Fri. mid-Mar.–Oct.* Ⓜ *6 to 96th St.*

Fodor's Choice ★ **Metropolitan Museum of Art.** *See highlighted listing in this chapter.*

Museum of the City of New York. In a Colonial Revival building designed for the museum in the 1930s, the city's history and many quirks are revealed through engaging exhibits here. The museum is currently in the last phase of a three-part, $90 million renovation that will upgrade and modernize the entire facility. Improvements to date include a new climate-control system, new flooring, an updated lobby and terrace, a redesigned gift shop, and restored historical elements throughout the

SOLOMON R GUGGENHEIM MUSEUM

1071 5th Ave., between E. 88th and E. 89th Sts., Upper East Side 212/423–3840 www.guggenheim.org $22 Sun.–Wed. 10–5:45, Fri. 10–5:45, Sat. 10–7:45. Closed Thurs. M 4, 5, 6 to 86th St.

TIPS

- Gallery talks provide richer understanding of the masterpieces in front of you. Tours are included in your admission fee, so be sure to take advantage.
- The museum often runs special programs—including lectures, conversations, and film screenings—in conjunction with major exhibitions. Check the Public Programs page on the museum's website for details of upcoming events.
- Take it from the top: Escape the crowded lobby and keep your legs fresh for the rest of the museum by taking the elevator to the top and working your way down the spiral.
- The museum is pay-what-you-wish on Saturday from 5:45 to 7:45. Lines can be long, so arrive early. The last tickets are handed out at 7:15.
- Eat before you visit; restaurants on Lexington Avenue offer more varied fare than the museum's small Café 3 espresso and snack bar on the third floor.

Frank Lloyd Wright's landmark nautilus-like museum building is renowned as much for its famous architecture as for its superlative collection of art and its well-curated shows. Opened in 1959, shortly after Wright's death, the Guggenheim is acclaimed as one of the greatest buildings of the 20th century. Inside, under a 92-foot-high glass dome, a ramp spirals down past the artworks of the current exhibits (the ramp is just over a quarter mile long, if you're wondering). The museum has strong holdings of Wassily Kandinsky, Paul Klee, Marc Chagall, Pablo Picasso, and Robert Mapplethorpe.

Highlights

Wright's design was criticized by some who believed that the distinctive building detracted from the art within, but the interior nautilus design allows artworks to be viewed from several different angles and distances. Be sure to notice not only what's in front of you but also what's across the spiral from you.

Even if you aren't planning to eat, stop at the museum's modern American restaurant, the Wright, for its stunning design created by Andre Kikoski.

On permanent display, the museum's Thannhauser Collection is made up primarily of works by French impressionists and postimpressionists van Gogh, Toulouse-Lautrec, Cézanne, and Matisse. Perhaps more than any other 20th-century painter, Wassily Kandinsky, one of the first "pure" abstract artists, has been closely linked to the museum's history: beginning with the acquisition of his masterpiece *Composition 8* (1923) in 1930, the collection has grown to encompass more than 150 works.

WHITNEY MUSEUM OF AMERICAN ART

945 Madison Ave., at E. 75th St., Upper East Side 212/570–3600 www.whitney.org $18 Wed., Thurs., and weekends 11–6; Fri. 1–9 M 6 to 77th St.

TIPS

- After 6 pm on Friday the price of admission is pay-what-you-wish. On some of those nights the Whitney Live series presents new artists and reinterpretations of American classics. Be forewarned that this combination may result in long lines.
- The Untitled restaurant in the basement (by Danny Meyer of the Union Square Café), serves updated diner classics; it's open for breakfast and lunch Tuesday through Saturday, and for dinner Thursday through Saturday.

With its bold collection of 20th- and 21st-century contemporary American art, the Whitney presents an eclectic mix drawn from more than 19,000 works in its permanent collection. The museum was originally a gallery in the studio of sculptor and collector Gertrude Vanderbilt Whitney, whose talent and taste were accompanied by the money of two wealthy families. In 1930, after the Met turned down Whitney's offer to donate her collection of 20th-century American art, she established an independent museum in Greenwich Village. The museum moved uptown in 1996, into this minimalist gray-granite building designed by Marcel Breuer and Hamilton Smith. In 2015, the Whitney will head downtown to an exciting new space, designed by architect Renzo Piano, and situated between the High Line (New York's beloved elevated park) and the Hudson River. Exhibits will continue at the uptown location until late 2014.

Highlights

Start your visit on the fifth floor, where the galleries house rotating exhibitions of postwar and contemporary works from the permanent collection by artists such as Jackson Pollock, Jim Dine, Jasper Johns, Mark Rothko, Chuck Close, Cindy Sherman, and Roy Lichtenstein.

Although the collection on display constantly changes, notable pieces often on view include Hopper's *Early Sunday Morning* (1930), Bellows's *Dempsey and Firpo* (1924), Alexander Calder's beloved *Circus,* and several of Georgia O'Keeffe's dazzling flower paintings.

The often-controversial Whitney Biennial, which showcases the most important developments in American art over the previous two years, takes place in the spring of even-numbered years—2014 is the next.

building. The third phase of the modernization includes renovating the North Wing to create three continuous floors of gallery space, a state-of-the-art auditorium, and a new café. Renovations are expected to be complete in 2015. In the meantime, the museum remains open, and rotating exhibits on subjects such as architecture, fashion, history, and politics are still on display. Don't miss *Timescapes,* a 25-minute media projection that innovatively illustrates New York's physical expansion and population changes, or *Activist New York,* an ongoing exploration of the city's history of social activism. The museum hosts New York–centric lectures, films, and walking tours. **TIP→ When you're finished touring the museum, cross the street and stroll through the Vanderbilt Gates to enter the Conservatory Garden, one of Central Park's hidden gems.** ✉ *1220 5th Ave., at E. 103rd St., Upper East Side* ☎ *212/534–1672* 🌐 *www.mcny.org* *$10 suggested donation* ⏲ *Daily 10–6* Ⓜ *6 to 103rd St.*

Neue Galerie New York. Early-20th-century German and Austrian art and design are the focus here, with works by Gustav Klimt, Wassily Kandinsky, Paul Klee, Egon Schiele, Josef Hoffman, and other designers from the Wiener Werkstätte taking center stage. The Neue Galerie was founded by the late art dealer Serge Sabarsky and cosmetics heir and art collector Ronald S. Lauder. It's situated in a 1914 wood- and marble-floored mansion designed by Carrère and Hastings, which was once home to Mrs. Cornelius Vanderbilt III. An audio guide is included with admission. Note that children under 12 are not admitted, and teens 12–16 must be accompanied by an adult. **Café Sabarsky**, in an elegant, high-ceiling space below the Neue Galerie, is a destination in its own right, for their Viennese coffee, cakes, strudels, and Sacher tortes (Monday and Wednesday 9–6, Thursday–Sunday 9–9). If you seek something more than a sugar fix, the savory menu includes trout crepes and Hungarian goulash. Café Fledermaus, on the lower level of the museum, offers the same menu as Café Sabarsky. Admission is free from 6–8 pm on the first Friday of every month. ✉ *1048 5th Ave., at E. 86th St., Upper East Side* ☎ *212/628–6200* 🌐 *www.neuegalerie.org* *$20* ⏲ *Thurs.–Mon. 11–6* Ⓜ *4, 5, 6 to 86th St.* ☞ *Children under 12 not admitted.*

10

WORTH NOTING

Acquavella Galleries. The 19th- and 20th-century art shown inside this five-story marble-floored French neo-classical mansion tends to be by the big names, from Impressionists through Pop artists, including Picasso, Lucian Freud, James Rosenquist, and Wayne Thiebaud. ✉ *18 E. 79th St., between 5th and Madison Aves., Upper East Side* ☎ *212/734–6300* 🌐 *www.acquavellagalleries.com* ⏲ *Mon.–Sat. 10–5* Ⓜ *6 to 77th St.*

FAMILY **Carl Schurz Park.** Facing the East River, this park, named for a German immigrant who was a prominent newspaper editor in the 19th century, is so tranquil you'd never guess you're directly above FDR Drive. Walk along the promenade, where you can take in views of the river and the Roosevelt Island Lighthouse across the way. To the north are Randall's and Wards islands and the RFK Bridge (aka the Triborough Bridge). If you enter the park at its 86th Street entrance or if you're exiting there, you'll find yourself approaching the grounds

Continued on page 159

Mesmerizing carvings in the ancient Egyptian Temple of Dendur.

THE METROPOLITAN MUSEUM OF ART

If the city held no other museum than the colossal Metropolitan Museum of Art, you could still occupy yourself for days roaming its labyrinthine corridors. Because the Metropolitan Museum has more than 2 million works of art representing 5,000 years of history, you're going to have to make tough choices. Looking at everything here could take a week.

Before you begin exploring the museum, check the museum's floor plan, available at all entrances, for location of the major wings and collections. Google Maps will help you find your way through the museum. The service tracks your location with a blue dot and guides you through exhibits, across floors, and to bathrooms and exits. It can even help you avoid the gift shop if you're visiting with kids!

The posted adult admission, though only a suggestion, is one that's strongly encouraged. Whatever you choose to pay, admission includes all special exhibits and same-day entrance to the Cloisters (see Chapter 12). The Met's audio guide costs an additional $7, and if you intend to stay more than an hour or so, it's worth it. The generally perceptive commentary covers museum highlights and directors' picks, with separate commentary tracks directed at kids.

If you want to avoid the crowds, visit weekday mornings. Also good are Friday and Saturday evenings, when live classical music plays from the Great Hall balcony. If the Great Hall (the main entrance) is mobbed, avoid the chaos by heading to the street-level entrance to the left of the main stairs, near 81st Street. Ticket lines and coat checks are much less ferocious here.

What to see? Check out the museum highlights on the following pages.

- 5th Ave. at 82nd St., Upper East Side
- Subway: 4, 5, 6 to 86th St.
- 212/535-7710
- www.metmuseum.org
- $25 suggested donation
- Tues.–Thurs. and Sun. 9:30–5:30, Fri. and Sat. 9:30–9

Left, Great Hall

MUSEUM HIGHLIGHTS

Egyptian Art

A major star is the **Temple of Dendur** (circa 15 BC), in a huge atrium to itself and with a moatlike pool of water to represent its original location near the Nile. The temple was commissioned by the Roman emperor Augustus to honor the goddess Isis and the sons of a Nubian chieftain. Look for the scratched-in graffiti from 19th-century Western explorers on the inside. Egypt gave the temple as a gift to the U.S. in 1965; it would have been submerged after the construction of the Aswan High Dam.

The Egyptian collection as a whole covers 4,000 years of history, with papyrus pages from the Egyptian Book of the Dead, stone sarcophagi inscribed with hieroglyphics, and tombs. The galleries should be walked through counterclockwise from the Ancient Kingdom (2650–2150 BC), to the period under Roman rule (30 BC–400 AD). In the latter, keep an eye out for the enormous, bulbous **Sarcophagus of Horkhebil,** sculpted from basalt.

Greek and Roman Art

Today's tabloids have nothing on ancient Greece and Rome. They had it all—sex, cults, drugs, unrelenting violence, and, of course, stunning art. The recently redone Greek and Roman galleries encompass 6,000 works of art that reveal aspects of everyday life in these influential cultures.

The urnlike terracotta kraters were used by the Greeks for mixing wine and water at parties and other events. Given that, it's not surprising that most depict slightly racy scenes. Some of the most impressive can be found in the gallery covering 5th century BC.

On the mezzanine of the Roman galleries, the Etruscan bronze chariot from 650 BC depicts scenes from the life of Achilles. Notice how the simplistic Etruscan style in combination with the Greek influence evolved into the naturalistic Roman statues below.

The frescoes from a bedroom in the Villa of P. Fannius Synistor preserved by the explosion of Mt. Vesuvius in 79 AD give us a glimpse into the stylistic achievement of perspective in Roman painting.

Temple of Dendur

ART TO TAKE HOME

You don't have to pay admission to get to the mammoth gift shop on the first floor. One of the better souvenirs here is also one of the more reasonable: the Met's own **illustrated guide** to 869 of the best items in its collection ($19.95).

Engelhard Court

An artifact from ancient Greece.

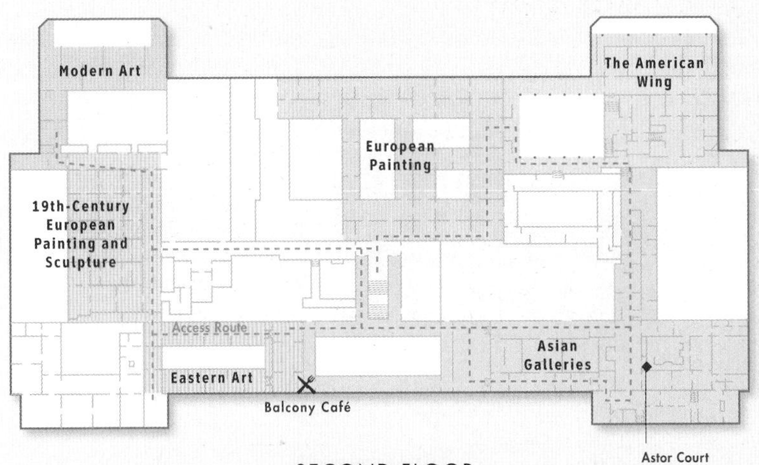
Modern Art
The American Wing
European Painting
19th-Century European Painting and Sculpture
Access Route
Asian Galleries
Eastern Art
Balcony Café
Astor Court

SECOND FLOOR

MEZZANINES

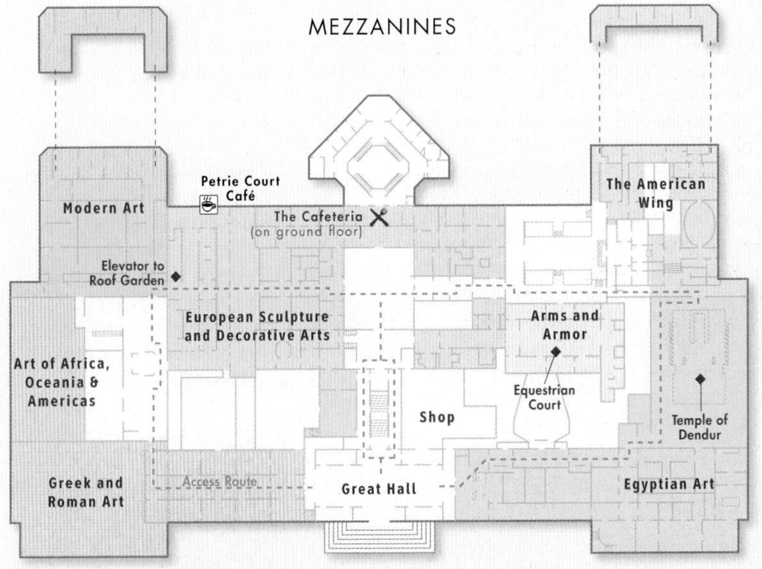
Petrie Court Café
Modern Art
The Cafeteria (on ground floor)
The American Wing
Elevator to Roof Garden
European Sculpture and Decorative Arts
Arms and Armor
Art of Africa, Oceania & Americas
Equestrian Court
Temple of Dendur
Shop
Greek and Roman Art
Access Route
Great Hall
Egyptian Art

FIRST FLOOR

5th Avenue

The American Wing of the Metropolitan Museum of Art.

American Wing

After years of extensive renovations, the Met's revitalized **New American Wing Galleries for Paintings, Sculpture, and Decorative Arts** reopened in 2012 with 30,000 square feet of skylit space to showcase one of the best and largest collections of American art in the country.

There's much to see, from Colonial furniture to the works of the great masters, including John Singleton Copley, Gilbert Stuart, Thomas Cole, Frederic Edwin Church, Winslow Homer, and Thomas Eakins, among others. The highlight of the new installation is Emanuel Gottlieb Leutze's magnificent 1851 painting, *Washington Crossing the Delaware*. Hung in an immense gilded frame (recreated from an 1864 photograph of the painting), Leutze's iconic work is displayed just as it was at a fundraiser for Union soldiers in 1864—flanked by Frederic Church's *Heart of the Andes* and Albert Bierstadt's *Rocky Mountains*.

Also not to be missed are John Singer Sargent's *Madame X*, a once-scandalous portrait of a Parisian socialite; the recreation of the entrance hall of the 18th Century Van Rensselaer Manor House in Albany, New York; and the collection of portrait miniatures—detailed watercolors to be carried or gifted as tokens of love.

TIME TO EAT? INSIDE THE MUSEUM

The **Petrie Court Café**, at the back of the 1st-floor European Sculpture Court, has waiter service. Prices range from $12 for a sandwich to $21 for organic chicken salad. Tea, sweets, and savories are served from 2:30 PM to 4:30 PM during the week.

The **Great Hall Balcony Bar** is located on the second floor belcony overlooking the Great Hall. On Fridays and Saturdays, 4 PM TO 8:30 PM waiters serve appetizers and cocktails accompanied by live classical music.

The **cafeteria** on the ground floor has stations for pasta, main courses, antipasti, and sandwiches.

Looking for one of the best views in town? The **Roof Garden** (open May–Oct.) exhibits contemporary sculpture, but most people take the elevator here to have a drink or snack while checking out Central Park and the skyline.

Tiffany

Arms and Armor

The **Equestrian Court,** where the knights are mounted on armored models of horses, is one of the most dramatic rooms in the museum. For a bird's-eye view, check it out again from the balconies in the Musical Instruments collection on the second floor.

European Sculpture and Decorative Arts

Among the many sculptures in the sun-filled Petrie Court, ***Ugolino and His Sons*** still stands out for the despairing poses of its subjects. Ugolino, a nobleman whose family's tragic story is told in Dante's *Inferno,* was punished for treason by being left to starve to death with his grandsons and sons in a locked tower. (It's not clear if putting such a sculpture so near the Petrie Court's café is some curator's idea of a joke or not.) By the way, the redbrick and granite wall on the court's north side is the museum's original entrance.

The newly renovated Wrightsman Galleries for French Decorative Arts on the first floor displays the opulence that caused Louis the XVI to lose his head. The blindingly golden Boiserie from the Hotel de Cabris, a remnant of French 18th century Neo-classical interiors, represents the finest collection of French decorative arts in the country.

Modern Art

The museum's most famous Picasso is probably his 1906 portrait ***Gertrude Stein*** in which the writer's face is stern and masklike. The portrait was bequeathed to the museum by Stein herself.

Of the Georgia O'Keeffes on view, 1931's ***Red, White, and Blue*** painting of a cow skull is a standout. The color, composition, and natural motif work together to create a work with religious as well as nationalist overtones.

European Paintings

On the second floor, the 13th- to 18th-century paintings are grouped at the top of the Great Hall's stairs.

Recently, the Met spent about $45 million to buy Duccio di Buoninsegna's ***Madonna and Child,*** painted circa 1300. The last remaining Duccio in private hands, this painting, the size of a piece of typewriter paper, is unimpressive at first glance. The work, though rigid, represents a revolution in Byzantine art. The humanity reflected in the baby Jesus grabbing his mother's veil changed European painting.

TIME TO EAT?
OUTSIDE THE MUSEUM

Because museum admission is good all day, you can always leave for lunch and come back later. A block from the museum, **Caffee Grazie** (26 E. 84th St., between Madison and Fifth Aves., 212/717–4407) offers casual Italian dining in a lovely townhouse. Options include omelets, pizzas, sandwiches, and salads, but they're best known for the Italian Bento-Box with its tastings of savory and sweets. At the fairly inexpensive sit-down eatery **Le Pain Quotidien** (1131 Madison Ave., at 84th St., 212/327–4900), the hungry dine at long communal tables on high-quality sandwiches (around $9), salads, and pastries.

Equestrian Court (1930)

Rembrandt's masterful ***Aristotle with a Bust of Homer*** (1653) shows a philosopher contemplating worldly gains versus values through its play of light and use of symbols. Around Aristotle is a gold medal of Alexander the Great, one of the philosopher's students.

In the room dedicated to **Monet** you can get to all his greatest hits—poplar trees, haystacks, water lilies, and the Rouen Cathedral. The muted tones of Pissaro are followed by a room full of bright and garish colors announcing works by Gauguin, Matisse, and Van Gogh.

Vincent van Gogh, *Wheatfield with Cypresses*

Islamic Galleries

In late 2011, after an eight-year renovation, the Met reopened its Islamic galleries, a suite of 15 galleries housing one of the world's premier collections of Islamic art. Now known as the "Art of the Arab Lands, Turkey, Iran, Central Asia, and Later South Asia," the collection comprises more than 12,000 works of art and traces the course of Islamic Civilization over a span of 13 centuries. Highlights include an 11-foot-high 14th century mihrab, or prayer niche, decorated with glazed ceramic tiles; the recently restored Emperor's Carpet—a 16th century Persian carpet that was presented to the Hapsburg Emperor Leopold I by Peter the Great of Russia; the Damascus Room—a Syrian Ottoman reception room decorated with poetic verses; and glass, ceramics, and metalwork from Egypt, Syria, Iraq, and Iran.

WHAT'S TO COME

The front steps of the Met are one of Manhattan's iconic meeting places, but the area has been under construction for almost two years. In late 2014, the new outdoor David H. Koch Plaza will reopen with public seating, a fountain, landscaping, and improved museum access.

Asian Galleries

The serene **Astor Court,** which has its own skylight and pond of real-life koi (goldfish), is a model of a scholar's court garden in Soochow, China.

The Han dynasty (206 BC–220 AD) introduced the practice of sending the dead on to the afterlife with small objects to help them there. Keep an eye out for these **small clay figures,** which include farm animals (enclosed in barnyards) and dancing entertainers.

On display in a glass case in the center of an early-Chinese gallery is a complete set of 14 **bronze altar vessels.** Dating 1100 BC—800 AD, these green and slightly crusty pieces were used for worshipping ancestors.The Met displays some of its finest **Asian stoneware and porcelain** along the balcony overlooking the Great Hall.

The teak dome and minature balconies from a **Jain meeting hall** in western India were carved in the 16th century. Just about the entire surface is covered with musicians, animals, gods, and servants.

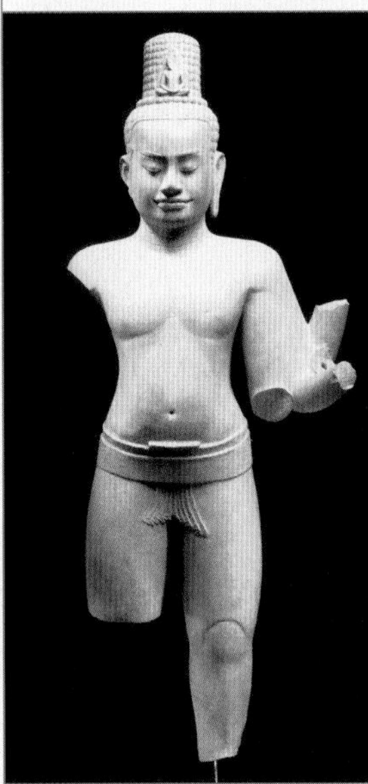

Standing eight-armed Avalokiteshvara

of a Federal-style wood-frame house that belies the grandeur of its name—Gracie Mansion.

TIP→ If you exit the park at 86th Street, cross East End Avenue for a stroll through Henderson Place, a miniature historic district of 24 connected Queen Anne–style houses in a dead end. The small redbrick houses, built in 1881 "for persons of moderate means," have turrets marking the corner of each block and symmetrical roof gables, pediments, parapets, chimneys, and dormer windows. ✉ *Carl Schurz Park spans East End Ave. to the East River, E. 84th to E. 90th Sts., Upper East Side* ☎ *212/459–4455* 🌐 *www.carlschurzparknyc.org* Ⓜ *4, 5, 6 to 86th St.*

Jane Kahan. This welcoming gallery represents some lofty works. In addition to tapestries by modern masters like Pablo Picasso, Joan Miró, and Alexander Calder—one of this gallery's specialties—you'll see works by late-19th- and early-20th-century modern artists such as Fernand Léger and Marc Chagall. ✉ *922 Madison Ave., 2nd fl., between E. 73rd and E. 74th Sts., Upper East Side* ☎ *212/744–1490* 🌐 *www.janekahan.com* ⏲ *Mon.–Sat. 10–6; weekdays 11–5 Memorial Day–Labor Day* Ⓜ *6 to 77th St.*

Leo Castelli. Castelli was one of the most influential dealers of the 20th century. He helped foster the careers of many important artists, including one of his first discoveries, Jasper Johns. The gallery continues to show works by Roy Lichtenstein, Andy Warhol, Ed Ruscha, Jackson Pollock, Robert Morris, and other heavies. ✉ *18 E. 77th St., between 5th and Madison Aves., Upper East Side* ☎ *212/249–4470* 🌐 *www.castelligallery.com* ⏲ *Tues.–Sat. 10–6* Ⓜ *6 to 77th St.*

Mitchell-Innes & Nash. This sleek spot represents the estates of Roy Lichtenstein and Jack Tworkov as well as other Impressionist, modern, and contemporary masters. ✉ *1018 Madison Ave., between 78th and 79th Sts., Upper East Side* ☎ *212/744–7400* 🌐 *www.miandn.com* ⏲ *Weekdays 10–5* Ⓜ *6 to 77th St.*

FAMILY **Mount Vernon Hotel Museum and Garden.** Built in 1799, this former carriage house (i.e., stable) became a day hotel (a sort of country club) in 1826. Now restored and owned by the Colonial Dames of America, it provides a glimpse of the days when the city ended at 14th Street and this area was a country escape for New Yorkers. A 45-minute tour passes through the eight rooms that display furniture and artifacts of the Federal and Empire periods. Many rooms have real artifacts such as clothes, hats, and fans that children can handle. There is a lovely adjoining garden, designed in an 18th-century style. ✉ *421 E. 61st St., between York and 1st Aves., Upper East Side* ☎ *212/838–6878* 🌐 *www.mvhm.org* 🎫 *$8* ⏲ *Tues.–Sun. 11–4* Ⓜ *4, 5, 6, F, N, R to Lexington Ave.–59th St.*

10

Museum of American Illustration. Founded in 1901, the museum of the Society of Illustrators presents its annual "Oscars," a juried, international competition, from January to March. The best in children's book illustrations is featured October through November. In between are eclectic exhibitions on science fiction, fashion, political, and historical illustrations. In 2012, the Society of Illustrators incorporated the holdings of the Museum of Comic and Cartoon Art (MoCCA) into its collections. MoCCA's collection has its own gallery on the second floor and continues its workshops, programs, and comic festival (MoCCA Fest). ✉ *128 E. 63rd St., between Lexington and Park Aves., Upper East Side* ☎ *212/838–2560* 🌐 *www.societyillustrators.org* 🎟 *Free* ⏲ *Tues. 10–8, Wed.–Fri. 10–5, Sat. noon–4* Ⓜ *F to 63rd St.; 4, 5, 6, N, R to Lexington Ave.–59th St.*

Peter Findlay Gallery. Covering 19th- and 20th-century works by European artists, this gallery shows pieces by Mary Cassatt, Paul Klee, and Alberto Giacometti. ✉ *16 E. 79th St., 2nd fl., Upper East Side* ☎ *212/644–4433* 🌐 *www.findlay.com* ⏲ *Weekdays 1:30–5* Ⓜ *6 to 77th St.*

FAMILY **Roosevelt Island.** The 2-mile-long East River slice of land that parallels Manhattan from East 48th to East 85th streets is now a quasi-suburb of more than 12,000 people, and the vestiges of its infamous asylums, hospitals, and prisons make this an offbeat trip for the historically curious. At the south tip are the eerie ruins of a **Smallpox Hospital,** built in 1854 in a Gothic Revival style by the prominent architect James Renwick Jr. (Renwick also designed St. Patrick's and the Smithsonian's Castle). Neighboring the hospital ruins is the recently opened **Four Freedoms Park**, a memorial to Franklin Delano Roosevelt designed by famed architect Louis I. Kahn. After decades of delays, the four-acre park—once just a landfill with wasted dramatic city views—opened in late 2012. The monument to President Roosevelt is essentially a large, open granite box with a giant bust of FDR, and a wall inscribed with the words of the wartime Four Freedoms speech, which the park honors. Visitors can stroll the stone walkways tree-lined pebble paths that run along the manicured lawn and enjoy views of the United Nations and East River. On a small park at the island's north tip is a lighthouse built in 1872 by island convicts. You can get here by subway, but it's more fun to take the five-minute ride on the **Roosevelt Island Tramway,** the only commuter cable car in North America, which lifts you 250 feet in the air, with impressive views of Queens and Manhattan. A visitor center, made from an old trolley kiosk, stands to your left as you exit the tram. Red buses service the island for 25¢ a ride. ✉ *Tramway entrance on 2nd Ave. at either 59th St. or 60th St., Upper East Side* ☎ *212/688–4836 Visitors Center* 🌐 *www.rioc.com* 🎟 *$2.25 (MetroCard accepted)* ⏲ *Tram Sun.–Thurs. 6 am–2 am, Fri. and Sat. 6 am–3:30 am; leaves approximately every 15 min* Ⓜ *F to Roosevelt Island.*

Sotheby's. Occupying its own 10-story building, this branch of the storied U.K. auction house is the site of more than a hundred auctions a year. You don't have to bid to view items on auction; most items are displayed for the general public in the days leading up to the event. A sizeable portion of these are extremely high-profile: a copy of the Magna Carta, Fabergé eggs, rare Tiffany lamps, and Norman Rockwell's 1943 painting *Rosie the Riveter* have all been sold through this Sotheby's. Call ahead for hours. ✉ *1334 York Ave., at E. 72nd St., Upper East Side* ☎ *212/606–7000* 🌐 *www.sothebys.com* ⏲ *Hrs vary* Ⓜ *6 to 77th St.*

Central Park

WORD OF MOUTH

"Central Park was fabulous! I love that this busy, bustling city has such a huge expanse of peaceful parkland."

— cathies

OUR BACKYARD

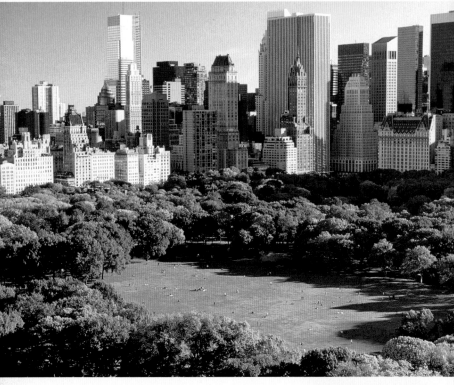

HOW A SWAMP BECAME AN OASIS

1855 Using the power of eminent domain, New York City acquires 843 acres of undeveloped swamp for the then-obscene sum of $5 million, displacing 1,600 people living there.

1857 The landscape architect Frederick Law Olmsted becomes superintendent of a park that does not yet exist. He spends days clearing dirt and evicting squatters and evenings working with architect Calvert Vaux on what will become the Greensward plan. The plan is the winning entry in the city's competition to develop a design for the park.

While the Panic of 1857 creates widespread unemployment, thousands of workers begin moving five million cubic yards of dirt and planting more than five million trees and plants. Beleaguered by bureaucrats, Olmsted and Vaux unsuccessfully submit resignations several times.

1873 The Greensward plan is completed. It has been the basic blueprint for Central Park ever since.

More than thirty-eight million people visit Central Park each year; on an average summer weekend day, a quarter of a million children and adults flood these precincts, frolicking in the 21 playgrounds and 26 ballfields, and collapsing on more than 9,000 benches, which would span seven miles if you lined them up. There are more than 55 monuments and sculptures in the park, and countless ways to have fun.

30 THINGS WE LOVE TO DO IN CENTRAL PARK

1 Take a rowboat out on the lake

2 Clap for the sea lions at the zoo

3 Jog around the Reservoir

4 Ice-skate at Wollman Rink

5 Watch rollerbladers show off

6 Go bird-watching at the Ramble

7 Doze in Sheep Meadow

8 Rent a bike at the Boathouse

9 Sit on the hill behind the Met Museum

10 See a free concert or play

11 Catch a softball game

12 Bask in fall foliage

13 Remember John Lennon at Strawberry Fields

14 Take a Central Park Conservancy Tour

15 Rent a gondola and a gondolier

16 Cross the park on the bridle path

17 Stand under the 72nd Street Wisteria Pergola

18 Hear the Delacorte Clock's musical chimes

19 Crunch the snow before anyone else

20 Pilot a model boat at Conservatory Water

21 Stroll through Shakespeare Garden

22 Fish at Harlem Meer

23 Sunbathe on Hernshead

24 Smell the Conservatory Garden tulips

25 Shoot photos from Bow Bridge

26 Ride the Carousel

27 People-watch at Bethesda Fountain

28 Picnic on the Great Lawn

29 Pet the bronze Balto statue

30 Climb to the top of Belvedere Castle

(top left) Monarch butterfly pollinates at Conservatory Garden (top center) Bethesda Fountain (top right) Chrysanthemums near Sheep Meadow (center) The skyline with some of the park's 26,000 trees (bottom) Park skaters in the 1860s.

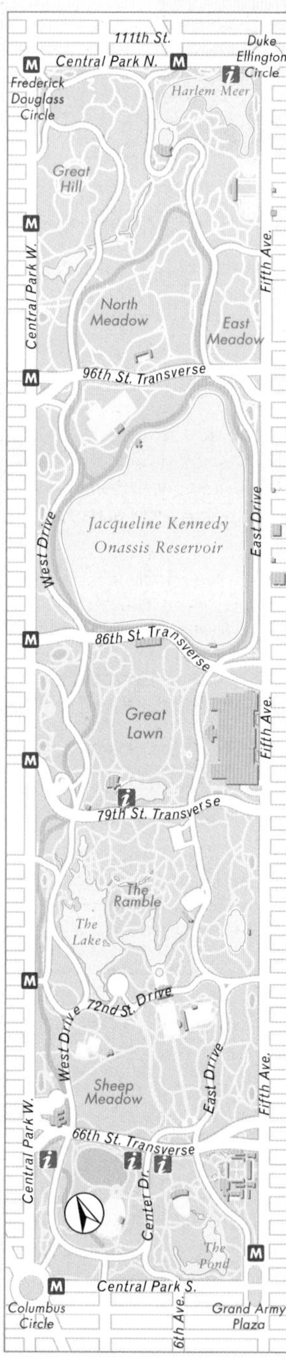

PARK BASICS

Several entrances lead into the park. You can enter from the east, west, south, and north by paved pedestrian walkways, just off Fifth Avenue, Central Park North (110th St.), Central Park West, and Central Park South (59th St.).

Four roads, or transverses, cut through the park from east to west—66th, 79th, 86th, and 96th streets. The East and West drives are both along the north–south axis; Center Drive enters the south edge of the park at Sixth Avenue and connects with East Drive around 66th Street.

There are five Visitor Centers—the Dairy (just south of the 66th St. transverse), Belvedere Castle (just north of the 79th Street transverse), the Chess & Checkers House (mid-park at 64th St.), and the Charles A. Dana Discovery Center (at the top of the park at Central Park North)—that have directions, park maps, event calendars, and volunteers who can guide you. Until a new restaurant opens in its place, the former Tavern on the Green (west side near 66th St.) is also serving as a visitor center, with food vendors as well.

TOURS

The **Central Park Conservancy** gives several different free walking tours of the park based on the season. Most tours are 60 to 90 minutes and explore the park's history, ecology, and design. Custom tours are also available. If you'd rather go it alone, the Conservancy also offers an audio guide you can follow on your cell phone. Each description is read by a different celebrity or NYC VIP. Self-guided tours of the Ramble and North Woods are available as PDFs for download. For more information, see *centralparknyc.org*.

WHERE AM I?

Along the main loop and some paths, lampposts are marked with location codes. Posts bear a letter—always "E" (for east) or "W" (for west)—and four numbers. The first two numbers tell you the nearest cross street. The second two tell you how far you are from either 5th Ave. or Central Park West (depending on whether it's an "E" or "W" post). So E7803 means you're near 78th St., three posts in from 5th Ave. For street numbers above 99, the initial "1" is omitted, for example, E0401 (near 104th St., one post in from 5th Ave.).

PERFORMERS AND THE PARK: SOULMATES

It was inevitable that Central Park, conceived to give so much and ask little in return, would attract artists and art lovers who feel the same way.

Be they superstars like Paul Simon, Diana Ross, or Barbra Streisand or one of the amateur musicians, animal handlers, or jugglers who delight passersby, they all share the urge to entertain and give back to the city, the park, and its visitors.

Information on scheduled events is provided, but if you can't catch one, don't fret: you'll be rewarded by the serendipitous, particularly on summer and autumn days. Just keep your ears peeled for the music, applause, and laughter. The Central Park Conservancy, in cooperation with other arts patrons, organizes a series of free events, including the Harlem Meer Performance Festival and the Great Lawn performances by the Metropolitan Opera and New York Philharmonic. SummerStage has yielded a cornucopia of international performers.

Perhaps the brass ring of park performances is Shakespeare in the Park, which celebrated its 50th year in 2012. Every summer's performances of works by the Bard (and others) wow as many as 90,000 New Yorkers and visitors. Free tickets (two per person) are given out starting at 1 PM for the performance that evening, but you need to line up by midmorning or earlier, depending on the show. Tickets are also distributed via online lottery on the show day at www.*shakespeareinthepark.org*. Either way, the trouble is worth it, as casts are often studded with stars like Meryl Streep, Philip Seymour Hoffman, Natalie Portman, Morgan Freeman, Denzel Washington, and Kevin Kline.

GOINGS ON

Central Park Conservancy Film Festival: Five nights at end of summer; Rumsey Playfield, near E. 72nd St. entrance.

Harlem Meer Performance Festival: Late June–early Sept., Sun.; at Dana Discovery Center, near Lenox Ave. entrance.

Jazz & Colors: Live jazz and fall foliage at this one-day concert in November.

New York Grand Opera: Performances July.–Aug.; Naumburg Bandshell; mid-park near 72nd St.

New York Philharmonic: Two performances in the summer; Great Lawn.

Shakespeare in the Park: June–early Aug., Tues.–Sun. evenings.

Storytelling: June–Sept., Sat. 11 AM; Hans Christian Andersen Statue at 72nd St. and 5th Ave.

SummerStage: Late May or June–early Sept.; Rumsey Playfield.

Swedish Cottage Marionette Theatre: Since 1947, puppeteers have entertained in this 1876 Swedish schoolhouse.

(center) N.Y. Philharmonic associate conductor Xian Zhang (right) Shakespeare's *Much Ado About Nothing*

FROM 59TH TO 72ND ST.

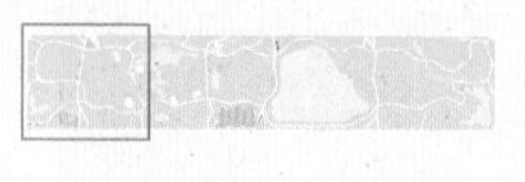

The busy southern section of Central Park is where most visitors get their first impression; it's also where most of the park's child-friendly attractions are centered. Artists line the entrances off Central Park South, and horse carriages await passengers. But no matter how many people gather here, you can always find a spot to picnic, ponder, or just take in the beauty, especially on a sunny day.

At the southeast corner of the park, you will come upon one of its prettiest areas, the **Pond.** Swans and ducks cruise on its calm waters, and if you follow the shore line to Gapstow Bridge and look southward, you'll see much of New York City's skyline: to the left (east) are the peak-roofed Sherry-Netherland Hotel, the black-and-white GM Building, the Chippendale-style top of the Sony Building, and the black-glass Trump Tower. In front of you is the château-style Plaza Hotel.

Opening in late October, **Trump Wollman Skating Rink** sits inside the park against a backdrop of Central Park South skyscrapers. You can rent skates, buy snacks, and have a perfect city-type outing. There's a lively feeling here with lots of great music playing and a terrace so you can watch if you're not into skating.

The **Friedsam Memorial Carousel,** also known as the Central Park Carousel, was built in 1908. It has 58 nearly life-size hand-carved horses and remains a favorite among young and old. Its original Wurlitzer organ plays calliope waltzes, polkas, and standards. Even if you don't need visitor infomation, the **Dairy** is worth a stop for its Swiss-chalet exterior.

If you saw the film *Madagascar,* you may recognize the **Central Park Zoo.** Here, the polar bears play at the Polar Circle, monkeys frolic in the open-air Temperate Territory, and the Rain Forest showcases flora and fauna that you wouldn't expect to see in Manhattan. An unusual exhibit is the ant colony—even New York City's zoo has a sense of humor. Stick around to see the sea lion feedings (call for times) and to watch the animal statues dance to a variety of nursery rhymes at the **Delacorte Musical Clock** just outside, on the hour and half-hour from 8 AM to 5 PM.

Wedged between the zoo and the clock is **The Arsenal,** the second-oldest building in the park. Inside are rotating exhibits that often cover park history and landscape art.

North of the clock is **Tisch Children's Zoo,** where kids can pet and feed sheep, goats, rabbits, cows, and pigs. Enter through the trunk of a make-believe tree and arrive at The Enchanted Forest, filled with huge "acorns,"

QUICK BITES

Zabar's, on 80th and Broadway, is a perennial pit stop for picnic fare, but there are many grab-and-go eateries and supermarkets on either side of the park. Your best bet for rations: west of Columbus Ave. and east of Park Ave.

The **Whole Foods** in the Time Warner Center at Columbus Circle is a good option at the southwest corner of the park.

The Mineral Springs Pavilion (mid-park at W. 69th St.) houses **Le Pain Quotidien,** serving sandwiches, soups, and pastries.

For even quicker bites, vendors sell snacks throughout the park.

If you prefer a more formal bite, try the **Boathouse Restaurant** (Midpark at 74th St.). An adjacent café dishes up good, cheap meals.

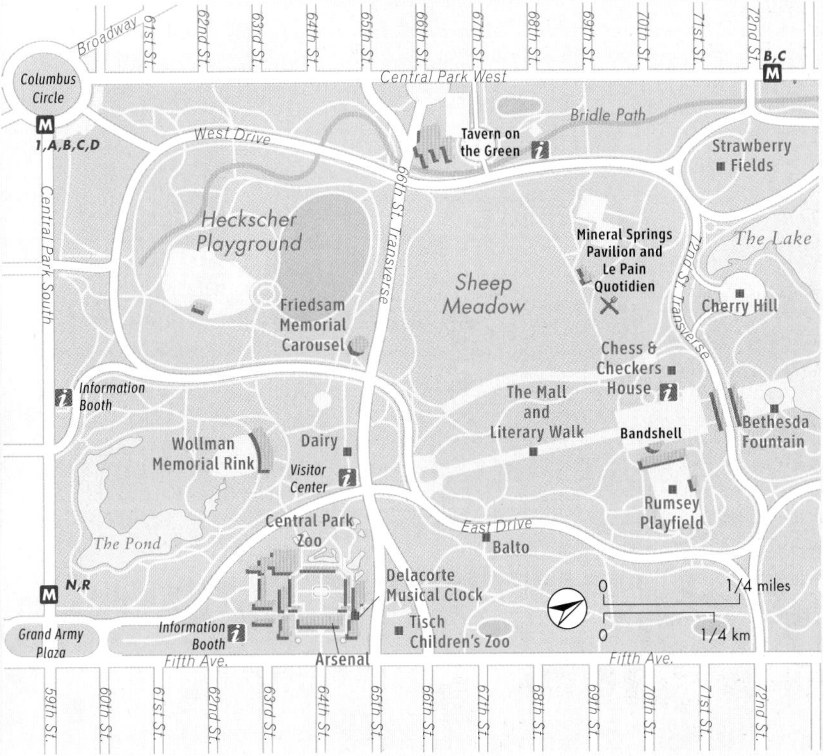

Broadway
61st St.
62nd St.
63rd St.
64th St.
65th St.
66th St.
67th St.
68th St.
69th St.
70th St.
71st St.
72nd St.
B,C
Columbus Circle
1,A,B,C,D
Central Park West
Bridle Path
West Drive
Tavern on the Green
Strawberry Fields
Central Park South
Heckscher Playground
66th St. Transverse
Sheep Meadow
Mineral Springs Pavilion and Le Pain Quotidien
72nd St. Transverse
The Lake
Cherry Hill
Friedsam Memorial Carousel
Chess & Checkers House
Information Booth
The Mall and Literary Walk
Bandshell
Bethesda Fountain
Wollman Memorial Rink
Dairy
Visitor Center
Rumsey Playfield
Central Park Zoo
East Drive
The Pond
Balto
N,R
Delacorte Musical Clock
0
1/4 miles
Tisch Children's Zoo
0
1/4 km
Grand Army Plaza
Information Booth
Fifth Ave.
Arsenal
Fifth Ave.
59th St.
60th St.
61st St.
62nd St.
63rd St.
64th St.
65th St.
66th St.
67th St.
68th St.
69th St.
70th St.
71st St.
72nd St.

a climbable "spider web," and hoppable "lily pads."

Perhaps more pettable than any of the zoo's occupants is a decidely more inert creature, perched on a rockpile at East Drive and 67th Street: **Balto.** Shiny in places from constant touching, this bronze statue commemorates a real-life sled dog who led a team of huskies that carried medicine for 674 mi across perilous ice to Nome, Alaska, during a 1925 diphtheria epidemic.

The Mall, at the intersection of Central Drive and East Drive, is arguably the most elegant area of Central Park. In the beginning of the 20th century, it was the place to see and be seen. Today, these formal walkways are still a wonderful place to stroll, meander, or sit and take in the "parade" under a canopy of the largest collection of American elms in North America. The mall's southern end, known as **Literary Walk,** is lined with statues of authors and artists such as Robert Burns and William Shakespeare.

(from left to right) Riding on the outside track (recommended) of the Carousel; Getting in a workout on a park drive loop; The Mall, where Dustin Hoffman's character famously teaches his son to ride a bike in *Kramer vs. Kramer.*

The large expanse to the west of the Mall is known as the **Sheep Meadow**, the only "beach" that some native New Yorkers have ever known. Join in on a Frisbee or football game, admire the tenacity of kite flyers, or indulge simultaneously in the three simplest meadow pleasures of them all—picnicking, sunbathing, and languorously reading a book or magazine.

There's a reason why the ornate **Bethesda Fountain**, off the 72nd Street transverse, shows up in so many movies set in New York City: the view from the staircase above is one of the most romantic in the city. The statue in the center of the fountain, **The Angel of the Waters**, designed by Emma Stebbins, is surrounded by four figures symbolizing Temperance, Purity, Health, and Peace. There's a good amount of New York–style street entertainment here, too, with break dancers, acrobats, and singers all vying for your spare change. It's also a great place to meet, sit, and admire the beautiful lake with its swans. For a glimpse of the West Side skyline, walk slightly west to **Cherry Hill**. Originally a watering area for horses, this circular plaza

has a small wrought-iron-and-gilt fountain. It's particularly beautiful in the spring when the cherry trees are in full pink-and-white bloom. Farther west are the Oak Bridge and the lovely Ladies Pavilion, emblematic of the park's past.

Across from the Dakota apartment building on Central Park West is **Strawberry Fields**, named for the Beatles' 1967 classic, "Strawberry Fields Forever." Sometimes called the "international garden of peace," this spot draws fans who come to reflect among its shrubs, trees, and flower beds, and lay flowers on the black-and-white "Imagine" mosaic. On December 8, hundreds of Beatles fans mark the anniversary of Lennon's death by gathering here.

(top from left to right) Horse-drawn carriages; Artist painting the oft-rendered Gapstow bridge, which spans the northeast end of the Pond; Cutting through the park is a classic midday timesaver and post-work respite; Seals at the Central Park Zoo (center left); Nighttime at Wollman Rink serves up twinkling skyscrapers and skaters of all abilities (center right); The late John Lennon and his widow, Yoko Ono, often visited the site of what would become Strawberry Fields.

FROM 72ND ST. TO THE RESERVOIR

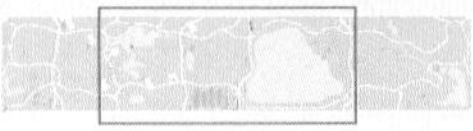

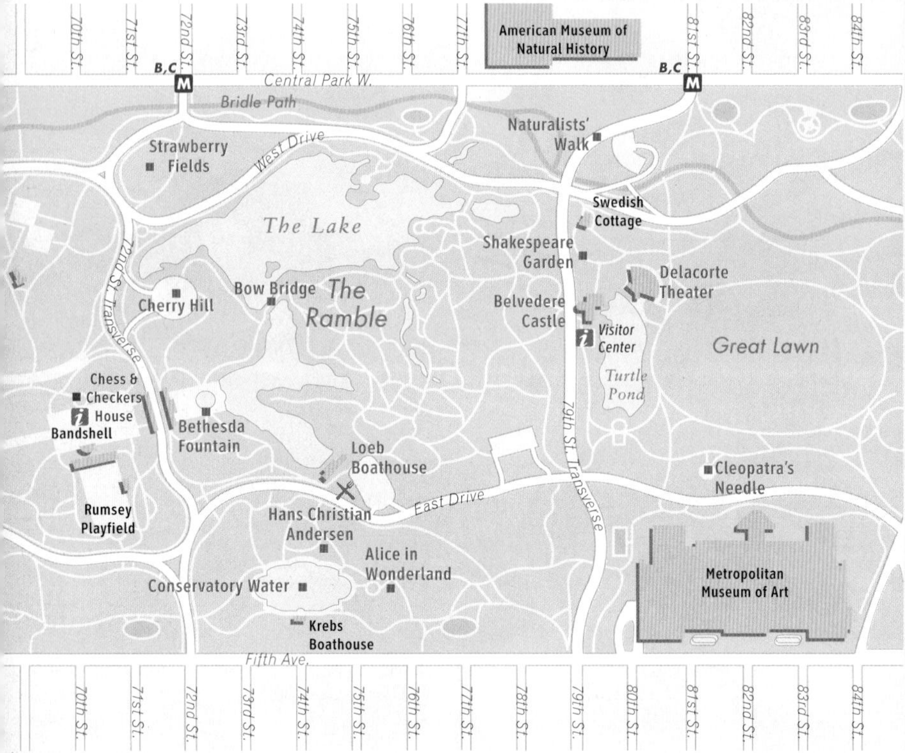

Playgrounds, lawns, jogging and biking paths, and striking buildings populate the midsection of the park. You can soak up the sun, have a picnic, or even play in a pick-up basketball or baseball game by the Great Lawn; get your cultural fix at the Metropolitan Museum of Art; or train for the next New York City Marathon along the Reservoir.

A block from Fifth Avenue, just north of the 72nd Street entrance, is a peaceful section of the park where you'll find the **Conservatory Water,** named for a conservatory that was never built. Generations of New Yorkers have grown up racing radio-controlled model sailboats here. It's a tradition that happens each Saturday at 10 AM from April through Oct. During those months smaller boats are available for rent daily. At the north end is the **Alice in Wonderland** statue; on the west side of the pond, a bronze statue of **Hans Christian Andersen,** the Ugly Duckling at his feet, is the site of Saturday storytelling hours during summer.

At the neo-Victorian **Loeb Boathouse** on the park's 18-acre Lake, you can rent a rowboat, kayak, bike, or ride in an authentic Venetian gondola. The attached café is a worthy pit stop.

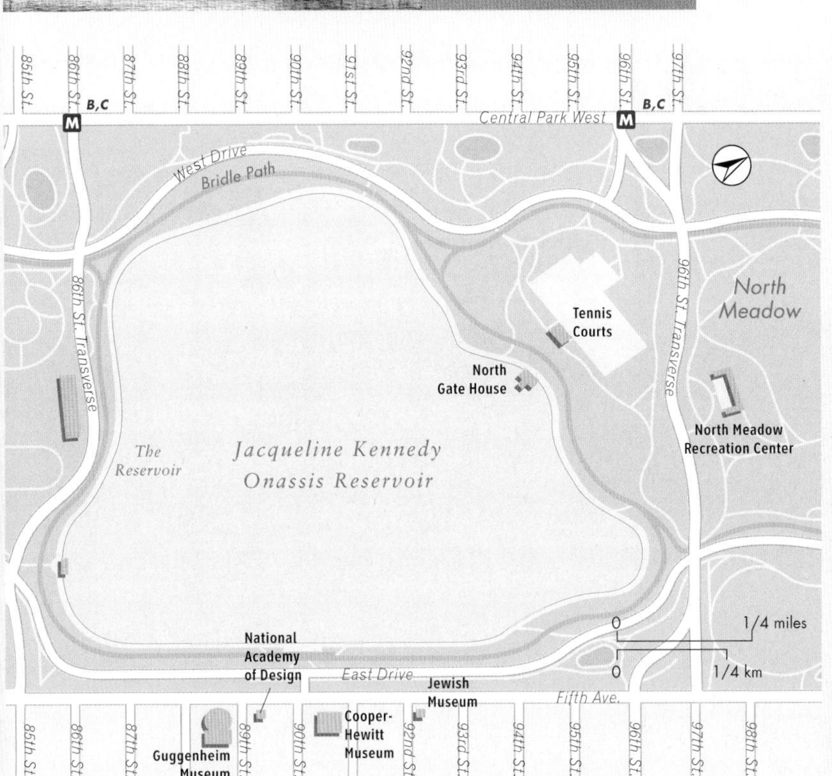

Designed to resemble upstate New York's Adirondack Mountain region, the **Ramble** covers 38 acres and is laced with twisting, climbing paths. This is prime bird-watching territory, since it's a rest stop along a major migratory route and a shelter for many of the more than 230 species of birds that have been sighted in the park; bring your binoculars. Because the Ramble is so dense and isolated, however, don't wander here alone, or after dark. Head south through the Ramble and you'll come to the beautiful cast-iron **Bow Bridge**, spanning part of the Lake between the Ramble and Bethesda Fountain. From the center of the bridge, you can get a sweeping view of the park as well as of the apartment buildings on both the East Side and the West Side.

North of the Ramble atop Vista Rock, **Belvedere Castle** is the second-highest natural point in the park. If you can't get tickets for Delacorte Theater, you can climb to one of the castle's

(from left to right) Belvedere means "beautiful view" in Italian, a clue to why we climb to the top of Belvedere Castle; Birders, photographers, and couples of all ages are drawn to Bow Bridge; Red-eared slider turtles frolic in Turtle Pond, at the base of Belvedere Castle.

three terraces and look down on the stage. You'll also get a fantastic view of the Great Lawn—it's particularly beautiful during the fall foliage months—and of the park's myriad bird visitors. Since 1919 the castle has served as a U.S. Weather Bureau station, and meteorological instruments are set on top of the tower. If you enter the Castle from the lower level, you can visit the Henry Luce Nature Observatory, which has nature exhibits, children's workshops, and educational programs.

Somewhat hidden behind Belvedere Castle, **Shakespeare Garden** is an informal jumble of flowers, trees, and pathways, inspired by the flora mentioned in Shakespeare's plays and poetry. Bronze plaques throughout the garden bear the bard's lines mentioning the plants.

The Great Lawn hums with action on weekends, on warm days, and on most summer evenings, when its baseball fields and picnic grounds fill with city folks and visitors alike. Its 13 acres have endured millions of footsteps, thousands of ball games, hundreds of downpours, dozens of concerts, fireworks displays, and even a papal mass. On a beautiful day, everyone seems to be here.

Chancing upon the 70-ft-tall **Cleopatra's Needle** always feels a bit serendipitous and delightfully jarring, even to the most cynical New Yorkers. This weathered hieroglyphic-covered obelisk began life in Heliopolis, Egypt, around 1500 BC, but has only a little to do with Cleopatra—it's just New York's nickname for the work. It was eventually carted off to Alexandria by the Romans in 12 BC, and it landed here on January 22, 1881, when the khedive of Egypt made it a gift to the city.

At the southwest corner of the Great Lawn is the fan-shaped **Delacorte Theater**, home to the summer Shakespeare in the Park festival.

If you want to take in several sites in a single brisk jaunt, consider walking the **Naturalists' Walk**. On this path you can wind your way toward the Swedish Cottage, the Shakespeare Garden, and Belvedere Castle on a landscaped nature

(top, from left to right) A female Canada goose and goslings on Turtle Pond; Cyclists make good use of the bike paths; Bikers as well as joggers boost their egos by outpacing the hansom carriages; Racing boats at Conservatory Water (center) In the 1930s, a flock of sheep was evicted from what would later be known as the Sheep Meadow.

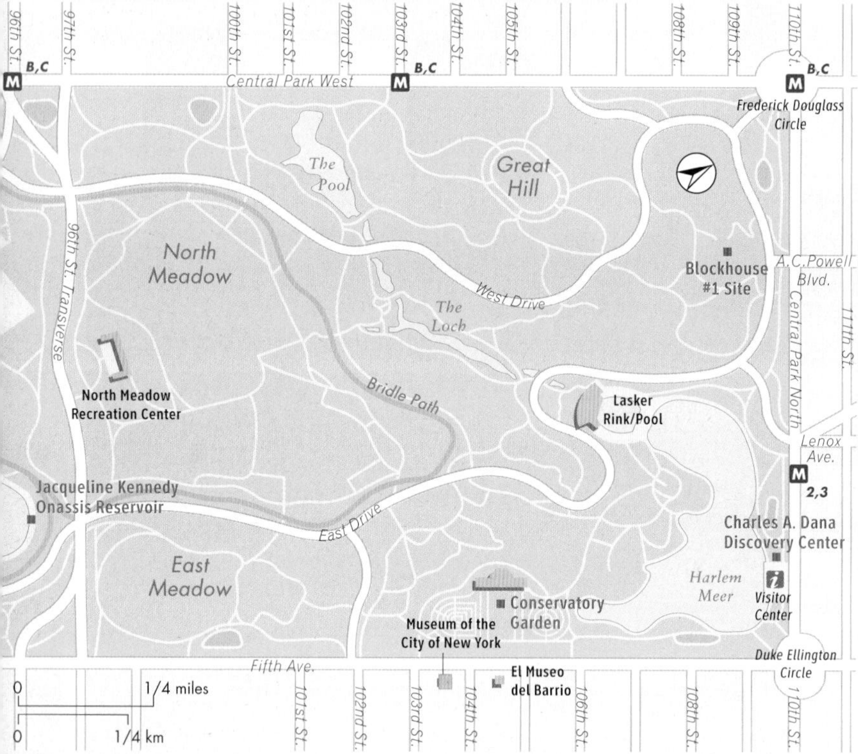

walk with spectacular rock outcrops, a stream that attracts bird life, a woodland area with various native trees, stepping-stone trails, and, thankfully, benches.

North of the Great Lawn and the 86th Street transverse is a popular gathering place for New Yorkers and visitors alike, the **Jacqueline Kennedy Onassis Reservoir**. Rain or shine, you'll see runners of all ages and paces heading counterclockwise around the 1.58-mi dirt path that encircles the water. The path in turn is surrounded by hundreds of trees that burst into color in the spring and fall. The 106-acre reservoir, finished in 1862, was a source of fresh water for Manhattanites. It holds more than a billion gallons, but it's no longer used for drinking water; the city's main reservoirs are upstate. From the top of the stairs at 90th Street just off 5th Avenue you have a 360-degree panorama of the city's exciting skyscrapers and often-brilliant sunsets. On the south side, there are benches so you can rest and recharge.

FROM THE RESERVOIR TO 110TH ST.

More locals than tourists know about the wilder-looking, less-crowded northern part of Central Park, and there are hidden gems lurking here that enable even the most tightly wound among us to decompress, at least for a short while.

Walking along Fifth Avenue to 105th Street, you'll see a magnificent wrought-iron gate—once part of the 5th Avenue mansion of Cornelius Vanderbilt II—that marks the entrance to the **Conservatory Garden.** As you walk through it, you enter a different world, a quiet place that's positively idyllic for reading and slowing down. The Italian-style **Central Garden** is a beauty, with an expansive lawn, a strikingly simple fountain, and a wisteria-draped pergola that just oozes romance.

The French-inspired **North Garden** is a colorful place with plants placed into elaborate patterns. Springtime is magical—thousands of tulips come to life in a circle around the garden's striking Untermyer Fountain and its three bronze dancers; in the fall, chrysanthemums take their place. The English-style **South Garden** conjures up images from the classic children's book *The Secret Garden.* The garden is a beautiful hodgepodge of trees, bushes, and flowers that bloom year-round. A free tour is conducted on Saturday at 11 AM, from April through October.

At **Harlem Meer,** the third-largest body of water in Central Park, you can borrow fishing poles (identification required) from mid-April through October and try your hand at catching (and releasing) the largemouth bass, catfish, golden shiners, and bluegills that are stocked in the water's 11 acres. You can also learn about the upper park's geography, ecology, and history at the Victorian-style **Charles A. Dana Discovery Center.**

Although only a shell of this stone building remains, **Blockhouse #1** serves as a historical marker: the structure was built in 1814 as a cliffside fortification against the British. The area is deserted and dense with trees, so go as a group here, and avoid it at night.

(left) A pensive raccoon in the park's northern reaches; (center) A jogger makes her counterclockwise progress along the reservoir; (right) Inside the Central Park Conservancy Garden.

CONTACT INFORMATION

Central Park Conservancy
☎ 212/310–6600
🌐 www.centralparknyc.org

Central Park SummerStage
☎ 212/360–2777
🌐 www.summerstage.org

Central Park Wildlife Center (Central Park Zoo)
☎ 212/439–6500
🌐 www.centralparkzoo.org

Central Park Visitor Centers
☎ 212/794–6564 (Dairy)
🌐 www.nycgovparks.org

Charles A. Dana Discovery Center
☎ 212/860–1370

Loeb Boathouse, Boathouse Restaurant
☎ 212/517–2233
🌐 www.thecentralparkboathouse.com

Shakespeare in the Park
☎ 212/539–8750 (Public Theater)
🌐 www.shakespeareinthepark.org

Swedish Cottage Marionette Theatre
☎ 212/988–9093
🌐 www.cityparksfoundation.org

Wollman Memorial Rink
☎ 212/439–6900
🌐 www.wollmanskatingrink.com

DID YOU KNOW?

Central Park is a major stopping point for migratory birds; more than 275 species have been spotted. Some of the common birds you can expect to see are the red-bellied woodpecker, the Canada goose, the blue jay, and the northern cardinal.

THE UPPER WEST SIDE

with the Cloisters

GETTING ORIENTED

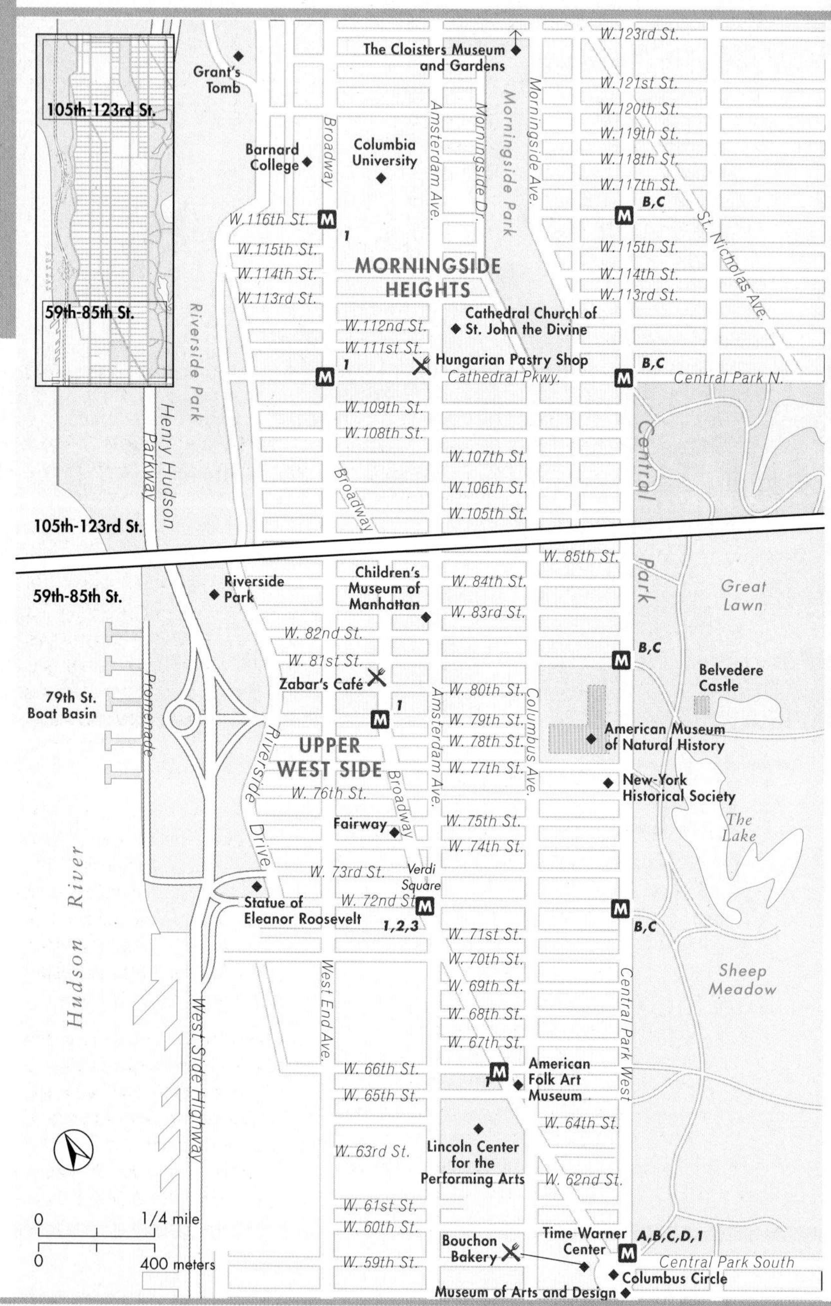

MAKING THE MOST OF YOUR TIME

Broadway is one of the most walkable and interesting thoroughfares on the Upper West Side because of its broad sidewalks and aggressive mix of retail stores, restaurants, and apartment buildings. If you head north from the Lincoln Center area (around 65th Street) to about 81st Street (about 1 mile), you'll get a feel for the neighborhood's local color, particularly above 72nd Street. Up here you'll encounter residents of every conceivable age and ethnicity either shambling or sprinting, street vendors hawking used and newish books, and such beloved landmarks as the 72nd Street subway station, the Beacon Theater, the produce mecca Fairway (the cause of perhaps the most perpetually congested block), and Zabar's (a food spot that launches a memorable assault on all five of your senses—and your wallet). The Upper West Side's other two main avenues—Columbus and Amsterdam—are more residential but also have myriad restaurants and shops.

If you're intrigued by having the city's only Ivy League school close at hand, hop the 1 train to 116th Street and emerge on the east side of the street, which puts you smack in front of Columbia University and its Graduate School of Journalism. Pass through the gates and up the walk for a look at a cluster of buildings so elegant you'll understand why it's an iconic NYC setting.

GETTING HERE

The A, B, C, D, and 1 subway lines will take you to Columbus Circle. From there, the B and C lines run along Central Park, stopping at 72nd, 81st, 86th, 96th, 103rd, and 110th streets. The 1 train runs up Broadway, making local stops at 66th, 72nd, 79th, 86th, 96th, 103rd, 110th, 116th, and 125th streets. The 2 and 3 trains, the express trains that also go along Broadway, stop at 72nd and 96th.

TOP EXPERIENCES

Walking along Broadway—for the shopping, people-watching, and snacking.

Grazing at Zabar's.

Strolling through Riverside Park past the boat basin.

Strolling in Central Park *(See Chapter 11)*

Standing below the gigantic blue whale at the Museum of Natural History.

Watching performers and students rushing to rehearsals and classes at Lincoln Center.

COFFEE AND QUICK BITES

Bouchon Bakery. Located in busy Columbus Circle shopping center this busy bakery serves excellent sandwiches, quiches, pastries, and coffee. ✉ *Time Warner Center, 10 Columbus Circle, 3rd fl., Upper West Side* ☎ *212/823-9363.*

Hungarian Pastry Shop. Linger over a Danish and bottomless cups of coffee with the Columbia kids and professors at this old-world café and bakery—if there's room. ✉ *1030 Amsterdam Ave., at 111th St., Upper West Side* ☎ *212/866-4230.*

Zabar's Cafe. Fast-track the Zabar's experience with a gourmet coffee and sandwich, pickled lox, or slice of cheesecake from Zabar's Cafe. ✉ *2245 Broadway, at 80th St., Upper West Side* ☎ *212/787-2000.*

Sightseeing ★★★
Nightlife ★★
Dining ★★
Lodging ★
Shopping ★★★★

The Upper West Side is one of the city's quieter, more family-oriented neighborhoods, with wide sidewalks, a relatively slower pace, and more of a residential feel than you'll find in many other parts of New York City. The Cloisters, in Inwood, has the Metropolitan Museum's medieval collection.

THE UPPER WEST SIDE

Updated by Jacinta O'Halloran

The tree-lined side streets of the Upper West Side are lovely, with high stoops leading up to stately brownstones. Central Park, of course, is one of the main attractions here, no matter the season or time of day, though residents know that Riverside Park, along the Hudson River, can be even more appealing, with smaller crowds.

The Upper West Side also has its share of cultural institutions, from the 16-acre **Lincoln Center** complex, to the impressive and quirky collection at the **New-York Historical Society,** to Columbus Circle's **Museum of Arts and Design** and the much-loved **American Museum of Natural History.**

Most people think the area north of 106th Street and south of 125th Street on the West Side is just an extension of the Upper West Side. But technically it's called Morningside Heights, and it's largely dominated by Columbia University, along with a cluster of academic, religious, and medical institutions, including Barnard College and the **Cathedral Church of St. John the Divine.**

TOP ATTRACTIONS

Fodor's Choice ★

American Museum of Natural History. *See highlighted feature in this chapter.*

Cathedral Church of St. John the Divine. The largest Gothic-style cathedral in the world, even with its towers and transepts still unfinished, this divine behemoth comfortably asserts its bulk in the country's most vertical city. The seat of the Episcopal diocese in New York, it acts as a sanctuary for all, giving special services that include a celebration of New York's gay and lesbian community as well as the annual

Blessing of the Bikes, when cyclists of all faiths bring their wheels for a holy-water benediction. The cathedral hosts **musical performances** (🌐 *www.stjohndivine.org*) and has held funerals and memorial services for such artists as Duke Ellington, Jim Henson, George Balanchine, James Baldwin, and Alvin Ailey. Built in two long spurts starting in 1892, the cathedral remains only two-thirds complete. What began as a Romanesque-Byzantine structure under the original architects George Heins and Christopher Grant Lafarge shifted (upon Heins's death in 1911) to French Gothic under the direction of Gothic Revival purist Ralph Adams Cram. You can spot the juxtaposition of the two medieval styles by comparing the finished Gothic arches, which are pointed, with the still-uncovered arches, which are rounded in the Byzantine style.

Above the 3-ton central bronze doors is the intricately carved **Portal of Paradise,** which depicts St. John witnessing the Transfiguration of Jesus, and 32 biblical characters. Then step inside to the cavernous nave. More than 600 feet long, it holds some 5,000 worshippers, and the 162-foot-tall dome crossing could comfortably contain the Statue of Liberty (minus its pedestal). Turn around to see the **Great Rose Window,** made from more than 10,000 pieces of colored glass, the largest stained-glass window in the United States.

At the end of the nave, surrounding the altar, are seven chapels expressing the cathedral's interfaith tradition and international mission—with menorahs, Shinto vases, and dedications to various ethnic groups. The **Saint Saviour Chapel** contains a three-panel bronze altar in white-gold leaf with religious scenes by artist Keith Haring (his last work before he died in 1990).

Outside in the cathedral's south grounds, the eye-catching **Peace Fountain** depicts the struggle of good and evil in the form of the archangel Michael decapitating Satan, whose head hangs from one side. Encircling it are whimsical animals cast in bronze from pieces sculpted by children.

On the first Sunday of October the Cathedral Church of St. John the Divine is truly a zoo. In honor of St. Francis of Assisi, the patron saint of animals, the church holds its usual Sunday service with a twist: the service is attended by men, women, children, dogs, cats, rabbits, hamsters, and the occasional horse, sheep, or ant farm. In past years upward of 3,500 New Yorkers have shown up to have their pets blessed. A procession is led by such guest animals as elephants, camels, llamas, and golden eagles. Seats are first-come, first-served for this popular event, so come at least an hour ahead of time. Sunday services are at 8, 9, 11, and 4. "Highlight Tours" and "Vertical Tours" are offered throughout the week: check the website for details and to reserve space. ✉ *1047 Amsterdam Ave., at W. 112th St., Upper West Side* ☎ *212/316–7540* 🌐 *www.stjohndivine.org* 🎫 *Tours $10–$20* ⏲ *Mon.–Sat. 7–6, Sun. 7–7; tours Tues.–Sat. at 11 and 1, Sun. at 2* Ⓜ *1 to Cathedral Pkwy.–110th St.*

FAMILY
Fodor's Choice ★

Central Park. *See Chapter 11.*

Continued on page 190

INSECTS AND MYRIAPODS

Theodore Roosevelt Memorial Hall

AMERICAN MUSEUM OF NATURAL HISTORY

The largest natural history museum in the world is also one of the most impressive sights in New York. Four city blocks make up its 45 exhibition halls, which hold more than 30 million artifacts and wonders from the land, the sea, and outer space. With all those wonders, you won't be able to see everything on a single visit, but you can easily hit the highlights in half a day.

Before you begin, plan a route before setting out. Be sure to pick up a map when you pay your admission. The museum's four floors (and lower level) are mazelike.

Visitors can use Google Maps to find their way through the museum. The service tracks your location and guides you through exhibits and even to bathrooms and exits. The free AMNH Explorer App for iPhone and iPod touch has turn-by-turn directions, profiles of iconic museum objects, and tours. The museum has devices you can borrow if you don't have an app-friendly phone.

Getting into the museum can be time consuming. For the shortest lines, use the below-street-level entrance connected to the 81st Street subway station (look for the subway entrance to the left of the museum's steps). The entrance on Central Park West, where the vast steps lead up into the impressive, barrel-ceilinged Theodore Roosevelt Rotunda, is central and a good starting place for exploring.

The Rose Center for Earth and Space is attached to the museum. Enter from West 81st Street, where a path slopes down to the entrance, after which elevators and stairs descend to the ticket line on the lower level.

What to see? Check out the museum highlights on the following pages.

✉ Central Park West at W. 79th St., Upper West Side

Ⓜ Subway: B, C to 81st St.

☎ 212/769–5100

🌐 www.amnh.org

🎟 $19 suggested donation, includes admission to Rose Center for Earth and Space

🕒 Daily 10–5:45.

Left, Spectrum of Life Wall

MUSEUM HIGHLIGHTS

Left, Woolly Mammoth
Above, Tyrannosaurus rex

Dinosaurs and Mammals

An amazing assembly of dinosaur and mammal fossils covers the entire fourth floor. The organization can be hard to grasp at first, so head to the **Wallace Orientation Center,** where a short film explains how each of the Fossil Halls lead into each other. You'll want to spend at least an hour here—the highlights include a *T. rex,* an *Apatosaurus* (formerly called a Brontosaurus), and the *Buettneria,* which resembles a modern-day crocodile.

The specimens are not in chronological order; they're put together based on their shared characteristics. Key branching-off points—a watertight egg, a grasping hand—are highlighted in the center of rooms and surrounded by related fossil groups. Check out the touch screens here; they make a complex topic more comprehensible.

Reptiles and Amphibians

Head for the Reptiles and Amphibians Hall on the third floor to check out the Komodo Dragon lizards and a 23-foot-long python skeleton. The weirdest display is the enlarged model of the Suriname toad *Pipa pipa,* whose young hatch from the female's back. The Primates Hall carries brief but interesting comparisons between apes, monkeys, and humans. Also on the third floor is the upper gallery of the famed Akeley Hall of African Mammals.

SPECIAL SHOWS AND NEW EXHIBITS

Special exhibits, the IMAX theater, and the Space Show cost extra. The timed tickets are available in advance at the museum's Web site and are sold same day at the door. Between October and May, don't miss the warm, plant-filled Butterfly Conservatory, where blue morphos, monarchs, and other butterflies flit and feed. Ten minutes is probably enough time to enjoy it.

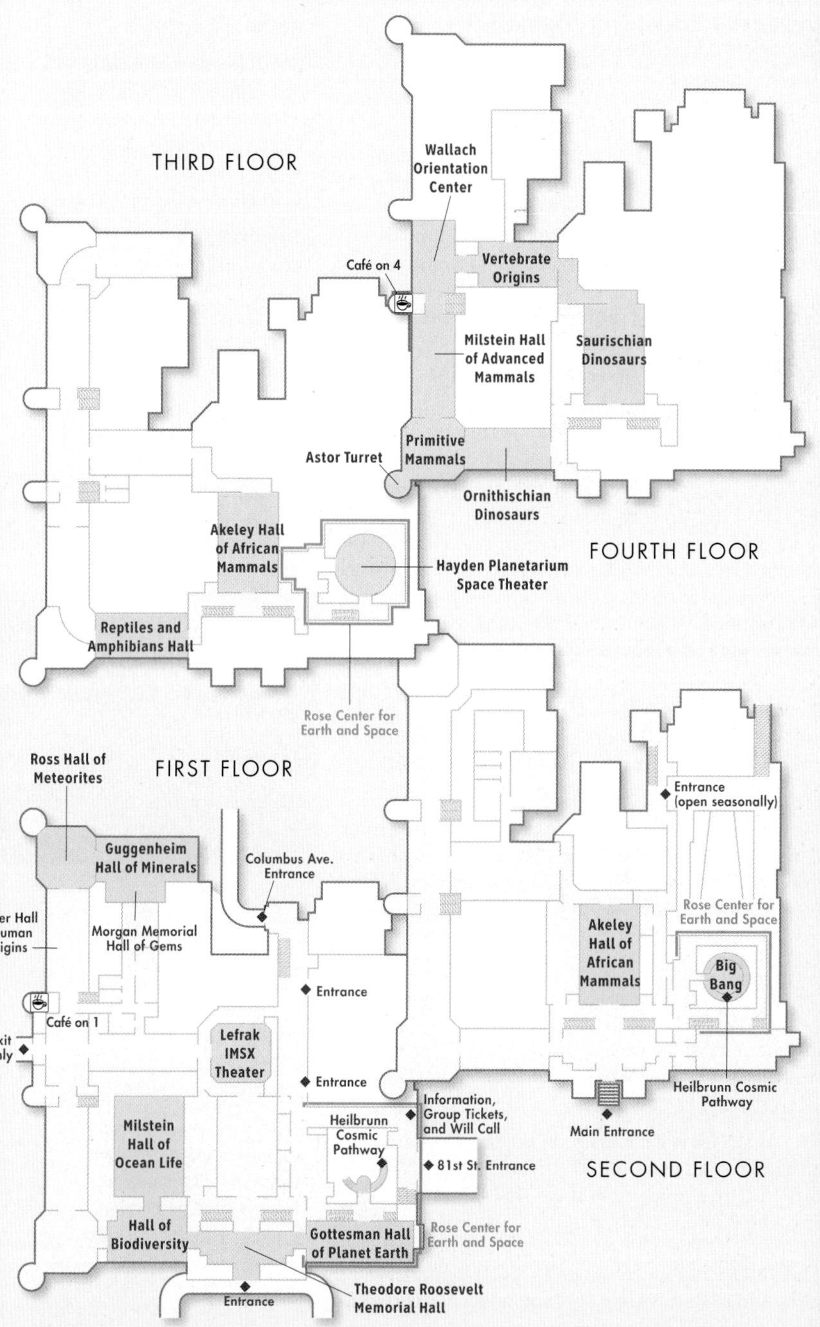
THIRD FLOOR
Wallach Orientation Center
Café on 4
Vertebrate Origins
Milstein Hall of Advanced Mammals
Saurischian Dinosaurs
Primitive Mammals
Astor Turret
Ornithischian Dinosaurs
Akeley Hall of African Mammals
Hayden Planetarium Space Theater
FOURTH FLOOR
Reptiles and Amphibians Hall
Rose Center for Earth and Space
FIRST FLOOR
Ross Hall of Meteorites
Guggenheim Hall of Minerals
Columbus Ave. Entrance
Entrance (open seasonally)
Morgan Memorial Hall of Gems
Rose Center for Earth and Space
Akeley Hall of African Mammals
Big Bang
Entrance
Café on 1
Exit only
Lefrak IMSX Theater
Entrance
Information, Group Tickets, and Will Call
Heilbrunn Cosmic Pathway
Main Entrance
Heilbrunn Cosmic Pathway
Milstein Hall of Ocean Life
81st St. Entrance
SECOND FLOOR
Hall of Biodiversity
Gottesman Hall of Planet Earth
Rose Center for Earth and Space
Theodore Roosevelt Memorial Hall
Entrance

Theodore Roosevelt Memorial

After a $40 million renovation, the two-story Theodore Roosevelt Memorial re-opened in late 2012. It includes the restored Central Park West entrance, the Theodore Roosevelt Rotunda, and the Theodore Roosevelt Memorial Hall. Highlights are a new bronze statue of a seated Roosevelt, celebratory murals honoring the Conservation President, touch-screen timelines, and film footage. The Hall of North American Mammals was also restored as part of the memorial to Roosevelt; the hall originally opened in 1942 and many of its displays feature scenes from National Parks that were signed into being by the president.

Akeley Hall of African Mammals

Opened in 1936, this hall on the third floor, its 28 dramatically lighted dioramas is one of the most beloved parts of the museum.

The hall was the life's work of the explorer Carl Akeley, who came up with the idea for the hall, raised the funds for the expeditions, gathered specimens, and sketched landscape studies for what would become the stunning backgrounds. (The backgrounds themselves were painted by James Perry Wilson, whose works can be found throughout the museum.)

Akeley died a decade before the hall opened on an expedition in what's now Rwanda. His gravesite is near the landscape portrayed in the gorilla diorama, completed after his death as a memorial to him and his work.

Hall of Human Origins

The Spitzer Hall of Human Origins on the first floor is a comprehensive exhibit that allows visitors to draw their own conclusions about human evolution by presenting both the scientific methods and the material evidence that goes into evolutionary theory.

The exhibit then traces the evolution of our species over six million years of fossil record and spells out our ancestors' physical and intellectual advancements. Highlights include casts of our famous hairy relative "Lucy," who walked the plains of Africa over 1.8 million years ago.

Hall of Biodiversity

The small **Hall of Biodiversity** on the first floor includes a shady replica of a Central African Republic rain forest. Nearby, the **Spectrum of Life Wall** showcases 1,500 specimens and models, helping show just how weird life can get. The wall opens into the gaping Milstein Hall of Ocean Life, designed to give it an underwater glow and to show off the 94-foot model of a **blue whale** that's suspended from the ceiling.

AMNH ON FILM

Does the inside of AMNH look familiar? It should. The museum is a popular location for movies filming in New York. Here are a few of its recent close ups:

Spider-Man 2: Peter Parker (Tobey Maguire) has yet another bad day wrestling with his secret identity while in the Rose Center.

Night at the Museum: Larry (Ben Stiller) is chased through the halls by a T. Rex and outsmarts a monkey in the Hall of African Mammals while working as a night security guard.

Blue Whale

The Squid & the Whale: Walt Berkman (Jesse Eisenberg) comes to a revelation that he is the squid and his father is the whale in front of the Hall of Ocean Life's famous diorama.

The Devil Wears Prada: Andrea (Anne Hathaway) wins over Miranda (Meryl Streep) by remembering the names of high society guests while attending a benefit here.

ROSE CENTER FOR EARTH AND SPACE

The vast expanses of space and time involved in the creation of the universe can be hard to grasp even with the guiding hand of a museum, so you may want to visit the center when you're at your sharpest. The stunning glass building's centerpiece is the aluminum-clad Hayden Sphere, 87 feet in diameter. Enclosed within are the planetarium, called the Space Theater, and an audiovisual Big Bang presentation consisting of four minutes of narration by Maya Angelou, indistinct washes of color, and frightening bursts of sound. The rock-filled **Hall of Planet Earth** is particularly timely given the earthquakes and other natural disasters of recent years: one section uses a working earthquake monitor to help explain just what causes such seismic violence.

The Space Theater

At the Space Theater, the stage is the dome above you and the actors, heavenly projections. One of the world's largest virtual reality simulators, the theater uses surround sound and slight vibrations in the seats, to immerse you in scenes of planets, star clusters, and galaxies. *Journey to the Stars*, narrated by actress Whoopi Goldberg, launches viewers through space and time; you'll never see the night sky in the same way again.

Tip: The Museum's Cosmic Discoveries app allows you to take the universe, and all its galaxies and planets, with you when you leave. The app offers images, findings, and bulletins all culled from the museum's archives and curated by the museum's astrophysicists. 🌐 *www.amnh.org/apps*

TIME TO EAT?

Inside the museum:
The **main food court** on the lower level serves sandwiches for about $7.95; hamburgers cost $5.50. The animal- and planet-shaped cookies are draws for kids; adults should check out the barbecue station.

The small **Café on 4**, in a turret next to the fossil halls, sells pre-made sandwiches and salads, and yogurt and desserts, but nothing warm.

The über-white **Café on 1**, tucked away beside the Hall of Human Origins, sells warm sandwiches, soup, salads, beer and wine at New York prices.

TIME TO PLAY

Nights at the museum aren't just for kids! Bust out your moonwalk and enjoy a few *cosmic*politans at the Rose Center's monthly One Step Beyond series, featuring live bands, DJs, VJs, cocktails, and dynamic visuals. Get tickets at amnh.org/rose/specials.

TIME TO WATCH

Each October, the AMNH hosts the Margaret Mead Film & Video Festival, the longest-running premiere showcase for international documentaries in the United States. Tickets are made available one month prior to the festival, and online at www.amnh.org/mead

AMNH TALKS TO FODOR'S

Interview with Ellen V. Futter, President of the American Museum of Natural History, conducted by Michelle Delio.

If You Only Have an Hour: The American Museum of Natural History has the world's finest collection of dinosaur fossils, so a visit to the fourth-floor's Fossil Halls, where more than 600 specimens are on display, is a must. An extraordinarily high percentage of the specimens on view—85%—are real fossilized bones as opposed to casts. At most museums those percentages are reversed, so here visitors have the chance to see the real thing including T. rex, velociraptor, and triceratops.

What to Hit Next? The museum also is renowned for its habitat dioramas, which are considered among the finest examples in the world. Visits to the Akeley Hall of African Mammals, the Hall of North American Mammals, and the Sanford Hall of North American Birds provide an overview of the diorama arts—pioneered and advanced at the museum—while allowing visitors to come face-to-face with some glorious and beautiful animals depicted in their natural habitats—habitats which in many cases no longer exist in such pristine conditions.

If You're Looking to Be Starstruck: Even if you don't have time to take in a space show in the Hayden Planetarium, the Rose Center for Earth and Space has lots of fascinating exhibits describing the vast range of sizes in the cosmos; the 13-billion-year history of the universe; the nature of galaxies, stars, and planets; and the dynamic features of our own unique planet Earth—all enclosed in a facility with spectacular award-winning architecture.

Hidden gems

The museum consists of 45 exhibition halls in 25 interconnected buildings so there are gems around every corner. Some lesser-known treasures include:

Star of India: The 563-carat Star of India, the largest and most famous star sapphire in the world, is displayed in the Morgan Memorial Hall of Gems.

Rose Center for Earth and Space

WHERE'S PLUTO?

With all the controversy about what constitutes a planet, some visitors enjoy hunting for Pluto in the Cullman Hall of the Universe in the Rose Center for Earth and Space. We'll give you a hint: it's not with the other planets.

Black Smokers: These sulfide chimneys—collected during groundbreaking museum expeditions to the Pacific Ocean—are the only such specimens exhibited anywhere. Black smokers form around hot springs on the deep ocean floor and support a microbial community that does not live off sunlight but instead on the chemical energy of the Earth. Some of these microbes are considered the most ancient forms of life on Earth and may offer clues to the development of life here and the possibility of life elsewhere. See them in the Gottesman Hall of Planet Earth.

Spectrum of Life: The Hall of Biodiversity aims to showcase the glorious diversity of life on Earth resulting from 3.5 billion years of evolution. The impressive "Spectrum of Life" display is a 100-foot-long installation of more than 1,500 specimens and models—microorganisms and mammals, bacteria and beetles, fungi and fish. Use the computer workstations to learn more about the species depicted in each area.

Dodo: One of the museum's rarest treasures is the skeleton of a dodo bird, displayed along with other endangered or extinct species in the "Endangered Case" in the Hall of Biodiversity.

Small Dioramas: Tucked along the sides of the Hall of North American Mammals are two easy-to-miss corridors displaying a number of exquisitely rendered dioramas. In these jewel-box-like displays, some a mere 3 feet deep, you will see the smaller animals such as wolves galloping through a snowy night, a Canada lynx stalking a snowshoe hare, and a spotted skunk standing on its hands, preparing to spray a cacomistle, to name just a few of the evocative scenes.

Dinosaur Eggs: In 1993 museum scientists working in the Gobi Desert of Mongolia were the first to unearth fossilized embryos in dinosaur eggs, as well as the fossil of an adult oviraptor in a brooding posture over its nest. This discovery provided invaluable information about dinosaur gestation and revolutionized thinking about dinosaur behavior. Look for the display in the museum's Fossil Halls on the fourth floor.

Ross Terrace: In warmer months the Ross Terrace, with its fountains and cosmic theme, offers a wonderful outdoor spot for resting and reflecting, while providing a spectacular view of the Rose Center for Earth and Space.

Star of India

A diorama featuring a Komodo Dragon, the largest and most powerful lizard in the world.

MOST INTERESTING OBJECT?

What's most interesting about the American Museum of Natural History is not any single object on exhibit, but the sheer range and scope of what you can experience here. Think of it is a field guide to the natural world, the universe, and the cultures of humanity—all under one roof. The experience of visiting the museum is ultimately about awakening a sense of discovery, wonder, awe, and stewardship of this Earth we call home.

Lincoln Center for the Performing Arts. *See the listing in Chapter 16, Performing Arts.*

New-York Historical Society. Manhattan's oldest museum, founded in 1804, has one of the city's finest research libraries and a collection of 6 million pieces of art, literature, and memorabilia. Special exhibitions shed light on America's—and, specifically, New York's—history, art, and architecture. Major exhibits have included Hudson River School landscapes and an examination of New York City's role in the slavery debate and the Civil War.

Visitors enter through the Great Hall, where kiosks and interactive exhibits explain original objects tied to key themes of American history, such as commerce and immigration. Special exhibits, like *WWII & NYC, Beer Here: Brewing New York's History,* and *AIDS in New York: The First Five Years* show off the museum's fresh approach and concentrated New York focus. The DiMenna Children's History Museum on the lower level invites children to become "history detectives" and to explore New York's past through interactive displays, hands-on activities, and the stories of iconic New York children through the centuries. The Historical Viewfinder allows kids to see how certain New York sites have changed over time. **TIP→ Unlike most other childrens' museums, this museum is geared to mature elementary school kids and middle schoolers, not toddlers.** Caffé Storico, the light-filled restaurant on the first floor serves upscale Italian food at lunch and dinner, and is open for brunch on the weekends. ✉ *170 Central Park West, Upper West Side* ☎ *212/873–3400* 🌐 *www.nyhistory.org* 🎟 *$15* 🕒 *Tues.–Thurs. and Sat. 10–6, Fri. 10–8, Sun. 11–5* Ⓜ *B, C to 81st St.–Museum of Natural History.*

WORTH NOTING

American Folk Art Museum. The focus of this museum is its incredible collection of contemporary self-taught artists of the 20th and 21st centuries, including the single largest collection of reclusive Chicago artist Henry Darger, known for his painstakingly detailed collage-paintings of fantasy worlds. The gift shop has interesting handcrafted items. ✉ *2 Lincoln Sq., Columbus Ave. at 66th St., Upper West Side* ☎ *212/595–9533* 🌐 *www.folkartmuseum.org* 🎟 *free* 🕒 *Tues.–Sat. noon–7:30, Sun. noon–6* Ⓜ *1 to 66th St.–Lincoln Center; A, B, C, D to 59th St.–Columbus Circle.*

FAMILY **Children's Museum of Manhattan.** In this five-story exploratorium, children ages one to seven are invited to paint their own masterpieces, float boats down a "stream" (weather permitting), join a mischievous Chinese monkey, and walk through giant interactive organs to explore the connections between food, sleep, and play. Other highlights include *Adventures with Dora and Diego,* an exhibition created in collaboration with Nickelodeon and "Bjork's Biophili," a workshop for older kids created in collaboration with the Icelandic singer, exploring the intersection of music, nature, and science. Art workshops, science programs, and storytelling sessions are held daily. **TIP→ Admission is free 5–8 pm on the first Friday of every month.** ✉ *212 W. 83rd St., between Broadway and*

Amsterdam Ave., Upper West Side ☎ *212/721–1223* 🌐 *www.cmom.org* 🎫 *$11* ⏲ *Tues.–Sun. 10–5, Sat. 10–7* Ⓜ *1 to 79th St. or 86th St.*

Columbus Circle. This busy traffic circle at Central Park's southwest corner anchors the Upper West Side. The central 700-ton granite monument (capped by a marble statue of Christopher Columbus) serves as a popular meeting place. To some people, Columbus Circle is synonymous with the **Time Warner Center** building and its several floors of shops and restaurants—including takeout-friendly Bouchon Bakery and Whole Foods, both perfect places to pick up picnic fixings to take to Central Park. ✉ *Broadway at 57th to 59th Sts.* Ⓜ *A, B, C, D, 1 to 59 St.–Columbus Circle.*

Grant's Tomb (*General Grant National Memorial*). Walk through upper Riverside Park and you're sure to notice this towering granite mausoleum (1897), the final resting place of Civil War general and two-term president Ulysses S. Grant and his wife, Julia Dent Grant. As the old joke goes, who's buried here? Nobody—they're *entombed* in a crypt beneath a domed rotunda, surrounded by photographs and Grant memorabilia. Once a more popular sight than the Statue of Liberty, this pillared Classical Revival edifice feels more like a relic of yesteryear, but it remains a moving tribute. The words engraved on the tomb, "Let Us Have Peace," recall Grant's speech to the Republican convention upon his presidential nomination. Surrounding the memorial are so-called "rolling benches," which are swoopy and covered with colorful mosaic tiles that bring to mind the works of architect Antonio Gaudí's Parque Güell, in Barcelona. Made in the 1970s as a public art project, they are now as beloved as they are incongruous with the grand memorial they surround. Free public talks are available in the visitor center (across the street from the tomb), Thursday through Monday at 11:15, 1:15, and 3:15. ✉ *Riverside Dr. at W. 122nd St., Upper West Side* ☎ *212/666–1640* 🌐 *www.nps.gov/gegr* 🎫 *Free* ⏲ *Thurs–Mon 9–5* Ⓜ *1 to 116th St.*

Museum of Arts and Design. In a funky-looking white building right across the street from the Time Warner Center, the Museum of Arts and Design celebrates joyful quirkiness and personal, sometimes even obsessive, artistic visions. The art is human-scale here, much of it neatly housed in display cases rather than on the walls, with a strong focus on contemporary jewelry, glass, ceramic, fiber, wood, and mixed-media works. Recent exhibits included *The Art of Scent,* which explored the design of olfactory art from 1889 to the present, and *The Home Front: American Design Now,* which featured more than 30 designers from throughout New York City. **TIP→ Thursday evening is pay-what-you-wish.** ✉ *2 Columbus Circle, 59th St. at 8th Ave., Upper West Side* ☎ *212/299–7777* 🌐 *www.madmuseum.org* 🎫 *$15* ⏲ *Tues., Wed., and weekends 11–6, Thurs. and Fri. 11–9* Ⓜ *A, B, C, D, 1 to Columbus Circle–59th St.; N, Q, R to 57th St.–7th Ave.; F to 57th St.*

FAMILY **Riverside Park.** Surrounded by concrete and skyscrapers all day, you might not realize that there is an expansive green space running along the water just blocks away. Riverside Park—which, along with the Riverside Park South extension, runs along the Hudson from 58th to 156th streets—dishes out a dose of tranquility. The original sections of Riverside Park, designed by Frederick Law Olmsted Law and Calvert Vaux of Central Park fame and laid out between 1873 and 1888, are outshone by Olmsted's "other" park—Central Park—but with its waterfront bike and walking paths and lighter crowds, this green space more than holds its own.

There are several access points to the park, including one at West 72nd Street and Riverside Drive (look for the **statue of Eleanor Roosevelt**) where you'll reach the waterfront path after heading through an underpass beneath the West Side Highway. You can then head north along the Hudson River, past the **79th Street Boat Basin,** where you can watch a flotilla of houseboats bobbing in the water. Above it, a ramp leads to the Rotunda, home in summer to the **Boat Basin Café**, an open-air café that's open for lunch and dinner in the warmer months (from about March through October). The **91st Street Garden,** planted by community gardeners, explodes with flowers in most seasons and is a level up from the water: leave the waterside path near 92nd Street by taking another underpass, then head up the path on the right. To the south, cresting a hill along Riverside Drive at West 89th Street, stands the Civil War **Soldiers' and Sailors' Monument** (1902), an imposing 96-foot-high circle of white-marble columns designed by Paul M. Duboy, who also designed the Ansonia Hotel. ✉ *W. 58th St. to W. 156th St. between Riverside Dr. and Hudson River, Upper West Side* 🌐 *www.nycgovparks.org* Ⓜ *1, 2, 3 to 72nd St.*

INWOOD

FAMILY
Fodor's Choice ★

The Cloisters Museum and Gardens. Perched on a wooded hill in Fort Tryon Park, near Manhattan's northwestern tip, the Cloisters Museum and Gardens, which shelters the medieval collection of the Metropolitan Museum of Art, is a scenic destination in its own right. Colonnaded walks connect authentic French and Spanish monastic cloisters, a French Romanesque chapel, a 12th-century chapter house, and a Romanesque apse. One room is devoted to the 15th- and 16th-century Unicorn Tapestries—must-see masterpieces of medieval mythology. The tomb effigies are another highlight. Two of the three enclosed gardens shelter more than 250 species of plants similar to those grown during the Middle Ages, including flowers, herbs, and medicinals; the third is an ornamental garden planted with both modern and medieval plants, providing color and fragrance from early spring until late fall. Concerts of medieval music are held here regularly (concert tickets include same-day admission to the museum). The outdoor Trie Café is open 10 to 4:15 daily except Monday, from April through October, and serves sandwiches, coffee, and snacks. **TIP→ Fee includes same-day admission to the Metropolitan Museum of Art's main building on 5th Ave.** ✉ *99 Margaret Corbin Dr., Fort Tryon Park, Upper West Side* ☎ *212/923–3700* 🌐 *www.metmuseum.org* 💳 *$25 suggested donation* ⏲ *Mar.–Oct., daily 10–5:15; Nov.–Feb., daily 10–4:45* Ⓜ *A to 190th St.*

13

HARLEM

GETTING ORIENTED

Highbridge Park
Morris-Jumel Mansion
555 Edgecombe Avenue
Hispanic Society of America Museum and Library
409 Edgecombe Avenue
Sugar Hill
345 Edgecombe Avenue
The Chipped Cup
HAMILTON HEIGHTS
Convent Avenue Baptist Church
Hamilton Terrace
Hamilton Grange
City College
Strivers' Row
Abyssinian Baptist Church
ST. NICHOLAS HISTORIC DISTRICT
St. Nicholas Park
Apollo Theater
African Sq.
125th St. Metro North Station
Studio Museum in Harlem
Greater Refuge Temple
HARLEM
Marcus Garvey Park
Morningside Park
Barnard College
Columbia University
Levain Bakery
Canaan Baptist Church of Christ
First Corinthian Baptist Church
Memorial Baptist Church
Masjid Malcolm Shabazz
Malcolm Shabazz Harlem Market
Cathedral Church of St. John the Divine
CENTRAL PARK
Harlem Meer
THE BRONX
Harlem River
Harlem River Dr.
145 St. Bridge
Madison Ave. Bridge
Henry Hudson Pkwy
Riverside Dr.
Riverside Park
Broadway
Amsterdam Ave.
Convent Ave.
St. Nicholas Ave.
Jackie Robinson Park
Edgecombe Ave
Frederick Douglass Blvd. (8th Ave.)
Adam Clayton Powell Jr. Blvd. (7th Ave.)
Lenox Ave./Malcolm X Blvd. (Sixth Ave.)
Mt. Morris Park West
Fifth Ave.
Madison Ave.
Park Ave.
Dr. Martin Luther King Jr. Blvd.
Dr. Martin Luther King Jr. Blvd. (125th St.)
Columbus Ave.
Central Park W.
Cathedral Pkwy.
Central Park North
0 1/4 mile
0 400 meters

MAKING THE MOST OF YOUR TIME

Harlem's simplest pleasures are free. Take time to walk the areas around Strivers' Row, Hamilton Heights, Sugar Hill, and 116th Street to see some impressive—and often fanciful—architecture. Hear the sweet sounds of a choir practice as you stroll by any of Harlem's churches (which number in the hundreds). See well-curated exhibits showcasing the work of contemporary artists of African descent at The Studio Museum in Harlem (open Thursday–Sunday), or visit the Morris-Jumel Mansion for a trip back in time to colonial New York.

GETTING HERE AND AROUND

The 2 and 3 subway lines stop on Lenox Avenue; the 1 goes along Broadway, to the west; and the A, B, C, and D trains travel along St. Nicholas and 8th avenues. And yes, as the song goes, the A train is still usually "the quickest way to Harlem."

The city's north–south avenues take on different names in Harlem: 6th Avenue is called both Malcolm X Boulevard *and* Lenox Avenue; 7th Avenue is Adam Clayton Powell Jr. Boulevard (it's named for the influential minister and congressman); and 8th Avenue is Frederick Douglass Boulevard. West 125th Street, the major east–west street and Harlem's commercial center, is also known as Dr. Martin Luther King Jr. Boulevard.

SAFETY

Harlem is more residential than many parts of the city and home to many families, so it gets quiet at night. Like everywhere else in New York, use common sense and steer clear of deserted side streets after dark.

TOP EXPERIENCES

Join Harlem's hippest for cocktails and music (live or DJ-spun) at Red Rooster/Ginny's Supper Club.

Attend a gospel service.

Visit The Studio Museum in Harlem.

Have fried chicken and waffles for breakfast, lunch, or dinner at a number of soul-food spots.

COFFEE AND QUICK BITES

The Chipped Cup. This coffeehouse offers fair-trade organic coffee, espresso drinks, tea, fresh pastries, and free Wi-Fi in a parlor-like atmosphere with a vibrant, neighborhood vibe. If the weather's nice, head to the garden patio out back. ✉ *3610 Broadway, between 148th and 149th Sts., Hamilton Heights* ✥ *Located below street level* ☎ *212/368–8881* 🌐 *www.chippedcupcoffee.com* Ⓜ *1 to 145th St.*

Levain Bakery. From coffee and cakes to breads and scones, this bakery has something for every sweet tooth. It's the cookies, however, that make them famous. Choose from varieties such as Chocolate Chip Walnut and Dark Chocolate Chocolate Chip; they're big enough to share, but after one bite you may not want to. ✉ *2167 Frederick Douglass Blvd., between 116th and 117th Sts.* ☎ *646/455–0952* 🌐 *www.levainbakery.com.*

Sightseeing ★★
Nightlife ★★★★
Dining ★★★
Lodging ★★
Shopping ★★

Harlem is known throughout the world as a center of African-American culture, music, and life. The neighborhood invites visitors to see historic jewels such as the Apollo Theater, architecturally splendid churches, cultural magnets like The Studio Museum in Harlem and the Schomburg Center for Research in Black Culture, as well as an ongoing list of new and renovated sites and buildings.

Updated by Anuja Madar

In Harlem, things are changing quickly. Luckily, its original charm and personalities are still around if you know where to look. While some iconic establishments have closed, newer spots aim to take their place by both paying homage to the area's roots and appealing to the young families and professionals who are buying up new, high-rise condos and restoring old brownstone and limestone buildings.

Harlem's 125th Street is at the heart of the neighborhood. Bill Clinton's New York office is at 55 West 125th Street, and the legendary Apollo Theater stands at No. 253. Growth has brought outposts of Starbucks, Old Navy, MAC Cosmetics, and H&M (overall welcome additions to the neighborhood), which make it hard to distinguish 125th Street from the city's other heavily commercialized areas. But there are still a few things that set it apart: an energy created by sidewalk vendors hawking bootleg DVDs, incense, and African shea butter; impromptu drum circles; and some of the best people-watching in Manhattan.

To get a taste of today's Harlem, spend time visiting its past and present. On 116th Street, particularly between St. Nicholas and Lenox Avenues (Malcolm X Boulevard), you'll find some of the area's most interesting religious buildings. Admire the ornate theatrical facade of the giant **First Corinthian Baptist Church,** or fill your soul with the mellifluous gospel music of the **Canaan Baptist Church of Christ's** choir during a Sunday service. Take a hint from the parishioners and follow up with smothered chicken and waffles at **Amy Ruth's,** at 113 W. 116th Street. After lunch, walk by the green-domed **Masjid Malcolm Shabazz**—a mosque attended primarily by West Africans and African-Americans. Finish at **Malcolm**

Shabazz Harlem Market where you can bargain for African and African-inspired jewelry, masks, crafts, and caftans at good prices.

Nowhere is the "new Harlem" more visible than along Lenox Avenue and Frederick Douglass Boulevard, between 110th and 126th Streets. Here you'll find restaurants, bars, and a few boutiques. Grab a bar stool at Red Rooster, where celebrity chef Marcus Samuelsson has created a restaurant-bar-lounge that draws tourists from across the globe and NYC residents from below 14th Street. While you might not be able to score a table, a visit here is more for the scene and creative cocktails than the food. Just west on 125th Street, check out contemporary African-American-oriented artworks at The **Studio Museum in Harlem.** If you're here on Thursday or Friday, exhibits are open until 9, and on Sunday admission is free.

TOP ATTRACTIONS

Abyssinian Baptist Church. This 1923 Gothic-style church holds one of Harlem's richest legacies, dating to 1808 when a group of parishioners defected from the segregated First Baptist Church of New York City and established the first African-American Baptist church in New York State. Among its legendary pastors was Adam Clayton Powell Jr., a powerful orator and civil rights leader and the first black U.S. congressman. Today sermons by Rev. Dr. Calvin O. Butts III are fiery, and the several choirs are excellent. Dress your best, remember to not take pictures or videos, and get there early—at least two hours ahead of time. ✉ *132 Odell Clark Pl., W. 138th St., between Adam Clayton Powell Jr. Blvd. (7th Ave.) and Malcolm X Blvd./Lenox Ave. (6th Ave.)* ✥ *Tourist entrance is on the southeast corner of 138th and Adam Clayton Powell, Jr. Blvd.* ☎ *212/862–7474* 🌐 *www.abyssinian.org* ⏲ *Visitor services Wed. 7 pm and Sun. 11 am; no visitor services on major holidays* Ⓜ *2, 3 to 135th St.*

Apollo Theater. *See the listing in Chapter 16 Performing Arts.*

Canaan Baptist Church of Christ. The heavenly gospel music during Rev. Dr. Thomas D. Johnson Jr.'s Sunday-morning services makes up for this church's unassuming, concrete-box-like exterior. Pastor emeritus Wyatt Tee Walker worked with Dr. Martin Luther King Jr., who delivered his famous "A Knock at Midnight" sermon here. Visitors may enter once parishioners are seated. To attend, arrive at least an hour before services. ✉ *132 W. 116th St., between Malcolm X and Adam Clayton Powell Jr. Blvds.* ☎ *212/866–0301* 🌐 *www.cbccnyc.org* ⏲ *Services Sun. at 8 and 11 am* Ⓜ *2, 3 to 116th St.*

Hamilton Heights. To taste this neighborhood's Harlem Renaissance days, walk down tree-lined Convent Avenue, detouring onto adjacent **Hamilton Terrace,** and see a time capsule of elegant stone row houses in mint condition. One of the neighborhood's most beautiful blocks, it's popular with film and TV crews. Continue down Convent Avenue and see the looming Gothic spires (1905) of City College. The stately Oxford-inspired buildings here are New York to the core: they are clad with the schist rock unearthed when the city was building what is now the 1 subway line. Walk down 141st Street and visit the ⇨ *Hamilton Grange*

CLOSE UP

D.I.Y. Harlem Gospel Tours

For the past decade, the popularity of Sunday gospel tours has surged. While some in the community see it as an opportunity to broaden horizons and encourage diversity, others find tours disruptive and complain that tourists take seats away from regular parishioners (churches regularly fill to capacity). If you plan on attending a service, here are some tips:

Most churches have Sunday services at 11, but you may need to arrive as much as two hours early (depending on the church) to get in. Dress nicely—no shorts, sneakers, or jeans—be as quiet as possible, do not leave in the middle of the service and do not take photos or videos or use your cell phone. Most important, remember that parishioners do not consider the service, or themselves, to be tourist attractions or entertainment.

A bus tour is generally an inauthentic (and more expensive) way to experience Harlem. Explore the neighborhood and churches on your own, or join a small tour like those offered by **Harlem Heritage Tours** (☎ *212/280-7888* 🌐 *www.harlemheritage.com*). Their tours ($39) get high marks from past clients and are run by guides who were born and raised in Harlem; groups are no larger than 25 people.

The following are some of the uptown churches with Sunday services:

Abyssinian Baptist Church is one of the few churches that does not allow tour groups. Service for visitors is at 11. Arrive at least two hours ahead of time for this service. **Canaan Baptist Church of Christ** has services at 8 and 11. **Convent Avenue Baptist Church** (✉ *420 W. 145th St., between Convent and St. Nicholas Aves., Harlem* ☎ *212/234-6767* 🌐 *www.conventchurch.org*) has services at 8, 11, and 5. **First Corinthian Baptist Church** has services at 8 and 10:45.

Greater Refuge Temple (✉ *2081 Adam Clayton Powell Jr. Blvd., at 124th St., Harlem* ☎ *212/866-1700* 🌐 *www.greaterrefugetemple.org*) has services at 11, 4, and 7:30. **Memorial Baptist Church** (✉ *141 W. 115th St., between Adam Clayton Powell Jr. and Malcolm X Blvds., Harlem* ☎ *212/663-8830* 🌐 *www.mbcvisionharlem.org*) has service at 11.

National Memorial, founding father Alexander Hamilton's Federal-style mansion.When you're ready to move on, head southeast, which will bring you to Strivers' Row. ✉ *Convent Ave., between 138th and 150th Sts.* Ⓜ *A, B, C, D to 145th St.*

Morris-Jumel Mansion. During the Revolutionary War, General Washington used this wooden, pillared 8,500-square-foot house (1765) as his headquarters, and when he visited as president in 1790, he brought along John Quincy Adams, Jefferson, and Hamilton. Inside are rooms furnished with period decorations—upstairs, keep an eye out for the hand-painted wallpaper (original to the house) and a "commode chair," stuck in a corner of the dressing room. Outside, behind the house, is a Colonial-era marker that says it's 11 miles to New York: a reminder of what a small sliver of Manhattan the city was at that time. East of the house is the block-long Sylvan Terrace, a row of crisp two-story clapboard houses built in 1882. ✉ *65 Jumel Terr., north of W. 160th St.*

Taking in Sunday gospel in Harlem.

between St. Nicholas and Edgecome Aves. ☎ *212/923–8008* 🌐 *www.morrisjumel.org* 🎟 *$5; guided tours $6* ⏲ *Wed.–Sun. 10–4; guided tours Sat. noon* Ⓜ *C to 163rd St.*

Strivers' Row. This block of gorgeous 1890s Georgian and neo-Italian homes earned its nickname in the 1920s from less affluent Harlemites who felt its residents were "striving" to become well-to-do. Some of the few remaining private service alleys, used when deliveries arrived via horse and cart, lie behind these houses and are visible through iron gates. Note the gatepost between Nos. 251 and 253 on West 138th Street that reads, "Private Road. Walk Your Horses." The houses were built by the contractor David H. King Jr., whose works also include the base for the Statue of Liberty and the oldest parts of the Cathedral Church of St. John the Divine. When the houses failed to sell to whites, the properties on these blocks were sold to African-American doctors, lawyers, and other professionals; the composers and musicians W. C. Handy and Eubie Blake were also among the residents. If you have the time, detour a block north to see the palazzo-style group of houses designed by Stanford White, on the north side of West 139th Street. ✉ *W. 138th and W. 139th Sts., between Adam Clayton Powell Jr. and Frederick Douglass Blvds.* Ⓜ *B, C to 135th St.*

The Studio Museum in Harlem. Contemporary art by African-American, Caribbean, and African artists is the focus of this small museum with a light-filled sculpture garden. Its changing exhibits included *The Bearden Project,* a year-long tribute to artist Romare Bearden featuring the works of one hundred artists inspired or influenced by Bearden. Three artists in residence present their works each year. The gift shop is small but packs a lot of punch; don't miss its fantastic collection of coffee table books. ✉ *144 W. 125th St., between Lenox Ave. and Adam Clayton Powell Jr. Blvd.* ☎ *212/864–4500* 🌐 *www.studiomuseum.org* 🎫 *$7 suggested donation, free on Sun.* ⏲ *Thurs. and Fri. noon–9, Sat. 10–6, Sun. noon–6* Ⓜ *2, 3 to 125th St.*

WORTH NOTING

First Corinthian Baptist Church. One of the most ornate structures in Harlem, this church kicked off its life in 1913 as the Regent Theatre, one of the country's early movie palaces that replaced the nickelodeons. Its elaborately columned and arched facade loosely resembles the Doges' Palace in Venice. The Regent was sold to the church in 1964. To attend services, arrive at least an hour ahead of time. ✉ *1912 Adam Clayton Powell Jr. Blvd., at 7th Ave.* ☎ *212/864–5976* 🌐 *www.fcbcsermons.com* ⏲ *Services Sun. at 8 and 10:45* Ⓜ *2, 3 to 116th St.*

Hamilton Grange National Memorial. Founding father Alexander Hamilton and his wife raised eight kids in this Federal-style country home, which he called his "sweet project." Located on Hamilton's 32 acres, the Grange, named after his father's childhood home in Scotland, has moved three times since it was built in 1802. It now stands in St. Nicholas Park and offers a lesson in Hamilton's life, from his illegitimate birth in the West Indies and his appointment as the nation's first Secretary of Treasury to his authoring of *The Federalist Papers* and his death following a duel with Vice President Aaron Burr. The house's ground floor, formerly servants quarters, hosts an interactive exhibit that includes a short film on Hamilton's life. Upstairs a parlor, study, dining room, and two guest rooms are open for viewing; notice the beautiful piano, which belonged to his daughter Angelica. ✉ *414 W. 141st St., between St. Nicholas and Convent Aves.* ☎ *646/548–2310* 🌐 *www.nps.gov/hagr/index.htm* 🎫 *Free* ⏲ *Wed.–Sun. 9–5* Ⓜ *1 to 137th St.–City College; A, B, C, D to 145th St.* ☞ *Self-guided tours of furnished rooms are 12–1 and 3–4 only. 30-min ranger-led tours are at 10, 11, 1, 2, and 4.*

The Hispanic Society of America Museum and Library. This is the best collection of Hispanic and Spanish art outside the Prado in Madrid, with paintings, sculptures, textiles, manuscripts, music, and decorative arts from ancient Iberia through the 20th century. There are notable pieces by Goya, El Greco, Murillo, Velázquez and Zurbarán. An entire room is filled with a collection of antique iron knockers. ✉ *613 West 155th St., Audubon Terr., Broadway between W. 155th and W. 156th Sts., entrance up steps to left* ☎ *212/926–2234* 🌐 *www.hispanicsociety.org* 🎫 *Free* ⏲ *Tues.–Sat. 10–4:30, Sun. 1–4* Ⓜ *1 to 157th St.*

Masjid Malcolm Shabazz (*Mosque*). Talk about religious conversions. In the mid-'60s, the Lenox Casino was transformed into this house of worship and cultural center, and given bright yellow arches and a huge green onion dome that loudly proclaims its presence in a neighborhood of churches. Once functioning as Temple No. 7 under the Nation of Islam with a message of pro-black racism, the mosque was bombed after the assassination of Malcolm X, who had preached here. It was then rebuilt and renamed in honor of the name Malcolm took at the end of his life, El-Hajj Malik Shabazz; its philosophy now is one of inclusion. These days the Sunni congregation has a large proportion of immigrants from Senegal, many of whom live in and around 116th Street. Next door is Graceline Court, a 16-story luxury condominium building that opened in 2008. Note how it cantilevers somewhat awkwardly over the mosque. Farther east on 116th Street is the outdoor **Malcolm Shabazz Harlem Market**, where you can find African and African-inspired jewelry, art, clothing and fabrics. On weekends with nice weather you'll find more vendors open. ⊠ *102 W. 116th St., at Malcolm X Blvd./Lenox Ave. (6th Ave.)* ☎ *212/662–2200* Ⓜ *2, 3 to 116th St.*

Sugar Hill. Standing on the bluff of Sugar Hill overlooking Jackie Robinson Park, outside the slightly run-down **409 Edgecombe Ave.** you'd never guess that here resided such influential African-Americans as NAACP founder W.E.B. DuBois and Supreme Court Justice Thurgood Marshall, or that farther north at **555 Edgecombe**, known as the "Triple Nickel," writers Langston Hughes and Zora Neale Hurston and jazz musicians Duke Ellington, Count Basie, and others lived and played. And it's also here that for nearly 20 years musician Marjorie Eliot has been hosting jazz concerts in her apartment, 3F, at 4pm every Sunday. Farther down, at 345 Edgecombe, you can't miss the **Benzinger House** with its flared mansard roof. Amidst all this history, the modern-looking **Sugar Hill Children's Museum of Art & Storytelling**, at 155th Street and St. Nicholas Avenue, is set to open in early 2014. Its design has earned it the nickname Sugar Cube Building. ⊠ *Bounded by 145th and 155th Sts. and Edgecombe and St. Nicholas Aves.* Ⓜ *A, B, C, D to 145th St.*

14

BROOKLYN

GETTING ORIENTED

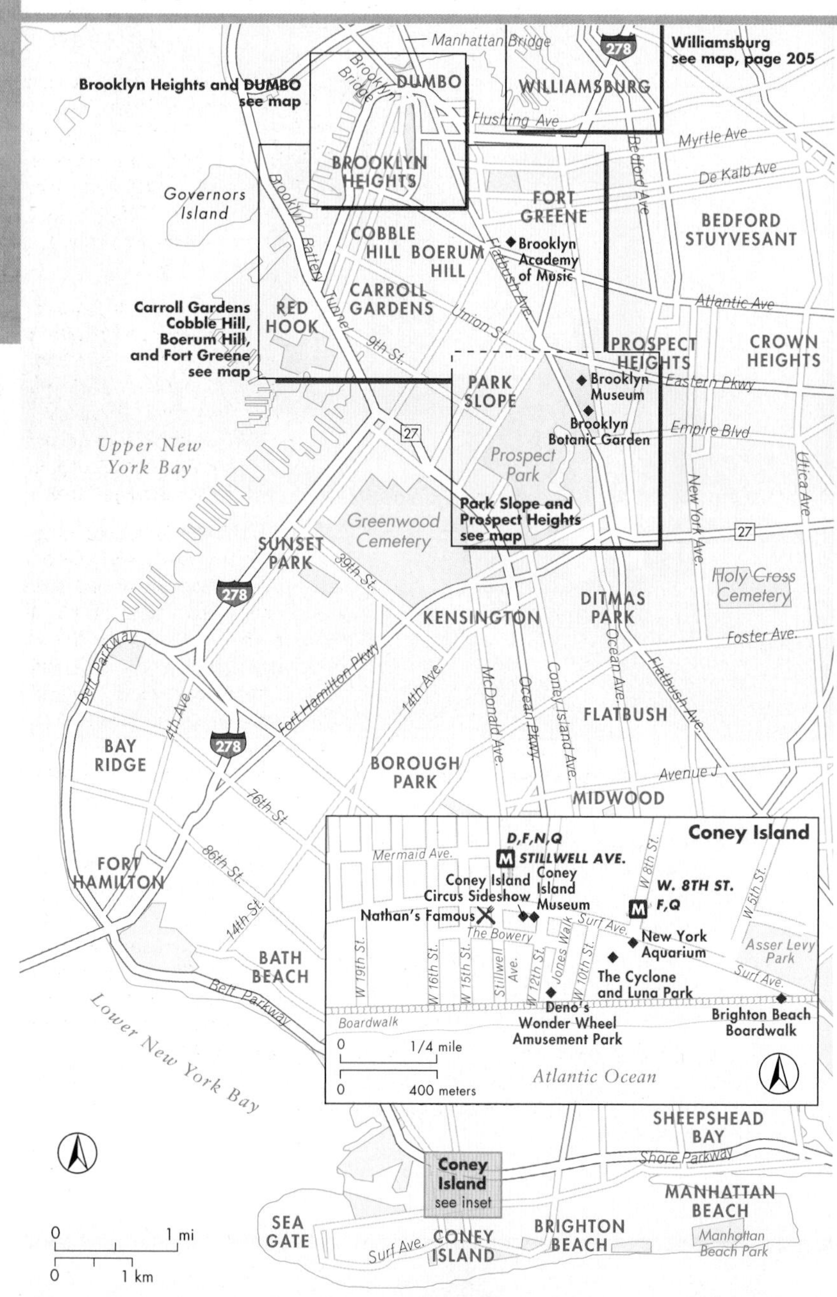
Manhattan Bridge
278
Williamsburg see map, page 205
Brooklyn Heights and DUMBO see map
Brooklyn Bridge
DUMBO
WILLIAMSBURG
Flushing Ave
Myrtle Ave
De Kalb Ave
Bedford Ave
BROOKLYN HEIGHTS
Governors Island
Brooklyn Battery Tunnel
FORT GREENE
BEDFORD STUYVESANT
COBBLE HILL
BOERUM HILL
Brooklyn Academy of Music
Flatbush Ave.
CARROLL GARDENS
Atlantic Ave
Carroll Gardens Cobble Hill, Boerum Hill, and Fort Greene see map
RED HOOK
Union St.
9th St.
PROSPECT HEIGHTS
CROWN HEIGHTS
PARK SLOPE
Brooklyn Museum
Eastern Pkwy
Brooklyn Botanic Garden
Empire Blvd
27
Upper New York Bay
Prospect Park
Utica Ave.
New York Ave.
Park Slope and Prospect Heights see map
Greenwood Cemetery
SUNSET PARK
39th St.
Holy Cross Cemetery
KENSINGTON
DITMAS PARK
Foster Ave.
Belt Parkway
Fort Hamilton Pkwy
14th Ave.
McDonald Ave.
Ocean Pkwy
Coney Island Ave.
Ocean Ave.
Flatbush Ave.
4th Ave.
FLATBUSH
BAY RIDGE
BOROUGH PARK
Avenue J
MIDWOOD
76th St.
86th St.
FORT HAMILTON
14th St.
BATH BEACH
Belt Parkway
Lower New York Bay
Coney Island
D,F,N,Q
Mermaid Ave.
STILLWELL AVE.
Coney Island Circus Sideshow
Coney Island Museum
W 8th St.
W. 8TH ST.
F,Q
W 5th St.
Nathan's Famous
Surf Ave.
The Bowery
New York Aquarium
Asser Levy Park
W 19th St.
W 16th St.
W 15th St.
Stillwell Ave.
W 12th St.
Jones Walk
W 10th St.
The Cyclone and Luna Park
Deno's Wonder Wheel Amusement Park
Brighton Beach Boardwalk
Boardwalk
0 1/4 mile
0 400 meters
Atlantic Ocean
SHEEPSHEAD BAY
Shore Parkway
Coney Island see inset
MANHATTAN BEACH
SEA GATE
CONEY ISLAND
BRIGHTON BEACH
Manhattan Beach Park
Surf Ave.
0 1 mi
0 1 km

TOP EXPERIENCES

Late-night music or bar-hopping in Williamsburg.

Screaming at the top of the Cyclone roller coaster.

Smelling the roses, and everything else, at the Brooklyn Botanic Garden.

Catching a show at BAM.

Pizza at Grimaldi's after a walk across the Brooklyn Bridge.

GETTING HERE

To get to Williamsburg, take the L train from any 14th Street station in Manhattan to Bedford Avenue, the first stop in Brooklyn.

You can reach Brooklyn Heights by the 2 or 3 train to Clark Street, the R to Court Street, or the 4 or 5 to Borough Hall.

To get to DUMBO, take the F train to York Street, the A or C to High Street, or walk from Brooklyn Heights.

The F train to 7th Avenue will take you to the center of Park Slope. From there, walk uphill to reach Prospect Park or walk north on 7th Avenue to get to the shops. The hipper boutiques and eateries are two long blocks west, on 5th Avenue, best accessed on the R train to Union Street.

To reach the Brooklyn Museum, Brooklyn Botanic Garden, and Prospect Park take the 2 or 3 train to Eastern Parkway–Brooklyn Museum.

Coney Island is the last stop on the D, F, N, and Q trains; the Q or B will take you to Brighton Beach. Allow a good part of the day for these, since it takes about an hour to reach the ocean from Manhattan.

COFFEE AND QUICK BITES

Bakeri. Sidle up to the wooden bar in this compact Williamsburg café and select from seasonal pastries, plus cakes, muffins, and cookies. ✉ *150 Wythe Ave., Williamsburg* ☎ *718/388-8037* 🌐 *www.bakeribrooklyn.com* Ⓜ *L to Bedford Ave.*

Gorilla Coffee. Pair your perfectly pulled espresso with a buttery, flaky pastry from Manhattan's Balthazar. ✉ *97 5th Ave., Park Slope* ☎ *718/230-3244* 🌐 *www.gorillacoffee.com* Ⓜ *2, 3, 4, 5, N, Q, R, W or M to Atlantic Ave.–Barclays Center.*

One Girl Cookies. Snag a window seat overlooking cobblestoned Main Street and tuck into whoopie pies, cakes, and cookies in flavors like chocolate-cinnamon-ganache and Thai-ginger-oatmeal, served with Stumptown Coffee. ✉ *33 Main St., DUMBO* ☎ *347/338-1268* 🌐 *www.onegirlcookies.com/dumbo* Ⓜ *F to York St.; A, C to High St.*

Red Horse Café. This Park Slope institution has a distinctly literary vibe. Cups of Crop to Cup coffee and Harney and Sons teas pair with locally sourced baked goods. ✉ *497 6th Ave., Park Slope* ☎ *718/499-4973* Ⓜ *F, G to 7th Ave.*

Sightseeing ★★★
Nightlife ★★★★
Dining ★★★★
Lodging ★
Shopping ★★★

To put it mildly, Brooklyn is exploding, and it has been for a while. Hardly Manhattan's wimpy sidekick, this is the largest and most populous of all the boroughs, with more than 2.5 million residents and a ton of cool places to eat, drink, shop, and explore, including a glamorous new arena, the Barclay's Center, home to the Brooklyn Nets NBA basketball team.

Updated by Sarah Amandolare

Brooklyn was a city itself until the end of the 19th century, with its own widely circulated newspaper (the *Brooklyn Eagle*), its own expansive park (Prospect Park), and its own baseball team that would eventually be called the Brooklyn Dodgers. And in 1883, it got its own bridge: the Brooklyn Bridge, which drew the attention of the entire country.

Aside from Brooklyn's mellow, family-friendly vibe in areas such as **Brooklyn Heights, Cobble Hill, Carroll Gardens,** and **Boerum Hill,** the borough is also home to hipsters. And if you're looking for the hipster hangouts, head to **Williamsburg,** where young artists started infiltrating the residential neighborhood back in the late 1990s. The area quickly became known for its galleries, and then for the funky bars, restaurants, and music venues.

Downtown Brooklyn encompasses multiple brownstone-filled neighborhoods, from **Fort Greene** to family-friendly **Park Slope,** and **Prospect Heights,** on the edge of Prospect Park, that are a joy to explore on foot. Indeed, with the exception of art exhibits at the Brooklyn Museum, the lush grounds of the Brooklyn Botanic Garden, and cutting-edge performances at the Brooklyn Academy of Music, so-called "sights" are thin on the ground here. Instead, the neighborhoods' real draws are their residential vibe, proudly local restaurants, and down-home shops and bars.

Hanging out in Brooklyn Bridge Park, with a view of the iconic bridge rising in the background.

BROOKLYN HEIGHTS

Brooklyn's toniest neighborhood offers residents something wealthy Manhattanites will never have: a stunning view of the Manhattan skyline from the **Brooklyn Heights Promenade.** First developed in the mid-1800s as the business center of the then-independent city of Brooklyn, Brooklyn Heights showcases historic cobblestone streets of pristine brownstones.

The majestic Brooklyn Bridge has one foot in Brooklyn Heights, and a walk across it either to or from Lower Manhattan is one of the quintessential New York experiences. Don't miss a stroll around leafy Pier 1, the newly expanded section of Brooklyn Bridge Park, accessible from Old Fulton Street.

There is a lot of history in Brooklyn Heights itself. In the early to mid-20th century the Heights was a bohemian haven, home to writers like Arthur Miller, Truman Capote, Alfred Kazin, Marianne Moore, Norman Mailer, and W. E. B. Du Bois. In the '80s a new generation of gentrifiers moved in, and—even with a softening real estate market—homes here are still as pricey as their Manhattan counterparts.

Much of Brooklyn Heights's early architecture has been preserved, thanks to its designation as New York's first historic district in the 1960s. Some 600 buildings built in the 19th century represent a wide range of American building styles. Many of the best line **Columbia Heights,** a residential street that runs parallel to the promenade, but any of its adjoining streets are also worth strolling. On **Willow Street** be

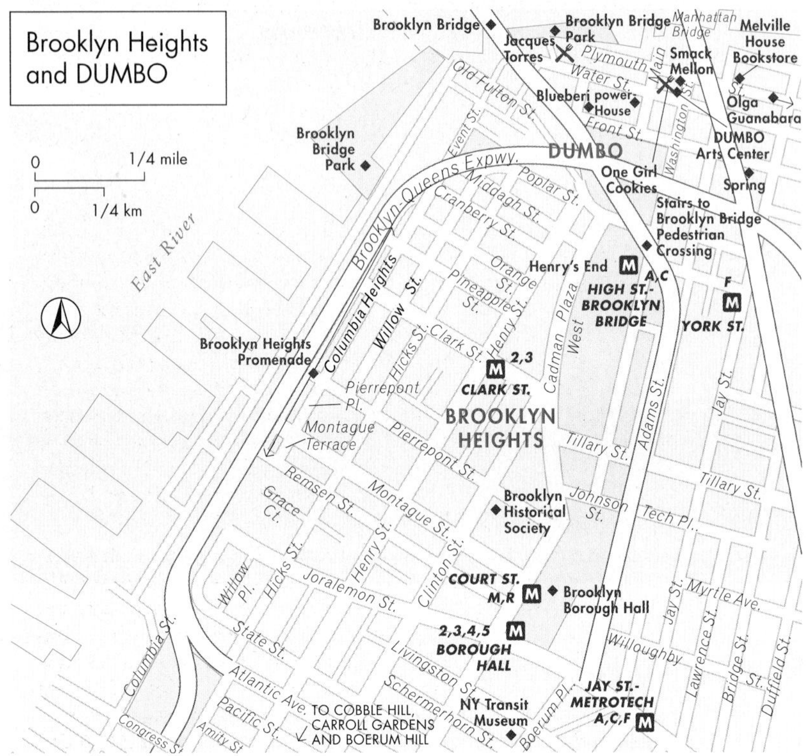

sure to note No. 22, Henry Ward Beecher's prim Greek Revival brownstone, and Nos. 155–159. These three brick Federal row houses are said to have been stops on the Underground Railroad. The skylight in the pavement by the gate to No. 157 provided the light for an underground tunnel leading to an 1880 carriage house.

TOP ATTRACTIONS

Fodor's Choice ★ **Brooklyn Bridge.** (⇨ *Chapter 2*) Ⓜ *4, 5, 6 to Brooklyn Bridge–City Hall; J, Z to Chambers St.; A, C to High St.*

FAMILY Fodor's Choice ★ **Brooklyn Heights Promenade.** Stretching from Orange Street to Remsen Street, the Brooklyn Heights esplanade provides enthralling views of Manhattan, especially in the evening when the lights of the city twinkle across the East River. Find a bench and take in the skyline, the Statue of Liberty, and the Brooklyn Bridge—an impressive 1883 steel suspension bridge designed by John Augustus Roebling. From under the bridge, Frank Gehry's majestic 8 Spruce Street, the city's tallest residential tower, is visible. Below the promenade is the Brooklyn–Queens Expressway and an industrial waterfront of warehouses, piers, and parking lots. Ⓜ *2, 3 to Clark St.; A, C to High St.*

FAMILY **New York Transit Museum.** Step down into a 1930s subway station, where you'll find more than 60,000 square feet devoted to the history of public transportation. Visitors can wander around the collection of vintage trains and turnstiles and sit behind the wheel of city buses. The old subway advertisements and signs are amusing. The gift store is a great place for NYC-theme souvenirs (there's also a shop at Grand Central). ✉ *Boerum Pl. at Schermerhorn St.,DUMBO* ☎ *718/694–1600* 🌐 *www.mta.info/museum* 🎟 *$7* 🕑 *Tues.–Fri. 10–4, weekends 11–5* Ⓜ *2, 3, 4, 5 to Borough Hall; A, C, G to Hoyt–Schemerhorn Sts.; A, C, F, R to Jay St.–MetroTech; R to Court St.*

WORTH NOTING

Brooklyn Borough Hall. Built in 1848 as Brooklyn's City Hall, this Greek Revival landmark is one of Brooklyn's handsomest buildings. Adorned with Tuckahoe marble, it features a hammered square rotunda and a two-story Beaux-Arts courtroom. Today the building serves as the office of Brooklyn's borough president and the home of the **Brooklyn Tourism & Visitors Center** (☎ *718/802–3846* 🌐 *www.visitbrooklyn.org*), which has historical exhibits, a gift shop, and helpful information. It's open weekdays 10–6. Each Tuesday and Saturday, as well as Thursday from April through December, a greenmarket sets up on the flagstone plaza in front. ✉ *209 Joralemon St., between Court and Adams Sts., DUMBO* ☎ *718/802–3700* 🌐 *www.brooklyn-usa.org* 🎟 *Free* Ⓜ *2, 3, 4, 5 to Borough Hall; A, C, F to Jay St.–MetroTech; R to Court St*

Brooklyn Historical Society. Housed in an 1881 Queen Anne–style National Landmark building (one of the gems of the neighborhood), the Brooklyn Historical Society displays memorabilia, artifacts, art, and interactive exhibitions. Upstairs, an impressive library—which contains an original copy of the Emancipation Proclamation—is invaluable to researchers. New renovations include two art galleries, a 200-seat event space, and a gift shop. The building's ornately carved front door has also been restored. ✉ *128 Pierrepont St., at Clinton St.,DUMBO* ☎ *718/222–4111* 🌐 *www.brooklynhistory.org* 🎟 *$6* 🕑 *Wed.–Fri. and Sun. noon–5, Sat. 10–5* Ⓜ *2, 3, 4, 5 to Borough Hall; A, C, F, R to Jay St.–MetroTech; R to Court St.*

DUMBO

Once home to bustling factories and dry-goods warehouses, DUMBO (*D*own *U*nder the *M*anhattan *B*ridge *O*verpass) is now among the chicest and most expensive neighborhoods in the city. Tucked downhill from Brooklyn Heights, beside the water and below thrumming subway lines, the scene is the epitome of old-meets-new. Warehouses that lured artists in the 1970s now house tech startups and indie book publishers. Luxury condos, high-end shops, and artisan coffee houses line cobblestone streets, lending tony energy to what was once known as Fulton Landing. Inventor and engineer Robert Fulton introduced steamboat ferry service from Brooklyn to Manhattan in 1814; expect to see wedding photo shoots at Fulton Ferry Landing, with its expansive views of Manhattan and the Brooklyn Bridge. The stroller set and nine-to-five lunch crowds also flock to the waterfront's playgrounds and benches. The blustery air will whet your appetite, so head uphill to perpetually packed Grimaldi's Pizzeria (✉ *1 Front St.* ☎ 718/858–4300

DID YOU KNOW?

The Brooklyn Heights Promenade has stunning views of the New York skyline.

www.grimaldis.com) and Brooklyn Ice Cream Factory (✉ *Old Fulton and Water Sts.* ☎ *718/246–3963* 🌐 *www.brooklynicecreamfactory.com*). Just leave some time for careless wandering—iconic views and beautiful people make the DUMBO streets worth exploring.

TOP ATTRACTIONS

FAMILY **Brooklyn Bridge Park.** On the waterfront between the Brooklyn Bridge and the Manhattan Bridge, this vast park is a great place for a riverside picnic or to just enjoy the view. There are several sections of the park, including Pier 1, Pier 6, the Main Street Lot (with DUMBO's free Wi-Fi network), and the newly renovated Empire-Fulton Ferry. The large playground at Pier 1 has a replica of a boat for make-believe voyages across the East River. In the Empire-Fulton Ferry part of the park is one of the park's new highlights, the fabulously restored **Jane Carousel**, originally built in 1922 and now housed in a pavilion designed by renowned French architect Jean Nouvel. The carousel runs all year but is closed on Tuesday; rides are $2, or you can buy 12 tickets for $20. From April to October the park is home to a wide range of arts performances, and on Thursday nights in July and August, Movies with a View projects New York classic films on an outdoor screen, free of charge. ✉ *New Dock St. at Water St., DUMBO* ☎ *718/222–9939* 🌐 *www.brooklynbridgepark.org* 🎟 *Free* ⏲ *Daily 6 am–1 am* Ⓜ *A, C to High St.; F to York St.*

WORTH NOTING

No trip to DUMBO would be complete without some gallery hopping—most are open afternoons, Wednesday or Thursday through Sunday.

DUMBO Arts Center (*DAC*). This 3,000-square-foot gallery draws visitors for contemporary art exhibits, workshops, and lectures. The annual DUMBO Arts Festival (🌐 *dumboartsfestival.com*) in September is three fabulous art-and-music-packed days in the area's galleries, open studios, warehouses, parks, and streets. ✉ *30 Washington St., between Water and Plymouth Sts.* ☎ *718/694–0831* 🌐 *www.dumboartscenter.org* 🎟 *$2* Ⓜ *F to York St.*

Smack Mellon. Inside a 12,000-square-foot restored boiler building with a 35-foot ceiling, Smack Mellon exhibits work by up-and-coming artists, and nurtures them with studio space and other support. ✉ *92 Plymouth St., at Washington St.,DUMBO* ☎ *718/834–8761* 🌐 *www.smackmellon.org* ⏲ *Wed.–Sun. 12–6* Ⓜ *F to York St.; A, C to High St..*

Spring. At this exhibition space and design shop you can view contemporary art, then satisfy your shopping urges with quirky home goods. ✉ *126a Front St., between Pearl and Jay Sts., DUMBO* ☎ *718/222–1054* 🌐 *www.spring3d.net* ⏲ *Tues.–Sat. 12–7* Ⓜ *F to York St.; A, C to High St.*

SHOPPING

Blueberi. Striking window displays will lure you into this sleek boutique where the vintage and contemporary designer wear, shoes, and accessories hail from the five boroughs as well as the faraway corners of the world. ✉ *143 Front St., between Pearl and Jay Sts., DUMBO* ☎ *718/422–7724* 🌐 *www.blueberi.net* ⏲ *Tues.–Sat. 11–8, Sun. 11–7* Ⓜ *F to York St.; A, C to High St.*

Jacques Torres Chocolate. You'll feel like Charlie getting a peek at the Oompa Loompas as you peer into the small chocolate factory while munching on an unusually flavored chocolate bonbon or sipping a cup of thick, rich hot chocolate. (For the latter, try the "wicked" flavor, spiked with chipotle peppers and cinnamon.) During summer months, the adjacent ice-cream shop serves scoops, sundaes, and ice-cream sandwiches, with flavors from salted caramel to black current sorbet. ✉ *66 Water St., DUMBO* ☎ *718/875–1269* 🌐 *www.mrchocolate.com* ⏲ *Mon.–Sat. 9–8, Sun. 10–6.*

Melville House Bookstore. Get a taste of the local literary scene inside this independent publisher's shop that hosts art exhibits and evening events, and stocks books from Brooklyn presses like Ugly Duckling and Akashic. ✉ *145 Plymouth St., DUMBO* ☎ *718/722–9205* 🌐 *www.mhpbooks.com* ⏲ *Weekdays 12–6* Ⓜ *F to York St.; A, C to High St.*

Olga Guanabara. São Paulo native Richard Velloso displays his beautifully minimalist furniture, inspired by New York City landscapes and architecture, inside a new, 14,000-square-foot DUMBO showroom. Make an appointment to view dining and coffee tables crafted from reclaimed wood and steel. And look out for Olga, Velloso's chocolate labrador. ✉ *215 Plymouth St., DUMBO* ☎ *646/812–1843* 🌐 *www.olgaguanabara.com* ⏲ *By appointment only* Ⓜ *F to York St.; A, C to High St.*

The powerHouse Arena. This stunning 5,000-square-foot space with soaring 24-foot ceilings, glass frontage, and amphitheater-style seating does multiple duty as gallery, boutique, bookstore, and performance space. It's a must-stop for culture hawks and bookworms. ✉ *37 Main St., DUMBO* ☎ *718/666–3049* 🌐 *www.powerhousearena.com* Ⓜ *F to York St.; A, C to High St.*

CARROLL GARDENS

Traditionally Italian Carroll Gardens began drawing Manhattan families in the 1990s, but still retains some of its old-school roots. Wedged between Gowanus and Red Hook, the scene is pleasantly less polished than northern neighbor Cobble Hill. Unpretentious delis, watch repair shops, and sweet-smelling Italian bakeries sit beside posh hair salons and a hipster version of a yacht club. Court and Smith Streets host most of the foot traffic, while the neighborhood's prettiest Italianate brownstone homes and namesake front gardens occupy First Place through Fourth Place. Break for Italian cookies and cheesecake at homey Monteleone Bakery (✉ *355 Court St.* ☎ 718/852–5600), where Italian shows flicker across a wall-mounted TV.

Store 518. Led by dancer-turned-designer Nadia Tarr, this playful Carroll Gardens shop holds a distinctive array of ladylike jewelry, playful home goods, and vintage toys that change seasonally. Items are stored in drawers and chests throughout the whimsical store, perfect for an afternoon browse. ✉ *518 Court St., Carroll Gardens* ☎ *646/256–5041* 🌐 *www.store518.com* ⏲ *Thurs. and Fri. 1–8, weekends 11–7* Ⓜ *F, G to Carroll St.*

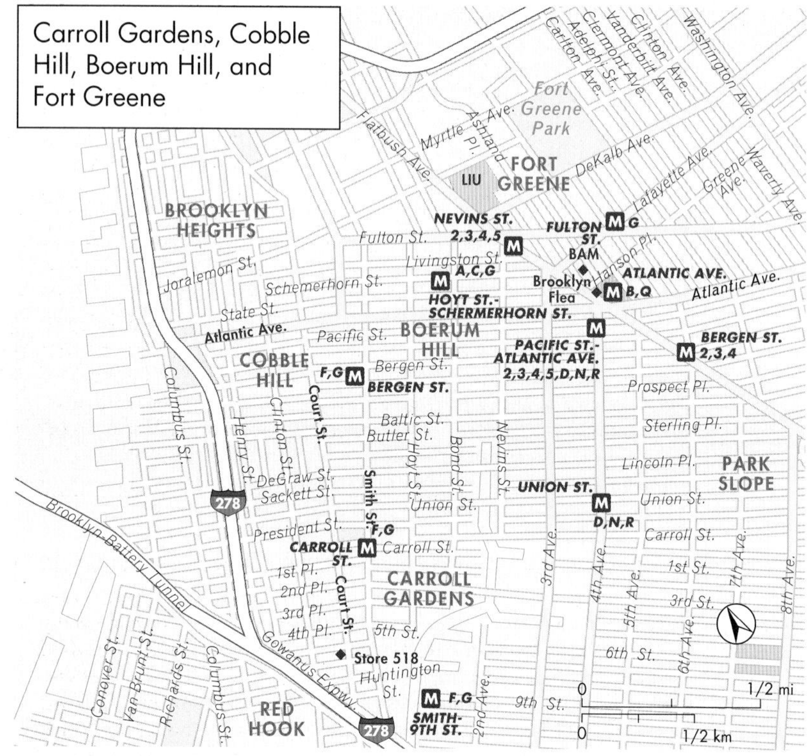

Carroll Gardens, Cobble Hill, Boerum Hill, and Fort Greene

COBBLE HILL

Set adjacent to Boerum Hill and to the north of Carroll Gardens, Cobble Hill stands out for its 19th-century architecture and leafy, compact parks. Dutch residents called the area Cobleshill in reference to a Revolutionary War–era land mound, which was flattened by British soldiers to prevent strategic use by George Washington's troops. These days, most of the 22-block neighborhood is landmarked as Brooklyn's second-oldest district, a mix of brick townhouses, brownstones, and Victorian schoolhouses, where only the Gothic revival churches exceed a 50-foot height limit. Historically working-class, the neighborhood has adopted all the trappings of haute Brooklyn, especially along busy Court Street: an independent bookstore, artisanal coffee shops, and a boutique devoted to vintage eyewear. But a quiet grace pervades the streets. Swing by the circular Cobble Hill Park, ringed by trees and edged by cozy Verandah Place, a narrow block that once held servants quarters. Stop for Stumptown coffee and people-watching at Café Pedlar (✉ *210 Court St.* ☎ *718/855–7129* 🌐 *www.cafepedlar.com*), all warm wood and soft lighting, or head to Bien Cuit (✉ *120 Smith St.* ☎ *718/852–0200* 🌐 *www.biencuit.com*), a husband-and-wife-led bakery with savory croissants and crusty breads.

BOERUM HILL

Understated elegance defines Boerum Hill, where redbrick townhouses and brownstones line quiet, leafy thoroughfares from 4th Avenue to Schemerhorn Street and Wyckoff to Warren. The neighborhood saw an influx of immigrants in the late 1800s, with completion of the Brooklyn Bridge and emergence of trolley cars, but fell into disrepair after World War II. Now fully gentrified, the setting is laden with beautiful cafés that are worth a visit; try local gathering place Building on Bond (⊠ *112 Bond St.* ☎ *347/853–8687* 🌐 *www.buildingonbond.com*) for coffee and Balthazar pastries, served amid the sort of repurposed furnishings that have come to define hipster Brooklyn decor. If you're looking for a cozy spot for a drink after hitting the shops on Atlantic Avenue and Smith Street, stop at Brooklyn Inn (⊠ *148 Hoyt St.* ☎ *718/522–2525*) and grab a seat at the carved wooden bar from 1870s Germany. Despite its air of sophistication, Boerum Hill presents moments of levity, namely artist Susan Gardner's sparkly mosaic-covered brownstone at 108 Wyckoff Street.

WILLIAMSBURG

These days, it's impossible to walk through North Brooklyn without encountering something new. Fabulously hip boutiques, vintage shops, and forward-thinking restaurants crop up constantly, lending an energy that verges on overwhelming. The neighborhood has certainly glossed itself up in recent years, evidenced by pricey cocktail bars, high-rise waterfront condos, and moneyed hipsters sauntering down Bedford Avenue. But Williamsburg's past is also endlessly intriguing: for much of the 20th century this industrial area on the East River was home to a mix of Latin Americans, Poles, and. Rising Manhattan rents in the 1990s sent an influx of artists and musicians to the L train, and since then the area has rapidly, albeit creatively, gentrified. And while some side streets may appear graffitied and creepy, rest assured that there's likely to be a DIY concert-gallery space in one of those seemingly abandoned former factories.

TOP ATTRACTIONS

Smorgasburg. The ultimate eating extravaganza, Smorgasburg does for local and regional culinary startups what the Brooklyn Flea does for independent designers and craftspeople. From April through mid-November, rain or shine, 75–100 food vendors sell prepared and packaged treats like gourmet s'mores, savory jams and Asian-influenced hot dogs. Bring your appetite to the Williamsburg Waterfront (at the East River between North 6th and North 7th Sts.) on Saturday, and on Sunday to DUMBO's historic Tobacco Warehouse (⊠ *26 New Dock St.*). ⊠ *Williamsburg* 🌐 *www.smorgasburg.com* ⏲ *April–mid-Nov., weekends 11–6* Ⓜ *Williamsburg location: L to Bedford Ave. DUMBO location: F to York St.; 2, 3 to Clark St.*

WORTH NOTING

Williamsburg's 70-plus galleries are distributed randomly, with no single main drag. Plan your trip ahead of time using the online **Brooklyn Art Guide** at ⊕ *www.wagmag.org*. (You can also pick up a copy at neighborhood galleries and some cafés.) Hours vary widely, but almost all are open weekends (call ahead). Although serendipitous poking is the best way to sample the art, two longtime galleries are must-sees.

Pierogi Gallery. Nope, it's not a restaurant, it's a hip art gallery. Check out the famous "Flat Files," an online collection of the portfolios of more than 700 young contemporary artists. The Boiler, a larger space nearby (✉ *191 North 14th St.* ☎ *718/599–2144*), has somewhat more limited hours. ✉ *177 N. 9th St., between Bedford and Driggs Aves., Williamsburg* ☎ *718/599–2144* ⊕ *www.pierogi2000.com* ⏲ *Pierogi, Tues.–Sun. 11–6; The Boiler, Thurs.–Sun. 12–6* Ⓜ *L to Bedford Ave.*

Sideshow Gallery. The focus is on local Williamsburg artists at this pioneering gallery, but there are traveling exhibits as well, and sometimes readings and concerts. ✉ *319 Bedford Ave. Williamsburg* ☎ *718/486–8180* ⊕ *www.sideshowgallery.com* Ⓜ *L to Bedford Ave.*

SHOPPING

Although the boutiques on Bedford Avenue are best for people-watching, you'll also find stores along Grand Street, and on many side streets, especially North 6th.

A&G Merch. Contemporary, stylish, and affordable home accessories with an urban bent, from large to small, are what you'll find at this Brooklyn shop. ✉ *111 N. 6th St. Williamsburg* ☎ *718/388–1779* ⊕ *www.aandgmerch.com* ⏲ *Weekdays 11–7* Ⓜ *L to Bedford Ave.*

Beacon's Closet. Local fashionistas and out-of-towners alike flock to Beacon's Closet for its huge selection of used and vintage clothing and accessories where real deals can be scored if you devote some time to browsing. ✉ *88 N. 11th St. Williamsburg* ☎ *718/486–0816* ⊕ *www.beaconscloset.com* ⏲ *Weekdays 12–9; weekends 11–8* Ⓜ *L to Bedford Ave.*

Bedford Cheese Shop. The small size of the Bedford Cheese Shop belies the fact that this is one of the city's best cheese stores, packed with an encyclopedic assortment of artisan cheeses as well as small-producer cured meats, gourmet imported oils, chocolates, and dry goods. The quirky and occasionally salacious descriptions of the cheeses ("looks like dirty scrimshaw but tastes like a peat-covered goat teat") add entertainment to your shopping experience. ✉ *229 Bedford Ave., at N. 4th St. Williamsburg* ☎ *718/599–7588* ⊕ *www.bedfordcheeseshop.com* ⏲ *Weekdays 11–9, Sat. 10–9, Sun. 10–8* Ⓜ *L to Bedford Ave.*

The Brooklyn Kitchen. The epicenter of Brooklyn culinary culture features classroom space and an on-site butcher, The Meat Hook, plus an incredibly thorough stash of kitchen tools and supplies fit for the most recreational or advanced gourmand. ✉ *100 Frost St., Williamsburg* ☎ *718/389–2982* ⊕ *www.thebrooklynkitchen.com* ⏲ *Mon.–Sat. 10–8, Sun. 12–6* Ⓜ *L to Metropolitan Ave.*

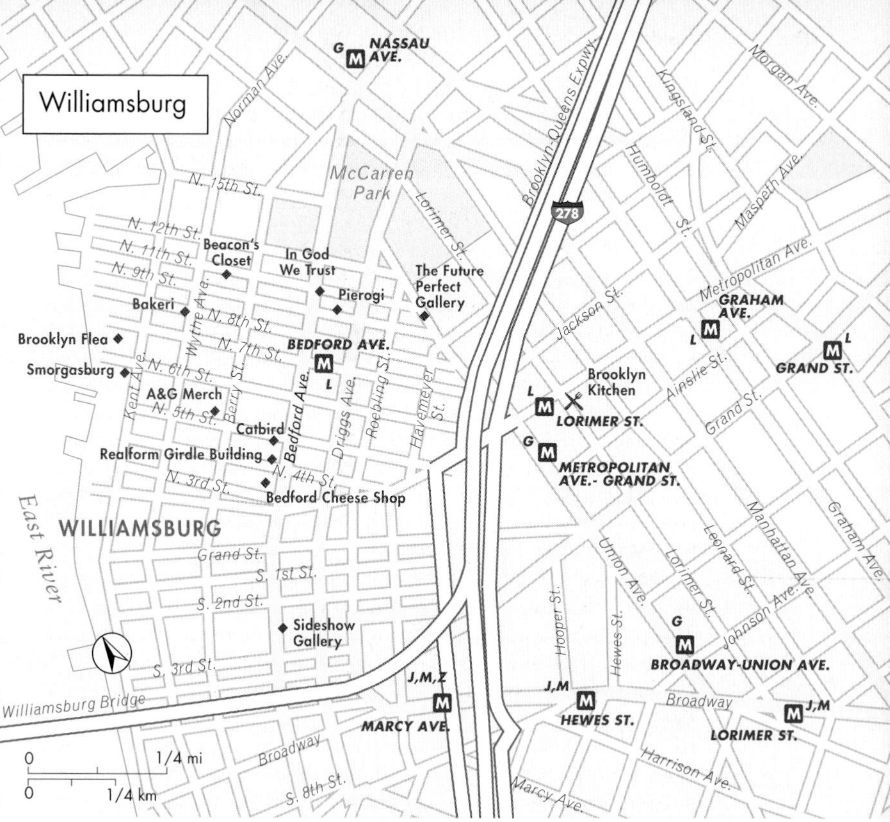

Catbird. One of the standout boutiques on Bedford, Catbird is a dollhouse-size shop with shelves filled with handmade jewelry, home accessories, and whimsical hats. ✉ *219 Bedford Ave., near N. 5th St. Williamsburg* ☎ *718/599–3457* 🌐 *www.catbirdnyc.com* ⏲ *Mon.–Sat. 12–8, Sun. 12–6* Ⓜ *L to Bedford Ave.*

The Future Perfect. Brooklyn's thriving home-design scene is often credited to The Future Perfect, which has since opened a Manhattan branch. Even if you're not planning on shipping home a Bone Chair made entirely of cow ribs, it's fun to browse the playful and often ironic furnishings from local Brooklyn and international designers. ✉ *115 N. 6th St., at Berry St. Williamsburg* ☎ *718/599–6278* 🌐 *www.thefutureperfect.com* ⏲ *Daily 11–7* Ⓜ *L to Bedford Ave.*

In God We Trust. Having mastered the distinctly Brooklyn, manicured-yet-rumpled combination, this clothing and accessories boutique draws a steady stream of cool kids to Bedford Avenue. Look for quietly elegant dresses from Brooklyn designer Samantha Pleet, and delicate utilitarian jewelry made locally by IGWT. Two other stores are located in Greenpoint (✉ *70 Greenpoint Ave.*) and lower Manhattan (✉ *265 Lafayette St.*). ✉ *129 Bedford Ave., Williamsburg* ☎ *718/384–0700* 🌐 *www.ingodwetrustnyc.com/stores/bedford* ⏲ *Mon.–Sat. 12–8, Sun. 12–7* Ⓜ *L to Bedford Ave.*

Realform Girdle Building. The Realform Girdle Building is the closest thing Williamsburg has to a mall; it houses a small café, a new/used record store, several hip yet inexpensive boutiques, and an art bookstore. ✉ *218 Bedford Ave. Williamsburg* Ⓜ *L to Bedford Ave.*

FORT GREENE

Thriving Fort Greene is one of the latest hot Brooklyn 'hoods, chock full of young professionals and families drawn by leafy streets and great food and drink venues. The bars here are just cool enough to rival Williamsburg's, but with a slightly older and less image-conscious crowd. It can be a trek to get to from Manhattan, but the rewards are many, including some of the best restaurants in Brooklyn, lovely brownstones, and beautiful Fort Greene Park. Fort Greene, as with many other areas of Brooklyn, has long been a home to famous writers and musicians, and fittingly it's also the locale of one of the city's top performing-arts powerhouses, the Brooklyn Academy of Music, known as BAM (⇨ *Chapter 16 Performing Arts*).

Fodor's Choice ★ **Brooklyn Flea.** Quirky, inclusive, and full of unclaimed treasures—that's Brooklyn in a nutshell, and it also aptly describes the Brooklyn Flea. This little-market-that-could is now one of Brooklyn's most popular shopping attractions, luring locals and bargain hunters from afar with vintage finds, hip crafts, and crazy-delicious eats.

The Flea is a hybrid of traditional flea market, garage sale, and crafts fair, a tumble of the expensive, the cheap, and the strange. Some vendors hawk high-end items like antique doors refashioned into tables, rescued fixtures from prewar houses, or midcentury lamps identical to those in *Mad Men*. The most "Brooklyn-y" component is the local artisans, and buying their one-of-a-kind handmade wares gives shoppers the altruistic feeling of supporting arts and crafts, whether that's silk-screen T-shirts of giant squid, tongue-in-cheek charm bracelets with little daggers, or hand-stitched stuffed elephants. You'll also find a number of oddly specialized booths like the vendor who sells nothing but oil paintings of bicycles. Why not? Finally, there is plenty of bric-a-brac to sift through: great stuff that may not be practical (mink stoles, nonfunctional alarm clocks, Star Wars collectibles), but that makes for fun browsing.

When you've exhausted the shopping side of things, the Flea boasts some fantastic food options. You'll find mini cupcakes from Kumquat Cupcakery, juicy sandwiches from Porchetta, gooey grilled cheese from Milk Truck, organic ice cream from Blue Marble, family-farmed coffee from Crop to Cup, and all sorts of pickled produce from popular McClure's Pickles.

The Flea takes place in two locations every weekend from mid-March to late November: On Saturday, in the parking lot of Bishop Laughlin Memorial High School, at 176 Lafayette Ave., between Clermont and Vanderbilt Aves., in Fort Greene. On Sunday, it's in the landmark Williamsburgh Savings Bank (now an event space known as Skylight One Hanson), at 1 Hanson Pl., Fort Greene. 🌐 *www.brooklynflea.com* 🎫 *Free* 🕓 *Mid-Mar. to late Nov., weekends 10–5* Ⓜ *C to Lafayette Ave.*

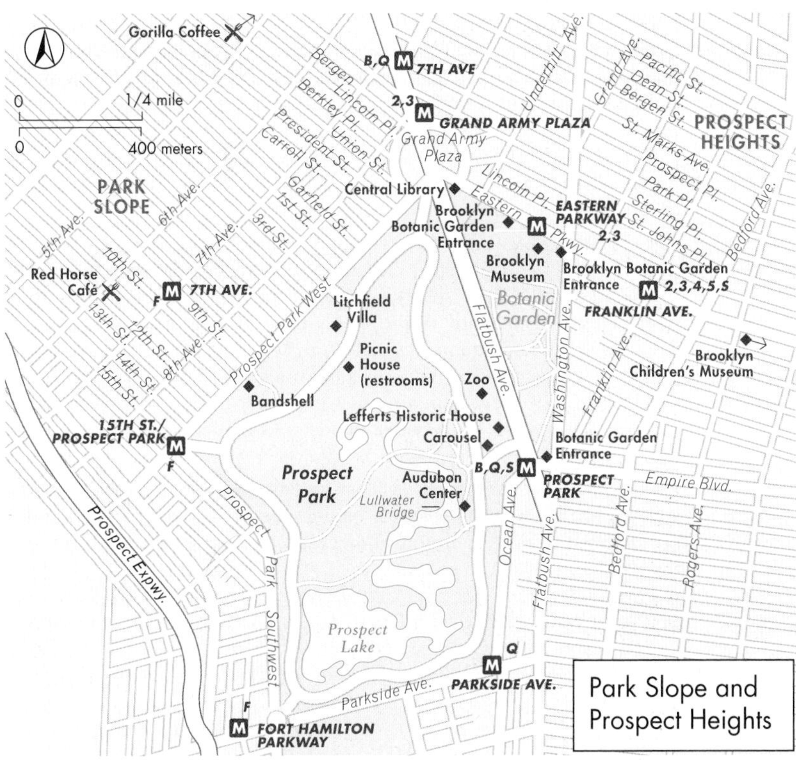

for school location. 2, 3, 4, 5, B, D, N, Q, R to Atlantic Ave.–Barclays Center for bank location.

PARK SLOPE

Full of young families, well-dressed dogwalkers, and impeccably curated shops, the neighborhood that literally slopes down from Prospect Park can feel like a veritable Norman Rockwell painting. Add to all that a slew of laptop-friendly coffeehouses and turn-of-the-20th-century brownstones—remnants of the days when Park Slope had the nation's highest per-capita income—and it's no surprise that academics and writers have flocked here. Park Slope's busiest drags, 5th and 7th avenues, present plenty of shopping and noshing opportunities, but side streets, especially between Sterling Place and 4th Street, also call for slow meandering. Head to the elegant, 585-acre Prospect Park for long strolls or bicycle rides past lazy meadows, shady forests, and lakes designed by Olmsted and Vaux of Central Park fame (look out for free summertime concerts). Adjacent is Brooklyn Botanic Garden, which features a variety of public classes and the springtime Cherry Blossom Festival. Also perched on the park is the Brooklyn Museum, lauded for collections of American, Egyptian, and feminist art.

TOP ATTRACTIONS

FAMILY **Brooklyn Botanic Garden.** The 52 acres of this beloved Brooklyn retreat, one of the finest botanic gardens in the country, are a must-see, especially in spring and summer. A major attraction is the beguiling Japanese Hill-and-Pond Garden—complete with a pond, blazing red *torii* gate, and Shinto shrine. Nearby, the Japanese cherry arbor turns into a breathtaking cloud of pink every spring; the Sakura Matsuri, a two-day cherry blossom festival, is a hugely popular event.

Also be sure to wander through the Cranford Rose Garden (5,000 plants, 1,200 varieties); the Fragrance Garden, designed especially for the blind; and the Shakespeare Garden, featuring more than 80 plants immortalized by the Bard. At the Steinhardt Conservatory, desert, tropical, temperate, and aquatic vegetation thrives. Don't miss the extraordinary C. V. Starr Bonsai Museum for close to 100 miniature Japanese specimens, some more than a century old. Near the conservatory are a café and a gift shop, with bulbs, plants, and gardening books as well as jewelry.

Entrances to the garden are on Eastern Parkway, next to the subway station; on Washington Avenue, behind the Brooklyn Museum; and on Flatbush Avenue at Empire Boulevard. Free garden tours meet at the front gate every weekend at 1. ✉ *900 Washington Ave., between Crown and Carroll Sts.Prospect Heights* ☎ *718/623–7200* 🌐 *www.bbg.org* 🎫 *$10; free all day Tues., Sat. before noon, and weekdays mid-Nov.–mid-Mar. Combo ticket with Brooklyn Museum $20* ⏲ *Mid-Mar.–late Oct.: grounds Tues.–Fri. 8–6, weekends 10–6; conservatory daily 10–5:30. Nov.–mid-Mar.: grounds Tues.–Fri. 8–4:30, weekends 10–4:30; conservatory daily 10–4. Closed Mon. except holidays* Ⓜ *2, 3 to Eastern Pkwy.–Brooklyn Museum; B, Q to Prospect Park.*

Brooklyn Museum. Although it may be overshadowed by the big-name museums in Manhattan, the Brooklyn Museum, with more than 1 million pieces in its permanent collection—from Rodin sculptures to Andean textiles and Assyrian wall reliefs—and a roster of consistently popular shows and neighborhood events, is a worthwhile and relatively peaceful museum-going experience.

Along with changing exhibitions, highlights include one of the best collections of Egyptian art in the world and impressive collections of African, pre-Columbian, and Native American art. It's also worth seeking out the museum's works by Georgia O'Keeffe, Winslow Homer, John Singer Sargent, George Bellows, Thomas Eakins, and Milton Avery—all stunners. The Elizabeth A. Sackler Center for Feminist Art hosts traveling exhibits in addition to serving as the permanent home to Judy Chicago's installation *The Dinner Party* (1974–79). On the first Saturday of each month (except September) the museum throws an extremely popular free evening of art, music, dancing, film screenings, and readings, from 5 to 11 pm. There are several cash bars. ✉ *200 Eastern Pkwy., at Washington Ave.Prospect Heights* ☎ *718/638–5000* 🌐 *www.brooklynmuseum.org* 🎫 *$12 suggested donation. Free, 1st Sat. of month, 5–11. Combo ticket with Brooklyn Botanic Garden $20*

A view of the pond at the Brooklyn Botanic Garden, seen through the blossoming cherry trees.

⏲ *Wed., Fri., and Sat., 11–6, Thurs. 11–10; 1st Sat. of month 11–11* Ⓜ *2, 3 to Eastern Pkwy–Brooklyn Museum.*

FAMILY **Prospect Park.** Brooklyn residents are fiercely passionate about Prospect Park, and with good reason. Gently curved paths beg for long walks and bike rides, while free summer concerts, winter sledding hills, and vivid autumn leaves make the park a year-round destination. Designed by Frederick Law Olmsted and Calvert Vaux, the park was completed in the late 1880s. Olmsted once said that he was prouder of it than of any of his other works—including Manhattan's Central Park.

A good way to experience the park is to walk along its 3.5-mile circular drive and make detours off it as you wish. The drive is closed to cars at all times except weekday rush hours. Families with children should head straight for the eastern side, where most kids' attractions are clustered.

The park's north entrance is at **Grand Army Plaza,** where the Soldiers' and Sailors' Memorial Arch honors Civil War veterans. (Look familiar? It's patterned after the Arc de Triomphe in Paris.) Three heroic sculptural groupings adorn the arch: atop, a dynamic four-horse chariot; to either side, the victorious Union Army and Navy of the Civil War. The inner arch has bas-reliefs of presidents Abraham Lincoln and Ulysses S. Grant, sculpted by Thomas Eakins and William O'Donovan, respectively. To the northwest of the arch, Neptune and a passel of debauched Tritons leer over the edges of the **Bailey Fountain.** On Saturday year-round, a greenmarket at the plaza sells produce, flowers and plants, cheese, and baked goods to throngs of locals. Other days, you can find a few vendors selling snacks here and at the 9th Street entrance. ✉ *450 Flatbush Ave.* ☎ *718/965–8951* 🌐 *www.prospectpark.org.*

Lefferts Historic House. This Dutch Colonial farmhouse was built in 1783 and moved to Prospect Park in 1918. Rooms of the historic house-museum are furnished with antiques and reproductions from the 1820s, when the house was last redecorated. The museum hosts all kinds of activities for kids; call for information. ☎ *718/789–2822* 🎫 *Free* ⏲ *Apr.–May, weekends noon–5; June and Sept., Thurs.–Sun. noon–5; July–Aug., Thurs.–Sun. noon–6; Oct., Thurs.–Sun. noon–4; Nov.–Dec., and Feb.–Mar., weekends noon–4*

Litchfield Villa. If you walk down the park's west drive from Grand Army Plaza, you'll first encounter Litchfield Villa, an Italianate hilltop mansion built in 1857 for a prominent railroad magnate. It has housed the park's headquarters since 1883; visitors are welcome to step inside and view the domed octagonal rotunda. ☎ *718/965–8951* 🎫 *Free* ⏲ *Weekdays 9–5*

Prospect Park Audubon Center and Visitor Center at the Boathouse. Styled after Sansovino's 16th-century Library at St. Mark's in Venice, the Prospect Park Audubon Center and Visitor Center at the Boathouse, built in 1904, sits opposite the Lullwater Bridge, creating an idyllic spot for watching pedal boats and wildlife, or just taking a break at the café. Interactive exhibits, park tours, and educational programs for kids make this a fun place to learn about nature. On a nice day, take a ride on the electric boat to tour the Lullwater and Prospect Lake. You can also sign up for a bird-watching tour to see some of the 200 species spotted here. ✉ *Just inside the Lincoln Rd./Ocean Ave. entrance, Prospect Park* ☎ *718/287–3400* 🌐 *www.prospectpark.org/audubon* 🎫 *Audubon Center free; electric-boat tours $10* ⏲ *Audubon Center: Apr.–June, Thurs.–Sun. noon–5; July–Aug., Thurs.–Sun. noon–6; Sept., weekends noon–5; Oct.–Mar., weekends noon–4; closed Jan.–Feb. except school holidays; call for program and tour times. Electric-boat tours every 30 mins: May–Aug., Thurs.–Sun. noon–4:30; Sept.–mid-Oct., weekends 12:30–4.*

Prospect Park Band Shell. The Prospect Park Band Shell is the home of the annual Celebrate Brooklyn Festival, which from early June through mid-August sponsors free films and concerts that have included Afro-Caribbean jazz, flamenco dance troupes from Spain, David Byrne, and the Brooklyn Philharmonic. Films are shown on a 50-foot-wide outdoor screen, one of the world's largest. ☎ *718/855–7882 for the Celebrate Brooklyn Festival* 🌐 *www.bricartsmedia.org*

Prospect Park Carousel. Climb aboard a giraffe or sit inside a dragon-pulled chariot at the immaculately restored Prospect Park Carousel, handcrafted in 1912 by master carver Charles Carmel. ☎ *718/282–7789* 🎫 *$2 per ride* ⏲ *Apr.–June, Sept., and Oct., Thurs.–Sun. noon–5; July–Labor Day, Thurs.–Sun. noon–6*

Prospect Park Zoo. Of the 400 inhabitants and 125 species at the small, friendly, Prospect Park Zoo, kids seem especially fond of the sea lions and the red pandas. An outdoor discovery trail has a simulated prairie-dog burrow, a duck pond, and kangaroos and wallabies in habitat. Be aware that there are no cafés, only vending machines. ✉ *450 Flatbush Ave.* ☎ *718/399–7339* 🌐 *www.prospectparkzoo.com*

$8 Apr.–Oct., weekdays 10–5, weekends 10–5:30; Nov.–Mar., daily 10–4:30; last ticket 30 mins before closing M 2, 3 to Eastern Pkwy.–Brooklyn Museum; B, Q to Prospect Park

WORTH NOTING

FAMILY **Brooklyn Children's Museum.** A mile east of Grand Army Plaza is the oldest children's museum in the world, now housed in a sparkling Rafael Viñoly–designed "green" building. Kids will have a blast, trekking through natural habitats found in the city, running a bakery, creating African-patterned fabric, and even becoming DJs, mixing the rhythms of the outdoors to make music. ✉ *145 Brooklyn Ave., at St. Marks Ave., Crown Heights* ☎ *718/735–4400* 🌐 *www.brooklynkids.org* *$9* *Tues.–Sun. 10–5* M *C to Kingston–Throop Aves.; 3 to Kingston Ave., A, C to Nostrand Ave.*

Central Library. Across Grand Army Plaza from the entrance to Prospect Park stands this sleek, modern temple of learning—the central location of the Brooklyn Public Library. The building resembles an open book, with the entrance at the book's spine; on the facade, gold-leaf figures celebrate art and science. Bright limestone walls and perfect proportions make this an impressive 20th-century New York building. Inside, more than 1.5 million books, public programs, and exhibitions in the lobby will keep you busy for at least a few hours. ✉ *10 Grand Army Plaza, Park Slope* ☎ *718/230–2100* 🌐 *www.brooklynpubliclibrary.org* *Mon.–Thurs. 9–9, Fri. and Sat. 10–6, Sun. 1–5* M *2, 3 to Grand Army Plaza; Q to 7th Ave.*

SHOPPING

Seventh Avenue is Park Slope's main shopping street, with long-established restaurants, bookstores, shops, cafés, bakeries, churches, and real-estate agents (one favorite neighborhood pastime is window-shopping for new apartments). More fun, however, are the newer restaurants and cute boutiques along 5th Avenue.

Bierkraft. Yes, this gourmet food store is all about the beer—there are nearly 1,000 craft beers available by the bottle—but there is also an impressive section of artisanal cheeses, boutique chocolates, olives, and other edible goodies, including delicious made-to-order sandwiches. Beer tastings are Tuesday at 7. There are also 16 different beers on tap daily, available in pints or growlers. ✉ *191 5th Ave., near Union St., Park Slope* ☎ *718/230–7600* 🌐 *www.bierkraft.com.*

Bird. Well-traveled owner Jen Mankins embodies Brooklyn's refined eclecticism, a vibe that's on full display inside her boutiques. An extremely well-curated selection of designers—think Band of Outsiders, Vena Cava, and 3.1 Phillip Lim—makes Bird one of the best of the many excellent women's clothing stores dotting the area. There are two other Brooklyn locations (in Cobble Hill, at 220 Smith Street, ☎ 718/797–3774, and the Ole Sondresen-designed store in Williamsburg, at 203 Grand Street, ☎ 718/388–1655). ✉ *316 5th Ave., between 2nd and 3rd Sts., Park Slope* ☎ *718/768–4940* 🌐 *www.shopbird.com.*

FAMILY **Brooklyn Superhero Supply Co.** Where else can young superheroes purchase capes, grappling hooks, secret identity kits, and more from staff who never drop the game of pretend? Proceeds benefit the free drop-in

Strolling on the boardwalk at Coney Island.

tutoring center (run by nonprofit organization 826NYC) in a "secret lair" behind a swinging bookcase. ⊠ *372 5th Ave., at 7th St., Park Slope* ☎ *718/499–9884* 🌐 *www.superherosupplies.com.*

CONEY ISLAND

Coney Island is practically synonymous with the sounds, smells, and sights of a New York City summer: hot dogs and ice cream, suntan lotion, excited crowds, and weathered old men fishing.

Named Konijn Eiland (Rabbit Island) by the Dutch for its wild rabbit population, the Coney Island peninsula has a boardwalk, a 2½-mile-long beach, amusement parks, and the **New York Aquarium,** which is set to reopen in late spring 2013, after sustaining damage from Hurricane Sandy. Nathan's Famous (⊠ *1310 Surf Ave.*), the quintessential hot dog spot, will also reopen before the summer 2013 season.

Among the other entertainments out here are the freakish attractions at **Coney Island Circus Sideshow** and the **Coney Island Museum,** and the heart-stopping plunge of the granddaddy of all roller coasters—the **Cyclone.** The minor-league baseball team, the Cyclones, plays at MCU Park, where music concerts are held in summer. The area's banner day is during the raucous Mermaid Parade, held in June. A fireworks display lights up the sky Friday night from late June through Labor Day.

TOP ATTRACTIONS

FAMILY **The Cyclone and Luna Park.** The highlight of Coney Island's amusement park will always be the Cyclone. One of the oldest roller coasters still operating, the world-famous, wood-and-steel colossus first roared around the tracks in 1927 and is still making riders scream. Luna Park is the amusement grounds that grew up in place of Astroland; it's fun if you keep your expectations in check—the rides are mostly for kids. ✉ *834 Surf Ave., at W. 10th St., Coney Island* ☎ *718/265–2100* 🌐 *www.lunaparknyc.com* 🎫 *Cyclone: $8 for first ride, $5 for additional rides* ⏲ *Luna Park & Cyclone: Apr.–May, weekends noon–8; June–Aug., daily noon–midnight. Schedule varies, so check website* Ⓜ *D, F, N, Q to Coney Island–Stillwell Ave.*

FAMILY **New York Aquarium.** Home to more than 8,000 creatures of the ocean, New York City's only aquarium is also the nation's oldest. Tropical fish, sea horses, and jellyfish luxuriate in large tanks; otters, walruses, penguins, and seals lounge on a replicated Pacific coast; and a 90,000-gallon tank is home to several different types of sharks. At press time, the aquarium is set to reopen in late spring 2013, after sustaining damage from Hurricane Sandy; call ahead for re-opening dates and times. ✉ *502 Surf Ave., at W. 8th St., Coney Island* ☎ *718/265–3474* 🌐 *www.nyaquarium.com* 🎫 *$14.95* ⏲ *Check website or call ahead for reopening dates and times* Ⓜ *F, Q to W. 8th St.; D, N to Coney Island–Stillwell Ave.*

14

WORTH NOTING

Coney Island Circus Sideshow. Step right up for lively circus-sideshow entertainment, complete with a fire-eater, sword swallower, snake charmer, and contortionist. Upstairs, the small museum has Coney Island memorabilia and lots of tourist information. ✉ *1208 Surf Ave., at W. 12th St., Coney Island* ☎ *718/372–5159* 🌐 *www.coneyisland.com/sideshow.shtml* 🎫 *Sideshow $10, museum $5* ⏲ *Sideshows: Memorial Day–Labor Day, daily; Sept.–May, some weekends. Museum: weekends 1–8.* Ⓜ *D, F, N, Q to Coney Island–Stillwell Ave.*

FAMILY **Deno's Wonder Wheel Amusement Park.** You'll get a wide perspective from atop the 150-foot-tall Wonder Wheel at Deno's Amusement Park. The Wonder Wheel was built in 1920 and although it appears tame, the swinging cars will quicken your heart rate. There are plenty of rides to amuse the kids at this park, which sits just beside the famed Cyclone. ✉ *3059 Denos Vourderis Pl., at W. 12th St., Coney Island* ☎ *718/372–2592* 🌐 *www.wonderwheel.com* 🎫 *$6 per ride, 5 rides for $25* ⏲ *Memorial Day–Labor Day, daily 11 am–midnight; Apr., May, Sept., and Oct., weekends noon–9* Ⓜ *D, F, N, Q to Coney Island–Stillwell Ave.*

BRIGHTON BEACH

A pleasant stroll down the boardwalk from Coney Island is Brighton Beach, named after Britain's beach resort. In the early 1900s Brighton Beach was a resort in its own right, with seaside hotels that catered to rich Manhattan families visiting for the summer. Since the 1970s and '80s Brighton Beach has been known for its 100,000 Soviet émigrés. To get to the heart of "Little Odessa" from Coney Island, walk about a mile east along the boardwalk to Brighton 1st Place, then head up to Brighton Beach Avenue. To get here from Manhattan directly, take the B or Q train to the Brighton Beach stop; the trip takes about an hour.

TOP ATTRACTIONS

Brighton Beach boardwalk. The Brighton Beach section of the boardwalk, especially between Brighton 3rd and 6th Streets, bustles with restaurants serving traditional Russian dishes. The beach tends to be slightly less crowded in summer than at Coney Island, filled with local sunbathers and Manhattanites who've come out for the day. Brighton Beach is about a mile from Coney Island. ✉ *Between Ocean Pkwy. and Coney Island Ave., Brighton Beach* Ⓜ *B, Q to Brighton Beach.*

Brighton Beach Avenue. The shops, bakeries, markets, and restaurants along Brighton Beach Avenue, the neighborhood's main artery, cater primarily to the neighborhood's Russian community but shopping along here is a primary reason to visit. This is the place to find knishes with every filling imaginable, borscht, *blinis* (small crepes or pancakes), fruit and veggies, Russian liquor, and cups of dark-roast coffee, plus caviar at prices that can put Manhattan purveyors to shame. Hurricane Sandy ravaged many restaurants and storefronts here in October 2012, but true to the neighborhood's toughness, business has slowly resumed. ✉ *Brighton Beach Ave. from Brighton 1st to Brighton 6th Sts., Brighton Beach* Ⓜ *Q to Brighton Beach.*

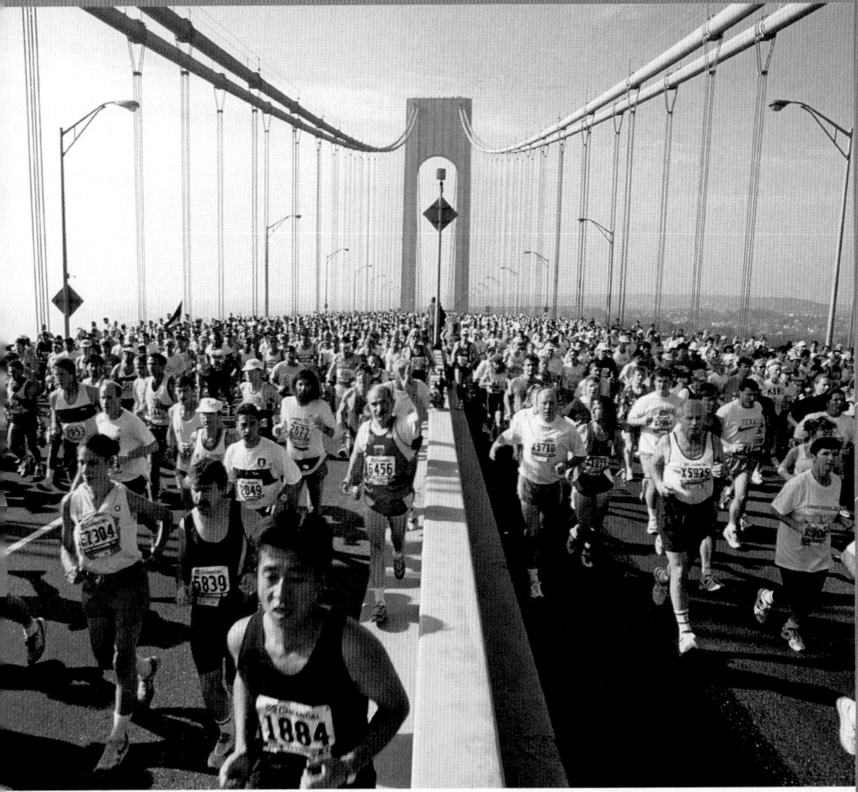

QUEENS, THE BRONX, AND STATEN ISLAND

GETTING ORIENTED

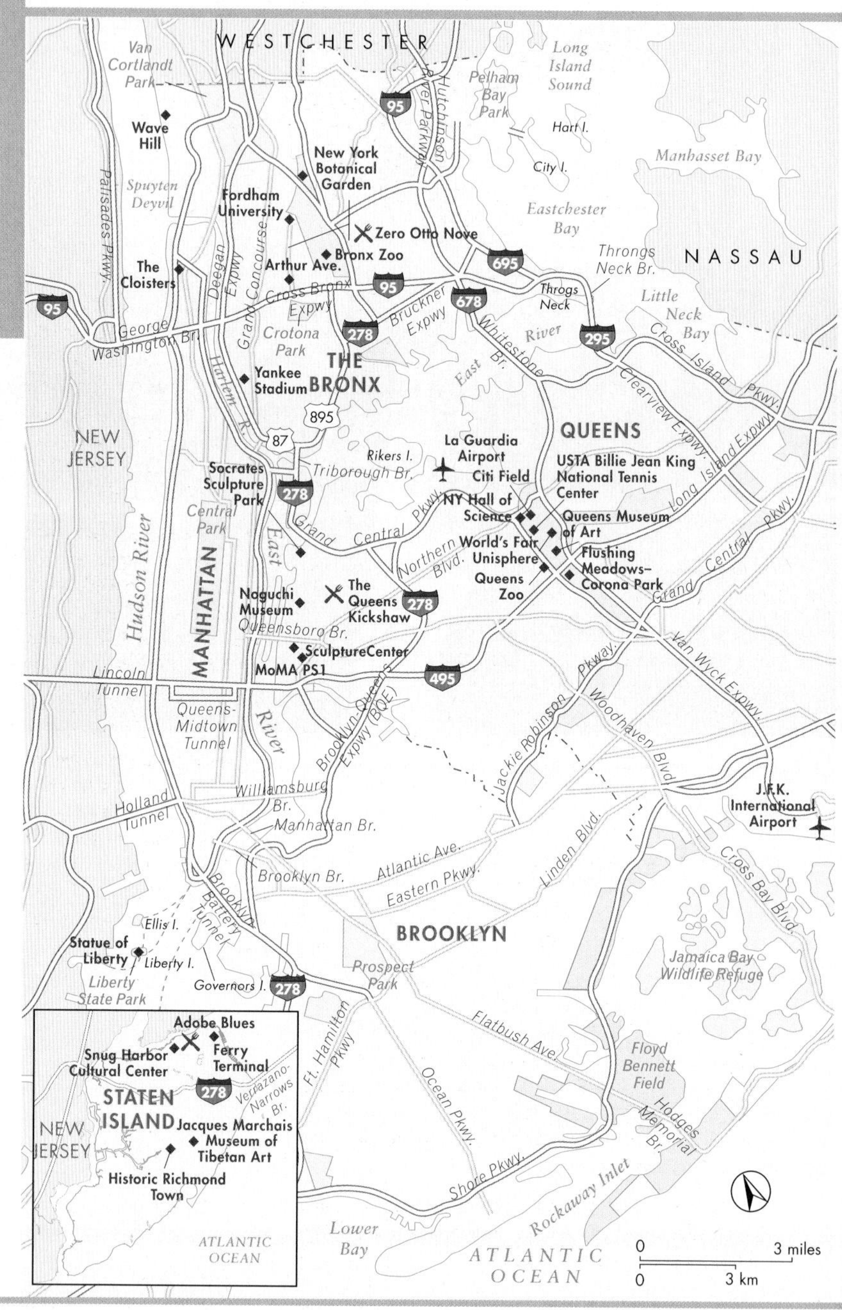
WESTCHESTER
Van Cortlandt Park
Wave Hill
New York Botanical Garden
Fordham University
Zero Otto Nove
Bronx Zoo
Arthur Ave.
The Cloisters
Long Island Sound
Pelham Bay Park
Hart I.
City I.
Manhasset Bay
Eastchester Bay
NASSAU
Throgs Neck Br.
Throgs Neck
Little Neck Bay
Yankee Stadium
THE BRONX
Crotona Park
Cross Bronx Expwy
Bruckner Expwy
Whitestone Br.
East River
Cross Island Pkwy.
Clearview Expwy.
QUEENS
NEW JERSEY
La Guardia Airport
Rikers I.
Triborough Br.
Socrates Sculpture Park
Citi Field
USTA Billie Jean King National Tennis Center
NY Hall of Science
Queens Museum of Art
World's Fair Unisphere
Flushing Meadows–Corona Park
Queens Zoo
Central Park
MANHATTAN
Hudson River
Noguchi Museum
The Queens Kickshaw
Queensboro Br.
SculptureCenter
MoMA PS1
Lincoln Tunnel
Queens-Midtown Tunnel
Long Island Expwy.
Grand Central Pkwy.
Van Wyck Expwy.
Jackie Robinson Pkwy.
Woodhaven Blvd.
Brooklyn-Queens Expwy (BQE)
Williamsburg Br.
Manhattan Br.
Holland Tunnel
J.F.K. International Airport
Brooklyn Br.
Atlantic Ave.
Eastern Pkwy.
Linden Blvd.
Cross Bay Blvd.
BROOKLYN
Ellis I.
Statue of Liberty
Liberty I.
Liberty State Park
Governors I.
Brooklyn Battery Tunnel
Prospect Park
Jamaica Bay Wildlife Refuge
Adobe Blues
Snug Harbor Cultural Center
Ferry Terminal
STATEN ISLAND
Verrazano-Narrows Br.
Jacques Marchais Museum of Tibetan Art
Historic Richmond Town
Ft. Hamilton Pkwy
Ocean Pkwy.
Flatbush Ave.
Floyd Bennett Field
Hodges Memorial Br.
Shore Pkwy.
Rockaway Inlet
Lower Bay
ATLANTIC OCEAN
0 3 miles
0 3 km

TOP EXPERIENCES

Ethnic eats in Queens.

Catching a game at Yankee Stadium or Citi Field.

Taking a free ride on the Staten Island Ferry.

MAKING THE MOST OF YOUR TIME

Queens is rich with superb museums. An afternoon in Long Island City and Astoria will enable you to take in the PS1 Contemporary Art Center, the Museum of the Moving Image, and the Noguchi Museum. After that, jump on the 7 train and have dinner in Jackson Heights or Flushing at one of the borough's excellent restaurants.

It is easy to spend a full day at either of the Bronx's treasures: the New York Botanical Garden or the Bronx Zoo. To visit both, start early and plan on a late lunch or early dinner in the Arthur Avenue area. The garden and the zoo are less crowded on weekdays during the school year.

Many tourists' only sight of Staten Island is during a round-trip ride on the ferry, but the borough also holds unexpected offerings in its small museums and historic villages. Set aside the better part of a day for Historic Richmond Town, and add on a couple of hours for the Museum of Tibetan Art.

GETTING HERE

Queens is served by many subway lines. To get to Astoria, take the N train. For Long Island City, take the E, M, or 7 train. To get to Jackson Heights, take the 7 train to the 74th Street–Broadway stop. You can also take the E, F, R, or M train to Jackson Heights–Roosevelt Avenue.

The Bronx is serviced by the 2, 4, 5, 6, B, and D trains. The attractions in the Bronx are spread out across the borough, so you'll need to take different lines to get where you want to go, and it's not necessarily convenient to make connections across town. The B, D, and 4 trains all go to Yankee Stadium, and the B and D continue uptown to the vicinity of Arthur Avenue. The 2 and 5 trains take you to the Bronx Zoo and to Arthur Avenue.

From the scenic (and free) Staten Island Ferry you can catch a local bus to attractions. Tell the driver where you're going, and ask about the return schedule.

COFFEE AND QUICK BITES

Abobe Blues. Just two blocks from Snug Harbor, this popular joint serves flavorful Mexican and Southwestern food and has a selection of nearly 200 varieties of beer. ✉ *63 Lafayette Ave., at Fillmore St., New Brighton* ☎ *718/720–2583.*

The Queens Kickshaw. Come here for specialty coffee, a variety of grilled cheese options, and craft ales. ✉ *40-17 Broadway, at 41st St., Astoria* ☎ *718/777–0913* 🌐 *www.thequeenskickshaw.com.*

Zero Otto Nove. For serious Neapolitan pizza, pasta, and fine wines, head to Zero Otto Nove. The cozy interior is reminiscent of a traditional restaurant in Italy. ✉ *2357 Arthur Ave, at E. 186th St., Belmont* ☎ *718/220–1027* 🌐 *www.089bx.roberto089.com.*

Sightseeing
★★★
Nightlife
★★★
Dining
★★★★
Lodging
★
Shopping
★★★★

Many tourists miss out on Queens, the Bronx, and Staten Island—the three boroughs of New York City other than the biggies, Manhattan and Brooklyn—and that's a shame. There are some noteworthy restaurants, museums, and attractions, and the subway's handful of express trains means that they're closer than you might think.

QUEENS

Updated by Megan Eileen McDonough

Just for the museums and restaurants alone, a short 15-minute trip on the 7 train from Grand Central or Times Square to **Long Island City** and **Astoria** is truly worth it. In Long Island City, major must-sees are **MoMA PS1** and the **Noguchi Museum.** No trip to Astoria—nicknamed "Little Athens"—would be complete without sampling Greek cuisine and stopping at the **Museum of the Moving Image.**

Jackson Heights is home to the city's largest Indian population. It's a wonderful place to spend an afternoon browsing its shops and dining in one of the many authentic ethnic restaurants.

Top reasons to trek out to **Flushing** and **Corona** include seeing the New York Mets' stadium, **Citi Field,** and spending time at the expansive **Flushing Meadows–Corona Park**—especially if traveling with kids.

ASTORIA

Astoria, nicknamed "Little Athens," was the center of Greek immigrant life in New York City for more than 60 years. An increase in Greek affluence has meant that many have left the borough, but they still return for authentic restaurants, grocery stores, and churches. Here you can buy kalamata olives and salty sheep's-milk feta from storeowners who can tell you where to go for the best spinach pie. Today substantial numbers of Asian, Eastern European, Irish, and Latino immigrants also live in Astoria. The heart of what remains of the Greek community is on Broadway, between 31st and Steinway streets. Thirtieth Avenue is

TIPS FOR QUEENS ADDRESSES

Addresses in Queens can seem confusing at first. Not only are there 30th Street and 30th Avenue, but there are also 30th Place and 30th Road, all next to one another. Then there are those hyphenated building numbers. But the system is actually logical. Sequentially numbered avenues run east-to-west, and sequentially numbered streets run north-to-south. If there are any smaller roads between avenues, they have the same number as the nearest avenue, and are called roads or drives. Similarly, smaller side roads between streets are called places or lanes. Thus, 30th Place is one block east of 30th Street. Most buildings have two pairs of numbers, separated by a hyphen. The first pair indicates the nearest cross street, and the second gives the location on the block. So 47-10 30th Place is 10 houses away from the corner of 47th Avenue and 30th Place. Logical, right? If this all still seems confusing to you, there's good news: locals are used to giving directions to visitors.

another busy thoroughfare, with almost every kind of food store imaginable. Astoria is also home to the nation's only museum devoted to the art, technology, and history of film, TV, and digital media. The **Museum of the Moving Image** has countless hands-on exhibits that allow visitors to edit, direct, and step into favorite movies and television shows.

TOP ATTRACTIONS

Museum of the Moving Image. Like switching to a widescreen television, the Museum of the Moving Image is twice as nice as it was before the 2011 expansion and renovation. The Thomas Lesser design includes a three-story addition and a panoramic entrance to this museum full of Hollywood and television memorabilia. Exhibitions range from "Behind the Screen" which demonstrates how movies are produced and shot to watching the live editing of Mets baseball games as they happen on the SNY network. Classic family films are shown as matinees on Saturday and Sunday, while the museum also has a section devoted to video artists for visitors looking for some culture. Film buffs will love the film retrospectives, lectures, and other special programs. ✉ *36-01 35th Ave., between 36th and 37th Sts., Astoria* ☎ *718/777–6888* 🌐 *www.movingimage.us* 🎟 *$12, free after 4 on Fri.* 🕒 *Wed. and Thurs. 10:30–5, Fri. 10:30–8, weekends 11:30–7* Ⓜ *M, R to Steinway St.; N, Q to 36th Ave.*

LONG ISLAND CITY

Long Island City (LIC for short) is the outer-borough art capital, with **MoMA PS1,** which presents experimental and formally innovative work; the **Noguchi Museum,** showcasing the work of Japanese-American sculptor Isamu Noguchi in a large, peaceful garden and galleries; and **Socrates Sculpture Park.**

TOP ATTRACTIONS

Fodor's Choice ★ **MoMA PS1.** A pioneer in the "alternative-space" movement, PS1 rose from the ruins of an abandoned school in 1976 as a sort of community arts center for the future. MoMA PS1 focuses on the work of currently

CLOSE UP

Filmmaking in Astoria

Hollywood may be the king of moviemaking now, but in the early days of sound, Queens was where it was at. In the 1920s such stars as Gloria Swanson, Rudolph Valentino, and Claudette Colbert all acted in one of the more than 100 films made at Astoria Studios. Opened in 1920 by the film company that would become Paramount, "the Big House" was the largest and most important filmmaking studio in the country.

Though Astoria's ideal location provided easy access to Broadway and vaudeville stars, Hollywood's weather soon lured most studios away. Astoria was able to hold its own for a while longer, creating such films as the Marx Brothers classics *The Cocoanuts* and *Animal Crackers*. But in 1942 the studio was sold to the U.S. Army. It became the Signal Corps Photographic Center, producing training films and documentaries, including Frank Capra's classic seven-film series *Why We Fight*. The army retained the studio until 1970.

In 1980 the city leased the studio to real-estate developer George S. Kaufman, in partnership with Alan King and Johnny Carson. Kaufman-Astoria Studios, with six stages, is a thriving operation once again, used for television series (*Sesame Street; Law & Order; Nurse Jackie*) as well as movies (*The Wiz; Eat, Pray, Love;* and *The Bourne Legacy*). Although the studio is not open to the public, movie buffs can hope to spot stars at the Studio Café and learn more about the craft next door at the fantastic Museum of the Moving Image.

active experimental and innovative artists. Long-term installations include work by Sol LeWitt and Pipilotti Rist. Every available corner of the enormous 100-room building is used; discover art not only in galleries but also on the rooftop, in the boiler room, and even in some bathrooms. On summer Saturdays, MoMA PS1 presents "Warm Up", an outdoor dance party series attracting a hip art-school crowd that's held in the courtyard from noon–9. Similarly, their "Summer Sessions" are held in the Dome and feature various artistic installations, scholarly lectures, and special performances. ✉ *22–25 Jackson Ave., at 46th Ave., Long Island City* ☎ *718/784–2084* 🌐 *www.momaps1.org* 🎫 *$10 suggested donation, free with MoMA entrance ticket* ⏲ *Thurs.–Mon. noon–6* Ⓜ *7 to Court Sq.; E, M to Court Sq.–23rd St.; G to 21st St.*

The Noguchi Museum. In 1985 the Japanese-American sculptor Isamu Noguchi (1904–88) transformed this former photo-engraving plant into a place to display his modernist and earlier works. A peaceful central garden is surrounded by gallery buildings, and there are more than 250 pieces done in stone, metal, clay, and other materials on view. Temporary exhibits have featured his collaborations with others, such as industrial designer Isamu Kenmochi. The museum is about a mile from subway stops; check the website for complete directions. On Sunday a shuttle bus leaves from the northeast corner of Park Avenue and 70th Street in Manhattan (in front of the Asia Society) hourly, beginning at 12:30 with return trips ending at 5; the round-trip costs $10. ✉ *9-01 33rd Rd., at Vernon Blvd., Long Island City* ☎ *718/204–7088* 🌐 *www.*

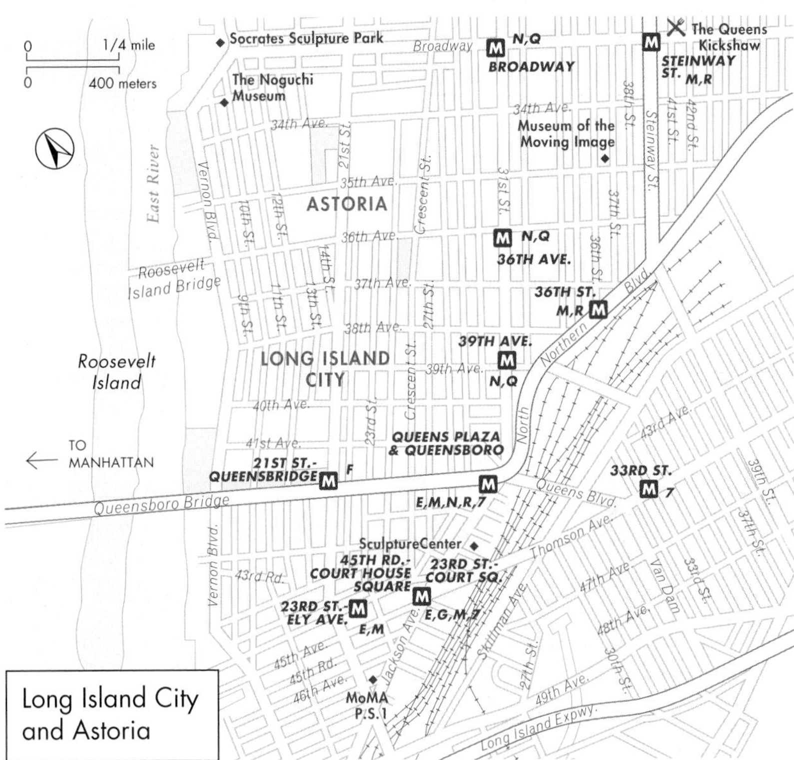

Long Island City and Astoria

noguchi.org 🎫 *$10; 1st Fri. of month, pay what you wish* 🕑 *Wed.–Fri. 10–5, weekends 11–6* Ⓜ *N, Q to Broadway.*

WORTH NOTING

SculptureCenter. Founded by artists in 1928 to exhibit innovative contemporary work, SculptureCenter now occupies a former trolley repair shop renovated by artist Maya Lin and architect David Hotson, not far from MoMA PS1. Their indoor and outdoor exhibition spaces sometimes close between shows; call ahead before visiting. ✉ *44-19 Purves St., at Jackson Ave., Long Island City* ☎ *718/361–1750* 🌐 *www.sculpture-center.org* 🎫 *$5 suggested donation* 🕑 *Thurs.–Mon. 11–6* Ⓜ *7, G to Court Sq.; E, M to Court Sq.–23rd St.; N, Q to Queensboro Plaza.*

FAMILY **Socrates Sculpture Park.** In 1986 local artist Mark di Suvero and other residents rallied to transform what had been an abandoned landfill and illegal dump site into this 4½-acre waterfront park devoted to public art. Today a superb view of the river and Manhattan frames changing exhibitions of contemporary sculptures and multimedia installations. Free public programs include art workshops and an annual outdoor international film series (July and August, Wednesday evenings). ✉ *32-01 Vernon Blvd., at Broadway, Long Island City* ☎ *718/956–1819* 🌐 *www.socratessculpturepark.org* 🎫 *Free* 🕑 *9 am–Sunset* Ⓜ *N, Q to*

Broadway, then walk 8 blocks west or take Q104 bus along Broadway to Vernon Blvd.

JACKSON HEIGHTS

Even in the diverse borough of Queens, Jackson Heights stands out for being a true polycultural neighborhood. In just a few blocks surrounding the three-way intersection of Roosevelt Avenue, 74th Street, and Broadway, you can find shops and restaurants catering to the area's strong Indian, Bangladeshi, Colombian, Mexican, and Ecuadorian communities. Built as a planned "garden community" in the late 1910s, the area boasts many prewar apartments with elaborate block-long interior gardens as well as English-style homes. Celebs who grew up in the area include Lucy Liu and Gene Simmons. It's also the birthplace of the board game Scrabble.

FLUSHING AND CORONA

Before it became a part of New York City, Queens consisted of many small independent townships. So it makes sense that the historic town of Flushing is today a microcosm of a larger city, including a bustling downtown area, fantastic restaurants, and bucolic suburbanlike streets nearby.

Flushing may seem like a strange name for a town, but it's an English adaptation of the original (and hard-to-pronounce) Dutch name Vlissingen. The Dutch named it for a favorite port city in the Netherlands.

Next door, quiet Corona could easily be overlooked, but that would be a mistake. Here you'll find two huge legacies: the music of Satchmo and the cooling simplicity of an Italian ice.

TOP ATTRACTIONS

Fodor's Choice ★ **Citi Field.** Opened in 2009, the Mets' newest stadium was designed to hark back to Ebbets Field (where the Dodgers played in Brooklyn) with a brick exterior and plenty of bells and whistles, from a batting cage and Wiffle ball field to the original giant apple taken from the team's old residence, Shea Stadium. Even those who aren't Mets fans but simply love baseball should come to see the Jackie Robinson Rotunda, a soaring multistory entrance and history exhibit dedicated to the Dodgers player who shattered baseball's color barrier. While here, don't miss making a stop at the more-than-fabulous food court behind center field, where you'll find Shake Shack burgers, surprisingly inexpensive beers such as Czechvar and Leffe, and even lobster rolls and tacos. Though it seats fewer people than Shea by about 10,000, tickets are not hard to come by, especially later in the season. Still feeling nostalgic for the old Shea? Pay your respects at the plaque in the parking lot. ✉ *126-01 Roosevelt Avenue, off Grand Central Pkwy., Flushing/Corona* ☎ *718/507–8499* 🌐 *newyork.mets.mlb.com* Ⓜ *7 to Mets–Willets Point.*

FAMILY **Flushing Meadows–Corona Park.** Standing in the lush grass of this park, you'd never imagine that it was once a swamp and dumping ground. But the gleaming Unisphere (an enormous 140-foot-high steel globe) might tip you off that this 1,255-acre park was also the site of two

World's Fairs. Take advantage of the park's barbecue pits and sports fields, but also don't forget that there's an art museum, a petting zoo, golf and minigolf, and even a model-plane field. There's way too much to see here to pack into a day, so aim to hit a few primary spots, noting that while several are clustered together on the northwest side of the park, visitors should be prepared for long peaceful walks in between. The flat grounds are ideal for family biking; rent bikes near the park entrance or Meadow Lake from March to October. **TIP→ Although the park is great in daytime, avoid visiting once it gets dark; there has been some crime in this area.** ✉ *Between 111th St./Grand Central Pkwy. and Van Wyck Expy. at 44th Ave., Flushing/Corona* 🌐 *www.nycgovparks.org/parks/fmcp* Ⓜ *7 to 111th St. or Mets–Willets Point.*

New York Hall of Science. At the northwestern edge of Flushing Meadows–Corona Park, the New York Hall of Science has more than 400 hands-on exhibits that make science a playground for inquisitive minds of all ages. Climb aboard a replica of John Glenn's space capsule, throw a fastball and investigate its speed, or explore Charles and Ray Eames's classic Mathematica exhibition. ✉ *Between 111th St./Grand Central Pkwy. and Van Wyck Expy. at 44th Ave., 47-01 111th St., Flushing/Corona* ☎ *718/699–0005* 🌐 *www.nysci.org* 🎟 *$11; free Fri. 2–5 and Sun. 10–11 Sept.–June* ⏲ *Feb.–March and Sept.–Jan. Tues.–Fri. 9:30–5, weekends 10–6; April–Aug., weekdays 9:30–5, weekends 10–6* Ⓜ *7 to 111th St.; walk 3 blocks south.*

Queens Museum of Art. Between the zoo and the Unisphere in Flushing Meadows–Corona Park, you'll find the Queens Museum of Art. Don't miss the astonishing Panorama, a nearly 900,000-building model of NYC made for the 1964 World's Fair. Many unsuspecting park visitors looking for a bathroom instead find themselves spending hours checking out the intricate structures that replicate every block in the city. There are also rotating exhibitions of contemporary art and a permanent collection of Louis Comfort Tiffany stained glass. The museum underwent a major expansion in 2013 which resulted in more exhibitions and education departments, a cafe, a bookstore, and places for children's activities. ✉ *Between 111th St./Grand Central Pkwy. and Van Wyck Expy. at 44th Ave., Flushing/Corona* ☎ *718/592–9700* 🌐 *www.queensmuseum.org* 🎟 *$8 suggested donation* ⏲ *Wed.–Sun. noon–6; call for extended hrs in July and Aug.* Ⓜ *7 to 111th St. or Mets–Willets Point.*

Queens Zoo. Behind the Hall of Science in Flushing Meadows–Corona Park lies the intimate Queens Zoo, whose small scale is especially well suited to easily tired young visitors. In only 11 acres you'll find North American animals such as bears, mountain lions, bald eagles, and pudu—the world's smallest deer. Buckminster Fuller's geodesic dome from the 1964 World's Fair is now the aviary. Across the street is a petting zoo. ✉ *53-51 111th St., at 53rd Ave., Flushing/Corona* ☎ *718/271–1500* 🌐 *www.queenszoo.com* 🎟 *$8* ⏲ *Apr.–Oct., weekdays 10–5, weekends 10–5:30; Nov.–March, daily 10–4:30; last ticket sold 30 mins before closing* Ⓜ *7 to 111th St. or Mets–Willets Point; Q58 to Corona Ave.*

USTA Billie Jean King National Tennis Center. Each August, 700,000 fans come here for the U.S. Open, which claims the title of highest-attended annual sporting event in the world. The rest of the year, the 33 courts (17 outdoor and 12 indoor, all Deco Turf II, plus 4 clay courts) are open to the public for $22–$66 hourly. Make reservations up to two days in advance. ✉ *Flushing Meadows–Corona Park, Flushing/Corona* ☎ *718/760–6200* 🌐 *www.usta.com* Ⓜ *7 to Mets–Willets Point.*

WORTH NOTING

Louis Armstrong House Museum. For the last 28 years of his life the famed jazz musician lived in this modest three-story house in Corona with his wife Lucille. Take a guided 40-minute tour and note the difference between the rooms vividly decorated by Lucille in charming midcentury style and Louis's dark den, cluttered with phonographs and reel-to-reel tape recorders. Although photographs and family mementos throughout the house impart knowledge about Satchmo's life, it's in his den that you'll really understand his spirit. ✉ *34-56 107th St., at 37th Ave., Flushing/Corona* ☎ *718/478–8274* 🌐 *www.louisarmstronghouse.org* 💵 *$10* 🕓 *Tours hourly Tues.–Fri. 10–5, weekends noon–5* Ⓜ *7 to 103rd St.–Corona Plaza.*

NEED A BREAK?

Lemon Ice King of Corona. If you're looking for an authentic Queens experience, there are few as true as eating an Italian ice from the Lemon Ice King of Corona on a hot summer day. There are no seats and the service can often be gruff at this neighborhood institution of more than 60 years, but none of that will matter after your first taste. And yes, there are plenty of flavors other than lemon. ✉ *52-02 108th St., at 52nd Ave., Flushing/Corona* ☎ *718/699–5133.*

THE BRONX

The Bronx is the city's most maligned and misunderstood borough. Its reputation as a gritty, down-and-out place is a little outdated, and there's lots of beauty to be found, if you know where to look. There is more parkland in the Bronx than in any other borough, as well as one of the world's finest botanical collections, the largest metropolitan zoo in the country, and, of course, Yankee Stadium. (The Bronx does cover a large area, though, so the attractions are spread out.) Whether you're relaxing at a ball game or scoping out exotic species at the zoo, there's plenty of fun to be had here.

TOP ATTRACTIONS

FAMILY
Fodor's Choice ★

The Bronx Zoo. When it opened its gates in 1899, the Bronx Zoo had only 843 animals. But today, with 265 acres and more than 4,000 animals (of more than 600 species), it's the largest metropolitan zoo in the United States. Get up close and personal with exotic creatures in outdoor settings that re-create natural habitats; you're often separated from them by no more than a moat or wall of glass. Don't miss the **Congo Gorilla Forest,** a 6.5-acre re-creation of a lush African rain forest with two troops of lowland gorillas, as well as white-bearded DeBrazza's monkeys, okapis, and red river hogs. At **Tiger Mountain**

The jungle habitat at the Bronx Zoo will make you forget the surrounding urban jungle.

an open viewing shelter lets you get incredibly close to Siberian tigers, who frolic in a pool, lounge outside (even in cold weather), and enjoy daily "enrichment sessions" with keepers. As the big cats are often napping at midday, aim to visit in the morning or evening. In the new $62 million exhibit **Madagascar!**, the formality of the old Lion House has been replaced with a verdant re-creation of one of the most threatened natural habitats in the world. Here you'll see adorable lemurs and far-from-adorable hissing cockroaches.

Go on a minisafari via the **Wild Asia Monorail**, open May–October, weather permitting. As you wend your way through the forest, see Asian elephants, Indo-Chinese tigers, Indian rhinoceroses, gaur (the world's largest cattle), Mongolian wild horses, and several deer and antelope species. **TIP→** Try to visit the most popular exhibits, such as Congo Gorilla Forest, early to avoid lines later in the day. In winter the outdoor exhibitions have fewer animals on view, but there are also fewer crowds, and plenty of indoor exhibits to savor. Also note that there is an extra charge for some exhibits. If you want to see everything, you'll save money by purchasing the Total Experience ticket. ✉ *2300 Southern Blvd., near E. 187 St., Bronx Park* ☎ *718/367–1010* 🌐 *www.bronxzoo.com* 🎟 *General admission: $16.95, extra charge for some exhibits. Total Experience: $20.95–$29.95. Entrance every Wed. is free (suggested donation of $16). Parking: $15 weekdays, $16 weekends* ⏲ *Apr.–Oct., weekdays 10–5, weekends 10–5:30; Nov.–Mar., daily 10–4:30; last ticket sold 30 mins before closing* Ⓜ *2, 5 to W. Farms Sq.–E. Tremont Ave., then walk 2 blocks up Boston Rd. to zoo's Asia entrance; Bx11 express bus to Bronx River entrance.*

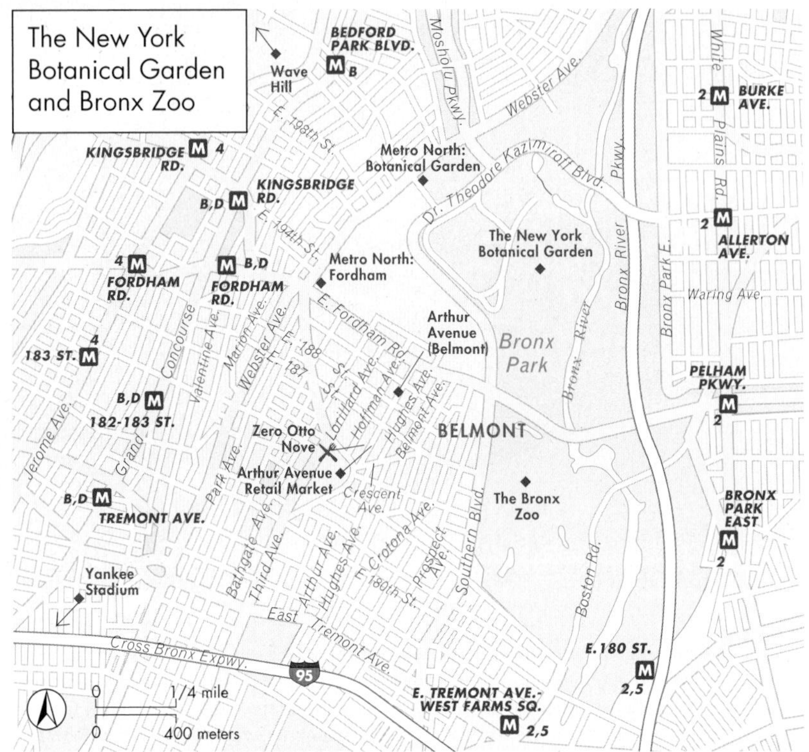

Fodor's Choice ★ **The New York Botanical Garden.** Considered one of the leading botany centers of the world, this 250-acre garden is one of the best reasons to make a trip to the Bronx. Built around the dramatic gorge of the Bronx River, the Garden offers lush indoor and outdoor gardens, and acres of natural forest, as well as classes, concerts, and special exhibits. Be astounded by the captivating fragrance of the Peggy Rockefeller Rose Garden's 2,700 plants of more than 250 varieties; see intricate orchids that look like the stuff of science fiction; relax in the quiet of the forest or the calm of the Conservatory; or take a jaunt through the Everett Children's Adventure Garden, a 12-acre, indoor-outdoor museum with a boulder maze, giant animal topiaries, and a plant discovery center.

The Garden's roses bloom in June and September, but there's plenty to see year-round. The Victorian-style **Enid A. Haupt Conservatory** houses re-creations of misty tropical rain forests and arid African and North American deserts as well as exhibitions, such as the annual Holiday Train Show and the Orchid Show. The **All-Garden Pass** (*$20*) gives you access to the Conservatory, Rock Garden, Native Plant Garden, Tram Tour, Everett Children's Adventure Garden, and exhibits in the library.

The most direct way to the Garden is via **Metro-North Railroad** (*www.mta.info/mnr*) from Grand Central Terminal (Harlem Local Line, Botanical Garden stop). Round-trip tickets are $11.50 to $15, depending on time of day. A cheaper alternative is to take the D or 4 train to Bedford Park Boulevard, then walk east. ✉ *2900 Southern Blvd., Fordham* ☎ *718/817–8700* 🌐 *www.nybg.org* 🎫 *Grounds only $10, free Sat. 10–11 and all day Wed.; All-Garden Pass $20; parking $12 weekdays, $15 weekends and during special events* ⏲ *Tues.–Sun. 10–5 (10–6 during special exhibitions)* Ⓜ *B, D, 4 to Bedford Park Blvd., then walk 8 blocks downhill to the garden; Metro-North to Botanical Garden.*

Fodor's Choice ★ **Yankee Stadium.** Fans are still mourning the original, legendary Yankee Stadium, which saw its last season in 2008. The new Yankee Stadium, however (right next to "The House That Ruth Built") got off to a good start, with the Yankees winning the World Series in its inaugural year. Tickets can be ridiculously expensive, but the experience is like watching baseball in Las Vegas's Bellagio hotel. It's incredibly opulent and over-the-top: traditional white frieze adorns the stadium's top; inside, limestone-and-marble hallways are lined with photos of past Yankee greats; lower-level seats have cushions, cup holders, and boffo meatery NYY Steak. Like the team, all the amenities don't come cheap. But the spirit of the original still remains. History buffs and hard-core fans should be sure to visit Monument Park, with plaques of past team members, by Center Field—it survived from the old stadium. Aside from the subway, you can also get here by taking Metro-North to the Yankees–153rd Street Station. ✉ *1 East 161st St., at River Ave., South Bronx* ☎ *718/293–6000* 🌐 *newyork.yankees.mlb.com* Ⓜ *B, D, or 4 to 161st St.–Yankee Stadium.*

15

WORTH NOTING

OFF THE BEATEN PATH

Wave Hill. Drawn by stunning views of the Hudson River and New Jersey's dramatic cliffs, 19th-century Manhattan millionaires built summer homes in the Bronx suburb of Riverdale. One of the most magnificent, Wave Hill, is now a 28-acre public garden and cultural center that attracts green thumbs from all over the world. Along with exquisite gardens, grand beech and oak trees adorn wide lawns, an elegant pergola overlooks the majestic river view, and benches on curving pathways provide quiet respite. Wave Hill House (1843) and Glyndor House (1927) are now home to art exhibitions, Sunday concerts, and gardening workshops. Even England's Queen Mother stayed here during a visit. It's worth the schlep. ✉ *Independence Ave. at W. 249th St., Riverdale* ☎ *718/549–3200* 🌐 *www.wavehill.org* 🎫 *$8; free Sat. 9–noon and some Tues. (check website)* ⏲ *Mid-Mar.–Oct., Tues.–Sun. 9–5:30; Nov.–mid-Mar., Tues.–Sun. 9–4:30; closed Mon. except holidays. Free garden tours Sun. at 2* Ⓜ *1 to 231st St., then Bx7 or Bx10 bus to 252nd St. and Riverdale Ave.; or free van service hourly from W. 242nd St. station between 9:10 am and 3:10 pm.*

STATEN ISLAND

Legally part of New York City, Staten Island is in many ways a world apart. The "Forgotten Borough," as some locals refer to it, is geographically more separate, less populous, politically more conservative, and ethnically more homogeneous than the rest of the city.

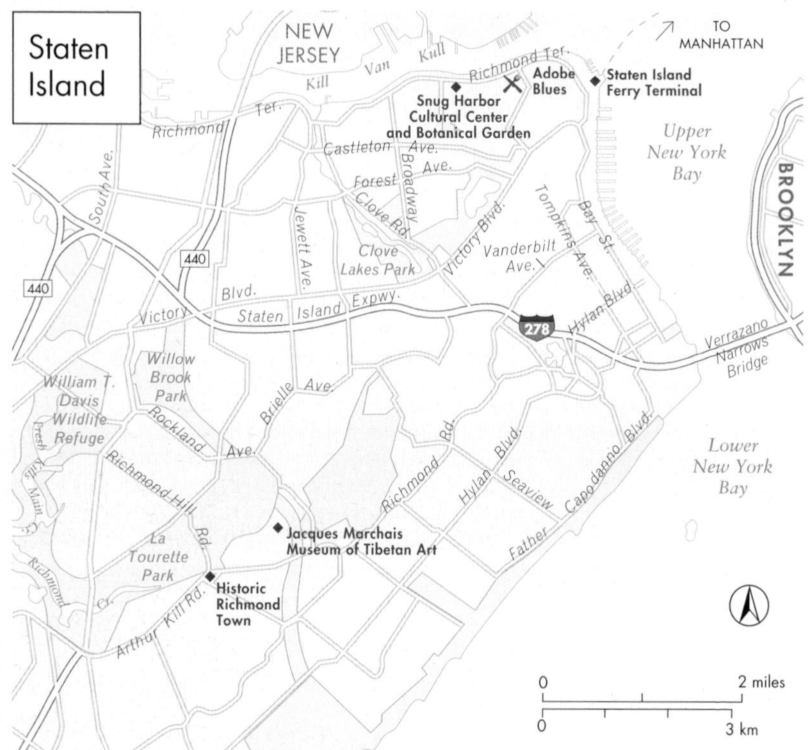

Hurricane Sandy hit New York City in October 2012 and Staten Island was among the hardest hit areas. Many residential properties and small neighborhood businesses were severely damaged, but all of the cultural and destination points survived fairly unharmed. Rebuilding is ongoing and it's expected that restoration efforts will continue into 2014.

Despite this setback, Staten Island is full of surprises. Along with suburban sprawl, there are wonderful small museums, including a premier collection of Tibetan art, walkable woodlands, and a historic village replicating New York's rural past. And for a view of the skyline and the Statue of Liberty, nothing beats the 25-minute free ferry trip to Staten Island. To explore the borough, take the Staten Island Ferry from the southern tip of Manhattan. After you disembark, grab an S40 bus to the **Snug Harbor Cultural Center** (about 10 minutes) or take the S74 and combine visits to the **Tibetan Museum** and **Historic Richmond Town.**

TOP ATTRACTIONS

FAMILY Fodor's Choice ★ **Historic Richmond Town.** Think of Virginia's Colonial Williamsburg (the polar opposite of Brooklyn's scene-y Williamsburg), and you'll understand the appeal of Richmond Town. This 100-acre village, constructed from 1695 to the 19th century, was the site of Staten Island's original county seat. Fifteen of the site's 27 historic buildings are open to the public. Highlights include the Gothic Revival **Courthouse**, the one-room

DID YOU KNOW?

Many New Yorkers consider the Staten Island Ferry the ultimate cheap date. Its decks provide romantic waterfront views of the Statue of Liberty and Lower Manhattan without costing a cent (and beers are really cheap!).

General Store, and the **Voorlezer's House,** one of the oldest buildings on the site. It served as a residence, a place of worship, and an elementary school. Also on-site is the **Staten Island Historical Society Museum,** built in 1848 as the second county clerk's and surrogate's office, which now houses Staten Island artifacts plus changing exhibits about the island. Audio tours are free with admission.

You may see staff in period dress demonstrate Early American crafts and trades such as tinsmithing or basket making, though the general era meant to be re-created is 1820–1860. December brings a monthlong Christmas celebration. Take the S74–Richmond Road bus (30 minutes) or a car service (about $15) from the ferry terminal. ✉ *441 Clarke Ave., Richmondtown* ☎ *718/351–1611* 🌐 *www.historicrichmondtown.org* 🎫 *$8* 🕘 *Year-round Wed.–Sun. 1–5; guided tours Wed.–Fri. 2:30, weekends 2 and 3:30* Ⓜ *S74 bus to St. Patrick's Pl.*

Jacques Marchais Museum of Tibetan Art. At the top of a hill sits this replica of a Tibetan monastery containing one of the largest collections of Tibetan and Himalayan sculpture, paintings, and artifacts outside Tibet. Meditate with visiting Buddhist monks, or just enjoy the peaceful views from the terraced garden. ✉ *338 Lighthouse Ave., Richmondtown* ☎ *718/987–3500* 🌐 *www.tibetanmuseum.org* 🎫 *$6* 🕘 *Apr.–Nov., Wed.–Sun. 1–5; Dec.–Mar., Fri.–Sun. 1–5* Ⓜ *S74 bus to Lighthouse Ave. and walk uphill 15 mins.*

WORTH NOTING

Snug Harbor Cultural Center and Botanical Garden. Once part of a sprawling farm, this 83-acre community is now a popular spot to see maritime art, frolic in the **Children's Museum**, or take a stroll through lush gardens.

Made up of 28 mostly restored historic buildings, Snug Harbor's center is a row of mid-19th-century Greek Revival temples. Main Hall—the oldest building on the property—is home to the **Eleanor Proske Visitors Center** (🎫 *$5, including Newhouse Center*), which has exhibits on art and Snug Harbor's history. The adjacent **Newhouse Center for Contemporary Art** (☎ *718/425–3524* 🎫 *$5, including visitor center*) shows multidisciplinary videos, mixed media, and performances. Next door at the **Noble Maritime Collection** (☎ *718/447–6490* 🌐 *www.noblemaritime.org* 🎫 *Entrance by donation*) an old seamen's dormitory is now a museum of ocean-inspired artwork.

From the Staten Island Ferry terminal, take the S40 bus two miles (about seven minutes) to the Snug Harbor Road stop. Or grab a car service at the ferry terminal. (The ride should cost you about $5.) ✉ *1000 Richmond Terr., between Snug Harbor Rd. and Tyson Ave., Livingston* ☎ *718/448–2500* 🌐 *www.snug-harbor.org* 🎫 *Free for grounds and gardens; $5 for New York Chinese Scholar's Garden; $8 Garden and Gallery combo ticket* 🕘 *Apr.–Sept., Tues.–Sun. 10–5; Oct.–Mar., Tues.–Sun. 10–4. Noble Maritime Thurs.–Sun. 1–5 or by appointment. Grounds dawn–dusk every day except major holidays.*

16

WHERE TO EAT

Updated by David Farley

Ready to take a bite out of New York? Hope you've come hungry. In a city where creativity is expressed in many ways, the food scene takes center stage, with literally thousands of ways to get an authentic taste of what Gotham is all about. Whether they're lining up at street stands, gobbling down legendary deli and diner grub, or chasing a coveted reservation at the latest celebrity-chef venue, New Yorkers are a demanding yet appreciative audience.

Every neighborhood offers temptations high, low, and in between, meaning there's truly something for every taste, whim, and budget. No matter how you approach dining out here, you can't go wrong. Planning a day of shopping among the glittering boutique flagships along 5th and Madison? Stop into one of the Upper East Side's storied restaurants for a repast among the "ladies who lunch." Clubbing in the Meatpacking District? Tuck into a meal at eateries as trendy as their patrons. Craving authentic ethnic? From food trucks to hidden joints, there are almost more choices than there are appetites. Recent years have also seen entire food categories, from ramen to meatballs to mac and cheese, riffed upon and turned into fetishistic obsessions.

Amid newfound economic realities, there's been a revived appreciation for value, meaning you can tap into wallet-friendly choices at every end of the spectrum. At many restaurants you'll also notice an almost religious reverence for seasonal, locally sourced cuisine. And don't forget—New York is still home to more celebrity chefs than any other city. Your chances of running into your favorite cookbook author, Food Network celeb, or paparazzi-friendly chef are higher, adding even more star wattage to a restaurant scene with an already through-the-roof glamour quotient. Ready, set, eat. Rest assured, this city will do its part to satisfy your appetite.

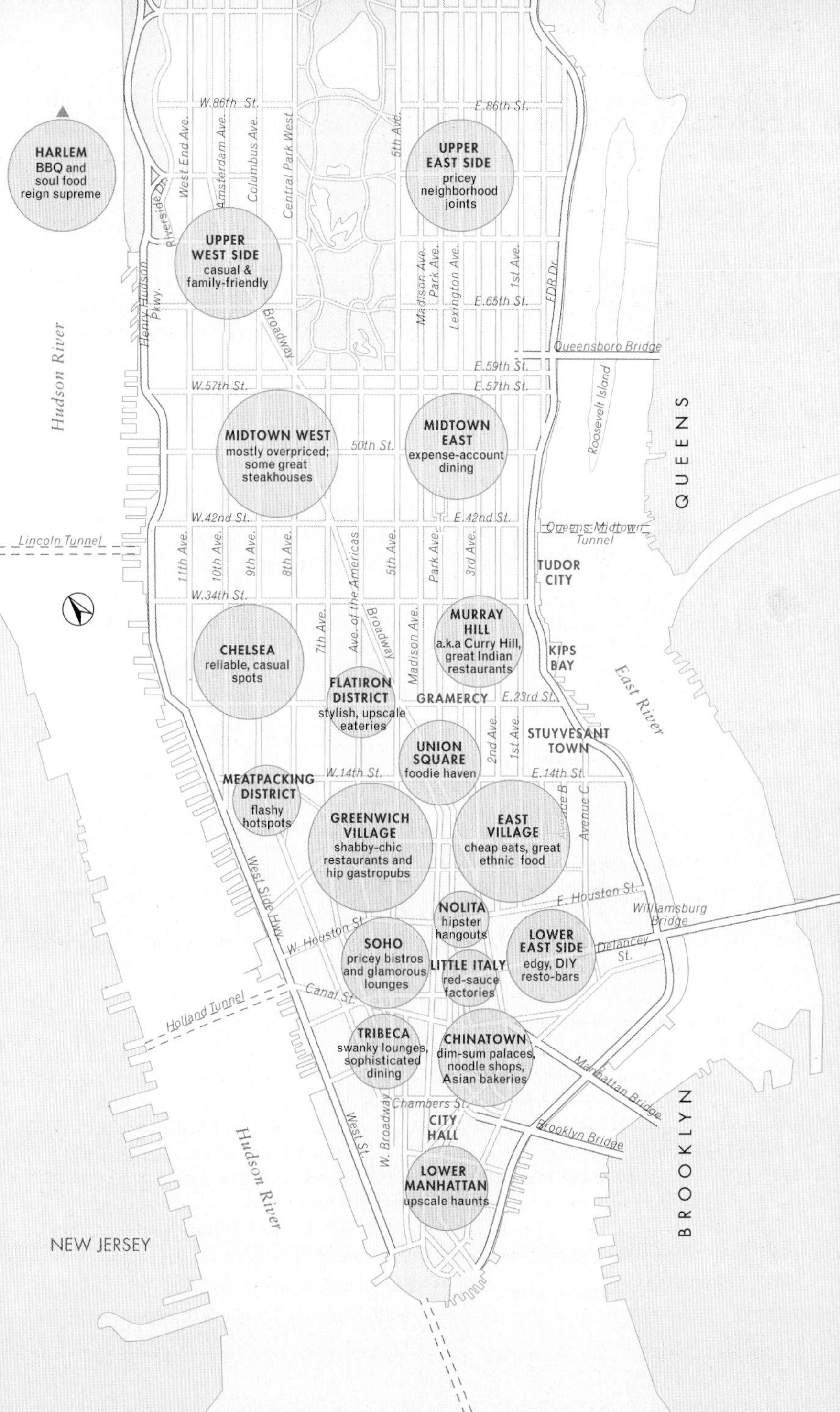
HARLEM
BBQ and soul food reign supreme
UPPER WEST SIDE
casual & family-friendly
UPPER EAST SIDE
pricey neighborhood joints
MIDTOWN WEST
mostly overpriced; some great steakhouses
MIDTOWN EAST
expense-account dining
TUDOR CITY
CHELSEA
reliable, casual spots
MURRAY HILL
a.k.a Curry Hill, great Indian restaurants
KIPS BAY
FLATIRON DISTRICT
stylish, upscale eateries
GRAMERCY
STUYVESANT TOWN
UNION SQUARE
foodie haven
MEATPACKING DISTRICT
flashy hotspots
GREENWICH VILLAGE
shabby-chic restaurants and hip gastropubs
EAST VILLAGE
cheap eats, great ethnic food
NOLITA
hipster hangouts
SOHO
pricey bistros and glamorous lounges
LITTLE ITALY
red-sauce factories
LOWER EAST SIDE
edgy, DIY resto-bars
TRIBECA
swanky lounges, sophisticated dining
CHINATOWN
dim-sum palaces, noodle shops, Asian bakeries
CITY HALL
LOWER MANHATTAN
upscale haunts
W.86th St.
E.86th St.
West End Ave.
Amsterdam Ave.
Columbus Ave.
Central Park West
5th Ave.
Riverside Dr.
Henry Hudson Pkwy.
Madison Ave.
Park Ave.
Lexington Ave.
1st Ave.
FDR Dr.
E.65th St.
Broadway
Queensboro Bridge
E.59th St.
W.57th St.
E.57th St.
Roosevelt Island
50th St.
W.42nd St.
E.42nd St.
Queens-Midtown Tunnel
Lincoln Tunnel
11th Ave.
10th Ave.
9th Ave.
8th Ave.
Ave. of the Americas
5th Ave.
Park Ave.
3rd Ave.
W.34th St.
7th Ave.
Broadway
Madison Ave.
E.23rd St.
2nd Ave.
1st Ave.
W.14th St.
E.14th St.
Avenue B
Avenue C
West Side Hwy.
E. Houston St.
W. Houston St.
Williamsburg Bridge
Delancey St.
Canal St.
Holland Tunnel
Manhattan Bridge
Chambers St.
Brooklyn Bridge
West St.
W. Broadway
Hudson River
East River
QUEENS
BROOKLYN
NEW JERSEY

BEST BETS FOR NEW YORK CITY DINING

With thousands of restaurants to choose from, how will you decide where to eat? Fodor's writers and editors have selected their favorite restaurants by price, cuisine, and experience in the Best Bets lists below.

Fodor's Choice ★

A Voce, $$$, p. 291
Aldea, $$$, p. 292
Babbo Ristorante, $$$, p. 278
Back Forty West, $$, p. 262
Bar Boulud, $$$, p. 316
The Breslin Bar and Dining Room, $$$, p. 292
Burger Joint, $, p. 306
Candle 79, $$, p. 313
The City Bakery, $, p. 293
Clinton St. Baking Co., $$, p. 273
Daniel, $$$$, p. 314
Danji, $$$, p. 306
Eleven Madison Park, $$$$, p. 294
Empellon Taqueria, $$$, p. 284
Emporio, $$, p. 258
Fatty Crab, $$, p. 284
Freeman's $$, p. 274
Gotham Bar & Grill, $$$$, p. 297
Hundred Acres, $$$, p. 263
I Sodi, $$$, p. 285
Katz's Delicatessen, $, p. 275
Le Bernardin, $$$$, p. 308
M. Wells Dinette, $$, p. 331
Marea, $$$$, p. 319
Momofuku Ko, $$$$, p. 270
Momofuku Noodle Bar, $$, p. 270
The NoMad, $$$$, p. 295
North End Grill, $$$, p. 254
Northern Spy Food Co., $$, p. 271
Osteria Morini, $$, p. 264
Per Se, $$$$, p. 320
Peter Luger, $$$$, p. 329
Reynards, $$$, p. 329
Saxon & Parole, $$$, p. 272
Shake Shack, $, p. 295
Tía Pol, $$, p. 289
Torrisi Italian Specialties, $$$, p. 261
Zabb Elee, $, p. 273

Best by Price

$

Bubby's, p. 253
Burger Joint, p. 306
Cascabel Taqueria, p. 313
City Bakery, p. 293
Gray's Papaya, p. 280
'inoteca, p. 274
Katz's Delicatessen, p. 275
Legend, p. 288
Mexicana Mama, p. 285
Mile End, p. 259
Shake Shack, p. 295

$$

Arturo's, p. 278
Candle 79, p. 313
Emporio, p. 258
Fatty Crab, p. 284
Mission Chinese Food, p. 276
Momofuku Noodle Bar, p. 270
Northern Spy Food Co., p. 271
Osteria Morini, p. 264
Tía Pol, p. 289

$$$

A Voce, p. 291
ABC Kitchen, p. 292
Babbo, p. 278
Balthazar, p. 262
Bar Boulud, p. 316
Craft, p. 293
Minetta Tavern, p. 281
The Modern and Bar Room, p. 310
The NoMad, p. 295
The Standard Grill, p. 291

$$$$

Eleven Madison Park, p. 294
Jean Georges, p. 318
Le Bernardin, p. 308
Marea, p. 319
Per Se, p. 320

Best by Cuisine

AMERICAN

ABC Kitchen, p. 292
Back Forty West, p. 262
Cookshop, p. 287
Gramercy Tavern, p. 294
Hundred Acres, p. 263
Northern Spy Food Co., p. 271
Park Avenue Seasonal, p. 315
Per Se, p. 320

CHINESE

Grand Sichuan, p. 268
Great New York Noodletown, p. 255
Joe's Shanghai, p. 256
Legend, p. 288
Mission Chinese Food, p. 276
Shun Lee Palace, p. 302
Tasty Hand-Pulled Noodles, p. 257

Best by Experience

NEW YORK FOOD TRENDS

A handful of foods are associated with New York City: apples (obviously), pizza, pastrami, hot dogs, bagels—the list of earthly delights is long and delicious. As with anything else, though, some food trends stick around around, while some vanish like, well, a flash in the pan. Some hibernate and return. These are some of the foodie things we've been talking about.

FOOD TRUCKS

The food-truck movement is officially on. It seems there's a special truck for everything from ethnic eats to fresh-baked sweets. The southern end of Washington Square, for example, near NYU, is a prime location, with trucks lined up serving the cuisines of Holland, Colombia, Cambodia, and Mexico, but you can find food trucks parked all over town, some with legendary followings and Twitter feeds to help you find them. Thompson Hotels, which has four properties in New York, even has a Food Truck Concierge.

PIZZA

There are few things more Big Apple than a slice of pizza, its bottom crust crispy from the coal oven. There are take-out joints for slices, and sit-down restaurants that only serve whole pies; some are thin-crust, some are thick, some even have fried dough. And everyone has a favorite. There's no question that pizza will always be synonymous with New York, but pizza crust is something that's being elevated to a real art form these days.

SOUL FOOD IN HARLEM

Sylvia Woods, the "Queen of Soul Food" and proprietor of the eponymous Harlem restaurant, may have ascended to that great soul food restaurant in the sky, but the cuisine lives on in this historic African American neighborhood—in fact, more now than ever, since celeb-chef Marcus Samuelsson moved into the area, opening the Red Rooster, a global eatery that gives a big nod to soul food.

CHINESE FOOD

There's Chinese food and then there's New York's downtown Chinatown Chinese food, which some visitors might find head-scratchingly unfamiliar. That's because Chinatown boasts a diverse population from China's many regions, which means menus are going to look deliciously foreign to the uninitiated. Go ahead, point and order something you've never heard of.

BURGERS

Hamburgers will forever be a part of the Big Apple dining landscape. But it so happens that it's never been a better time to be a burger eater, and nearly every restaurant—American or not—has some kind of burger on its menu. If you're a discriminating burger lover, look for the name Pat LaFrieda, a meat purveyor par excellence. Just don't expect to save any money; it's not unusual to see a $20 hamburger on a menu.

GASTROPUBS

The gastropub phenomenon, imported from London, began with the Spotted Pig in the West Village, and within a few years, every neighborhood had one. And why not? Blending a casual pub atmosphere with way-better-than-average pub grub is a fun and tasty combination that's hard to beat.

BANH MI SANDWICHES

The banh mi sandwich has grabbed the attention of Big Apple eaters and not let go in recent years. This French-influenced Vietnamese sandwich consists of pork, pâté, carrots, cilantro, and jalapeño peppers stuffed into a baguette. This is a delicacy worth seeking out, so check the menus at our top Asian restaurant picks.

LOCAVORE

The focus on local food and beverages took has definitely taken hold at NYC restaurants. Menus flaunt the nearby provenance of their meat and produce, whether it's from upstate New York or from the restaurant's rooftop garden. Wine lists frequently feature excellent Long Island wines, as well as bourbon and other spirits brewed as close as the Brooklyn Navy Yards or in the Hudson Valley.

Left: Lunch at the Spotted Pig, the gastropub that started it all. *Top right*: Thin crust pizza. *Bottom right*: Jewel-like dim sum.

PLANNING

CHILDREN

Though it's unusual to see children in the dining rooms of Manhattan's most elite restaurants, dining with youngsters in New York does not have to mean culinary exile. Many of the restaurants reviewed in this chapter are excellent choices for families, and are marked as such.

RESERVATIONS

It's always a good idea to plan ahead. Some renowned restaurants are booked weeks or even months in advance. If that's the case, you can get lucky at the last minute if you're flexible—and friendly. Most restaurants keep a few tables open for walk-ins and VIPs. Show up for dinner early (5:30) or late (after 10), and politely inquire about any last-minute vacancies or cancellations. Occasionally, an eatery may take your credit-card number and ask you to call the day before your scheduled meal to reconfirm: don't forget or you could lose out, or possibly be charged for your oversight.

WHAT TO WEAR

New Yorkers like to dress up, and so should you. Whatever your style, dial it up a notch. Have some fun while you're at it. Pull out the clothes you've been saving for a special occasion and get glamorous. Unfair as it is, the way you look can influence how you're treated—and where you're seated. Generally speaking, jeans and a button-down shirt will suffice at most table-service restaurants in the $ to $$ range. In reviews, we note dress only when a jacket or jacket and tie are required. If you have doubts, call the restaurant and ask.

TIPPING AND TAXES

In most restaurants, tip the waiter 15%–20%. (To figure out a 20% tip quickly, just move the decimal point one place to the left on your total and double that amount.) Bills for parties of six or more sometimes include the tip. Tip at least $1 per drink at the bar, and $1 for each coat checked. Never tip the maître d' unless you're out to impress your guests or expect to pay another visit soon.

SMOKING

Smoking is prohibited in all enclosed public spaces in New York City, including restaurants and bars.

HOURS

New Yorkers seem ready to eat at any hour. Many restaurants stay open between lunch and dinner, some offer late-night seating, and still others serve around the clock. Restaurants that serve breakfast often do so until noon or later. Restaurants in the East Village, the Lower East Side, SoHo, TriBeCa, and Greenwich Village are likely to remain open late, whereas Midtown spots and those in the Theater and Financial districts and uptown generally close earlier. Unless otherwise noted, the restaurants listed in this guide are open daily for lunch and dinner.

PRICES

Be sure to ask the price of the daily specials recited by the waiter. The charge for specials at some restaurants is noticeably out of line with the other prices on the menu. Beware of the $10 bottle of water; ask for tap water instead. And always review your bill.

If you eat early or late, you may be able to take advantage of a prix-fixe deal not offered at peak hours. Most upscale restaurants offer great lunch deals.

Credit cards are widely accepted, but many restaurants (particularly smaller ones downtown) accept only cash. If you plan to use a credit card, it's a good idea to confirm that it is acceptable when making reservations or before sitting down to eat.

Prices in the reviews are the average cost of a main course at dinner or, if dinner is not served, at lunch.

CHECK BEFORE YOU GO

The nature of the restaurant industry means that places open and close in a New York minute. It's always a good idea to phone ahead and make sure your restaurant is still turning tables.

RESTAURANT REVIEWS

Listed alphabetically within neighborhoods. Use the coordinate (⊕ 1:B2) at the end of each listing to locate a property on the corresponding map at the end of the chapter.

LOWER MANHATTAN

FINANCIAL DISTRICT

Post-9/11 development and attractive pricing have meant thousands of new residents in Lower Manhattan, fueling an up-and-coming—yet still slow-moving—neighborhood scene. The most visible changes? Restaurants in and around the Financial District no longer adhere to banker's hours, and formal dining rooms have been outnumbered by casual cafés and wine bars. On the pedestrian-only Stone Street, throngs of young professionals gather for after-work drinks and dinner at nearby bistros, oyster bars, and steakhouses.

$$ ITALIAN FAMILY

✕ **Adrienne's Pizza Bar.** They don't do slices, but this local lunch favorite on restaurant-packed Stone Street is the place for salads and shareables like the broccoli-rabe-and-sausage pie. ⓢ *Average main: $17* ✉ *54 Stone St., near Hanover Sq., Financial District* ☎ *212/248–3838* 🌐 *www.adriennespizzabar.com* Ⓜ *2, 3 to Wall St.; 1, R to South Ferry–Whitehall St.* ⊕ *1:E4.*

$$$$ STEAKHOUSE

✕ **Delmonico's.** The oldest continually operating restaurant in New York City (it opened in 1837), austere Delmonico's is steeped in cultural, political, and culinary history. Lobster Newburg and Baked Alaska were invented here—and are still served. Inside the stately mahogany-panel dining room, tuck into the classic Delmonico's steak, a 20-ounce boneless rib eye smothered with frizzled onions, and don't forget to order creamed spinach on the side. The cheesy spaetzle with pancetta is also sinfully sublime. The dining room gets busy early with an after-work Wall Street crowd, making reservations essential. *Average main: $37* *56 Beaver St., at William St., Financial District* *212/509–1144* *www.delmonicosny.com* *Reservations essential* *Closed Sun. No lunch Sat.* *2, 3 to Wall St.; R to South Ferry–Whitehall St.; 4, 5 to Bowling Green* *1:D4.*

$ CAFÉ **Financier Patisserie.** On the cobblestone pedestrian street that has become the Financial District's restaurant row, this charming patisserie serves excellent pastries and delicious savory foods, like mushroom bisque, salads, and hot or cold sandwiches (we have cravings for the panini pressed with prosciutto, fig jam, mascarpone, and arugula). After lunch, relax with a cappuccino and a *financier* (almond tea cake), or an elegant pastry. In warm weather, perch at an outdoor table and watch Manhattanites buzz by. There are locations all over town. *Average main: $7* *62 Stone St., between Mill La. and Hanover Sq., Financial District* *212/344–5600* *www.financierpastries.com* *Reservations not accepted* *Closed Sun.* *2, 3 to Wall St.; 4, 5 to Bowling Green.* *1:E4*

$$$ STEAKHOUSE **Harry's Café and Steak.** Its noise-dampening acoustics and maze of underground nooks combine to make Harry's Steak—the fine-dining half of the restaurant (Harry's Café is more casual, but the menu is the same)—one of the city's most intimate steakhouses. Settle in to one of the leather booths and start with a classic shrimp cocktail or the tomato trio, starring thick beefsteak slices topped with bacon and blue cheese, mozzarella and basil, and shaved onion with ranch dressing. The star attraction—prime aged porterhouse for two—is nicely encrusted with sea salt and a good match for buttery mashed potatoes infused with sweet roasted shallots and thick steak sauce spooned from Mason jars. Weekend brunch is popular, too. *Average main: $35* *1 Hanover Sq., between Stone and Pearl Sts., Financial District* *212/785–9200* *www.harrysnyc.com* *Reservations essential* *Closed Sun.* *4, 5 to Bowling Green; 2, 3 to Wall St.* *1:E4*

$ AMERICAN **Ulysses'.** Nestled alongside skyscrapers and the towering New York Stock Exchange, Stone Street is a two-block restaurant oasis that feels more like a village than the center of the financial universe. After the market closes, Wall Streeters head to Ulysses', a popular pub with 17 beers on tap and more than 50 bottled beers. *Average main: $9* *95 Pearl St., near Hanover Sq., Financial District* *212/482–0400* *www.ulyssesfolkhouse.com* *1:E4.*

TRIBECA

TriBeCa still holds an air of exclusivity, though glamorous dining rooms in converted warehouses have been joined by more casual spots with later hours. This is a great neighborhood to stop for a meal on your way to Lower Manhattan's many attractions.

$$$ AUSTRIAN FAMILY **Blaue Gans.** Chef Kurt Gutenbruner, one of the most lauded Austrian chefs in New York, runs this sprawling brasserie like an all-day clubhouse. Pop in for a late morning or early afternoon snack—the coffee comes topped with schlag, the donuts filled with apricot jam. Or swing by in the evening for sausage, schnitzel, and beer at the bar. *Average main: $25* *139 Duane St., near W. Broadway, TriBeCa*

PRICES

Be sure to ask the price of the daily specials recited by the waiter. The charge for specials at some restaurants is noticeably out of line with the other prices on the menu. Beware of the $10 bottle of water; ask for tap water instead. And always review your bill.

If you eat early or late, you may be able to take advantage of a prix-fixe deal not offered at peak hours. Most upscale restaurants offer great lunch deals.

Credit cards are widely accepted, but many restaurants (particularly smaller ones downtown) accept only cash. If you plan to use a credit card, it's a good idea to confirm that it is acceptable when making reservations or before sitting down to eat.

Prices in the reviews are the average cost of a main course at dinner or, if dinner is not served, at lunch.

CHECK BEFORE YOU GO

The nature of the restaurant industry means that places open and close in a New York minute. It's always a good idea to phone ahead and make sure your restaurant is still turning tables.

RESTAURANT REVIEWS

Listed alphabetically within neighborhoods. Use the coordinate (⊕ 1:B2) at the end of each listing to locate a property on the corresponding map at the end of the chapter.

LOWER MANHATTAN

FINANCIAL DISTRICT

Post-9/11 development and attractive pricing have meant thousands of new residents in Lower Manhattan, fueling an up-and-coming—yet still slow-moving—neighborhood scene. The most visible changes? Restaurants in and around the Financial District no longer adhere to banker's hours, and formal dining rooms have been outnumbered by casual cafés and wine bars. On the pedestrian-only Stone Street, throngs of young professionals gather for after-work drinks and dinner at nearby bistros, oyster bars, and steakhouses.

$$ ITALIAN FAMILY

✕ **Adrienne's Pizza Bar.** They don't do slices, but this local lunch favorite on restaurant-packed Stone Street is the place for salads and shareables like the broccoli-rabe-and-sausage pie. $ *Average main: $17* ✉ *54 Stone St., near Hanover Sq., Financial District* ☎ *212/248–3838* 🌐 *www.adriennespizzabar.com* Ⓜ *2, 3 to Wall St.; 1, R to South Ferry–Whitehall St.* ⊕ *1:E4.*

$$$$ STEAKHOUSE

✕ **Delmonico's.** The oldest continually operating restaurant in New York City (it opened in 1837), austere Delmonico's is steeped in cultural, political, and culinary history. Lobster Newburg and Baked Alaska were invented here—and are still served. Inside the stately mahogany-panel dining room, tuck into the classic Delmonico's steak, a 20-ounce boneless rib eye smothered with frizzled onions, and don't forget to order creamed spinach on the side. The cheesy spaetzle with pancetta is also sinfully sublime. The dining room gets busy early with an after-work Wall Street crowd, making reservations essential. *Average main: $37* *56 Beaver St., at William St., Financial District* *212/509–1144* *www.delmonicosny.com* *Reservations essential* *Closed Sun. No lunch Sat.* *2, 3 to Wall St.; R to South Ferry–Whitehall St.; 4, 5 to Bowling Green* *1:D4.*

$ CAFÉ **Financier Patisserie.** On the cobblestone pedestrian street that has become the Financial District's restaurant row, this charming patisserie serves excellent pastries and delicious savory foods, like mushroom bisque, salads, and hot or cold sandwiches (we have cravings for the panini pressed with prosciutto, fig jam, mascarpone, and arugula). After lunch, relax with a cappuccino and a *financier* (almond tea cake), or an elegant pastry. In warm weather, perch at an outdoor table and watch Manhattanites buzz by. There are locations all over town. *Average main: $7* *62 Stone St., between Mill La. and Hanover Sq., Financial District* *212/344–5600* *www.financierpastries.com* *Reservations not accepted* *Closed Sun.* *2, 3 to Wall St.; 4, 5 to Bowling Green.* *1:E4*

$$$ STEAKHOUSE **Harry's Café and Steak.** Its noise-dampening acoustics and maze of underground nooks combine to make Harry's Steak—the fine-dining half of the restaurant (Harry's Café is more casual, but the menu is the same)—one of the city's most intimate steakhouses. Settle in to one of the leather booths and start with a classic shrimp cocktail or the tomato trio, starring thick beefsteak slices topped with bacon and blue cheese, mozzarella and basil, and shaved onion with ranch dressing. The star attraction—prime aged porterhouse for two—is nicely encrusted with sea salt and a good match for buttery mashed potatoes infused with sweet roasted shallots and thick steak sauce spooned from Mason jars. Weekend brunch is popular, too. *Average main: $35* *1 Hanover Sq., between Stone and Pearl Sts., Financial District* *212/785–9200* *www.harrysnyc.com* *Reservations essential* *Closed Sun.* *4, 5 to Bowling Green; 2, 3 to Wall St.* *1:E4*

$ AMERICAN **Ulysses'.** Nestled alongside skyscrapers and the towering New York Stock Exchange, Stone Street is a two-block restaurant oasis that feels more like a village than the center of the financial universe. After the market closes, Wall Streeters head to Ulysses', a popular pub with 17 beers on tap and more than 50 bottled beers. *Average main: $9* *95 Pearl St., near Hanover Sq., Financial District* *212/482–0400* *www.ulyssesfolkhouse.com* *1:E4.*

TRIBECA

TriBeCa still holds an air of exclusivity, though glamorous dining rooms in converted warehouses have been joined by more casual spots with later hours. This is a great neighborhood to stop for a meal on your way to Lower Manhattan's many attractions.

$$$ AUSTRIAN FAMILY **Blaue Gans.** Chef Kurt Gutenbruner, one of the most lauded Austrian chefs in New York, runs this sprawling brasserie like an all-day clubhouse. Pop in for a late morning or early afternoon snack—the coffee comes topped with schlag, the donuts filled with apricot jam. Or swing by in the evening for sausage, schnitzel, and beer at the bar. *Average main: $25* *139 Duane St., near W. Broadway, TriBeCa*

212/571–8880 www.kg-ny.com 1, 2, 3, A, C to Chambers St. 1:C1

$ AMERICAN FAMILY **Bubby's.** Neighborhood crowds clamoring for coffee and freshly squeezed juice line up for brunch at this TriBeCa mainstay, but Bubby's is good for lunch and dinner, too, if you're in the mood for comfort food like mac 'n cheese or fried chicken. The dining room is homey and comfortable, with big windows; in summer, patrons sit at tables outside with their dogs. Brunch options include just about everything, including homemade granola, sour-cream pancakes with bananas and strawberries, and huevos rancheros with guacamole and grits. *Average main: $17 120 Hudson St., at N. Moore St., TriBeCa 212/219–0666 www.bubbys.com 1 to Franklin St. 1:C1*

$$$ FRENCH **Capsouto Frères.** If you're looking for an elegant atmosphere, try Capsouto Frères, a landmark French bistro that makes classic Gallic fare, including the city's best sweet and savory soufflés. We especially love the rich hazelnut dessert soufflé. *Average main: $26 451 Washington St., near Watts St., TriBeCa 212/966–4900 www.capsoutofreres.com Reservations essential A, C, E, 1 to Canal St. 2:B5.*

$$$$ FRENCH **Corton.** Über-restaurateur Drew Neiporent transformed the former Montrachet space into a spare, elegant dining room, the perfect stage for whiz-kid chef Paul Liebrandt's understated, mildly experimental cuisine. The walls are decorated with subtle white trompe-l'oeil designs of cherry blossoms and birds, but the real adornment is on the plate, where Liebrandt transports diners with dishes like his "from the garden" composition: an assemblage of nearly 20 vegetable components that redefines what produce can do. Heirloom eggs are presented at the table in a basket, then spirited back to the kitchen for a slow poach before being served with trumpet mushrooms and serrano gelée. Desserts include chocolate tart with grapefruit and hazelnuts. The well-curated wine list has a cost-conscious selection of "country French" bottles. *Average main: $90 239 W. Broadway, between Walker and White Sts., TriBeCa 212/219–2777 www.cortonnyc.com Reservations essential Closed Sun. No lunch 1 to Franklin St.; A, C, E to Canal St. 2:D5*

$$$ AMERICAN **The Harrison.** It's been more than a decade since Jimmy Bradley opened the Harrison, following his success with the Red Cat in Chelsea, but it's still a quintessential neighborhood eatery. The warm, woody room serves as a relaxed backdrop for the seasonal American food, like English-cut lamb loin with baby carrots and fennel, and malt-vinegar mayo. Desserts, including an ice cream–brownie sandwich with Sazerac caramel, are at once accessible and sophisticated. *Average main: $27 355 Greenwich St., at Harrison St., TriBeCa 212/274–9310 www.theharrison.com Reservations essential No lunch weeekends 1 to Franklin St. 2:C6*

$ AMERICAN FAMILY **Kitchenette.** This small, comfy restaurant lives up to its name with tables so close together, you're likely to make new friends. Indeed, the dining room pretty much feels like a breakfast nook, and the food tastes like your mom made it—provided she's a great cook. There are no frills, just solid cooking, friendly service, and a long line at peak times. At brunch don't miss the peach pancakes or the baked cinnamon-swirl

16

French toast. $ *Average main: $15* ✉ *156 Chambers St., near Greenwich St., TriBeCa* ☎ *212/267–6740* 🌐 *www.kitchenetterestaurant.com* Ⓜ *1, 2, 3, A, C to Chambers St.* ✢ *1:C2*

$$ ITALIAN ✕ **Locanda Verde.** Chef Andrew Carmellini, an acolyte of Daniel Boulud, has definitely made a name for himself in New York City with this Robert De Niro–backed restaurant, and then with the Dutch in SoHo. The space at Locanda Verde is warm and welcoming, with accents of brick and wood and large windows that open to the street, weather permitting, while the menu is full of inspired Italian comfort food that hits the mark. Standouts include small plates like blue crab crostino with jalapeños and the pumpkin agnolotti in brown sage butter that diners reminisce about. Several draft beers, along with more than a dozen wines by the glass, make an already hopping bar scene even more of a draw. $ *Average main: $26* ✉ *377 Greenwich St., at N. Moore St., TriBeCa* ☎ *212/925–3797* 🌐 *www.locandaverdenyc.com* ✍ *Reservations essential* Ⓜ *1 to Franklin St.* ✢ *1:B1*

$$$ AMERICAN ✕ **Marc Forgione.** Chef Marc Forgione has restaurant success in his blood (his father was one of the New York food scene megastars with his 1980s restaurant, An American Place) but he more than holds his own at this neighborhood restaurant that continues to attract crowds for the ambitious, creative New American cuisine. The menu changes frequently but whatever you order will be bold, flavorful, and inventive without a hint of preciousness. The bar scene hops with a sceney blend of neighborhood locals and Wall Street boys loosening their ties after work. Meat dishes are excellent and well-prepared but Forgione has a special way with seafood. His chili lobster appetizer, a take on a dish you'll find all over Asia, comes with Texas toast for mopping up the spicy, buttery sauce. Tartare (perhaps kingfish, hamachi, or salmon, depending on the day) is accented with avocado in a pool of sweet, soy-lashed sauce, accompanied by housemade chips. $ *Average main: $30* ✉ *134 Reade St., between Hudson and Greenwich Sts., TriBeCa* ☎ *212/941–9401* 🌐 *www.marcforgione.com* ✍ *Reservations essential* ⏲ *No lunch* Ⓜ *1, 2, 3 to Chambers St.* ✢ *1:C1*

$$$ JAPANESE ✕ **Nobu.** At this large, bustling TriBeCa dining room (or its sister location uptown), you might just spot a celeb or two. New York's famed Japanese restaurant has gained a lot of competition in recent years, but this is still the destination for the innovative Japanese cuisine Nobu Matsuhisa made famous (though he's rarely in attendance these days). Dishes like fresh yellowtail sashimi with jalapeño, rock shrimp tempura, or miso-marinated Chilean sea bass continue to draw huge crowds. Put yourself in the hands of the chef by ordering the tasting menu, the *omakase,* and specify how much you want to spend, then let the kitchen do the rest. Can't get reservations? Try your luck at the first-come, first-served **Nobu Next Door** (literally next door), with a similar menu plus a sushi bar. $ *Average main: $35* ✉ *105 Hudson St., at Franklin St., TriBeCa* ☎ *212/219–0500* 🌐 *www.myriadrestaurantgroup.com* ✍ *Reservations essential* ⏲ *No lunch weekends* Ⓜ *1 to Franklin St.* ✢ *1:B1*

$$$ SEAFOOD Fodor's Choice ★ ✕ **North End Grill.** The movers and shakers who frequent this handsome, seafood-heavy restaurant in the Financial District are in good hands. Floyd Cardoz, who made a name for himself at the now-shuttered elevated Indian eatery, Tabla, mans the stoves, churning out inspired fare

like memorable grilled octopus, pumpkin soup bobbing with crab, and succulent whole fish (for two). Carnivores can dig into a juicy Berkshire pork chop, lamb loin topped with a minty chickpea puree, or the whopping 16-ounce rib eye. Save some stomach space for a sweet ending: the sticky toffee pudding with vanilla bourbon ice cream is sublime. *Average main: $26 ✉ 104 North End Ave., at Murray St., Financial District ☎ 646/747–1600 www.northendgrillnyc.com* Ⓜ *1, 2, 3 to Chambers St.; E to World Trade Center ⊕ 1:B2.*

$$$ FRENCH FAMILY **Odeon.** New Yorkers change hangouts faster than they can press speed-dial, but this spot has managed to maintain its quality and flair for more than 30 years. The neo–art deco room is still packed nightly with revelers, and the pleasant service and well-chosen wine list are always in style. The bistro-menu highlights include *frisée aux lardons* (bacon-enhanced frisee salad) with poached farm egg, grilled NY strip steak, and slow-cooked cod with baby leeks and fennel confit. *Average main: $28 ✉ 145 West Broadway, between Duane and Thomas Sts., TriBeCa ☎ 212/233–0507 www.theodeonrestaurant.com* Ⓜ *1, 2, 3, A, C to Chambers St. ⊕ 1:C1*

SOHO, NOLITA, LITTLE ITALY, AND CHINATOWN

16

CHINATOWN

Chinatown beckons adventurous diners with restaurants representing numerous regional cuisines of China, including Cantonese-, Szechuan-, Hunan-, Fujian-, Shanghai-, and Hong Kong–style cooking. Malaysian and Vietnamese restaurants also have taken root here, and the neighborhood continues to grow rapidly, encroaching into what was Little Italy.

$ CHINESE **456 Shanghai Cuisine.** Come to this Chinatown eatery for above-average Chinese fare, such as General Tso's chicken, pork buns, and cold sesame noodles, but do yourself a favor and ask for an order of soup dumplings (*xiao long bao*) as soon as you sit down. You won't regret it. The dumplings, doughy and thin on the outside, encase morsels of crab swimming in a bold pork-y broth, and are truly a wonder of the culinary world—456 does them as well (or better) as anyone in the city. *Average main: $14 ✉ 69 Mott St., between Canal and Bayard Sts., Chinatown ☎ 212/964–0003* Ⓜ *6, J, N, Q, R, Z to Canal St. ⊕ 2:F5*

$ CHINESE FAMILY **Great New York Noodletown.** Although the soups and noodles are unbeatable at this no-frills restaurant, what you should really order are the window decorations—the hanging lacquered ducks and roasted pork, which are listed on a simple board hung on the wall and superb served with pungent garlic-and-ginger sauce on the side. Seasonal specialties like duck with flowering chives and salt-baked soft-shell crabs are excellent. So is the *congee*, or rice porridge, available with any number of garnishes. Solo diners may end up at a communal table. Noodletown is open late—till 4 am—on Friday and Saturday. *Average main: $10 ✉ 28 Bowery, at Bayard St., Chinatown ☎ 212/349–0923 No credit cards* Ⓜ *6, J, N, Q, R, Z to Canal St.; B, D to Grand St. ⊕ 2:G5*

$ CHINESE FAMILY **Jing Fong.** On weekend mornings people pack this vast dim sum palace so be prepared to wait. Once your number is called you'll take the escalator up to the carnivalesque third-floor dining room, where servers

Head to Chinatown for some authentic taste experiences.

push carts of steamed dumplings, barbecue pork buns, and shrimp balls. For adventurous eaters, there's chicken feet, tripe, and snails. Arrive early for the best selection, and save room for mango pudding. [$] *Average main: $14* ✉ *20 Elizabeth St., 2nd fl., between Bayard and Canal Sts., Chinatown* ☎ *212/964–5256* [M] *6, J, N, Q, R, Z to Canal St.* ✥ *2:F5*

$ CHINESE FAMILY

✕ **Joe's Shanghai.** Joe opened his first Shanghai restaurant in Queens in 1995 but, buoyed by the accolades accorded his steamed soup dumplings—filled with a rich, fragrant broth and ground pork or pork-crabmeat mixture—several Manhattan outposts soon followed. The trick is to take a bite of the dumpling and slurp out the soup, then eat the rest. There's almost always a wait, but the line moves fast. The soup dumplings are a must but you can fill out your order from the extensive menu. There's another Joe's Shanghai in Midtown West, at 24 W. 56th Street, between 5th and 6th avenues (where credit cards are accepted). [$] *Average main: $16* ✉ *9 Pell St., between Bowery and Mott St., Chinatown* ☎ *212/233–8888* 🌐 *www.joeshanghairestaurants.com* ▭ *No credit cards* [M] *6, J, N, Q, R, Z to Canal St.* ✥ *2:F5*

$ MALAYSIAN

✕ **New Malaysia.** This Malaysian restaurant is a real find. Literally. You could stroll right by it and never know it existed. That's because it's in a passageway between Bowery and Elizabeth Street. It's worth the trouble, though, as the menu is loaded with Malaysian favorites like roti flatbread with curry and delicious red-bean and coconut-milk drinks. The atmosphere is casual and table service is relaxed, which means you might need to flag down your server. [$] *Average main: $13* ✉ *48 Bowery, near Canal St., Chinatown* ☎ *212/964–0284* [M] *B, D to Grand St.; 6, J, N, Q, R to Canal St.* ✥ *2:G5.*

$$ CHINESE ✕ **Peking Duck House.** This Chinatown institution is the place to go in New York for authentic Peking duck. Although the restaurant offers a full Chinese menu, everyone—and we mean everyone—orders the duck. Begin, as most tables do, with an order of Shanghai soup dumplings, then move on to the bird. It's carved tableside with plenty of fanfare—crisp burnished skin separated from moist flesh. Roll up the duck, with hoisin and scallions, in tender steamed pancakes. The menu at the Midtown East location (✉ *236 E. 53rd St.*) is a bit pricier. $ *Average main: $18* ✉ *28 Mott St., at Mosco St., Chinatown* ☎ *212/227–1810* 🌐 *www.pekingduckhousenyc.com* Ⓜ *6, J, N, Q, R, Z to Canal St.* ✥ *2:F6*

$ CHINESE ✕ **Tasty Hand-Pulled Noodles.** The name says it all. And it doesn't lie. The open kitchen at this salt-of-the-earth Chinatown restaurant (located on the charming Doyers Street), means you can watch the noodle slinger in action while awaiting your bowl of, um, tasty hand-pulled noodles. Just choose your ingredients—beef, pork, oxtail, eel, chicken, lamb, or shrimp, among others—and prepare to eat the most delicious bowl of $5 noodles since that last trip to Shanghai. $ *Average main: $5* ✉ *1 Doyers St., at Bowery, Chinatown* ☎ *212/791–1817* 🌐 *www.tastyhandpullednoodles.com* ▭ *No credit cards* Ⓜ *6, J, N, Q, R, Z to Canal St.* ✥ *2:G6*

$ CHINESE ✕ **Vanessa's Dumpling House.** One of the best deals in Chinatown can be found at Vanessa's Dumpling House: sizzling pork-and-chive dumplings are four for a buck. The restaurant is very casual: order at the counter and then grab a seat at a table, if you can find one. $ *Average main: $8* ✉ *118 Eldridge St., near Broome St., Chinatown* ☎ *212/625–8008* ✍ *Reservations not accepted* ▭ *No credit cards* Ⓜ *B, D to Grand St.* ✥ *2:G4.*

$ VIETNAMESE ✕ **Xe Lua.** A good Vietnamese restaurant in Manhattan is hard to find, which is why you should seek out Xe Lua, in Chinatown just below Little Italy. Quick service and the marathon-length menu should satisfy any palate but the real standouts are the clay pot dishes: cooked and served in—you guessed it—a clay pot, the pork, chicken, veggies, or whatever you order become slightly caramelized, giving a subtle sweetness to the dish. The *pho* (the soupy national dish of Vietnam) is also a good bet, as the broth seems to have a bolder taste here than at other places. $ *Average main: $11* ✉ *86 Mulberry St., between Canal and Bayard Sts., Chinatown* ☎ *212/577–8887* Ⓜ *B, D to Grand St.* ✥ *2:F5.*

$ CHINESE ✕ **Xi'an Famous Foods.** Serving the very unrepresented cuisine of far western China, Xi'an Famous Foods serves Chinese food like you might not have tasted before. The restaurant first made a name for itself at its original location, in the dingy basement food court of a mall in Flushing, Queens, but this spot—shinier, brighter, and cleaner—offers the same exciting fare. First-timers should try the spicy cumin lamb burger, which is mouth-wateringly delicious. Some of the dishes challenge the bounds of adventurousness in eating (lamb offal soup, anyone?) but don't let that scare you off. It's cheap enough to experiment, so tuck into that bowl of oxtail noodle soup and enjoy. $ *Average main: $10* ✉ *67 Bayard St., Chinatown* ☎ *212/608–4170* Ⓜ *B, D to Grand St.* ✥ *2:F5.*

LITTLE ITALY

Little Italy is, these days, a tourist trap of pasta factories that just aren't very good. Don't despair, though: there is seriously good Italian food to be found in just about every neighborhood in Manhattan . . . and Brooklyn, too, of course. Right nearby, in NoLIta, check out Torrisi's and Rubirosa for some of the best Italian around.

NOLITA

In NoLIta, SoHo's trendy next-door neighborhood of indie boutiques and restaurants, the spirit of old SoHo prevails. Modest eateries are squeezed between boutiques featuring products from up-and-coming designers.

$ FRENCH **Café Gitane.** Specializing in simple salads, sandwiches, and a selection of hot mains, this French-Moroccan café draws models and model-gazers to its rather cramped NoLIta location (which is cash only). The clientele and the waitstaff seem to have wandered in fresh off the runway. The scene is quietest in the morning, when there are flaky croissants and big bowls of café au lait. There's a larger branch on the far edge of the West Village. *$ Average main: $14 ✉ 242 Mott St., near Prince St., NoLIta ☎ 212/334–9552 🌐 www.cafegitanenyc.com Reservations not accepted ▭ No credit cards Ⓜ 6 to Spring St., N, R, to Prince St. $ Average main: $14 ✉ Jane Hotel, 113 Jane St., near West St., West Village ☎ 212/334–9552 Ⓜ A, C, E, L to 14th St.–8th Ave. ✣ 2:F3*

$ ECLECTIC FAMILY **Café Habana.** The Mexican-style grilled corn, liberally sprinkled with chili powder, lime, and cotija cheese is undoubtedly worth getting your hands dirty at this crowded hip luncheonette. Follow up with a classic Cuban sandwich (roast pork, ham, Swiss cheese, pickles, and chipotle mayo), fish tacos, or one of the innovative salads. Be prepared for a wait at lunchtime or on weekend afternoons. The cocktails are good, too. There's a take-out shop around the corner at 229 Elizabeth, with a few seats, too. *$ Average main: $12 ✉ 17 Prince St., at Elizabeth St., NoLIta ☎ 212/625–2001 🌐 www.cafehabana.com Reservations not accepted Ⓜ 6 to Spring St., N, R, to Prince St. ✣ 2:F3.*

$$ ITALIAN Fodor's Choice ★ **Emporio.** In a neighborhood where the long, boutique-lined blocks can feel deserted after dark, Roman-accented Emporio is a chic, welcoming hangout with warmth to spare. The brick-lined front room is a gathering spot for happy hour at the bar, where you'll find an appetizing selection of free small bites like frittata, white-bean salad, and ham-and-spinach *tramezzini* (finger sandwiches). The centerpiece of the large, skylighted back room is a wood-fired oven that turns out crisp, thin-crusted pizzas topped with quality ingredients like prosciutto and buffalo mozzarella. Service is solicitous but not speedy, so you can linger over a bottle of wine from the copious selection. House-made pastas like garganelli with pork sausage and house-made ragù, and entrées like whole roasted fish with grilled lemon, are also excellent. *$ Average main: $18 ✉ 231 Mott St., between Prince and Spring Sts., NoLIta ☎ 212/966–1234 🌐 www.auroraristorante.com Ⓜ A, B, C, D, E, F, M to W. 4th St.–Washington Sq., 6 to Bleecker St. ✣ 2:F4*

$$ MEXICAN **La Esquina.** Anchoring a downtown corner under a bright neon sign, La Esquina looks like nothing more than a fast-food taqueria, with cheap tacos sold to-go until 2 in the morning. Just around the corner,

though, is a modestly priced café serving those same tacos along with more ambitious fare like *chiles rellenos* (stuffed peppers) and *carne asada* (grilled meat). The real hipster draw, however, is hidden from sight: the basement brasserie, like a Mexican speakeasy, is accessible by reservation only, through an unmarked door just inside the ground-floor taqueria. Once inside, you'll discover a buzzy subterranean scene with pretty people drinking potent margaritas, dining on upscale Mexican fare. Prices downstairs are high, but portions are large. $ *Average main: $18 ✉ 106 Kenmare, between Cleveland Pl. and Lafayette St., NoLIta ☎ 646/613–7100 🌐 www.esquinanyc.com* Ⓜ *6 to Spring St. ✥ 2:F4*

$ PIZZA FAMILY ✕ **Lombardi's Pizza.** Brick walls, red-and-white checkered tablecloths, and the aroma of thin-crust pies emerging from the coal oven set the mood for dining on some of the best pizza in Manhattan. Lombardi's has served pizza since 1905 (though not in the same location), and business doesn't seem to have died down a bit. The mozzarella is always fresh, resulting in an almost greaseless slice, and the toppings, such as meatballs, pancetta, or imported anchovies, are also top quality. The clam pizza, with freshly shucked clams, garlic oil, Pecorino Romano cheese, and parsley, is well known among aficionados. $ *Average main: $16 ✉ 32 Spring St., at Mott St., NoLIta ☎ 212/941–7994 🌐 www.firstpizza.com* ▭ *No credit cards* Ⓜ *6 to Spring St.; B, D, F, M to Broadway–Lafayette St. ✥ 2:F4*

$ DELI ✕ **Mile End.** Named for a neighborhood in Montréal where the city's famed bagel bakeries exist, Mile End became the darling of the city's fooderati when it opened in January 2010 in Brooklyn. By the time this NoHo location began rolling out its light, chewy, and slightly sweet Montréal bagels in May 2012, the place was already an institution. The bagels are authentic but the real reason to come here is for the impressive deli fare, including pastrami, roast beef, and smoked meat sandwiches. The poutine—french fries with cheese curds and gravy—is a delicious mess. The Manhattan location's narrow room is simply bedecked, consisting only of a long zig-zag communal table. Dinner is served at the original Brooklyn location in Boerum Hill, at 97A Hoyt Street. $ *Average main: $10 ✉ 53 Bond St., near Bowery, NoLIta ☎ 212/529–2990 🌐 www.mileenddeli.com ⏲ No dinner* Ⓜ *6 to Bleecker St. ✥ 2:F2*

$$$ ITALIAN ✕ **Peasant.** The crowd at this rustic restaurant is stylishly urban. Inspired by the proverbial "peasant" cuisine where meals were prepared in the kitchen hearth, chef-owner Frank DeCarlo cooks all of his wonderful food in a bank of wood- or charcoal-burning ovens, from which the heady aroma of garlic perfumes the room. Don't fill up on the crusty bread and fresh ricotta or you'll miss out on flavorful Italian fare like sizzling sardines that arrive in terra-cotta pots, or spit-roasted leg of lamb with bitter *trevisano* lettuce and polenta. $ *Average main: $25 ✉ 194 Elizabeth St., between Spring and Prince Sts., NoLIta ☎ 212/965–9511 🌐 www.peasantnyc.com ✍ Reservations essential ⏲ Closed Mon. No lunch* Ⓜ *6 to Spring St.; N, R to Prince St. ✥ 2:F3*

$$$ ECLECTIC ✕ **Public.** To start with, the space here is complex and sophisticated, with soaring ceilings and whitewashed brick walls, skylights, fireplaces, three dining areas, and a vast bar. You've come for the food, though,

16

You can order tasty tacos from La Esquina's counter-service taqueria, or squeeze into the small café around the corner for a sit-down meal.

and you won't be disappointed. The menu flaunts its nonconformity, and dishes like Australian barramundi fish, served with vanilla-celeriac puree and braised garlic greens, demonstrates a light yet adventurous touch. Brunch at Public is a local favorite, with exotic dishes like coconut pancakes topped with fresh ricotta, mango, and lime syrup, and a juicy venison burger. Standout desserts include a chocolate mousse with tahini ice cream and sesame candy. $ *Average main: $25* ✉ *210 Elizabeth St., between Prince and Spring Sts., NoLIta* ☎ *212/343–7011* 🌐 *www.public-nyc.com* ⏲ *No lunch weekdays* Ⓜ *6 to Spring St.; N, R to Prince St.; J, M to Bowery* ✧ *2:F3.*

$ AMERICAN ✕ **The Smile.** Subterranean and almost hidden, The Smile will turn your frown upside down if you like hipsters, celebrities, and, most especially, hipster celebrities. Lounge among the fashionably conscious clientele (who are trying oh so hard to not look that way) and munch on breakfast-y items (breakfast is served until 4:30 pm) like chunky granola, or go for one of the giant sandwiches or spaghetti with heirloom tomato sauce. Dinner options, like whole trout, brisket, hangar steak, or roasted chicken, are more ambitious. Just be sure you wear shoes that scream "this season." $ *Average main: $15* ✉ *26 Bond St., between Lafayette St. and Bowery, NoLIta* ☎ *646/329–5836* 🌐 *www.thesmilenyc.com* Ⓜ *B, D, F, M to Broadway–Lafayette St.; 6 to Astor Pl.* ✧ *2:F2*

$ MEXICAN FAMILY ✕ **Pinche Taqueria.** Offshoots of a popular Tijuana taco shop established in 1973 and still going strong, these slim taquerias (the word "pinche" can be translated as "tiny") do fish tacos the West Coast way, with lightly battered fish, crunchy cabbage, and a dollop of cilantro *crema*. The tacos *al pastor*—filled with succulent pork slow-roasted on a rotating spit—are of a similarly superior caliber, stuffed into warm, house-made corn tortillas and generously anointed with fresh guacamole. There's another location just around the corner at 227 Mott Street (near Prince); both these spots get busy at prime meal times. $ *Average main: $6 ✉ 333 Lafayette St., near Bleecker St., NoLIta ☎ 212/343–9977 🌐 www.pinchetaqueria.us ✍ Reservations not accepted Ⓜ B, D, F, M to Broadway–Lafayette St. ⊕ 2:E3*

$$ ITALIAN

✕ **Rubirosa.** Named for a jet-setting Dominican playboy, this Rubirosa is only Latin and lascivious in name. Owner Angelo "A. J." Pappalardo has created an exciting Italian-American eatery that locals have shown an insatiable appetite for (so be prepared to wait). The kitchen isn't trying to reinvent anything here, they simply serve high-quality classic Italian dishes: from pasta with red sauce or a fork-tender veal chop Milanese to the thin-crust pizza—the recipe for the latter comes from Mr. Pappalardo's parents who have run the popular Staten Island pizza joint, Joe & Pat's, since anyone can remember. You don't have to be a jet-setter or a playboy to love this place; just come hungry. $ *Average main: $17 ✉ 235 Mulberry St., between Prince and Spring Sts., NoLIta ☎ 212/965–0500 Ⓜ 6 to Spring St. ⊕ 2:F4*

$$$$ ITALIAN FAMILY Fodor's Choice ★

✕ **Torrisi Italian Specialties.** Italian-American cuisine is in style, and this hot spot is bringing locals back to Mulberry, a street otherwise flanked by mediocre, touristy Italian restaurants. Run by chefs Mario Carbone and Rich Torrisi (both of whom have logged time in the kitchens of some of the city's most lauded Italian eateries), this 25-seat restaurant isn't easy to get into, so reserve ahead. The $75 seven-course prix fixe is available at lunch (except Saturday) and dinner nightly; or, for a truly decadent experience, there's a nightly 20-course dinner (for $160). Either way, your feast might include Italian-American staples like devil's chicken, a crunchy pork chop, or spaghetti with clams. For a simpler meal, head next door to Torrisi spinoff Parm for great Italian-accented sandwiches, served at lunch and dinner. $ *Average main: $75 ✉ 250 Mulberry St., near Prince St., NoLIta ☎ 212/965–0955 🌐 www.torrisinyc.com ✍ Reservations essential ⏲ No lunch Mon.–Thurs. Ⓜ N, R to Prince St. ⊕ 2:F3*

SOHO

Longtime New Yorkers lament that SoHo has evolved from a red-hot art district into a big-brand outdoor mall. Shoppers engulf the neighborhood on weekends like angry bees, turning Lafayette Street into a buzzing hive of commerce. As a result, popular spots can be tough to get into during prime times.

$$$ SEAFOOD

✕ **Aquagrill.** A SoHo standard for fresh seafood, this lively neighborhood eatery also makes its own pastries and baked goods—including the bread for its brunchtime challah French toast with cinnamon apples and pecan butter. Fans rave about the lunchtime $23 prix-fixe Shucker Special—a half-dozen oysters with homemade soup or chowder and a salad. Dinner specialties include roasted Dungeness crab cake napoleon with sundried tomato oil, and falafel-crusted salmon. Desserts are excellent, too, especially the chocolate tasting plate with its molten chocolate cake, milk chocolate ice cream, and white chocolate mousse. Service is warm and welcoming. $ *Average main: $27 ✉ 210 Spring St., at 6th*

Ave., SoHo ☎ 212/274–0505 🌐 www.aquagrill.com ✍ Reservations essential Ⓜ *C, E to Spring St. ⊕ 2:D4*

$$ AMERICAN Fodor's Choice ★ ✕ **Back Forty West.** The SoHo spinoff of the popular East Village restaurant, Back Forty, where chef Peter Hoffman was doing sustainable farm-to-table fare long before it became a near-obligatory restaurant trend in the Big Apple, outdoes the original. Neighborhood denizens and shoppers flock here for well-executed comfort food. The menu changes with the season but expect dishes like coconut-milk-spiked scallop ceviche, pumpkin hummus, a very good grass-fed burger, and grilled trout from the Catskills, served alongside quality cocktails and a short but excellent list of beer and wine. Add in rustic, homey decor and you'll feel like you're hundreds of miles form that shopping mecca known as SoHo. $ *Average main: $17 ✉ 70 Prince St., at Crosby St., SoHo ☎ 212/219–8570 🌐 www.backfortynyc.com ⏲ No dinner Sun.* Ⓜ *B, D, F, M, to Broadway–Lafayette St. ⊕ 2:E3*

$ CAFÉ ✕ **Balthazar Bakery.** Follow the beguiling scent of fresh-baked bread to Balthazar Bakery, next door to Keith McNally's always-packed Balthazar restaurant. Choices include fresh baked baguettes and other varieties of French breads, as well as gourmet sandwiches, soups, and memorable pastries to take out (there is no seating). Try the berry noisette tart or coconut cake, or keep it simple with an eggy cannele or a buttery lemon or chocolate madeleine. $ *Average main: $23 ✉ 80 Spring St., near Crosby St., SoHo ☎ 212/965–1785 🌐 www.balthazarbakery.com ✍ Reservations not accepted ⏲ No dinner* Ⓜ *B, D, F, M, to Broadway–Lafayette St. ⊕ 2:E4.*

$$$ FRENCH ✕ **Balthazar.** Even with long waits and excruciating noise levels, most out-of-towners agree that it's worth making reservations to experience restaurateur Keith McNally's flagship, a painstakingly accurate reproduction of a Parisian brasserie with an insider New York feel. Like the decor, entrées re-create French classics: Gruyère-topped onion soup, steak frites, and icy tiers of crab, oysters, and other pristine shellfish. Brunch is still one of the toughest tables in town. The best strategy to experience this perennial fave is to go at off-hours, or on weekdays for breakfast, to miss the crush. $ *Average main: $28 ✉ 80 Spring St., between Broadway and Crosby St., SoHo ☎ 212/965–1414 🌐 www.balthazarny.com ✍ Reservations essential* Ⓜ *6 to Spring St.; N, R to Prince St.; B, D, F, M to Broadway–Lafayette St. ⊕ 2:E4*

$$$ MODERN AMERICAN ✕ **Blue Ribbon.** After 20 years, Blue Ribbon still has a reputation not just for top-notch seafood and eclectic menu items, but also as a serious late-night foodie hangout. Join the genial hubbub for midnight noshing, namely the beef marrow with oxtail marmalade and the renowned raw-bar platters. Trustafarians, literary types, chefs, designers—a good-looking gang—generally fill this dark box of a room until 4 am. The menu appears standard at first blush, but it's not. Try the duck club sandwich or the matzo ball soup; the latter is a heady brew filled with the sacrilegious combo of seafood and traditional Jewish dumplings. $ *Average main: $32 ✉ 97 Sullivan St., between Prince and Spring Sts., SoHo ☎ 212/274–0404 🌐 www.blueribbonrestaurants.com ✍ Reservations not accepted ⏲ No lunch* Ⓜ *C, E to Spring St.; N, R to Prince St. ⊕ 2:D4*

$$$ JAPANESE

Blue Ribbon Sushi. Sushi, like pizza, attracts plenty of opinionated fanatics, and Blue Ribbon Sushi gets consistent raves for their über-fresh sushi and sashimi. Stick to the excellent raw fish and specials here if you're a purist, or branch out and try one of the experimental rolls: the Blue Ribbon—lobster, *shiso* (Japanese basil), and black caviar—is popular. The dark, intimate nooks, minimalist design, and servers with downtown attitude attract a stylish crowd that doesn't mind waiting for a table or for chilled sake. As expected from the quality and the location, it's not cheap. *Average main: $24* *119 Sullivan St., between Prince and Spring Sts., SoHo* *212/343–0404* *www.blueribbonrestaurants.com* *Reservations not accepted* *C, E to Spring St.; N, R to Prince St.* *2:D3*

$$$ AMERICAN

The Dutch. Perpetually packed with the "see and be seen" crowd, chef Andrew Carmellini's homage to American cuisine is really an encapsulation of recent food and dining trends: there's an excellent burger (and at $17 it should be), a Kentucky-size bourbon collection behind the bar, greenmarket-driven comfort food dishes like fried chicken, and bacon paired with things you would have not likely seen a couple decades ago (in this case, scallops with bacon jam). And it all works well at this SoHo restaurant. So much so, you might consider returning for weekend brunch when the fried bologna sandwich or cornmeal flapjacks make appearances on the menu. *Average main: $25* *131 Sullivan St., at Prince St., SoHo* *212/677–6200* *Reservations essential* *C, E to Spring St.* *2:D3*

$$$ MODERN AMERICAN Fodor's Choice ★

Hundred Acres. Set on a quiet block of Greenwich Village, this rustic, farmhouse-slash-greenhouse is a lovely place to while away a long lunch or quiet dinner. The market-driven creative comfort food keeps the neighborhood patrons and out-of-towners-in-the-know coming back again and again. Mains run the gamut from fish to meat: think a luscious pork shank with polenta and rhubarb chutney; shrimp and grits; or a classic burger made from pasture-raised beef, topped with Vermont cheddar and served with fries and Vidalia onion mayonnaise. It's a cozy spot, though more relaxing at lunch. *Average main: $26* *38 MacDougal St., between Houston and Prince Sts., SoHo* *212/475–7500* *hundredacresnyc.com* *1 to Houston St.; C, E to Spring St.; N, R to Prince St.* *2:D3*

$$ BISTRO

Lucky Strike. Whether you're lucky enough to nab a table at this sceney SoHo bistro at 1 pm or 1 am, Lucky Strike always seems like the place to be. Bedecked in classic bistro trappings—copper hammered stools, mirrors with menu items scrawled on them—the restaurant would look just as perfect in the Bastille neighborhood of Paris as it does in this swanky part of the Big Apple. The kitchen offerings are a straightfoward affair: croque monsieur, grilled salmon, and salade Niçoise are old standbys, with a turkey burger thrown in to accommodate the *Americain* palate. *Average main: $16* *59 Grand St., between W. Broadway and Wooster St., SoHo* *212/941–0772* *1 to Canal St.* *2:D4*

$$$ SEAFOOD

Lure Fishbar. Decorated like the clubby interior of a sleek luxury liner, Lure's menu offers oceanic fare prepared in multiple culinary styles. From the sushi bar, you can feast on options like the Lure House

Roll—a shrimp tempura roll crowned with spicy tuna and Japanese tartar sauce—or you can opt for creative dishes from the kitchen, like steamed branzino with oyster mushrooms, scallions, and ponzu sauce, or Manila clams over pancetta-studded linguine. For an all-American treat, you can't go wrong with a classic lobster roll on brioche. The dark subterranean bar is a good spot for cocktails and a snack. Brunch is served on weekends. *Average main: $29 142 Mercer St., at Prince St., SoHo 212/431–7676 www.lurefishbar.com No lunch weekends 6 to Bleecker St.; B, D, F, M to Broadway–Lafayette St.; N, R to Prince St. 2:E3*

$ CAFÉ FAMILY **MarieBelle.** Practically invisible from the front of the chocolate emporium, the back entry to the Cacao Bar opens into a sweet, high-ceiling, 12-table hot-chocolate shop. Most people order the Aztec, European-style (that's 60% Colombian chocolate mixed with hot water—no cocoa powder here!). The first sip is startlingly rich but not too dense. American-style, made with milk, is sweeter. And not to worry if you're visiting in spring or summer: you can opt for Aztec iced chocolate—the warm-weather version of her decadent cacao elixir—or the house-made chocolate gelato. For more substantial snacking, choose a salad or sandwich from the dainty lunch menu. *Average main: $12 484 Broome St., between W. Broadway and Wooster St., SoHo 212/925–6999 www.mariebelle.com Reservations not accepted No dinner 6 to Spring St.; A, C, E to Canal St. 2:D4*

$$$ ASIAN FUSION **The Mercer Kitchen.** Part of Alsatian superchef Jean-Georges Vongerichten's culinary empire, the celebrity-laden front room of this SoHo spot in the Mercer Hotel is as much about scene as about cuisine—which isn't a bad thing. Dishes here look toward Asia (as is the proclivity of Mr. Vongerichten), using simple ingredients and pairings to create deliciousness for the taste buds. Think scallops with lentils and pancetta or crispy squid with black olive tartar sauce. It's all good enough to make you feign disinterest over the A-list celeb who just walked in. *Average main: $28 Mercer Hotel, 99 Prince St., at Mercer St., SoHo 212/966–5454 www.jean-georges.com 6 to Spring St.; N, R to Prince St. 2:E3*

$$ ITALIAN Fodor's Choice ★ **Osteria Morini.** Less formal than chef Michael White's other renowned Italian restaurants (like Marea in Midtown West), the atmosphere at Osteria Morini is lively and upbeat, with communal tables at the center and a rock-and-roll soundtrack. The food still steals the show, though. Start with a selection of cheeses and cured meats, then move on to hearty pastas—a lusty ragu Bolognese or garganelli with prosciutto and truffle butter, for example—and main courses like oven-baked polenta accompanied by either sausage or mushrooms. Waits can be long, so try to come early or late, or grab one of the few bar seats for an inventive cocktail or a glass of Italian wine. Brunch is served on the weekends. *Average main: $24 218 Lafayette St., between Spring and Broome Sts., SoHo 212/965–8777 www.osteriamorini.com Reservations essential No lunch weekends 6 to Spring St. 2:E4*

$$$ FRENCH **Raoul's.** One of the first trendy spots in SoHo, this arty French restaurant has yet to lose its touch, either in the kitchen or with the atmosphere. Expect a chic bar scene—especially late at night—filled with

polished PYTs, amazing photos on every piece of available wall space, and a lovely back room that you reach through the kitchen. The winding stairs to the upstairs dining room are narrow and a bit treacherous if you're wearing your highest heels. Food-wise, it's bistro-inspired, with oysters and salads to start, and pastas, fish, and meat options for mains. *Average main: $29 180 Prince St., between Sullivan and Thompson Sts., SoHo 212/966–3518 www.raouls.com No lunch* M *C, E to Spring St. 2:D3*

$$ GREEK **Snack.** This SoHo cubbyhole may look like just another drop-in café, but the food served inside will transport you to Greece. Typical mezes like tzakiki, taramosalata, hummus, and skordalia are several notches better than what you'd get elsewhere, but the menu options range beyond snacks: pop in at lunch for a braised-lamb sandwich or spinach pie, or linger in the evenings over votive-lighted tables and pastitsio or stuffed peppers. The light-filled West Village location, Snack Taverna, is somewhat roomier and also serves breakfast daily and brunch on weekends. *Average main: $19 105 Thompson St, near Prince St., SoHo 212/925–1040 www.snackny.com Reservations not accepted* M *C, E to Spring St. 2:D3*

16

$$ AMERICAN **Spring Street Natural.** When this SoHo spot first fired up its burners in 1973, restaurants emphasizing organic, whole, and natural ingredients were mostly limited to San Francisco and college towns. The dining landscape may have caught up, but Spring Street Natural is still going strong, powered by a loyal clientele who come here for healthy food that actually tastes good. Start with the creamy organic hummus (and warm pita bread) before moving on to pan-roasted free-range chicken (accompanied by sweet-potato-poblano-pepper gratin) or the pancetta-laced pumpkin ravioli. If you're too full for dessert, order a glass of organic wine, sit back and stare out the floor-to-ceiling windows, gawking at the occasional celebrity and the SoHo shoppers. *Average main: $18 62 Spring St., at Lafayette St., SoHo 212/966–0290* M *6 to Spring St. 2:E4*

EAST VILLAGE AND LOWER EAST SIDE

EAST VILLAGE

With luxury condos on Avenue C and the continued glamification of the formerly seedy Bowery, the East Village—once Manhattan's edgiest enclave—has become yet another high-rent neighborhood. But it still offers some of the best deals in the city, and the influx of flush new residents has steadily raised the bar on high-quality eats. There's something for every budget and craving, from yakitori parlors to midprice trattorias, as well as splurges like Momofuku Ko. St. Marks Place is the center of New York's downtown Little Tokyo, and 6th Street is its Indian row.

$ PIZZA FAMILY **Artichoke Pizza.** Grab a gargantuan slice at this popular take-out joint, or order whole pies in the small adjacent dining room. In the wee hours, lines often snake for the artichoke-spinach slice, which tastes like cheesy dip on crackers. Those in the know opt for the less greasy Margherita slice. *Average main: $4 328 E. 14th St., between 1st and 2nd Aves., East Village 212/228–2004 Reservations not accepted* M *L to 1st Ave. 3:H4.*

CLOSE UP

Restaurant Chains Worth a Taste

When you're on the go or don't have time for a leisurely meal, there are several very good chain restaurants and sandwich bars that have popped up around New York City. The ones listed below are usually reasonably priced and are the best in their category.

Le Pain Quotidien. Part bakery, part café, this Belgian chain with locations throughout the city serves fresh salads and sandwiches at lunch and is great for breakfast. You can grab a snack to go or stay and eat breakfast, lunch, or dinner with waiter service. There are more than 20 locations throughout Manhattan, including in Central Park. *www.lepainquotidien.com.*

Pret a Manger. This sandwich shop started in London in 1986 and opened their first American outpost in 2000. These days you can find them in various locations around NYC—there are several in Midtown, catering to the bustling lunch crowds. The sandwiches are excellent, and the salads are good too. *www.pret.com.*

'Wichcraft. Tom Colicchio may be best known these days as head judge of Bravo's *Top Chef*, but his fine dining restaurants Craft and Craftbar are also well-known around Manhattan and beyond. At 'wichcraft, the sandwich shop he started with several partners back in 2003, the creations have a deliciously distinctive chef's touch. *www.wichcraftnyc.com.*

$$ AMERICAN **Back Forty.** Pioneering chef Peter Hoffman, a longtime leader in promoting local, sustainable food, attracts a devoted crowd to this casual neighborhood restaurant, where the homey decor features a pastoral mural behind the bar and rusty farm tools on the walls. The simply prepared dinner selections include a perfect grilled trout, moist pan-roasted chicken, and a wide array of seasonal sides, perhaps including roasted Brussels sprouts with maple-cider vinegar. Wash it all down with a house cocktail like the excellent, bourbon-based "Back Forty." Don't miss the house-made doughnuts with seasonal glazes for dessert. Brunch is served on Saturday and there are frequent seasonal special events like crab-boil dinners in summer. Weather permitting, snag a table in the leafy garden out back. The new Back Forty West, on Prince Street, between Lafayette and Crosby, is garnering equally stellar reviews. *Average main: $19* *190 Ave. B, at 12th St., East Village* *212/388–1990* *www.backfortynyc.com* *No lunch Mon.–Sat.* *L to 1st Ave.* *3:H4*

$$ MOROCCAN **Cafe Mogador.** An East Village dining institution if there ever was one, Cafe Mogador is a frequent stop for locals and, for some, a hip place to be seen. Since 1983, the restaurant has been serving above-average Morrocan cuisine in a date-friendly candlelight atmosphere. Finish off that creamy hummus before the chicken tagine arrives, nurse that glass of Italian wine, and ponder the fact that most of the people around you were 3-feet tall when this family-run restaurant first fired up its couscous-cooking burners. *Average main: $14* *101 St. Marks Pl., near 2nd Ave., East Village* *212/677–2226* *www.cafemogador.com* *F to 2nd Ave.; L to 1st Ave.* *2:G1*

$ FAST FOOD FAMILY **Crif Dogs.** Gluttony reigns at Crif Dogs, where you can indulge in creative—and delicous—hot dog creations. Try the Chihuahua, bacon-wrapped and layered with avocado and sour cream. There are vegetarian dogs, too, for those who are into that kind of thing. The tater tots will banish all memories of the high school cafeteria. *Average main: $5 113 St. Marks Pl., at Ave. A, East Village 212/614–2728 www.crifdogs.com F to 2nd Ave.; L to 1st Ave. 3:H5.*

$$ FRENCH **DBGB Kitchen & Bar.** The downtown arm of Daniel Boulud's New York City restaurant fleet, DBGB forgoes the white tablecloths, formal service, and steep prices found at the famed chef's fancier digs, and instead pays homage to the grittier, younger feel of its Lower East Side location. (The name is a wink to the legendary rock club CBGB.) Lined with shelves of pots, plates, and pans (not to mention copperware donated by renowned chefs from around the world), the dining room gives way to a partially open kitchen where you can catch the chefs preparing Boulud's take on French- and German-inspired pub fare. The menu features 14 different varieties of sausages (the *tunisienne,* a spicy lamb-and-mint merguez, is a particular standout), decadent burgers (the aptly named "piggy" burger—a juicy beef patty topped with a generous portion of pulled pork, jalapeño mayonnaise, and mustard-vinegar slaw on a cheddar bun—is not for the weak-willed), and classic entrées like steak frites and lemon-and-rosemary roasted chicken. The $27 three-course, prix-fixe lunch is quite a steal. *Average main: $23 299 Bowery, between Houston and 1st Sts., East Village 212/933–5300 www.danielnyc.com Reservations essential F to 2nd Ave. 2:F2*

$$$ AUSTRIAN Fodor's Choice ★ **Edi & the Wolf.** For those who have always wanted to spend an evening in a countryside Austrian pub—and who hasn't?—but don't have the means to hop on a plane to Vienna, there's Edi & the Wolf, an outstanding restaurant deep in the section of the East Village called Alphabet City. The rustic interior (usually crammed with stylish thirtysomethings) is the perfect venue to sample dishes like honey-and-beer-accented ribs, pork belly–laced poached eggs, and, of course, wienerschnitzel, which is refreshingly free of grease and super tender. The well-edited beer selection focuses on central Europe. Try the dark Czech brew, Krusovice (pronounced Kroo-sho-vitzay) *Average main: $20 102 Ave. C, at E. 7th St., East Village 212/598–1040 F to 2nd Ave.; L to 1st Ave. 2:H1*

$$ BRITISH Fodor's Choice ★ **The Fat Radish.** The phrase "seasonal British" might have once seemed puzzling but with seasonal ingredients very much in vogue and British cuisine making a name for itself, this handsome, hip, and sceney Lower East Side (almost Chinatown) restaurant is very much of the moment. The menu is eclectic but full of excellent choices. Think green curried monkfish, a cheeseburger served with duck fat fries, and, as the name vaguely suggests, plenty of farm-to-table fresh veggie dishes. Match that with quality craft British brews and potent cocktails and you'll be championing English cuisine in no time. *Average main: $18 17 Orchard St., near Canal St., Lower East Side 212/300–4053 thefatradishnyc.com F to E. Broadway 2:G5.*

$$ AMERICAN **Five Points.** Describing a menu in terms of "seasonal" and "market-driven" might be old news but chef Marc Meyer really makes the most

16

of the greenmarket, and showcases it in a cozy, convivial dining room. Expect plump chilled oysters, exemplary Caesar salad, and splendid house-made pasta, followed by the likes of pan-seared day-boat halibut with cucumber gazpacho and chopped tomato salsa, and grilled baby lamb chops with rosemary potatoes, mint-yogurt sauce, and black-olive-stuffed tomato. Weekend brunch is one of the best in the city, and prices are quite friendly. Weekday lunch is served, too, usually without the wait that hungry stomachs have come to expect at other times. *Average main: $24 ✉ 31 Great Jones St., between Lafayette St. and Bowery, East Village ☎ 212/253–5700 ⊕ www.fivepointsrestaurant.com Ⓜ 6 to Bleecker St.; B, D, F, M to Broadway–Lafayette St. ✣ 2:F2*

$$ ITALIAN **Gemma.** There's something almost formulaic about this restaurant on the ground floor of the hip Bowery Hotel: from the rustic, wood-bedecked interior to the stone-wall interior facade to the see-and-be-seen crowd who frequent the place and the menu of above-average Italian staples (from pizza to pastas mains). But the food here is good, the service is attentive, and nabbing an outside table may make you feel cooler than you are for a couple of hours, so what difference does it make? Answer: no difference, until it's time to pay the bill. Weekend brunch is also a good bet. *Average main: $19 ✉ 335 Bowery, at E. 3rd St., East Village ☎ 212/505–9100 ⊕ theboweryhotel.com/dining ✍ Reservations not accepted Ⓜ F to 2nd Ave. ✣ 2:F2*

$$ ITALIAN **Gnocco.** Owners Pierluigi Palazzo and Gianluca Giavonetti named their restaurant not after gnocchi but after a regional Italian specialty—deep-fried dough bites typically served with Northern Italian sliced meats like capicola, salami, and aged prosciutto. The *gnocco* are certainly good, but the menu has so many other options you'll be forgiven if you skip them in favor of the salads, house-made pasta specials, pizza topped with mozzarella, truffles, and mushrooms, and hearty entrées like pork tenderloin in a balsamic emulsion with flakes of Grana Padano cheese—preferably all enjoyed in the roomy, canopied garden out back. *Average main: $20 ✉ 337 E. 10th St., between Aves. A and B, East Village ☎ 212/677–1913 ⊕ www.gnocco.com Ⓜ L to 1st Ave.; 6 to Astor Pl. ✣ 2:H1*

$$ CHINESE **Grand Sichuan.** Yes, it's a local Chinese chainlet, and no, you don't come here for the ambience, but the food—like fiery Sichuan *dan dan* noodles or crab soup dumplings—is good and inexpensive. Check the website for other locations around town. *Average main: $18 ✉ 19–23 St. Marks Pl., near 3rd Ave., East Village ☎ 212/529–4800 ⊕ www.thegrandsichuan.com Ⓜ 6 to Astor Pl. ✣ 2:F1*

$$ MEXICAN **Hecho en Dumbo.** "Made in Dumbo"—referring to the restaurant's former location in the Brooklyn neighborhood DUMBO—specializes in *antojitos,* or "little cravings." The result is something equivalent to Mexican comfort food for the hip thirtysomethings who frequent this restaurant on the ever-happening Bowery. Variations on the theme of tacos may dominate the menu, but Hecho shines with house dishes like roasted kid and wine-braised oxtail served over Oaxacan mole sauce. Pair your meal with one of their delicious margaritas (no bottled mix used here), sangria, or perhaps a michelada—beer on ice with lime and a salted rim. *Average main: $16 ✉ 354 Bowery, between Great Jones*

and W. 4th Sts., East Village ☎ *212/937–4245* 🌐 *www.hechoendumbo.com* Ⓜ *6 to Astor Pl.* ✣ *2:F2*

$$$ ITALIAN ✕ **Il Buco.** The unabashed clutter of vintage kitchen gadgets and tableware harks back to Il Buco's past as an antiques store and the effect is a romantic country-house feel with excellent food. This is a favorite for a cozy, intimate meal. The menu focuses on meat and produce from local farms, with several excellent pasta choices, and a variety of Mediterranean tapas-like appetizers. Call ahead to book the intimate wine cellar for dinner. The Il Buco Alimentari & Vineria, around the corner at 53 Great Jones St., is a more casual setting, with a small market up front selling gourmet cheese and house-cured meats, and a wine bar in the back. Ⓢ *Average main: $28* ✉ *47 Bond St., between Bowery and Lafayette St., NoHo* ☎ *212/533–1932* 🌐 *www.ilbuco.com* ⏲ *No lunch Sun.* Ⓜ *6 to Bleecker St.; B, D, F, M to Broadway–Lafayette St.* ✣ *2:F2*

$ JAPANESE ✕ **Ippudo.** Crowds wait hours for the ramen noodles at Ippudo, the first American branch of the Japanese chain, and if you ask, loyal patrons will say it's all about the rich, pork-based broth—there is a vegetarian version available but it lacks the depth of flavor. Those really in the know, though, make sure to order the sleeper hit appetizers like the peppery chicken wings or the pork buns. It's not a hole in the wall ramen spot, so although a meal here is relatively inexpensive, it's not dirt cheap. Ⓢ *Average main: $15* ✉ *65 4th Ave., between 9th and 10th Sts., East Village* ☎ *212/388–0088* 🌐 *www.ippudony.com* ✍ *Reservations not accepted* Ⓜ *L, N, Q, R, 4, 5, 6 to Union Sq.* ✣ *3:G5.*

$$$$ JAPANESE ✕ **Jewel Bako.** Tiny Jewel Bako is arguably the best sushi restaurant in the East Village, gleaming in a minefield of cheap, often inferior sushi houses. The futuristic bamboo tunnel of a dining room is gorgeous, but try to nab a place at the sushi bar and put yourself in the hands of sushi master Yoshi Kousaka. The five-course *omakase,* or chef's menu, starts at $95. (A less-expensive sushi or sashimi omakase is $55.) You'll be served only what's freshest and best. Ⓢ *Average main: $40* ✉ *239 E. 5th St., between 2nd and 3rd Aves., East Village* ☎ *212/979–1012* ✍ *Reservations essential* ⏲ *Closed Sun. No lunch* Ⓜ *6 to Astor Pl.* ✣ *3:G6*

$ MIDDLE EASTERN FAMILY ✕ **Mamoun's Falafel.** Mamoun's is an institution. Bustling day and night, this hole-in-the-wall is the place to go for speedy, hot, super-cheap, and delicious Middle Eastern food. Tahini-topped pitas are packed with fresh, green-on-the-inside falafel balls. Be warned: the hot sauce is incendiary. The small space has a few tables, but this is food you can easily eat on the go. The original Mamoun's is still on MacDougal Street, near Washington Square Park in Greenwich Village. Ⓢ *Average main: $7* ✉ *22 St. Marks Pl., between 2nd and 3rd Aves., East Village* ☎ *212/387–7747* 🌐 *mamouns.com* ✍ *Reservations not accepted* ▭ *No credit cards* Ⓜ *6 to Astor Pl.* ✣ *3:G5.*

$ JAPANESE ✕ **Minca.** It may have received less fanfare than some other East Village noodle bars, but the ramen at this tiny, cramped spot is among the best in the city; the fact that visiting Japanese students eat here is a good sign. Try to get a seat at the bar, where you can watch the chefs prepare your food. Start with homemade gyoza dumplings, then dive your spoon and chopsticks into one of the many types of ramen. The *shoyu* (soy sauce) Minca ramen is unfailingly good, but anything with pork is a good bet.

$ Average main: $13 ✉ 536 E. 5th St., between Ave. A and Ave. B, East Village ☎ 212/505–8001 ⊕ www.newyorkramen.com ✍ Reservations not accepted ▬ No credit cards Ⓜ F to 2nd Ave. ✣ 2:G2.

$$$$ ASIAN Fodor's Choice ★ ✕ **Momofuku Ko.** A seasonal tasting menu full of clever combinations and esoteric ingredients explains the deafening buzz for James Beard Award–winning chef David Chang's most formal dining option. Ko's small, intimate space is sparsely furnished with a counter of blonde wood and only a dozen stools. Diners get to see Ko's chefs in action as they prepare all manner of inventive dishes, including a signature preparation of frozen foie gras torchon grated over lychee fruits and white wine gelee. Reservations can be made only online, no more than 7 days ahead for dinner and 14 days ahead for lunch, and are extremely difficult to get. Log on at 10 am (credit-card number needed just to get in the system) when new reservations are available, and keep hitting reload. *$ Average main: $60 ✉ 163 1st Ave., at E. 10th St., East Village ⊕ www.momofuku.com ✍ Reservations essential ⏲ No lunch Mon.–Thurs. Ⓜ L to 1st Ave.; 6 to Astor Pl. ✣ 3:H5*

$$ ASIAN Fodor's Choice ★ ✕ **Momofuku Noodle Bar.** Chef-owner David Chang has created a shrine to ramen with this stylish 70-seat restaurant. His riff on the Japanese classic features haute ingredients like Berkshire pork, free-range chicken, and organic produce—though there are plenty of other innovative options on the menu. His modern take on pork buns with cucumber and scallions is phenomenal—worth the trip alone. You'll probably have to wait if you go at regular meal times, but seats at the long counter open up fairly quickly, and the lively atmosphere is part of the fun. The excellent fried-chicken meal, featuring triple-fried Korean-style chicken and Old Bay southern-style, with a variety of accoutrements feeds four-to-eight people and is available by special reservations only on the website. *$ Average main: $15 ✉ 171 1st Ave., between E. 10th and E. 11 Sts., East Village ☎ 212/777–7773 ⊕ www.momofuku.com ✍ Reservations not accepted Ⓜ L to 1st Ave. ✣ 3:H5*

$$ ASIAN ✕ **Momofuku Ssäm Bar.** New York foodies have been salivating over chef David Chang's Asian-influenced fare since he opened his first restaurant, Momofuku, a Japanese noodle shop, in 2004, and Ssäm Bar, with a more extensive menu, is equally worth the raves. The restaurant is packed nightly with downtown diners cut from the same cloth as the pierced and tattooed waitstaff and cooks, and the no-reservation policy (except for large parties or special dinners) means you'll likely have to wait for a chance to try Chang's truly inventive flavor combinations. The menu is constantly changing but the not-to-be-missed riff on the classic Chinese steamed pork bun is almost always available. You can make reservations for the festive Bo Ssäm dinner (6 to 10 people), featuring a slow-roasted pork shoulder, oysters, kimchi, and a variety of sauces, or the rotisserie duck dinner (3 to 6 people) through their website. *$ Average main: $23 ✉ 207 2nd Ave., at 13th St., East Village ☎ 212/254–3500 ⊕ www.momofuku.com/ssam Ⓜ L to 1st Ave. ✣ 3:G4*

$ KOREAN ✕ **Mono+Mono.** Live jazz and Korean fried chicken? Yes, please. After a visit to this dimly lit, wood-bedecked East Village restaurant you'll think the two are as harmonious as blues and barbeque. If live jazz is not on the agenda, there's a DJ tucked away on the second-floor balustrade spinning records from the floor-to-ceiling 30,000-strong record collection on the side wall. The restaurant claims it serves the best Korean fried chicken in the city. And they may not be lying. It's spicy, it's cripsy, and it often inspires a second order. The rest of the Korean-accented menu includes kimchi pancakes and skewered grilled meat. [$] *Average main: $14* ✉ *116 E. 4th St., East Village* ☎ *212/466–6660* 🌐 *www.monomononyc.com* Ⓜ *F to 2nd Ave.* ✧ *2:G2.*

$ PIZZA ✕ **Motorino Pizza.** The Manhattan branch of the now-closed Williamsburg original has brought its high standards—and long lines—to a new borough. The authentic Neapolitan pies are made with glutinous double-zero flour and San Marzano tomatoes, and the crusts are lightly charred. You can't go wrong with any of the signature traditional pizzas, like marinara; margherita with fresh tomatoes, mozzarella, and basil; or a pie with spicy sopressata, sausage and garlic; but the seasonal selections are also tempting. Check out the brunch pizza (with egg and pancetta) on the weekends. Antipasti like octopus and fingerling potato salad with celery-chili oil, and cockle-clam crostini round out the menu. The weekday, lunchtime prix fixe means pizza and salad is a bargain at $12 per person. [$] *Average main: $15* ✉ *349 E. 12th St., at 1st Ave., East Village* ☎ *212/777–2644* 🌐 *www.motorinopizza.com* ✍ *Reservations not accepted* Ⓜ *L to 1st Ave.* ✧ *3:H4*

16

$$ AMERICAN Fodor's Choice ★ ✕ **Northern Spy Food Co.** A gem in the East Village, named for an apple variety, Northern Spy is run by two San Francisco transplants who have a West Coast perspective on the farm-to-table movement. Start your meal with the freekeh risotto, a traditional dish made with a quirky little-known grain, or a giant mound of shredded kale tossed with cheddar, pecorino, and toasted almonds. Main courses are winners, too—choose tender meatballs in marinara sauce, roast chicken for two, or baked polenta, eggs, and mushrooms topped with crème fraîche. There is also an interesting, reasonably priced list of wines and beers, and a selection of housemade desserts like chocolate cake with sea salt and caramel. [$] *Average main: $22* ✉ *511 E. 12th St., between 1st Ave. and Ave. A, East Village* ☎ *212/228–5100* 🌐 *www.northernspyfoodco.com* ✍ *Reservations not accepted* Ⓜ *L to 1st Ave.* ✧ *3:H4*

$$ SOUTHERN FAMILY ✕ **Peels Restaurant.** Imagine a Southern-flair eatery in one of the hippest parts of Manhattan, and you might come up with Peels, a grits-and-all spot from the people who gave NYC the trendsetting Freemans. As one might expect, the buttermilk biscuit egg sandwich is a delightful way to start any day. And the buttery grits are done right. Peels really excels with more original fare, though: the andouille corn dogs with sweet Dijon mustard and the root vegetable pot pie are good enough to name your next child Cletus. [$] *Average main: $26* ✉ *325 Bowery, near 2nd St., East Village* ☎ *646/602–7015* 🌐 *peelsnyc.com* ✍ *Reservations not accepted* Ⓜ *4, 6 to Bleecker St.* ✧ *3:G6*

$ ITALIAN ✕ **Porchetta.** Super-succulent Italian roast pork—dusted in fennel pollen and covered in crisp cracklin' skin—is the star attraction here. It is, in fact, just about the only thing this tiny spot offers. Order your pork in a sandwich or as a platter with stewed greens and roasted potatoes. There's not much room inside for dining on-site, but the benches out front are ideal when the weather cooperates. [$] *Average main: $10*

☒ *110 E. 7th St., near 1st Ave., East Village* ☎ *212/777–2151* 🌐 *www.porchettanyc.com* ✍ *Reservations not accepted* Ⓜ *6 to Astor Pl.* ✥ *3:H5*

$$ AMERICAN ✕ **Prune.** There's just something very right-on about the food at Prune, a cozy treasure of a restaurant serving eclectic, well-executed American food from cult chef Gabrielle Hamilton. The choices change with the season, but you might find braised rabbit legs in vinegar sauce, whole grilled fish with fennel oil and chunky sea salt, or roasted marrow bones with parsley salad and toast points. If they're on the menu, try the pillowy, fired sweetbreads. There's usually a wait, and the quarters are very cramped, so don't expect to feel comfortable lingering at your rickety wooden table. Desserts, like ricotta ice cream with salted-caramel croutons, are irresistible, and on weekends lines form early for the restaurant's deservedly popular brunch. $ *Average main: $20* ☒ *54 E. 1st St., between 1st and 2nd Aves., East Village* ☎ *212/677–6221* 🌐 *www.prunerestaurant.com* ✍ *Reservations essential* Ⓜ *F to 2nd Ave.* ✥ *2:G2*

$$$ GREEK ✕ **Pylos.** The perfect setting for a relaxed dinner or an intimate special occasion, this tastefully refined, light-filled East Village restaurant emphasizes rustic Greek cooking from all over Greece. There are delicious versions of hearty comfort food dishes like pastitsio and moussaka on the menu but the lighter dishes—especially fish—let the flavors shine through. There is an extensive selection of interesting hot and cold mezes—start with the traditional trio of *tzatkziki* (garlicky yogurt dip), *taramosalata* (lemony fish roe dip), and *melitzanosalta* (an eggplant-based dip) and explore from there. Accompany your meal with some vino from the all-Greek wine list; the light white Atlantis wine from the island of Santorini is particularly enjoyable—and affordable. $ *Average main: $25* ☒ *128 E. 7th St., near Ave. A, East Village* ☎ *212/473–0220* 🌐 *www.pylosrestaurant.com* Ⓜ *F to 2nd Ave.; L to 1st Ave.* ✥ *3:H5*

$$ AMERICAN Fodor's Choice ★ ✕ **Saxon & Parole.** One of the hottest spots on this burgeoning stretch of the Bowery, this eatery may be named for two 19th century racehorses but the food—and the extremely good-looking crowd—is nothing that you'd find in a barnyard. Settle into this cozy, sceney spot, order a cocktail, and peruse a menu loaded with the zeitgeist dishes of New York dining: roasted bone marrow, Brussels sprouts, pork belly, chicken-liver mousse, and, of course, an overpriced-but-excellent burger. The kitchen executes it all to complete deliciousness. The bar scene is lively, so plan to come early for a cocktail. $ *Average main: $22* ☒ *316 Bowery, at Bleecker St., East Village* ☎ *212/254–0350* 🌐 *saxonandparole.com* Ⓜ *B, D, F, M to Broadway–Lafayette St.* ✥ *2:F2*

$ PIZZA ✕ **South Brooklyn Pizza.** This outpost of the famed Brooklyn pizza spot has expanded from it's original tiny storefront and now has seating next door (but currently no table service), and also serves beer. Yes, you'll pay a a bit more than at other take-out joints, but this is some of the most memorable pizza you'll eat in the Big Apple—especially if you spread your slice with the roasted garlic and pickled peppers available on the counter. If you're wandering the East Village late at night and have the munchies, take note, it's open until 5 am. $ *Average main: $4* ☒ *122 1st Ave., at 7th St., East Village, New York* ☎ *212/533–2879* 🌐 *www.southbrooklynpizza.com* Ⓜ *F to 2nd Ave.* ✥ *2:G1.*

$ CAFÉ FAMILY ✕ **Veniero's Pasticceria.** More than a century old, this bustling bakery-café sells every kind of Italian *dolce* (sweet), from cherry-topped cookies to creamy cannoli and flaky *sfogliatelle* pastry. A wine license means you can top off an evening with a bottle of red. $ *Average main: $5* ✉ *342 E. 11th St., near 1st Ave., East Village* ☎ *212/674–7070* 🌐 *www.venierospastry.com* ✍ *Reservations not accepted* Ⓜ *6 to Astor Pl.; L to 1st Ave.* ✣ *3:H5*

$ EASTERN EUROPEAN FAMILY ✕ **Veselka.** The name means "rainbow" in Ukrainian, and you can order potato pierogis 24 hours a day at this East Village stalwart. The authentic Ukrainian-cuisine-slash-diner-food is the perfect stick-to-your-ribs end to a night on the town. It's a neighborhood experience, with tables of families sharing space with the hipsters. $ *Average main: $11* ✉ *144 2nd Ave., at 9th St., East Village* ☎ *212/228–9682* 🌐 *www.veselka.com* ✍ *Reservations not accepted* Ⓜ *F to 2nd Ave.* ✣ *3:H5.*

Westville East. *Branch location at 173 Avenue A, near 11th Street. See West Village for full review.*

$ THAI Fodor's Choice ★ ✕ **Zabb Elee.** Don't expect to find pad thai on the menu at this comfortable but simply bedecked subterranean East Village restaurant. An outpost of a popular Queens restaurant of the same name, Zabb Elee is one of the few very good Thai restaurants in Manhattan. The long menu is a showecase for the cuisine of Isan, a region in northeastern Thailand that emphasizes simplicity and spiciness. Order a plate of *larb*—ground meat with mint, scallions, cilantro, and chili—or *som tam*, spicy papaya salad. Fish lovers will dig the herb-stuffed grilled tilapia. Just be sure to tell the server the level of hotness you prefer (one means mild, four means very spicy, and "Thai" means out-of-this-world hot). $ *Average main: $9* ✉ *75 2nd Ave., between E. 4th and E. 5th Sts., East Village* ☎ *212/505–9533* Ⓜ *F to 2nd Ave.* ✣ *2:F1.*

$ GERMAN ✕ **Zum Schneider.** Located in Alphabet City—the wilds of the East Village—this garrulous Tuetonic spot will teach you the ABCs of beer drinking and hearty eating. Grab a table outside when the weather's nice, among the young hipsters who frequent the spot, and get ready for some kraut-laden fun. After quaffing a huge liter stein of the sudsy stuff, you may want to eat and the menu, naturally, is a veritable sausage-palooza. In addition to the usual meaty fare, such as Wiener schnitzel and goulash, there are, well, more sausages. The crispy potato pancakes are a good bet, too. $ *Average main: $16* ✉ *107 Ave. C, at E. 7th St., East Village* ☎ *212/598–1098* 🌐 *www.zumschneider.com* Ⓜ *L to 1st Ave.; F to 2nd Ave.* ✣ *2:H1*

LOWER EAST SIDE

The Lower East Side, home to generations of immigrant newcomers, is undergoing a transformation into a high-rent neighborhood. Cute little bistros have been inching into newly gentrified stretches south of Delancey Street. And the neighborhood has even given birth to its own homegrown star chefs, wildly creative renegades with cultish followings like **wd~50**'s Wylie Dufresne.

$$ AMERICAN Fodor's Choice ★ ✕ **Clinton St. Baking Co.** There once was a time when this Lower East Side restaurant was *the* place to come for brunch. Specifically, it was *the* place to eat blueberry pancakes, which many regulars professed were the best in the city, if not the state, or the whole country. But all

16

that changed when owners Neil Kleinberg and DeDe Lahman opened their beloved eatery for lunch and dinner. Oh, it's still a great place for brunch, but now you can eat those pancakes (along with a good Black Angus burger or a crab cake sandwich) any time of day you like. February is pancake month, when, in addition to the blueberry pancakes, every weekday brings a special incarnation of the pancake. *Average main: $17* *4 Clinton St., near E. Houston St., Lower East Side* *646/602–6263* *www.clintonstreetbaking.com* *No dinner on Sunday* *F to 2nd Ave.* *2:H2*

$ CHINESE **Congee Village.** Don't be put off by the name—this boisterous Chinatown icon serves much more than the eponymous rice porridge. Indeed, the menu is enormous, covering an encyclopedic range of unusual Cantonese classics. The bamboo-cloaked dining room is great with a group of people, but being wedged in at a communal table with a boisterous family is part of the experience. If you're feeling adventurous, try the duck tongues in XO sauce or salt-and-pepper frog, or stick to familiar classics. Either way, the congee is a great way to start. *Average main: $15* *100 Allen St., near Delancey St., Lower East Side* *212/941–1818* *www.congeevillagerestaurants.com* *F, J, M, Z to Delancey St.–Essex St.* *2:G4*

$ CAFÉ FAMILY **Doughnut Plant.** If the cupcake craze is getting you down, head to the Doughnut Plant, where the all-American junk food staple is elevated to high art. Fresh seasonal ingredients go into these treats, with real fruit and imported chocolate mixed into the batter. Purists will croon over the vanilla bean doughnut but there are plenty of exotic flavors to tempt tastebuds: the dense, fudgy blackout is covered in crumb topping; carrot cake doughnuts have a cream-cheese filling. The Lower East Side location is open every day from 6:30 am to 8 pm. There's a second location in Chelsea, next to the Chelsea Hotel; doughnuts are also available around the city at Dean & Deluca and Zabar's. *Average main: $5* *379 Grand St., near Essex St., Lower East Side* *212/505–3700* *www.doughnutplant.com* *Reservations not accepted* *No credit cards* *F, J, M, Z to Delancey St.–Essex St.* *2:G4*

$$ AMERICAN Fodor's Choice ★ **Freemans.** It's hard to believe now but there was once a time when New York restaurant interiors looked like they were trying hard not to look cool, when there was no taxidermy or ironic tchotchkes littered around the room, when the menu wasn't filled with old-school (albeit very good) lodge-ish dishes like hunters stew, potted pork, and grilled trout with an equally inspired cocktails menu. But we have Freemans to thank for that. Down a little-used alleyway on the Lower East Side, trendsetting Freemans is as hip and popular as when it opened in 2004. Just don't try too hard to look cool. The hot artichoke dip is still the best way to start any meal. *Average main: $18* *End of Freeman Alley, near Rivington St., Lower East Side* *212/420–0012* *www.freemansrestaurant.com* *F to 2nd Ave.* *2:F3.*

$ ITALIAN **'inoteca.** The Italian terms on the menu may be unfamiliar (*tramezzini* just means "soft bread sandwiches") but the food is not daunting in the least—this is real Italian comfort food. An Italian small-plates concept with an excellent by-the-glass wine list, this rustic eatery is perpetually packed. (Reservations are accepted for parties of six or more.) Come

For an authentic deli experience, you can't beat Katz's.

for cheese and charcuterie plates, the famous truffled-egg toast, and delicious paninis filled with cured meat, runny cheeses, and hot peppers. Menu staples include fresh salads and creative entrées like linguine with sea urchin, shrimp, and fennel, as well as an unctuous Wagyu beef sandwich with horseradish and arugula. $ *Average main: $13* ✉ *98 Rivington St., at Ludlow St., Lower East Side* ☎ *212/614–0473* 🌐 *www.inotecanyc.com* Ⓜ *F, J, M, Z to Delancey St.–Essex St.* ✢ *2:G3*

$ DELI Fodor's Choice ★

✕ **Katz's Delicatessen.** Everything and nothing has changed at Katz's since it first opened in 1888, when the neighborhood was dominated by Jewish immigrants. The rows of Formica tables, the long self-service counter, and such signs as "Send a salami to your boy in the army" are all completely authentic. The lines still form on the weekends for giant, succulent hand-carved corned beef and pastrami sandwiches, soul-warming soups, juicy hot dogs, and crisp half-sour pickles. Weeknights are more laid back. You'll get a ticket when you walk in and then get it punched at the various stations where you pick up your food; don't lose your ticket or you'll have to pay the lost ticket fee. $ *Average main: $15* ✉ *205 E. Houston St., at Ludlow St., Lower East Side* ☎ *212/254–2246* 🌐 *www.katzdeli.com* Ⓜ *F to 2nd Ave.* ✢ *2:G2*

$$ GERMAN

✕ **Loreley Restaurant & Biergarten.** Once upon a time, beer gardens dotted the New York City landscape in the way that Starbucks does now, but after World War I and Prohibition, most of these outdoor drinking spots vanished. And then in 2003 came Loreley (which eventually kicked off a new beer garden craze in the city). But don't mistake this Lower East Side hotspot for a place where geriatrics in lederhosen swing their plus-size steins of beer to polka music. Instead, there's a better than good chance that you'll find a gaggle of hipsters nursing German craft beers while bobbing their heads to the new Radiohead album and munching on plates of sausage, meatballs, or schnitzel. The space out back may be more concrete than garden, but it's a pleasure on a mild evening. $ *Average main: $15* ✉ *7 Rivington St., near Bowery, Lower East Side* ☎ *212/253–7077* 🌐 *www.loreleynyc.com* Ⓜ *J, Z to Bowery; B, D to Grand St.; F to 2nd Ave.* ✣ *2:F3*

$ ITALIAN FAMILY

✕ **The Meatball Shop.** New York's first full-service meatball restaurant has a pedigree chef, a wine list, and a hip crowd. And the meatballs, oh, the meatballs. Choose beef, pork, chicken, or veggie, or "special" ball options that range from chili-cheese balls to Greek lamb balls to Buffalo chicken balls, then decide if you want them served simple as is, in sliders or a hero, as a salad, or as a platter; all with an appropriate choice of sauce and cheese. The meatball concept quickly caught on and there are now three locations: two in Manhattan and one in Williamsburg. Mix 'n' match ice-cream sandwiches are worth saving room for. $ *Average main: $9* ✉ *84 Stanton St., near Allen St., Lower East Side* ☎ *212/982–8895* 🌐 *www.themeatballshop.com* ✍ *Reservations not accepted* Ⓜ *F to 2nd Ave.* ✣ *2:G3*

$ CHINESE Fodor's Choice ★

✕ **Mission Chinese Food.** When the news spread that chef Danny Bowien was bringing his popular San Franisco Chinese spot to the Lower East Side, you could almost hear a collective shout of blogosphere glee. And it hasn't disappointed. The food here, cheaper than it really should be, is billed as Szechuan but is really at the chef's whim. As an homage to the Lower East Side neighborhood, for example, he's added pastrami to *kung pao* (and the pairing tastes like it should have been there all along); the thrice-cooked bacon, while not necessarily for the Lipitor crowd, is nearly revelatory in its unctuous flavor; the spicy chicken wings are fabulous, and *really* spicy. $ *Average main: $15* ✉ *154 Orchard St., Lower East Side* ☎ *212/529–8800* 🌐 *www.missionchinesefood.com* Ⓜ *F to 2nd Ave.* ✣ *2:G3.*

$ CAFÉ FAMILY

✕ **Momofuku Milk Bar.** This combination bakery, ice cream parlor, and sandwich shop offers quick-serve access to chef David Chang's cultish pork buns, along with some truly psychedelic treats by pastry whiz Christina Tosi. Swing by for a kimchee croissant and a glass of "cereal milk," or for treats like the curiously flavored soft-serve ice cream (cereal milk, lemon verbena), "candy bar pie" (a sweet bomb of caramel, peanut-butter nougat, and pretzels atop a chocolate-cookie crust), one of the addictive cookies (try the "compost" cookies, with pretzels, chocolate chips, and whatever inspires the bakers that day), or any of the intriguing savories (the "volcano" is a cheese-and-potato pastry that is impossible to eat daintily). $ *Average main: $6* ✉ *251 E. 13th St., East Village* ☎ *347/577–9505* 🌐 *www.milkbarstore.com* ✍ *Reservations not accepted* Ⓜ *L to 3rd Ave.* ✣ *3:G4.*

$$$ LATIN AMERICAN

✕ **Rayuela.** There's a young, sexy vibe at this vibrant Lower East Side restaurant where diners come for creative Latin cuisine courtesy of Máximo Tejada, the chef who built his reputation cooking at the popular (now closed) Lucy's Latin Kitchen. The bilevel eatery has a dining area, a ceviche bar, and—growing in the center of the restaurant—an olive tree. Ceviches are excellent, and there are several to choose from, as well as a selection of tapas. The kitchen excels with fish but the rice dishes are worthy of acclaim, too. For maximum enjoyment, come early for a predinner drink at the bar: standout cocktails include the pisco made with sour lime juice and foamy egg white. Latin-inspired brunch is served on weekends. *Average main: $28* *165 Allen St., between Rivington and Stanton Sts., Lower East Side* *212/253–8840* *www.rayuelanyc.com* *No lunch* *F to 2nd Ave.; J, M, Z to Delancey St.–Essex St.* *2:G3*

$$ BISTRO FAMILY **Schiller's Liquor Bar.** It may not be as hard to get in as it was back in 2003 when Keith McNally first opened this sceney hangout on the Lower East Side but it still has the allure, with excellent bistro fare, sexy cocktails, and the kind of atmosphere that is as comfortable for celebrities or parents with a strollers. This is vintage Parisian à la McNally: verdigris mirrored panels, forever-in-style subway tiles, a tin ceiling, and a checkered floor, while Cuban sandwiches and steak frites reveal a steady hand in the kitchen. This is also the place for a late-night bite, since the kitchen is open until midnight every night except Friday and Saturday, when food is served until 3 am. Breakfast is served weekdays until 4 pm, with brunch on the weekends. *Average main: $20* *131 Rivington St., at Norfolk St., Lower East Side* *212/260–4555* *www.schillersny.com* *F, J, M, Z to Delancey St.–Essex St.* *2:G3*

16

$ ECLECTIC FAMILY **Shopsin's.** Don't ask for substitutions or sauce on the side at New York's most eccentric eatery because Kenny Shopsin, owner and chef, really may toss you out or ban you for life; somehow the attitude is part of the appeal here. Though the eclectic menu runs to literally hundreds of items—from pumpkin pancakes to chilaquiles, and from chili cheeseburgers to lamb-curry soups—even the strangest foods conjured up in his tight diner kitchen taste pretty great. The mac-and-cheese pancakes have loyal followers (they're even better with hot sauce). The space in the Essex market is tiny, so expect to wait. Parties of more than four aren't accepted. *Average main: $17* *120 Essex St., near Rivington St., in Essex Market, Lower East Side* *www.shopsins.com* *Reservations not accepted* *No credit cards* *Closed Mon. and Tues. No dinner* *F, J, M, Z to Delancey St.–Essex St.* *2:G3*

$$ ECLECTIC **The Stanton Social.** This swanky Lower East Side favorite lures the crowds with an expansive and eclectic small-plates menu, accompanied by a perfectly calibrated cocktail list. Come before 7 if you want to be able to hear your fellow diners speak, but the people-watching and shared dishes are good at any hour. Try the gooey, Gruyère-topped onion soup dumplings, juicy Kobe-beef sliders, and wasabi-crusted salmon. Downstairs feels like a more traditional dining room, whereas the second level features a buzzy bar. The late-night lounge area, decorated with cherry-blossom wallpaper and red leather upholstery, turns more nightclubby the later it gets. Brunch—with options like spicy lobster Benedict, and appropriate cocktails—might blow your mind. Whatever time you come, save room for the fresh doughnuts. *Average main: $20* *99 Stanton St., between Ludlow and Orchard Sts., Lower East Side* *212/995–0099* *www.thestantonsocial.com* *Reservations essential* *No lunch* *F to 2nd Ave.* *2:G3*

$ CAFÉ FAMILY **Sugar Sweet Sunshine.** The brainchild of two former Magnolia Bakery employees, Sugar Sweet's cupcakes are far superior; try the chocolate-almond Gooey Gooey, or the cream-cheese-frosting-topped pumpkin flavor. The real showstopper? Swoon-inducing banana pudding incorporating slices of ripe fruit and crumbled Nilla wafers suspended in decadent vanilla pudding. Cupcakes are the perfect on-the-go treat but if you prefer to hang out, there are cozy couches for lounging. *Average main: $5 ✉ 126 Rivington St., between Essex and Norfolk Sts., Lower East Side ☎ 212/995–1960 Reservations not accepted* Ⓜ *F to 2nd Ave. ⊕ 2:G3.*

$$$ MODERN AMERICAN **wd~50.** Chef Wylie Dufresne—the mad genius and early progenitor of the molecular gastronomy trend—mixes colors, flavors, and textures with a masterful hand, and the staff encourages diners to feel at ease trying the deconstructed interpretations of modern food. You might think you know what an everything bagel with lox and cream cheese, or eggs Benedict might look like but you're in for a surprise. Expect the unexpected when it comes to taste combinations like corned duck with rye crisp and purple mustard, or lamb shoulder with pistachio "polenta." This style of cooking isn't news anymore, but dinner here is still an eye-opening experience, although presentation and conceptualization sometimes outshine the flavors. Tasting menus (including a dessert-tasting one) allow you to really experience the chef's creativity. *Average main: $34 ✉ 50 Clinton St., between Rivington and Stanton Sts., Lower East Side ☎ 212/477–2900 ⊕ www.wd-50.com No lunch.* Ⓜ *F, J, M, Z to Delancey St–Essex St. ⊕ 2:H3*

GREENWICH VILLAGE AND THE WEST VILLAGE

GREENWICH VILLAGE

Greenwich Village's bohemian days may have faded with the Beatnik era, but the romantic allure of its tiny bistros, bars, and cafés remains. Around New York University, shabby-chic eateries and take-out joints line the streets and are patronized by a student clientele, but there are a growing number of more sophisticated dining spots, too. Avoid heavily trafficked thoroughfares like Bleecker Street (unless you're tapping into the artisan pizza craze).

$$ PIZZA FAMILY **Arturo's.** Few guidebooks list this classic pizzeria, but the packed room and pleasantly smoky scent foreshadow a satisfying meal. There's a full menu of Italian classics, but don't be fooled: pizza is the main event. The thin-crust beauties are cooked in a coal oven, and emerge sizzling with simple toppings like pepperoni, sausage, and eggplant. Monday to Thursday you can call ahead to reserve a table; weekends, be prepared to wait and salivate. *Average main: $18 ✉ 106 W. Houston St., near Thompson St., Greenwich Village ☎ 212/677–3820 No lunch* Ⓜ *1 to Houston St.; B, D, F, M to Broadway–Lafayette St. ⊕ 2:D3*

$$$ ITALIAN Fodor's Choice ★ **Babbo Ristorante.** It shouldn't take more than one bite of the ethereal homemade pasta or tender barbecued squab with roast beet farrotto for you to understand why it's so hard to get a reservation at Mario Batali's casually elegant restaurant. The menu strays widely from Italian standards and hits numerous high points, in particular with the "mint love letters": ravioli filled with pureed peas, ricotta, and fresh mint, finished with spicy lamb sausage ragout; and rabbit with Brussels sprouts, house-made pancetta, and carrot vinaigrette. This is the perfect spot for

FOOD COURT RENAISSANCE

Everywhere you turn, a new food court is opening. But these are not shopping-mall-style clusters of franchised eateries. Because we're talking New York, you can expect high-quality dining, a boon for hungry pavement-pounders looking for food, fast—not fast food.

At the **Plaza Food Hall** (✉ *1 W. 59th St., at 5th Ave.* ☎ *212/986–9260* ✣ *4:E1*) in the basement of the Plaza Hotel, celeb chef Todd English oversees a series of mini-restaurants, each with its own counter with seating ideal for a quick snack or a full-fledged meal. Entry is a little confusing; though the place is made up of individual food concepts, you'll be seated by a hostess at any available counter. Once you're settled, get up and survey your choices, then sit down and place one order from your waiter. There's a glistening raw bar, a burger joint, and a wood-burning pizza station where you can sample some of English's iconic pies, such as fig and prosciutto. It's one of the most varied and affordable daytime food options in an area of town that can still feel like a lunchtime wasteland.

The cavernous **Eataly** (✉ *200 5th Ave., at 23rd St.* ☎ *646/398–5100* ✣ *3:E2*), from Mario Batali & Co., is a temple of all things Italian. *(See the full listing in the Flatiron District.)*

16

a raucous celebratory dinner with flowing wine and festive banter. But be forewarned: if anyone in your party is hard of hearing, or bothered by loud rock music, choose someplace more sedate. [$] *Average main: $29* ✉ *110 Waverly Pl., between MacDougal St. and 6th Ave., Greenwich Village* ☎ *212/777–0303* 🌐 *www.babbonyc.com* *Reservations essential* ⏲ *No lunch Sun.–Mon.* [M] *A, B, C, D, E, F, M to W. 4th St.–Washington Sq.* ✣ *2:C1*

$ PIZZA FAMILY ✕ **Bleecker Street Pizza.** Flavor reigns at this bustling corner pizzeria. It's the perfect place to stop for a stand-up slice at the counter: the thin-crusted Nonna Maria is topped with garlicky marinara, grated and fresh mozzarella, and freshly grated Parmesan. [$] *Average main: $4* ✉ *69 7th Ave. S, at Bleecker St., West Village* ☎ *212/924–4466* 🌐 *bleekerstreetpizza.net* *Reservations not accepted* [M] *A, B, C, D, E, F, M to W. 4th St.–Washington Sq.* ✣ *2:C2.*

$$$ MODERN AMERICAN ✕ **Blue Hill.** This tasteful, sophisticated den of a restaurant—formerly a speakeasy—on a quiet side street maintains an impeccable reputation for excellence and consistency under the leadership of chef Dan Barber. The Obamas even stopped by here for dinner, shutting down the street for one of their "date nights." Part of the slow-food, sustainable-agriculture movement, Blue Hill mostly uses ingredients grown or raised within 200 miles, including the Four Season Farm at Stone Barns Center for Food and Agriculture, Barber's second culinary project in nearby Westchester County. The chefs produce precisely cooked and elegantly constructed food such as wild striped bass with potato-and-clam chowder and house-cured *guanciale* (pork jowl), and a smoked-tomato soup with American caviar. [$] *Average main: $29* ✉ *75 Washington Pl., between Washington Sq. W and 6th Ave., Greenwich Village* ☎ *212/539–1776*

www.bluehillfarm.com *Reservations essential* *No lunch* M *A, B, C, D, E, F, M to W. 4th St.–Washington Sq.* *2:C1*

$ AMERICAN **Gray's Papaya.** It's a stand-up, takeout dive. And, yes, limos do sometimes stop here for these legendary hot dogs. These traditional, juicy all-beef dogs are delicious, and quite the economical meal. The recession special is two hot dogs and a drink for $5. There are cheap breakfast offerings, too, like the quintessential egg-and-cheese on a roll. There is also a location at 72nd Street and Broadway, on the Upper West Side. $ *Average main: $6* *402 6th Ave., at W. 8th St., Greenwich Village* *212/260–3532* *Reservations not accepted* *No credit cards* M *A, B, C, D, E, F, M to W. 4th St.–Washington Sq.* *3:D5*

$ INDIAN **Kati Roll Company.** You can think of a kati roll as a South Asian taco: griddled parathas stuffed with savory-spiced grilled meat, shrimp, paneer, chickpea mash, or spiced mashed potato. They're the only things sold at this tiny, popular lunch spot cheerfully festooned with Bollywood posters. This is an excellent and inexpensive lunch option but be warned that lines often form at weekday lunch, and there are only a few seats, so a good plan is to take your kati roll to a nearby park bench. There's also a location at 39th Street and 6th Avenue. $ *Average main: $6* *99 MacDougal St., near Bleecker St., Greenwich Village* *212/730–4280* *www.thekatirollcompany.com* *Reservations not accepted* *No credit cards* M *A, C, B, D, E, F, M to W. 4th St.–Washington Sq.* *2:D2*

$ PIZZA **Keste Pizza & Vino.** At the back of the long, narrow Keste Pizza & Vino restaurant is a beautiful, tiled, wood-fired oven that cooks what might be Manhattan's most authentic Neapolitan pies at 1,000 degrees. Blistered and chewy around the edges, the Margherita pie gives way to a softer center pooled with San Marzano tomato sauce and house-made mozzarella. There are numerous pizza options, including white pies and ones with gluten-free crusts. This is a definite contender for best pizza in New York. The dining room is casual and the location means it's almost always busy. $ *Average main: $14* *271 Bleecker St., between 6th and 7th Aves., West Village* *212/243–1500* *www.kestepizzeria.com* *Reservations not accepted* M *A, B, C, D, E, F, M to W. 4th St.–Washington Sq.* *2:C2.*

$$ ITALIAN **Lupa.** Even the most hard-to-please connoisseurs have a soft spot for Lupa, Mario Batali and Joseph Bastianich's "downscale" Roman trattoria. Rough-hewn wood, great Italian wines, and simple preparations with top-quality ingredients define the restaurant, along with the "gentle" prices. People come repeatedly for dishes such as ricotta gnocchi with sweet-sausage ragout, house-made salumi, and sardines with golden raisins and pine nuts. The restaurant is split into two rooms: a boisterous space up front, where walk-ins are welcome; the back room is more intimate, for those with reservations, and feels something like you're dining in a culinary cocoon, in the best sense. $ *Average main: $22* *170 Thompson St., between Bleecker and W. Houston Sts., Greenwich Village* *212/982–5089* *www.luparestaurant.com* M *A, B, C, D, E, F, M to W. 4th St.–Washington Sq.* *2:D3*

$$ SEAFOOD **Mermaid Oyster Bar.** If you're craving a great raw bar, lobster roll, or soft-shell crab sandwich (in season), Mermaid Oyster Bar gives nearby

classics Mary's Fish Camp and Pearl Oyster Bar a run for their money. Almost every dish is a winner here, but the lobster bisque laced with Manzanilla sherry and toasted pumpkin seeds, the blackened striped bass with roasted squash and Swiss chard, and the spicy seafood bucatini fra diavolo are all standouts. From the bar, try something from the list of pitch-perfect cocktails, like a Dark and Stormy, made with black rum and ginger beer, or a Pimm's cooler with refreshing pieces of fresh cucumber. There are two other locations in Manhattan: on the Upper West Side and in the East Village. *Average main: $21 ⊠ 79 MacDougal St., at W. Houston St., Greenwich Village ☎ 212/260–0100 www.themermaidnyc.com No lunch* M *1 to Houston St.; C, E to Spring St. ⊕ 2:D2*

$$$ MODERN AMERICAN

✕ **Minetta Tavern.** By converting a moribund 80-year-old Italian restaurant into a cozy hot spot, restaurateur Keith McNally has created yet another hit. Try early and often to score reservations, so that you can sample creations like buttery trout meunière, bone marrow on toast, expertly aged steaks, and the celebrated Black Label burger, a gorgeous assembly of meat topped with caramelized onions and—for the brave—an added layer of cheese. The bar room, with its original details intact, is great for people watching. Landing a table in the back room, with its original mural depicting West Village life and wall-to-wall photos of famous and infamous customers from eras gone by, makes sweet-talking the reservationist worth your while. *Average main: HK$26 ⊠ 113 MacDougal St., between Bleecker and West 3rd Sts., Greenwich Village ☎ 212/475–3850 www.minettatavernny.com Reservations essential No lunch Mon.–Tues.* M *A, B, C, D, E, F, M to W. 4th St.–Washington Sq. ⊕ 2:D2*

16

$ AMERICAN FAMILY

✕ **Peanut Butter & Co. Sandwich Shop.** For a childhood classic kicked up a notch, head to Peanut Butter & Co. Sandwich Shop. You can go with a standard PB&J, or explore any of the menu's 20 options, including the Elvis (grilled with peanut butter, bananas, and honey), the Pregnant Lady (peanut butter and pickles), or the sandwich of the week, with expertly paired ingredients such as cherry jam, cream cheese, and Crunch Time peanut butter. Pair your sandwich with a milkshake—there are traditional flavors as well as more innovative combos. And of course there are peanut butter cookies for dessert, as well as sundaes. *Average main: $7 ⊠ 240 Sullivan St., near W. 3rd St., Greenwich Village ☎ 212/677–3995 ilovepeanutbutter.com Reservations not accepted* M *A, B, C, D, E, F, M to W. 4th St.–Washington Sq. ⊕ 2:D2.*

$ MIDDLE EASTERN

✕ **Taïm.** There's a real chef behind this tiny sliver of a restaurant, New York's only gourmet falafel stand. Taïm means "tasty" in Hebrew, and Tel Aviv transplant Einat Admony's fried chickpea balls are delicious, and available in several beguiling flavors (try them infused with spicy harissa sauce) along with a tantalizing display of à la carte salads (the carrots with Moroccan spices is a standout). There's also a location in NoLIta, on Spring Street between Mott and Mulberry, as well as a food truck that makes its way around the city (you can find it via Twitter). *Average main: $9 ⊠ 222 Waverly Pl., near Perry St., West Village ☎ 212/691–1287 www.taimfalafel.com Reservations not accepted No credit cards* M *1 to Christopher St.–Sheridan Sq. ⊕ 2:B1*

WEST VILLAGE

Many of the Village's culinary gems lie tucked away on side streets and alleyways, especially west of 7th Avenue, in the West Village. The vibe here is low-key and friendly, with patrons squeezed together at tiny tables in matchbox-size eateries.

$$$ MODERN ASIAN ✕ **Annisa.** After a fire gutted this chic West Village restaurant in 2009, celebrity chef and co-owner Anita Lo has bounced back stronger than ever. "Annisa" may mean "the women" in Arabic, but the food here is inspired by Asia. And it's top notch. Foie gras soup dumplings, barbequed squid with basil and peanuts, and Japanese curry-spiked rabbit are just a few winning examples you might find on the menu here. But be sure to save room for dessert: the pecan and salted butterscotch beignets with bourbon ice cream are good enough to make you enroll in the fire academy to protect the place from another fire. *Average main: $30 ✉ 13 Barrow St., between W. 4th and 7th Ave. S, West Village ☎ 212/741–6699 🌐 www.annisarestaurant.com Ⓜ 1 to Christopher St.–Sheridan Sq. ✥ 2:C2*

$$$ EUROPEAN ✕ **August.** Rustic simplicity is the theme at this bustling West Village eatery, where many of the dishes come from the wood-burning oven in the dining room. Fish is always a good choice here, be it baked skate or pan-roasted cod, and meaty entrées like the pork chop or dry-aged sirloin are excellently cooked. Starters are more inventive; try the tarte flambé, an Alsatian flatbread topped with onion, bacon, and crème fraîche. Wood floors and an arched cork ceiling envelop the busy 40-seat dining room; you can also dine at the bar. For a quieter meal, ask for a table in the glass-enclosed 15-seat atrium in back. *Average main: $34 ✉ 359 Bleecker St., at Charles St., West Village ☎ 212/929–8727 🌐 www.augustny.com Reservations essential Ⓜ 1 to Christopher St.–Sheridan Sq.; A, B, C, D, E, F, M to W. 4th St.–Washington Sq. ✥ 3:C5*

$$ ITALIAN ✕ **Barbuto.** Chef Jonathan Waxman made a name for himself with his French-inspired California cuisine. Barbuto specializes in rustic preparations with bright flavors, like house-made duck sausage with creamy polenta, red-wine-braised short ribs, and pasta carbonara, though the menu changes daily, depending on what's available. The chef's acclaimed roasted chicken is usually on the menu in one form or another. The airy, sophisticated space continues to get busy so make a reservation. The restaurant is particularly pleasant in nice weather when the giant garage-door-like windows open onto the street and you can watch the neighborhood go by. *Average main: $17 ✉ 775 Washington St., between Jane and W. 12th Sts., West Village ☎ 212/924–9700 🌐 www.barbutonyc.com Ⓜ A, C, E to 14th St.; L to 8th Ave.; 1 to Christopher St.–Sheridan Sq. ✥ 3:B5*

$$$ ECLECTIC ✕ **Blue Ribbon Bakery.** A neighborhood standard for good, if expensive, food, this outpost of the Blue Ribbon empire has an eclectic menu featuring substantial sandwiches on homemade bread (freshly baked on site), small plates, legendary bread pudding, and entrées that span the globe, from hummus to grilled catfish with sautéed collards and sweet potatoes. The cavelike basement dining room is dark and intimate; upstairs is more open, with large windows looking out onto a pretty West Village corner. Brunch is notoriously crowded. *Average main:*

$25 ✉ 35 Downing St., at Bedford St., Greenwich Village ☎ 212/337–0404 🌐 www.blueribbonrestaurants.com Ⓜ 1 to Houston St.; A, B, C, D, E, F, M to W. 4th St.–Washington Sq. ✣ 2:C2

$$$$ MODERN AMERICAN **Commerce.** This former speakeasy harks back to days gone by with its Diego Rivera–style murals, vintage sconces, and restored subway tiles, but the crowd really comes for chef Harold Moore's seasonal cuisine. Appetizers range from a red cabbage, apple, and pecan salad to yuzu-marinated hamachi ceviche. Entrées are just as vibrant: bright, sweet peas offset pristine halibut, and the shareable roast chicken, presented table-side, is served with foie-gras bread stuffing. Brunch has a Middle Eastern influence, with scrambled eggs and hummus atop a pillowy pita, and a mean *shakshuka*—baked eggs nestled in a pepper, onion, and tomato sauce. Even the contents of the bread basket are a pleasure here. For a quieter meal, choose one of the booths near the bar. *$ Average main: $36 ✉ 50 Commerce St., West Village ☎ 212/524–2301 🌐 www.commercerestaurant.com ⏲ No lunch Ⓜ 1 to Christopher St.–Sheridan Sq.; A, B, C, D, E, F, M to W. 4th St.–Washington Sq. ✣ 2:B2*

$$$ ITALIAN **dell'anima.** Lines still snake out the door of this neighborhood favorite so it's a good idea to make a reservation. Once you're in, check out the open kitchen, where the stylish crowd converges to watch chefs prepare authentic Italian dishes with a modern twist. Starters might include sweetbreads, bone marrow, or charred octopus with chorizo, while traditional first courses like pasta alla carbonara with *speck* (smoked and cured pork), egg, and pecorino are impeccable. The signature *pollo al diavolo* (spicy chicken) with broccoli rabe, garlic, and chili is seared with enough smoke and heat for all seasons. Anfora, their wine bar next door, is good for an after-dinner drink if you want to linger. Brunch is served on weekends. *$ Average main: $26 ✉ 38 8th Ave., at Jane St., West Village ☎ 212/366–6633 🌐 www.dellanima.com ⏲ No lunch weekdays Ⓜ A, C, E to 14th St.; L to 8th Ave. ✣ 3:C5*

$ SEAFOOD **Ditch Plains.** Named for a surf spot in Montauk, this laid-back neighborhood restaurant serves an eclectic bill of beachfront fare—from fish tacos, lobster rolls, and fish-and-chips to clam chowder and crab dip. There are options for landlubbers and vegetarians, too. It's not quite a beach shack, but the food and the setting, with an upbeat rock soundtrack, are designed for conviviality, and the wine-list prices are extremely friendly, with whole and half bottles sold just above cost. The bloody marys are recommended, too. Breakfast or brunch is served every day from 11 am. *$ Average main: $14 ✉ 29 Bedford St., near Downing St., West Village ☎ 212/633–0202 🌐 www.ditch-plains.com ✍ Reservations not accepted Ⓜ 1 to Houston St. ✣ 2:C3*

$$ KOREAN **Do Hwa.** If anyone in New York is responsible for making Korean food cool, it is the mother-daughter team behind this chic and popular restaurant and its East Village sister, Dok Suni's. Jenny Kwak and her mother, Myung Ja, serve home cooking in the form of *kalbi jim* (braised short ribs), *bibimbop* (a spicy, mix-it-yourself vegetable-and-rice dish), and other favorites that may not be as pungent as they are in Little Korea but are satisfying nevertheless—and the atmosphere is definitely more sophisticated. The bar, where movies are projected onto the side wall, gets pretty happening, too. *$ Average main: $23 ✉ 55 Carmine*

16

St., between Bedford St. and 7th Ave., West Village ☎ *212/414–1224* 🌐 *www.dohwanyc.com* ⏲ *No lunch weekends* Ⓜ *1 to Houston St.; A, B, C, D, E, F, M to W. 4th St.–Washington Sq.* ✣ *2:C2*

$$ MEXICAN Fodor'sChoice ★ ✕ **Empellón Taqueria.** Chef Alex Stupak worked for years as the wizard-like pastry chef at wd~50, New York's premier home to molecular gastronomy, so when he departed that restaurant to open—wait for it—a taqueria, many Manhattan diners either scratched their heads or wondered if they'd be served deconstructed tacos. Instead, they got simple yet well-executed tacos using top-notch ingredients. There are straightforward options—fish tempura, lamb, steak—as well as surprising (as in surprisingly good) variations, like tacos with sweetbreads and chorizo gravy, or with pork and masa spaetzle. There are, of course, also several variations on the margarita theme, too, including one using the Japanese citrus, *yuzu*. Empellon isn't really south-of-the-border in its authenticity but when it's this good, who cares? $ *Average main: $20* ✉ *230 W. 4th St., at W. 10th St., West Village* ☎ *212/367 0999* 🌐 *www.empellon.com* Ⓜ *1 to Christopher St.–Sheridan Sq.* ✣ *2:B1*

$ MALAYSIAN Fodor'sChoice ★ ✕ **Fatty Crab.** This rustic Malaysian cantina showcases the exciting cuisine of chef Zak Pelaccio, who spent years cooking at famous French restaurants before escaping to Southeast Asia for a year, where he fell in love with the flavors of the region. Start with the addictive pickled watermelon and crispy pork salad, an improbable combination that's both refreshing and decadent. The can't-miss signature dish is chili crab—cracked Dungeness crab in a pool of rich, spicy chili sauce, served with bread for dipping. It's messy for sure, but worth rolling up your sleeves. The small space fills up quickly and be warned that the tables are practically on top of each other, but it's lots of fun. $ *Average main: $15* ✉ *643 Hudson St., between Gansevoort and Horatio Sts., West Village* ☎ *212/352–3592* 🌐 *www.fattycrab.com* ✍ *Reservations not accepted* Ⓜ *A, C, E to 14th St.; L to 8th Ave.* ✣ *3:B4*

$$$ ECLECTIC ✕ **Fedora.** Up until 2011, subterranean Fedora was an ancient, little-patronized restaurant with an even more ancient owner (for whom the restaurant was named). But charming Fedora has left the building and restaurateur Gabe Stulman took over the spot, vowing to keep the place largely intact—or at least the decor. Now, see-and-be-scene folk cram the long narrow space munching on French Canadian–accented fare like garlic cream–topped duck breast and scallops paired with bone marrow and sipping cocktails such as the signature Fedora Dorato, named for the erstwhile owner: Scotch, Cynar, and Cocchi Americano. Fedora (the restaurant) will never be the same and that may be a good thing. $ *Average main: $25* ✉ *239 W. 4th St., between Charles and W. 10th Sts., West Village* ☎ *646/449–9336* 🌐 *www.fedoranyc.com* Ⓜ *1 to Christopher St.–Sheridan Sq.* ✣ *2:B1*

$$ ITALIAN ✕ **Frankies Spuntino.** The Frankies—that is, owners and chefs Frank Falcinelli and Frank Castronovo—have a winning formula and their fourth New York restaurant seems to exemplify it best: serve hearty, not-necessarily-by-the-book, Italian-inflected fare using local, organic, and humanely raised ingredients in a laid-back atmosphere. Most menu items change seasonally but expect pasta dishes with standout sauces like almond pesto or ravioli stuffed with sweet potato. The large menu

also includes crostini, fresh salads, cured meats, and cheese plates. It's a casual, family-friendly, neighborhood spot. *Average main: $18* ✉ *570 Hudson St., at W. 11th St., West Village* ☎ *212/924–0818* 🌐 *www.frankiesspuntino.com* Ⓜ *A, C, E to 14th St.; L to 8th Ave.* ✥ *2:B1*

$$$ ITALIAN Fodor's Choice ★ **I Sodi.** In a city of what seems like a million Italian restaurants, this minimalist-designed, Tuscan-focused eatery in the West Village is a real find. Spikey-haired owner, Rita Sodi, a Florentine who formerly worked in the fashion industry, ensures the traditional fare coming from the kitchen is satisfying. The menu changes weekly based on seasonal ingredients but expect a bevy of pasta dishes topped with good stuff like duck ragu and artichoke-laced lasagna, as well as not-very-Lipitor-friendly pancetta-wrapped pork and rabbit. Hoist a glass of grappa at the end of the meal and be happy you're in the right place. *Average main: $25* ✉ *105 Christopher St., between Bleecker and Hudson Sts., West Village* ☎ *212/414–5774* 🌐 *www.isodinyc.com* Ⓜ *1 to Christopher St.–Sheridan Sq.* ✥ *2:B2*

$$ MODERN AMERICAN **The Little Owl.** This tiny neighborhood joint, with seating for 28 people, is exceptionally eager to please—and attitude, along with the food, is a winning combination. The menu is congruently small, which actually makes it easier to decide what you want. And what you want are the pork-veal-beef-pecorino-cheese meatball "sliders," or miniburgers. The unusually juicy pork loin chop, served with Parmesan butter beans and wild dandelion greens, is gigantic, and hugely satisfying. Raspberry-filled beignets, served with a ramekin of warm Nutella, are otherworldly. It's quintessential West Village: quirky and wonderful. *Average main: $24* ✉ *90 Bedford St., at Grove St., West Village* ☎ *212/741–4695* 🌐 *www.thelittleowlnyc.com* *Reservations essential* Ⓜ *1 to Christopher St.–Sheridan Sq.; A, B, C, D, E, F, M to W. 4th St.–Washington Sq.* ✥ *3:C6*

$$ SEAFOOD **Mary's Fish Camp.** Diners still line up down the street before the restaurant opens for dinner to get a table at this small but bustling seafood shack. The result of a split between Pearl Oyster Bar's partners, Mary's is a more intimate space, but the two have similar menus: excellent fried oysters, chowders, and, of course, the sweet lobster roll with crisp fries, all of which will have you licking your fingers. The killer hot fudge sundae is worth saving room for. The staff here are warm and friendly, too. This is the kind of place everyone wishes was in their neighborhood. *Average main: $21* ✉ *64 Charles St., at W. 4th St., West Village* ☎ *646/486–2185* 🌐 *marysfishcamp.com* *Reservations not accepted* *Closed Sun.* Ⓜ *1 to Christopher St.–Sheridan Sq.* ✥ *2:B1*

$ MEXICAN **Mexicana Mama.** This small, colorful, and popular space serves vividly flavored fare and the kitchen is serious enough to create four different salsas daily. The tomato-habanero salsa is simply unforgettable; cream tames the habaneros, but only slightly. Three chili-roasted pork tacos are also filled with piquant Chihuahua cheese and black beans, and served over Mexican rice and avocado cubes. Quesadillas are made with fresh corn tortillas, filled with that melted Chihuahua cheese and your choice of chicken, barbacoa beef, chicken mole, or a daily special vegetable filling. For dessert, look no further than the eggy flan in flavors like caramel or cinnamon. *Average main: $13* ✉ *525 Hudson*

16

St., near Charles St., West Village ☎ 212/924–4119 ▭ No credit cards ⏲ Closed Mon. Ⓜ 1 to Christopher St.–Sheridan Sq.; A, B, C, D, E, F, M to W. 4th St.–Washington Sq. ✣ 3:C6

$ MIDDLE EASTERN **Moustache.** There's typically a crowd waiting outside for one of the copper-top tables at this casual Middle Eastern neighborhood restaurant. The focal point is the perfect pita that accompanies tasty salads like lemony chickpea and spinach, hearty lentil and bulgur, or falafel. Also delicious is *lahambajin,* spicy ground lamb on a crispy flat crust. For entrées, try the leg of lamb or merguez sausage sandwiches. Service is slow but friendly. There are also locations in the East Village and in East Harlem. *$ Average main: $12 ✉ 90 Bedford St., between Barrow and Grove Sts., West Village ☎ 212/229–2220 🌐 moustachepitza.com ✍ Reservations not accepted ▭ No credit cards Ⓜ 1 to Christopher St.–Sheridan Sq. ✣ 2:B2*

$$$ SEAFOOD **Pearl Oyster Bar.** There have been many imitators and few real competitors to this West Village seafood institution. Since 1997, Rebecca Charles has been serving arguably the best lobster roll in New York City in a no-frills space down charming, restaurant-lined Cornelia Street—and expanded next door to accommodate the throngs. But that's not the only reason you should cast your net here. Pan-roasted sea scallops and plus-size crab cakes may compete with the legendary lobster roll for your taste buds' attention. Service is very efficient; you might even say rushed. *$ Average main: $25 ✉ 18 Cornelia St., between W. 4th and Bleecker Sts., West Village ☎ 212/691–8211 🌐 www.pearloysterbar.com ⏲ Closed Sun. Ⓜ A, B, C, D, E, F, M to W. 4th St.–Washington Sq. ✣ 2:C2*

$$$ CHINESE **RedFarm.** Conceived and run by Ed Schoenfeld, an expert on Chinese cuisine, and Joe Ng, known as the dumpling king of New York, this second-floor West Village restaurant specializes in—you guessed it—Chinese-style dumplings. At least partly. The menu focuses mostly on dim sum—small plates and snacks (often in dumpling form)—as well as Chinese-American dishes like three-chili chicken and chicken in garlic sauce. The lobster dumplings and the crab and pork soup dumplings are culinary wonders and nearly obligatory for first timers. But come with a wallet the size of China itself because the dishes add up. *$ Average main: $29 ✉ 529 Hudson St., between W. 10th and Charles Sts., West Village ☎ 212/792–9700 🌐 redfarmnyc.com Ⓜ 1 to Christopher St.–Sheridan Sq.; A, C, E to 14th St.; L to 8th Ave. ✣ 2:B2*

Snack Taverna. *Branch location at 63 Bedford Street, at Morton. See SoHo for full review.*

$$ BRITISH **The Spotted Pig.** Part cozy English pub, part laid-back neighborhood hangout, part gastronome's lure, the Spotted Pig showcases the impeccable food of the now legendary London chef April Bloomfield (Mario Batali and his partners consulted). Pair the tang of radishes in a salad with plenty of Parmesan and arugula, or smoked haddock–and-corn chowder with homemade crackers for studies in contrasts in texture and flavor. Shoestring potatoes accompany the Roquefort cheeseburger. Chase it with a glass of foam-dripping Old Speckled Hen. This neighborhood hangout still packs it in, so come early, or late. The Breslin is another of Bloomfield's standout New York restaurants with an

überclubby feel. *Average main: $23 ✉ 314 W. 11th St., at Greenwich St., West Village ☎ 212/620–0393 www.thespottedpig.com Reservations not accepted* Ⓜ *A, C, E to 14th St.; L to 8th Ave. ⊕ 2:A1*

$$$ AUSTRIAN **Wallsé.** The modern Austrian menu at Kurt Gutenbrunner's lovely, light-filled neighborhood restaurant has a strong emphasis on Austrian tradition and urban New York attitude. It's hard to argue with such dishes as Wiener schnitzel with potato-cucumber salad and lingonberries, or venison goulash with spaetzle and Brussels sprouts, and it's often lighter than you'd think Austrian food would be. Desserts do Vienna proud: apple-walnut strudel is served with apple sorbet. The atmosphere is casual but sophisticated—perfect for either a week night dinner or a special occasion. *Average main: $33 ✉ 344 W. 11th St., at Washington St., West Village ☎ 212/352–2300 www.wallse.com Reservations essential No lunch weekdays* Ⓜ *1 to Christopher St.–Sheridan Sq.; A, C, E to 14th St.; L to 8th Ave. ⊕ 3:B6*

$ AMERICAN FAMILY **Westville.** If New York's neighborhoods were small country towns, they'd all have restaurants just like Westville. These adorable spots—with branches in the East and West Village, Chelsea, and west SoHo—serve simple wholesome fare, at reasonable prices. Salads, grilled chicken, burgers, and chops are all good, but the seasonal sides, which change daily based on what's fresh at the market, are the real star attractions (the "Market Plate" with any three sides is a popular dinner option). Dessert is worth saving room for, too, especially the daily pie selections. *Average main: $11 ✉ 210 W. 10th St., near Bleecker St., West Village ☎ 212/741–7971 www.westvillenyc.com* Ⓜ *1 to Christopher St.–Sheridan Sq. ⊕ 3:C6*

16

CHELSEA AND THE MEATPACKING DISTRICT

CHELSEA

Chelsea is a calm neighborhood filled with art galleries and casual eateries. Subway stops are few and far between once you get west of 8th Avenue, so be prepared to walk or take a cab. One of the neighborhood's main highlights is the High Line, an elevated park that towers over the neighborhood.

$ PIZZA Fodor's Choice ★ **Co.** "Company," as it's pronounced, took the New York pizza scene by red-sauce-scented storm when it opened in early 2009. Bread master Jim Lahey, who made a name for himself at the Sullivan Street Baking Company, crafts simple but memorable pies, the dough and crust of which play a starring role. The simple Margherita (tomato sauce, mozzarella, basil) is a good way to sample Co.'s fare, but diners are always tempted by unorthodox pizzas like the caramelized-onion-walnut-puree pie, or the béchamel-and-Parmesan-topped version. If you can, take a few friends, so you can order several pies. This casual Chelsea pizzeria is anything but half baked. *Average main: $15 ✉ 230 9th Ave., at W. 24th St., Chelsea ☎ 212/243–1105 www.co-pane.com No lunch Mon.* Ⓜ *C, E to 23rd St. ⊕ 3:B2*

$$$ AMERICAN **Cookshop.** One of far-west Chelsea's first hot restaurants, Cookshop (from the same team as Five Points and Hundred Acres) manages a casual elegance while focusing on seasonal, farm-fresh cuisine that

continues to wow. Outdoor seating on 10th Avenue is quite peaceful in the evening; during the day you can survey a cross-section of gallery-hoppers and shoppers. Divine cocktails, made with fresh fruit juices, are veritable elixirs of well-being. Line up early for brunch; it's worth the wait for dishes like baked eggs over duck and Swiss chard, or the fluffiest pancakes in town. Dinner is also a triumph, with a variety of perfectly prepared dishes like whitefish with lemony asparagus and hen-of-the-woods mushrooms or a simply roasted chicken. $ *Average main: $26* ✉ *156 10th Ave., at 20th St., Chelsea* ☎ *212/924–4440* 🌐 *www.cookshopny.com* M *A, C, E to 23rd St.* ⊕ *3:A3*

WORD OF MOUTH

"On our last trip one of the highlights was sitting outside on the patio (actually, the sidewalk) of a restaurant in Chelsea, eating and people-watching. We would have sat in that seat for hours if they'd let us!"—Austin

$ ECLECTIC ✕ **Coppelia.** Named for a legendary ice cream shop in Havana, Coppelia is neither Cuban nor an ice cream parlor. At least not strictly speaking. Chef Julian Medina has created a 24-hour pan-Latin diner that works on many levels—for a quick breakfast, a casual lunch, or a post-club late-night bite. The continent-sized menu emphasizes comfort food, with satisfying dishes like the pork belly spiked mac 'n' cheese, mountainous nachos, grilled cheese with jalapeño and bacon, and even kimchi-stuffed tacos. And if you had your *corazon* set on ice cream, there's plenty of it on the dessert menu. $ *Average main: $15* ✉ *207 W. 14th St., between 7th and 8th Aves., Chelsea, New York* ☎ *212/858–5001* 🌐 *www.ybandco.com* M *1, 2, 3 to 14th St.* ⊕ *3:C4*

$ CHINESE ✕ **Legend.** Sure, there's nothing Chinese about the generic name; and the location, on a stretch of 7th Avenue in Chelsea, is flanked by forgettable eating options. But do your taste buds a favor and eat at this affordable Sichuan spot, whose quiet opening was followed by a lot of buzz among New York's fooderati. The long menu is not for the indecisive but nearly anything is a hit, including the double-cooked bacon, the massive and flaky whole roasted fish, and the ultra-spicy ma po tofu. Dishes here lean toward the fiery side so be prepared. $ *Average main: $14* ✉ *88 7th Ave., between 15th and 16th Sts., Chelsea, New York* ☎ *212/929–1778* 🌐 *www.legendrestaurant88.com* M *1, 2, 3 to 14th St.* ⊕ *3:C4*

$$$ MODERN AMERICAN ✕ **The Red Cat.** Elegant yet unpretentious, a lovely neighborhood spot *and* a destination restaurant, the Red Cat and its American-meets-Mediterranean menu is a great place for a long chat with a friend, to celebrate an auspicious occasion, to have a business dinner, or just the kind of place to go for an excellent meal. The menu changes frequently, based on what's in season, but expect an eclectic menu of well-executed pastas, burgers, saffron-laced seafood, and meaty numbers. Factor in the affordable wine list and you'll most definitely feel like one lucky cat. $ *Average main: $25* ✉ *227 10th Ave., between W. 23rd and W. 24th Sts., Chelsea* ☎ *212/242–1122* 🌐 *www.redcatrestaurants.com* M *C, E to 23rd St.* ⊕ *3:A2*

$$ SWISS ✕ **Trestle on Tenth.** Cozy and warm with an inviting exposed brick interior, this Swiss brasserie is a true west Chelsea neighborhood spot.

Locals and gallery hoppers quaff foamy beers or glasses of wine from the reasonable list while awaiting hearty Alpine-inspired dishes. Crispy duck necks, calves' liver with potato rösti and butter lettuce with bacon are fan favorites here. It's not art—for that, hit up one of the many galleries in the neighborhood—but it will make you yearn for Alpine landscapes. The location is convenient to the High Line. *Average main: $20 ✉ 242 10th Ave., at W. 24th St., Chelsea ☎ 212/645–5659 www.trestleontenth.com* Ⓜ *C, E to 23rd St. ⊕ 3:A2*

$ SPANISH Fodor's Choice ★

Tía Pol. It may be small, dark, and somewhat out-of-the-way, but none of that stops this popular tapas bar from being packed most nights (a sardine-can metaphor would be particularly apt here), with good reason. This is one of the best tapas spots in town, with a welcoming vibe, a dozen reasonably priced Spanish wines by the glass, and charm to spare. One of their most original tapas has become a signature here: bittersweet chocolate smeared on a baguette disc and topped with salty Spanish chorizo. *Patatas bravas* (rough-cut potatoes served with spicy aioli) are so addictive, you won't want to share them. The pork loin, piquillo pepper, and mild tetilla cheese sandwich is scrumptious, and so is the Galician octopus terrine. In fact, everything on the menu is delicious. *Average main: $12 ✉ 205 10th Ave., between 22nd and 23rd Sts., Chelsea ☎ 212/675–8805 www.tiapol.com Reservations essential No lunch Mon.* Ⓜ *C, E to 23rd St. ⊕ 3:A2*

$$ SOUTHERN

Tipsy Parson. If New York's Chelsea neighborhood were magically transported to the American South, it might taste something like the Tipsy Parson, a hip southern-accented eatery with a menu of artery-hardening delights. Named for a boozy southern dessert, the TP and its menu are all about comfort in the belly and soul: fried pickles, homemade peanut butter with crackers, bourbon-laced chicken liver mouse, and seafood pot pie are designed to make you leave full and happy. The restaurant's close proximity to the High Line means you can walk it all off afterward. *Average main: $24 ✉ 156 9th Ave., between W. 19th and W. 20th Sts., Chelsea ☎ 212/620–4545 www.tipsyparson.com* Ⓜ *C, E to 23rd St. ⊕ 3:B3*

MEATPACKING DISTRICT

For a glitzy scene, head to the Meatpacking District, which has transformed in recent years from a gritty commercial warehouse area to the celebrity chef–driven epicenter of the city's dining scene. The vibe is flashy, favored by Europeans, actors, models, and their suitors.

$$$$ ITALIAN

Del Posto. Much more formal than Babbo, Del Posto is Mario Batali's grown-up venue (in partnership with Lidia and Joe Bastianich), and the dining room—with its sweeping staircase, formal decor, and live tinkling from a baby grand—has the feel of an opulent hotel lobby. This is one of the most consistently dazzling special-occasion spots in the city and the food is stellar. There are a variety of set menus to choose from (no à la carte): pitch-perfect risotto is made fresh to order for two people or more; meat dishes like roasted veal chops are standout, and pastas are ethereal—all with Old World table-side service. For a smaller taste of the experience, come for a cocktail and sample the bargain bar menu. *Average main: $60 ✉ 85 10th Ave., between 15th*

Francophiles and fashionistas flock to Pastis, a brasserie in the Meatpacking District.

and 16th Sts., Meatpacking District ☎ *212/497–8090* 🌐 *www.delposto.com* ⏲ *No lunch Tues.–Sat.* Ⓜ *A, C, E to 14th St.; L to 8th Ave.* ✥ *3:A4*

$$$ BISTRO Fodor's Choice ★ ✕ **Pastis.** Long a mainstay in the Meatpacking District, Pastis looks like it was shipped in, tile by nicotine-stained tile, from Paris's Pigalle neighborhood. French favorites are front-and-center, including toothsome steak frites with béarnaise, mussels steamed in Pernod, and a tasty apple tartlet with phyllo crust. The people-watching is stellar, and there's a still a good chance you'll see a local celebrity or two. Tables outside in nice weather are prime real estate. Locals and visitors are still drawn to this neighborhood mainstay so it gets busy at mealtimes. At press time, there was talk that Pastis will be closed for renovations between January and September of 2014. 💲 *Average main: $27* ✉ *9 9th Ave., at Little W. 12th St., Meatpacking District* ☎ *212/929–4844* 🌐 *www.pastisny.com* Ⓜ *A, C, E to 14th St.; L to 8th Ave.* ✥ *3:B4*

$$$ ITALIAN ✕ **Scarpetta.** Chef Scott Conant left L'Impero and Alto to open Scarpetta, a critical darling since day one, adjacent to the glitz of the Meatpacking District. Walk past the bar into the polished dining room, where orange belts loop around mirrors and a retractable roof ushers in natural light. For a rousing start, try the creamy, rich polenta and mushrooms before enjoying one of the house-made pastas, like the al dente tagliatelle laced with strands of tender lamb ragout or his signature spaghetti with tomato sauce. Save room for dessert: the Amadei chcocolate cake with burnt-caramel gelato brings à la mode to a whole new level. 💲 *Average main: $29* ✉ *355 W. 14th St., at 9th Ave., Meatpacking District* ☎ *212/691–0555* 🌐 *www.scarpettanyc.com* ⏲ *No lunch* Ⓜ *A, C, E to 14th St.; L to 8th Ave.* ✥ *3:B4*

$$ ASIAN **Spice Market.** Set in a cavernous space amid embroidered curtains and artifacts from Burma, India, and Malaysia, chef Jean-Georges Vongerichten's playful take on Southeast Asian street food will keep you asking the waiters for information: what exactly was in that? Sometimes the playfulness works, sometimes it doesn't, but don't miss the steamed lobster with garlic, ginger, and dried chili, or the squid salad with papaya and cashews. This may not be the hottest new restaurant on the block anymore but it's still a fun Meatpacking venue with food that doesn't disappoint. *Average main: $22 ⊠ 403 W. 13th St., at 9th Ave., Meatpacking District ☎ 212/675–2322 www.spicemarketnewyork.com Reservations essential M A, C, E to 14th St.; L to 8th Ave. ⊕ 3:B4*

$$$$ AMERICAN **The Standard Grill.** Hotelier Andre Balasz created a scene for celebs, fashion-industry insiders, and the common folk, too, who all cluster at this buzzy restaurant inside the Standard Hotel. In warm weather the spacious outdoor seating area is perfect for sampling creative cocktails; there's an indoor bar too, and two dining rooms—a casual one in front and a larger room in back, with a floor whimsically made up of thousands of glittering pennies. The menu is comfort-luxe, with dishes like roast chicken for two in a cast-iron skillet and delicious moist trout with a currant-and-pine nut relish. For dessert, there's a nearly obscene chocolate mousse that comes with four silicone spatulas in lieu of spoons. A late-night menu is offered until 4 am. *Average main: $57 ⊠ 848 Washington St., between Little W. 12th and 13th Sts., Meatpacking District ☎ 212/645–4100 www.thestandardgrill.com M A, C, E to 14th St.; L to 8th Ave. ⊕ 3:B4*

16

UNION SQUARE WITH THE FLATIRON DISTRICT AND GRAMERCY

FLATIRON DISTRICT

Some of the city's most popular restaurants are in the area northwest of Union Square, called the Flatiron District. The neighborhood is also a hot shopping destination, with plenty of refueling spots like City Bakery, a gourmet deli and sweets spot that's a standby for many New Yorkers.

$$$ ITALIAN Fodor's Choice ★ **A Voce.** Executive chef Missy Robbins has a passion for Italian cuisine, and it shows. The American-born Robbins honed her Italian chops in northern Italy at the acclaimed Agli Amici restaurant in Friuli and also spent five years as the executive chef at Chicago's Spiaggia. At A Voce, her menu is inspired by regional dishes from all over Italy. The pasta is prepared fresh every day, and the fish and meat dishes are exceptional. The *agnello in due modi* entrée is especially well prepared, with tender lamb chops and a flavorful vegetable *soffrito*. For dessert, try the Tuscan doughnuts with dark-chocolate dipping sauce. The attentive staff add to the pleasurable dining experience. The dining room has a retro Italian feel to it—with pale green leather-top tables and Eames chairs—and additional seating on the patio when weather permits. *Average main: $27 ⊠ 41 Madison Ave., between 25th and 26th Sts., Flatiron District ☎ 212/545–8555 www.avocerestaurant.com M N, R to 23rd St. ⊕ 3:F2*

$$$ AMERICAN

ABC Kitchen. Much more than a shopping break, Jean Georges Vongerichten's popular restaurant, inside posh housewares emporium ABC Carpet and Home, is more like a love letter to greenmarket cuisine. Underneath the exposed concrete beams, a chic crowd devours fresh, flavorful appetizers like the roasted carrot salad with avocado, crème fraîche, and toasted pumpkin seeds or sweet baby Maine shrimp with a sprinkling of sea salt and horseradish. There are whole-wheat pizzas as well as entrées like a well-charred steak served with a lusty red-wine-and-carrot puree or a pristine fillet of arctic char served with Romanesco cauliflower. The restaurant is committed to all the right causes—environmentalism, sustainability, supporting local farmers—all of which are announced in a near manifesto-length list on the back of the menu; thankfully, ABC Kitchen pulls it off without seeming patronizing or preachy. *Average main: $27 35 E. 18th St., between Broadway and Park Ave. S, Flatiron District 212/475–5829 www.abckitchennyc.com Reservations essential L, N, Q, R, 4, 5, 6 to 14th St.–Union Square 3:F3.*

$$$ MEDITERRANEAN Fodor's Choice ★

Aldea. Bouley alumnus George Mendes has opened a restaurant that uses his Portuguese heritage as inspiration and rises to new heights. Although there are no bad seats in this sleek bilevel space decorated with touches of wood, glass, and blue accents, watching Mendes work in his spotless tiled kitchen from one of the seats at the chef's counter in the back is undeniably exciting. *Petiscos* (small bites) like cubes of crisp pork belly with apple cider and caramelized endive and an earthy pork-and-duck terrine reveal sophisticated cooking techniques and flavors. A delicate matsutake mushroom broth floated with a slow-poached egg is edged with a subtle brace of pine. On the $85 six-course chef's tasting menu, the sea urchin on a crispy toast flat is a standout, as is the duck confit with chorizo and crunchy duck-skin cracklings. *Average main: $31 31 W. 17th St., between 5th and 6th Aves., Flatiron District 212/675–7223 www.aldearestaurant.com Reservations essential Closed Sun. No lunch Sat. L, N, Q, R, 4, 5, 6 to 14th St.–Union Sq.; F, M to 14th St. 3:E3*

$$ SPANISH

Boqueria. Perenially packed, this convivial tapas spot has leather banquettes lining the main room but if you want to make friends, opt for the communal table running down the center of the dining room—if you can get a seat. There are a few seats at the bar, too. Fried quail eggs and chorizo on roasted bread are even better than they sound, and the mushroom and ham croquettes are a mainstay. Traditional churros come with a thick hot chocolate for dipping. The original spot in the Flatiron District was so popular it spawned an offshoot in SoHo, at 171 Spring Street. *Average main: $19 53 W. 19th St., between 5th and 6th Aves., Flatiron District 212/255–4160 www.boquerianyc.com Reservations not accepted 6, F, M, N, R to 23rd St. 3:E3*

$$$ BRITISH Fodor's Choice ★

The Breslin Bar and Dining Room. A sceney meatopia inside the ever-trendy Ace Hotel, the Breslin is not for the Lipitor crowd. English chef April Bloomfield, who also runs the John Dory right next door and the excellent Spotted Pig in the West Village, hardens arteries with peanuts fried in pork fat, whipped lardo on pizza bianca, blood sausage accompanied by a fried duck egg, and a delicious feta-topped lamb burger. The dimly lighted, wood-bedecked interior is like a culinary womb, inspiring thoughts of planting yourself there all day or night nursing pints of cask-conditioned ale or Scotch-based cocktails. And you wouldn't be the first (or last) to have actually done it. *Average main: $30* *20 W. 29th St., at Broadway, Flatiron District* *212/679–1939* *N, R to 28th St.* *3:E1*

$ AMERICAN FAMILY Fodor's Choice ★ **The City Bakery.** This self-service bakery-restaurant has the urban aesthetic to match its name. Chef-owner Maury Rubin's baked goods—giant cookies; addictively flaky, salty-sweet pretzel croissants; elegant caramel tarts—are unfailingly rich and outstandingly delicious, but another major draw is the salad bar. It may seem overpriced, but the large selection of impeccably fresh food, including whole sides of baked salmon, roasted vegetables, soups, and several Asian-accented dishes, delivers bang for the buck. Much of the produce comes from the nearby farmers' market. In winter the bakery hosts a hot-chocolate festival; in summer it's lemonade time. *Average main: $12* *3 W. 18th St., between 5th and 6th Aves., Flatiron District* *212/366–1414* *www.thecitybakery.com* *Reservations not accepted* *No dinner* *L, N, Q, R, 4, 5, 6 to 14th St.–Union Sq.; F, M to 14th St.* *3:E3*

$$$ MODERN AMERICAN **Craft.** A meal here is like a luscious choose-your-own-adventure game since every delectable dish comes à la carte, including sides for your roasted guinea hen or braised monkfish. Craft is *Top Chef* head judge Tom Colicchio's flagship of a mini-empire of excellent restaurants around the country, including the upscale Craftbar and Craftsteak brands, as well as grab-and-go sandwich bars called 'wichcraft. Just about everything here is exceptionally prepared with little fuss, from simple yet intriguing starters (like harissa-spiked octopus) and sides (including the justly famous variety of roasted mushrooms, including oysters, trumpets, chanterelles, and hen-of-the-woods) to desserts (warm chocolate tart with buttermilk ice cream, cinnamon custard, and cashews). The serene dining room of burnished dark wood and dangling radiant bulbs is more welcoming than it sounds. *Average main: $33* *43 E. 19th St., between Broadway and Park Ave. S, Flatiron District* *212/780–0880* *www.craftrestaurant.com* *Reservations essential* *No lunch* *L, N, Q, R, 4, 5, 6 to 14th St.–Union Sq.* *3:F3*

$$ MODERN AMERICAN **Craftbar.** The casual sibling to Tom Colicchio's Craft is a bargain in comparison, but still not cheap, though the food continues to garner raves and the service is consistently excellent. The menu features assertive seasonal cooking similar to what you can find at the upscale flagship just around the corner. The small-plates category on the menu elevates tiny nibbles like sausage-stuffed fried sage leaves or addictive fluffy salt-cod croquettes to temptations that make you forget the main course entirely. The rest of the menu is eclectic enough to satisfy. *Average main: $18* *900 Broadway, between 19th and 20th Sts., Flatiron District* *212/461–4300* *www.craftbarnyc.com* *Reservations essential* *L, N, Q, R, 4, 5, 6 to 14th St.–Union Sq.* *3:F3*

$$$ ITALIAN **Eataly.** The cavernous Eataly, from Mario Batali & Co., is a temple of all things Italian. Ignore the overpriced produce market by the front entrance and make a beeline for La Piazza for sandwiches made with meticulously sourced ingredients (you can eat at the standup tables

nearby). There's also a full-service pizza and pasta restaurant, a raw bar and fish eatery, and a wine bar for quaffing wines by the glass and beers on tap. Gourmet Italian chocolates, coffees, gelati, and pastries are all delicious to take away, too, though none of this is cheap. Upstairs, the covered, rooftop birrerria is open in all weather and serves hearty Austrian and German food as well as Italian specialties, and excellent beer, of course. *Average main: $25* *200 5th Ave., at 23rd St., Flatiron* *646/398–5100* *www.eatalyny.com* *Reservations not accepted* *N, R to 23rd St.* *3:E2.*

$$$$ MODERN AMERICAN Fodor's Choice ★ **Eleven Madison Park.** Luxury, precision, and creativity are the driving forces at this internationally renowned restaurant overlooking Madison Park. Swiss-born chef Daniel Humm oversees the kitchen, concocting unexpected dishes that change often. It's a tasting-menu-only format, and dishes are kept minimalist, giving Humm and company maximum latitude to work their magic on the plate. Not that they're resting on their laurels and accolades; the restaurant seems to reinvent itself when you least expect it, its most recent incarnation a focus on elevated versions of classic New York fare. Think cognac-doused, truffle-sprinkled foie gras and Sichuan peppercorn–encrusted duck. Reservations should be made two months in advance. *Average main: $195* *11 Madison Ave., at 24th St., Flatiron District* *212/889–0905* *www.elevenmadisonpark.com* *Reservations essential* *Closed Sun. No lunch Sat.* *6, N, R to 23rd St.* *3:F2*

$$$$ AMERICAN **Gramercy Tavern.** Danny Meyer's intensely popular restaurant tops many a New Yorker's list of favorite dining spots. In front, the first-come, first-served tavern has a lighter menu—including a value-packed three-course prix-fixe—along with great craft beers and cocktails scrawled on a board at the bar. The more formal dining room has a prix-fixe American menu, where choices include seasonal dishes such as marinated sea scallops with pickled peppers and fresh grapes, and rack of lamb with sunchokes, hazelnuts, and exotic mushrooms. Meyer's restaurants—he owns several well-regarded eateries in the city—are renowned for their food and hospitality, and Gramercy Tavern sets the standard. *Average main: $35* *42 E. 20th St., between Broadway and Park Ave. S, Gramercy* *212/477–0777* *www.gramercytavern.com* *Reservations essential* *No lunch weekends* *6, N, R to 23rd St.* *3:F3*

$$ SEAFOOD **The John Dory.** Chef April Bloomfield and former rock-band-manager-turned-restaurateur Ken Friedman can do no wrong. Their third restaurant—after the gastropub-y Spotted Pig and the Breslin—turns its attention to the sea. Fish tanks with brightly colored reefs and floor-to-ceiling windows create an eye-pleasing venue for the seafood feast that awaits those who snagged tables at this restaurant off the lobby of the hip Ace Hotel. The menu is dominated by small plates—chorizo-stuffed squid, an excellent lobster roll—but focuses on the *crudo* (raw) dishes. The happy-hour special of a half-dozen oysters or clams and a choice of sparkling wine or a pint of ale for $15 is the perfect start to an evening. *Average main: $19* *1196 Broadway, at W. 29th St., Flatiron District* *212/792–9000* *thejohndory.com* *Reservations not accepted* *N, R to 28th St.* *3:E1*

$$$ MODERN AMERICAN Fodor's Choice ★ **The NoMad.** Named for the hotel, which itself is named for the up-and-coming neighborhood, north of Madison Square Park, the NoMad is brought to you by Daniel Humm and Will Guidara, the masterminds behind much-lauded Eleven Madison Park. The menu here, more affordable than its sister a few blocks away, is chef Humm's take on American cuisine, but the inspiration for the restaurant as a whole is the Rolling Stones, a photo of whom graces a wall in the kitchen—the connection isn't explicit but it comes through in the philospphy of the dishes, which are casual yet dynamic, alive yet simple. A whole roasted chicken for two, for example, looks basic until the foie gras and black truffles are uncovered. Likewise the poached egg and quinoa dish unexpectedly transforms into a stew once the yokes are broken. It's only-rock-and roll-inspired food . . . and we like it. *$ Average main: $32 ✉ 1170 Broadway, at 28th St., Flatiron District ☎ 347/472–5660 ⊕ www.thenomadhotel.com Reservations essential M N, R to 28th St. ✣ 3:E2*

$$$ ITALIAN **SD26.** The charming father-daughter restaurant team of Tony and Marisa May closed uptown's San Domenico to open this more casual, yet still impressive, Italian spot. The cavernous main dining room, decorated with a constellation of pinpoint lights and ringed with more intimate tables and banquettes, speaks to a fresher, more modern approach than its predecessor. The food—pappardelle with wild boar ragù, smoked lobster with porcini mushrooms and orange segments—is a refreshing mix of classic and forward-thinking. Expect a personal greeting from either father or daughter before your meal comes to an end. *$ Average main: $26 ✉ 19 E. 26th St., between 5th and Madison Aves., Flatiron District ☎ 212/265–5959 ⊕ www.sd26ny.com Reservations essential M N, R to 23rd St. ✣ 3:E2*

16

$ AMERICAN Fodor's Choice ★ **Shake Shack.** Although there are other locations of Danny Meyer's patties 'n' shakes joint around town (including Brooklyn), this is where it all began. Here in Madison Square Park there's no indoor seating—just snaking outdoor lines. **TIP→ Check the "Shack Cam" from their Web site to gauge your wait.** Fresh Angus beef burgers are ground daily, and a single will run you from $3.55 to $6.25, depending on what you want on it. For a burger on the go, they're decidedly tasty. For a few more bucks you can order a double, a Shack Stack, or a vegetarian 'Shroom Burger—a super-rich, melty-Muenster-and-cheddar-cheese–stuffed, fried portobello, topped with lettuce, tomato, and Shack sauce. The menu also offers beef and bird (chicken) hot dogs, french fries, and a variety of delicious frozen custard desserts, and—of course—shakes! *$ Average main: $5 ✉ Madison Square Park near Madison Ave. and E. 23rd St., Flatiron District ☎ 212/889–6600 ⊕ www.shakeshack.com M N, R, 6 to 23rd St. ✣ 3:F2*

$$$ INDIAN **Tamarind.** Many consider Tamarind Manhattan's best Indian restaurant. Forsaking the usual brass, beads, sitar, and darkness, you'll find a lustrous skylighted dining room awash in soothing neutral colors and awaft with tantalizing fragrances. Your welcoming hosts, owner Avtar Walia and his nephew, general manager Gary, practically reinvent charm. The busy kitchen offers multiregional dishes, some familiar (tandoori chicken, a searing lamb vindaloo), some unique (succulent

venison chops in a vigorously spiced cranberry sauce, she-crab soup with saffron, nutmeg, and ginger juice). The more intriguing a dish sounds, the better it turns out to be. *Average main: $25* *41–43 E. 22nd St., between Broadway and Park Ave. S, Flatiron District* *212/674–7400* *www.tamarinde22.com* *Reservations essential* *N, R, 6 to 23rd St.* *3:F2*

GRAMERCY

This leafy, high-rent neighborhood is anchored by Gramercy Park, a locked, private park that takes up a city block. Access to the park is restricted to nearby residents and businesses, including guests of the Gramercy Park Hotel. With its historic homes and tucked-away bars and restaurants, it is a scenic, interesting neighborhood for an afternoon stroll.

$$$$ STEAKHOUSE **BLT Prime.** A masculine, vivacious space is the showcase for bold, appealing Franco-American cuisine. Menu specials are scrawled on a blackboard. Everything is served à la carte, and prices are high, but so is the quality of every dish. Although there are poultry, veal, and lamb dishes on the menu—from lemon-rosemary chicken to a lamb T-bone—steaks are the main event. The dry-aged USDA prime steaks—pulled from a 30-foot-wide dry-aging room—are broiled at 1,700 degrees, spread lightly with herb butter and offered with a choice of sauce (the béarnaise is perfection). *Average main: $38* *111 E. 22nd St., between Lexington and Park Aves., Gramercy* *212/995–8500* *www.bltprime.com* *Reservations essential* *No lunch* *N, R, 6 to 23rd St.* *3:F2*

$$ SPANISH **Casa Mono.** Andy Nusser put in his time cooking Italian under Mario Batali at Babbo before an obsession with Spain landed him his own acclaimed Iberian niche. The perennially cramped and crowded Casa Mono sends patrons to Bar Jamón, the annex wine-and-ham bar next door, where you can pick at plates of jamon serrano while awaiting the main feature. Our favorites seats are at the Casa Mono counter overlooking the chef's open kitchen. Though most menu items are delectably shareable, of particular note are all things seared à la plancha, including blistered peppers and garlic-kissed mushrooms. Like his mentor, Nusser has a weakness for the neglected cuts of meat so check your food fears at the door and try the blood sausage, cockscombs, or tripe. *Average main: $18* *52 Irving Pl., at E. 17th St., Gramercy* *212/253–2773* *www.casamononyc.com* *L, N, Q, R, 4, 5, 6 to 14th St.–Union Sq.* *3:G3*

$$ ROMAN **Maialino.** Named for its signature dish—suckling pig—the perpetually packed restaurant in the Gramercy Park Hotel has benefited from New York diners' growing interest in all things Roman but the suckling pig *is* worth every penny (and it's not cheap) for the taste of the crispy skin that gives way to juicy pork. And if you haven't been to the Eternal City in a while, there's plenty to reintroduce your taste buds to La Dolce Vita: excellent fried artichokes, spaghetti alla carbonara (made with *guanciale,* or pig cheek, just like in Rome), and sausage-studded pasta dish *lumaconi alla Norcia.* It's enough to make a toast to the good life—that is, if your dining companions can hear you over the chatter of the fashion models and bankers at surrounding tables.

Average main: $24 ✉ 2 Lexington Ave., at E. 21st St., Gramercy ☎ 212/777–2410 www.maialinonyc.com Reservations essential M 6 to 23rd St. ⊕ 3:G3

UNION SQUARE

The blocks around Union Square and its open-air greenmarket are filled with upscale foodie havens featuring market-driven menus. But fancy seasonal fare isn't all the area offers. With excellent shopping nearby, there are also plenty of spots to duck in for a quick lunch or snack on the go.

$$$$ AMERICAN Fodor's Choice ★

Gotham Bar & Grill. A culinary landmark, Gotham Bar & Grill is every bit as thrilling as it was when it opened in 1984. Celebrated chef Alfred Portale, who made the blueprint for "architectural food"—that is, towers of stacked ingredients—builds on a foundation of simple, clean flavors. People come for Portale's transcendent preparations: no rack of lamb is more tender, no seafood salad sweeter. The stellar 20,000-bottle cellar provides the perfect accompaniments—though at a price. The three-course $34 greenmarket-driven prix-fixe lunch from noon to 2:30 weekdays is a steal, even if it's not as sophisticated as dinner. Take a stroll through the Union Square greenmarket before or after lunch to see the chef's inspirations. Desserts are also memorable. *Average main: $41 ✉ 12 E. 12th St., between 5th Ave. and University Pl., Union Square ☎ 212/620–4020 www.gothambarandgrill.com No lunch weekends M L, N, Q, R, 4, 5, 6 to 14th St.–Union Sq. ⊕ 3:E4*

$ ASIAN

Republic. When Republic first opened, it was one of very few places to get an Asian-style noodle bowl with a stylish edge. Many have followed in its footsteps—and some are better—but for window shoppers, greenmarketeers, and anyone else in the Union Square area, this is a fun stop for a meal. The look is a cross between a downtown art gallery and a Japanese school cafeteria, and the young waitstaff dressed in black T-shirts and jeans hold remote-control ordering devices to accelerate the already speedy service. Sit at the long, bluestone bar or at the picnic-style tables and order appetizers such as smoky grilled eggplant and luscious fried wontons. Spicy coconut chicken soup and Vietnamese-style barbecued pork are menu standouts. *Average main: $14 ✉ 37 Union Sq. W, between E. 16th and E. 17th Sts., Union Square ☎ 212/627–7172 www.thinknoodles.com Reservations not accepted M L, N, Q, R, 4, 5, 6 to 14th St.–Union Sq. ⊕ 3:F4*

$$$ MODERN MEXICAN

Rosa Mexicano. The idea that you can't find good south-of-the-border cuisine in the Big Apple is quickly fading, thanks in part to this Union Square restaurant (there are two other locations, at Lincoln Center and Midtown East). Although the spacious, colorfully lighted interior might tip you off that if authenticity is what you seek, you should look elsewhere, but if you're looking for high-quality, well-executed Mex-flavored fare, step right up, hombre. Start with an order of guac (made tableside) and dig in, moving on, perhaps, to the pork belly and scallop tacos, soul-comforting chicken tortilla pie, or the crispy pork shank. All of which taste better with a margarita. Happy hour at the bar is a great deal but it gets crowded. *Average main: $28 ✉ 9 E. 18th St., between 5th Ave. and Union Sq. W, Flatiron District ☎ 212/533–3350 www.rosamexicano.com M L, N, Q, R, 4, 5, 6 to 14th St.–Union Sq. ⊕ 3:F3*

16

Get an idea of what produce is in season at the Union Square greenmarket, then look for it on menus around town.

$$$ MODERN AMERICAN **Tocqueville.** Hidden just steps from busy Union Square, Tocqueville is a refined dining oasis that's a secret even to many New York foodies. Enter through the austere reception area, past the heavy curtains and a six-seat bar, and you'll find the intimate dining area where chef-owner Marco Moreira's signature starter is the unctuous sea urchin angel-hair carbonara. Main courses are steeped in French tradition, but with international flavors like saffron-and-fennel-spiked grilled octopus, and smoked duck breast paired with baby bok choy and Asian pear. The three-course $29 prix-fixe lunch is the ultimate deal. *Average main: $28* *1 E. 15th St., between 5th Ave. and Union Sq. W, Union Square* *212/647–1515* *www.tocquevillerestaurant.com* *Reservations essential* *L, N, Q, R, 4, 5, 6 to 14th St.–Union Sq.* *3:E4*

$$$ AMERICAN **Union Square Cafe.** When he opened Union Square Cafe in 1985, Danny Meyer changed the American restaurant landscape: his combination of upscale food and unpretentious but focused service sparked a revolution. This landmark spot still draws devotees with the crowd-pleasing menu, warm atmosphere, and, of course, the service. Wood paneling and white walls are hung with splashy modern paintings; in addition to the three dining areas, there's a long bar ideal for solo diners. The cuisine is American with a thick Italian accent—hearty pastas, seafood, and meat, as well as an excellent roast chicken—and the lunchtime burger is a perennial favorite. *Average main: $29* *21 E. 16th St., between 5th Ave. and Union Sq. W, Union Square* *212/243–4020* *www.unionsquarecafe.com* *Reservations essential* *L, N, Q, R, 4, 5, 6 to 14th St.–Union Sq.* *3:F4*

$ BURGER FAMILY

Stand4. A pioneer on the gourmet-burger scene, this spiffy full-service restaurant serves its bespoke patties with a wide variety of upmarket toppings, from applewood-smoked bacon and onion marmalade to porcini-mushroom and green-peppercorn sauces. Even the classic burgers here are a better breed than most, fat and juicy on a great eggy bun—options include chicken, turkey, veggie, salmon, and "crabbie" burgers. Accompany your meal with a premium gelato milkshake, virgin or spiked. *Average main: $14 24 E. 12th St., near University Pl., Union Square 212/488–5900 www.standburger.com Reservations not accepted L, N, Q, R, 4, 5, 6 to 14th St.–Union Sq. 3:E4.*

MIDTOWN EAST WITH MURRAY HILL

MIDTOWN EAST

Midtown East's streets are relatively quiet at night and on weekends, but the restaurants are filled with expense-account diners celebrating their successes. Some of the most formal dining rooms and most expensive meals in town can be found here, at restaurants like the landmark Four Seasons and Le Cirque.

16

$$$$ SCANDINAVIAN

Aquavit and Aquavit Café. Celebrity chef and co-owner Marcus Samuelsson may no longer be in the kitchen here, but you'd never know it from the impeccable cuisine and service at this fine-dining restaurant and upscale café, now in the hands of able executive chef Marcus Jenmark. The elegant atmosphere features warm woods and modern decor from a Scandinavian design team. Dishes can be ordered à la carte or you can opt for the $85 four-course dinner. Standout dishes include scallops paired with sea urchin, gravlax topped with shaved foie gras, and wild mushrooms in a polenta emulsion. Head to the sumptuous bar area to sample housemade aquavit. *Average main: $60 65 E. 55th St., between Madison and Park Aves., Midtown East 212/307–7311 www.aquavit.org Reservations essential Closed Sun. No lunch Sat. E, M to 5th Ave./53rd St. 4:F2*

$$$ STEAKHOUSE

BLT Steak. Chef Laurent Tourondel may no longer be involved with his namesake steak house, but this classy space, decked out in beige with resin-top black tables, still draws crowds. As soon as you're settled, puffy Gruyère popovers arrive still steaming. The no-muss, no-fuss menu is nonetheless large, and so are the portions of supple crab cakes with celery-infused mayonnaise and luscious ruby tuna tartare with avocado, ramped up with soy-lime dressing. A veal chop crusted with rosemary and Parmesan lends new depth to the meat. Sides and desserts, like a killer peanut butter–chocolate mousse with banana ice cream, are all superior. *Average main: $33 106 E. 57th St., between Lexington and Park Aves., Midtown East 212/752–7470 www.bltsteak.com Reservations essential No lunch weekends 4, 5, 6 to 59th St.; N, Q, R to Lexington Ave./59th St. 4:F1*

$$$$ AMERICAN

The Four Seasons. The landmark Seagram Building houses one of America's most famous restaurants, truly an only-in–New York experience. Owners Alex Von Bider and Julian Niccolini supervise the seating chart like hawks, placing power players in finance, entertainment, and New York society in prime positions for maximum visibility. The

Dinner at the Four Seasons is always a special occasion.

stark Grill Room, birthplace of the power lunch, has one of the best bars in New York. Illuminated trees and a gurgling Carrara marble pool characterize the more romantic Pool Room. The menu changes seasonally; there's a $75 prix-fixe pretheater dinner—a delicious indulgence. You can't go wrong with classic dishes like Dover sole, filet mignon, or crispy duck, but the restaurant moves with the times, so expect seasonal specials featuring luxe ingredients and preparations. *Average main: $57 ✉ 99 E. 52nd St., between Park and Lexington Aves., Midtown East ☎ 212/754–9494 🌐 www.fourseasonsrestaurant.com Reservations essential. Jacket required ⊙ Closed Sun. No lunch Sat. Ⓜ E, M to Lexington Ave./53rd St.; 6 to 51st St. ✣ 4:F2*

$$$ SEAFOOD **Grand Central Oyster Bar & Restaurant.** Nestled deep in the belly of Grand Central Station, the vast Oyster Bar has been a worthy seafood destination since 1913, and it's still a worthy destination, whether you're about to catch a train or craving seafood. Sit at the counter for the fried oyster po'boy or to slurp an assortment of bracingly fresh oysters before having a steaming bowl of clam chowder washed down with an ice-cold beer. This is also the place to experience the pleasure of fresh, unadorned seafood such as lobster with drawn butter or grilled herring in season—generally a better option than anything that sounds too complicated, like cream-smothered seafood pan roasts. *Average main: $30 ✉ Grand Central Terminal, Lower Level, E. 42nd St. at Vanderbilt Ave., Midtown East ☎ 212/490–6650 🌐 www.oysterbarny.com ⊙ Closed Sun. Ⓜ 4, 5, 6, 7, S to Grand Central–42nd St. ✣ 4:F4.*

$$$$ JAPANESE **Kuruma Zushi.** Only a small sign in Japanese indicates the location of this extraordinary restaurant that serves only sushi and sashimi. Bypass the tables, sit at the sushi bar, and put yourself in the hands

of Toshishiro Uezu, the chef-owner. Among the selections are hard-to-find fish that Uezu imports directly from Japan. The most attentive, pampering service staff in the city completes the wildly expensive experience. The showstopping chef's omakase, priced at whatever the market dictates and the type of fish being offered, could run as much as $250 but it's a multicourse feast you'll never forget. $ *Average main: $155* ✉ *7 E. 47th St., 2nd Floor, Midtown East* ☎ *212/317–2802* 🌐 *www.kurumazushi.com* ✍ *Reservations essential* ⊙ *Closed Sun.* Ⓜ *4, 5, 6, 7, S to Grand Central–42nd St.* ✥ *4:E3.*

WORD OF MOUTH

"My wife and I love to go to the Grand Central Oyster Bar and have a dozen oysters, bottle of champagne, chowder and split a fish entree and then head to the Campbell Apartment for cocktails. Great way to spend an evening." —ksucat

$$$$ FRENCH ✕ **Le Cirque.** Impresario-owner Sirio Maccioni still presides over this dining room, filled nightly with a who's who of political, business, and society circles—regulars who've table-hopped from Le Cirque's first incarnation to its latest, in a glass-enclosed aerie on the ground floor of the Bloomberg headquarters. The menu strikes a balance between the creative and classic: Dover sole, filleted table-side, gives way to more avant-garde preparations like foie gras ravioli. Desserts, too, have a split personality, with the menu divided into the "classic" and "new." The foot-tall napoleon that seems to arrive at every second table is an old favorite, but newer creations like the praline tortellini with exotic fruit also satisfy. Though jackets are still required in the dining room, things are more relaxed in the casual wine lounge. $ *Average main: $59* ✉ *151 E. 58th St., at Lexington Ave., Midtown East* ☎ *212/644–0202* 🌐 *www.lecirque.com* ✍ *Reservations essential* ⊙ *Closed Sun. No lunch Sat.* Ⓜ *4, 5, 6 to 59th St.; N, Q, R to Lexington Ave./59th St.* ✥ *4:G1*

$$$ STEAKHOUSE ✕ **Michael Jordan's The Steakhouse NYC.** Don't be dissuaded by the fact that this place is technically part of a chain: there's nowhere remotely like it. The handsomely appointed space in Grand Central Terminal, hung with gracious filigree chandeliers, overlooks one of the most famous interiors in America. Start with the stack of soft, toasted bread soldiers in a pool of hot Gorgonzola fondue. Pristine oysters make a great prelude for a prime dry-aged rib eye or a 2½-pound lobster, grilled, steamed, sautéed, or broiled. Sides, like creamy mac 'n' cheese and a crispy rosemary hash-brown cake, are equally tempting. $ *Average main: $30* ✉ *Grand Central Terminal, West Balcony, 23 Vanderbilt Ave., between E. 43rd and E. 44th Sts., Midtown East* ☎ *212/655–2300* 🌐 *www.michaeljordansnyc.com* ✍ *Reservations essential* Ⓜ *4, 5, 6, 7 to Grand Central–42nd St.* ✥ *4:F4.*

$$ INDIAN ✕ **Mint Restaurant & Lounge.** With a delightful dining room splashed with bright colors and flattering lighting, and executive chef and owner Gary Sikka's brightly seasoned dishes, Mint has joined the ranks of the best Indian restaurants in town. The large menu includes rarely encountered specialties from Goa and Sikkim. Freshly grilled, moist ground lamb kebabs deliver a slow burn to the palate. Chili heat punctuates other spices in the lamb vindaloo, resulting in a well-rounded array

16

of savory flavors. Finish with carrot pudding with saffron and coconut flakes. *Average main: $20 ✉ 150 E. 50th St., Midtown East ☎ 516/307–8677 🌐 mintny.com* Ⓜ *E, M to Lexington Ave./53rd St.; 6 to 51st St. ✥ 4:G3*

$$$ STEAKHOUSE **The Palm Restaurant.** They may have added tablecloths, but it would take more than that to hide the brusque, no-nonsense nature of this legendary steakhouse. The steak is always impeccable, and the Nova Scotia lobsters are so big—3 pounds and up—that there may not be room at the table for such classic side dishes as rich creamed spinach, served family-style for two or more. The "half-and-half" side combination of cottage-fried potatoes and fried onions is particularly addictive. There are other locations (the original, Palm 1, is on 2nd Ave, at 58th St., there's one in the mid 50s, one in TriBeca, and one in JFK), but because of its perch near the Theater District and Midtown businesses, this is the one with the most action. *Average main: $30 ✉ 837 2nd Ave., between 44th and 45th Sts., Midtown East ☎ 212/687–2953 🌐 www.thepalm.com ⏲ No lunch Sun.* Ⓜ *4, 5, 6, 7, S to Grand Central–42nd St. ✥ 4:G4.*

$$ AMERICAN **P. J. Clarke's.** This East Side institution has been dispensing burgers and beer for more than a century. Despite renovations and several different owners over the years, the original P. J. Clarke's (there's also an offshoot in Midtown West, on 63rd Street at Broadway) maintains the beveled-glass and scuffed-wood look of an old-time saloon. Many of the bartenders and patrons are as much a fixture as the decor. More civilized at lunchtime, the bar area heaves with an after-work mob on weekday evenings. Pull up a stool if you can for superlative bar food, like clams casino and the signature burger smothered in creamy béarnaise. *Average main: $18 ✉ 915 3rd Ave., at 55th St., Midtown East ☎ 212/317–1616 🌐 www.pjclarkes.com* Ⓜ *E, M to Lexington Ave./53rd St.; 4, 5, 6 to 59th St.; N, Q, R to Lexington Ave./59th St. ✥ 4:G2*

$$$ CHINESE **Shun Lee Palace.** If you want inexpensive Cantonese food without pretensions, head to Chinatown; but if you prefer to be pampered and don't mind spending a lot of money, this is the place. The cuisine is absolutely classic Chinese. Beijing panfried dumplings make a good starter, and rack of lamb Szechuan-style, grilled with scallions and garlic, is a popular entrée. Beijing duck is sure to please. *Average main: $28 ✉ 155 E. 55th St., between Lexington and 3rd Aves., Midtown East ☎ 212/371–8844 🌐 www.shunleepalace.com ✍ Reservations essential* Ⓜ *4, 5, 6 to 59th St.; N, Q, R to Lexington Ave./59th St. ✥ 4:G2*

$$$$ STEAKHOUSE **Sparks Steakhouse.** Magnums of wines that cost more than most people earn in a week festoon the large dining rooms of this classic New York steakhouse. Although seafood is given more than fair play on the menu, Sparks is really about dry-aged steak. The extra-thick lamb and veal chops are also noteworthy. Classic sides of hash browns, creamed spinach, sautéed mushrooms, and grilled onions are all you need to complete the experience. *Average main: $38 ✉ 210 E. 46th St., between 2nd and 3rd Aves., Midtown East ☎ 212/687–4855 🌐 www.sparkssteakhouse.com ✍ Reservations essential ⏲ Closed Sun. No lunch Sat.* Ⓜ *4, 5, 6, 7, S to Grand Central–42nd St. ✥ 4:G4.*

$$$ JAPANESE

✕ **Sushi Yasuda.** Devotees mourned the return to Japan of namesake chef Naomichi Yasuda, but things are in able hands with his handpicked successor, Misturu Tamura. Here, the sleek bamboo-lined interior is as elegant as the food. Whether using fish flown in daily from Japan or the creamiest sea urchin, the chef makes sushi so fresh and delicate, it melts in your mouth. A number of special appetizers change daily (crispy fried eel backbone is a surprising treat), and a fine selection of sake and beer complements the lovely food. Try to sit at the bar, which was handcrafted Yasuda out of imported Japanese materials. *Average main: $30 ✉ 204 E. 43rd St., between 2nd and 3rd Aves., Midtown East ☎ 212/972–1001 🌐 www.sushiyasuda.com ⏲ Closed Sun. No lunch Sat. Ⓜ 4, 5, 6, 7, S to Grand Central–42nd St. ✥ 4:G4.*

MURRAY HILL

This area has a residential feel with plenty of bistros perfect for a casual meal. Lexington Avenue's "Curry Hill" section between East 27th and East 29th streets is home to Indian spice shops, cafés, and restaurants.

$$ DELI

✕ **2nd Ave Deli.** It may no longer be on 2nd Avenue, but the new incarnation of this East Village institution—about a mile uptown, in midtown—is still delivering on its longtime traditional matzo-ball soup, overstuffed three-decker sandwiches filled with house-cured pastrami, and other old-world specialties. Hot open sandwiches, like juicy beef brisket served with gravy and french fries, may be a heart attack on a plate, but hey, you only live once. Even better, you can now get your fill of kasha *varnishkes,* carrot tzimmes, and potato kugel until the wee hours of the night. There's also an outpost on the Upper East Side. *Average main: $23 ✉ 162 E. 33rd St., between Lexington and 3rd Aves., Midtown East ☎ 212/689–9000 🌐 www.2ndavedeli.com Ⓜ 6 to 33rd St. ✥ 4:G6*

16

$$$ BRASSERIE

✕ **Artisanal.** This spacious brasserie is a shrine to cheese, the passion of chef-owner Terrance Brennan. Though service can be spotty, gastronomes and business lunchers still flock here for the more than 150 cheeses—available for on-site sampling or retail sale—then stay to enjoy their selections with one of 160 wines by the glass. Hot *fromage*-imbued fare also is satisfying, with preparations like addictive gougère cheese puffs, onion soup gratiné, and several types of fondue. For curd-adverse customers, steak frites or selections from the raw bar should satisfy. *Average main: $27 ✉ 2 Park Ave., at E. 32nd St., Midtown East ☎ 212/725–8585 🌐 www.artisanalbistro.com ✍ Reservations essential Ⓜ 6 to 33rd St. ✥ 3:F1*

$$ FRENCH FAMILY

✕ **Les Halles.** This local hangout, owned by Philippe Lajaunie since 1990 and benefiting from the celebrity of former executive chef and writer Anthony Bourdain (although he has little to do with the restaurant these days), is boisterous and unpretentious—just like a true French brasserie. A good bet is steak frites—with fries regarded by some as the best in New York. Other prime choices include crispy duck-leg confit with frisée salad, blood sausage with caramelized apples, and steak tartare, prepared tableside. Another Les Halles is in Lower Manhattan at 15 John St. *Average main: $22 ✉ 411 Park Ave. S, between E. 28th and E. 29th Sts., Flatiron District ☎ 212/679–4111 🌐 www.leshalles.net Ⓜ 6 to 28th St. ✥ 3:F1*

MIDTOWN WEST

Big is the buzz in Times Square and neighboring 'hoods in Midtown West, where neon-lighted billboards, towering skyscrapers, and Broadway theaters play starring roles. But watch out for restaurant rip-offs in this urban-theme-park environment.

It's true that tourist traps abound on the Great White Way, but fortunately you needn't head far from Times Square to score a stellar meal. Just move away from the bright lights and unrelenting foot traffic that clogs the area. On calmer side streets and in adjoining Hell's Kitchen there are excellent dining options for budget travelers and expense-account diners alike. Some of the best steak houses and Italian restaurants are here, and many eateries offer budget pretheater dinners and prix-fixe lunch menus to draw in new business.

$$$$ AMERICAN ✕ **'21' Club.** Tradition's the thing at this town-house landmark, a former speakeasy that opened in 1929. Chef John Greeley tries to satisfy everyone with standards like the famous '21' burger and Dover sole with brown butter, and more modern dishes, such as smoked Berkshire pork belly with maple-glazed Brussels sprouts, but the food is almost secondary to the restaurant's storied past. Belongings donated by famous patrons—for example, John McEnroe's tennis racket or Howard Hughes's model plane—hang from the ceiling. Men, a jacket is required, but you can leave your tie at home. *Average main: $41 ✉ 21 W. 52nd St., between 5th and 6th Aves., Midtown West ☎ 212/582–7200 🌐 www.21club.com Jacket required Closed Sun. No lunch Sat. and Mon. Ⓜ E, M to 5th Ave./ 53rd St.; B, D, F, M to 47th–50th Sts./Rockefeller Center ✣ 4:D2.*

$$$$ MODERN AMERICAN ✕ **Aureole.** An island of fine dining just a stone's throw from bustling Times Square, Aureole is the second act of a New York classic from Charlie Palmer and his executive chef, Marcus Gleadow. From the street, a curved second-story corridor hosting the restaurant's storied wine collection beckons. A welcoming front bar room serves a more casual, yet refined, menu with dishes like a cheddar-bacon burger with pickled ramp mayonnaise. The dining room, with its abundance of flowers, is the place to hobnob with expense-account diners and pretheater revelers. For dinner, starters like the sea-scallop "sandwich" topped with foie gras and passion-fruit coulis is a treat, and the $118 "parallel tasting" offers the menu's greatest hits, with an optional wine pairing. There is no à la carte option in the main dining room. *Average main: $50 ✉ 135 W. 42nd St., between Broadway and 6th Ave., Midtown West ☎ 212/319–1660 🌐 www.charliepalmer.com Reservations essential Ⓜ B, D, F, M to 42nd St.–Bryant Park; 1, 2, 3, 9, N, Q, R to Times Sq.–42nd St. ✣ 4:D4*

$$$ SOUTHERN ✕ **Bar Americain.** Celeb chef Bobby Flay's largest Manhattan restaurant is the soaring Bar Americain. The 200-seat two-story space looks like a dining room on a luxury liner (complete with a gift shop: you can purchase his many cookbooks in the front). This is not food for the faint-of-heart: Flay piles on the butter, cream, and endless varieties of bacon. Southern-inflected brasserie fare includes deviled eggs with smoked shrimp, chicken with Hatch-green-chili spoonbread and

black-pepper vinegar sauce, and duck confit flavored with a bourbon-based sauce and fig chutney. Slightly naughtier are the éclairs piped with whiskey-infused pastry cream and burnished with a burnt-sugar glaze. Brunch, featuring dishes like biscuits and cream gravy with sausage and scrambled eggs, is delicious. *$ Average main: $34 ✉ 152 W. 52nd St., between 6th and 7th Aves., Midtown West ☎ 212/265–9700 ⊕ www.baramericain.com ✍ Reservations essential Ⓜ B, D, E to 7th Ave.; 1, C, E to 50th St.; N, Q, R to 49th St. ✣ 4:C2*

WORD OF MOUTH

"It's true that the downtown area is much more hip and trendy than midtown, but it doesn't mean you can't find good food in midtown—perhaps more traditional than 'hip.' For one, you might try the Bar Americain on West 52 St." —nytraveler

$$ ITALIAN

✕ **Becco.** An ingenious concept makes Becco a prime Restaurant Row choice for time-constrained theatergoers. There are two pricing scenarios: one includes an all-you-can-eat selection of antipasti and three pastas served hot out of pans that waiters circulate around the dining room; the other adds a generous entrée to the mix. The pasta selection changes daily, but often includes gnocchi, fresh ravioli, and fettuccine in a cream sauce. The entrées include braised veal shank, grilled double-cut pork chop, and rack of lamb, among other selections. *$ Average main: $23 ✉ 355 W. 46th St., between 8th and 9th Aves., Midtown West ☎ 212/397–7597 ⊕ www.becco-nyc.com Ⓜ A, C, E to 42nd St.–Port Authority ✣ 4:B3*

$$$ FRENCH

✕ **Benoit.** Who needs to go to Paris when the world's most famous French chef, Alain Ducasse, can come to you? Ducasse imported his famous Right Bank bistro to the Big Apple in 2008 and it's been a hit with Gallic-loving eaters ever since. The decor—cozy red velour banquettes and wall lamps illuminating each table—is plucked straight from the City of Light. So is the menu, which doesn't reinvent anything as much as it replicates. And that's okay, especially when the fennel-inflected *loup de mer* (also known as sea bass) or the tender leg of lamb are so well executed. It's not exactly cheap for simple bisto fare. Then again, neither is a round-trip ticket to Paris. *$ Average main: $25 ✉ 60 W. 55th St., between 5th and 6th Aves., Midtown West ☎ 646/943–7373 ⊕ www.benoitny.com Ⓜ B, D, E to 7th Ave.; N, Q, R to 57th St. ✣ 4:D2*

$$$ BRASSERIE

✕ **Brasserie Ruhlmann.** In a plush 120-seat dining room with just enough art deco touches to harmonize with its Rockefeller Center setting, the sublime French bistro cookery, courtesy of Laurent Tourondel, is on display. The room has a refined air but the staff is so friendly that the place could never be stuffy. The raw bar, with its selection of pedigreed oysters, is a great way to begin, or opt for a blue crab salad over mâche with a honey-lime vinaigrette. If it's on the menu, order braised rabbit nestled in mustard cream on a bed of fresh pappardelle, sprinkled with pitted cherries. Desserts like Floating Island—delicately baked meringue floating on a pond of crème anglaise—are embellished with a flurry of spun sugar. *$ Average main: $28 ✉ 45 Rockefeller Plaza, 50th St. between 5th and 6th Aves., Midtown West ☎ 212/974–2020 ⊕ www.*

16

brasserieruhlmann.com ✍ *Reservations essential* ⊙ *No dinner Sun.* Ⓜ *B, D, F, M to 47th–50th Sts./Rockefeller Center* ✥ *4:D3.*

$ BURGER Fodor's Choice ★ ✕ **Burger Joint.** What's a college burger bar, done up in particleboard and rec-room decor straight out of a *Happy Days* episode, doing hidden inside a five-star Midtown hotel? This tongue-in-cheek lunch spot, hidden behind a heavy red velvet curtain in the Parker Meridien hotel, does such boisterous midweek business that lines often snake through the lobby (which means you're best off coming at noon or earlier). Stepping behind the curtain, you can find baseball cap–wearing, grease-spattered cooks dispensing paper-wrapped cheeseburgers and crisp, thin fries. Forget Kobe beef or foie gras—these burgers are straightforward, cheap, and delicious. Ⓢ *Average main: $7* ✉ *Parker Meridien, 118 W. 57th St., between 6th and 7th Aves., Midtown West* ☎ *212/245–5000* 🌐 *www.parkermeridien.com* ▭ *No credit cards* Ⓜ *F to 57th St.; N, Q, R to 57th St.–7th Ave.* ✥ *4:D1*

$$ ITALIAN FAMILY ✕ **Carmine's.** Savvy New Yorkers line up early for the affordable family-style meals at this large, busy Midtown eatery. Family photos line the walls, and there's a convivial feeling amid all the Times Square hubbub. Don't be fooled: Carmine's may be huge, but it fills up with families carbo-loading for a day of sightseeing or a night of theater on Broadway. There are no reservations taken for parties of fewer than six people after 7 pm, but those who wait are rewarded with mountains of such popular, toothsome viands as fried calamari, linguine with white clam sauce, chicken parmigiana, and veal saltimbocca. Ⓢ *Average main: $24* ✉ *200 W. 44th St., between Broadway and 8th Ave., Midtown West* ☎ *212/221–3800* 🌐 *www.carminesnyc.com* Ⓜ *A, C, E to 42nd St.–Port Authority; N, Q, R, S, 1, 2, 3, 7 to Times Sq.–42nd St.* ✥ *4:C4*

$ KOREAN Fodor's Choice ★ ✕ **Danji.** Diminutive and dark, Danji is no ordinary Korean restaurant. Helmed by talented chef Hooni Kim, this Hell's Kitchen spot is a standout among the rows of restaurants that attract theater-going tourists in the neighborhood. That's because Kim's take on Korean cuisine is inventive and inspired. The menu is split in two, and both sides contain a number of winning dishes. Start with the scallion and pepper pancake and the trio of kimchi from the "traditional" side of the page, then set your taste buds singing with Korean chicken wings and unctuous pork belly sliders from the "modern" side of the menu. Then count your blessings that you're not eating a mediocre meal like the rest of the out-of-town visitors in the neighborhood. Ⓢ *Average main: $14* ✉ *346 W. 52nd St., between 8th and 9th Aves., Midtown West* ☎ *212/586–2880* 🌐 *www.danjinyc.com* ⊙ *Closed Sun.* Ⓜ *C, E to 50th St.* ✥ *4:B2*

$$$ FRENCH ✕ **db Bistro Moderne.** Daniel Boulud's "casual bistro" (it's neither, actually) consists of two elegantly appointed dining rooms. The menu features classic dishes like Nantucket Bay scallops or hanger steak exquisitely prepared. Ever the trendsetter, Boulud's $32 db hamburger stuffed with braised short ribs, foie gras, and black truffles, is the patty credited with kick-starting the whole gourmet burger trend. And, yes, it's worth every penny. Although it may not be the trendy destination it once was, it's still a treat, and the service is friendly without being overbearing. Ⓢ *Average main: $31* ✉ *55 W. 44th St., between 5th and 6th Aves., Midtown West* ☎ *212/391–2400* 🌐 *www.danielnyc.com*

Reservations essential Ⓜ *B, D, F, M to 42nd St.–Bryant Park; 7 to 5th Ave.* ✣ *4:D4.*

$$ AMERICAN FAMILY ✕ **Ellen's Stardust Diner.** If you haven't had enough Broadway singing and dancing, you'll get a kick out of Ellen's, a retro, 1950s-style diner, complete with a singing waitstaff. The menu focuses on all-American classics like meat loaf and chicken potpie, and the waiters and waitresses serenading you on roller skates have the talent to prove this restaurant is right on Broadway. It's the kind of over-the-top family-style fun that you'd expect from the close-to-Times-Square location so don't expect a sophisticated—or quiet—dining experience. *Average main: $20* ✉ *1650 Broadway, at 51st St., Midtown West* ☎ *212/956–5151* *www.ellensstardustdiner.com* Ⓜ *1 to 50th St.; B, D, E to 7th Ave.* ✣ *4:C2.*

$$$ SEAFOOD ✕ **Esca.** The name is Italian for "bait," and this restaurant, courtesy of partners Mario Batali, Joe Bastianich, and longtime chef David Pasternack, lures diners in with delectable raw preparations called *crudo*—such as tilefish with orange and Sardinian oil or pink snapper with a sprinkle of crunchy red clay salt—and hooks them with such entrées as whole, salt-crusted branzino, sea bass for two, or bucatini pasta with spicy baby octopus. The menu changes daily. Bastianich is in charge of the wine cellar, so you can expect an adventurous list of Italian bottles. *Average main: $30* ✉ *402 W. 43rd St., at 9th Ave., Midtown West* ☎ *212/564–7272* *www.esca-nyc.com* *Reservations essential* *No lunch Sun.* Ⓜ *A, C, E to 42nd St.–Port Authority.* ✣ *4:A4*

16

$ AMERICAN ✕ **Five Napkin Burger.** This perennially packed Hell's Kitchen burger place–brasserie has been a magnet for burger lovers since day one. Bottles of Maker's Mark line the sleek, alluringly lighted bar in the back, a collection of antique butcher's scales hangs on a tile wall near the kitchen, and meat hooks dangle from the ceiling between the light fixtures. Though there are many menu distractions—deep-fried pickles, warm artichoke dip, to name a few—the main attractions are the juicy burgers, like the original 10-ounce chuck with a tangle of onions, Gruyère cheese, and rosemary aioli. There's a patty variety for everyone, including a ground lamb kofta and an onion ring–topped ahi tuna burger. For dessert, have an über-thick black-and-white malted milkshake. *Average main: $16* ✉ *630 9th Ave., at 45th St, Midtown West* ☎ *212/757–2277* *www.5napkinburger.com* Ⓜ *A, C, E to 42nd St.–Port Authority.* ✣ *4:B4*

$ KOREAN ✕ **Gahm Mi Oak.** The deconstructed industrial design, inexpensive 24-hour menu, and late-night hours attract a young, stylish crowd—there are even photos on the menu to help bleary-eyed revelers order. Every item on the limited menu goes well with *soju,* a Korean spirit, or beer. Korean-style fried mung-bean pancakes with scallions, onions, carrots, and ground pork are addictive, and the kimchi is renowned. Try the *sul long tang,* a milky ox-bone soup with thin slices of beef, rice, and noodles that is reputed to be an effective hangover cure. *Average main: $14* ✉ *43 W. 32nd St., between 5th Ave. and Broadway, Midtown West* ☎ *212/695–4113* *www.gahmmioak.com* *Reservations not accepted* Ⓜ *B, D, F, M, N, Q, R, to 34th St.–Herald Sq.* ✣ *3:E1*

$$ CUBAN ✕ **Havana Central.** This is a great place for reasonably priced group dining and for sampling Cuban-Latino standards like garlicky chicken and

well-seasoned skirt steak with a cucumber-and-mango salad. There's a full menu of tropical-flavored mojitos, including coconut, blueberry, and passion fruit. *Average main: $18* ✉ *151 W. 46th St., between 6th and 7th Aves., Midtown West* ☎ *212/398–7440* 🌐 *www.havanacentral.com* Ⓜ *B, D, F, M to 47–50th Sts./Rockefeller Ctr.; N, R to 49th St.* ✣ *4:C3.*

$ JAPANESE FAMILY
Kyotofu. Even if you're not crazy about tofu, the soy-based delights at Kyotofu—New York's preeminent dessert bar—will make you reconsider the merits of the soybean. The signature sweet tofu with Kuromitsu black sugar syrup is so creamy and delicious, you'd think it was a traditional panna cotta. The strawberry shortcake with strawberry sake sorbet and the warm miso chocolate cake with chocolate soybean ganache are two more compelling favorites. The menu is full of intriguing options so your best bet, on your first visit, is to go for the Kaiseki prix-fixe, a three-course tasting menu that lets you try six different minidesserts. The menu changes seasonally, and it also includes savory brunch, lunch, and dinner options as well as desserts. *Average main: $15* ✉ *705 9th Ave., near 48th St., Midtown West* ☎ *212/974–6012* 🌐 *www.kyotofu-nyc.com* ⊙ *No lunch Mon.* Ⓜ *C, E to 50th St.* ✣ *4:A3*

$ FRENCH
La Bonne Soupe. Midtown office workers and in-the-know out-of-towners keep this French restaurant bustling for the ever-popular La Bonne Soupe special—you get a bowl of their excellent soup with bread, salad, a beverage (house wine, beer, soda, or coffee), and dessert for $19.50. À la carte options include bistro classics like crepes, omelets, salads, quiche, and croque madame and monsieur. There's often a line at lunchtime but there are two floors of tables so you won't go hungry for long. *Average main: $15* ✉ *48 W. 55th St., between 5th and 6th Aves., Midtown West* ☎ *212/586–7650* 🌐 *www.labonnesoupe.com* Ⓜ *B, D, F, M to 47–50 Sts.–Rockefeller Center* ✣ *4:E2.*

$$$ MODERN AMERICAN
The Lambs Club. Restaurateur Geoffrey Zakarian's opulent supper club on the ground floor of the Chatwal Hotel has superb art deco detailing, blood-red leather banquettes, and a roaring fireplace. Cocktails are concocted by hipster mixologist Sasha Petraske, who eschews experimental in favor of classics like the sidecar and the martini, done well. The food is typical Zakarian, meaning New American cuisine with luxe touches in dishes like veal sweetbreads with peppered jus and grilled treviso lettuce, or seared scallops with porcini mushrooms and Indian-spiced sauce. The lunchtime menu is padded with appealing choices, but the sleeper meal here is breakfast. Dishes like a house-made biscuit with fried egg, bacon, and cheddar, or fluffy lemon-ricotta pancakes, may just fill you up for the rest of the day. *Average main: $36* ✉ *132 W. 44th St., between 6th Ave. and Broadway, Midtown West* ☎ *212/997–5262* 🌐 *www.thelambsclub.com* Ⓜ *N, Q, R, S, 1, 2, 3, 7 to Times Sq.–42nd St., B, D, F, M to 47th–50th Sts./Rockefeller Center.* ✣ *4:C4*

$$$$ FRENCH Fodor's Choice ★
Le Bernardin. Owner Maguy LeCoze presides over the teak-panel dining room at this trendsetting French seafood restaurant, and chef-partner Eric Ripert works magic with anything that swims—preferring at times not to cook it at all. Deceptively simple dishes such as poached lobster in rich coconut-ginger soup or crispy spiced black bass in a

Peking duck bouillon are typical of his style. It's widely agreed that there's no beating Le Bernardin for thrilling cuisine, seafood or otherwise, coupled with some of the finest desserts in town and a wine list as deep as the Atlantic. It's prix fixe only, and there are nonfish options (pasta and meat) by request. *Average main: $155 155 W. 51st St., between 6th and 7th Aves., Midtown West 212/554–1515 www.le-bernardin.com Jacket required Closed Sun. No lunch Sat. 1 to 50th St.; N, R to 49th St.; B, D, F, M to 47th–50th Sts./Rockefeller Center 4:C2.*

$ BAKERY **Le Pain Quotidien.** This international Belgian chain brings its homeland ingredients with it, treating New Yorkers to crusty organic breads, jams, chocolate, and other specialty products. You can grab a snack to go or stay and eat breakfast, lunch, or dinner at communal or private tables with waiter service. Come for a steaming latte and croissant in the morning or a tartine (open-faced sandwich) at noon. There are more than 20 locations throughout Manhattan, including in Central Park. *Average main: $13 1271 Ave. of the Americas, at 50th St., Midtown West 646/462–4165 www.lepainquotidien.com B, D, F, M to 47–50th Sts.–Rockefeller Center 4:D2*

16

$$ ITALIAN **Lugo Caffé.** The area around Madison Square Garden is a restaurant wasteland with the rare sparkling exception of Lugo Caffé, founded by an Italian menswear line. Locals rejoiced at the introduction of this spacious Italian "brasserie" offering comfort food with a *Dolce Vita* twist all day long. Stop by for an espresso and pastry in the morning. Later, a single menu presents lunch, *aperitivo*, and dinner options, which include grazing portions of salumi, cheeses, and vegetable dishes like eggplant caponata, Tuscan bean salad, and grilled zucchini with pine nuts. Fuller meals of Neapolitan-style pizzas, house-made pastas, and grilled meats and fish also are commendable. *Average main: $24 1 Penn Plaza, 33rd St. and 8th Ave., Midtown West 212/760–2700 www.lugocaffe.com Closed Sun. (except on some MSG game days) A, C, E, 1, 2, 3 to 34th St.–Penn Station. 4:C6*

$$$ ASIAN **Má Pêche.** Starkly decorated and set in the basement of the Chambers Hotel, Má Pêche is just blocks from MoMA. And as the largest restaurant in David Chang's empire, you've got a better shot of nabbing a seat. The menus are a bit more refined (and expensive) than those at Momofuku Noodle Bar and Ssäm Bar, with elegantly composed plates that might include lamb shank accompanied by eggplant, raisins, and rice, or seared swordfish with black beans, braised celery, and crisped shallots. At lunchtime, there are also tasty banh mi filled with pork and vegetables. On the way out you can pick up sweets from the uptown offshoot of Momofuku Milk Bar, like the addictive, buttery Crack Pie or intriguingly flavored soft-serve. *Average main: $25 15 West 56th St., between 5th and 6th Aves., Midtown West 212/757–5878 www.momofuku.com/ma-peche No lunch Sun F to 57th St.; N, R to 5th Ave.–59th St. 4:E1.*

$$ MEDITERRANEAN **Marseille.** With great food and a convenient location near several Broadway theaters, Marseille is perpetually packed. The Mediterranean creations are continually impressive, including the bouillabaisse, the signature dish of the region for which the restaurant is named—a

mélange of mussels, shrimp, and white fish in a fragrant broth, topped with a garlicky crouton and served with rouille on the side. Leave room for the spongy beignets with chocolate and raspberry dipping sauces. *Average main: $22 ✉ 630 9th Ave., at W. 44th St., Midtown West ☎ 212/333–2323 ⊕ www.marseillenyc.com ✍ Reservations essential* Ⓜ *A, C, E to 42nd St.–Port Authority ✣ 4:A4.*

$$$ FRENCH — ✕ **The Modern and Bar Room.** Both spots competing for the title of the country's best museum restaurant sit side by side on the ground floor of the New York MoMA. The Modern, run by restaurateur Danny Meyer, is two restaurants in one, and both offer the dazzling food of Alsatian chef Gabriel Kreuther. The formal dining room features a view of the museum's sculpture garden and an ambitious, pricey, prix-fixe menu with standouts like chorizo-crusted codfish with white coco-bean puree. The far more accessible and popular Bar Room lies just beyond a partition, and this is where you can find a dizzying collection of shareable plates, like the refreshing arctic char tartare and oysters with leeks and caviar. Two or three make a fine if extravagant afternoon snack—double that number and you have a full meal. *Average main: $45 ✉ 9 W. 53rd St., between 5th and 6th Aves., Midtown West ☎ 212/333–1220 ⊕ www.themodernnyc.com ⊙ Closed Sun.* Ⓜ *E, M to 5th Ave./53rd St. ✣ 4:D2*

$$$ SEAFOOD — ✕ **Oceana.** Entering Oceana is like walking into the dressy stateroom of a modern luxury ocean liner. Floor-to-ceiling windows look out both north and west, and the arrestingly designed raw bar backed with Mediterranean-hue ceramics offers stunningly fresh choices—you would expect gorgeous oysters at a restaurant called Oceana, and you get them. Chef Ben Pollinger has all the skill and confidence necessary to serve some of the most vivid and delicious seafood in town. A "contemporary appetizer" section features items like marinated cucumber with cucumber, apple, and toasted spices. Grilled whole fish like halibut, swordfish, and crispy wild striped bass are served with a perfect rotating roster of sauces like classic romesco and grilled pineapple salsa. Thai-style red snapper comes with tender silk squash, crisp jicama, and a kaffir-saffron broth. *Average main: $32 ✉ 120 W. 49th St., at 6th Ave., Midtown West ☎ 212/759–5941 ⊕ www.oceanarestaurant.com ✍ Reservations essential ⊙ No lunch weekends* Ⓜ *E, M to 5th Ave./53rd St. ✣ 4:D3*

$$$ BRAZILIAN — Fodor's Choice ★ — ✕ **Plataforma Churrascaria Rodizio.** This sprawling, boisterous shrine to meat, with its all-you-can-eat prix-fixe menu, is best experienced with a group of ravenous friends. A *caipirinha,* featuring cachaça sugarcane liquor, sugar, and lime, will kick things off nicely. Follow up with a trip to the fabulous salad bar, piled with vegetables, meats, and cheeses—but remember, there's about to be a parade of all manner of grilled meats and poultry, from pork ribs to chicken hearts, delivered to the table on long skewers. Everyone at the table gets a coaster-sized disc that's red on one side and green on the other: turn the green side up when you're ready for more; pace yourself so you can try all the different delicacies. It's definitely a fun evening, but make sure to come hungry. *Average main: $33 ✉ 316 W. 49th St., between 8th and 9th Aves., Midtown*

West ☎ *212/245–0505* 🌐 *www.plataformaonline.com* ✍ *Reservations essential* Ⓜ *C, E to 50th St.* ✣ *4:B3*

$$ ECLECTIC ✕ **Plaza Food Hall by Todd English.** At the Plaza Food Hall in the basement of the Plaza Hotel, celeb chef Todd English oversees a series of mini-restaurants, each with its own counter with seating ideal for a quick snack or a full-fledged meal. Entry is a little confusing; though the place is made up of individual food concepts, you'll be seated by a hostess at any available counter. One you're settled, get up and survey your choices, then sit down and place one order from your waiter. There's a glistening raw bar, a burger joint, and a wood-burning pizza station where you can sample some of English's iconic pies, such as fig and prosciutto. It's one of the most varied and affordable daytime food options in an area of town that can still feel like a lunchtime wasteland. Ⓢ *Average main: $18* ✉ *1 W. 59th St., at 5th Ave., Midtown East* ☎ *212/986–9260* 🌐 *theplazafoodhall.com* Ⓜ *N, Q, R to 5th Ave./59th St.* ✣ *4:E1*

$$$ AUSTRIAN ✕ **Seäsonal Restaurant and Weinbar.** Partners and executive chefs Wolfgang Ban and Eduard Frauneder have brought something *neu* to Midtown: a swanky Austrian-German restaurant and Weinbar. With its sculptural ceiling lighting, elliptical bar, and contemporary Austrian and German art, Seäsonal feels more "downtown" than you'd expect from such central Midtown digs. The cuisine is sophisticated and contemporary, yet still steeped in regional traditions. Appetizers like the foie-gras terrine and the cheese ravioli with smoked chanterelle mushrooms delight with their contrasting lightness and intensity of flavor. Mains, such as the pumpkin seed–crusted black sea bass with butternut squash and black truffles, and the classic Wiener schnitzel served with a crescent potato-cucumber salad, will definitely please your palate. Seäsonal's Weinbar features a distinctive selection of wines from emerging Austrian and German winemakers. Ⓢ *Average main: $27* ✉ *132 W. 58th St., between 6th and 7th Aves., Midtown West* ☎ *212/957–5550* 🌐 *www.seasonalnyc.com* Ⓜ *F to 57th St.* ✣ *4:D1*

$ BURGER ✕ **Shake Shack.** Local restaurant legend Danny Meyer has gone a little low-brow with his fast-ish food venture, Shake Shack—and New Yorkers are loving it. Area-wise, this Theater District location is the largest and with the most seating, but be warned: lines still snake out the door, especially at prime mealtimes. Still, the grub is good and well priced. Fresh steer burgers are ground daily, and a single will run you from $4.55 to $6.25, depending on what you want on it. For a few more bucks you can also order doubles and Shack Stacks or a vegetarian 'Shroom Burger—a melty-Muenster-and-cheddar-cheese-stuffed portobello. The Shake Shack also offers beef and bird (chicken) hot dogs, french fries, and a variety of delicious frozen custard desserts and—of course—thick shakes! Ⓢ *Average main: $6* ✉ *691 8th Ave., at W. 44th St., Midtown West* ☎ *646/435–0135* 🌐 *www.shakeshacknyc.com* Ⓜ *A, C, E to 42nd St.–Port Authority* ✣ *4:C4.*

$$ ITALIAN ✕ **Sosa Borella.** This is one of the Theater District's top spots for reliable food at a reasonable cost. The bilevel, casual Argentine-Italian eatery is an inviting and friendly space where diners choose from a wide range of options. The lunch menu features staples like warm sandwiches and entrée-size salads, whereas the dinner menu is slightly gussied up with

meat, fish, and pasta dishes (the rich agnolotti with lamb Bolognese sauce, topped with a wedge of grilled pecorino cheese, is a must-try). The freshly baked bread served at the beginning of the meal with pesto dipping sauce is a nice touch as you wait for your meal. The service can be slow at times, so leave yourself plenty of time before the show. *$ Average main: $25 ✉ 832 8th Ave., between 50th and 51st Sts., Midtown West ☎ 212/262–8282 🌐 www.sosaborella.com Ⓜ C, E, 1 to 50th St. ✣ 4:B2*

$$ MEXICAN ✕ **Toloache.** Make a quick detour off heavily trafficked Broadway into this pleasantly bustling Mexican cantina for one of the best dining options around Times Square. The bilevel eatery has a festive, celebratory vibe, with several seating options: bar, balcony, main dining room, and ceviche bar. Foodies flock here for three types of guacamole (traditional, fruited, and spicy), a trio of well-executed ceviches, and dishes like the Mexico City–style tacos with Negra Modelo–braised brisket, and quesadillas studded with black truffle and *huitlacoche* (a corn fungus). There's an extensive tequila selection—upward of 100 brands. Adventurous palates will be drawn to tacos featuring chili-studded dried grasshoppers, lobes of seared foie gras, and caramelized veal sweetbreads. *$ Average main: $19 ✉ 251 W. 50th St., near 8th Ave., Midtown West ☎ 212/581–1818 🌐 www.toloachenyc.com Ⓜ 1, C, E to 50th St.; N, Q, R to 49th St. ✣ 4:B3*

UPPER EAST SIDE

The Upper East Side is jam-packed with pricey neighborhood eateries that cater to the area's well-heeled residents. Long viewed as an enclave of the privileged, these neighborhoods have plenty of elegant restaurants that serve the society "ladies who lunch" and bankers looking forward to a steak and single-malt scotch at the end of the day. However, visitors to Museum Mile and 5th Avenue shopping areas need not be put off. Whether you're looking to celebrate a special occasion or just want to grab a quick bite, you're sure to find something here for almost any budget.

$$$$ ITALIAN ✕ **Alloro.** Italian chef Salvatore Corea and his wife, Gina, a native New Yorker, are living their dream of opening an old-fashioned family-run restaurant here on the Upper East Side. It's not Corea's first New York restaurant endeavor—he's opened three other successful venues in the city (Cacio e Pepe, Spiga, and Bocca), but Alloro is his first venture with his wife, and judging by the friendly vibe and the delicious dishes coming out of Corea's *cucina,* it's working swimmingly well. Chef Corea's creative take on traditional, regional Italian cuisines leads the way for delicious dishes, like creamy Parmesan risotto with Lambrusco-wine caramel. Both the sliced rib eye over corn puree and the fillet of sole in pumpkin-Amaretto crust are fantastic. Gluten-free pasta selections are also available. *$ Average main: $38 ✉ 307 E. 77th St., near 2nd Ave., Upper East Side ☎ 212/535–2866 🌐 www.alloronyc.com Ⓜ 6 to 77th St. ✣ 5:H2*

$$$$ FRENCH ✕ **Café Boulud.** Manhattan's "who's who" in business, politics, and the art world come to hobnob at Daniel Boulud's café-in-name-only, where the food and service are top-notch. The menu, overseen by Boulud

protégé Gavin Kaysen, is divided into four parts: under La Tradition you can find classic French dishes such as roasted duck breast Montmorency with cherry chutney, green Swiss chard, and baby turnips; Le Potager tempts with lemon ricotta ravioli; La Saison follows the rhythms of the season; and Le Voyage reinterprets cuisines of the world. Start with a drink at the chic Bar Pleiades. [$] *Average main: $36* ✉ *Surrey Hotel, 20 E. 76th St., between 5th and Madison Aves., Upper East Side* ☎ *212/772–2600* 🌐 *www.danielnyc.com* ✍ *Reservations essential* [M] *6 to 77th St.* ✣ *5:F3*

$$ BRASSERIE ✕ **Café d'Alsace.** Unusually comfortable burgundy banquettes, huge antiqued mirrors, and low lighting that makes everyone look fabulous characterize this Alsatian gem. Start with a house cocktail—say, L'Alsacien, in which the aperitif Belle de Brillet meets cognac, pear, and fresh lemon in a happy union. Standouts include the *tarte flambé*, a *fromage blanc*–topped flatbread scattered with tawny caramelized onions and hunks of bacon. The *choucroute garnie* entrée comes in a cast-iron kettle that keeps it piping hot. Sausages, smoked pork breast, and pork belly are so carefully braised that everything comes out in perfect harmony. Delicious bread pudding is studded with strawberries. [$] *Average main: $22* ✉ *1695 2nd Ave., at 88th St., Upper East Side* ☎ *212/722–5133* 🌐 *www.cafedalsace.com* [M] *4, 5, 6 to 86th St.* ✣ *6:G6*

16

$$ AUSTRIAN Fodor's Choice ★ ✕ **Café Sabarsky.** In the Neue Galerie, this stately coffeehouse is meant to duplicate the Viennese café experience. And it does a good job, with art deco furnishings and cases filled with cakes, strudels, and Sacher tortes. Museumgoers and locals love to linger here over coffee. There is also a menu of heartier fare—created by Michelin-starred chef Kurt Gutenbrunner—of sausage, sandwiches, and goulash. [$] *Average main: $18* ✉ *Neue Galerie, 1048 5th Ave., near 86th St., Upper East Side* ☎ *212/240–9557* 🌐 *kg-ny.com* ✍ *Reservations not accepted* [M] *4, 5, 6 to 86th St.* ✣ *6:E6*

$$ VEGETARIAN Fodor's Choice ★ ✕ **Candle 79.** The Upper East Side may seem like an unlikely place for gourmet vegan fare, but the people behind Candle 79 have found a formula that would work in any neighborhood. The elegant, bi-level space, done in warm, autumnal tones with touches of wood and rich fabric, is far from the health-food stereotype. Try for a second-floor table overlooking the street, and refresh yourself with an inventive cocktail. Appetizers like rice balls with tempeh bacon may sound like hippie throwbacks, but they taste more like well-executed trattoria fare. Signature dishes include the seitan piccata, which replaces the usual protein with a vegetarian substitute and is so well made and well seasoned that you would never miss the meat. Salads, soups, desserts, and entrées are all stunningly fresh and made with local, organic, seasonal produce. There's also an impressive list of organic wines and sakes. [$] *Average main: $22* ✉ *154 E. 79th St., at Lexington Ave., Upper East Side* ☎ *212/537–7179* 🌐 *www.candle79.com* [M] *6 to 77th St.* ✣ *5:G2*

$ MEXICAN ✕ **Cascabel Taqueria.** At Cascabel, the wrestling-theme decor is a whimsical backdrop for delicious, reasonably priced Mexican food. Tacos, which come two to an order, are inventive without veering too far from the comfort-food norm. The Camaron taco scatters plump roasted shrimp among fresh oregano, garlic oil, and black beans. The beef tongue is slow-braised, then topped with spring onion and serrano chiles. There's also fresh, creamy guacamole with house-fried chips, pert tortilla soup with queso fresco cheese and chicken, and dinner-only platters like adobe-marinated Berkshire pork butt. At lunchtime, sandwiches—like shredded chicken with mango and smashed avocado—hit the spot with a cold Mexican beer. Inside seating is limited, but in temperate weather the outdoor tables expand your possibilities. $ *Average main: $13* ✉ *1538 2nd Ave., between 80th and 81st Sts., Upper East Side* ☎ *212/717–8226* 🌐 *www.nyctacos.com* Ⓜ *6 to 77th St.* ✥ *5:H2*

$$$ AMERICAN **Central Park Boathouse Restaurant.** There are plenty of pushcarts offering hot dogs and sodas, but if you're looking to soak up Central Park's magical ambience in an elegant setting, head for the Central Park Boathouse, which overlooks the gondola lake. There you can relax on the outdoor deck with a glass of wine and a cheese plate, or go for a more formal meal inside the restaurant. In warmer months the restaurant can get crowded: go for a late lunch or early-evening cocktail. Note that dinner is not served in the winter months. $ *Average main: $30* ✉ *E. 72nd St., at Park Dr. N, Upper East Side* ☎ *212/517–2233* 🌐 *www.thecentralparkboathouse.com* *Reservations not accepted* ⏲ *No dinner Dec.–Mar.* Ⓜ *6 to 77th St.* ✥ *5:E3*

$$$$ FRENCH Fodor's Choice ★ **Daniel.** Celebrity-chef Daniel Boulud has created one of the most elegant dining experiences in Manhattan. The prix fixe–only menu (there are à la carte selections in the elegant lounge and bar) is predominantly French, with such modern classics as turbot on Himalayan salt with an ale-and-gingerbread sauce, and a duo of dry-aged Angus black beef featuring meltingly tender red wine–braised short ribs and seared rib eye with black trumpet mushrooms and Gorgonzola cream. Equally impressive are the serious artwork, professional service, extensive wine list, and masterful cocktails. Don't forget the decadent desserts and overflowing cheese trolley. A three-course vegetarian menu is also available. $ *Average main: $60* ✉ *60 E. 65th St., between Madison and Park Aves., Upper East Side* ☎ *212/288–0033* 🌐 *www.danielnyc.com* *Reservations essential. Jacket required* ⏲ *Closed Sun. No lunch* Ⓜ *6 to 68th St.–Hunter College* ✥ *5:F5.*

$$$ EASTERN EUROPEAN **Hospoda.** The word may mean "pub" in Czech, but this chic Upper East Side, Central Europe–inspired spot is far from the dingy Prague drinking holes of years past. On the ground floor of the Bohemian National Hall, a Czech cultural center, the interior is dominated by artsy, backlit wall engravings, while in the kitchen Chef Oldrich Sehajdak, who has been at the forefront in revolutionizing Czech cuisine at Prague's acclaimed restaurant La Degustation, has created a menu of updated European and Czech fare. The menu changes based on seasonal ingredients but expect dishes like grilled hen of the woods mushrooms with chicken jus or duck leg confit with roasted apple and cabbage. The Pilsner Urquell, shipped from the brewery in Plzen, is especially bold in its taste. Remember to say "*Na zdravi*," cheers, before your first sip. $ *Average main: $25* ✉ *321 E. 73rd St., between 1st and 2nd Aves., Upper East Side* ☎ *212/861–1038* 🌐 *www.hospodanyc.com* ⏲ *No lunch* Ⓜ *4, 5, 6 to 68th St.* ✥ *5:H3*

$$ MEXICAN ✕ **Maya.** The upscale-hacienda appearance of this justifiably popular restaurant showcases some of the best Mexican food in the city, courtesy of pioneering Mexican chef Richard Sandoval. Begin with a fresh mango mojito, then tuck into delicious roasted corn soup with huitlacoche dumplings, stuffed poblano peppers, and a smoky filet mignon taco with jalapeño escabeche. The bottomless brunch on the weekends can get loud but the local Upper East Siders still enjoy it. *$ Average main: $24 ✉ 1191 1st Ave., between 64th and 65th Sts., Upper East Side ☎ 212/585–1818 🌐 www.modernmexican.com ⏲ No lunch M 6 to 68th St.–Hunter College ✣ 5:H5.*

$$$$ AMERICAN ✕ **Park Avenue Seasonal.** New York's most self-consciously seasonal restaurant swaps out much more than its menu as temperatures change. Four times a year the restaurant—the formerly staid Park Avenue Café—shuts its doors for a head-to-toe makeover, switching, for instance, from a summery blond-wood beach-house motif to dark-wood-and-copper fall-foliage tones. Chef Craig Koketsu's seasonal food lives up to the striking surroundings. Summer brings a bounty of fresh-shucked corn, with a big, juicy veal chop and heirloom tomatoes. Come autumn the kitchen turns its focus to mushrooms, truffles (on a flaky halibut fillet accompanied by a brioche-crusted poached egg), and game (local quail, venison chops scattered with pomegranate and pumpkin seeds). Desserts include hard-to-resist elegant creations like sweet-corn ice cream with rhubarb, warm caramel, and popcorn. *$ Average main: $39 ✉ 100 E. 63rd St., at Park Ave., Upper East Side ☎ 212/644–1900 🌐 www.parkavenyc.com ✍ Reservations essential M F to Lexington Ave.–63rd St.; 4, 5, 6 to 59th St.; N, Q, R to 5th Ave./59th St. ✣ 5:F6*

$$ JAPANESE ✕ **Sushi of Gari.** Options at this popular sushi spot range from the ordinary (California roll) to such exotic choices as tuna with creamy tofu sauce, miso-marinated cod, or Japanese yellowtail with jalapeño. Japanese noodles (udon or soba) and meat dishes such as teriyaki and *negimaki* (scallions rolled in thinly sliced beef) are well prepared. Reservations are recommended. Another location at 370 Columbus Avenue gives Upper West Siders their udon and raw fish fix. *$ Average main: $24 ✉ 402 E. 78th St., at 1st Ave., Upper East Side ☎ 212/517–5340 🌐 www.sushiofgari.com ⏲ No lunch M 6 to 77th St. ✣ 5:H2*

16

UPPER WEST SIDE

Anchoring the dining experience in this section of town are the high-end restaurants at the Time Warner Center, which some call a "fine-dining food court." Head farther uptown for both cheaper eats as well as a burgeoning gourmet dining scene.

With Lincoln Center theatergoers, hungry shoppers, and visitors to Central Park nearby, chefs are finally waking up to the captive built-in audience of tourists and locals alike. The main avenues are indeed lined with restaurants, but until recently many of them had been mediocre. Now the better-known destination-dining spots beyond the Time Warner Center—among them **Jean-Georges, Picholine, Telepan,** and **Dovetail**—have been joined by newcomers like **Salumeria Rossi, Fishtag,** and **Ed's Chowder,** all second or third restaurants from well-known chefs. Brunch is still a good bet, too. The flaky scones and fluffy omelets at **Sarabeth's,** not to mention blintzes and bagels at **Barney Greengrass,** are worth seeking out.

$$$$ ASIAN

Asiate. The unparalleled view is reason enough to visit Asiate's pristine dining room, perched on the 35th floor of the Time Warner Center in the Mandarin Oriental Hotel. Artfully positioned tables and minimalist decor help direct eyes to the windows, which peer over Central Park. At night crystalline lights reflect in the glass, creating a magical effect. The kitchen turns out contemporary dishes with an Asian influence, such as the great surf-and-turf dish: pork belly and octopus or butter-poached lobster in a Kaffir lime emulsion. Another standout is Wagyu beef tenderloin with smoked potato puree. Professional, attentive service helps foster an atmosphere of dreamlike luxury. The restaurant has prix-fixe menus only, and an illustrious wine collection housing 2,000 bottles. *Average main: $85 Mandarin Oriental Hotel, 80 Columbus Circle, 35th fl., at 60th St., Upper West Side 212/805–8881 www.mandarinoriental.com A, B, C, D, 1 to 59th St.–Columbus Circle 5:C6.*

$$$ FRENCH

Fodor's Choice ★

Bar Boulud. Acclaimed French chef Daniel Boulud, known for upscale New York City eateries Daniel and Café Boulud, shows diners his more casual side with this lively contemporary bistro and wine bar. The long, narrow space accommodates 100 people and has a 14-seat round table for special wine-theme tastings. An additional level has three rooms for larger parties. The menu emphasizes charcuterie, including terrines and pâtés designed by Parisian charcutier Gilles Verot, who relocated just to work with Boulud, as well as traditional French bistro dishes like steak frîtes and *poulet rôti à l'ail* (roast chicken with garlic mashed potatoes). The 500-bottle wine list is heavy on wines from Burgundy and the Rhône Valley. Wallet watchers won't feel left out: a pretheater three-course menu starts at $45, and weekend brunch has four courses plus coffee for $32. *Average main: $26 1900 Broadway, between 63rd and 64th Sts., Upper West Side 212/595–0303 www.barboulud.com 1 to 66th St.–Lincoln Center; A, C, B, D, 1 to 59th St.–Columbus Circle. 5:B5*

$$ AMERICAN

Barney Greengrass. At this Upper West Side landmark, brusque waiters send out stellar smoked salmon, sturgeon, and whitefish to a happy crowd packed to the gills at small Formica tables. Split a fish platter with bagels, cream cheese, and other fixings, or get your velvety nova scrambled with eggs and buttery caramelized onions. If you're still hungry, go for a plate of cheese blintzes or the to-die-for chopped liver. Be warned that the weekend brunch wait can exceed an hour, so you're better off coming during the week. *Average main: $18 541 Amsterdam Ave., between 86th and 87th Sts., Upper West Side 212/724–4707 www.barneygreengrass.com Reservations not accepted No credit cards Closed Mon. No dinner B, C, 1 to 86th St. 6:B6*

$ DINER

Big Nick's Burger Joint & Pizza Joint. This cramped, 24-hour neighborhood diner is quintessential divey New York, decorated with photographs of the celebrities who've visited, but the primary draw is the burgers, which are huge and juicy. It's a neighborhood institution and the seemingly endless menu has just about anything you might be craving, including every conceivable burger topping, from avocado and bacon to Greek tzatziki sauce. The classic Bistro Burger has mushrooms, Swiss, and fried onions on toasted challah bread. *Average main: $11 ✉ 2175 Broadway, between 76th and 77th Sts., Upper West Side ☎ 212/362–9238 🌐 www.bignicksnyc.com Ⓜ 1 to 79th St.; 1, 2, 3 to 72nd St. ⊕ 5:A3*

$ CAFÉ **Bouchon Bakery.** Never mind that you're in the middle of a shopping mall under a Samsung sign, soups and sandwiches don't get much more luxurious than this. Acclaimed chef Thomas Keller's low-key lunch spot (one floor down from his extravagant flagship, Per Se) draws long lines for good reason. Share a mason jar of salmon rillettes—an unctuous spread of cooked and smoked salmon folded around crème fraîche and butter—then move on to one of the fork-and-knife open-faced tartines, like the tuna niçoise. When a sandwich has this much pedigree, $13.50 is actually a bargain. Grab dessert to go, a fresh macaroon or éclair, from the nearby bakery window. *Average main: $14 ✉ Time Warner Center, 10 Columbus Circle, 3rd fl., Upper West Side ☎ 212/823–9366 🌐 www.bouchonbakery.com Ⓜ A, B, C, D, 1 to 59th St.–Columbus Circle ⊕ 5:C6.*

16

$$ FRENCH **Café Luxembourg.** The old soul of the Lincoln Center neighborhood seems to inhabit the tiled and mirrored walls of this lively, cramped restaurant, where West End Avenue regulars—including lots of on-air talent from nearby ABC News—are greeted with kisses, and musicians and audience members pack the room after a concert. The bar's always hopping, and the menu (served until 11 pm Sunday through Tuesday and until midnight from Wednesday through Saturday) includes dishes like steak tartare and lobster roll alongside dishes with a more contemporary spin like pan-seared trout with haricots verts, hazelnuts, and tomato-caper compote. *Average main: $18 ✉ 200 W. 70th St., between Amsterdam and West End Aves., Upper West Side ☎ 212/873–7411 🌐 www.cafeluxembourg.com ✍ Reservations essential Ⓜ 1, 2, 3, B, C to 72nd St. ⊕ 5:A4*

$$ ITALIAN FAMILY **Carmine's.** Set on a nondescript block of Broadway, this branch of the Italian family-style mainstay is a favorite for families celebrating special occasions, pre-prom groups of teens, and plain folks who come for the tried-and-true menu items like fried calamari, linguine with white clam sauce, chicken parmigiana, and veal saltimbocca, all served in mountainous portions. Family photos line the walls, there's a groaning antipasti table filled with savory meats, cheese, and salads, and there's a convivial feeling amid the organized chaos. On weekends, only parties of six or more can make dinner reservations. *Average main: $24 ✉ 2450 Broadway, between 90th and 91st Sts., Upper West Side ☎ 212/362–2200 🌐 www.carminesnyc.com Ⓜ 1, 2, 3, to 96th St. ⊕ 6:A6*

$$$$ AMERICAN **Dovetail.** Inside Dovetail, chef-owner John Fraser's subdued townhouse and restaurant, cream-color walls and maple panels create a warm atmosphere, and a recent expansion allows for more dining space and a larger bar area. The menu, which changes daily, features refined but hearty dishes. Seek solace from winter temperatures with the earthy gnocchi topped with matsutake mushrooms, poppy seeds, and lemon.

Tender lamb is heightened by potatoes, artichokes, and olives. The savory feast continues with pastry chef Michael Shelkowitz's Earl Grey pumpkin cake with lemon curd and cinnamon-toast ice cream. *Average main: $37* ✉ *103 W. 77th St., at Columbus Ave., Upper West Side* ☎ *212/362–3800* 🌐 *www.dovetailnyc.com* ⏲ *No lunch* Ⓜ *1 to 79th St.; B, C to 81st St.–Museum of Natural History.* ✥ *5:B2*

$$ CAFÉ **Fairway Café.** Fairway Supermarket is a neighborhood institution, living up to its reputation for great prices on gourmet products—and shopping-cart jockeying down the narrow aisles. Upstairs, though, is the respite of Fairway Café, a large, brick-walled room with windows overlooking Broadway. Up front you can grab a pastry and coffee to go, but there's a full menu of fairly priced entrées as well. The place is run by Mitchell London, who's known for his juicy, well-marbled steaks—try the rib eye and you may never go back to Brooklyn's Peter Luger steak house again. *Average main: $20* ✉ *2127 Broadway, between 74th and 75th Sts., Upper West Side* ☎ *212/994–9555* 🌐 *www.fairwaymarket.com* Ⓜ *1, 2 3 to 72nd St.* ✥ *5:A3*

$$ MEDITERRANEAN **Fishtag.** Upper West Siders aren't going to be throwing chef Michael Psilakis and his Greek-heavy Mediterranean fare back into the water any time soon. At Anthos, a big-box Midtown eatery that shuttered a few years ago, Psilakis was lauded for his prowess on the grill. He brings the same skills to Fishtag with dishes like grilled striped bass and grilled swordfish. Fanatics of Anthos' insanely good lamb burger can breath easy, as it's on the menu here. The wine list is long and categorized with subtitles like "Funky & Earthy" and "Explosive & Bold" and brew imbibers will declare Fishtag a good catch when they see 20 craft beers on the menu. *Average main: $19* ✉ *222 W. 79th St., between Broadway and Amsterdam Ave., Upper West Side* ☎ *212/362–7470* 🌐 *www.michaelpsilakis.com* Ⓜ *1 to 79th St.* ✥ *5:A2*

$$ AMERICAN FAMILY **Isabella's.** Set in the shadow of the Museum of Natural History, Isabella's has been a brunch-and-beyond stalwart for decades. Brunch is especially busy, even though the restaurant is large; lunch is less crowded, and a great time to try salads like the seafood-loaded Cobb or grilled artichoke hearts with Parmesan and lemon-thyme vinaigrette. Another winner: the crab cake sandwich layered with lush avocado. Try for a table outside when the weather's nice; it's a great perspective on the neighborhood. *Average main: $20* ✉ *359 Columbus Ave., at 77th St., Upper West Side* ☎ *212/724–2100* 🌐 *www.isabellas.com* Ⓜ *B, C to 81st St.–Museum of Natural History* ✥ *5:B3.*

$$$$ FRENCH **Jean Georges.** This culinary temple in the Trump International Hotel and Towers focuses wholly on *chef celebre* Jean-Georges Vongerichten's spectacular creations. The chef may now have restaurants sprinkled around the globe but this is the spot in his culinary empire you want to be at. Some dishes approach the limits of the taste universe, like foie gras brûlée with spiced fig jam and ice-wine reduction. Others are models of simplicity, like slow-cooked cod with warm vegetable vinaigrette. Exceedingly personalized service and a well-selected wine list contribute to an unforgettable meal. It's prix-fixe only. For Jean Georges on a budget, try the prix-fixe lunch in the front room, Nougatine. *Average main: $100* ✉ *1 Central Park W, at 59th St., Upper West Side*

☏ *212/299–3900* 🌐 *www.jean-georges.com* ✍ *Reservations essential. Jacket required* Ⓜ *A, B, C, D, 1 to 59th St.–Columbus Circle* ⊕ *5:C6.*

$ GREEK ✕ **Kefi.** "Kefi" is Greek for the bliss that accompanies a bacchanalia. And at Michael Psilakis's Upper West Side eatery—a giant homage to his grandmother's Greek cooking—it's not hard to achieve such a culinary state. Among the mezes, the meatballs with roasted garlic, olives, and tomato is a standout; the flavorful roast chicken, potatoes, red peppers, garlic, and thyme makes for a winning entrée; and the béchamel-rich Kefi mac 'n' cheese is irresistible. Reasonable prices make it easy to stick around for a piece of traditional walnut cake with walnut ice cream. Ⓢ *Average main: $14* ✉ *505 Columbus Ave., between 84th and 85th Sts., Upper West Side* ☏ *212/873–0200* 🌐 *www.kefirestaurant.com* Ⓜ *1 to 86th St.; B, C to 86th St.* ⊕ *5:B1*

$ BAKERY FAMILY ✕ **Levain Bakery.** Completely unpretentious and utterly delicious, Levain Bakery's cookies are rich and hefty. In fact, they clock in at 6 ounces each! Choose from the chocolate-chip walnut, dark-chocolate chocolate chip, dark-chocolate peanut-butter chip, or oatmeal raisin. Batches are baked fresh daily, and they taste best when they're warm and melty right out of the oven, so it's definitely worth seeking out this small basement bakery for a cookie craving. Levain's also bakes artisanal breads, including banana chocolate chip and pumpkin ginger spice, sour cream coffee cake, chocolate-chip and cinnamon brioche, sourdough rolls stuffed with Valrhona chocolate, blueberry muffins, a variety of scones, and *bomboloncini*—their unique jelly doughnuts. Ⓢ *Average main: $9* ✉ *167 W. 74th St., near Amsterdam Ave., Upper West Side* ☏ *212/874–6080* 🌐 *www.levainbakery.com* ⏲ *No dinner* Ⓜ *1, 2, 3 to 72nd St.* ⊕ *5:B3*

$$$$ SEAFOOD Fodor's Choice ★ ✕ **Marea.** Carefully sourced, meticulously prepared fish and seafood take center stage at this well-pedigreed restaurant. Large picture windows in the dining room offer expansive views of Central Park South, and silver-dipped shells on pedestals decorate the dining room. No expense is spared in importing the very best of the ocean's bounty, beginning with raw *crudo* dishes—think scallops with orange, wild fennel, and arugula—that is becoming the restaurant's signature and can be enjoyed in the main dining room or at the small bar at the end of the front room's shimmering onyx wall. You'd be remiss, though, if you skipped the pastas that made chef Michael White famous. They're served here in lusty iterations like rich fusilli with octopus and bone marrow and spaghetti with sea urchin. Whole fish like roasted turbot and salt-baked snapper are equally showstopping. Service is flawless. Ⓢ *Average main: $20* ✉ *240 Central Park S, between Broadway and 7th Ave., Midtown West* ☏ *212/582–5100* 🌐 *www.marea-nyc.com* ✍ *Reservations essential* Ⓜ *A, B, C, D, 1 to 59th St.–Columbus Circle* ⊕ *4:C1.*

$$ BISTRO FAMILY ✕ **Nice Matin.** If the Upper West Side and the French Riviera collided, it might look a little bit like Nice Matin. This is a longtime neighborhood favorite, particularly in the warm weather months, when regulars plant themselves at sidewalk tables and gawk at passersby while munching on Gallic fare like monkfish wading in sweet potato puree and garlicky mussels, and, of course, steak frites. The novel-size wine list boasts more than 2,000 bottles, so bring your reading glasses. And be sure to dress

The views from Per Se are spectacular, but so is the food.

for the people-watching occasion, particularly at the popular weekend brunch. *Average main: $24* ✉ *201 W. 79th St., at Amsterdam Ave., Upper West Side* ☎ *212/873–6423* 🌐 *www.nicematinnyc.com* Ⓜ *1 to 79th St.* ✣ *5:A2*

$$$$ AMERICAN Fodor's Choice ★ **Per Se.** The New York interpretation of what many consider America's finest restaurant, Napa Valley's French Laundry, Per Se is chef Thomas Keller's Broadway stage. The large dining room is understated and elegant, with touches of wood, towering florals, and sweeping views of Central Park. Keller embraces seasonality and a playfulness that speaks to his confidence in the kitchen, and some of his dishes are now world renowned, such as the tiny cones of tuna tartare topped with crème frâiche, and the "oysters and pearls"—tiny mollusks suspended in a creamy custard with tapioca. Dessert service is a multicourse celebration of all things sweet, including a choice of 27 house-made chocolates. Service is sublime, as you'd expect. An à la carte "salon" menu is available in the front bar room, but let's face it: if you manage to snag a reservation, there's nothing else to do but submit to the $295 prix-fixe. *Average main: $77* ✉ *Time Warner Center, 10 Columbus Circle, 4th fl., at 60th St., Upper West Side* ☎ *212/823–9335* 🌐 *www.perseny.com* *Reservations essential. Jacket required* ⊙ *No lunch Mon.–Thurs.* Ⓜ *A, B, C, D, 1 to 59th St.–Columbus Circle* ✣ *5:C6.*

$$$$ MEDITERRANEAN **Picholine.** Terrence Brennan's classic French restaurant has maintained its dignified atmosphere over the years, as well as the emphasis on contemporary Mediterranean cuisine, sourced from artisanal farmers and food producers. The menu is divided into options for a three-course and a twelve-course tasting menu, though it is also possible to order á la carte. The sweetbreads saltimboca, with prosciutto from the rich and

rare mangalitsa pig, is particularly tasty. So is the caviar-sprinkled sea urchin panna cotta. But whatever you do, don't miss the famous cheese course, which Brennan practically invented here. The atmosphere is refined but not stuffy. *Average main: $42 ✉ 35 W. 64th St., between Broadway and Central Park W, Upper West Side ☎ 212/724–8585 🌐 www.picholinenyc.com Reservations essential Closed Sun. No lunch.* Ⓜ *1 to 66th St.–Lincoln Center ✣ 5:C5.*

$$$$ STEAKHOUSE **Porter House New York.** With clubby interiors by Jeffrey Beers and an adjoining lounge area, Porter House marks the splashy return to the scene of former Windows on the World chef Michael Lomonaco. Filling the meat-and-potatoes slot in the Time Warner Center's upscale "Restaurant Collection," the masculine throwback highlights American wines and pedigreed super-size meat. The neighborhood, long underserved on the steakhouse front, has quickly warmed to Lomonaco's simple, solid American fare. Begin with his smoky clams casino or rich roasted marrow bones. Steaks are huge and expertly seasoned, and come with the usual battery of à la carte sides—creamed spinach, roasted mushrooms, and truffle mashed potatoes. *Average main: $40 ✉ Time Warner Center, 10 Columbus Circle, at 60th St., 4th fl., Upper West Side ☎ 212/823–9500 🌐 www.porterhousenewyork.com No lunch weekends* Ⓜ *A, B, C, D, 1 to 59th St.–Columbus Circle ✣ 5:C6.*

16

$ ITALIAN **Salumeria Rosi Parmacotto.** Just up the block from Gray's Papaya is this compact temple to a whole different subset of cured meats. Chef Cesare Casella has created a showcase for dozens of varieties of prosciutto, coppa, mortadella, and more, carved from a professional slicer for consumption on the spot or as indulgent takeout. There's also a more ambitious menu, including salads and a lusty osso buco over creamy mashed potatoes. If you're lucky, you might catch a glimpse of the avuncular chef with his signature rosemary sprig peeking out from his breast pocket. There's a spin-off with a more elaborate menu on the Upper East Side. *Average main: $13 ✉ 283 Amsterdam Ave., between 73rd and 74th Sts., Upper West Side ☎ 212/877–4800 🌐 www.salumeriarosi.com* Ⓜ *1, 2, 3 to 72nd St. ✣ 5:B3*

$$ AMERICAN **Sarabeth's Kitchen.** Lining up for brunch here is as much an Upper West Side tradition as taking a sunny Sunday afternoon stroll in nearby Riverside Park. Locals love the bric-a-brac-filled restaurant for sweet morningtime dishes like lemon ricotta pancakes, as well as for the comforting dinners. The afternoon tea includes buttery scones with Sarabeth's signature jams, savory nibbles, and outstanding baked goods. Dinner entrées include chicken potpie and truffle mac 'n' cheese. There are several other locations around town, including in the Lord & Taylor department store on 5th Avenue at 39th St. *Average main: $18 ✉ 423 Amsterdam Ave., at 80th St., Upper West Side ☎ 800/773–7378 🌐 www.sarabeth.com* Ⓜ *1 to 79th St. ✣ 5:B2*

$$$ AMERICAN **Telepan.** Chef-owner Bill Telepan is a regular at the neighborhood greenmarket, and it shows in his seasonal, produce-driven menu, which is divided into three courses: appetizers of salads, light fish dishes, and soups; middle courses of eggs, pasta, or vegetables; and main courses of meat and fish. A trio of tiny *amuses-bouches* such as wild mushroom cappuccino arrive to tease your palate, and the servers are refreshingly

well versed on the wine list. The menu features brook trout, served on celery-root blini with green-apple sour cream, a well-deserved favorite, as is anything on the menu that contains eggs, like the "egg-in-a-hole" served with spinach and hen-of-the-woods mushrooms. For dessert, a crunchy peanut-butter and milk-chocolate gianduja duo with peanut-brittle ice cream is sublime. $ *Average main: $29* ✉ *72 W. 69th St., between Columbus Ave. and Central Park W, Upper West Side* ☎ *212/580–4300* 🌐 *www.telepan-ny.com* ⊙ *No lunch Mon. and Tues.* Ⓜ *1 to 66th St.–Lincoln Center; 1, 2, 3 to 72nd St.; B, C to 72nd St.* ✥ *B:C4*

HARLEM

For more adventurous eating, head up to Harlem for the city's best Southern cooking. This is a neighborhood that takes pride in its food, and in addition to plates of collard greens, mac and cheese and smothered chicken, an infusion of wine bars, restaurants, and lounges is changing the landscape. This is where renowned chef Marcus Samuelsson lives and his high-profile restaurant, Red Rooster, is helping to encourage the beginning of a new Harlem dining renaissance.

$$ BISTRO ✕ **Chez Lucienne.** French Harlem? Not exactly, but Chez Lucienne is about as close as you'll get to France without leaving the comfortable confines of this historic neighborhood. And if you can't get into the Red Rooster next door, then grab a seat at the baby blue banquette or relax at an outdoor table where locals come to sip coffee or wine, dogs at their side. The menu looks to Lyon with classics like sauteed foie gras and steak au poivre by a chef who logged time in the kitchen with famed chef Daniel Boulud. $ *Average main: $18* ✉ *308 Lenox Ave., between 125th and 126th Sts., Harlem* ☎ *212/289–5555* 🌐 *www.chezlucienne.com* Ⓜ *2, 3 to 116th St.* ✥ *6:D1*

$$$ AMERICAN ✕ **Red Rooster Harlem.** Marcus Samuelsson, who earned his celebrity chefdom at Aquavit in Midtown for his take on Ethiopian-accented Scandinavian cuisine (fusing the food of his birthplace with that of where he grew up), moves way uptown to Harlem, where he has created a culinary hot spot for the ages. The comfort food menu jumps all over the place, reflecting the ethnic diversity that is modern-day New York City (and the patrons who regularly come here), from plantain-loaded oxtail to fried chicken to the tender meatballs (with lingonberry sauce) that he served at Aquavit. Expect a wait for Sunday brunch, with its gospel music, boozy cocktails, and modern takes on dishes like chicken and waffles. $ *Average main: $26* ✉ *310 Lenox Ave., between 125th and 126th, Harlem* ☎ *212/792–9001* 🌐 *www.redroosterharlem.com* Ⓜ *2, 3 to 125th St.* ✥ *6:D1*

$$ SOUTHERN FAMILY ✕ **Sylvia's.** This Harlem mainstay has been serving soul-food favorites like smothered chicken, barbecue ribs, collard greens, and mashed potatoes to a dedicated crowd of locals, tourists, and college students since 1962. Owner Sylvia Woods may have passed away in the summer of 2012 but her restaurant and the signature sauces that are jarred and sold online and in the restaurant are more popular than ever. Some say it's overly touristy—and the bus loads attest, but it's still an experience. For the ultimate, come for Sunday gospel brunch. Singing and eating were

never a more delicious combination. [$] *Average main: $24* ✉ *328 Lenox Ave., near 127th St., Harlem* ☎ *212/996–0660* 🌐 *www.sylviassoulfood.com* [M] *2, 3 to 125th St.* ⊕ *6:D1*

BROOKLYN

BRIGHTON BEACH

The subway trains that shuttle people out to this beachside neighborhood could be nicknamed the "time machine" because strolling the wide boardwalk along the sea feels like you've dropped into another time and space. Odessa in the 1980s comes to mind. After all, it was around that time when a mass migration of Russian immigrants settled in Brighton Beach. Today you'll hear more Slavic than English and you'll most certainly be tempted by the vodka and highly entertaining Russian restaurants that line the boardwalk.

$ RUSSIAN ✕ **Tatiana Grill.** It's open year-round, but Tatiana's, right on the boardwalk, really bustles in the summer when the outdoor tables fill with Russian-speaking couples and families, as well as day trippers out from Manhattan for a day at the beach. The menu has pages and pages of options that range from sushi to Ukrainian dishes. The excellent Greek salad is a refreshing choice after a day at the beach, and the grilled chicken skewers are simple but good. Order a Russian beer to go with your meal. [$] *Average main: $15* ✉ *3152 Brighton 6th St., on boardwalk, Brighton Beach* ☎ *718/891–5151* 🌐 *www.tatianagrill.com* [M] *B, Q to Brighton Beach* ⊕ *7:H6.*

16

BROOKLYN HEIGHTS

$$ AMERICAN ✕ **Henry's End.** At this nearly 40-year-old neighborhood favorite, the casual decor belies the quality of the food and wine. Wild game such as elk, kangaroo, and ostrich take center stage in the winter months and during the Wild Game Festival in the late fall; seasonal seafood and foraged vegetables star in the springtime. If duck is your thing, there are usually several preparations on the menu. At the end of Henry Street, the small space still fills up quickly at dinnertime. [$] *Average main: $18* ✉ *44 Henry St., near Cranberry St., Brooklyn Heights* ☎ *718/834–1776* 🌐 *www.henrysend.com* ⏲ *No lunch* [M] *2, 3 to Clark St.; A, C to High St.* ⊕ *7:B3*

CARROLL GARDENS

If you look closely, you can still see some elements of old Brooklyn in this leafy neighborhood: the older Italian men parked on lawn chairs speaking a southern Italian dialect, the meat market with its archaic sign a relic from the 1950s. But Carroll Gardens is anything but old-fashioned. Walk down Smith or Court Street to find blocks flanked by hip, crowded bars and restaurants good enough to lure even travel-finicky Manhattanites.

$$ AMERICAN ✕ **Buttermilk Channel.** This cozy restaurant is like a spirited slice of down-home Americana. Locals swear by comfort-food mainstays with emphasis on local and organic, especially the all-time fave: buttermilk-fried chicken with cheddar waffles. Other standouts include the house-made charcuterie and snacks like handmade mozzarella. Specials include a

Monday night, three-course dinner for $25. It's a bit of a trek if you're taking the subway but you'll be rewarded with a homey, Brooklyn dining experience. *Average main: $19 524 Court St., at Huntington St., Carroll Gardens 718/852–8490 www.buttermilkchannelnyc.com No lunch weekdays F to Carroll St. 7:A5*

$$ AMERICAN **Char No. 4.** With 300-plus whiskeys to choose from—the focus is on American labels—Char No. 4 is a connoisseur's dream (the name refers to barrels in which the golden liquor is aged). Naturally, there are also plenty of bourbon-accented cocktails (try the Noreaster, with ginger beer and maple syrup). To complement your tipple, there are updated dishes from south of the Mason-Dixon line. Many of the appetizers involve bacon; don't miss the thick-cut bacon with peas and carrots, lamb pastrami, the BLT, or the cheese curds with pimento sauce. *Average main: $20 196 Smith St., between Baltic and Warren Sts., Carroll Gardens 718/643–2106 www.charno4.com No lunch Mon.–Thurs. F to Bergen St. 7:B4*

$$$ AMERICAN **SAUL restaurant.** Owner Saul Bolton, who logged time in the kitchens of Le Bernardin and Bouley, and was one of the first to include seasonal local ingredients on his plates. More than a decade later, this Smith Street restaurant is still a favorite eating destination for the culinary cognoscenti. Saul is particularly good at mixing surf and turf, in dishes like caramelized scallops paired with chorizo and grilled octopus with slow-roasted pork belly—the resulting delights are well executed without being overly precious. *Average main: $31 140 Smith St., near Bergen, Carroll Gardens 718/935–9844 www.saulrestaurant.com No lunch F to Bergen St. 7:B4*

CONEY ISLAND

It's no longer an island but this amusement park on the sea is salt-of-the-earth paradise. Think pizza and hot dogs and calorie-laden carnival fare. If you're in town during the Fourth of July, a Big Apple must-see is the annual Nathan's Famous hot dog eating contest where hundreds of people gather to watch "professional" eaters scarf down tubular meat.

$ AMERICAN **Nathan's Famous.** No visit to Coney Island would be complete without a hot dog from this stand that opened in 1916—although as of press time, Nathan's was closed due to damage from Hurricane Sandy but expected to reopen by summer 2013. On the Fourth of July thousands come to see their world-famous hot dog–eating contest; the record stands at 68 in 10 minutes. *Average main: $4 1310 Surf Ave., at Stillwell Ave., Coney Island 718/946–2705 www.nathansfamous.com D, F, N, Q to Coney Island–Stillwell Ave. 7:G6*

DOWNTOWN BROOKLYN

Filled with Neoclassical courthouse buildings and glass skyscrapers, there isn't much reason to come to downtown Brooklyn—unless, of course, you managed to nab a reservation at the borough's only three-Michelin-starred restaurant, Brooklyn Fare.

$$$$ ECLECTIC **Brooklyn Fare.** At Brooklyn's only restaurant with three coveted Michelin stars, local star chef César Ramirez and his sous-chefs offer a culinary performance during three nightly seatings. At each, 20 dainty, often seafood-focused concoctions are presented to 18 diners seated at

a semicircular steel counter. Dishes might include king salmon parfait with basil gelée, avocado, maple syrup, and mustard; or fresh tofu and king crab blended with matsutake mushrooms and dashi sauce. Getting a reservation is a complicated ordeal so plan in advance. And make sure you're wearing your best: formal wear is required. *$ Average main: $135 ✉ 200 Schermerhorn St., near Hoyt St., Downtown ☎ 718/243–0050 🌐 www.brooklynfare.com ✍ Reservations essential ⏲ Closed Sun. No lunch Ⓜ A, C, G to Hoyt–Schermerhorn Sts.; 2, 3 to Hoyt St.; 4, 5 to Nevins St.; B, Q, R to Dekalb Ave. ✣ 7:B4*

DUMBO

Once upon a time, the primary reason for a hungry person to come to DUMBO was to eat pizza at Grimaldi's. The past few years have seen the growing gentrification of the loft-strewn cobblestone streets, though, which are now sprinkled with toothsome eateries and cute boutiques, and now that the Brooklyn waterfront has been fully developed you can walk off your meal with a romantic stroll.

$ PIZZA

✕ Grimaldi's. This legendary New York–style parlor serves excellent pizza pies from its coal ovens. Although sometimes inconsistent, when they're good, the thin crisp crust is slightly blackened, and the fresh mozzarella oozes satisfyingly. Grimaldi's is still one of the city's premier pizza spots and, paired with a walk across the Brooklyn Bridge, this is a top-notch New York experience. Grimaldi's popularity allows them to be picky: no slices, no reservations, no credit cards; and there are usually no empty tables so expect a wait. Impatient foodies have been known to phone in a to-go order, swoop past the lines, and then enjoy their pizza in the nearby Brooklyn Bridge Park. *$ Average main: $14 ✉ 1 Front St., near Water St., DUMBO ☎ 718/858–4300 🌐 www.grimaldis.com ✍ Reservations not accepted ▭ No credit cards Ⓜ A, C to High St.; 2, 3 to Clark St.; F to York St. ✣ 7:B3*

$$$$ MODERN AMERICAN

✕ River Café. The River Café's incredible views of the Manhattan skyline, lush flowers, and live piano music make it a waterfront favorite for romantic meals, marriage proposals, fancy birthdays, and special celebrations. The menu offers a contemporary take on local and exotic ingredients—it's fixed-price-only at dinner; lunch has à la carte options. For the ultimate experience, snag a window seat and try the chef's six-course tasting menu ($135 per person). Gentlemen: jackets are required after 5 pm. The restaurant was hit hard by Hurricane Sandy in October 2012 and was still shuttered at press time so check back before you plan a visit. *$ Average main: $100 ✉ 1 Water St., near Old Fulton St., DUMBO ☎ 718/522–5200 🌐 www.rivercafe.com Ⓜ F to York St.; A, C to High St.; 2, 3 to Clark St. ✣ 7:B3*

$$ MODERN AMERICAN

✕ Vinegar Hill House. In an offbeat enclave on the edge of DUMBO called Vinegar Hill, this intimate eatery has been a hit with Brooklynites since the day it first fired up its burners in 2008. Foodies trek out to the rustic-chic dining room for well-prepared seasonal food, the cozy ambience, and expertly prepared cocktails. Favorites from the small menu include the moist, crispy-skinned cast-iron chicken and the giant pork chop. The homey, vintage-y decor and the clientele are quintessential modern-urban Brooklyn. Brunch is served on the weekends. *$ Average main: $24 ✉ 72 Hudson Ave., between Front and Water Sts., DUMBO*

16

718/522–1018 www.vinegarhillhouse.com Reservations not accepted No lunch weekdays M *F to York St. 7:C2*

FORT GREENE

Fort Greene has lately become one of the most desirable neighborhoods in Brooklyn, the lovely brownstone apartments attracting young professionals and many of the borough's established and up-and-coming writers and artists. It's also a garden of culinary delights with restaurants leading the locavore farm-to-table movement. And who knows? Maybe even a famous director or author will be sitting at the table next to you.

$$ AMERICAN **The General Greene.** Hearty, locally sourced fare seems to keep the crowds happy these days no matter where you are, but this neighborhood darling outdoes much of the competition. The menu changes with the season but here's a sampling of what you might find: buttermilk biscuits or seven-spice onion rings, a very memorable (and crispy) fried chicken, whole trout, or short-rib stroganoff with organic rigatoni. Vegetable sides like steamed red kale or Brussels sprouts with bacon and mushrooms are just the other side of virtuous. Waiting for a table is part of the experience, especially at brunch on weekends, as are the cocktails and the famous salted-caramel sundae. $ *Average main: $18 229 DeKalb Ave., Fort Greene 718/222–1510 www.thegeneralgreene.com* M *C to Lafayette Ave.; B, Q, R to DeKalb Ave. 7:C4*

$$ MODERN AMERICAN **No. 7.** Perch at the marble-topped bar or lounge at one of the banquettes in the back at this buzzy neighborhood bistro lighted up by Edison bulbs. The frequently changing menu takes American classics and throws them for a global spin. The result is nouveau fusion that pulls in droves of local diners and makes vegetarians happy. Highlights might include anything from crispy eggplant with tofu in a tomato vinaigrette to skirt steak with baked potato, Chinese sausage, and chimichurri sauce. Brunch dishes are similarly innovative but delicious—think fried eggs with nachos and jalapeños, or pork loin with fried eggs, buttermilk pancake, and pineapple maple syrup. On Monday nights, the dining room is closed but the bar is still open. $ *Average main: $20 7 Greene Ave., Fort Greene 718/522–6370 www.no7restaurant.com No lunch weekdays, no dinner Mon.* M *C to Lafayette Ave.; 2, 3, 4, 5, B, Q to Atlantic Ave.–Barclays Center. 7:C4*

$$ ITALIAN Fodor's Choice ★ **Roman's.** When the masterminds behind Marlow & Sons opened this locavore Italian restaurant in Fort Greene, neighborhood foodies rejoiced, and the consistently excellent food, convivial atmosphere, and friendly service still has them clamoring for a table or a spot at the refinished marble bar. The small menu changes nightly and showcases refined interpretations using top of the line produce and proteins. Think appetizers like roasted rabbit loins with lentils; a salad of radishes with anchovy and a boiled egg; innovative pastas; and main courses that might include chicken al diavolo or whole fish. Weekend brunch is a hit—if they're on the menu, don't skip the homemade doughnuts. $ *Average main: $17 243 Dekalb Ave., near Vanderbilt Ave., Fort Greene 718/622–5300 www.romansnyc.com Reservations not accepted No lunch weekdays* M *C to Lafayette Ave. 7:D4.*

$$ MODERN AMERICAN **Stonehome Wine Bar and Restaurant.** Just down the street from BAM, Stonehome is the place to go before or after a show for sophisticated food and wine at reasonable prices. This dim basement hideaway has excellent tasting flights—three samples for $18—and 35 wines by the glass, perfect to pair with cheese, charcuterie, and housemade pâtés. The uncomplicated menu focuses on market-fresh new American fare like pan-roasted chicken with cheddar grits and greens. The back garden is a delight in nice weather. *Average main: $19 87 Lafayette Ave., at S. Portland Ave., Fort Greene 718/624–9443 www.stonehomewinebar.com No lunch C to Lafayette Ave. 7:C4*

PARK SLOPE

Park Slope's reputation precedes it: known as a gay-friendly family neighborhood, this handsome neighborhood also happens to be a great place to fill the tummy. Stroll down 5th Avenue, a no-go zone about 15 years ago, where each block clamors with intriguing eateries.

$$ ITALIAN **al di là.** This Northern Italian hot spot has been consistently packed since it first opened back in 1998, and it's easy to understand why: affordable prices, a relaxed and charming environment, and simple yet soulfully comforting dishes from the Veneto region of Italy. Expect to find homemade pastas like black spaghetti with crab or tortellini filled with roasted squash, as well as meaty mains such as braised rabbit, or hanger steak. The dessert fritters are legendary. The no-reservations policy ensures that the place always has a buzz around it from waiting patrons. *Average main: $21 248 5th Ave., at Carroll St., Park Slope 718/783–4565 www.aldilatrattoria.com Reservations not accepted F, G, R to 4th Ave.–9th St.; R to Union St. 7:C5*

$ PIZZA **Franny's.** Though many swear by Grimaldi's for Brooklyn's best pie, this Park Slope pizza shop has developed quite a following of its own. The crisp, thin-crust pizzas run the gamut from a "naked" pie with olive oil and salt to their justly talked-up clam-and-garlic iteration. Many of the toppings are seasonal and locally sourced. In the years since Franny's has opened, several other excellent artisanal pizza shops have opened in the neighborhood and around, but Franny's still draws lines at dinnertime. *Average main: $16 348 Flatbush Ave., Park Slope 718/230–0221 www.frannysbrooklyn.com Reservations not accepted No lunch weekdays B, Q to 7th Ave.; 2, 3 to Bergen St.; 4, 5, N, R to Pacific St. 7:C5*

$$ ASIAN **Talde.** Fans of *Top Chef* will recognize the name of chef Dale Talde (from season 4) but even if you're not familiar with the show it's worth making a culinary pilgrimage to Park Slope to eat here. Chef Talde churns out impressive dishes that span most of Asia. Standouts on the menu include inventive, fun fare like the sticky kung pao chicken wings, the pretzel pork and chive dumplings, and peanut-sprinkled smoked *char siu* pork. Be sure to save some room for the finale: chocolate pudding with Campari-candied grapefruit rind and Sichuan-spiced peanuts is a real showstopper. *Average main: $20 369 7th Ave., at 11th St., Park Slope 347/916–0031 www.taldebrooklyn.com Reservations not accepted F, G to 7th Ave. 7:C6*

16

PROSPECT HEIGHTS

$ DINER ✕ **Tom's Restaurant.** For friendly service and great diner fare—especially the excellent fluffy lemon-ricotta pancakes served with homemade flavored butters—head three blocks north of the Brooklyn Museum to this family-owned restaurant, which opened in 1936. Lines are long on weekends. *Average main: $8 ✉ 782 Washington Ave., at Sterling Pl., Prospect Heights ☎ 718/636–9738 Reservations not accepted No credit cards No dinner Ⓜ 2, 3 to Grand Army Plaza ✢ 7:D5.*

WILLIAMSBURG

Still probably the hippest, happening-est neighborhood in the five boroughs, Williamsburg is also one of the hottest destinations on the culinary landscape. Peter Luger's, the classic steak house, has been serving customers since 1887, but the past few years has seen the opening of ground-breaking dining destinations like Dressler, Fette Sau, Marlow & Sons, Roberta's (which is technically across the border in Bushwick), and, most recently, Reynards and Gwynnett St.

$$ AMERICAN ✕ **Diner.** Tucked inside a 1927 dining car, this restaurant serves simple seasonal fare and so many specials that your waiter will scrawl their names on the paper tablecloth to help you remember them all. It's more upscale than the name implies but still casual. Save room for the intense flourless chocolate cake. *Average main: $20 ✉ 85 Broadway, at Berry St., Williamsburg ☎ 718/486–3077 www.dinernyc.com Reservations not accepted Ⓜ J, M, Z to Marcy Ave.; L to Bedford Ave. ✢ 7:D2*

$$$ AMERICAN ✕ **Dressler.** Williamsburg has become one of the tastiest parts of the Big Apple and handsome, dark-wood-and-exposed-brick-bedecked restaurants like Dressler are exactly what have given the neighborhood its culinary star status. Famed, old-school steak house Peter Luger may be just across the street, but food-loving hipsters are hitting Dressler for American seasonal cuisine like house-smoked sturgeon and braised veal cheeks. And if that's not enough to make a hipster's skinny jeans tighter, the legendary burger from sister restaurant, DuMont, is also on the menu. Brunch is served on Sunday. *Average main: $31 ✉ 149 Broadway, between Bedford and Driggs Aves., Williamsburg ☎ 718/384–6343 www.dresslernyc.com Ⓜ J, M, Z to Marcy Ave.; L to Bedford Ave. ✢ 7:D2*

$$ AMERICAN ✕ **DuMont.** Slide into a leather booth or sit outside in the charming garden and peruse the menu of seasonal salads, pasta, and main courses. This is the place for inspired cocktails and cuisine in a laid-back atmosphere. Classic menu items include a swoon-inducing mac 'n' cheese and juicy burgers that inspired a separate restaurant, DuMont Burger, nearby (314 Bedford Avenue). *Average main: $20 ✉ 432 Union Ave., between Metropolitan Ave. and Devoe St., Williamsburg ☎ 718/486–7717 www.dumontrestaurant.com Ⓜ L to Lorimer St. ✢ 7:E2*

$ AMERICAN ✕ **Fette Sau.** It might seem odd to go to a former auto-body repair shop to eat meat, but the funky building and outside courtyard seem just right for the serious 'cue served here. A huge wood-and-gas smoker delivers well-smoked brisket, sausages, ribs, and even duck, all ordered by the pound. Avoid the disappointing salads and sides, and instead choose from among the more than 40 American whiskeys and 10 microbrews. Come early, as tables fill up quickly, and even with 700 pounds of meat a night, the good stuff sometimes runs out by 9 pm. There's limited indoor seating. *Average main: $12 354 Metropolitan Ave., between Havemeyer and Roebling Sts., Williamsburg 718/963–3404 fettesaubbq.com Reservations not accepted No lunch weekdays M L to Lorimer St. 7:E2*

$$ AMERICAN **Gwynnett St.** Named for a street that ran through 19th-century Williamsburg, connecting the neighborhood to other parts of Brooklyn, Gwynnett St. has been the darling of New York restaurant critics since the ovens were fired up in late 2011, and the popularity has not waned. And why should it? The fare is New American, ordered as either small or large plates, and along the lines of chicken paired with ginger, liver, and pear or halibut with roasted pine nuts. Factor in a killer cocktail list and an affordable but nicely selected wine list and you have all the makings of an excellent dinner. *Average main: $20 312 Graham Ave., at Ainslie St., Williamsburg 347/889–7002 www.gwynnettst.com Reservations essential M L to Graham Ave. 7:E2*

$ MEXICAN **La Superior.** Serving some of Brooklyn's best Mexican grub this side of the Red Hook ball fields, La Superior is Mexican street food with a Williamsburg ethic. The service is slapdash and the decor is unremarkable, but the food—from beef-tongue tacos to pescadillas (fish quesadillas)—really delivers. Don't be surprised if your waiter has a seat at your table while discussing the menu. *Average main: $10 295 Berry St., Williamsburg 718/388–5988 lasuperiornyc.com Reservations not accepted No credit cards M L to Bedford Ave.; J, M, Z to Marcy Ave. 7:D2*

$$ AMERICAN **Marlow & Sons.** It may look like a gourmet food store but it's also a buzzy restaurant with a wood-paneled dining room, started by the people behind Diner next door, and Roman's in Fort Greene. Start with oysters or a wedge of delicate tortilla Española or choose one of many daily specials. Don't miss the adventurous cocktails, so good they'll almost make you forget about the uncomfortable wooden seating. After dinner, you can shop for delicacies like wildflower honey and aromatic bitters. *Average main: $23 81 Broadway, at Berry St., Williamsburg 718/384–1441 www.marlowandsons.com Reservations not accepted M J, M, Z to Marcy Ave.; L to Bedford Ave. 7:D2*

$$$$ STEAKHOUSE Fodor's Choice ★ **Peter Luger Steak House.** Long before Brooklyn was chic, even the snobbiest Manhattanites flocked to Peter Luger's. Other steak houses have more elegant ambience, bigger wine lists, and less brusque service, but the meat here makes the trip undeniably worth it. Three tips: bring a meat-eating buddy or several (individual steaks are available, but porterhouse is served only for two, three, or four), make a reservation (prime slots fill up more than a month in advance), and bring lots of cash—Luger's doesn't take plastic. The lunch-only burger is beloved among locals, as is the bacon appetizer, available by the slice. *Average main: $50 178 Broadway, at Driggs Ave., Williamsburg 718/387–7400 www.peterluger.com Reservations essential No credit cards M J, M, Z to Marcy Ave. 7:D2*

$$ Fodor's Choice ★ **Reynards.** In the hip Wythe Hotel, Reynards opened in 2012 and quickly became part of the increasingly upscale side of the Williamsburg scene, serving sophisticated fare at Manhattan prices. The restaurant is

from the team who brought Brooklyn the much-lauded Diner and Marlow & Sons, so the pedigree is there and so is the follow-through. The high-ceilinged, exposed-brick dining room is a fitting venue for artisanal cocktails and a menu that encapsulates most of the food trends of the last couple years—from a kale salad to Brussels sprouts to intriguing takes on surf and turf (sea urchin and foie gras, anyone?). It's all enough to make you want to sprout a beard and plant a vegetable garden on your roof. *Average main: $20 ✉ Wythe Hotel, 80 Wythe Ave., at N. 11th St., Williamsburg ☎ 718/460–8004 🌐 www.reynardsnyc.com Ⓜ L to Bedford Ave. ⊕ 7:D1*

$$ ITALIAN Fodor's Choice ★ **Roberta's.** Roberta's gets Manhattan-dwelling food lovers to get on the subway and go across the East River to the buddingly hip neighborhood of Bushwick, which lies just beyond Williamsburg (some people just call it East Williamsburg). Rustic-looking Roberta's is worth the trek. The menu, which is something like "Brooklyn Italian" with its emphasis on using very local ingredients (there's a garden on the roof!) changes regularly but expect duck-prosciutto pizza, goat-spiked pasta, and variations on the theme of snout-to-tail dining. And, of course, a supercool soundtrack that's music to any hipster's ears. For a more elegant "Roberta's" experience, check out the adjacent offshoot, Blanca, which serves upscale fixed-price multi-course meals (reservations are essential and hard to get). *Average main: $20 ✉ 261 Moore St., at Bogart St., Williamsburg ☎ 718/417–1118 Ⓜ L to Morgan Ave. ⊕ 7:F2*

$$ AMERICAN **Rye.** Delicious bistro classics and creative American fare are on the menu at this dark, moody speakeasy-style hideaway on a little-trodden block. Enter through the unmarked door and you'll find yourself in a world of leather cushions, pressed-tin ceilings, dark wood, mosaic floors, and a 100-year-old oak bar. The signature meatloaf sandwich is daydream-worthy, served with crispy buttermilk onions and horseradish sauce. Cocktails are also excellent; try the Havemayer with overproof rye whiskey. The happy hour special—$5 cheeseburgers and Manhattans—is worth the trip alone, but only available at the bar. *Average main: $25 ✉ 247 S. 1st St., at Havemeyer St., Williamsburg ☎ 718/218–8047 🌐 www.ryerestaurant.com ⏲ No lunch weekdays Ⓜ L to Lorimer St.; J, M, Z to Marcy Ave. ⊕ 7:E2*

QUEENS

ASTORIA

After you're finished with the sights, why head back to Manhattan? End your day with dinner at one of Astoria's legendary Greek restaurants (on or near Broadway), or venture to the Middle Eastern restaurants farther out on Steinway Street.

$ MIDDLE EASTERN **Kabab Café.** Middle Eastern restaurants are a dime a dozen in NYC, but Egyptian-Mediterranean spots are rarer, attracting foodies like celebrity chef Anthony Bourdain. This charming 16-seat café, which excels at interesting homestyle dishes, is a true hidden treasure. The menu changes nightly, but exceedingly tender lamb stuffed with pomegranate is always great. *Average main: $16 ✉ 25-12 Steinway St., Astoria ☎ 718/728–9858 Reservations not accepted No credit cards ⏲ Closed Mon. Ⓜ N, Q to Astoria–Ditmars Blvd. ⊕ 7:F1*

$ VEGETARIAN **Taverna Kyclades.** The current powerhouse of Hellenic eats in the neighborhood, Taverna Kyclades offers Greek classics at a higher level than you'd expect, given the simple decor and unassuming location. Fried calamari and grilled octopus make appearances at rock-bottom prices, despite their obvious quality, as do more out-of-the-ordinary dishes like "caviar dip" and swordfish kebabs. Be prepared to wait for a table at peak times, as they don't take reservations. *Average main: $12 33-07 Ditmars Blvd., Astoria 718/545–8666 tavernakyclades.com Reservations not accepted N, Q to Astoria–Ditmars Blvd. 7:F1*

FLUSHING

Manhattan may be known for its fine four-star restaurants, but food lovers know there's one train line to take to some of the best eats in the city. The 7 train snakes its way through the middle of Queens, and conveniently through some of the best eating neighborhoods in New York. At the end of the line is Flushing, home to the second-largest Chinatown in the United States. (First is San Francisco's.) Wide streets have few tourists and many interesting stores and restaurants, making the long trip worth it. A couple tips: bring cash, because not many of these restaurants accept credit cards, and be prepared to encounter language difficulties, as English speakers are in the minority. In Manhattan, catch the 7 train at Times Square or Grand Central Terminal.

16

$ CHINESE **Spicy and Tasty.** For standout Chinese, head to Spicy and Tasty, which lives up to its name with numbing Szechuan peppercorns and slicks of red chili oil. Tea-smoked duck has crispy skin and smoky, salty meat. Eggplant with garlic sauce tastes of ginger, tomatoes, and red chilies. Cool it all down with a Tsingtao beer. *Average main: $10 39-07 Prince St., at 39th Ave., Flushing 718/359–1601 Reservations not accepted 7 to Flushing–Main St. 7:H1*

LONG ISLAND CITY

$ CANADIAN Fodor's Choice ★ **M. Wells Dinette.** When the original version of this beloved and experimental restaurant in Long Island City lost its lease and had to shut down, a swath of New York eaters let out a collective groan. But they didn't have to go too long without their foie gras fix because in Fall 2012, French-Canadian chef Hugue Dufour reopened the restaurant at MoMA's PS1. As at the previous incarnation Dufour serves an array of dishes so unctuous you might want to come with a prescription for Lipitor. The menu changes depending on the season but diners might find dishes like veal cheek stroganoff, using thick bucatini as the noodles, or bone marrow and escargot. Finish off with a slice of maple pie and a shot of maple bourbon. Then wander the gallery trying to make sense of the art (and your meal). At press time, the restaurant was only serving lunch but dinner service is expected in the future so check the website. *Average main: $17 MoMA PS1, 22-25 Jackson Ave., at 46th Ave., Long Island City 718/786–1800 www.momaps1.org/about/mwells Reservations not accepted No dinner. Closed Tues. and Wed. E, M to 23rd St.–Ely Ave.; G, 7 to Court Sq. 7:F1*

JACKSON HEIGHTS

$ INDIAN **Jackson Diner.** Neighborhood folk and Manhattanites alike flock to Jackson Diner for the spicy, authentic fare served in generous portions. Popular choices include chicken tandoori, South Indian lentil doughnuts in a tangy broth, and any of the curry dishes, as well as the many vegetarian specialties. There's now a location in Manhattan at 72 University Place, but it's not quite the same experience as when you make the trip out to Jackson Heights. *Average main: $15 37-47 74th St., between Roosevelt and 37th Aves., Jackson Heights 718/672–1232 E, F, M, R to Jackson Heights–Roosevelt Ave.; 7 to 74th St.–Broadway 7:F1.*

WOODSIDE

$ THAI **SriPraPhai.** The main reason foodies flock to Woodside is to go to SriPraPhai, ronounced See-PRA-pie. It's widely considered the best Thai restaurant in New York. Don't miss the crispy watercress salad and the *larb* (ground pork with mint, lime juice, and onions). It's closed Wednesday. *Average main: $12 64-13 39th Ave. Woodside 718/899–9599 7 to 69th St. 7:H1*

THE BRONX

$$ ITALIAN **Antonio's Trattoria.** Antonio's bills itself as "an Italian restaurant serving simple food," but that's underselling it by far. Fantastic classic Italian fare is dished out here; do not miss the baked clams, the house-made ravioli, and the excellent pizzas. It's a bit off the main Arthur Avenue strip, but worth the trek. *Average main: $20 2370 Belmont Ave., Belmont, Bronx 718/733–6630 www.antoniostrattoria.com B, D to 182nd–183rd Sts.*

$ ITALIAN **Zero Otto Nove.** Though insiders who can get a table swear by Rao's on E. 114th Street in Manhattan, Zero Otto Nove chugs along as one of the best Italian restaurants north of 96th Street. The draw? Wood oven–fired pizza, perfectly chewy and larded with buffalo mozzarella. The San Matteo, which adds broccoli rabe to the mix, is just as addictive as the plain Jane margherita. *Average main: $15 2357 Arthur Ave., Belmont 718/220–1027 www.roberto089.com/ Reservations not accepted Closed Mon. B, D to 182nd–183rd Sts.*

NEW YORK CITY DINING AND LODGING ATLAS

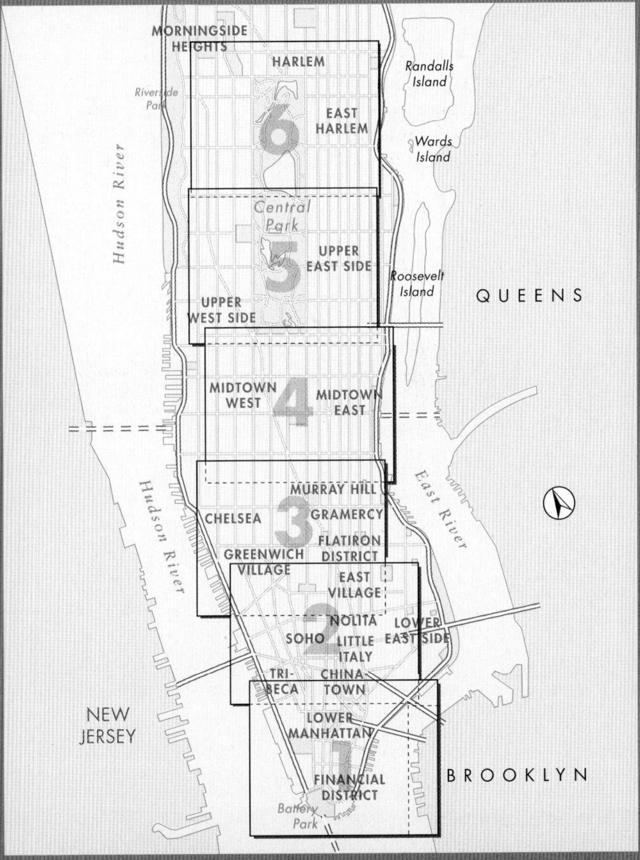

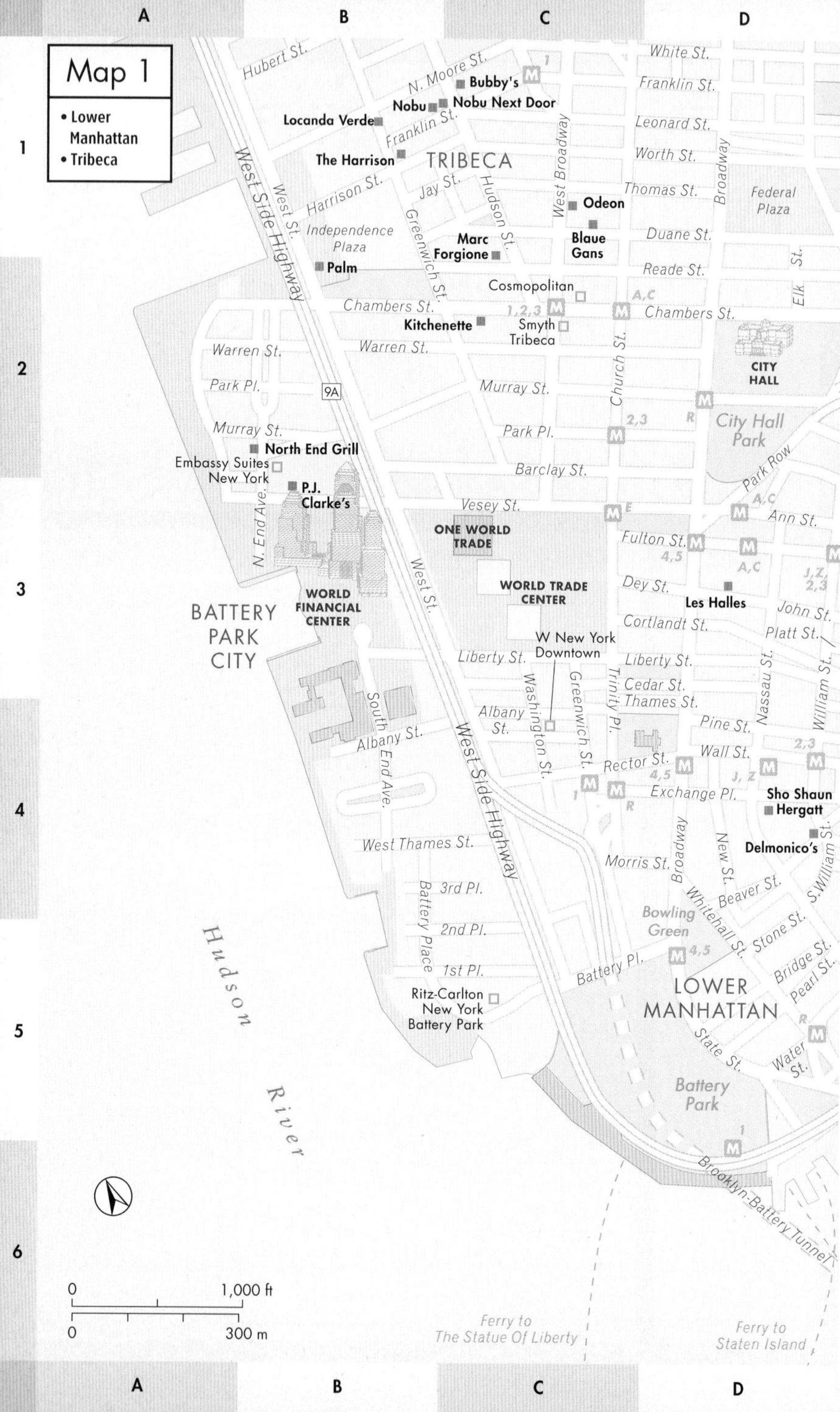

Map 1
• Lower Manhattan
• Tribeca
A
B
C
D
1
2
3
4
5
6
TRIBECA
BATTERY PARK CITY
LOWER MANHATTAN
Hudson River
Bubby's
Nobu
Nobu Next Door
Locanda Verde
The Harrison
Odeon
Blaue Gans
Marc Forgione
Palm
Cosmopolitan
Kitchenette
Smyth Tribeca
North End Grill
Embassy Suites New York
P.J. Clarke's
ONE WORLD TRADE
WORLD TRADE CENTER
WORLD FINANCIAL CENTER
Les Halles
W New York Downtown
Sho Shaun Hergatt
Delmonico's
Ritz-Carlton New York Battery Park
CITY HALL
City Hall Park
Federal Plaza
Independence Plaza
Bowling Green
Battery Park
Brooklyn-Battery Tunnel
Ferry to The Statue Of Liberty
Ferry to Staten Island
0
1,000 ft
0
300 m
9A

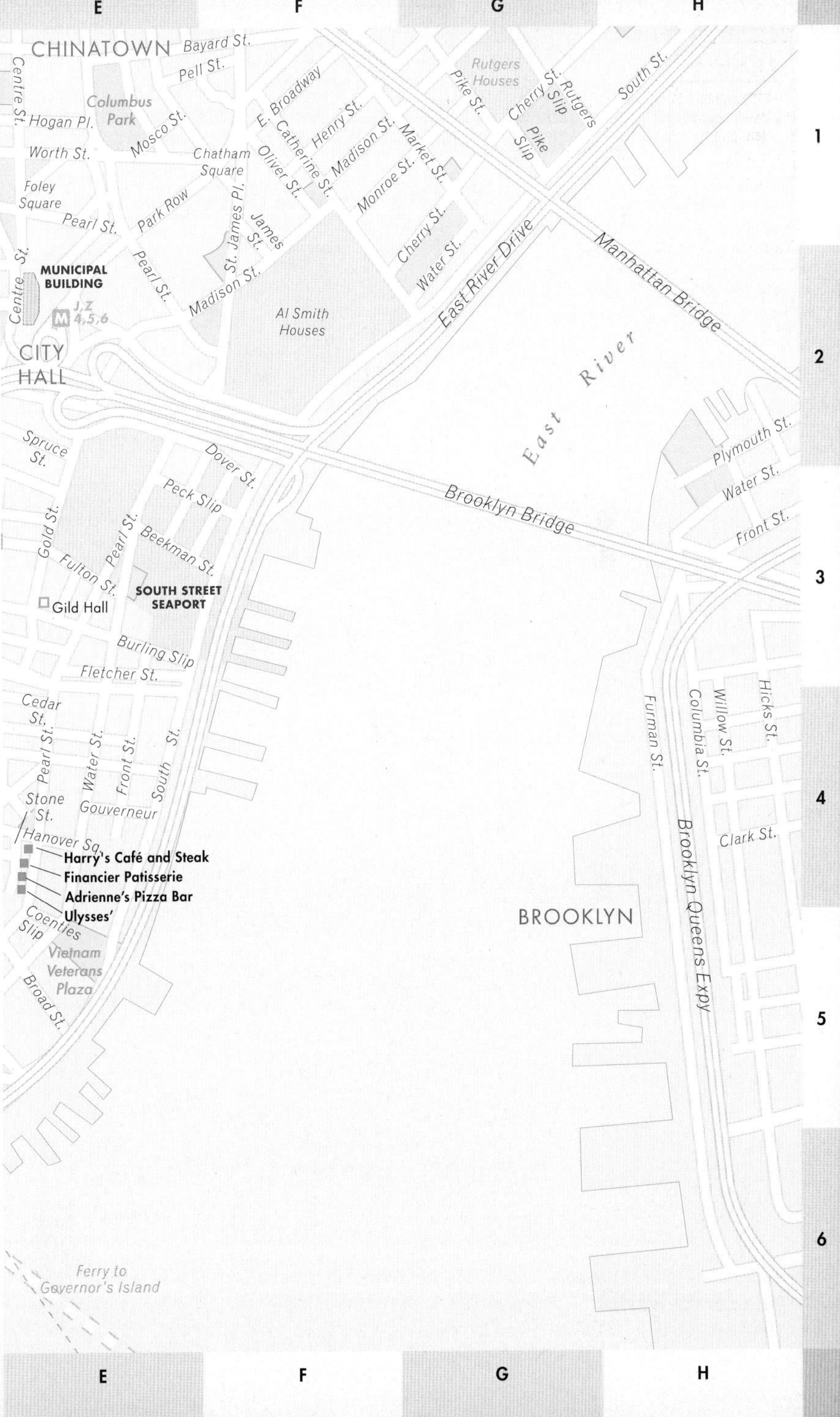
E
F
G
H
1
2
3
4
5
6
CHINATOWN
Bayard St.
Pell St.
Centre St.
Hogan Pl.
Columbus Park
Mosco St.
Worth St.
Chatham Square
Foley Square
Pearl St.
Park Row
E. Broadway
Catherine St.
Henry St.
Oliver St.
Madison St.
Market St.
Monroe St.
Rutgers Houses
Pike St.
Cherry St.
Rutgers Slip
Pike Slip
South St.
St. James Pl.
James St.
Madison St.
Cherry St.
Water St.
MUNICIPAL BUILDING
Centre St.
J,Z 4,5,6
Al Smith Houses
East River Drive
Manhattan Bridge
CITY HALL
East River
Spruce St.
Dover St.
Peck Slip
Plymouth St.
Water St.
Brooklyn Bridge
Front St.
Gold St.
Pearl St.
Beekman St.
Fulton St.
SOUTH STREET SEAPORT
Gild Hall
Burling Slip
Fletcher St.
Cedar St.
Pearl St.
Water St.
Front St.
South St.
Furman St.
Columbia St.
Willow St.
Hicks St.
Stone St.
Gouverneur
Hanover Sq.
Brooklyn Queens Expy
Clark St.
Harry's Café and Steak
Financier Patisserie
Adrienne's Pizza Bar
Ulysses'
BROOKLYN
Coenties Slip
Vietnam Veterans Plaza
Broad St.
Ferry to Governor's Island

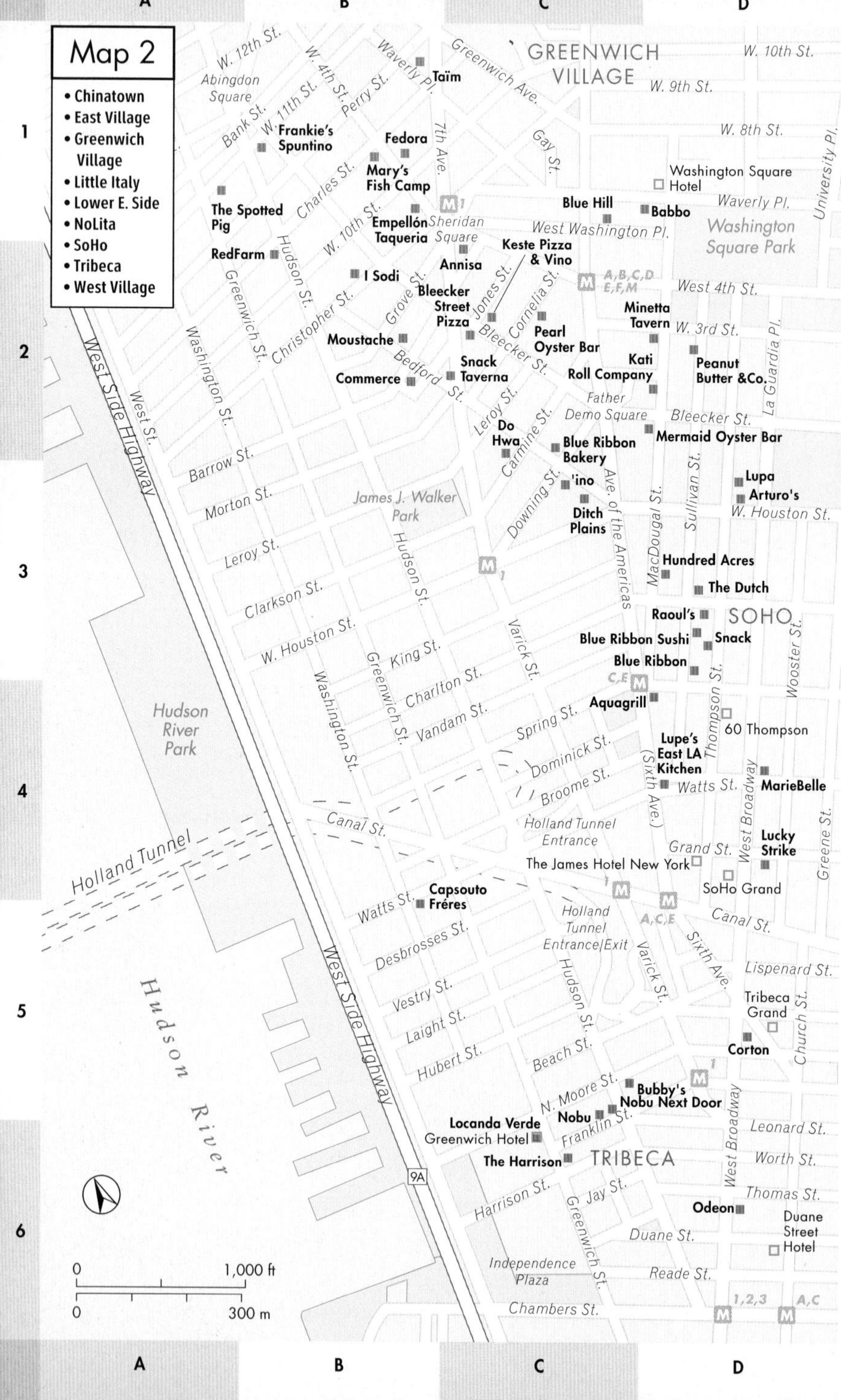
Map 2
• Chinatown
• East Village
• Greenwich Village
• Little Italy
• Lower E. Side
• NoLita
• SoHo
• Tribeca
• West Village
A
B
C
D
1
2
3
4
5
6
GREENWICH VILLAGE
SOHO
TRIBECA
Taïm
Frankie's Spuntino
Fedora
Mary's Fish Camp
The Spotted Pig
Empellón Taqueria
RedFarm
I Sodi
Annisa
Keste Pizza & Vino
Bleecker Street Pizza
Blue Hill
Babbo
Washington Square Hotel
Moustache
Commerce
Snack Taverna
Pearl Oyster Bar
Minetta Tavern
Kati Roll Company
Peanut Butter &Co.
Do Hwa
Blue Ribbon Bakery
'ino
Ditch Plains
Mermaid Oyster Bar
Lupa
Arturo's
Hundred Acres
The Dutch
Raoul's
Blue Ribbon Sushi
Snack
Blue Ribbon
Aquagrill
60 Thompson
Lupe's East LA Kitchen
MarieBelle
Lucky Strike
The James Hotel New York
SoHo Grand
Capsouto Fréres
Tribeca Grand
Corton
Bubby's
Nobu Next Door
Nobu
Locanda Verde
Greenwich Hotel
The Harrison
Odeon
Duane Street Hotel
Abingdon Square
Sheridan Square
Washington Square Park
Father Demo Square
James J. Walker Park
Hudson River Park
Hudson River
Holland Tunnel
Holland Tunnel Entrance
Holland Tunnel Entrance/Exit
Independence Plaza
West Side Highway
9A
W. 12th St.
W. 4th St.
Waverly Pl.
Greenwich Ave.
W. 10th St.
W. 9th St.
W. 8th St.
University Pl.
Bank St.
W. 11th St.
Perry St.
7th Ave.
Gay St.
Charles St.
W. 10th St.
Waverly Pl.
West Washington Pl.
Hudson St.
Greenwich St.
Christopher St.
Grove St.
Jones St.
Cornelia St.
West 4th St.
W. 3rd St.
La Guardia Pl.
Washington St.
West St.
Bedford St.
Bleecker St.
Leroy St.
Carmine St.
Bleecker St.
Barrow St.
Morton St.
Downing St.
Ave. of the Americas (Sixth Ave.)
MacDougal St.
Sullivan St.
W. Houston St.
Leroy St.
Clarkson St.
W. Houston St.
King St.
Varick St.
Thompson St.
Wooster St.
Charlton St.
Vandam St.
Spring St.
Dominick St.
Broome St.
Watts St.
West Broadway
Greene St.
Canal St.
Grand St.
Watts St.
Desbrosses St.
Vestry St.
Laight St.
Hubert St.
Beach St.
Varick St.
Sixth Ave.
Canal St.
Lispenard St.
Church St.
N. Moore St.
Franklin St.
Leonard St.
Worth St.
Harrison St.
Jay St.
Greenwich St.
Thomas St.
Duane St.
Reade St.
Chambers St.
A,B,C,D E,F,M
C,E
A,C,E
1,2,3
A,C
0
1,000 ft
300 m

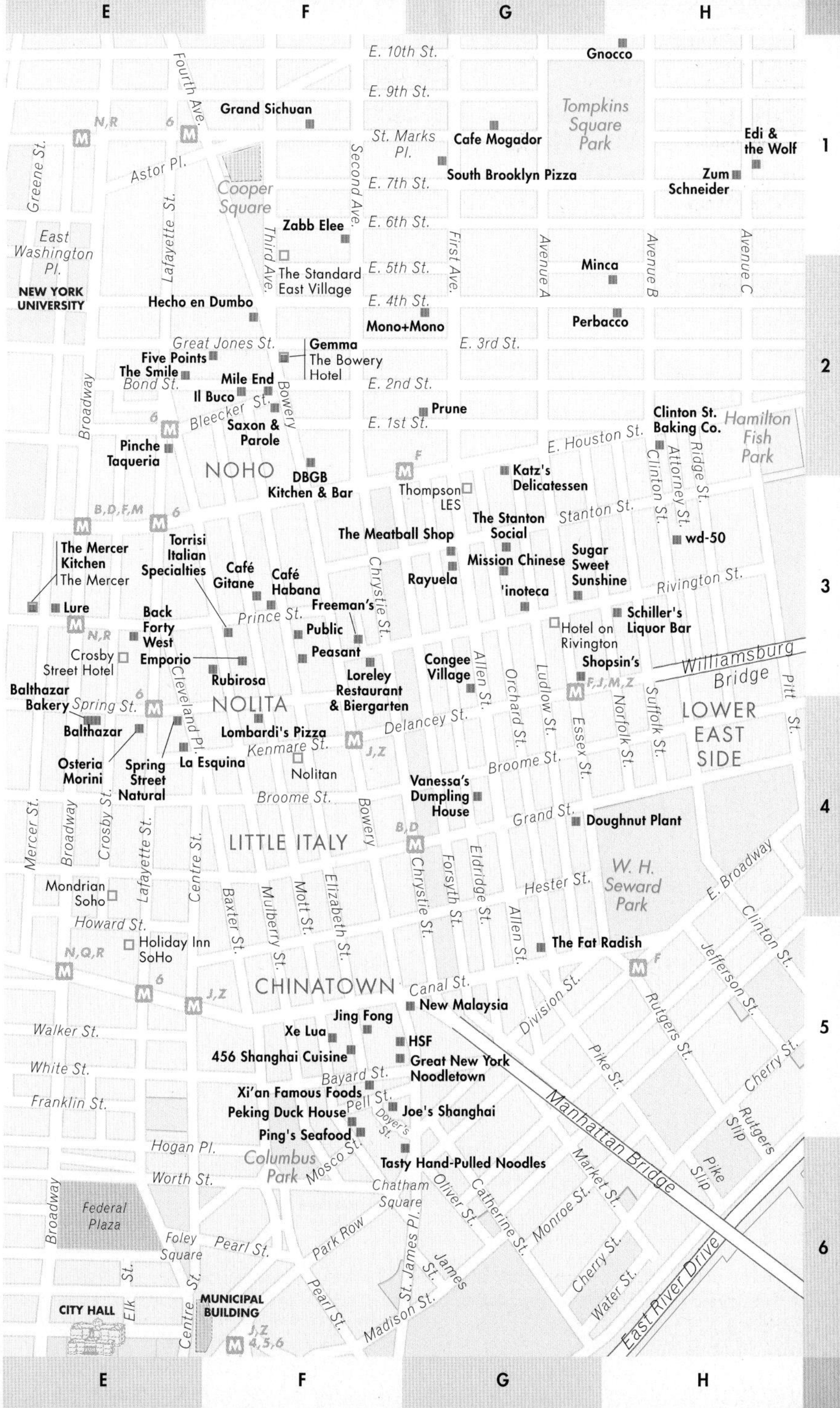

E
F
G
H
1
2
3
4
5
6
NOHO
NOLITA
LITTLE ITALY
CHINATOWN
LOWER EAST SIDE
NEW YORK UNIVERSITY
CITY HALL
MUNICIPAL BUILDING
Tompkins Square Park
Cooper Square
Hamilton Fish Park
W. H. Seward Park
Columbus Park
Federal Plaza
Gnocco
Grand Sichuan
Cafe Mogador
South Brooklyn Pizza
Edi & the Wolf
Zum Schneider
Zabb Elee
The Standard East Village
Minca
Hecho en Dumbo
Mono+Mono
Perbacco
Gemma
The Bowery Hotel
Five Points
The Smile
Mile End
Il Buco
Saxon & Parole
Prune
Clinton St. Baking Co.
Pinche Taqueria
DBGB Kitchen & Bar
Thompson LES
Katz's Delicatessen
The Stanton Social
wd-50
The Meatball Shop
Mission Chinese
Sugar Sweet Sunshine
Rayuela
'inoteca
The Mercer Kitchen
The Mercer
Torrisi Italian Specialties
Café Gitane
Café Habana
Freeman's
Lure
Back Forty West
Public
Schiller's Liquor Bar
Hotel on Rivington
Crosby Street Hotel
Emporio
Peasant
Congee Village
Shopsin's
Rubirosa
Loreley Restaurant & Biergarten
Balthazar Bakery
Balthazar
Lombardi's Pizza
Osteria Morini
Spring Street Natural
La Esquina
Nolitan
Vanessa's Dumpling House
Doughnut Plant
Mondrian Soho
Holiday Inn SoHo
The Fat Radish
New Malaysia
Jing Fong
Xe Lua
HSF
456 Shanghai Cuisine
Great New York Noodletown
Xi'an Famous Foods
Joe's Shanghai
Peking Duck House
Ping's Seafood
Tasty Hand-Pulled Noodles
E. 10th St.
E. 9th St.
St. Marks Pl.
E. 7th St.
E. 6th St.
E. 5th St.
E. 4th St.
E. 3rd St.
E. 2nd St.
E. 1st St.
E. Houston St.
Stanton St.
Rivington St.
Delancey St.
Broome St.
Grand St.
Hester St.
Canal St.
Division St.
Fourth Ave.
Astor Pl.
Greene St.
Lafayette St.
Third Ave.
Second Ave.
First Ave.
Avenue A
Avenue B
Avenue C
East Washington Pl.
Great Jones St.
Bond St.
Bleecker St.
Bowery
Broadway
Chrystie St.
Clinton St.
Attorney St.
Ridge St.
Prince St.
Spring St.
Kenmare St.
Cleveland Pl.
Allen St.
Orchard St.
Ludlow St.
Essex St.
Norfolk St.
Suffolk St.
Pitt St.
Williamsburg Bridge
Mercer St.
Crosby St.
Centre St.
Baxter St.
Mulberry St.
Mott St.
Elizabeth St.
Forsyth St.
Eldridge St.
Howard St.
E. Broadway
Jefferson St.
Rutgers St.
Walker St.
White St.
Franklin St.
Bayard St.
Pell St.
Doyer's St.
Mosco St.
Hogan Pl.
Worth St.
Pike St.
Cherry St.
Rutgers Slip
Pike Slip
Manhattan Bridge
Market St.
Monroe St.
Catherine St.
Oliver St.
Chatham Square
Foley Square
Pearl St.
Park Row
St. James Pl.
James St.
Madison St.
Water St.
East River Drive
Elk St.
N,R
6
B,D,F,M
F
F,J,M,Z
J,Z
B,D
N,Q,R
J,Z 4,5,6

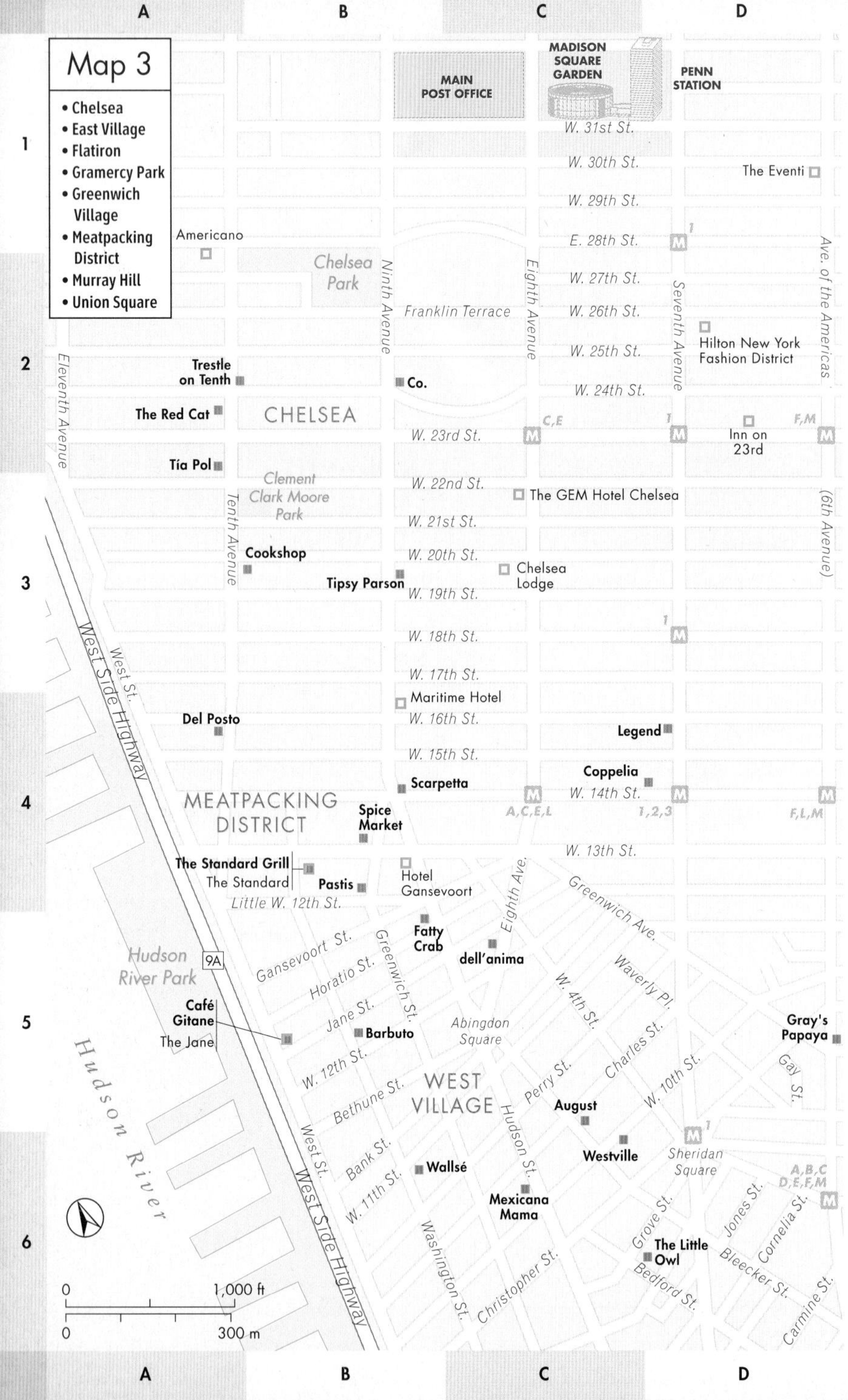
A
B
C
D
1
2
3
4
5
6
Map 3
• Chelsea
• East Village
• Flatiron
• Gramercy Park
• Greenwich Village
• Meatpacking District
• Murray Hill
• Union Square
MAIN POST OFFICE
MADISON SQUARE GARDEN
PENN STATION
W. 31st St.
W. 30th St.
The Eventi
W. 29th St.
Americano
E. 28th St.
Chelsea Park
Ninth Avenue
Eighth Avenue
W. 27th St.
Seventh Avenue
Ave. of the Americas
Franklin Terrace
W. 26th St.
Hilton New York Fashion District
W. 25th St.
Eleventh Avenue
Trestle on Tenth
Co.
W. 24th St.
The Red Cat
CHELSEA
C,E
F,M
W. 23rd St.
Inn on 23rd
Tía Pol
Clement Clark Moore Park
W. 22nd St.
The GEM Hotel Chelsea
Tenth Avenue
W. 21st St.
(6th Avenue)
Cookshop
W. 20th St.
Chelsea Lodge
Tipsy Parson
W. 19th St.
W. 18th St.
West Side Highway
West St.
W. 17th St.
Maritime Hotel
Del Posto
W. 16th St.
Legend
W. 15th St.
Coppelia
Scarpetta
W. 14th St.
MEATPACKING DISTRICT
Spice Market
A,C,E,L
1,2,3
F,L,M
W. 13th St.
The Standard Grill
The Standard
Pastis
Hotel Gansevoort
Little W. 12th St.
Greenwich Ave.
Eighth Ave.
Fatty Crab
Gansevoort St.
Greenwich St.
dell'anima
Hudson River Park
9A
Horatio St.
Waverly Pl.
W. 4th St.
Café Gitane
The Jane
Jane St.
Barbuto
Abingdon Square
Gray's Papaya
Hudson River
W. 12th St.
Charles St.
Gay St.
WEST VILLAGE
Bethune St.
Perry St.
W. 10th St.
August
Hudson St.
West St.
Westville
Sheridan Square
Bank St.
Wallsé
West Side Highway
A,B,C D,E,F,M
W. 11th St.
Mexicana Mama
Washington St.
Grove St.
Jones St.
Cornelia St.
The Little Owl
Christopher St.
Bleecker St.
Bedford St.
Carmine St.
0
1,000 ft
0
300 m

E
F
G
H
1
2
3
4
5
6
E. 10th St.
Gnocco
Fourth Ave.
E. 9th St.
Grand Sichuan
Tompkins Square Park
N,R
6
St. Marks Pl.
Cafe Mogador
Edi & the Wolf
Greene St.
Astor Pl.
South Brooklyn Pizza
Zum Schneider
Cooper Square
Second Ave.
E. 7th St.
Lafayette St.
Zabb Elee
E. 6th St.
East Washington Pl.
Third Ave.
First Ave.
Avenue A
Avenue B
Avenue C
The Standard East Village
E. 5th St.
Minca
NEW YORK UNIVERSITY
Hecho en Dumbo
E. 4th St.
Mono+Mono
Perbacco
Great Jones St.
Gemma
The Bowery Hotel
E. 3rd St.
Five Points
The Smile
Bond St.
Mile End
E. 2nd St.
Broadway
Il Buco
Bowery
Bleecker St.
Prune
E. 1st St.
Saxon & Parole
Clinton St. Baking Co.
Hamilton Fish Park
Pinche Taqueria
E. Houston St.
NOHO
DBGB Kitchen & Bar
Katz's Delicatessen
Thompson LES
Clinton St.
Attorney St.
Ridge St.
B,D,F,M
Stanton St.
The Stanton Social
The Mercer Kitchen
The Mercer
Torrisi Italian Specialties
The Meatball Shop
wd-50
Sugar Sweet Sunshine
Mission Chinese
Café Gitane
Café Habana
Chrystie St.
Rayuela
Rivington St.
'inoteca
Lure
Back Forty West
Prince St.
Freeman's
Schiller's Liquor Bar
Hotel on Rivington
Public
Crosby Street Hotel
Emporio
Peasant
Congee Village
Allen St.
Williamsburg Bridge
Shopsin's
Rubirosa
Loreley Restaurant & Biergarten
Orchard St.
Ludlow St.
F,J,M,Z
Pitt St.
Balthazar Bakery
Spring St.
Cleveland Pl.
NOLITA
Delancey St.
Essex St.
Norfolk St.
Suffolk St.
LOWER EAST SIDE
Balthazar
Lombardi's Pizza
Kenmare St.
J,Z
Osteria Morini
Spring Street Natural
La Esquina
Nolitan
Broome St.
Vanessa's Dumpling House
Mercer St.
Crosby St.
Lafayette St.
Centre St.
Broome St.
Grand St.
Doughnut Plant
B,D
LITTLE ITALY
Chrystie St.
Forsyth St.
Eldridge St.
W. H. Seward Park
E. Broadway
Mondrian Soho
Baxter St.
Mulberry St.
Mott St.
Elizabeth St.
Hester St.
Howard St.
Holiday Inn SoHo
Allen St.
The Fat Radish
Clinton St.
N,Q,R
Jefferson St.
CHINATOWN
Canal St.
Division St.
New Malaysia
Jing Fong
Rutgers St.
Walker St.
Xe Lua
HSF
456 Shanghai Cuisine
Great New York Noodletown
Pike St.
Cherry St.
White St.
Bayard St.
Xi'an Famous Foods
Franklin St.
Pell St.
Joe's Shanghai
Manhattan Bridge
Peking Duck House
Doyer's St.
Rutgers Slip
Ping's Seafood
Hogan Pl.
Mosco St.
Columbus Park
Tasty Hand-Pulled Noodles
Market St.
Pike Slip
Worth St.
Chatham Square
Oliver St.
Catherine St.
Federal Plaza
Monroe St.
Foley Square
Pearl St.
Park Row
St. James Pl.
James St.
Cherry St.
Elk St.
Water St.
East River Drive
CITY HALL
MUNICIPAL BUILDING
Pearl St.
Madison St.
Centre St.
J,Z 4,5,6

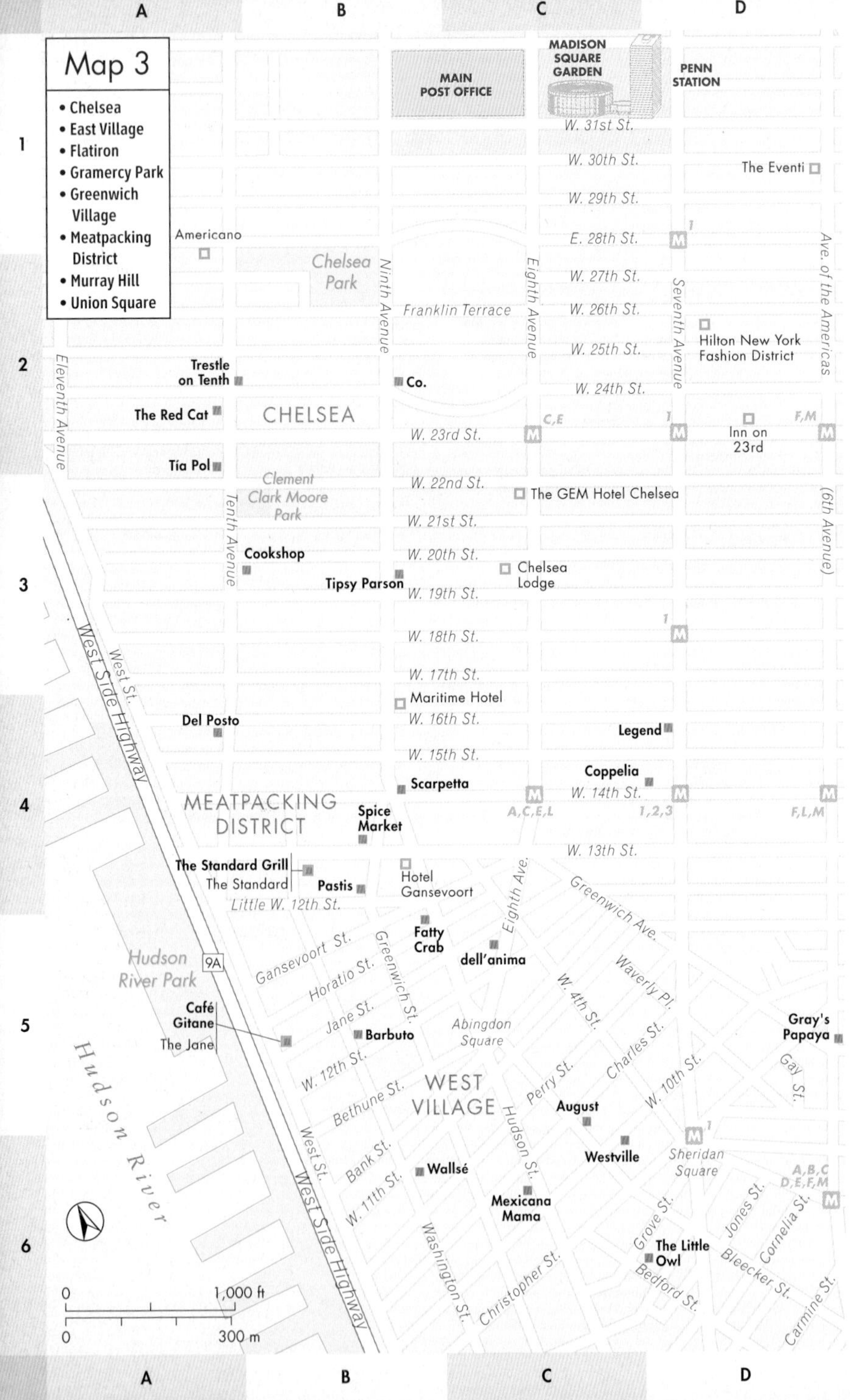

Map 3
• Chelsea
• East Village
• Flatiron
• Gramercy Park
• Greenwich Village
• Meatpacking District
• Murray Hill
• Union Square
MAIN POST OFFICE
MADISON SQUARE GARDEN
PENN STATION
W. 31st St.
W. 30th St.
The Eventi
W. 29th St.
Americano
E. 28th St.
Chelsea Park
Ninth Avenue
Eighth Avenue
W. 27th St.
Seventh Avenue
Ave. of the Americas
Franklin Terrace
W. 26th St.
Hilton New York Fashion District
W. 25th St.
Eleventh Avenue
Trestle on Tenth
Co.
W. 24th St.
The Red Cat
CHELSEA
C,E
F,M
Inn on 23rd
W. 23rd St.
Tía Pol
Clement Clark Moore Park
W. 22nd St.
The GEM Hotel Chelsea
(6th Avenue)
W. 21st St.
Tenth Avenue
Cookshop
W. 20th St.
Chelsea Lodge
Tipsy Parson
W. 19th St.
W. 18th St.
West Side Highway
West St.
W. 17th St.
Maritime Hotel
Del Posto
W. 16th St.
Legend
W. 15th St.
Coppelia
Scarpetta
W. 14th St.
MEATPACKING DISTRICT
Spice Market
A,C,E,L
1,2,3
F,L,M
W. 13th St.
The Standard Grill
The Standard
Pastis
Hotel Gansevoort
Little W. 12th St.
Eighth Ave.
Greenwich Ave.
Gansevoort St.
Greenwich St.
Fatty Crab
dell'anima
Hudson River Park
9A
Horatio St.
Waverly Pl.
W. 4th St.
Café Gitane
The Jane
Jane St.
Barbuto
Abingdon Square
Gray's Papaya
Hudson River
W. 12th St.
Charles St.
Gay St.
WEST VILLAGE
Bethune St.
Perry St.
W. 10th St.
August
Hudson St.
Westville
Sheridan Square
Bank St.
Wallsé
A,B,C
D,E,F,M
W. 11th St.
Mexicana Mama
Jones St.
Grove St.
Cornelia St.
Washington St.
The Little Owl
Bleecker St.
Christopher St.
Bedford St.
Carmine St.
0
1,000 ft
0
300 m
A
B
C
D
1
2
3
4
5
6

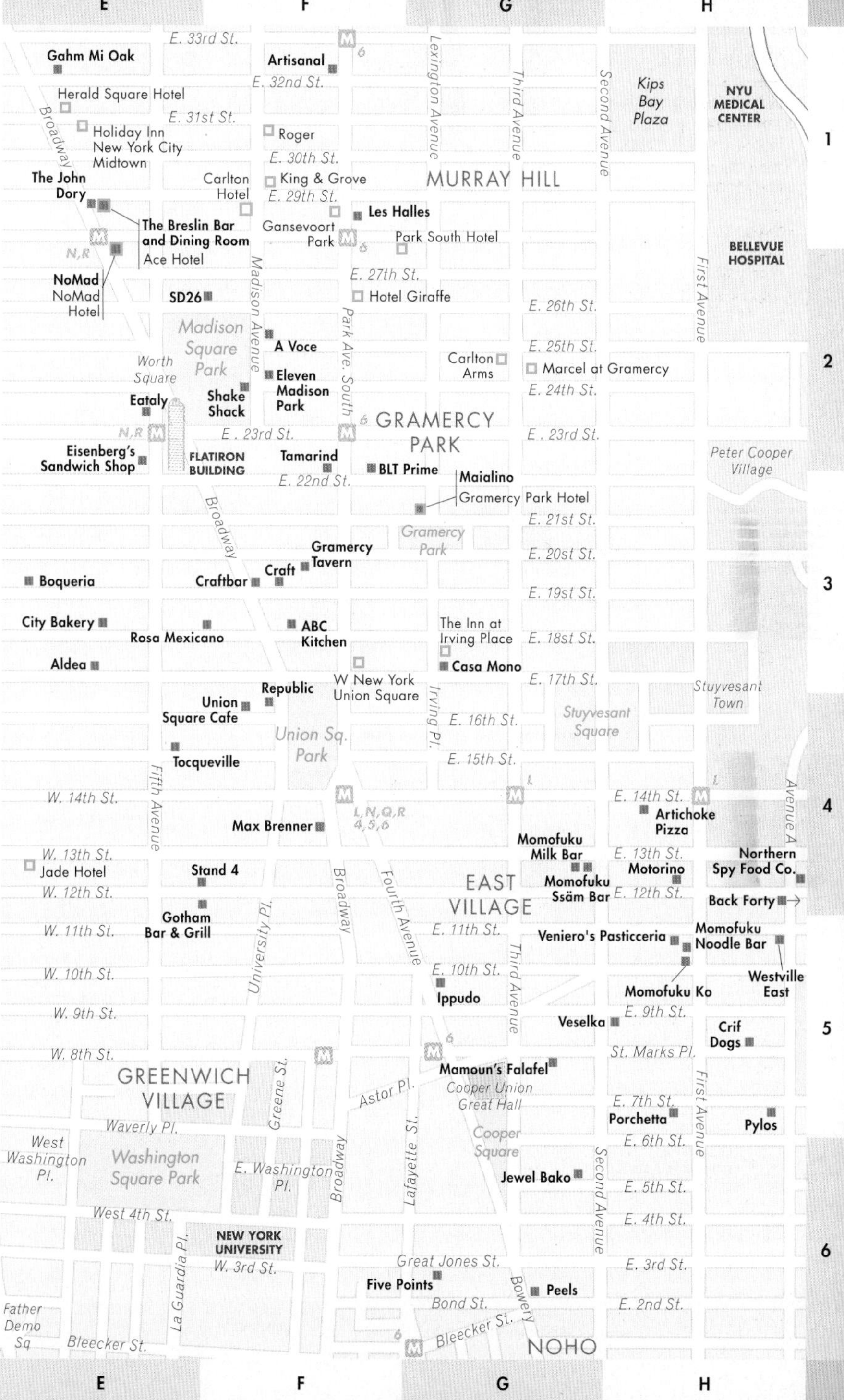

E
F
G
H
1
2
3
4
5
6
E. 33rd St.
Gahm Mi Oak
Artisanal
E. 32nd St.
Herald Square Hotel
Broadway
E. 31st St.
Holiday Inn New York City Midtown
Roger
E. 30th St.
Lexington Avenue
Third Avenue
Second Avenue
Kips Bay Plaza
NYU MEDICAL CENTER
MURRAY HILL
The John Dory
Carlton Hotel
King & Grove
E. 29th St.
Les Halles
The Breslin Bar and Dining Room
Ace Hotel
Gansevoort Park
Park South Hotel
N,R
BELLEVUE HOSPITAL
NoMad
NoMad Hotel
E. 27th St.
SD26
Hotel Giraffe
Madison Avenue
Park Ave. South
E. 26th St.
First Avenue
Madison Square Park
A Voce
E. 25th St.
Worth Square
Eleven Madison Park
Carlton Arms
Marcel at Gramercy
Eataly
Shake Shack
E. 24th St.
GRAMERCY PARK
N,R
E. 23rd St.
E. 23rd St.
Eisenberg's Sandwich Shop
FLATIRON BUILDING
Tamarind
BLT Prime
Peter Cooper Village
E. 22nd St.
Maialino
Gramercy Park Hotel
E. 21st St.
Gramercy Park
Gramercy Tavern
E. 20st St.
Broadway
Craft
Boqueria
Craftbar
E. 19st St.
City Bakery
ABC Kitchen
The Inn at Irving Place
Rosa Mexicano
E. 18st St.
Aldea
Casa Mono
E. 17th St.
W New York Union Square
Republic
Stuyvesant Town
Union Square Cafe
Stuyvesant Square
Irving Pl.
E. 16th St.
Union Sq. Park
Tocqueville
E. 15th St.
Fifth Avenue
L
L
W. 14th St.
E. 14th St.
L,N,Q,R 4,5,6
Artichoke Pizza
Avenue A
Max Brenner
Momofuku Milk Bar
W. 13th St.
E. 13th St.
Northern Spy Food Co.
Jade Hotel
Stand 4
Motorino
EAST VILLAGE
Momofuku Ssäm Bar
W. 12th St.
E. 12th St.
Broadway
Fourth Avenue
Back Forty
Gotham Bar & Grill
University Pl.
W. 11th St.
E. 11th St.
Veniero's Pasticceria
Momofuku Noodle Bar
W. 10th St.
E. 10th St.
Westville East
Third Avenue
Ippudo
Momofuku Ko
W. 9th St.
Veselka
E. 9th St.
Crif Dogs
W. 8th St.
St. Marks Pl.
GREENWICH VILLAGE
Mamoun's Falafel
Greene St.
Cooper Union Great Hall
Astor Pl.
E. 7th St.
Porchetta
Pylos
Waverly Pl.
West Washington Pl.
Washington Square Park
Cooper Square
E. 6th St.
Lafayette St.
E. Washington Pl.
Broadway
Jewel Bako
Second Avenue
E. 5th St.
West 4th St.
E. 4th St.
NEW YORK UNIVERSITY
La Guardia Pl.
W. 3rd St.
Great Jones St.
E. 3rd St.
Five Points
Bowery
Peels
Bond St.
E. 2nd St.
Father Demo Sq
Bleecker St.
Bleecker St.
NOHO
E
F
G
H

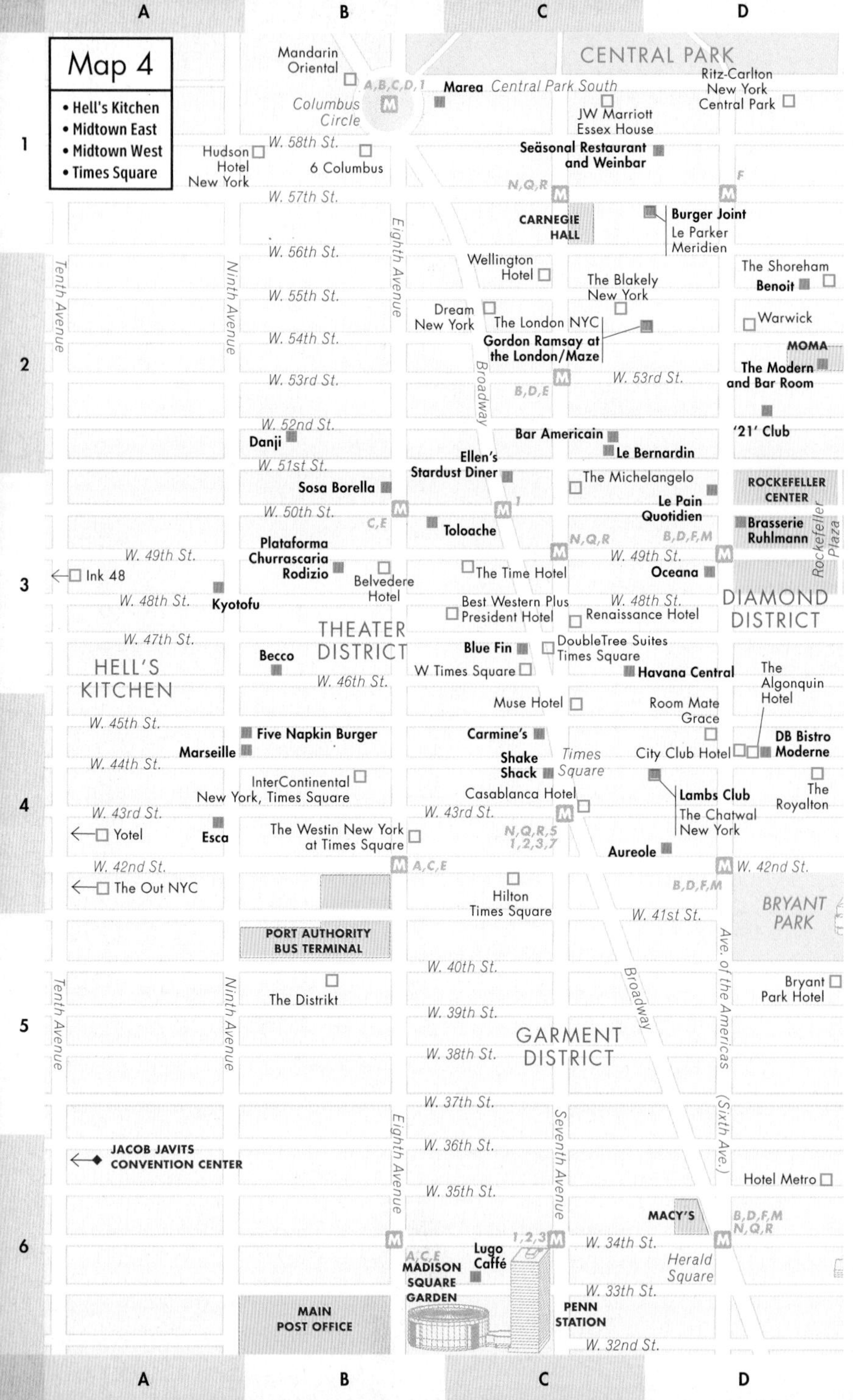

Map 4
• Hell's Kitchen
• Midtown East
• Midtown West
• Times Square
A
B
C
D
1
2
3
4
5
6
CENTRAL PARK
Mandarin Oriental
A,B,C,D,1
Columbus Circle
Marea
Central Park South
Ritz-Carlton New York Central Park
JW Marriott Essex House
Hudson Hotel New York
W. 58th St.
6 Columbus
Seäsonal Restaurant and Weinbar
N,Q,R
F
W. 57th St.
CARNEGIE HALL
Burger Joint
Le Parker Meridien
Eighth Avenue
W. 56th St.
Wellington Hotel
The Shoreham
Tenth Avenue
Ninth Avenue
The Blakely New York
Benoit
W. 55th St.
Dream New York
The London NYC
Warwick
W. 54th St.
Gordon Ramsay at the London/Maze
MOMA
Broadway
The Modern and Bar Room
W. 53rd St.
B,D,E
W. 53rd St.
W. 52nd St.
Danji
Bar Americain
'21' Club
Ellen's Stardust Diner
Le Bernardin
W. 51st St.
The Michelangelo
ROCKEFELLER CENTER
Sosa Borella
Le Pain Quotidien
W. 50th St.
C,E
1
Toloache
Brasserie Ruhlmann
N,Q,R
B,D,F,M
Rockefeller Plaza
Plataforma Churrascaria Rodizio
W. 49th St.
W. 49th St.
Ink 48
The Time Hotel
Oceana
Belvedere Hotel
Kyotofu
W. 48th St.
Best Western Plus President Hotel
W. 48th St.
Renaissance Hotel
DIAMOND DISTRICT
THEATER DISTRICT
W. 47th St.
Blue Fin
DoubleTree Suites Times Square
HELL'S KITCHEN
Becco
W Times Square
Havana Central
The Algonquin Hotel
W. 46th St.
Muse Hotel
Room Mate Grace
W. 45th St.
Five Napkin Burger
Carmine's
DB Bistro Moderne
Marseille
Times Square
City Club Hotel
W. 44th St.
Shake Shack
InterContinental New York, Times Square
The Royalton
Casablanca Hotel
Lambs Club
W. 43rd St.
W. 43rd St.
The Chatwal New York
Yotel
Esca
The Westin New York at Times Square
N,Q,R,S 1,2,3,7
Aureole
W. 42nd St.
A,C,E
W. 42nd St.
The Out NYC
Hilton Times Square
B,D,F,M
BRYANT PARK
W. 41st St.
PORT AUTHORITY BUS TERMINAL
Ave. of the Americas (Sixth Ave.)
W. 40th St.
Broadway
Bryant Park Hotel
The Distrikt
W. 39th St.
GARMENT DISTRICT
W. 38th St.
W. 37th St.
Seventh Avenue
JACOB JAVITS CONVENTION CENTER
W. 36th St.
Hotel Metro
W. 35th St.
MACY'S
B,D,F,M N,Q,R
1,2,3
W. 34th St.
A,C,E
Lugo Caffé
Herald Square
MADISON SQUARE GARDEN
W. 33rd St.
MAIN POST OFFICE
PENN STATION
W. 32nd St.

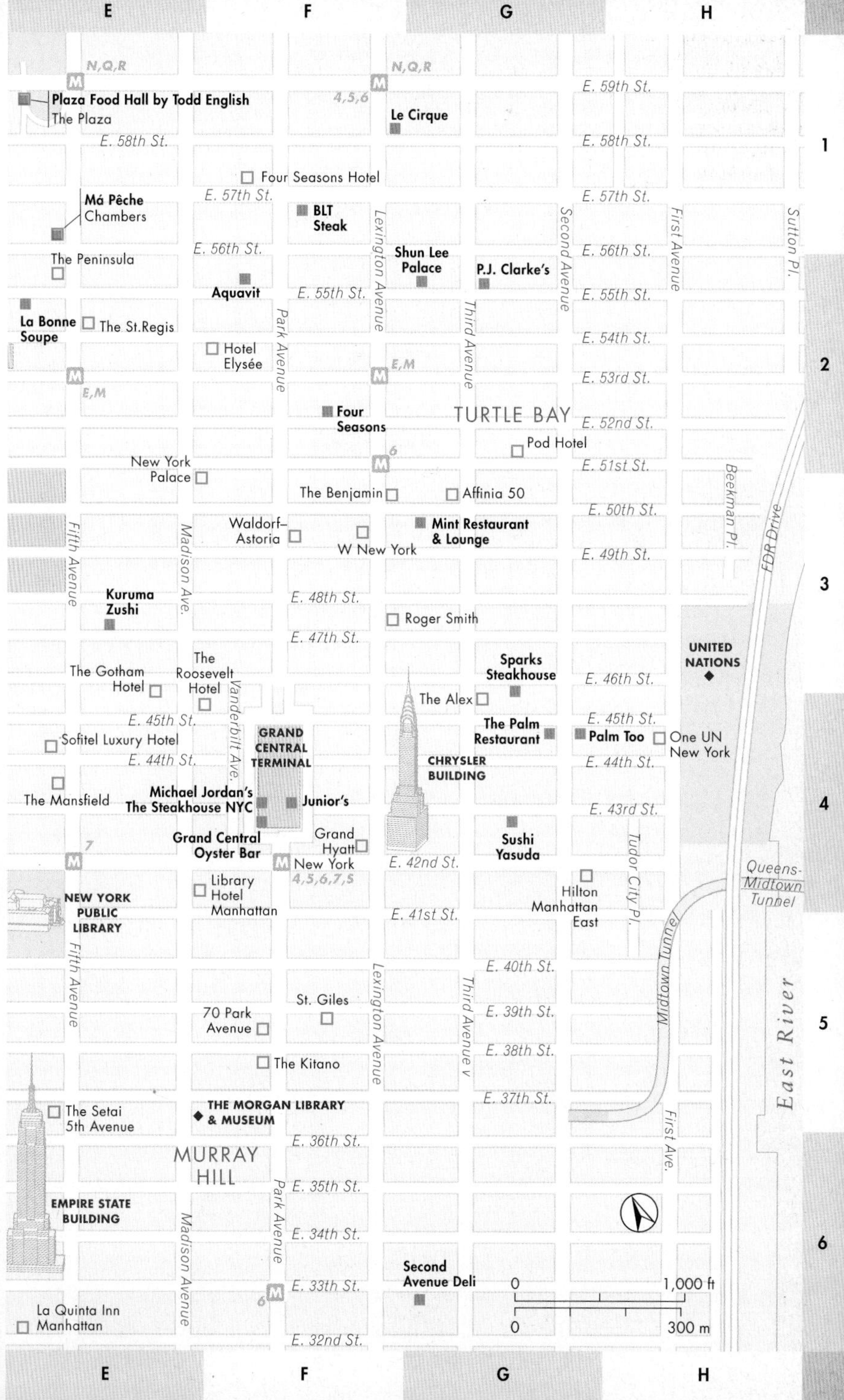

E
F
G
H
1
2
3
4
5
6
N,Q,R
4,5,6
Plaza Food Hall by Todd English
The Plaza
Le Cirque
E. 59th St.
E. 58th St.
Four Seasons Hotel
E. 57th St.
Má Pêche
Chambers
BLT Steak
Lexington Avenue
Second Avenue
First Avenue
Sutton Pl.
E. 56th St.
The Peninsula
Shun Lee Palace
P.J. Clarke's
Aquavit
E. 55th St.
Third Avenue
La Bonne Soupe
The St.Regis
Park Avenue
E. 54th St.
Hotel Elysée
E,M
E. 53rd St.
Four Seasons
TURTLE BAY
E. 52nd St.
Pod Hotel
6
New York Palace
E. 51st St.
Beekman Pl.
The Benjamin
Affinia 50
E. 50th St.
FDR Drive
Fifth Avenue
Madison Ave.
Waldorf–Astoria
W New York
Mint Restaurant & Lounge
E. 49th St.
Kuruma Zushi
E. 48th St.
Roger Smith
E. 47th St.
UNITED NATIONS
The Gotham Hotel
The Roosevelt Hotel
Vanderbilt Ave.
Sparks Steakhouse
E. 46th St.
The Alex
E. 45th St.
GRAND CENTRAL TERMINAL
The Palm Restaurant
Palm Too
One UN New York
Sofitel Luxury Hotel
E. 44th St.
CHRYSLER BUILDING
The Mansfield
Michael Jordan's The Steakhouse NYC
Junior's
E. 43rd St.
Grand Central Oyster Bar
Grand Hyatt New York
Sushi Yasuda
7
E. 42nd St.
Tudor City Pl.
Queens-Midtown Tunnel
4,5,6,7,S
Library Hotel Manhattan
Hilton Manhattan East
NEW YORK PUBLIC LIBRARY
E. 41st St.
Midtown Tunnel
E. 40th St.
St. Giles
E. 39th St.
70 Park Avenue
East River
E. 38th St.
The Kitano
E. 37th St.
The Setai 5th Avenue
THE MORGAN LIBRARY & MUSEUM
E. 36th St.
First Ave.
MURRAY HILL
E. 35th St.
EMPIRE STATE BUILDING
Madison Avenue
E. 34th St.
Second Avenue Deli
0
1,000 ft
E. 33rd St.
300 m
La Quinta Inn Manhattan
E. 32nd St.

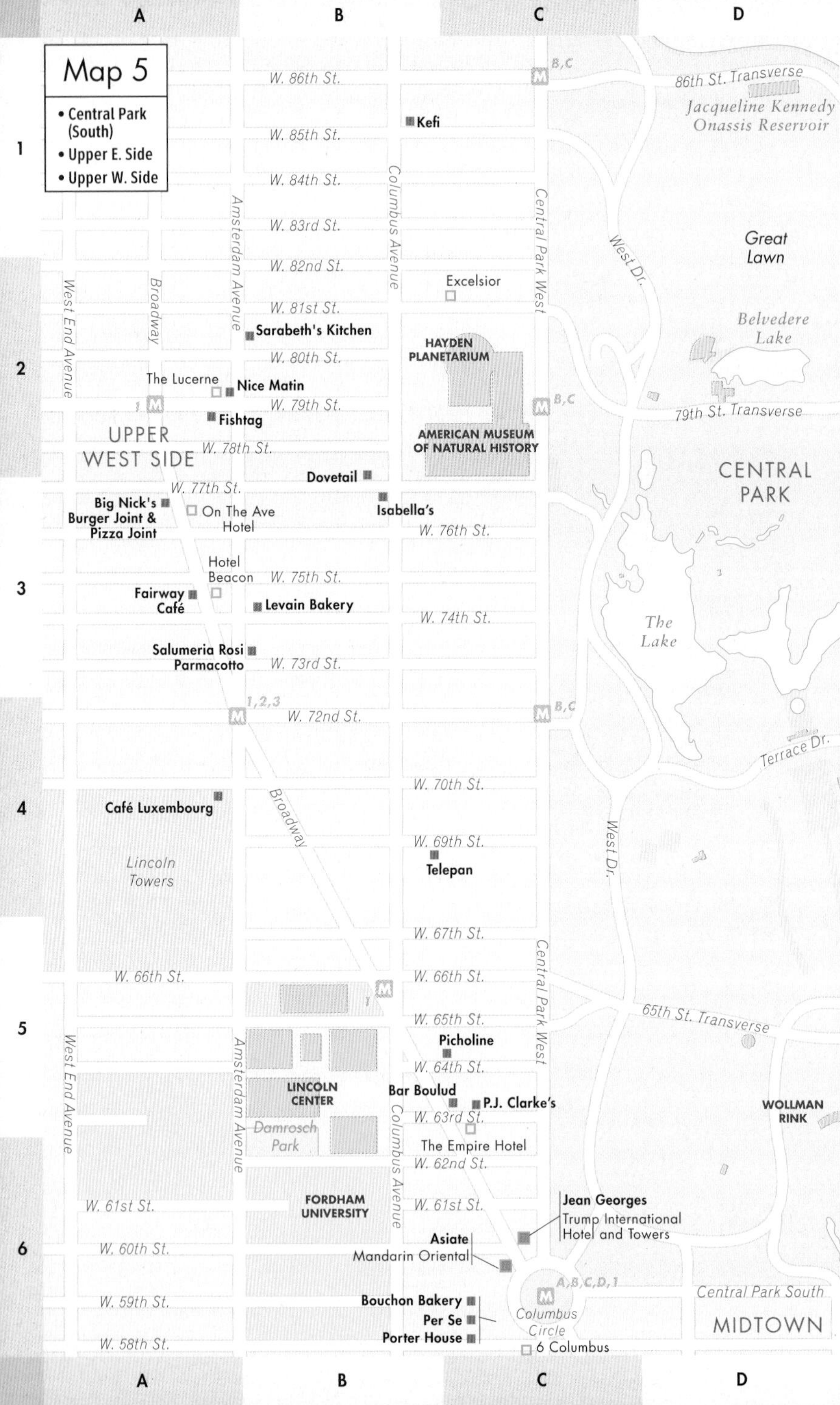

A
B
C
D
Map 5
• Central Park (South)
• Upper E. Side
• Upper W. Side
1
2
3
4
5
6
W. 86th St.
W. 85th St.
W. 84th St.
W. 83rd St.
W. 82nd St.
W. 81st St.
W. 80th St.
W. 79th St.
W. 78th St.
W. 77th St.
W. 76th St.
W. 75th St.
W. 74th St.
W. 73rd St.
W. 72nd St.
W. 70th St.
W. 69th St.
W. 67th St.
W. 66th St.
W. 65th St.
W. 64th St.
W. 63rd St.
W. 62nd St.
W. 61st St.
W. 60th St.
W. 59th St.
W. 58th St.
Kefi
86th St. Transverse
Jacqueline Kennedy Onassis Reservoir
Columbus Avenue
Amsterdam Avenue
Central Park West
West End Avenue
Broadway
West Dr.
Great Lawn
Excelsior
Belvedere Lake
Sarabeth's Kitchen
HAYDEN PLANETARIUM
The Lucerne
Nice Matin
79th St. Transverse
Fishtag
UPPER WEST SIDE
AMERICAN MUSEUM OF NATURAL HISTORY
CENTRAL PARK
Dovetail
Big Nick's Burger Joint & Pizza Joint
On The Ave Hotel
Isabella's
Hotel Beacon
Fairway Café
Levain Bakery
The Lake
Salumeria Rosi Parmacotto
Terrace Dr.
Café Luxembourg
Lincoln Towers
Telepan
65th St. Transverse
Picholine
Bar Boulud
P.J. Clarke's
LINCOLN CENTER
Damrosch Park
The Empire Hotel
WOLLMAN RINK
FORDHAM UNIVERSITY
Jean Georges
Trump International Hotel and Towers
Asiate
Mandarin Oriental
Bouchon Bakery
Per Se
Porter House
Columbus Circle
Central Park South
MIDTOWN
6 Columbus

E
F
G
H
1
2
3
4
5
6
0
1,000 ft
0
300 m
E. 86th St.
4,5,6
E. 85th St.
E. 84th St.
E. 83rd St.
E. 82nd St.
E. 81st St.
E. 80th St.
E. 79th St.
E. 78th St.
E. 77th St.
E. 76th St.
E. 75th St.
E. 74th St.
E. 73rd St.
E. 72nd St.
E. 71st St.
E. 70th St.
E. 69th St.
E. 68th St.
E. 67th St.
E. 66th St.
E. 65th St.
E. 64th St.
E. 63rd St.
E. 62nd St.
E. 61st St.
E. 60th St.
E. 59th St.
E. 58th St.
East Dr.
Central Park East (Fifth Avenue)
Madison Avenue
Lexington Avenue
Third Avenue
Second Avenue
First Avenue
Park Avenue
Fifth Avenue
METROPOLITAN MUSEUM OF ART
Cascabel Taqueria
UPPER EAST SIDE
Candle 79
Sushi of Gari
The Mark
6
Alloro
The Carlyle
LENOX HILL HOSPITAL
Café Boulud
Central Park Boathouse Restaurant
WHITNEY MUSEUM
Hospoda
Hunter College
6
Daniel
Hôtel Plaza Athénée
Maya
CENTRAL PARK ZOO/ WILDLIFE CONSERVATION CENTER
The Lowell
F
Park Avenue Seasonal
Loews Regency Hotel
ROOSEVELT ISLAND TRAMWAY
Queensboro Bridge
Sherry-Netherland
Grand Army Plaza
N,Q,R
N,Q,R,4,5,6
E
F
G
H

A
B
C
D
Map 6
• Central Park (North)
• East Harlem
• Harlem
• Upper E. Side
• Upper W. Side
COLUMBIA UNIVERSITY
W. 115th St.
Aloft Harlem
Red Rooster Harlem
Chez Lucienne
Sylvia's
W. 114th St.
W. 113th St.
W. 112th St.
W. 111th St.
Morningside Ave.
Morningside Drive
Morningside Park
CATHEDRAL CHURCH OF ST. JOHN THE DIVINE
Frederick Douglass Blvd.
Adam Clayton Powell Blvd.
St. Nicholas Ave.
Lenox Avenue
Cathedral Parkway
Central Park North
B,C
2,3
1
W. 109th St.
W. 108th St.
W. 107th St.
W. 106th St.
W. 105th St.
W. 104th St.
W. 103rd St.
W. 102nd St.
W. 101st St.
W. 100th St.
W. 99th St.
W. 98th St.
Broadway
Amsterdam Avenue
Columbus Avenue
Manhattan Avenue
Central Park West
LASKER RINK/POOL
The Loch
The Pool
Frederick Douglass Houses
CENTRAL PARK
100th St. Transverse
North Meadow
VISITOR CENTER
West Dr.
Park West Village
96th St. Transverse
W. 97th St.
W. 96th St.
1,2,3
Tennis Courts
W. 95th St.
W. 94th St.
W. 93rd St.
W. 92nd St.
W. 91st St.
W. 90th St.
W. 89th St.
W. 88th St.
W. 87th St.
W. 86th St.
West End Avenue
Columbus Ave.
UPPER WEST SIDE
Carmine's
Barney Greengrass
Jacqueline Kennedy Onassis Reservoir
86th St. Transverse
1
2
3
4
5
6

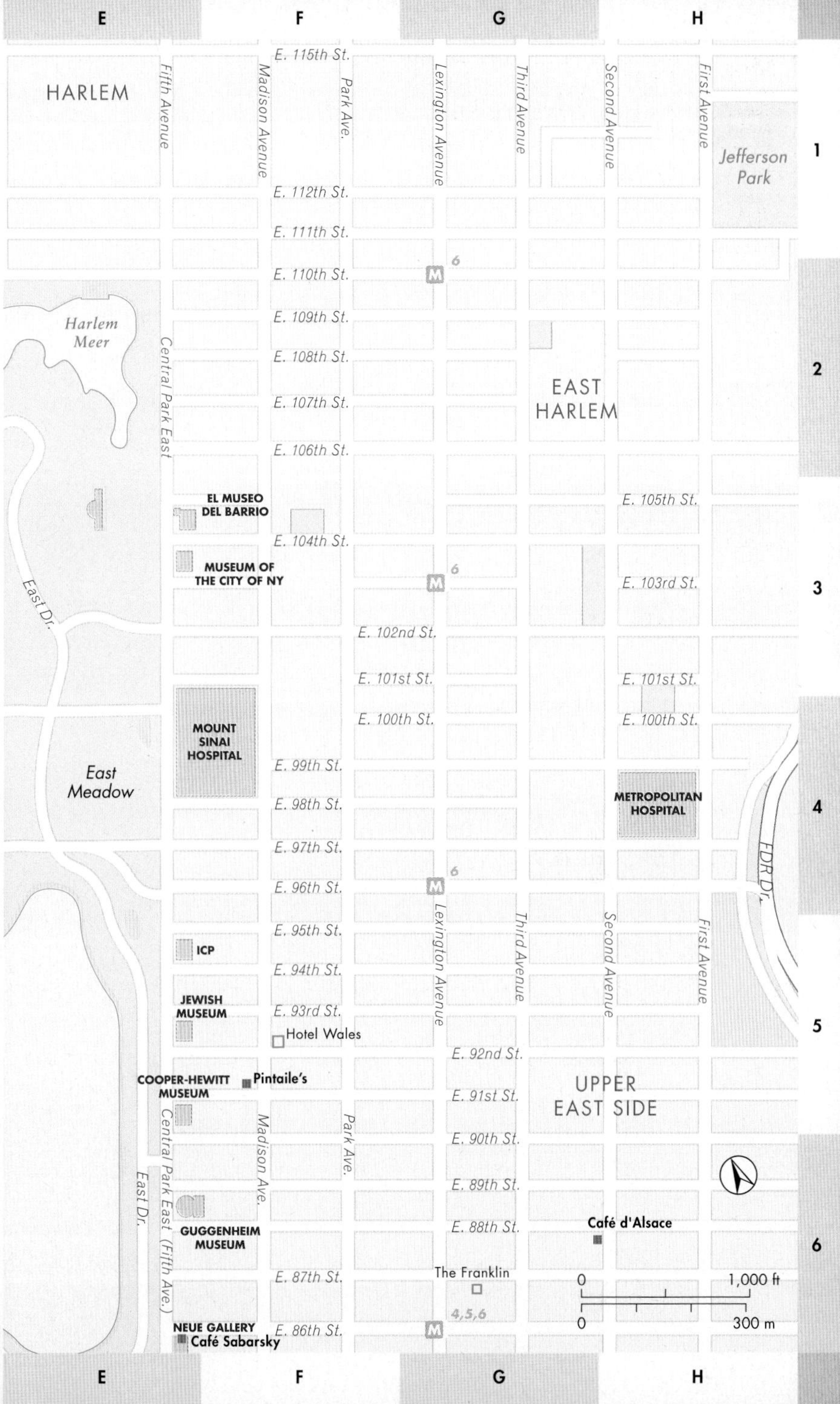
E
F
G
H
1
2
3
4
5
6
HARLEM
EAST HARLEM
UPPER EAST SIDE
Jefferson Park
Harlem Meer
East Meadow
E. 115th St.
E. 112th St.
E. 111th St.
E. 110th St.
E. 109th St.
E. 108th St.
E. 107th St.
E. 106th St.
E. 105th St.
E. 104th St.
E. 103rd St.
E. 102nd St.
E. 101st St.
E. 100th St.
E. 99th St.
E. 98th St.
E. 97th St.
E. 96th St.
E. 95th St.
E. 94th St.
E. 93rd St.
E. 92nd St.
E. 91st St.
E. 90th St.
E. 89th St.
E. 88th St.
E. 87th St.
E. 86th St.
Fifth Avenue
Madison Avenue
Park Ave.
Lexington Avenue
Third Avenue
Second Avenue
First Avenue
Central Park East
Central Park East (Fifth Ave.)
Madison Ave.
East Dr.
FDR Dr.
EL MUSEO DEL BARRIO
MUSEUM OF THE CITY OF NY
MOUNT SINAI HOSPITAL
METROPOLITAN HOSPITAL
ICP
JEWISH MUSEUM
Hotel Wales
COOPER-HEWITT MUSEUM
Pintaile's
GUGGENHEIM MUSEUM
Café d'Alsace
The Franklin
NEUE GALLERY
Café Sabarsky
6
4,5,6
0
1,000 ft
300 m

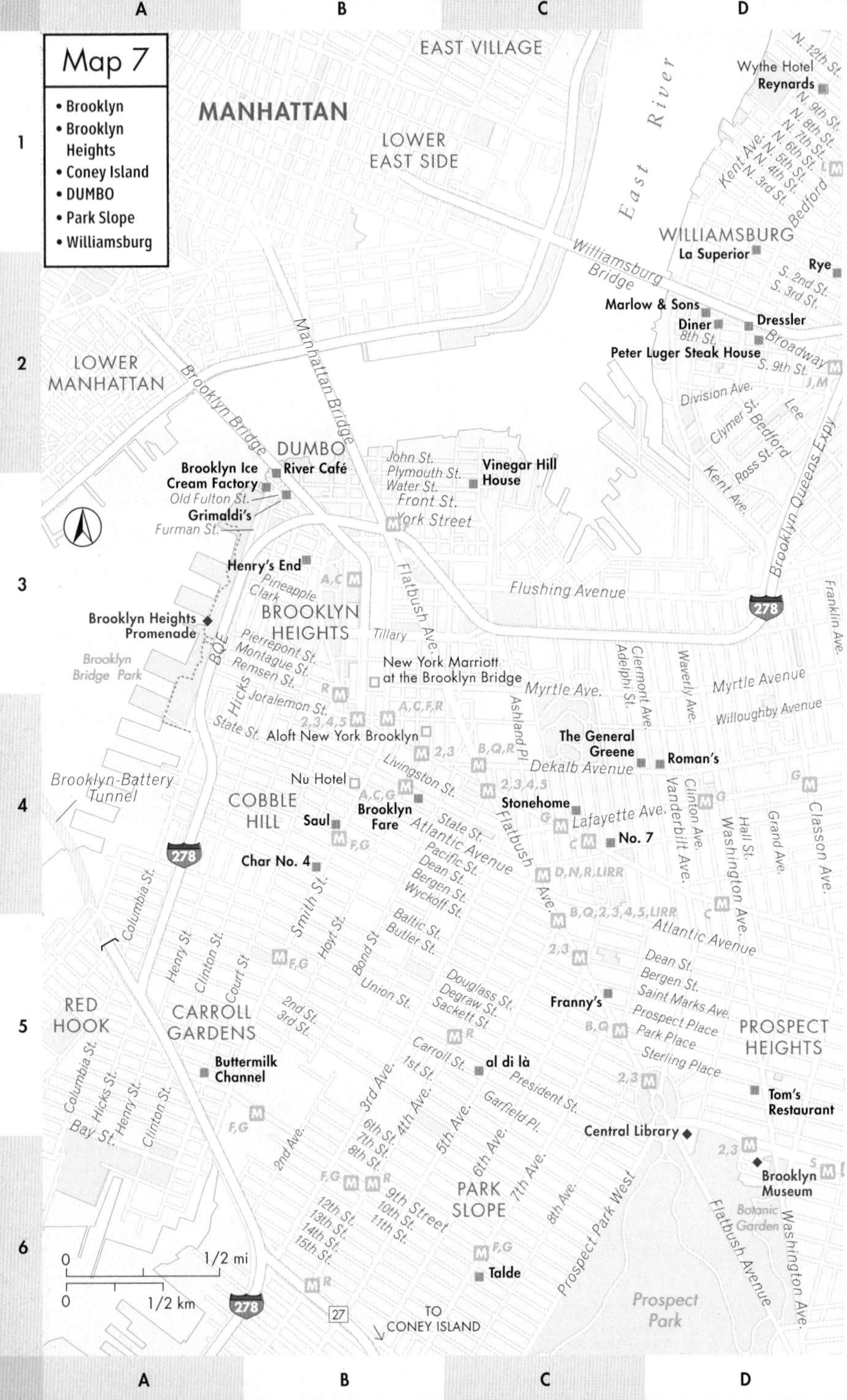

A
B
C
D
Map 7
• Brooklyn
• Brooklyn Heights
• Coney Island
• DUMBO
• Park Slope
• Williamsburg
EAST VILLAGE
MANHATTAN
LOWER EAST SIDE
East River
Wythe Hotel
Reynards
WILLIAMSBURG
La Superior
Rye
Williamsburg Bridge
Marlow & Sons
Diner
Dressler
Peter Luger Steak House
LOWER MANHATTAN
Brooklyn Bridge
Manhattan Bridge
DUMBO
Brooklyn Ice Cream Factory
River Café
Grimaldi's
Vinegar Hill House
Henry's End
Brooklyn Heights Promenade
Brooklyn Bridge Park
BROOKLYN HEIGHTS
New York Marriott at the Brooklyn Bridge
Flushing Avenue
Myrtle Avenue
Aloft New York Brooklyn
The General Greene
Roman's
Brooklyn-Battery Tunnel
Nu Hotel
COBBLE HILL
Saul
Brooklyn Fare
Stonehome
No. 7
Char No. 4
Atlantic Avenue
Franny's
RED HOOK
CARROLL GARDENS
PROSPECT HEIGHTS
Buttermilk Channel
al di là
Tom's Restaurant
Central Library
Brooklyn Museum
PARK SLOPE
Talde
Prospect Park
Botanic Garden
TO CONEY ISLAND
1
2
3
4
5
6

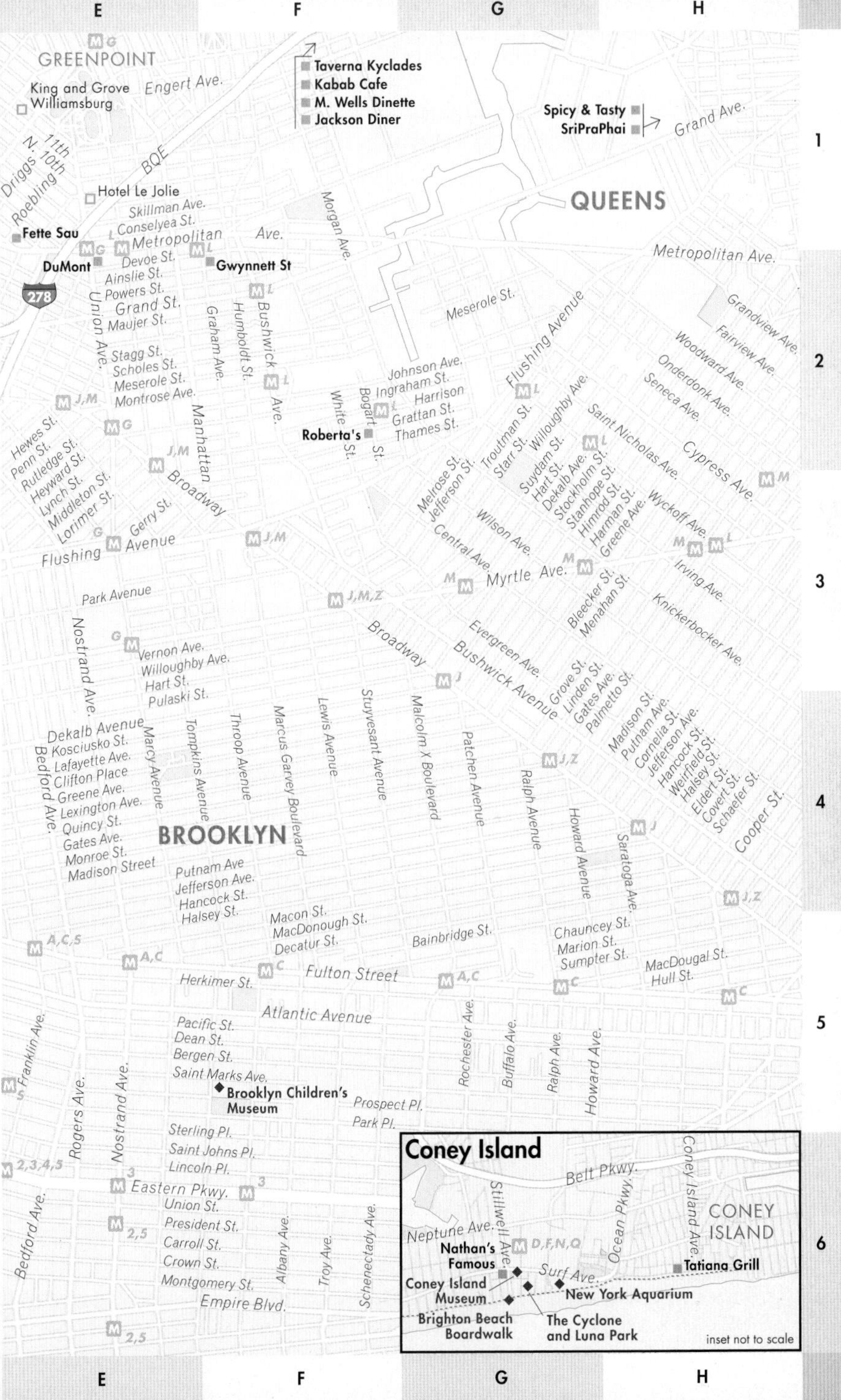
E
F
G
H
GREENPOINT
King and Grove Williamsburg
Engert Ave.
Taverna Kyclades
Kabab Cafe
M. Wells Dinette
Jackson Diner
Spicy & Tasty
SriPraPhai
Grand Ave.
1
QUEENS
Hotel Le Jolie
Fette Sau
DuMont
Gwynnett St
Metropolitan Ave.
BQE
278
BROOKLYN
Roberta's
Brooklyn Children's Museum
2
3
4
5
6
Coney Island
Belt Pkwy.
Neptune Ave.
Surf Ave.
Stillwell Ave.
Ocean Pkwy.
Coney Island Ave.
CONEY ISLAND
Nathan's Famous
Coney Island Museum
Brighton Beach Boardwalk
The Cyclone and Luna Park
New York Aquarium
Tatiana Grill
inset not to scale
Flushing Avenue
Broadway
Myrtle Ave.
Bushwick Avenue
Fulton Street
Atlantic Avenue
Eastern Pkwy.
Empire Blvd.

Dining

Lodging

WHERE TO STAY

Updated by
Jessica Colley

There are more hotel rooms than ever in New York City, as exciting new properties continue to open their doors not only in Manhattan proper, but in Brooklyn and the outer boroughs as well. But does that mean that New York is cheap? Well, we wouldn't say *cheap,* but you can still find some deals, especially if you're not set on a specific property or neighborhood, and if you don't mind a few extra minutes of commuting time.

Hotels continue to slash rates based on market sensitivity—especially if you and all of those other Internet-savvy room shoppers are willing to wait until the last minute. That said, if you want to stay in a specific place and the rate seems reasonable, book it—it's just as likely to go up, especially during peak seasons (spring and fall).

And how to choose? The first thing to consider is location (*check out our "Where Should I Stay?" chart*). Many New York City visitors insist on staying in the hectic Midtown area—and options are improving there—but other neighborhoods are often just as convenient. Less-touristy areas, such as Gramercy, the Lower East Side, the Upper West Side—even Brooklyn—offer a far more realistic sense of New York life.

Also consider timing: the least expensive months to book rooms in the city are January and February. If you're flexible on dates, ask the reservationist if there's a cheaper time to stay during your preferred traveling month—that way you can avoid peak dates, like Fashion Week and the New York City Marathon. And be sure to ask about possible weekend packages that could include a third night free. (The Financial District in particular can be a discount gold mine on the weekend.)

Another source of bargains? Chain hotels. Many have moved into the city, offering reasonable room rates. In addition to favorites like the Sheraton, Hilton, and Hyatt brands, there are Best Westerns, Days Inns, and Comfort Inns. These rates aren't as low as you'll find outside Manhattan, but they're certainly getting closer.

WHERE SHOULD I STAY?

	NEIGHBORHOOD VIBE	PROS	CONS
Brooklyn	Brooklyn has a bit of everything so it depends on where you end up. Williamsburg is all about hipsters, while downtown Brooklyn and around are quite residential.	You'll find generally smaller boutique-style hotels with personalized service and character, and rates worth traveling for. Plus, a whole new borough to explore.	If you're out late in the city and you want to get back to Brooklyn, it's either the subway or a relatively pricey taxi.
Lower Manhattan	Mostly skyscraper hotels in an area that buzzes with activity during weekday hours but can be eerily quiet at night.	Low crime area; easy subway access to uptown sights; great walking paths along the waterfront and in Battery Park.	Construction and congestion near World Trade Center site; limited choice of restaurants and shopping.
SoHo and Little Italy (with NoLIta)	Swanky, high-end hotels with hip restaurants and lounges patronized by New Yorkers and travelers alike.	Scores of upscale clothing boutiques and art galleries nearby; safe area for meandering walks; easy subway access.	Not budget-friendly; streets are crowded on weekends; few major monuments nearby.
Greenwich Village and the West Village	Hotels in this part of town are few and far between. The ones that are here are small and boutiquey.	Easy subway access to anywhere in town; great shopping, dining, and drinking venues.	Winding streets can be tough to navigate; most hotels are on the pricey side.
Chelsea (with the Meatpacking District)	More hotels are opening in one of the city's trendiest restaurant and nightlife areas.	See and be seen, and lots of great shopping.	This is a trendy and pricey neighborhood for hotels. Most hotel bars are a real scene.
Union Square, with the Flatiron District and Gramercy	A relatively quiet residential area.	Patches of calm respite from the hustle-and-bustle of downtown and midtown; low crime area.	Limited subway access; Gramercy may be too quiet for some.
East Village and the Lower East Side	The epicenter of edgy New York, great for travelers looking to party.	Great low-cost options for young generation. Great restaurants and independent boutiques.	One of the least subway-accessible Manhattan 'hoods; expect late-night noise.
Midtown East and West, and Murray Hill	Mostly big-name hotel chains and luxury business suites around Times Square; lots of tourists.	Near Broadway theaters; budget options are available in chain hotels and indies alike.	Streets are often packed with pedestrians; area around Port Authority can feel gritty. Murray Hill is pretty quiet.
Upper East Side	Well-heeled residential neighborhood near many museums.	Removed from Midtown hustle; near tourist attractions like Central Park.	Streets are quiet after 9 pm; few budget dining options; limited subway access (just the 6 line).
Upper West Side	Hotels in a residential neighborhood near Central Park, Lincoln Center, and some museums.	Lovely tree-lined streets; laid-back neighborhood eateries.	Weekend trains can be slow; most hotels are on the pricey side.

BEST BETS FOR NEW YORK CITY LODGING

Fodor's offers a selective listing of high-quality lodging in every price range, from the city's best budget motel to its most sophisticated luxury hotel. Here we've compiled our top picks by price and experience.

Fodor's Choice ★

Ace Hotel, $, p. 365
Crosby Street Hotel, $$$, p. 359
The Inn at Irving Place, $$$, p. 367
Inn on 23rd, $, p. 363
James Hotel, $$$, p. 359
Library Hotel, $$, p. 370
Mandarin Oriental, $$$$, p. 378
NoMad, $$$, p. 366
The Out NYC, $$$, p. 381
The Peninsula, $$$$, p. 370
Ritz-Carlton New York, Central Park, $$$$, p. 382
The St. Regis, $$$$, p. 371
The Standard, $, p. 365
The Wythe Hotel, $$, p. 388

Best by Price

$

Ace Hotel, p. 365
Best Western Plus President Hotel, p. 375
Carlton Arms, p. 366
The Herald Square Hotel, p. 372
Holiday Inn SoHo, p. 359
Hotel Beacon, p. 385
Hotel Metro, p. 377
Inn on 23rd, p. 363
La Quinta Inn, p. 378
Pod Hotel, p. 371
Yotel, p. 383

$$

Casablanca Hotel, p. 376
Library Hotel, p. 370
The Mansfield, p. 381
The Maritime Hotel, p. 364
The Michelangelo, p. 381
Room Mate Grace, p. 382
W Hotel New York, p. 372
The Standard, p. 365

$$$

Gramercy Park Hotel, p. 366
The Inn at Irving Place, p. 367
The James Hotel New York, p. 359
The Mercer, p. 361
Thompson LES, p. 362

$$$$

The Carlyle, p. 384
The Chatwal, p. 376
Mandarin Oriental, p. 378
The Mark, p. 385
The Peninsula, p. 370
Ritz-Carlton New York, Central Park, p. 382
The St. Regis, p. 371

Best by Experience

BEST BEDS

Four Seasons, p. 369
Ink48, p. 377
The Inn at Irving Place, p. 367
The Mansfield, p. 381
The Mark, p. 385
The Nolitan Hotel, p. 359
Ritz-Carlton, p. 358
The Langham, Fifth Avenue, p. 371

BEST FOR BUSINESS

Bryant Park Hotel, p. 375
The Chatwal, p. 376
The Peninsula, p. 370
Ritz-Carlton New York, Battery Park, p. 358
The Langham, Fifth Avenue, p. 371
Trump International Hotel and Towers, p. 387

BEST CELEBRITY RETREAT

Ace Hotel, p. 365
Four Seasons, p. 369
The Lowell, p. 384
Mandarin Oriental, p. 378
The Mark, p. 385
The Mercer, p. 361
The Standard, p. 365

BEST CONCIERGE

Four Seasons, p. 369
Le Parker Meridien, p. 378
The London NYC, p. 378
Mandarin Oriental, p. 378
Ritz-Carlton New York, Battery Park, p. 358

BEST GYM

The Grand Hyatt New York, p. 369
The James Hotel New York, p. 359
Le Parker Meridien, p. 378
The London NYC, p. 378
The Mark, p. 385
Trump International Hotel and Towers, p. 387

BEST HIPSTER HOTELS

Ace Hotel, p. 365

The Bowery Hotel, p. 361

Gramercy Park Hotel, p. 366

The Jade, p. 362

The Nolitan Hotel, p. 359

Nu Hotel Brooklyn, p. 388

The Standard, p. 365

Thompson LES, p. 362

BEST FOR HISTORY BUFFS

The Carlyle, p. 384

The Chatwal, p. 376

The Inn at Irving Place, p. 367

Plaza Hotel, p. 381

The St. Regis, p. 371

BEST HOTEL BAR

Bemelmans Bar at the Carlyle, p. 384

The Biergarten at the Standard, p. 365

Breslin Bar at the Ace Hotel, p. 364

The Gansevoort Park, p. 365

Jimmy at the James Hotel, p. 359

King Cole Bar at St. Regis, p. 371

Lobby Bar at the Bowery Hotel, p. 364

Oak Bar at the Plaza Hotel, p. 381

Print Lounge at Ink48, p. 377

Rose Bar at the Gramercy Park Hotel, p. 366

BEST FOR KIDS

Affinia 50, p. 367

Aloft New York Brooklyn, p. 387

Ink48, p. 377

Le Parker Meridien, p. 378

Plaza Hotel, p. 381

BEST-KEPT SECRET

Best Western Plus President, p. 375

The Franklin, p. 384

The Inn at Irving Place, p. 367

Inn on 23rd, p. 363

The Lowell, p. 384

BEST LOBBY

Ace Hotel, p. 365

Four Seasons, p. 369

Gramercy Park Hotel, p. 366

Mandarin Oriental, p. 378

The Peninsula, p. 370

The St. Regis, p. 371

BEST NEIGHBORHOOD EXPERIENCE

The Bowery Hotel, p. 361

The Carlyle, p. 384

The Franklin, p. 384

The Greenwich Hotel, p. 358

The Inn at Irving Place, p. 367

The Mark, p. 385

The Standard, p. 365

BEST NEW HOTELS

Ace Hotel, p. 365

Aloft New York Brooklyn, p. 387

Hotel Americano, p. 363

NoMad, p. 366

The Out NYC, p. 381

Wythe Hotel, p. 388

Yotel, p. 383

BEST POOL

Hotel Gansevoort, p. 365

Mandarin Oriental, p. 378

ONE UN Plaza, p. 370

The Peninsula, p. 370

Thompson LES, p. 362

Trump International Hotel and Towers, p. 387

BEST SERVICE

The Carlyle, p. 384

The Chatwal, p. 376

Four Seasons, p. 369

The James Hotel New York, p. 359

The Peninsula, p. 370

The Mark, p. 385

Plaza Hotel, p. 381

Ritz-Carlton New York, Battery Park, p. 358

SoHo Grand, p. 361

BEST TOILETRIES

Aloft New York Brooklyn and Harlem, p. 387

The Carlyle, p. 384

The Eventi, p. 365

The Gotham Hotel, p. 369

Gramercy Park Hotel, p. 366

The James Hotel New York, p. 359

The Peninsula, p. 370

SoHo Grand, p. 361

The St. Regis, p. 371

TriBeCa Grand, p. 358

BEST VIEWS

The Carlyle, p. 384

Ritz Carlton New York, Central Park, p. 382

The Standard East Village, p. 361

The Standard, p. 365

Trump International Hotel and Towers, p. 387

MOST ROMANTIC

The Inn at Irving Place, p. 367

Library Hotel, p. 370

The Lowell, p. 384

Ritz-Carlton New York, Battery Park, p. 358

The Standard, p. 365

PLANNER

STRATEGY

Manhattan has hundreds of hotels, so making a choice may seem daunting. But fret not—our expert writers and editors have done most of the legwork. The 120-plus selections here represent the best this city has to offer—from the best budget motels to the sleekest designer boutiques. Scan "Best Bets" on the previous pages for top recommendations by price and experience. Or find a review quickly in the listings—search by neighborhood, then alphabetically. Happy hunting!

NEED A RESERVATION?

Hotel reservations are an absolute necessity when planning your trip to New York—although rooms are easier to come by these days. Competition for clients also means properties must undergo frequent improvements, especially during July and August, so when booking, ask about any renovations, lest you get a room within earshot of construction. In this ever-changing city travelers can find themselves temporarily, and most inconveniently, without commonplace amenities such as room service or spa access if their hotel is upgrading.

SERVICES

Unless otherwise noted in the individual descriptions, all hotels listed have private baths, central heating, air-conditioning, and private phones. Almost all hotels have data ports and phones with voice mail, as well as valet service. Many now have wireless Internet (Wi-Fi) available, although it's not always free. Most large hotels have video or high-speed checkout capability, and many can arrange babysitting. Pools are a rarity, but most properties have gyms or health clubs, and sometimes full-scale spas; hotels without facilities usually have arrangements for guests at nearby gyms, sometimes for a fee.

PARKING

Bringing a car to Manhattan can add significantly to your expenses. Many properties in all price ranges do have parking facilities, but they are often at independent garages that charge as much as $20 or more per day, and valet parking can cost up to $60 a day. The city's exorbitant 18.375% parking tax can turn any car you drive into the Big Apple into a lemon.

FAMILY TRAVEL

New York has gone to great lengths to attract family vacationers, and hotels have followed the family-friendly trend. Some properties provide such diversions as Web TV and in-room video games; others have suites with kitchenettes and foldout sofa beds. Most full-service Manhattan hotels provide rollaway beds, babysitting, and stroller rental, but be sure to make arrangements when booking the room, not when you arrive.

DOES SIZE MATTER?

If room size is important to you, ask the reservationist how many square feet a room has, not just if it's big. A hotel room in New York is considered quite large if it's 500 square feet. Very large rooms, such as those at the Four Seasons, are 600 square feet. To stay anywhere larger you'll have to get a multiroom suite. Small rooms are a tight 150 to 200 square feet, and sometimes even less. Very small rooms are less than 100 square feet; you'll find these at inns and lodges, and they're sold as a single for only one person. There are studio apartments in the city that are 250 square feet and include a kitchen; 1,000 square feet is considered a huge abode in this very compact and crowded urban playland.

PRICES

There's no denying that New York City hotels are expensive, but rates run the full range. For high-end hotels like the Mandarin Oriental at Central Park, prices start at $895 a night for a standard room in high season, which runs from September through December. At the low end of the spending spectrum, a bunk at the Jane starts at $99 for a single. But don't be put off by the prices printed here—many hotels slash their rates significantly for promotions and Web-only deals.

Prices in the reviews are the lowest cost of a standard double room in high season.

HOTEL REVIEWS

Listed alphabetically within neighborhoods. Please visit Fodors.com for expanded reviews. Use the coordinate (✣ 1:B2) at the end of each listing to locate a property on the corresponding map preceding this chapter.

17

LOWER MANHATTAN

FINANCIAL DISTRICT

$$ HOTEL **Gild Hall.** Captains of Industry, here's a boutique hotel for you: operated by the owners of the several Thompson hotels around the United States and elsewhere, Gild Hall aggressively courts those clientele with a Y chromosome: beds have padded leather headboards and tartan throw blankets. **Pros:** central Financial District location; eye-popping lobby; stylish room design. **Cons:** small rooms for the price; untraditional location. $ *Rooms from: $409* ✉ *15 Gold St., at Platt St., Financial District* ☎ *212/232–7700, 800/268–0700* 🌐 *www.thompsonhotels.com* *116 rooms, 10 suites* 🍴 *No meals* Ⓜ *2, 3, 4, 5, A, C, J, Z to Fulton St.* ✣ *1:E3.*

$$ HOTEL **The W New York Downtown.** In the heart of the Financial District, this W outpost juxtaposes the gritty feel of the Financial District with sleek surfaces. **Pros:** near popular tourist attractions; restaurant offers some surprisingly affordable fare; modern workout room. **Cons:** scaffolding-dense neighborhood; construction of World Trade Center nearby; partially obstructed views; not family-friendly. $ *Rooms from: $409* ✉ *123 Washington St., at Albany St., Financial District* ☎ *646/826–8600* 🌐 *www.starwoodhotels.com* *214 rooms, 3 suites* 🍴 *No meals* Ⓜ *1 to Rector St.; R to Rector St.* ✣ *1:C4*

TRIBECA

$$$$ HOTEL **Conrad New York.** A pleasant surprise in a quiet Battery Park City location, the Conrad New York offers many coveted amenities: significant square footage, a breezy rooftop bar, and access to green space in

nearby Hudson River Park. **Pros:** huge rooms with separate bedroom and living area; emphasis on art and design; movie theater and restaurants in same complex; near downtown attractions like 9/11 Memorial. **Cons:** daily fee for Wi-Fi; removed from midtown attractions; expensive. *Rooms from: $699 ✉ 102 North End Ave., between Vesey and Murray Sts., TriBeCa ☎ 212/945–0100 www.conradnewyork.com 463 suites No meals Ⓜ 1, 2, 3 to Chambers St.; A, C to Chambers St. ✣ 1:B3.*

$$ HOTEL **The Cosmopolitan Hotel.** For a bargain room in a great downtown neighborhood, it's hard to beat this cost-conscious favorite. **Pros:** friendly staff; great location for power shoppers. **Cons:** noisy location; spartan rooms; slow elevators; no gym. *Rooms from: $379 ✉ 95 West Broadway, at Chambers St., TriBeCa ☎ 212/566–1900 www.cosmohotel.com 129 rooms No meals Ⓜ 1, 2, 3 to Chambers St.; A, C to Chambers St. ✣ 1:C2*

$$ HOTEL **Duane Street Hotel.** Amid TriBeCa's historic warehouses and trendy art galleries sits the Duane Street Hotel, a fashionable addition to the neighborhood. **Pros:** great location; in-room spa treatments available through Euphoria Spa TriBeCa. **Cons:** noisy; off-site gym. *Rooms from: $430 ✉ 130 Duane St., TriBeCa ☎ 212/964–4600 www.duanestreethotel.com 45 rooms No meals Ⓜ 1, 2, 3 to Chambers St.; A, C to Chambers St. ✣ 1:C1*

$$$ HOTEL **The Greenwich Hotel.** You talkin' to me? Yes, Robert De Niro is an owner of the Greenwich Hotel in TriBeCa, De Niro's backyard and a neighborhood he's helped put on the map as a culinary and cultural benchmark. **Pros:** varied yet clever room decoration; great restaurant; gorgeous pool. **Cons:** odd lobby; price is high for what you get. *Rooms from: $525 ✉ 377 Greenwich St., TriBeCa ☎ 212/941–8900 www.thegreenwichhotel.com 75 rooms, 13 suites No meals Ⓜ 1 to Franklin St. ✣ 1:B1*

$$$ HOTEL **The Ritz-Carlton New York, Battery Park.** If you're staying this far downtown, the Ritz is your top choice. **Pros:** excellent service; best base for downtown exploring; pet- and kid-friendly; Statue of Liberty views. **Cons:** removed from midtown tourist sights; limited nighttime activities; few neighborhood options for dining and entertainment. *Rooms from: $545 ✉ 2 West St., at Battery Park, Battery Park ☎ 212/344–0800, 800/241–3333 www.ritzcarlton.com/batterypark 259 rooms, 39 suites No meals Ⓜ 1 to Rector St.; R to Rector St. ✣ 1:C5*

$$ HOTEL **Smyth Tribeca.** Resting almost on top of a convenient subway stop, this thoroughly modern hotel makes TriBeCa a welcoming landing spot for visitors. **Pros:** great service; good restaurant; excellent subway access. **Cons:** Wi-Fi not free; only a frosted glass partition divides bathroom from sleeping area; bathrooms could have better lighting. *Rooms from: $299 ✉ 85 W. Broadway, between Chambers and Warren Sts., TriBeCa ☎ 212/587–7000 www.thompsonhotels.com 84 rooms, 16 suites No meals Ⓜ 1, 2, 3 to Chambers St.; A, C to Chambers St. ✣ 1:C2.*

$$$ HOTEL **Tribeca Grand.** Still popular with the glitterati, the scene at the Tribeca Grand centers on the eight-story atrium's Church Lounge bar and café. **Pros:** great dining and bar scene; central downtown location; fun social

atrium; pet-friendly. **Cons:** rooms get noise from restaurant below; bathroom has slightly cold design. *Rooms from: $499* ✉ *2 Ave. of the Americas (6th Ave.), between Walker and White Sts., TriBeCa* ☎ *212/519–6600, 800/965–3000* 📠 *212/519-6700* 🌐 *www.tribecagrand.com* *187 rooms, 14 suites* 🍽 *No meals* Ⓜ *A, C, E to Canal St.* ⊕ *1:D5*

WORD OF MOUTH

"[The SoHo Grand] is definitely funky, yet nice. The bar is always packed but a good place to people watch. I have found the rooms small but comfortable and the staff helpful. I find it less pretentious than some 'W' hotels at which I have stayed." —A2

SOHO AND NOLITA

NOLITA

$$ HOTEL **The Nolitan Hotel.** A welcome addition to an underserved area, the Nolitan combines a hip, slightly gritty, city feel with some luxe touches, but don't expect a lot of space to spread out. **Pros:** cool vibe; fun location convenient to lower Manhattan and Brooklyn. **Cons:** small rooms; blasé concierge; gym access five-minute walk away; street noise from other balconies. *Rooms from: $409* ✉ *30 Kenmare St., NoLIta* ☎ *212/925–2555* *54 rooms, 1 suite* 🍽 *No meals* Ⓜ *6 to Spring St.* ⊕ *2:F4.*

SOHO

$$$$ HOTEL **60 Thompson.** It may no longer be the center of the universe, scene-wise, but that's been a blessing for guests at 60 Thompson, improving the service and toning down the attitude of hotel staffers. **Pros:** supercentral for SoHo nightlife; good gym; some rooms have balconies. **Cons:** not family-oriented; no pets allowed. *Rooms from: $719* ✉ *60 Thompson St., between Broome and Spring Sts., SoHo* ☎ *212/431–0400, 877/431–0400* 🌐 *www.thompsonhotels.com* *100 rooms, 10 suites* 🍽 *No meals* Ⓜ *C, E to Spring St.* ⊕ *2:D4*

$$$ HOTEL Fodor's Choice ★ **Crosby Street Hotel.** The first branch of the UK's Firmdale Hotels to open in the United States, the Crosby Street Hotel is a whimsical boutique property with excellent SoHo views. **Pros:** unique design; big, bright rooms; great bar. **Cons:** breakfast not included; small gym. *Rooms from: $555* ✉ *79 Crosby St., between Prince and Spring Sts., SoHo* ☎ *212/226–6400* 🌐 *www.firmdale.com* *68 rooms, 18 suites* 🍽 *No meals* Ⓜ *6 to Spring St.; N, R to Prince St.* ⊕ *2:E3*

$ HOTEL **Holiday Inn SoHo.** "SoHo" and "Holiday Inn" may not sound right together, but here they are. **Pros:** well-priced SoHo solution; well-trained staff. **Cons:** nothing stylish; closer to Chinatown than to SoHo. *Rooms from: $270* ✉ *138 Lafayette St., near Canal St., SoHo* ☎ *212/966–8898, 800/465–4329* 🌐 *www.hidowntown-nyc.com* *215 rooms, 12 suites* 🍽 *No meals* Ⓜ *6, J, N, Q, R, Z to Canal St.* ⊕ *2:E5*

$$$ HOTEL FAMILY Fodor's Choice ★ **The James Hotel New York.** A favorite of creative-types, businesspeople, fashionistas, and deep-pocketed regular Joes, the James, right on the edge of SoHo, never sacrifices comfort for style, so it's no wonder there's a high percentage of return customers. **Pros:** stellar service; fabulous views. **Cons:** the upstairs Jimmy bar is expensive and sometimes too-cool-for-school. *Rooms from: $539* ✉ *27 Grand St., between Thomp-*

Fodor's Choice ★

Crosby Street Hotel

The Chatwal

The Standard

son St. and 6th Ave., SoHo ☎ 212/465–2000 🌐 www.jameshotels.com ⇆ 108 rooms, 6 suites 🍴 No meals Ⓜ A, C, E, 1 to Canal St. ✧ 2:D4.

$$$ HOTEL **The Mercer.** Owner André Balazs has a knack for dating Hollywood starlets and channeling a neighborhood sensibility, and here it's SoHo loft all the way. **Pros:** great location; sophisticated design touches; celebrity sightings in lobby. **Cons:** service inconsistent; some tight rooms. *$ Rooms from: $595 ✉ 147 Mercer St., at Prince St., SoHo ☎ 212/966–6060, 888/918–6060 🌐 www.mercerhotel.com ⇆ 68 rooms, 7 suites 🍴 No meals Ⓜ R to Prince St. ✧ 2:E3*

$$ HOTEL Fodor's Choice ★ **Mondrian Soho.** Snazzy style and a chic SoHo vibe make the Mondrian a winner for anyone looking for a real downtown New York experience. **Pros:** great design; friendly to electronics addicts. **Cons:** dark elevators; standard rooms are small; charge for Internet. *$ Rooms from: $399 ✉ 9 Crosby St., SoHo ☎ 212/389–1000 📠 212/389-1001 🌐 www.mondriansoho.com ⇆ 217 rooms, 43 suites 🍴 No meals Ⓜ 6, J, N, Q, R, Z to Canal St. ✧ 2:E4.*

$$ HOTEL **SoHo Grand.** The SoHo Grand defines what SoHo is today—once pioneering, now expensive, and with a vaguely creative vibe. **Pros:** fashionable, laid-back sophistication; great service; surprisingly discreet setting; diverse eating and drinking options. **Cons:** closer to Canal Street than prime SoHo; rooms on small side. *$ Rooms from: $329 ✉ 310 West Broadway, at Grand St., SoHo ☎ 212/965–3000, 800/965–3000 🌐 www.sohogrand.com ⇆ 341 rooms, 12 suites 🍴 No meals Ⓜ A, C, E to Canal St.; 6, J, N, Q, R, Z to Canal St. ✧ 2:D4*

EAST VILLAGE AND THE LOWER EAST SIDE

EAST VILLAGE

$$$ HOTEL Fodor's Choice ★ **The Bowery Hotel.** The Bowery Hotel is like an English hunting lodge in Manhattan, warmed by rich tapestries, fireplaces, and chandeliers—and there's no shortage of Brits, who flock to the property; the only thing missing is a trusty hound. **Pros:** quirky, fun location; happening bar and lobby-lounge area; celebrity sightings; interesting views. **Cons:** gritty neighbors; rooms aren't luxurious. *$ Rooms from: $495 ✉ 335 Bowery, at 3rd St., East Village ☎ 212/505–9100 🌐 www.theboweryhotel.com ⇆ 135 rooms, 25 suites 🍴 No meals Ⓜ 6 to Bleecker St.; B, D, F, M to Broadway–Lafayette St. ✧ 2:F2*

$$$ HOTEL **Standard East Village.** A jarring, 21-story glass-and-steel finger rising up in the low-rise East Village, this hotel was never going to pass under the radar—and that's guaranteed now that André Balasz and company have taken over. **Pros:** stylish rooms; central location. **Cons:** out of character with the area; restaurant seems constantly in flux. *$ Rooms from: $525 ✉ 25 Cooper Sq., between 5th and 6th Sts., East Village ☎ 212/475–5700 🌐 www.standardhotels.com/eastvillage ⇆ 141 rooms, 4 suites 🍴 No meals Ⓜ 6 to Astor Pl.; N, R to 8th. St.–NYU ✧ 2:F2.*

LOWER EAST SIDE

$$ HOTEL **Hotel on Rivington.** A pioneer when it opened in 2004, this glass-walled hotel on the Lower East Side is still a go-to choice, especially if being in the thick of the neighborhood's nightlife and dining action is a priority. **Pros:** cool location and vibe; huge windows with wonderful

views; many rooms have balconies. **Cons:** feels like a club on weekends; spotty service; small rooms and suites. *Rooms from: $380 ✉ 107 Rivington St., between Ludlow and Essex Sts., Lower East Side ☎ 212/475–2600, 800/915–1537 www.hotelonrivington.com 91 rooms, 17 suites No meals M F, J, M, Z to Delancey St.–Essex St. ⊕ 2:G3*

> **WORD OF MOUTH**
>
> "The Gansevoort (and its location) is young, hip, and fun but can also be loud. The rooftop bar is extremely popular; there are often lines outside the hotel to get into the bar at night. The rooms are nice, albeit not large. I live in Manhattan but have still stayed there on a couple of occasions for bachelor parties of friends. The few times I've hung out by the pool, we met several other Manhattanites who were staying there as a one- or two-day getaway from their apartment. —JarredK

$$$ HOTEL **Thompson LES.** With its smoked glass tower and central location, the Thompson LES is a great embodiment of the neighborhood inhabitants: hip, but friendly when you get to know it. **Pros:** in the heart of downtown; great views from suites; hip rooftop bar and pool. **Cons:** occasionally snobby staff; rooms stylish but dark. *Rooms from: $529 ✉ 190 Allen St., between Houston and Stanton Sts., Lower East Side ☎ 212/460–5300 www.thompsonhotels.com 124 rooms, 17 suites No meals M F, J, M, Z to Delancey St.–Essex St. ⊕ 2:G3*

GREENWICH VILLAGE AND THE WEST VILLAGE

GREENWICH VILLAGE

$$ HOTEL **The Jade.** Among the ghosts of the literary salons and speakeasies of Greenwich Village is the Jade, a new boutique property on a tree-lined street with an art deco sensibility. **Pros:** delivers a true Greenwich Village experience; cozy fireplaces; fresh, brand-new property. **Cons:** small rooms; no connecting rooms. *Rooms from: $400 ✉ 52 W. 13th St., between 5th and 6th Aves., Greenwich Village ☎ 212/375–1300 www.thejadenyc.com 109 rooms, 4 suites No meals M F, M to 14th St. ⊕ 3:E4.*

$ HOTEL **Washington Square Hotel.** This low-key hotel in Greenwich Village is popular with visiting New York University parents—the location near Washington Square Park and its magnificent arch (and just down the street from Mario Batali's Babbo Ristorante) is just a bonus. **Pros:** park-front location; deluxe rooms are charming; great hotel bar. **Cons:** NYU students everywhere in the neighborhood; rooms are small. *Rooms from: $285 ✉ 103 Waverly Pl., at MacDougal St., Greenwich Village ☎ 212/777–9515, 800/222–0418 www.washingtonsquarehotel.com 150 rooms Breakfast M A, B, C, D, E, F, M to W. 4th St.–Washington Sq. ⊕ 2:D1*

WEST VILLAGE

$ HOTEL **The Jane.** To some, it's impossibly chic; to others, the rooms are reminiscent of Sing Sing—welcome to the Jane hotel, a sister property to the hip Bowery Hotel on the Lower East Side. **Pros:** cheap; hot bar scene; amazing decor in lounge; great branch of weekend brunch favorite

Café Gitane; convenient neighborhood for downtown sightseeing. **Cons:** impossibly tiny standard rooms; shared bathrooms; noise from the bar. *Rooms from: $125 ✉ 113 Jane St., at West St., West Village ☎ 212/924–6700 ⊕ www.thejanenyc.com ↬ 141 rooms, 30 suites ¶ No meals Ⓜ A, C, E to 14th St.; L to 8th Ave. ✣ 3:B5*

CHELSEA AND THE MEATPACKING DISTRICT

CHELSEA

$ HOTEL **Chelsea Lodge.** Popular with Europeans and budget-conscious visitors, the Chelsea Lodge is a great location for guests who don't insist on a lot of amenities. **Pros:** on a gorgeous Chelsea block; residential feel; great bang for the buck. **Cons:** not romantic; shared bathrooms. *Rooms from: $144 ✉ 318 W. 20th St., between 8th and 9th Aves., Chelsea ☎ 212/243–4499 ⊕ www.chelsealodge.com ↬ 18 rooms, 4 suites ¶ No meals Ⓜ C, E to 23rd St.; 1 to 18th St. ✣ 3:C3*

$$ HOTEL **The GEM Hotel Chelsea.** At this stylish, well-priced boutique hotel, the modern rooms are small but designed to make the most of limited space. **Pros:** great Chelsea location; close to several subway lines; coffeemakers in the room. **Cons:** gym and business center, both on the lower level, feel like a work in progress; rooms may be too small for some. *Rooms from: $329 ✉ 300 W. 22nd St., Chelsea ☎ 212/675–1911 ⊕ www.thegemhotel.com ↬ 81 rooms ¶ No meals Ⓜ C, E to 23rd St.; 1 to 23rd St. ✣ 3:C3*

$ HOTEL **Hilton New York Fashion District.** This addition to the Hilton chain is part of the emerging Fashion District neighborhood, previously known as the garment district, on the upper edge of Chelsea, and fashion is the theme here—the lobby is done in rich textiles with multicolor spools mounted on a white board behind the front desk. **Pros:** reasonable prices for a great location. **Cons:** small closets; trying to be trendier than it is. *Rooms from: $249 ✉ 152 W. 26th St., between 6th and 7th Aves., Chelsea ☎ 212/858–5888 📠 212/858–5889 ⊕ www3.hilton.com ↬ 280 rooms ¶ No meals Ⓜ 1, 2, 3 to 34th St.–Penn Station; A, C, E to 34th St.–Penn Station; B, D, F, M, N, Q, R to 34th St.–Herald Sq. ✣ 3:D2*

$$ HOTEL **Hotel Americano.** Capturing the artistic and stylish spirit of Chelsea, the Hotel Americano is a boutique property with an industrial edge overlooking the High Line. **Pros:** all-year rooftop pool and bar; views overlooking the High Line; near the thriving gallery scene in Chelsea. **Cons:** low beds; bathrooms lack privacy; some furniture is form over function. *Rooms from: $395 ✉ 518 W. 27th St., between 10th and 11th Aves., Chelsea ☎ 212/525–0000 ⊕ www.hotel-americano.com ↬ 49 rooms, 7 suites ¶ No meals Ⓜ C, E to 23rd St. ✣ 3:A1.*

$ B&B/INN FAMILY Fodor's Choice ★ **The Inn on 23rd.** Friendly innkeepers Annette and Barry Fisherman welcome guests to this five-floor, 19th-century building, which also comes with its own cat-mascot. **Pros:** charming innkeepers; comfy and relaxed library; affordable, given location. **Cons:** few business services; some older amenities; beware if you have cat allergies. *Rooms from: $279 ✉ 131 W. 23rd St., between 6th and 7th Aves., Chelsea ☎ 212/463–0330 ⊕ www.innon23rd.com ↬ 13 rooms, 1 suite ¶ Breakfast Ⓜ F, M to 23rd St. ✣ 3:D2*

17

CLOSE UP

Hotel Hot Spots

Some of the city's most stylish bars and lounges are in hotels. These boîtes occasionally require crossing a velvet-roped entrance, but most extend automatic entry to hotel guests.

Downtown, the swank bar at the **Mondrian** (⇨ *SoHo)* is a treat, and the Jimmy bar at the **James Hotel** (⇨ *SoHo)* has some of the best views in town. On the Lower East Side, the Lobby Bar in the **Bowery Hotel** (⇨ *Lower East Side*) is a Wes Anderson movie come to life, with worn velvet furniture, Persian rugs, an assortment of taxidermy, and a back patio that harbors some of the most coveted summertime tables in the neighborhood.

Mega-hotelier Ian Schrager's properties are design temples, with chic lounges favored by jet-setters and locals alike. The new "haute Bohemian" **Gramercy Park Hotel** (⇨ *Gramercy)* is Schrager's latest offering, with its popular—and pricey—Rose Bar and Jade Bar. The hotel also has a private members-and-guests-only Roof Club. The **Ace Hotel** (⇨ *Flatiron)* is the sweet spot du jour, with one bar in the eclectic lobby and another at the trendy Breslin restaurant. The **Standard** (⇨ *Meatpacking District)* has a happening bar scene at the Standard Grill. It's hard to get in to the 18th-floor lounge but the outdoor beer garden downstairs is more egalitarian and, frankly, more fun—they even have Ping-Pong. It's also open year-round now.

In Midtown, the art deco–designed **Chatwal** (⇨ *Midtown West*) has a hopping lobby scene with drinks by cocktail guru Sasha Petraske and an elegant second-floor bar decorated with whimsical touches that are a paean to classic New York (look for the shimmering light fixtures shaped like the Chrysler Building).

Print at the Ink48 (⇨ *Midtown West*) is an elegant place to catch an early bite and a drink—later you can dance to views of the Hudson to the west and the glittering city to the east. The **Room Mate Grace** (⇨ *Midtown West)* in Times Square has a bar that's adjacent to its lobby-level pool; you can see all the underwater action through voyeur windows above the bar. Just make sure to pay attention at the end of the evening, or you might be the hotel's next swimming sensation. At the **Mandarin Oriental** on Columbus Circle (⇨ *Midtown West*), the 35th-floor lounge is the place to soak in views of Central Park. Come summertime, **Yotel** (⇨ *Midtown West*) offers one of the city's most expansive outdoor patios, with happening DJs and Latin-inspired cocktails.

$$ HOTEL **The Maritime Hotel.** The Maritime's white-ceramic tower, the former HQ for the National Maritime Union, was the first luxury hotel to be built in the Chelsea gallery district and the property still feels a bit nautical: the small rooms resemble modern ship's cabins, with burnished teak paneling, sea-blue drapes and bed accents, and 5-foot "portholes" that face the Hudson River skyline. **Pros:** fun rooms with big porthole windows; great location near Chelsea Market and the Chelsea galleries. **Cons:** Street noise; small rooms. $ *Rooms from: $435* ✉ *363 W. 16th St., at 9th Ave., Chelsea* ☎ *212/242–4300* 🌐 *www.themaritimehotel.*

com 121 *rooms, 5 suites* No meals Ⓜ *A, C, E to 14th St.; L to 8th Ave.* ✣ *3:B4*

MEATPACKING DISTRICT

$$ HOTEL **Hotel Gansevoort.** Though the nearby Standard New York has stolen some of its thunder, there's plenty to draw guests to this chic Meatpacking District pioneer, starting with the sleek rooms that overlook the city or the Hudson River and the rooftop deck with a 45-foot heated pool that remains a draw for locals and tourists alike. **Pros:** rooftop pool; wonderful art collection; great location for restaurants and shopping. **Cons:** location can seem too trendy, especially at night; service can be slipshod. *Rooms from: $425* ✉ *18 9th Ave., at 13th St., Meatpacking District* ☎ *212/206–6700* ⊕ *www.hotelgansevoort.com* *165 rooms, 21 suites* *No meals* Ⓜ *A, C, E to 14th St.; L to 8th Ave.* ✣ *3:B4*

$$ HOTEL Fodor's Choice ★ **The Standard.** André Balazs's architectural statement on the West Side is still one of New York's hottest hotels. **Pros:** beautiful building; beautiful people; impressive restaurant space. **Cons:** noisy at night; tight rooms; can be too sceney. *Rooms from: $395* ✉ *848 Washington St., between W. 13th and Little W. 12th Sts., Meatpacking District* ☎ *212/645–4646* ⊕ *www.standardhotels.com* *321 rooms, 4 suites, 13 studios* *No meals* Ⓜ *A, C, E to 14th St.; L to 8th Ave.* ✣ *3:B4*

UNION SQUARE, FLATIRON DISTRICT, AND GRAMERCY

17

FLATIRON DISTRICT

$$ HOTEL Fodor's Choice ★ **Ace Hotel.** Stepping into Ace Hotel is something of a revelation: you'll immediately be hit with the thought that this is not an ordinary boutique hotel. **Pros:** in-house restaurants are destination worthy in their own right; supercool but friendly vibe. **Cons:** dark lobby; caters to a young crowd; may be too sceney for some; neighborhood itself isn't the most exciting. *Rooms from: $399* ✉ *20 W. 29th St., at Broadway, Flatiron District* ☎ *212/679–2222* ⊕ *www.acehotel.com* *266 rooms, 8 suites* *No meals* Ⓜ *N, R to 28th St.; 1 to 28th St.* ✣ *3:E1*

$$ HOTEL FAMILY **The Eventi.** One of the new Kimpton properties to grace New York City, the Eventi adds a touch of hotel style just below Penn Station in an area desperately in need of new hotel options. **Pros:** great location; fun dining options; nice gym. **Cons:** crowded lobby; dark rooms. *Rooms from: $350* ✉ *851 Avenue of the Americas, at 30th St., Flatiron District* ☎ *866/996–8396* ⊕ *www.eventihotel.com* *236 rooms, 56 suites* *No meals* Ⓜ *N, R to 28th St.* ✣ *3:D1*

$$ HOTEL **Gansevoort Park.** A downtown-hip hotel on the edge of lower Midtown, the Gansevoort Park improves upon its hard-living Meatpacking District sibling by several degrees. **Pros:** happening bar; location convenient to Union Square; friendly staff. **Cons:** if you want peace and quiet this hotel is not for you. *Rooms from: $395* ✉ *420 Park Avenue S, at 29th St., Flatiron District* ☎ *212/317-2900* ⊕ *www.gansevoortpark.com* *212 rooms, 37 suites* *No meals* Ⓜ *6 to 28th St.* ✣ *3:F1*

$$$ HOTEL **Hotel Giraffe.** The decade-old Giraffe remains a consistent property with friendly service, large rooms, and lots of repeat customers, particularly business travelers. **Pros:** rooftop terrace for guests; quiet hotel. **Cons:** street noise near lower levels; pricey for the quality you get.

$ Rooms from: $449 ⊠ 365 Park Ave. S, at 26th St., Flatiron District ☎ 212/685–7700, 877/296–0009 ⊕ www.hotelgiraffe.com ⇆ 52 rooms, 21 suites ¦◎¦ Breakfast M 6 to 28th St. ⊕ 3:F2

$ **King & Grove.** Convenient to the action without being smack in the middle of it is King & Grove, a sleek new hotel with a sister property in Williamsburg, Brooklyn. **Pros:** up and coming neighborhood; trendy but not over the top; cozy single rooms are a great option for solo travelers. **Cons:** dark entryway; lower floors lack views and can feel a bit basement-y. *$ Rooms from: $279 ⊠ 29 E. 29th St., between Park and Madison Aves., Flatiron District ☎ 212/689–1900 ⊕ www.kingandgrove.com ⇆ 276 rooms ¦◎¦ No meals M 6 to 28th St. ⊕ 3:F1*

$$$ HOTEL Fodor's Choice ★ **The NoMad Hotel.** Named for the emerging "North of Madison" (i.e., Madison Square Park) neighborhood in which it's located, this upscale-bohemian property was one of the most buzzed-about hotel openings of 2012. **Pros:** 24-hr room service; free Wi-Fi; rooftop terrace; central location. **Cons:** those sharing a room with a friend may wish for more privacy than the exposed bathtubs provide. *$ Rooms from: $445 ⊠ 1170 Broadway, at 28th St., Flatiron District ☎ 212/796-1500 ⊕ www.thenomadhotel.com ⇆ 168 rooms ¦◎¦ No meals M N, R to 28th St. ⊕ 3:E2*

$ HOTEL **Park South Hotel.** In this beautifully transformed 1906 office building, rooms feel smartly contemporary, though they've retained some period details; request one that doesn't overlook noisy 27th Street and isn't too close to the bar on the ground floor—ask instead for a view of the Chrysler Building. **Pros:** free breakfast and Internet; turndown service; good value. **Cons:** rooms can feel a bit worn; small rooms and bathrooms. *$ Rooms from: $269 ⊠ 124 E. 28th St., between Lexington and Park Aves., Flatiron District ☎ 212/448–0888, 800/315–4642 ⊕ www.parksouthhotel.com ⇆ 139 rooms, 2 suites ¦◎¦ Breakfast M 6 to 28th St. ⊕ 3:G2*

$$ HOTEL **The Roger.** A colorful choice in a rather plain neighborhood, the Roger continues to have a following among repeat visitors to New York, especially since its 2012 redesign. **Pros:** colorful room decor; friendly service; good value. **Cons:** no room service; tiny bathrooms. *$ Rooms from: $399 ⊠ 131 Madison Ave., at 31st St., Flatiron District ☎ 212/448–7000, 877/847–4444 ⊕ www.therogernewyork.com ⇆ 194 rooms ¦◎¦ Breakfast M 6 to 33rd St. ⊕ 3:F1*

GRAMERCY

$ HOTEL **Carlton Arms.** Europeans and students know about the chipper, winning attitude of this friendly, no-frills hotel, where the rooms are painted by artists on a rotating basis. **Pros:** rock-bottom prices; friendly attitude; quieter residential Murray Hill location. **Cons:** no elevator; many rooms have shared baths. *$ Rooms from: $130 ⊠ 160 E. 25th St., at 3rd Ave., Gramercy ☎ 212/684–8337, 212/679–0680 for reservations ⊕ www.carltonarms.com ⇆ 54 rooms, 20 with bath M N, R to 28th St. ⊕ 3:G2*

$$$ HOTEL **Gramercy Park Hotel.** Ian Schrager, boutique hotelier extraordinaire, decorated this property with contemporary art by the likes of Andy Warhol and Jean-Michel Basquiat. **Pros:** trendy bar scene; opulent rooms; great restaurant; parkside location. **Cons:** inconsistent service; form-over-function rooms; expensive bar. *$ Rooms from: $595 ⊠ 2*

Lexington Ave., at Gramercy Park, Gramercy ☎ 212/920–3300 🌐 www.gramercyparkhotel.com ⇨ 139 rooms, 46 suites Ⓜ 6 to 23rd St. ✥ 3:G3

$$$ HOTEL Fodor's Choice ★ **The Inn at Irving Place.** Fantasies of Old New York—Manhattan straight from the pages of Edith Wharton and Henry James, an era of genteel brick town houses and Tiffany lamps—spring to life at this discreet, romantic inn. **Pros:** romantic; charming property; big rooms; excellent breakfast and tea service; Mario Batali's Casa Mono is downstairs. **Cons:** rooms aren't flawless, with imperfections like older grouting; street noise. *$ Rooms from: $449 ✉ 56 Irving Pl., between 17th and 18th Sts., Gramercy ☎ 212/533–4600, 800/685–1447 🌐 www.innatirving.com ⇨ 5 rooms, 4 suites, 3 apartments 🍴 Breakfast Ⓜ 4, 5, 6, L, N, Q, R to 14th St.–Union Sq. ✥ 3:G3*

$$ HOTEL **Marcel at Gramercy.** The chic, affordable Marcel gives guests both style and substance in a prime location. **Pros:** outdoor patio has spectacular views of the city; good value. **Cons:** elevators are slow; some rooms are tight on space; decor not to everyone's taste. *$ Rooms from: $299 ✉ 201 E. 24th St., Gramercy ☎ 212/696–3800 🌐 www.themarcelatgramercy.com ⇨ 134 rooms, 2 suites 🍴 No meals Ⓜ 6 to 23rd St. ✥ 3:G2*

UNION SQUARE

$$$$ HOTEL **W New York Union Square.** The W chain's iconic New York City property continues to attract a mix of trendsetters and tourists, thanks to the downtown location and its funky style. **Pros:** fashionable location; great restaurant. **Cons:** noisy lobby; expensive Wi-Fi. *$ Rooms from: $650 ✉ 201 Park Ave. S, at 17th St., Union Square ☎ 212/253–9119, 877/946–8357 🌐 www.wnewyorkunionsquare.com ⇨ 254 rooms, 16 suites 🍴 No meals Ⓜ 4, 5, 6, L, N, Q, R to 14th St.–Union Sq. ✥ 3:G3*

MIDTOWN EAST AND MURRAY HILL

MIDTOWN EAST

$$ HOTEL **70 Park Avenue.** A multimillion-dollar refresh in 2012 brought new life to this Midtown business-traveler favorite, infusing the lobby and rooms with a bright color palette and modern furniture. **Pros:** weekday wine reception; polite service; simple, not overdesigned rooms and hotel layout. **Cons:** small rooms; small fitness center. *$ Rooms from: $299 ✉ 70 Park Ave., at 38th St., Midtown East ☎ 212/973–2400, 800/707–2752 🌐 www.70parkave.com ⇨ 201 rooms, 4 suites 🍴 No meals Ⓜ 6 to 33rd St. ✥ 4:F5*

$$ HOTEL FAMILY **Affinia 50.** This popular hotel attracts business travelers but it's also comfortable for families or leisure travelers—especially the studios and suites, which have plenty of space to stretch out in, with full kitchens and a clean, playful design that incorporates oversize chairs and couches. **Pros:** apartment-style living; large rooms; good value; kid- and pet-friendly. **Cons:** Pricey Wi-Fi. *$ Rooms from: $449 ✉ 155 E. 50th St., at 3rd Ave., Midtown East ☎ 212/751–5710, 800/637–8483 🌐 www.affinia.com ⇨ 75 rooms, 134 suites 🍴 No meals Ⓜ 6 to 51st St.; E, M to Lexington Ave./53rd St. ✥ 4:G3*

$$ HOTEL **The Alex.** Often overlooked in a part of the city that's heavy with office buildings, the Alex is a sleek oasis of style on Manhattan's East

Fodor's Choice ★

Mandarin Oriental

The Mark

Ritz-Carlton New York, Central Park South

Side. **Pros:** all suites have kitchens; good service; on-site gym. **Cons:** cramped lobby; small bathrooms; expensive Wi-Fi. *Rooms from: $405 205 E. 45th St., between 2nd and 3rd Aves., Midtown East 212/867–5100 www.thealexhotel.com 73 rooms, 130 suites No meals 4, 5, 6, 7, S to 42nd St.–Grand Central 4:G4.*

$$ HOTEL FAMILY **The Benjamin.** NYC is often called the City That Never Sleeps, but if a good night's rest is essential for your visit, the Benjamin may be your choice accommodation—with a menu of 12 pillows to choose from (including buckwheat, water, and Swedish memory varieties), white-noise machines, and 400-thread-count sheets, they've got it covered. **Pros:** sleep-friendly; great location; gracious staff; kitchenettes in big rooms, pets stay for free **Cons:** paid Internet and Wi-Fi; boring views; dull neighborhood after dark. *Rooms from: $329 125 E. 50th St., at Lexington Ave., Midtown East 212/715–2500 www.thebenjamin.com 112 rooms, 97 suites No meals 6 to 51st St.; E, M to Lexington Ave./53rd St. 4:F3*

$$$$ HOTEL **Four Seasons Hotel.** It's the Four Seasons and, for better or worse, it remains the blueprint for what a Manhattan luxury hotel should be—sure, that means it's outrageously expensive, but you get a fair amount of bang for your buck, including stellar service, an imposing lobby done in marble and blond wood, and a well-connected concierge who can get reservations at most of New York's hot tables. **Pros:** spacious and comfortable rooms; perfect concierge and staff service; afternoon tea in the lobby lounge. **Cons:** pricey; confusing room controls; some furniture could use updating. *Rooms from: $950 57 E. 57th St., between Park and Madison Aves., Midtown East 212/758–5700, 800/487–3769 www.fourseasons.com 300 rooms, 68 suites No meals 4, 5, 6 to 59th St.; N, Q, R to Lexington Ave./59th St. 4:F1*

$$ HOTEL **The Gotham Hotel.** This sleek hotel has a lot going for it, but a clincher for some is the fact that every room has an outdoor space. **Pros:** welcoming staff; central location; every room has a balcony. **Cons:** no on-site gym. *Rooms from: $350 16 E. 46 St., between 5th and 6th Aves., Midtown East 212/490–8500 www.thegothamhotelny.com 66 rooms No meals B, D, F, M to 47th–50th Sts./Rockefeller Center 4:E4.*

$$ HOTEL **Grand Hyatt New York.** A recent renovation reinvented this historic Grand Central mainstay into a sleek, modern behemoth, making it a desireable central hub once again. **Pros:** Comfy beds, light-filled gym on a high floor; refreshing modern design; large rooms. **Cons:** No in-room minibar; Wi-Fi not free. *Rooms from: $359 109 E. 42nd St., Between Park and Lexington Aves., Midtown East 212/833–1234, 800/233–1234 www.grandnewyork.hyatt.com 1,255 rooms, 50 suites No meals 4, 5, 6, 7 to 42nd St. 4:F4.*

$$$ HOTEL **Hotel Elysée.** A relative bargain given its location, this intimate hotel is a favorite for travelers looking for great location without breaking the bank. **Pros:** complimentary snacks and Wi-Fi; individually decorated rooms; cute library. **Cons:** underwhelming lobby; slightly outdated decor. *Rooms from: $495 60 E. 54th St., between Madison and Park Aves., Midtown East 212/753–1066, 800/535–9733 www.*

17

elyseehotel.com 87 *rooms, 16 suites* *Breakfast* *E, M to 5th Ave./53rd St.* *4:F2*

$$$ HOTEL **The Kitano.** As you might guess from the name, the Kitano imports much of its sensibility from Japan, with touches that include a bilingual concierge and a high-concept Japanese restaurant—and it also makes for a notably service-oriented stay. **Pros:** extra soundproofing in guest rooms; cute mezzanine bar area; guest pass to great local New York Sports Club; good value. **Cons:** lower-floor views are limited; expensive restaurant. *Rooms from: $499* *66 Park Ave., at 38th St., Midtown East* *212/885–7000, 800/548–2666* *www.kitano.com* *149 rooms, 18 suites* *No meals* *6 to 33rd St.* *4:F5*

$$ HOTEL Fodor's Choice ★ **Library Hotel Manhattan.** Bookishly handsome, this stately landmark brownstone, built in 1900, is inspired by the nearby New York Public Library—each of its 10 floors is dedicated to one of the 10 categories of the Dewey Decimal System and is stocked with art and books relevant to a subtopic such as erotica, astronomy, or biography—let your interests guide your choice. **Pros:** fun rooftop bar; playful book themes; stylish rooms. **Cons:** rooftop sometimes reserved for events; more books in rooms themselves would be nice. *Rooms from: $379* *299 Madison Ave., at 41st Street, Midtown East* *212/983–4500, 212/983–4500* *www.libraryhotel.com* *52 rooms, 8 suites* *Breakfast* *4, 5, 6, 7, S to 42nd St.–Grand Central* *4:F4.*

$$$ HOTEL **Loews Regency Hotel.** The Loews Regency started renovations in January 2013 and is expected to be closed for 11 months. *Rooms from: $509* *540 Park Ave., at E. 61st St., Midtown East* *212/759-4100, 800/233–2356* *www.loewshotels.com* *267 rooms, 87 suites* *No meals* *4, 5, 6 to 59th St.; N, Q, R to Lexington Ave./59th St.* *5:F6*

$$$ HOTEL **New York Palace.** From the moment you enter the gilded gates of these connected mansions, originally built in the 1880s by railroad baron Henry Villard, you know you're somewhere special; there's a reason this is called the Palace. **Pros:** gorgeous courtyard with 15th-century Italian-style motifs; great service; unmatched views of St. Patrick's Cathedral. **Cons:** high prices; harried staff. *Rooms from: $599* *455 Madison Ave., at 50th St., Midtown East* *212/888–7000, 800/697–2522* *www.newyorkpalace.com* *811 rooms, 88 suites* *No meals* *6 to 51st St.; E, M to Lexington Ave./53rd St.* *4:F3*

$$ HOTEL **ONE UN New York.** In a sky-high tower near the landmark United Nations building, the ONE UN New York starts on the 28th floor, offering fabulous views—ask for a room facing west, toward Manhattan's skyline—and a multilingual staff that caters to a discerning clientele including heads of state. **Pros:** unbeatable East River and city views; good value; great front-door and bell staff. **Cons:** a walk to the subway; pricey Internet access. *Rooms from: $220* *1 United Nations Plaza, at E. 44th St. and 1st Ave., Midtown East* *212/758–1234, 866/866–8086* *www.millenniumhotels.com* *439 rooms, 34 suites* *No meals* *4, 5, 6, 7, S to 42nd St.–Grand Central* *4:H4.*

$$$$ HOTEL Fodor's Choice ★ **The Peninsula.** Stepping through the Peninsula's Beaux-Arts facade onto the grand staircase overhung with a monumental chandelier, you know you're in for a glitzy treat. **Pros:** brilliant service; fabulous rooms, with the best lighting of all city hotels (good angles, easy to use); unforgettable rooftop bar. **Cons:** expensive. *Rooms from: $995* *700*

5th Ave., at 55th St., Midtown East ☎ 212/956–2888, 800/262–9467 🌐 www.peninsula.com ⇨ 185 rooms, 54 suites 🍴 No meals Ⓜ E, M to 5th Ave./53rd St. ✥ 4:E2

$ HOTEL **The Pod Hotel.** This is the hotel that made bunk beds cool again. **Pros:** great prices; fun design. **Cons:** if you're prone to claustrophobia, you may want to reconsider. 💲 *Rooms from: $179 ✉ 230 E. 51st St., between 2nd and 3rd Aves., Midtown East ☎ 212/355–0300, 800/742–5945 🌐 www.thepodhotel.com ⇨ 350 rooms, 195 with bath 🍴 No meals Ⓜ 6 to 51st St.; E, M to Lexington Ave./53rd St. ✥ 4:G2*

$$ HOTEL **Roger Smith.** This quirky choice is one of the better budget stays in the city and the art-filled rooms, matched by the murals in the lobby, are homey and comfortable, with down pillows and quilts on the beds. **Pros:** good location near Grand Central; intimate atmosphere; free Wi-Fi. **Cons:** street noise; small bathrooms. 💲 *Rooms from: $369 ✉ 501 Lexington Ave., between 47th and 48th Sts., Midtown East ☎ 212/755–1400, 800/445–0277 🌐 www.rogersmith.com ⇨ 102 rooms, 28 suites 🍴 No meals Ⓜ 6 to 51st St.; E, M to Lexington Ave./53rd St. ✥ 4:G3*

$ HOTEL **The Roosevelt Hotel.** Named after Teddy, not Franklin, this Midtown icon just steps from Grand Central has an ornate lobby with cushy couches and an old-school bar with heavy wood detailing that makes the place feel like it's from another time, and it should—the property dates from 1924. **Pros:** great public areas; big bathrooms. **Cons:** dated decor; limited in-room amenities. 💲 *Rooms from: $299 ✉ 45 E. 45th St., at Madison Ave., Midtown East ☎ 888/833–3969, 212/661–9600 🌐 www.therooseveltthotel.com ⇨ 982 rooms, 33 suites 🍴 No meals Ⓜ 4, 5, 6, 7, S to 42nd St.–Grand Central. ✥ 4:F4*

17

$$$$ HOTEL **The Langham, Fifth Avenue.** Setting new standards for luxury, the towering, limestone-clad The Langham was conceived as an opulent crash pad for wealthy overseas tourists, captains of industry on long-term stays, and anyone in need of some serious pampering. **Pros:** attentive service; gorgeous spa; great location. **Cons:** street noise reported by guests on lower floors. 💲 *Rooms from: $745 ✉ 400 5th Ave., Midtown East ☎ 212/695–4005 🌐 www.newyork.langhamplacehotels.com ⇨ 157 rooms, 57 suites 🍴 No meals Ⓜ B, D, F, M, N, Q, R to 34th St.–Herald Sq. ✥ 4:E6*

$$$$ HOTEL **The Sherry-Netherland.** The Sherry is a stately part of the New York landscape so it may come as a surprise to learn that it's essentially a tall, luxurious apartment building that also has 50 hotel rooms and suites. **Pros:** gorgeous lobby; commanding, impeccable location; Cipriani access. **Cons:** small check-in area; rooms vary in taste and decor; nonsuites are on the small side; interior rooms lack views; guests sometimes feel the cold shoulder from the full-time residents. 💲 *Rooms from: $649 ✉ 781 5th Ave., at 59th St., Midtown East ☎ 212/355–2800, 800/247–4377 🌐 www.sherrynetherland.com ⇨ 26 rooms, 24 suites 🍴 No meals Ⓜ N, Q, R to 5th Ave./59th St. ✥ 5:E6*

$$$$ HOTEL Fodor's Choice ★ **The St. Regis.** World-class from head to toe, this 5th Avenue Beaux-Arts landmark comes as close to flawless as any hotel in New York. **Pros:** rooms combine true luxury with helpful technology; easy-access butler service; superb in-house dining; prestigious location. **Cons:** expensive; too serious for families seeking fun. 💲 *Rooms from: $1045*

2 E. 55th St., at 5th Ave., Midtown East 212/753-4500, 877/787-3447 www.stregisnewyork.com 164 rooms, 65 suites No meals M E, M to 5th Ave./53rd St. 4:E2

$$ HOTEL **Hilton Manhattan East.** This traditional-style, 20-story Tudor City hotel is a stone's throw from the United Nations and Grand Central Terminal, making it fairly convenient but not very glamorous. **Pros:** near UN; some balconies; convenient location for getting to major sights. **Cons:** long walk to subway; unexciting room decor. *Rooms from: $405 304 E. 42nd St., between 1st and 2nd Aves., Midtown East 212/986–8800, 800/879–8836 www3.hilton.com 286 rooms, 14 suites No meals M 4, 5, 6, 7, S to 42nd St.–Grand Central 4:H4.*

$$$ HOTEL **Waldorf-Astoria.** The Waldorf is undeniably historic, and presidents usually stay here thanks to the security of the drive-in entrance, but we'd recommend having a cocktail at the classic Bull and Bear Bar downstairs rather than spending the night in one of the small standard rooms, which top out at a tight 250 square feet and can feel a bit oppressive with their extensive floral patterns. **Pros:** historic Art Deco building filled with NYC's aristocratic, gangster, and jazz histories; best Waldorf salad in town; knowledgeable doormen. **Cons:** rooms not up-to-date; more about the name than the experience; in-hotel Starbucks costs twice as much as ones around the corner. *Rooms from: $549 301 Park Ave., between 49th and 50th Sts., Midtown East 212/355–3000, 800/925–3673 www.waldorfastoria.com 1,183 rooms, 230 suites No meals M 6 to 51st St.; E, M to Lexington Ave./53rd St. 4:F3*

$$ HOTEL **W Hotel New York.** A hopping bar and sunken lounge in the reception area, superfunky decor touches like window boxes filled with grass, and guest rooms that hew to the classic brand formula—they're small but they look good—make this a quintessential W property. **Pros:** central location; great-looking rooms; Bliss Spa in hotel. **Cons:** thin walls; small rooms; inconsistent service. *Rooms from: $279 541 Lexington Ave., between 49th and 50th Sts., Midtown East 212/755–1200, 877/946–8357 www.whotels.com 629 rooms, 62 suites No meals M 6 to 51st St.; E, M to Lexington Ave./53rd St. 4:F3*

MURRAY HILL

$$ HOTEL **The Carlton Hotel.** From the two-story lobby designed by David Rockwell to still-intact, original 1904 Beaux-Arts details such as the stained-glass dome (created by workers from the Tiffany glass factory), a 40-foot ceiling in the lobby, and a soaring crystal chandelier, the Carlton is a refurbished gem. **Pros:** spectacular lobby; stylish rooms. **Cons:** expensive bar; small rooms. *Rooms from: $449 88 Madison Ave., between 28th and 29th Sts., Murray Hill 212/532–4100, 800/601–8500 www.carltonhotelny.com 294 rooms, 23 suites No meals M 6 to 28th St. 3:F1*

$ HOTEL **The Herald Square Hotel.** The sculpted cherubs on the facade and the vintage magazine covers adorning the common areas give good hints that the great value Herald Square Hotel used to be *Life* magazine's headquarters. **Pros:** cheap; centrally located. **Cons:** unattractive lobby; readers report inconsistent service. *Rooms from: $199 19 W. 31st St., between 5th Ave. and Broadway, Murray Hill 212/279–4017,*

Inn at Irving Place

The Peninsula

The St. Regis

CLOSE UP

Romantic Retreats

As the English explorer Sir Walter Raleigh once wrote, "Romance is a love affair in other than domestic surroundings." Indeed, many high-end hotels seem custom-built for romance, with plush feather beds, silky linens, and ultrasoft robes. But some properties go above and beyond in catering to couples, offering services like bath butlers and in-room massages. Here's our pick of the city's best spots for an intimate getaway.

At the **Ritz-Carlton New York, Battery Park** (⇨ *Lower Manhattan*), your wish is their command. Take advantage of lower-than-normal weekend rates to book a Liberty Suite, with sweeping views of the Statue of Liberty. With a quick call to the concierge you can arrange to have champagne and strawberries waiting in your room when you arrive. A bath butler can then fill your marble tub with a potion of bath oils and flower petals. If you're here in February, don't miss a trip to the penthouse Chocolate Bar, with its aphrodisiac chocolate-and-champagne buffet.

The **Inn at Irving Place** (⇨ *Union Square/Gramercy*) does romance the old-fashioned way, with four-poster beds, fireplaces, fur throws, and plenty of privacy in an elegant 1800s brownstone. The complimentary breakfast is served on fine bone china either in the cozy sitting room or in bed.

Few things are as romantic as taking a bath, and at the Carlyle (⇨ *Upper East Side*) every room has one. Fill the tub with steaming water and some Kiehl's bubble bath, take a soak, then lounge with your lover in a plush terrycloth robe while looking out at some of the City's best views. The 23,000-square-foot Bliss Spa at **W New York** (⇨ *Midtown East and Upper East Side*), on Lexington Avenue, is an urban oasis, with men's and women's lounges, a gym, and a full menu of facial and body treatments, massage, waxing, and nail services. Couples can spend a full day being pampered in the spa or unwind in their rooms with an in-room massage, offered 24 hours a day.

All the rooms at the **Library Hotel** (⇨ *Midtown East and Upper East Side*) have an inviting charm that makes them a good choice for a romantic weekend away, but if you're looking for a little mood reading, ask for the Erotic Literature room or the Love Room, curated by Dr. Ruth.

800/727–1888 🌐 *www.heraldnyc.com* *100 rooms* *No meals* Ⓜ *B, D, F, M, N, Q, R to 34th St.–Herald Sq.* ✥ *3:E1*

$$$ HOTEL FAMILY **St. Giles New York—The Tuscany.** After a complete gut renovation in 2012, some of the most spacious rooms in New York are back and refreshed at the St. Giles's Tuscany. **Pros:** very generous room space for New York; brand-new, fresh decor and furnishings; art installations featuring local artists. **Cons:** on the expensive side. Ⓢ *Rooms from: $495* ✉ *120 E. 39th St., between Park and Lexington Aves., Murray Hill* ☎ *212/686–1600* 🌐 *www.tuscany.stgilesnewyork.com* *116 rooms, 8 suites* *No meals* Ⓜ *4, 5, 6, 7 to 42nd St.* ✥ *4:F5.*

MIDTOWN WEST

$$ **6 Columbus.** A boutique-style hotel nestled in the shadow of the towering Time Warner Center, 6 Columbus—part of the ever-proliferating Thompson Hotels group—offers the vibe and amenities of downtown lodging with the convenience of a more central midtown location. **Pros:** convenient location; fun in-hotel restaurant; reasonably priced for neighborhood; family-friendly. **Cons:** rooms on lower floors facing 58th Street can be noisy. *Rooms from: $295* *6 Columbus Circle, 58th St. between 8th and 9th Aves., Midtown West* *212/204–3000* *www.thompsonhotels.com* *70 rooms, 18 suites* *No meals* *1, A, B, C, D to 59th St.–Columbus Circle* *4:B1.*

$$$ HOTEL **The Algonquin.** One of Manhattan's most historic properties, the Algonquin is a landmark of literary history. **Pros:** free Internet; friendly, knowledgeable staff; central location. **Cons:** some small rooms. *Rooms from: $550* *59 W. 44th St., between 5th and 6th Aves., Midtown West* *212/840–6800, 800/555–8000* *www.algonquinhotel.com* *156 rooms, 25 suites* *No meals* *B, D, F, M to 42nd St.–Bryant Park.* *4:D4*

$ HOTEL **Belvedere Hotel.** Built during the 1920's, the Belvedere's main draw is its Times Square/Theater District location; the rooms tend to be dark and don't stand out design-wise, although they are spacious and have kitchenettes with a microwave, mini-refrigerator, and coffeemaker. **Pros:** good rates available; renovated rooms are good value. **Cons:** can be loud with street noise; slow elevators; Wi-Fi free in only some room categories. *Rooms from: $239* *319 W. 48th St., between 8th and 9th Aves., Midtown West* *212/245–7000, 888/468–3558* *www.belvederehotelnyc.com* *345 rooms* *No meals* *C, E to 50th St.* *4:B3*

17

$ HOTEL **Best Western Plus President Hotel.** The President is the only politically themed hotel in the city, starting with the purple color scheme, a combination of Republican red and Democratic blue. **Pros:** sleek rooms for the price; convenient location; unique theme. **Cons:** cramped lobby; dark bathrooms; poor views. *Rooms from: $249* *234 W. 48th St., between 8th Ave. and Broadway, Midtown West* *212/246–8800, 800/828–4667* *www.bestwestern.com* *334 rooms* *No meals* *C, E to 50th St.* *4:C3*

$$$ HOTEL **The Blakely New York.** It may be a tried-and-true design motif, but it's hard to resist the English gentlemen's club when it's done right. **Pros:** all rooms have kitchenettes; central location; good-size rooms; acclaimed restaurant. **Cons:** rooms facing 54th Street can be noisy; some rooms have little natural light; expensive. *Rooms from: $525* *136 W. 55th St., between 6th and 7th Aves., Midtown West* *212/245–1800, 800/735–0710* *www.blakelynewyork.com* *60 rooms, 58 suites* *Breakfast* *N, Q, R to 57th St.–7th Ave.* *4:C2*

$$ HOTEL **Bryant Park Hotel.** A New York landmark in brown brick that towers over the New York Public Library and Bryant Park, this sleek hotel is still a Midtown hot spot. **Pros:** gorgeous building; fashionable crowd and setting; across from Bryant Park. **Cons:** expensive; Cellar Bar frequently booked for events. *Rooms from: $445* *40 W. 40th St., between 5th and 6th Aves., Midtown West* *212/869–0100, 877/640–*

9300 ⊕ www.bryantparkhotel.com ⇆ 114 rooms, 14 suites ✕ No meals Ⓜ B, D, F, M to 42nd St.–Bryant Park; 7 to 5th Ave. ✣ 4:D5

$$ HOTEL Fodor's Choice ★ **Casablanca Hotel.** A favorite for the comfortable rooms and great location, the Casablanca evokes the sultry Mediterranean. **Pros:** great access to the Theater District; free continental breakfast and evening wine/cheese reception. **Cons:** exercise facilities at nearby New York Sports Club, not on premises; heavy tourist foot traffic. $ *Rooms from: $439 ✉ 147 W. 43rd St., Midtown West ☎ 212/869–1212 ⊕ www.casablancahotel.com ⇆ 42 rooms, 6 suites ✕ Breakfast Ⓜ 1, 2, 3, 7, N, Q, R, S to Times Sq.–42nd St. ✣ 4:C4*

$$$$ HOTEL Fodor's Choice ★ **The Chatwal New York.** A lavishly refurbished reincarnation of a classic Manhattan theater club that lay fallow for decades, the Chatwal New York delivers the luxury experience in style, with the price tag to match. **Pros:** gorgeous lobby; state-of-the-art room controls and amenities; excellent service. **Cons:** expensive—some visitors may find justifying such high prices for a Times Square locale difficult. $ *Rooms from: $795 ✉ 130 W. 44th St., between 5th and 6th Aves., Midtown West ☎ 212/764–6200 ⊕ www.thechatwalny.com ⇆ 50 rooms, 26 suites ✕ No meals Ⓜ B, D, F, M to 42nd St.–Bryant Park; 7 to 5th Ave. ✣ 4:D4*

$$ HOTEL **City Club Hotel.** The City Club's ocean liner–inspired rooms are brisk, bright, and masculine: they're also about the same size as a room on a cruise ship—that means tight quarters, matey, no matter how much you enjoy sharing space with Jonathan Adler ceramics. **Pros:** free Wi-Fi; great restaurant; personal service. **Cons:** no gym; occasionally dim lighting; tiny lobby. $ *Rooms from: $400 ✉ 55 W. 44th St., between 5th and 6th Aves., Midtown West ☎ 212/921–5500 ⊕ www.cityclubhotel.com ⇆ 62 rooms, 3 suites ✕ No meals Ⓜ B, D, F, M to 42nd St.–Bryant Park; 1, 2, 3, 7, N, Q, R, S to Times Sq.–42nd St. ✣ 4:D4*

$$ HOTEL **The Distrikt.** Rising high above Port Authority, the Distrikt tries to approximate the boutique hotel experience in an area of town better known for its bus depot and, for the most part, it succeeds. **Pros:** great central location; friendly staff; good Midtown views from higher floors. **Cons:** on a gritty block right across from Port Authority; noisy on lower floors. $ *Rooms from: $329 ✉ 342 W. 40th St., between 8th and 9th Aves., Midtown West ☎ 212/706–6100 ⊕ www.distrikthotel.com ⇆ 155 rooms ✕ No meals Ⓜ A, C, E to 42nd St.–Port Authority. ✣ 4:B5*

$$ HOTEL FAMILY **DoubleTree Suites by Hilton Hotel New York City–Times Square.** Space is the draw at this all-suites, 45-story Times Square top dog, where rooms are twice the size of New York City's average one-bedroom apartment. **Pros:** free 24-hour gym and Wi-Fi in public areas; helpful, informed concierge; convenient to the Theater District; quiet considering the Times Square location. **Cons:** paid Wi-Fi in guest rooms; pricey for a DoubleTree. $ *Rooms from: $349 ✉ 1568 Broadway, at 47th St., Midtown West ☎ 212/719–1600 ⊕ www.doubletree3.hilton.com ⇆ 460 suites ✕ No meals Ⓜ B, D, F, M to 42nd St.–Bryant Park. ✣ 4:C3*

$$ HOTEL **Dream New York.** Part hotel, part Kafkaesque dream, this Midtown experience is brought to you by hotelier Vikram Chatwal; it specializes in style over comfort but is still quite livable, despite some over-the-top design features—and noise from the scenesters headed to the rooftop bar. **Pros:** Ava Lounge penthouse bar; large spa; up-to-the-minute

electronics. **Cons:** small rooms; spotty service; might be too sceney for some. *Rooms from: $279 210 W. 55th St., at Broadway, Midtown West 212/247–2000, 212/247–2000 www.dreamny.com 204 rooms, 12 suites No meals N, Q, R to 57th St.–7th Ave. 4:C2*

$$$ HOTEL **Hilton Times Square.** A glass-and-steel skyscraper atop a 335,000-square-foot retail complex that includes a movie theater and Madame Tussaud's Wax Museum, the Hilton Times Square soars 44 stories above Manhattan and overlooks New York City's famous skyline and the Hudson River. **Pros:** great location for Times Square entertainment; convenient to public transportation; big rooms. **Cons:** impersonal feel; nickel-and-dime charges and overpriced food and drink, including a $26 buffet breakfast. *Rooms from: $549 234 W. 42nd St., between 7th and 8th Aves., Midtown West 212/840–8222, 800/445–8667 www.hilton.com 460 rooms, 2 suites No meals 1, 2, 3, 7, N, Q, R, S to Times Sq.–42nd St. 4:C4*

$ HOTEL **Holiday Inn New York City Midtown.** Business travelers, tourists, and families alike appreciate this good value option a stone's throw from Penn Station, but understand that it's not the most exciting hotel experience New York has to offer. **Pros:** good value; friendly and efficient service; location in the thick of it. **Cons:** small workout room; not much character. *Rooms from: $219 30 W. 31st St., between 5th Ave. and Broadway, Midtown West 212/695–7401 www.holidayinn.com 120 rooms, 2 suites No meals B D, F, M, N, Q, R to 34th St. 3:E1.*

$ HOTEL **Hotel Metro.** With mirrored columns and elegant black-and-white photos in the lobby, the Hotel Metro feels distinctively retro. **Pros:** complimentary coffee and tea 24/7; renovated exercise room has flat-screen TVs; free Wi-Fi in rooms. **Cons:** noise seeps in from outside; rooms are tasteful but spartan. *Rooms from: $275 45 W. 35th St., between 5th and 6th Aves., Midtown West 212/947 2500 www.hotelmetronyc.com 162 rooms, 19 suites Breakfast B, D, F, M, N, Q, R to 34th St.–Herald Sq. 4:D6*

$$ HOTEL **Hudson New York Hotel.** Budget fashionistas are once again drawn to the Hudson after a dramatic renovation of every single room in 2012. **Pros:** fabulous, elegant bar; gorgeous Francesco Clemente fresco in lobby; breathtaking Sky Terrace. **Cons:** staff can be condescending; tiny rooms; overpriced cocktails. *Rooms from: $339 356 W. 58th St., between 8th and 9th Aves., Midtown West 212/554–6000 www.hudsonhotel.com 791 rooms, 75 suites suites No meals 1, A, B, C, D to 59th St.–Columbus Circle 4:B1.*

$ HOTEL FAMILY **Ink48.** If you want convenience to central Midtown but some remove from the hustle and bustle (not to mention a breathtaking rooftop space), this Kimpton property is an excellent option. **Pros:** friendly staff; great views; large rooms; beautiful rooftop **Cons:** off-the-beaten-track location; lobby can feel overly quiet at times; street noise in lower-floor rooms. *Rooms from: $259 653 11th Ave., at 48th St., Midtown West 212/757–0088 www.ink48.com 195 rooms, 28 suites No meals C, E to 50th St. 4:A3*

$$ HOTEL **InterContinental New York Times Square.** A central location mere blocks from the heart of Broadway, Times Square, and restaurant-rich Hell's

Kitchen makes the city's newest InterContinental a conveniently located draw. **Pros:** central for transportation and entertainment; in-house restaurant helmed by celebrity chef; attentive staff. **Cons:** fee for Internet. *Rooms from: $399 ✉ 300 W. 44th St., Midtown West ☎ 877/331–5888 📠 212/315–2535 www.interconny.com 578 rooms, 4 suites, 25 studios No meals Ⓜ A, C, E to 42nd St.–Port Authority ✥ 4:B4.*

$$ HOTEL **JW Marriott Essex House.** With Central Park views and an art deco masterpiece of a lobby, the JW Marriott Essex House is a comfortable Midtown hotel that is full of character. **Pros:** great service; amazing views; impressive restaurant. **Cons:** overly complex room gadgetry; expensive bar. *Rooms from: $399 ✉ 160 Central Park S, between 6th and 7th Aves., Midtown West ☎ 212/247–0300, 800/937–8461 www.marriott.com 509 rooms, 117 suites No meals Ⓜ F to 57th St.; N, Q, R to 57th St.–7th Ave. ✥ 4:C1*

$ HOTEL **La Quinta Inn Manhattan.** Smack in the middle of Koreatown and close to Penn Station, this budget-friendly hotel in a cheerful old Beaux-Arts building may be one of the best deals in town. **Pros:** self-check-in machines; gift shop on the premises for necessities; relaxed rooftop bar. **Cons:** no room service; no frills. *Rooms from: $225 ✉ 17 W. 32nd St., between 5th Ave. and Broadway, Midtown West ☎ 212/736–1600 www.lq.com 182 rooms Breakfast Ⓜ B, D, F, M, N, Q, R to 34th St.–Herald Sq. ✥ 4:E6*

$$$ HOTEL FAMILY **Le Parker Meridien.** A splash of kookiness in otherwise staid Midtown, the Parker Meridian combines the comforts of a dependable large hotel with elements of whimsy that keep visitors coming back. **Pros:** lively, animated spirit; best hotel gym in the city; fun eating options; tech-friendly rooms. **Cons:** lobby is a public space; small bathrooms. *Rooms from: $450 ✉ 119 W. 56th St., between 6th and 7th Aves., Midtown West ☎ 212/245–5000, 800/543–4300 www.parkermeridien.com 511 rooms, 215 suites No meals Ⓜ B, D, E to 7th Ave.; N, Q, R to 57th St.–7th Ave. ✥ 4:D1*

$$$ HOTEL **The London NYC.** Stylish and sophisticated, the London NYC merges the flair of both its namesake cities, with the added bonus of Gordon Ramsay's first stateside restaurant. **Pros:** posh atmosphere without prissiness; Gordon Ramsay restaurants; great fitness club. **Cons:** inconsistent service; no bathtubs in most rooms; expensive dining options. *Rooms from: $599 ✉ 151 W. 54th St., between 6th and 7th Aves., Midtown West ☎ 866/690–2029, 212/307–5000 www.thelondonnyc.com 562 suites No meals Ⓜ B, D, E to 7th Ave.; N, Q, R to 57th St.–7th Ave. ✥ 4:C2*

$$$$ HOTEL Fodor's Choice ★ **Mandarin Oriental.** The Mandarin's lobby, 280 feet above ground on the Time Warner Center's 35th floor, features dramatic floor-to-ceiling windows, setting the tone for the rest of the luxurious hotel experience. **Pros:** fantastic views from rooms and pool; all the resources of the Time Warner Center; expansive suites. **Cons:** Trump hotel blocks some park views; expensive; mall-like surroundings. *Rooms from: $955 ✉ 80 Columbus Circle, at 60th St., Midtown West ☎ 212/805–8800 www.mandarinoriental.com/newyork 198 rooms, 46 suites No meals Ⓜ A, B, C, D, 1 to 59th St.–Columbus Circle ✥ 4:B1.*

CLOSE UP

Kids in Tow

Many New York hotels go out of their way to accommodate families, with special amenities and family-size rooms. However, a hotel claiming that it's child-friendly doesn't always translate to true kid-welcoming style. Ask if cribs come with linens, whether there are high chairs and children's menus in the dining room, and if there are in-house babysitters. Some hotels will even clear out the minibar (for bottle or baby-food storage), baby-proof a room, or provide baby-proofing materials. Here are some of the top picks for traveling with kids.

IN THE BAG. At Aloft hotels in Harlem and Brooklyn, kids receive a sleeping bag, coloring tools, and even popcorn in their own bag. And many rooms at Aloft New York Brooklyn can be conjoined to create family-friendly suites.

SUITE LIFE. Space is at a premium in New York hotels, and if you have more than two people in a standard room, you'll really start to feel the squeeze. The answer? A suite, where you can spread out in style. The **Conrad New York** (⇨ *TriBeCa)* is an all-suite property that's in the same building as a multiplex movie theater and several reasonably priced dining options—including Shake Shack. With renovated, spacious suites, **Affinia 50** (⇨ *Midtown East and Upper East Side)* is the family hotel of choice on the residential East Side.

PURE PAMPERING. Just because you have children in tow doesn't mean your dream of a pampering vacation needs to go down the drain. Several top New York hotels go out of their way to accommodate families. The **Mandarin Oriental** (⇨ *Midtown West)* offers complimentary kids' DVDs and video games, and free coloring books and crayons for kids.

FUN FLAVOR. Room Mate Grace (⇨ *Midtown West)* might make the perfect respite if you have teens in tow. There's a funky lobby pool, a kiosk that stocks sweets with which to fill the in-room refrigerators, and rooms with bunk beds that levitate out of the walls and have their own plasma TVs. At the hip **Hotel on Rivington** (⇨ *East Village and Lower East Side)* a special family suite has two full bedrooms, one with two sets of bunk beds and a big bin of toys, two full baths, and a Japanese tub. Bonus points: the hotel is across from Economy Candy.

KID KARMA. Family-friendly **Le Parker Meridien** (⇨ *Midtown West and Chelsea)* has a large pool, a restaurant that serves decadent breakfast foods such as chocolate French toast until 3 pm, and a casual dining spot, Burger Joint, that serves nothing but burgers and shakes.

KID-SIZE. At **70 Park, Eventi,** and **Ink48** (all Kimpton Hotels), kids get their own minisize animal-print robes (also available for purchase) so they can feel just like their grown-up travel companions.

TEA FOR TWO. At the **Plaza,** fanciful children of all ages will revel in dress-up clothes, formal tea service, and film screenings that are all part of the Eloise-theme experiences that seek to re-create the fictional character's time at the iconic hotel.

Fodor's Choice ★

Ace Hotel

Library Hotel, Inn on 23rd

$$ HOTEL **The Mansfield.** They sweat the small stuff at the Mansfield: Wi-Fi is free, bathroom products are from Aveda, and even the key cards are snazzily embossed with scenes of old-timey New York. **Pros:** complimentary Wi-Fi; business center; 24-hour gym; great bar. **Cons:** small rooms and bathrooms; air conditioners are window units. *Rooms from: $319 ✉ 12 W. 44th St., between 5th and 6th Aves., Midtown West ☎ 212/277–8700, 800/255–5167 www.mansfieldhotel.com 99 rooms, 27 suites No meals M B, D, F, M to 42nd St.–Bryant Park. ✥ 4:E4*

$$ HOTEL **The Michelangelo.** Italophiles will feel like they've been transported to the good life in the Mediterranean at this deluxe hotel, where the long, wide lobby lounge is clad with multihue marble and Veronese-style oil paintings. **Pros:** good location and restaurant; spacious rooms. **Cons:** noisy air-conditioning units; some rooms have limited views; small closets; in-room fixtures need some updating. *Rooms from: $399 ✉ 152 W. 51st St., at 7th Ave., Midtown West ☎ 212/765–1900, 800/237–0990 www.michelangelohotel.com 123 rooms, 56 suites Breakfast M B, D, E to 7th Ave.; 1 to 50th St.; B, D, F, M to 47th–50th Sts./Rockefeller Center ✥ 4:C3.*

$$ HOTEL **Muse Hotel.** Surrealist prints and busts of Thalia, the muse of comedy, adorn the lobby of this polished Kimpton property that pleases guests looking for a Midtown boutique hotel experience. **Pros:** contemporary interiors; good Midtown location; pet-friendly. **Cons:** street noise; small gym. *Rooms from: $389 ✉ 130 W. 46th St., between 6th and 7th Aves., Midtown West ☎ 212/485–2400, 877/692–6873 www.themusehotel.com 181 rooms, 19 suites No meals M B, D, F, M to 47th–50th Sts./Rockefeller Center ✥ 4:C4.*

17

$$$ HOTEL Fodor's Choice ★ **The Out NYC.** Opened in 2012 and billed as a straight-friendly "urban resort" in one of New York's most happening gay neighborhoods, this 103-room hotel is the incarnation of all things hip and modern. **Pros:** centrally located; affordable; friendly staff. **Cons:** can be noisy at night. *Rooms from: $360 ✉ 510 W. 42nd St., Midtown West ☎ 212/947–2999 www.theoutnyc.com 91 rooms, 4 suites, 8 quads No meals M A, C, E at 42nd St.–Port Authority. ✥ 4:A4*

$$$$ HOTEL **The Plaza.** Eloise's adopted home on the corner of Central Park, the Plaza is one of New York's most storied hotels, hosting all manner of dignitaries, moneymakers, and royalty. **Pros:** historic property; great hotel bar; lavish rooms. **Cons:** rooms aren't that big for the money; Oak Room restaurant is pricey and inconsistent. *Rooms from: $895 ✉ 768 5th Ave., at Central Park S, Midtown West ☎ 212/759–3000 www.theplazany.com 180 rooms, 102 suites No meals M N, Q, R to 5th Ave./59th St. ✥ 4:E1*

$$$ HOTEL **Renaissance Hotel.** After a shift from all-business to a more design-centric approach, the Renaissance is enjoying a renaissance of its own. **Pros:** contemporary design; latest in-room technology. **Cons:** rooms can be a bit noisy; high occupancy means rooms can wear out fast. *Rooms from: $539 ✉ 714 7th Ave., between 47th and 48th Sts., Midtown West ☎ 212/765–7676, 800/628–5222 www.renaissancehotels.com 305 rooms, 5 suites No meals M N, Q, R to 49th St.; 1 to 50th St. ✥ 4:C3*

$$$$ HOTEL FAMILY Fodor's Choice ★ **The Ritz-Carlton New York, Central Park.** It's all about the park views here, though the above-and-beyond service, accommodating to a fault, makes this renowned property popular with celebs and other demanding guests. **Pros:** great concierge; personalized service; stellar location; views. **Cons:** pricey; limited common areas. *Rooms from: $895 ✉ 50 Central Park S, at 6th Ave., Midtown West ☎ 212/308–9100, 866/671–6008 ⊕ www.ritzcarlton.com 259 rooms, 47 suites No meals M F to 57th St. ⊕ 4:D1*

WORD OF MOUTH

"If you could afford any hotel in Midtown, Upper West Side NYC, where would you stay?" —Vivid01

"The attention and service at the Mandarin Oriental are unsurpassed. I've done several meetings there with extremely high level international clinical investigators and they were able to easily satisfy even the prima donnas. However, it is VERY modern. If you want something traditional, this isn't for you." —nytraveler

$$ HOTEL FAMILY **Room Mate Grace.** A favorite of European visitors and business travelers who work in fashion and entertainment, Grace delivers high-design lodgings on a budget. **Pros:** cool swimming pool lounge; friendly, helpful staff. **Cons:** small rooms; little in-room privacy (no door separating shower from main room). *Rooms from: $319 ✉ 125 W. 45th St., Midtown West ☎ 212/354–2323 ⊕ www.room-matehotels.com 139 rooms No meals M B, D, F, M to 42nd St.–Bryant Park. ⊕ 4:D4*

$$ HOTEL **The Royalton.** Back in the 1990s, the Royalton's lobby bar was one of the prime meeting spots for local A-listers and a redesign now attracts a new generation of movers and shakers—so be prepared to run the gauntlet of the buzzing lounge before reaching your room—but the helpful staff ensures the process goes smoothly. **Pros:** hip lobby scene; luxurious beds and bathrooms; helpful service. **Cons:** dark hallways; lighting verges on eye-strainingly dim. *Rooms from: $399 ✉ 44 W. 44th St., between 5th and 6th Aves., Midtown West ☎ 212/869–4400, 800/697–1791 ⊕ www.royaltonhotel.com 141 rooms, 27 suites No meals M B, D, F, M to 42nd St.–Bryant Park. ⊕ 4:D4*

$$ HOTEL **The Shoreham.** In a neighborhood packed with generic hotels, the Shoreham offers a welcome dose of style, along with a location central to the best of Midtown's attractions. **Pros:** tech-friendly; pet-friendly attitude; stylish decor. **Cons:** not designed for families; limited space. *Rooms from: $399 ✉ 33 W. 55th St., between 5th and 6th Aves., Midtown West ☎ 212/247–6700, 877/847–4444 ⊕ www.shorehamhotel.com 174 rooms, 37 suites Breakfast M E, M to 5th Ave./53rd St. ⊕ 4:D2*

$$ HOTEL **Sofitel Luxury Hotel.** With bilingual signage throughout the hotel, plenty of velvet in the lobby, and European modern design in the rooms—think blond wood and fresh flowers—the Sofitel brings a Gallic flair to Midtown West. **Pros:** central location; great beds; some suites with terraces and views. **Cons:** pricey; room views vary. *Rooms from: $350 ✉ 45 W. 44th St., between 5th and 6th Aves., Midtown West ☎ 212/354–8844 ⊕ www.sofitel.com 346 rooms, 52 suites No meals M B, D, F, M to 42nd St.–Bryant Park. ⊕ 4:E4*

$ HOTEL **The Time Hotel.** One of the neighborhood's first boutique hotels, this spot half a block from the din of Times Square tempers trendiness with a touch of humor. **Pros:** acclaimed and popular Serafina restaurant downstairs; surprisingly quiet for Times Square location; good turndown service. **Cons:** decor makes the rooms a little dated; service is inconsistent; water pressure is lacking. *Rooms from: $275 ✉ 224 W. 49th St., between Broadway and 8th Ave., Midtown West ☎ 212/246–5252, 877/846–3692 🌐 www.thetimeny.com 164 rooms, 29 suites No meals Ⓜ 1 to 50th St.; C, E to 50th St. ✢ 4:C3*

$$ HOTEL **W Times Square.** Although it opened back in 2001, the W Times Square still stands out in the the craziness of Times Square, thanks to its iconic, 57-story exterior—and if you want to be in the thick of the action, this is a fun place to stay. **Pros:** bustling nightlife and happy-hour scene; sleek rooms. **Cons:** if you want quiet, head elsewhere; no bathtubs in the smaller rooms. *Rooms from: $359 ✉ 1567 Broadway, at 47th St., Midtown West ☎ 212/930–7400, 877/946–8357 🌐 www.whotels.com 453 rooms, 56 suites No meals Ⓜ 1, 2, 3, 7, N, Q, R, S to Times Sq.–42nd St. ✢ 4:C3*

$$ HOTEL **Warwick.** This grande dame was built by William Randolph Hearst in 1926 for his mistress, Hollywood actress Marion Davies, and it's hosted many from Tinseltown since then including Cary Grant in the Presidential Suite for 12 years. **Pros:** excellent restaurant and bar; historic property; spacious suites. **Cons:** some rooms could use a refresh; no a/c in the hallways. *Rooms from: $299 ✉ 65 W. 54th St., at 6th Ave., Midtown West ☎ 212/247–2700, 800/223–4099 🌐 www.warwickhotelny.com 359 rooms, 67 suites No meals Ⓜ E, M to 57th St.; N, Q, R to 57th St.–7th Ave. ✢ 4:D2*

17

$ HOTEL FAMILY **Wellington Hotel.** A few blocks south of Central Park and Columbus Circle, the Wellington is a good base for visitors who want to see the sights in Midtown and the Upper West Side. **Pros:** central location; chipper, helpful staff; good for big families. **Cons:** dark, often small bathrooms; limited breakfast options. *Rooms from: $275 ✉ 871 7th Ave., at 55th St., Midtown West ☎ 212/247–3900, 800/652–1212 🌐 www.wellingtonhotel.com 515 rooms, 85 suites No meals Ⓜ N, Q, R to 57th St. ✢ 4:C2*

$$ HOTEL **Westin New York at Times Square.** This giant Midtown hotel has all the amenities and service you would expect from a reliable brand, at fairly reasonable prices, though without much style. **Pros:** central for midtown attractions; big rooms; great gym. **Cons:** congested area near Port Authority; small bathroom sinks; some rooms need to be refreshed. *Rooms from: $319 ✉ 270 W. 43rd St., at 8th Ave., Midtown West ☎ 212/201–2700, 866/837–4183 🌐 www.westinny.com 834 rooms, 29 suites No meals Ⓜ A, C, E to 42nd St.–Port Authority. ✢ 4:B4*

$ HOTEL Fodor's Choice ★ **Yotel.** Look beyond the gimmicks (a luggage-storing robot, the futuristic white design scheme) of this Midtown West hotel and you'll discover one of New York's best-run, most functional lodgings, though note that it's pretty far west. **Pros:** great value; large common outdoor space; access to West Side piers and Javits Center. **Cons:** rooms may be small for some; limited luggage storage and hanging space; 10th Avenue may be stretching "Times Square" a bit far for some. *Rooms from:*

$149 ✉ 570 10th Ave., at 42nd St., Midtown West ☎ 646/449–7700 🌐 www.yotel.com 647 rooms, 22 suites 🍽 Breakfast Ⓜ A, C, E to 42nd St. ✣ 4:A4.

UPPER EAST SIDE

$$$$ HOTEL Fodor's Choice ★ **The Carlyle, A Rosewood Hotel.** On the well-heeled corner of Madison Avenue and 76th Street, the Carlyle's fusion of venerable elegance and Manhattan swank calls for the aplomb of entering a Chanel boutique: walk in chin-high, wallet out, and ready to be impressed. **Pros:** perhaps NYC's best Central Park views; refined service; delightful array of dining and bar options; chic shopping in the neighborhood; great bathtubs. **Cons:** removed from touristy Manhattan; stuffy vibe may not work for families; every room is different, limiting consistency. *$ Rooms from: $800 ✉ 35 E. 76th St., between Madison and Park Aves., Upper East Side ☎ 212/744–1600 🌐 www.thecarlyle.com 124 rooms, 64 suites 🍽 No meals Ⓜ 6 to 77th St. ✣ 5:F3*

$ HOTEL **The Franklin.** The best luxury boutique hotel north of 57th Street, the Franklin, in a nine-story town house, is a gem nestled in a decidedly residential neighborhood. **Pros:** neighborhood-y location; free Wi-Fi and generous breakfast; pet-friendly. **Cons:** far from many tourist sights except Museum Mile; small rooms. *$ Rooms from: $279 ✉ 164 E. 87th St., between Lexington and 3rd Aves., Upper East Side ☎ 212/369–1000, 800/607–4009 🌐 www.franklinhotel.com 50 rooms 🍽 Breakfast Ⓜ 4, 5, 6 to 86th St. ✣ 6:G6*

$$$$ HOTEL **Hôtel Plaza Athénée.** Positioned unobtrusively by Central Park on the Upper East Side, the Plaza Athénée (now related in name only to its Parisian cousin) makes stellar service a priority, with a personal sit-down check-in off to the side of the lobby, and extravagant in-room dining service with an old-world feel: white tablecloths, candles, and flowers are part of the deal. **Pros:** discerning service; fabulous hotel bar. **Cons:** lobby can feel dark; Wi-Fi costs extra; expensive. *$ Rooms from: $895 ✉ 37 E. 64th St., at Madison Ave., Upper East Side ☎ 212/734–9100, 212/606–4600 🌐 www.plaza-athenee.com 117 rooms, 25 suites 🍽 No meals Ⓜ 6 to 68th St.–Hunter College ✣ 5:F5.*

$$$ HOTEL FAMILY **Hotel Wales.** A favorite for in-the-know travelers, the Wales is pleasant if unassuming in a sedate neighbhorhood. **Pros:** on-site fitness facilities; great neighborhood feel; roof garden. **Cons:** standard rooms are tight on space; if seeking nightlife go elsewhere. *$ Rooms from: $395 ✉ 1295 Madison Ave., between 92nd and 93rd Sts., Upper East Side ☎ 212/876–6000, 212/876–6000 🌐 www.hotelwalesnyc.com 46 rooms, 43 suites 🍽 No meals Ⓜ 4, 5, 6 to 86th St. ✣ 6:F5*

$$$$ HOTEL **The Lowell.** This old-money refuge was built as an upscale apartment hotel in the 1920s and it still delivers genteel sophistication and pampering service in an unbeatable location. **Pros:** great location; service with a personal touch; charming decor. **Cons:** cramped lobby; expensive. *$ Rooms from: $775 ✉ 28 E. 63rd St., between Madison and Park Aves., Upper East Side ☎ 212/838–1400, 800/221–4444 🌐 www.lowellhotel.com 23 rooms, 49 suites 🍽 No meals Ⓜ 4, 5, 6 to 59th St.; N, Q, R to Lexington Ave./59th St.; F to Lexington Ave./63rd St. ✣ 5:F6*

$$$$ HOTEL Fodor's Choice ★ **The Mark.** If you took every Upper East Side real estate fantasy and condensed it into a modern hotel, you'd come up with the Mark, the perfect representation of uptown panache infused with a healthy dose of downtown chic. **Pros:** hip design; cavernous closet space; great service; scene-making restaurant and bar. **Cons:** expensive; limited budget dining options in neighborhood. *Rooms from: $600 ✉ 25 E. 77th St., at Madison Ave., Upper East Side ☎ 212/744–4300 www.themarkhotel.com 100 rooms, 50 suites No meals* Ⓜ *6 to 77th St. ✣ 5:F2*

UPPER WEST SIDE

$$ HOTEL **The Empire Hotel.** In a prime Upper West Side spot, the sophisticated Empire Hotel attracts locals for views from the rooftop pool and lounge area underneath the hotel's iconic red neon sign, while guests appreciate the rooms, which are a comfortable and chic escape from the bustle of the city. **Pros:** great location next to Lincoln Center and blocks from Central Park; beautiful rooftop pool and bar; nice turndown service. **Cons:** rooftop bar brings foot traffic through hotel lobby, plus noise to some rooms; some rooms could use a refresh; bathrooms are nicely designed but tiny; pool is quite small. *Rooms from: $329 ✉ 44 W. 63rd St., at Columbus Ave., Upper West Side ☎ 212/265–7400 www.empirehotelnyc.com 370 rooms, 50 suites No meals* Ⓜ *1, A, B, C to 59th St.–Columbus Circle ✣ 5:C5.*

$$ HOTEL **The Excelsior Hotel.** Directly across the street from the American Museum of Natural History, this well-kept, old-school spot is comfortable but has occasionally inconsistent staff. **Pros:** excellent neighborhoody Upper West Side location near Central Park; near foodie mecca Zabar's and popular burger joint Shake Shack; tranquil environment. **Cons:** spotty front-desk staff; rooms are inconsistent; Wi-Fi is not free. *Rooms from: $329 ✉ 45 W. 81st St., between Central Park W and Columbus Ave., Upper West Side ☎ 212/362–9200 www.excelsiorhotelny.com 118 rooms, 80 suites No meals* Ⓜ *B, C to 81st St.–Museum of Natural History. ✣ 5:C2*

$ HOTEL **Hotel Beacon.** A neighborhood favorite for a reason, the Upper West Side's best buy for the price is three blocks from Central Park, 10 blocks from Lincoln Center, and footsteps from the neighborhood's best gourmet grocery stores—Zabar's, Fairway, and Citarella. **Pros:** kitchenettes in all rooms; heart of UWS location; affordable; great service. **Cons:** rooms emphasize comfort over style; gym passes to local Equinox $20/day per guest. *Rooms from: $245 ✉ 2130 Broadway, at 75th St., Upper West Side ☎ 212/787–1100, 800/572–4969 www.beaconhotel.com 134 rooms, 133 suites No meals* Ⓜ *1, 2, 3 to 72nd St. ✣ 5:A3*

$$ HOTEL **The Lucerne.** Service is the strong suit at this landmark-façaded hotel, whose exterior has more pizzazz than the predictable guest rooms decorated with dark-wood reproduction furniture and chintzy bedspreads. **Pros:** free Wi-Fi; clean; great gym; close to Central Park. **Cons:** inconsistent room size; some guests report uncomfortable pillows. *Rooms from: $309 ✉ 201 W. 79th St., at Amsterdam Ave., Upper West Side ☎ 212/875–1000, 800/492–8122 www.thelucernehotel.com 163 rooms, 37 suites No meals* Ⓜ *1 to 79th St. ✣ 5:A2*

CLOSE UP

Lodging Alternatives

APARTMENT RENTALS VS. SUITE HOTELS

For your trip to New York, you may want a little more space than the city's typically tiny hotel rooms provide. Some travelers consider apartment rentals, but there are many good reasons to stick to hotel suites instead. Why? First, apartment rentals of less than 30 days are now—with some very limited exceptions—illegal in New York City. Furthermore, apartment-rental scams are prevalent. In some published reports, potential guests have arrived to find that the apartment they rented does not exist, or that they are paying for an illegal sublet. In some cases, travelers have lost their deposit money, or their prepaid rent (note: never wire money to an individual's account).

There are a few reputable providers of short-term rentals,. But many Fodorites have turned to suite hotels and bed-and-breakfasts with apartmentlike accommodations to guard themselves from possible scams. We've noted some of their most enthusiastic recommendations.

Local rental agencies that arrange rentals of furnished apartments:

Abode Limited ☎ *800/835–8880, 212/472–2000* 🌐 *www.abodenyc.com.*

Manhattan Getaways ☎ *212/956–2010* 🌐 *www.manhattangetaways.com.*

Suite suggestions from **Fodor's Forums** (🌐 *www.fodors.com/forums*):

"For a week or less, there's no need to risk being scammed or renting something illegal by renting a private apt. There are *loads* of suite hotels and B&Bs at all price levels that will provide the space and convenience of an apartment, many with the amenities of a hotel including the ability to be able to read reviews of them before you book and know what you're getting. **Affinia** (🌐 *www.Affinia.com*) is a group of seven suite hotels at various prices that's well regarded. **Milburn Hotel** (🌐 *www.milburnhotel.com*) and the **Salisbury Hotel** (🌐 *www.nycsalisbury.com*) are some of the more popular independent budget options." —mclaurie

BED-AND-BREAKFASTS

B&Bs booked through a service may be either hosted (you're the guest in someone's quarters) or unhosted (you have full use of someone's vacated apartment, including kitchen privileges). Reservation services:

Bed-and-Breakfast Network of New York ✉ *134 W. 32nd St., Suite 602, between 6th and 7th Aves.* ☎ *212/645–8134, 888/707–4626* 🌐 *www.bedandbreakfastnetwork.com.*

City Lights Bed-and-Breakfast ☎ *212/737–7049* 🌐 *www.citylightsbedandbreakfast.com.*

"**West Eleventh** (🌐 *www.west-eleventh.com*) and **Abingdon Guest House** (🌐 *www.abingdonguesthouse.com*) are two of many B&Bs in the village with some charm, but are only good for two people." —mclaurie

"Also try **B&B Manhattan** (🌐 *www.bandbmanhattan.com*) which has very nice studio and 1-bed apartments in Chelsea and GV. A friend stayed with them last year and liked it a lot." —tomassocroccante

$ HOTEL **On the Ave Hotel.** At this tranquil Upper West Side property just off Broadway, decor is tasteful and modern and service is purposeful and professional. **Pros:** great dining options; excellent value. **Cons:** small charges add up; location not ideal for all NYC visitors. *Rooms from: $279 ✉ 2178 Broadway, at 77th St., Upper West Side ☎ 800/509–7598, 212/362–1100 www.ontheave-nyc.com 282 rooms, 23 suites No meals Ⓜ 1 to 79th St. ✣ 5:A3*

$$$$ HOTEL **Trump International Hotel and Towers.** This iconic New York property with incomparable views of Central Park has interior design and decor—much conceived with the help of the Donald's equally famous daughter, Ivanka—in line with the rest of the hotel's stellar standards for personalized service and attention to detail. **Pros:** fine service; stellar views; discerning treatment. **Cons:** expensive. *Rooms from: $995 ✉ 1 Central Park W, between 59th and 60th Sts., Upper West Side ☎ 212/299–1000, 888/448–7867 www.trumpintl.com 33 rooms, 143 suites No meals Ⓜ 1, A, B, C, D to 59th St.–Columbus Circle ✣ 5:C6.*

HARLEM

$ HOTEL **Aloft Harlem.** A reasonably priced option in an increasingly popular area of Harlem (Marcus Samuelsson's hot Red Rooster restaurant is within walking distance), this branch of the Aloft chain delivers with cheerful service and a fun atmosphere, once you get past the confusing front entrance. **Pros:** good room size for the price; convenient to subways, ever-increasing local shopping, and dining options. **Cons:** rooms have minimal space for hanging clothes; rooms get some street noise. *Rooms from: $199 ✉ 2296 Frederick Douglass Blvd., between 124th and 125th Sts., Harlem ☎ 212/749–4000 www.alofthariem.com 124 rooms No meals Ⓜ A, B, C, D to 125th St. ✣ 6:C1.*

BROOKLYN

DOWNTOWN BROOKLYN

$$ HOTEL FAMILY Fodor's Choice ★ **Aloft New York Brooklyn.** A funky boutique in the heart of downtown Brooklyn, the Aloft is a lively yet comfortable space, with world music pumping in the lobby lounge and the quality beds Starwood properties are known for in the relatively spacious rooms upstairs. **Pros:** Pet- and family-friendly; good subway access; fab rooftop bar; reasonable prices; guests have access to Sheraton's indoor swimming pool and room service. **Cons:** rumored construction on back side of hotel could mean noisy construction in years to come. *Rooms from: $359 ✉ 216 Duffield St., between Wiloughby St. and Fulton Mall, Downtown Brooklyn ☎ 718/256–3833 www.alofthotel.com 170 rooms, 6 suites No meals Ⓜ 2, 3 to Hoyt St.; A, C, F to Jay St.–Metrotech ✣ 7:B4.*

$$ HOTEL **New York Marriott at the Brooklyn Bridge.** You'll find, like many New Yorkers before you, that one virtue of staying in Brooklyn is all the extra space; what Manhattan hotel has room for an Olympic-length lap pool, an 1,100-car garage, and even a dedicated kosher kitchen? **Pros:** near some of New York's hipper neighborhoods; traditional-style full-service hotel, stylish rooms. **Cons:** on a busy street in downtown Brooklyn. *Rooms from: $369 ✉ 333 Adams St., between Johnson*

and Willoughby Sts., Downtown Brooklyn ☎ *718/246–7000* 🌐 *www.marriott.com/nycbk* 638 *rooms, 28 suites* 🍽 *No meals* Ⓜ *2, 3, 4, 5 to Borough Hall* ✥ *7:B4.*

COBBLE HILL

$ HOTEL **NU Hotel Brooklyn.** The hip-yet-affordable NU, on one of Brooklyn's main nightlife and shopping streets, is perfect for visitors seeking a manageable taste of outer-borough New York—and the staff is eager to highlight the neighborhood's charms. **Pros:** great Brooklyn launching pad; knowledgeable staff; fitness center open 24 hours. **Cons:** subway or cab ride to anything in Manhattan; bar area can be a little too quiet; limited in-room amenities. $ *Rooms from: $269* ✉ *85 Smith St., Cobble Hill* ☎ *718/852–8585* 🌐 *www.nuhotelbrooklyn.com* *87 rooms, 6 suites* 🍽 *Breakfast* Ⓜ *F to Bergen St.; A, C, G to Hoyt–Schermerhorn Sts.* ✥ *7:B4*

WILLIAMSBURG

$ HOTEL **Hotel Le Jolie.** This no-frills favorite has excellent service and is convenient not only to the arts, culture, and dining scenes that Williamsburg has become known for—but also to several subway lines and the Bronx-Queens Expressway, in case you want to get into the city. **Pros:** good value; free parking on a first-come, first-served basis; convenient part of Brooklyn. **Cons:** location next to highway can mean noise; can feel remote even though convenient to subways. $ *Rooms from: $199* ✉ *235 Meeker Ave., between Lorimer and Union Aves., Williamsburg* ☎ *718/625–2100* 🌐 *www.hotellejolie.com* *52 rooms, 2 suites* 🍽 *Breakfast* Ⓜ *L to Lorimer* ✥ *7:E1.*

$$ HOTEL **King & Grove Williamsburg.** With funky design details like an underfoot, glass-encased river in the lobby (plus a fireplace), and a plum location overlooking Brooklyn's McCarren Park, King & Grove Williamsburg succeeds in scenester savvy. **Pros:** high hip factor; in-house restaurant/bar, complimentary coffee/tea/water on request; close to main thoroughfare Bedford Avenue. **Cons:** potential for noise from concerts in McCarren Park; some room details like lighting controls could be more user-friendly. $ *Rooms from: $315* ✉ *160 N. 12th St., between Bedford Ave. and Berry St., Williamsburg* ☎ *718/218–7500* 🌐 *www.kingandgrove.com* *60 rooms, 4 suites* 🍽 *No meals* Ⓜ *L to Bedford* ✥ *7:E1.*

$$ HOTEL Fodor's Choice ★ **Wythe Hotel.** An old factory on the Brooklyn waterfront has found new life as the Wythe Hotel, one of the hottest hotels opening in 2012 and with just cause—the Manhattan skyline views are stunning. **Pros:** excellent entry into fun neighborhood; local Brooklyn-based design and environmentally friendly products; fabulous Manhattan skyline views from rooms or rooftop bar; destination-worthy restaurant with wood-fired stove. **Cons:** somewhat isolated from the subway; no room service. $ *Rooms from: $320* ✉ *80 Wythe Ave., at N. 11th St., Williamsburg* ☎ *718/460–8001* 🌐 *www.wythehotel.com* *68 rooms, 4 suites* 🍽 *No meals* Ⓜ *L to Lorimer* ✥ *7:D1.*

18

SHOPPING

The Big Apple is one of the best shopping destinations in the world, rivaled perhaps only by London, Paris, and Tokyo. Its compact size, convenient subway system, and plentiful cabs (unless it's raining) make it easy to navigate with plenty of bags in tow. But what it really comes down to is the staggering number and variety of stores. If you can't find it in New York, it probably doesn't exist.

Updated by Christina Valhouli

If you like elegant flagships and money is no object, head to Midtown, where you'll find international megabrands like Louis Vuitton, Yves Saint Laurent, and Gucci, as well as famed department stores Bergdorf Goodman and Barneys. Nearby Madison Avenue offers couture from Carolina Herrera and Vera Wang, and 5th Avenue is lined with famous jewelry stores like Tiffany, Van Cleef & Arpels, and Harry Winston. This is also the neighborhood to indulge in bespoke goods, such as ordering handmade shoes from John Lobb. If you like designer pieces but can't afford them, don't despair—there are plenty of upscale consignment shops dotted around the city where you can find last season's Chanel suit or a vintage YSL jacket.

The small, independent shops that once lined SoHo have largely been swallowed up by J. Crew and Uniqlo, but if you want to hit the chains, this is a great place to do it, since SoHo also provides high-quality people-watching and superb lunches. If you're craving some of SoHo's artistic spirit, don't discount the street vendors' stalls, which sell handmade jewelry and simple cotton dresses. You never know—you might buy something from a soon-to-be-famous designer.

The East Village and Lower East Side are hotbeds of creativity and quirky coolness, with little boutiques selling everything from retro furniture to industrial-inspired jewelry tucked among bars and tenement apartments. The Meatpacking District is another great shopping destination, where you'll find chic stores like Diane Von Furstenberg and Catherine Malandrino.

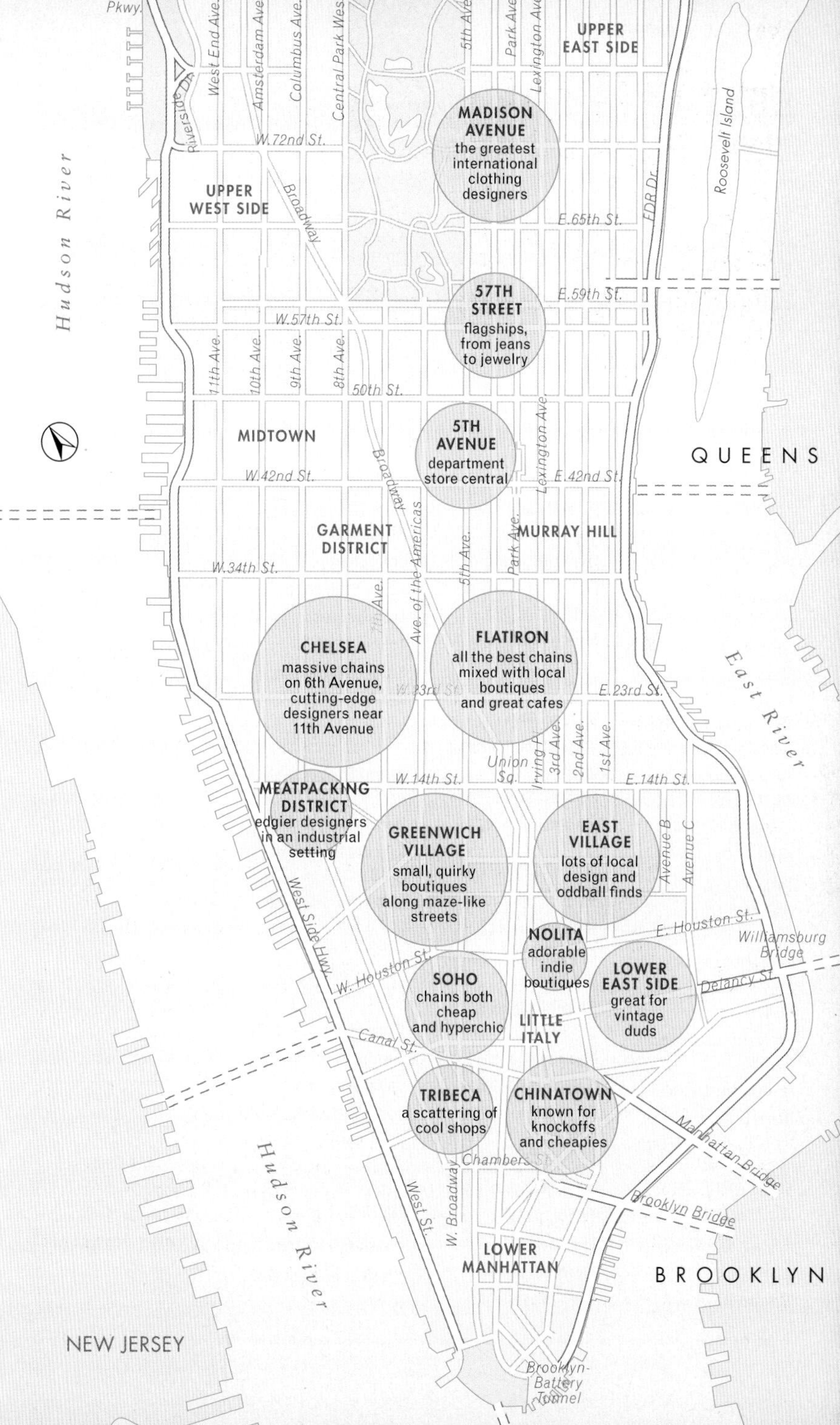

Henry Hudson Pkwy.
West End Ave.
Amsterdam Ave.
Columbus Ave.
Central Park West
5th Ave.
Park Ave.
Lexington Ave.
UPPER EAST SIDE
Riverside Dr.
W.72nd St.
MADISON AVENUE
the greatest international clothing designers
Roosevelt Island
Hudson River
UPPER WEST SIDE
Broadway
FDR Dr.
E.65th St.
57TH STREET
flagships, from jeans to jewelry
E.59th St.
W.57th St.
11th Ave.
10th Ave.
9th Ave.
8th Ave.
50th St.
MIDTOWN
5TH AVENUE
department store central
Lexington Ave.
QUEENS
W.42nd St.
E.42nd St.
GARMENT DISTRICT
Ave. of the Americas
5th Ave.
Park Ave.
MURRAY HILL
W.34th St.
7th Ave.
CHELSEA
massive chains on 6th Avenue, cutting-edge designers near 11th Avenue
FLATIRON
all the best chains mixed with local boutiques and great cafes
W.23rd St.
E.23rd St.
East River
Union Sq.
Irving Pl.
3rd Ave.
2nd Ave.
1st Ave.
W.14th St.
E.14th St.
MEATPACKING DISTRICT
edgier designers in an industrial setting
GREENWICH VILLAGE
small, quirky boutiques along maze-like streets
EAST VILLAGE
lots of local design and oddball finds
Avenue B
Avenue C
West Side Hwy.
E. Houston St.
NOLITA
adorable indie boutiques
Williamsburg Bridge
W. Houston St.
SOHO
chains both cheap and hyperchic
LOWER EAST SIDE
great for vintage duds
Delancy St.
LITTLE ITALY
Canal St.
TRIBECA
a scattering of cool shops
CHINATOWN
known for knockoffs and cheapies
Manhattan Bridge
Chambers St.
Hudson River
West St.
W. Broadway
Brooklyn Bridge
LOWER MANHATTAN
BROOKLYN
NEW JERSEY
Brooklyn-Battery Tunnel

BEST BETS FOR NYC SHOPPING

With thousands of shops to choose from, how will you decide where to go? Below you'll find some of Fodor's writers and editors favorites to help you get started. You can also search by category within each neighborhood for noteworthy shops, and peruse the spotlights about specific neighborhoods.

Fodor's Choice ★

ABC Carpet & Home, p. 424
Agent Provocateur, p. 400
Alexis Bittar, p. 406
Bloomingdale's, p. 429
Diane von Furstenberg, p. 422
FAO Schwarz Fifth Avenue, p. 432
Fishs Eddy, p. 425
Flight 001, p. 419
Intermix, p. 401
Jacques Torres Chocolates, p. 405
Kidrobot, p. 408
La Petite Coquette, p. 416
McNally Jackson, p. 409
The Strand, p. 426
Tani, p. 446
Tiffany & Co., p. 430

BEST CHILDREN'S CLOTHING

A Time for Children, p. 445
Bonpoint, p. 438
Bundle, p. 397
Giggle, p. 397
Les Petits Chapelais, p. 398
Shoofly, p. 395
Space Kiddets, p. 424

BEST DENIM

3X1, p. 399
7 for all Mankind, p. 399
Earnest Sewn, p. TK
Madewell, p. 424

BEST DEPARTMENT STORES

Barneys, p. 442
Bergdorf Goodman, p. 434
Bloomingdale's, p. 429
Macy's, p. 435
Saks Fifth Avenue, p. 429

BEST HANDBAGS

Devi Kroell, p. 444
Fendi, p. 431
Furla, p. 431
Hermès, p. 444
High Way, p. 411
Kate Spade, p. 408
Khirma Eliazov, p. 419
Longchamp, p. 408
Louis Vuitton, p. 431
Lulu Guiness, p. 420
Token, p. 412
Stuart Weitzman, p. 432

BEST LINGERIE

Agent Provocateur, p. 400
Bra Smyth, p. 439
Kiki di Montparnasse, p. 401
La Petite Coquette, p. 416

BEST MEN'S BOUTIQUES

Duncan Quinn, p. 409
Dunhill, p. 428
Jay Kos, p. 410
John Varvatos, p. 413
Paul Smith, p. 403
Reiss, p. 403

BEST SHOES

Camper, p. 407
Charlotte Olympia, p. 444
Christian Louboutin, p. 444
Jimmy Choo, p. 444
John Fluevog Shoes, p. 411
John Lobb, p. 445
Leffot, p. 419
Matt Bernson, p. 396
Tod's, p. 445

BEST SOUVENIRS

City Store, p. 395
New York City Transit Museum Gift Shop, p. 429

BEST TOY STORES

American Girl Place, p. 432
Dinosaur Hill, p. 415
FAO Schwarz, p. 432
Kidrobot, p. 408

BEST VINTAGE SHOPS

INA, p. 410
Frock, p. 410
New York Vintage, p. 420
Resurrection, p. 411
What Goes Around Comes Around, p. 405

BEST WOMEN'S BOUTIQUES

Alexander Wang, p. 400
Anna Sui, p. 400
Comptoir des Cotonniers, p. 400

Creatures of Comfort, p. 409
Intermix, p. 401
Isabel Marant, p. 401
Kate Spade, p. 408
Kirna Zabête, p. 402
Marni, p. 402
Milly, p. 441
Mint, p. 446
Miu Miu, p. 402
Nanette Lepore, p. 410
Opening Ceremony, p. 402
Reiss, p. 403
Tory Burch, p. 441
UNIQLO, p. 434

BEST FOR BARGAINS

Century 21, p. 394
Joe Fresh, p. 434
Loehmann's, p. 420
Pearl River Mart, p. 397
Topshop, p. 404
UNIQLO, p. 434
Zara, p. 434

BEST BEAUTY AND PERFUME STORES

Aedes De Venustas, p. 417
C.O. Bigelow, p. 416
Fresh, p. 426
Kiehl's since 1851, p. 412
Lafco NY/Santa Maria Novella, p. 409
MiN, p. 397

BEST BOOKSTORES

Books of Wonder, p. 420
Idlewild, p. 423
McNally Jackson, p. 409
Shakespeare & Co. Booksellers, p. 437
The Strand, p. 426

BEST CHOCOLATE

Jacques Torres Chocolate Haven, p. 405
La Maison du Chocolat, p. 443
MarieBelle, p. 405
Vosges Haut-Chocolat, p. 405

BEST-DESIGNED STORES

Alexander Wang, p. 400
Issey Miyake, p. 396
Polo Ralph Lauren, p. 441
Prada, p. 403

BEST FOR HOME DECOR

ABC Carpet & Home, p. 424
Jonathan Adler, p. 443
Kiosk, p. 406
Las Venus, pg. 416
Marimekko, p. 425
Matter, p. 406

BEST JEWELRY

Alexis Bittar, p. 406
Erica Weiner, p. 411
Fragments, p. 407
Me & Ro, p. 411
Swarovski Crystallized, p. 407
Versani, p. 407

BEST MUSEUM SHOPS

Cooper-Hewitt, National Design Museum, p. 443
Metropolitan Museum of Art Shop, p. 443
Museum of Arts and Design, p. 436
Museum of the City of New York, p. 444
Museum of Modern Art Design and Book Store, p. 436
Neue Gallery, p. 444
New York Transit Museum Gift Shop, p. 429

BEST MUSIC STORES

Jazz Record Center, p. 421
Other Music, p. 415

CLOSE UP

Deals and Steals

Everyone loves a bargain—including a temporary New Yorker. Scoring a good deal is a rite of passage, and the city offers everything from low-cost department stores like Century 21 to hawkers of pseudo-Rolex watches and Kate Spade bags stationed at street corners and in Canal Street stalls. And then there are the sample sales.

If a seasonal sale makes New Yorkers' eyes gleam, a sample sale throws shoppers into a frenzy. With so many designer flagships and corporate headquarters in town, merchandise fallout periodically leads to tremendous deals. Although technically the term sample sale refers to stock that's a sample design, a show model, a leftover, or is already discounted, the term is now also used for sales of current-season goods. Location adds a bit of an illicit thrill to the event: sales are held in hotels, warehouses, offices, or loft spaces, where items both incredible and unfortunate jam a motley assortment of racks, tables, and bins. Generally, there is a makeshift communal dressing room, but mirrors are scarce, so veteran sample-sale shoppers come prepared for wriggling in the aisles; some wear tank tops with tights or leggings for modest quick changes. Two rules of thumb: grab first and inspect later, and call in advance to find out what methods of payment are accepted. One of the ultimate experiences is the Barneys Warehouse Sale, held in February and August in Chelsea. Other luscious sales range from the Vera Wang bridal-gown sale (early winter) to Dwell Studio (spring and late fall).

How to find out about these events? The level of publicity and regularity of sales vary. The print and online versions of *New York* magazine are always worth checking for sample sale tip-offs, as are regular bulletins on Racked (🌐 *racked.com*) and Daily Candy (🌐 *www.dailycandy.com*). If you're interested in specific designers, call their shops and inquire—you may get lucky.

LOWER MANHATTAN AND TRIBECA

FINANCIAL DISTRICT

Although it is known primarily as the home of Wall Street, Lower Manhattan—especially TriBeCa—is a hotbed for interesting boutiques and shopping icons. Come here for downtown fixtures, including Century 21 and J&R, the electronics megastore.

BARGAIN SHOPPING

Fodor's Choice ★ **Century 21.** For many New Yorkers this downtown fixture—right across the street from the former World Trade Center site—remains the mother lode of discount shopping. Four floors are crammed with everything from Marc Jacobs shoes and half-price cashmere sweaters to Donna Karan sheets, though you'll have to sift through racks and fight the crowds to find the gems. Best bets for men are shoes and designer briefs; the full floor of designer women's wear can yield some dazzling finds, such as a Calvin Klein leather trench coat for less than $600. Don't miss the children's section, either, for brands like Ralph Lauren and Ed Hardy. ■ **TIP→ Since lines for the communal dressing rooms** can be prohibitively long, do what the locals do: wear leggings and change discreetly in the aisles. ✉ *22 Cortlandt St., between Broadway and Church St., TiBeCa* ☎ *212/227–9092* 🌐 *www.c21stores.com* Ⓜ *R to Cortlandt St.* ✉ *1972 Broadway, between 66th and 67th Sts., Upper West Side* ☎ *212/518 2121* 🌐 *www.c21stores.com/lincoln-square*

WORD OF MOUTH

"Century 21 is great over the holidays, lots of gifty stuff and holiday decorations for home. I am often found downstairs in the home section of the store looking for tabletop [stuff]. You can find some really interesting accessories there." —travelbuff

CAMERAS AND ELECTRONICS

J&R. Just south of City Hall, J&R is one of the city's most competitively priced one-stop electronics outlets, with an enormous selection of video equipment, cameras, computers, and stereos. The hands-on staff is super-knowledgeable; many of them are A/V wizards who've worked here since the early 1990s. The store occupies an entire city block on Park Row: home-office supplies are at No. 1, computers at No. 15, small appliances at No. 27. Got kids? Don't miss J&R Jr. at 1 Ann Street which stocks all kinds of kids' gear and also hosts story time, concerts, and events. ✉ *23 Park Row, between Beekman and Ann Sts., Financial District* ☎ *212/238–9000* Ⓜ *4, 5, 6 to Brooklyn Bridge–City Hall.*

CLOTHING

Abercrombie & Fitch. This brand is known for its casual preppy clothes for men, women, and kids—but brace yourself for the thumping club music and dim lighting. ✉ *199 Water St.* ☎ *212/809–9000* 🌐 *www.abercrombie.com* Ⓜ *2, 3 to Fulton St.* ✉ *720 Fifth Ave., Midtown East* ☎ *212/306–0936* .

18

GIFTS AND SOUVENIRS

City Store. The official store of NYC sells anything and everything having to do with the city, from books and pamphlets to fun gift ideas. Pick up NYPD T-shirts, taxicab medallions, garbage truck toys, and dishtowels silk-screened with the skyline. The store shuts at 5 pm on weekdays and is closed weekends. ✉ *1 Centre St., at Chambers St., Financial District* ☎ *212/669–8246* 🌐 *a856-citystore.nyc.gov* Ⓜ *4, 5, 6 to Brooklyn Bridge–City Hall..*

TRIBECA

Known for its multimillion dollar lofts and Hollywood residents (don't be surprised if you see Justin Timberlake or Naomi Watts), TriBeCa is home to some of the most interesting boutiques in the city. Although there aren't many stores here, specialty shops such as Korin or J. Crew Men's Shop at the Liquor Store are worth a visit.

CHILDREN'S CLOTHING

Shoofly. Children's shoes and accessories imported from all over the world are the name of the game here. Choose from Mary Janes, trendy sneakers, and motorcycle boots along with pom-pom hats, brightly patterned socks, eclectic toys, and jewelry. ✉ *42 Hudson St., between Thomas and Duane Sts., TriBeCa* ☎ *212/406–3270* 🌐 *www.shooflynyc.com* Ⓜ *1 to Franklin St.*

CLOTHING

Fodor's Choice ★ **Issey Miyake.** This flagship, designed by Frank Gehry, attracts a non-fashion crowd who come just to gawp at his undulating 25-foot high titanium sculpture, *The Tornado*. Miyake's signature style offers clothes that are sleek and slim-fitting, and made from polyester or ultrahigh-tech textiles. This flagship carries the entire runway collection, as well as Pleats Please and Issey Miyake Fete. ✉ *119 Hudson St., at N. Moore St., TriBeCa* ☎ *212/226–0100* 🌐 *www.tribecaisseymiyake.com* Ⓜ *1 to Franklin St.*

J.Crew Men's Shop at the Liquor Store. It would be easy to walk right past this place and think it's a bar rather than an outpost of J.Crew for men, because it's filled with manly knickknacks like old Jack Kerouac books and vintage photographs. Some of the best finds are the limited-edition suits and cashmere sweaters, as well as non–J.Crew items like Barbour jackets and vintage Timex watches. ✉ *235 W. Broadway, at White St., TriBeCa* ☎ *212/226–5476* 🌐 *www.jcrew.com* Ⓜ *1 to Franklin St.*

HOME DECOR

Korin. If you're serious about cooking, head to this specialty knife store in TriBeCa. Previously only open to the trade, it is one of the best places to shop for top-quality knives imported from Japan. ✉ *57 Warren St., between W. Broadway and Church St., TriBeCa* ☎ *212/587–7021* 🌐 *www.korin.com* Ⓜ *1, 2, 3 to Chambers St.*

SHOES

Matt Bernson. Thankfully, the footwear at designer Matt Bernson's new TriBeCa store is both beautiful and blister-proof. Though the native New Yorker's comfy, affordable sandals are staples at Bergdorf's, Scoop and Madewell, this shop is his first stand-alone venture. With the help of his father, Bernson renovated the 1820s carriage house he now calls a showroom, giving it an at-home feel with antique furniture he refurbished himself. (Another store fixture is the designer's dog, Abraham, who accompanies him to work every day.) ✉ *20 Harrison St., between Greenwich and Staple Sts., TriBeCa* ☎ *212/941–7634* 🌐 *www.mattbernson.com* Ⓜ *1 to Franklin St.*

SOHO AND NOLITA

SOHO

Head to SoHo for both the cheap and the hyperchic. The narrow sidewalks get very busy, especially on the weekends but this is a fun see-and-be-seen neighborhood. You'll see plenty of familiar high fashion names like Prada, Chanel, and Louis Vuitton and several less expensive chains, like Banana Republic and Sephora, which have made land grabs on Broadway. But you can still hit a few clothing and housewares boutiques you won't find elsewhere in this country. The hottest shopping area runs west from Broadway over to 6th Avenue, between West Houston and Grand Streets. Don't overlook a couple of streets east of Broadway: Crosby and Lafayette each have a handful of intriguing shops.

ANTIQUES AND COLLECTIBLES

Jacques Carcanagues Gallery. Crammed with goods from Japan to India, this SoHo gallery offers an eclectic array of objects, from pillboxes to 18th-century Burmese Buddhas and teak tables. ✉ *21 Greene St., between Grand and Canal Sts., SoHo* ☎ *212/925–8110* 🌐 *www.jacquescarcanagues.com* Ⓜ *J, N, Q, R, Z, 6 to Canal St.*

BARGAIN SHOPPING

Pearl River Mart. Whether you're looking for a decorative birdcage or a massive bag of jasmine rice, this mega–department store has everything Asian under one roof—at bargain prices. Browse through housewares like bamboo rice steamers and ceramic tea sets, or decorate your apartment with paper lanterns and porcelain stools. On the main floor, under a ceiling festooned with dragon kites and rice-paper parasols, you can buy kimono-style robes, pajamas, and embroidered satin slippers for the whole family. There's also a dry-goods section, where you can load up on ginger candy, jasmine tea, and cellophane noodles. ✉ *477 Broadway, between Broome and Grand Sts., SoHo* ☎ *212/431–4770* 🌐 *www.pearlriver.com* Ⓜ *J, N, Q, R, Z, 6 to Canal St.*

BEAUTY

MiN. If the selection of grooming products at Duane Reade doesn't cut it for you, head to MiN. This wood-paneled shop is decidedly male-friendly, with leather couches and exposed brick walls. Shop for unusual scents from Santa Maria Novella and L'Artisan Parfumeur, shaving products from Old Bond Street, or quirky items like mustache wax. ✉ *117 Crosby St., between Prince and Houston Sts., SoHo* ☎ *212/206–6366* Ⓜ *N, R to Prince St.*

18

BOOKS AND STATIONERY

Scholastic Store. Kids and the young at heart will be delighted by the whimsical design here, including an 11-foot orange dinosaur, a life-size Magic School Bus, and a massive Harry Potter. In addition to the thousands of books, kids can amuse themselves with games, toys, DVDs, computers, and arts-and-crafts workshops. It is so kid-friendly that parents will find a separate entrance just for strollers (at 130 Mercer Street). ✉ *557 Broadway, at Prince St., SoHo* ☎ *212/343–6166* 🌐 *www.scholastic.com/sohostore* Ⓜ *N, R to Prince St.*

CAMERAS AND ELECTRONICS

Apple Store. Branch location at 103 Prince Street, between Greene and Spring Streets. *See Midtown East for full review.*

CHILDREN'S CLOTHING

Bundle. This SoHo boutique goes above and beyond selling fashionable onesies by offering a concierge service. If you can't make it to the store to choose a gift, just email them and they'll reply with suggestions. Visit and choose adorable clothes from brands including Kissy Kissy, Baby CZ, and Tea. ✉ *128 Thompson St., between Prince and Houston Sts., SoHo* ☎ *212/982–9465* 🌐 *www.bundlenyc.com* Ⓜ *C, E to Spring St.*

Giggle. This high-end baby store is often crammed with stroller gridlock, but it stocks nearly everything a stylish parent (and baby) could ever need. The Giggle flagship carries all the gear and accessories to build a chic nursery, including Dwell bedding, plush toys, and funky

CLOSE UP

Street Vendor Shopping

If you're looking for original or reproduced artwork, the two areas to visit for street vendors are the stretch of 5th Avenue in front of the Metropolitan Museum of Art (roughly between 81st and 82nd Streets) and the SoHo area of West Broadway, between Houston and Broome Streets. In both areas you'll find dozens of artists selling original paintings, drawings, and photographs (some lovely, some lurid), as well as photo reproductions of famous New York scenes (the Chrysler building, South Street Seaport). Prices can start as low as $10, but be sure to haggle.

The east–west streets in SoHo are an excellent place to look for handmade crafts: Spring and Prince Streets, especially, are jammed with tables full of beaded jewelry, tooled leather belts, cotton sundresses, and homemade hats and purses. These streets are also great places to find deals on art books; several vendors have titles featuring the work of artists from Diego Rivera to Annie Leibovitz, all for about 20% less than you'd pay at a chain. It's best to know which books you want ahead of time, though; street vendors wrap theirs in clear plastic, and can get testy if you unwrap them but don't wind up buying.

Faux-designer handbags, sunglasses, wallets, and watches are some of the most popular street buys in town—but crackdowns on knockoffs have made them harder to find. The hub used to be Canal Street, roughly between Greene and Lafayette Streets, but many vendors there have swept their booths clean of fake Vuitton, Prada, Gucci, and Fendi merchandise. You might have better luck finding a Faux-lex near Herald Square or Madison Square Garden, and good old-fashioned fake handbags are still sold by isolated vendors around such shopping areas as Rockefeller Center and the stretch of lower 5th near Union Square. If you're looking for cheap luggage, skip Canal Street, as the bags there might not last beyond the flight home, and instead pick up a bargain at Marshalls, TJ Maxx, or Loehmann's.

kids' clothing. Basic gear such as highchairs and strollers are also sold, and staff will make sure parents know how to fold that complicated stroller before leaving the store. Additional Giggle outlets are located on the Upper West and Upper East Sides. ✉ *120 Wooster St., between Spring and Prince Sts., SoHo* ☎ *212/334–5817* 🌐 *www.giggle.com* Ⓜ N, *R to Prince St.*

J.Crew Crewcuts. If you don't like to dress your child in clothes that are too cute or painfully trendy, head to J.Crew's children's store, Crewcuts. Offering pint-size versions of the preppy classic clothes the brand is famous for, this shop is stocked with cords, cashmere sweaters, and blazers for the junior set. ✉ *99 Prince St., between Greene and Mercer Sts., SoHo* ☎ *212/343–1227* 🌐 *www.jcrew.com* Ⓜ *C, E to Spring St.* ✉ *1190 Madison Ave., Upper East Side* ☎ *212/348–9803*.

Les Petits Chapelais. Designed and made in France, these kids' clothes (from newborn up to age 12) are cute and stylish but also practical. Corduroy outfits have details like embroidered flowers and contrasting cuffs, and soft, fleecy jackets are reversible. There's also a line of sailor-inspired

Luxe shops line the streets of SoHo.

clothes. ✉ *86 Thompson St., between Spring and Prince Sts., SoHo* ☎ *212/625–1023* 🌐 *www.lespetitschapelaisnyc.com* Ⓜ *C, E to Spring St.*

CLOTHING

Fodor's Choice ★ **3X1.** In this huge denim shop, which doubles as a factory, customers can watch their bespoke jeans being made. The walls of the pristine white space are lined with more than 100 bolts of denim. After you select the perfect fabric, jeans are hand cut and sewn by the in-house seamstresses, who work in a glass-enclosed space. Shoppers can also buy off-the-rack jeans; unfinished hems are tailored on the spot (starting at $295). ✉ *15 Mercer St., SoHo* ☎ *212/391–6969* 🌐 *3x1.us* Ⓜ *J, N, Q, R, 6 to Canal St.*

7 for All Mankind. Whether you're hunting for super skinny, high-waisted, or boot-cut jeans in a dark or distressed finish, this temple to denim offers it all. The jeans are a firm celebrity favorite (Cameron Diaz is a fan), but be warned: although they are guaranteed to make your derriere look good, they don't come cheap. You'll also find stylish and sexy dresses here, plus sweaters and jackets for men and women. ✉ *394 West Broadway, between Broome and Spring Sts., SoHo* ☎ *212/226–8615* 🌐 *www.7forallmankind.com* Ⓜ *C, E to Spring St.*

A Bathing Ape. Known simply as BAPE to devotees, this exclusive label has a cult following in its native Tokyo. At first it may be hard to see what the fuss is about. A small selection of camouflage gear and limited-edition T-shirts is placed throughout the minimalist space; the real scene stealers are the flashy retro-style sneakers in neon colors. ✉ *91 Greene St., between Prince and Spring Sts., SoHo* ☎ *212/925–0222* 🌐 *www.bape.com* Ⓜ *N, R to Prince St.*

Fodor's Choice ★ **Agent Provocateur.** If Victoria's Secret is too tame for you, try this British lingerie shop, which has a naughty twist. Showpieces include boned corsets, lace sets with contrast-color trim, bottoms tied with satin ribbons, and a few fetish-type leather ensembles. A great selection of stockings is complemented by the garter belts to secure them. ✉ *133 Mercer St., between Prince and Spring Sts., SoHo* ☎ *212/965–0229* 🌐 *www.agentprovocateur.com* Ⓜ *N, R to Prince St.*

Alexander Wang. *Vogue* darling Alexander Wang's boutique is as unfussy—but cool—as his clothes. Shoppers can take a break on a fur hammock in between browsing for perfectly slouchy tank tops, sheath dresses, or edgy ankle boots. ✉ *103 Grand St., between Greene and Mercer Sts., SoHo* ☎ *212/977–9683* 🌐 *www.alexanderwang.com* Ⓜ *A, C, E, N, Q, R, 6 to Canal St.*

Allan & Suzi. The duo behind Allan & Suzi have been selling their pristine vintage clothing to celebrities for years—and have also outfitted the cast of *Sex and the City*. Their downtown store offers a mix of new and vintage finds, ranging from the elegant to the wacky. Dig and you may find a Gaultier gown or a Pauline Trigere dress, along with crazy disco gear. ✉ *237 Centre St., between Grand and Broome Sts., SoHo* ☎ *212/724–7445* 🌐 *www.allanandsuzi.net* Ⓜ *J, N, Q, R, Z, 6 to Canal St.*

Anna Sui. The violet-and-black salon, with its Victorian rock-chick vibe, is the ideal setting for Sui's bohemian and rocker-influenced designs and colorful beauty products. ✉ *113 Greene St., between Prince and Spring Sts., SoHo* ☎ *212/941–8406* 🌐 *www.annasui.com* Ⓜ *N, R to Prince St.*

A.P.C. This hip French boutique sells deceptively simple clothes in an equally understated setting. Watch your step on the uneven wooden floorboards while choosing narrow gabardine and corduroy suits or dark denim jeans and jackets. For women, best bets include striped sweaters and skinny jeans. ✉ *131 Mercer St., between Prince and Spring Sts., SoHo* ☎ *212/966–9685* 🌐 *www.apc.fr* Ⓜ *6 to Spring St.; N, R to Prince St.*

Bloomingdale's. Branch location at 504 Broadway, between Broome and Spring Streets. *See Midtown East for full listing.*

Christopher Fischer. Featherweight cashmere sweaters, wraps, and throws in every hue from Easter-egg pastels to rich jewel tones have made Fischer the darling of the preppy set. His shop also carries leather accessories, home wares such as throw pillows, and baby clothes. ✉ *80 Wooster St., between Spring and Broome Sts., SoHo* ☎ *212/965–9009* 🌐 *www.christopherfischer.com* Ⓜ *N, R to Prince St.*

Fodor's Choice ★ **Comptoir des Cotonniers.** The "cotton counter" angles for multigenerational shopping, lining up stylish, comfortable basics for babies, twentysomethings, ladies of a certain age, and everyone in between. There's a subtle Parisian vibe to the understated tunics, dresses, and separates; colors tend to be earthy. The brand's first US branch has a nature-friendly minimalist look, with pale-wood floors and lots of natural light. ✉ *155 Spring St., at W. Broadway, SoHo* ☎ *212/274–0830* 🌐 *www.comptoirdescotonniers.com* Ⓜ *C, E to Spring St.*

Costume National. Everything about this boutique is sexy and minimalist, with an edge. The clothes—and lighting—are dark. Shoppers will find sharply tailored wool pants for men and silky tops for women in muted shades of black, gray, and charcoal, along with motorcycle boots and leather gloves. ✉ *160 Mercer St., between Prince and W. Houston Sts., SoHo* ☎ *212/431–1530* 🌐 *www.costumenational.com* Ⓜ *C, E to Spring St.*

C. Wonder. This lifestyle boutique, founded by Tory Burch's ex-husband, offers preppy clothing with a bohemian vibe (think embroidered caftans) as well as home goods, all at surprisingly affordable prices. Just about everything in sight, from tote bags to cuffs and pillows, can be monogrammed on the spot. ✉ *72 Spring St., at Crosby St., SoHo* ☎ *212/219-3500* 🌐 *www.cwonder.com* Ⓜ *6 to Spring St.*

Emporio Armani. At this middle child of the Armani trio, the clothes are dressy without quite being formal, and are frequently offered in cream, muted blues, and ever-cool shades of taupe. ✉ *410 W. Broadway, at Spring St., SoHo* ☎ *646/613–8099* 🌐 *www.armani.com/us/emporioarmani* Ⓜ *C, E to Spring St.*

Etro. This Italian fashion house is known for its trademark paisleys and bold patterns, which cover everything from suits and dresses to lustrous pillows. Etro's flagship combines the best of Italy with a Soho loft; it boasts high tin ceilings, brightly colored rugs, and industrial lighting. ✉ *89 Greene St., between Spring and Prince Sts., SoHo* ☎ *646/329–6929* 🌐 *www.etro.com* Ⓜ *N, R to Prince St.*

French Connection. This British-owned company stocks an impressive collection of on-trend clothing for men and women at reasonable prices. Some of the best bets are the sharply tailored trench coats and jeans, as well as dresses. For men, try the cashmere sweaters and skinny trousers. ✉ *435 W. Broadway* ☎ *212/219–1197* 🌐 *www.frenchconnection.com* Ⓜ *C, E to Prince St.* ✉ *700 Broadway, East Village* ☎ *212/473–4486.*

18

Fodor's Choice ★ **Intermix.** This boutique is stocked with a healthy mid- to high-range lineup of established and emerging designers—think Stella McCartney, Mulberry, and Yigal Azrouel. You'll find everything from denim to silk frocks, along with stylish outerwear. ✉ *98 Prince St., between Greene and Mercer Sts., SoHo* ☎ *212/249–7858* 🌐 *www.intermixonline.com* Ⓜ *N, R to Prince St.*

Fodor's Choice ★ **Isabel Marant.** If you're after that casually glamorous Parisian vibe, look no further than Isabel Marant. Long a favorite of globe-trotting fashionistas, this location is the French designer's first US retail store. The tailored jackets, shorts, and flirty dresses are eclectic and sophisticated, with textured, deeply hued fabrics. ✉ *469 Broome St., at Greene St., SoHo* ☎ *212/219–2284* 🌐 *www.isabelmarant.tm.fr* Ⓜ *N, R to Prince St.*

Kiki de Montparnasse. Named for Man Ray's mistress and muse from the 1940s, this upscale lingerie store serves up decadent styles in a seductive but artistic setting. Shoppers will find exquisitely made corsets and bra and underwear sets, but a large portion of the store is used as a rotating art gallery for erotic art. ✉ *79 Greene St., at Spring St., SoHo* ☎ *212/965–8150* 🌐 *www.kikidm.com* Ⓜ *N, R to Prince St.*

Kirna Zabête. A heavy-hitting lineup of prestigious designers—Balenciaga, Alexander Wang, Lanvin, Proenza Schouler—is managed with an exceptionally cheerful flair. Step downstairs for dog apparel, coffee-table books, and hip infant gear from Kit and Lili. ✉ *96 Greene St., between Spring and Prince Sts., SoHo* ☎ *212/941–9656* 🌐 *www.kirnazabete.com* Ⓜ *N, R to Prince St.*

Marc Jacobs. One of Marc Jacobs' various NYC boutiques, this location, housed in a former garage, offers crisply tailored designs for men and women in luxurious fabrics: silk, cashmere, wool bouclé, and tweeds ranging from the demure to the flamboyant. The details, though—oversize buttons, circular patch pockets, and military-style grommet belts—add a sartorial wink. The shoe selection is not to be missed. ✉ *163 Mercer St., between W. Houston and Prince Sts., SoHo* ☎ *212/343–1490* 🌐 *www.marcjacobs.com* Ⓜ *N, R to Prince St.*

Marni. If you're a fan of the boho chic look, stock up on Consuelo Castiglioni's brightly-colored, happy clothes here. The collection features dresses and jackets in quirky prints and many of the silhouettes are vintage-inspired. Accessories are also eye-popping. ✉ *161 Mercer St., between W. Houston and Prince Sts., SoHo* ☎ *212/343–3912* 🌐 *www.marni.com* Ⓜ *N, R to Prince St.*

Miu Miu. Prada front woman Miuccia Prada established a secondary line (bearing her childhood nickname, Miu Miu) to showcase her more experimental ideas. Look for Prada-esque styles in more daring colors and cuts, such as high-waist skirts with scalloped edges, Peter Pan–collar dresses in trippy patterns, and patent-leather pumps. ✉ *100 Prince St., between Mercer and Greene Sts., SoHo* ☎ *212/334–5156* 🌐 *www.miumiu.com* Ⓜ *N, R to Prince St.*

Moncler. Many New York women swear by Moncler coats to keep them warm but still looking stylish throughout the brutal winters. This store is the Italian brand's first foray into New York. The knee-length puffer is a firm favorite, but there are stylish ski jackets and accessories, along with pieces created in collaboration with designers like Giambattista Valli. ✉ *90 Prince St., between Mercer St. and Broadway, SoHo* ☎ *646/350–3620* 🌐 *www.moncler.com* Ⓜ *N, R to Prince St.*

Fodor's Choice ★ **Opening Ceremony.** Just like Colette in Paris, Opening Ceremony bills itself as a concept store, which means you never know what you will find. The owners are constantly globetrotting to soak up the style and designers in a foreign country, and bring back the best clothing, products, and vintage items to showcase in their store. Hong Kong, Japan, Brazil, and the United Kingdom have all been represented. There's also a gallery space here. ✉ *35 Howard St., between Broadway and Lafeyette St., SoHo* ☎ *212/219–2688* 🌐 *www.openingceremony.us* Ⓜ *J, N, Q, R, Z, 6 to Canal St.*

Odin. Men, if you're tired of the corporate look, head to Odin to spruce up your weekend wardrobe. This boutique, which caters only to men, carries separates from cool brands including Rag & Bone, Engineered Garments, and Band Of Outsiders. The cheerful staff will guarantee you will leave looking hip—but not as if you're trying too hard. ✉ *199 Lafayette St., between Broome and Kenmare Sts., SoHo* ☎ *212/966–0026* 🌐 *www.odinnewyork.com* Ⓜ *6 to Spring St.*

Paul Smith. Fans love Paul Smith for his classic-with-a-twist clothes, and his 5,000-square-foot flagship is a temple to his design ethos and inspirations. Victorian mahogany cases complement the dandyish British styles they hold. Embroidered vests; brightly striped socks, scarves, and shirts; and tongue-in-cheek cuff links leaven the classic, double-back-vent suits for men. Women head for the tailored suits and separates, classic outerwear, and dresses. Plus, you'll find furniture and a selection of photography books and ephemera. ✉ *142 Greene St., between Prince and W. Houston Sts., SoHo* ☎ *646/613–3060* 🌐 *www.paulsmith.co.uk* Ⓜ *N, R to Prince St.*

Philosophy di Alberta Ferretti. The designer's eye for delicate detailing and soft, feminine design is evident in the perforated hemlines, embroidery, and sprinkling of beads across gauzy fabrics and knits. ✉ *452 W. Broadway, between W. Houston and Prince Sts., SoHo* ☎ *212/460–5500* 🌐 *www.albertaferretti.com* Ⓜ *B, D, F, M to Broadway–Lafayette St.*

Fodor's Choice ★ **Piperlime.** This popular e-tailer now has its first brick and mortar store. The large loft-like space, which is accented with lime green, carries clothing from designers like Rachel Roy and Rebecca Taylor, shoes from Zac Posen, and a multitude of accessories. A smattering of kiosks allow shoppers to purchase items online as well. ✉ *121 Wooster St., between Prince and Spring Sts., SoHo* ☎ *212/343–4284* 🌐 *www.piperlime.com* Ⓜ *N, R to Prince St.*

Prada. This ultramodern space, designed by Rem Koolhaas, incorporates so many technological innovations that it was written up in *Popular Science*. The dressing-room gadgets alone include liquid crystal displays, changeable lighting, and scanners that link you to the store's database. ✉ *575 Broadway, at Prince St., SoHo* ☎ *212/334–8888* 🌐 *www.prada.com* Ⓜ *N, R to Prince St.*

R by 45rpm. Shopping at this Japanese clothing store is a Zen-like experience, thanks to a stone pathway, limestone dressing rooms, and denim dangling from wooden trees. Although it's pricey, fans love the label for its attention to detail, like hand-dyed denim that has been woven on antique looms. The T-shirts are particularly funky. ✉ *169 Mercer St., between W. Houston and Prince Sts., SoHo* ☎ *917/237–0045* 🌐 *www.rby45rpm.com* Ⓜ *RN, R to Prince St.*

Reiss. Think of Reiss as the Banana Republic of Britain—a go-to place for casual-but-tailored clothes at a relatively gentle price. Kate Middleton is a loyal customer. Standouts for women include cowl-neck sweater dresses and A-line skirts. Men's wool combat trousers are complemented by shrunken blazers, military-inspired pea coats, and trim leather jackets. ✉ *387 W. Broadway, between Spring and Broome Sts., SoHo* ☎ *212/925–5707* 🌐 *www.reissonline.com* Ⓜ *N, R to Prince St.*

Sean. This French-pedigreed shop carries classic, understated menswear imported from Europe at reasonable prices. Linen and corduroy painter's coats are best sellers, along with V-neck sweaters and a respectable collection of slim cut suits. ✉ *199 Prince St., between Sullivan and*

18

MacDougal Sts., SoHo ☎ *212/598–5980* 🌐 *www.seanstore.com* Ⓜ *N, R to Prince St.*

Seize sur Vingt. Head to this boutique if you're ready to splurge on an exquisitely tailored shirt or suit. Men and women can pick out an off-the-rack item and have it custom tailored in house for a perfect fit, or create a fully bespoke shirt from a mind-boggling array of fabrics (linen, broadcloth oxford, flannel). To complete the look, sweaters, shoes, and accessories are also available. ✉ *78 Greene St., between Spring and Broome Sts., SoHo* ☎ *212/625–1620* 🌐 *www.16sur20.com* Ⓜ *N, R to Prince St.*

Stella McCartney. McCartney's flagship store has a luxe look, thanks to parquet flooring and touches of gold found in the art deco sculptures and clothing racks. Her main collection, done mostly in gauzy, muted colors, is on the top floor, while children's, Adidas by Stella McCartney, and lingerie are on the lower level. In keeping with McCartney's vegetarianism, fur and leather are verboten. ✉ *112 Greene St., between Spring and Prince Sts., SoHo* ☎ *212/255–1556* 🌐 *www.stellamccartney.com* Ⓜ *N, R to Prince St.*

Tess Giberson. This Rhode Island School of Design graduate is making waves for her eponymous women's collection. The boutique has an airy, minimalist feel, with whitewashed walls and rotating art exhibits that perfectly match the clothing's pared down aesthetic. The best bets are floaty silk dresses and draped trousers. ✉ *97 Crosby St., between Prince and Spring Sts., SoHo* ☎ *212/226–1932* 🌐 *www.tessgiberson.com* Ⓜ *N, R to Prince St.*

Topshop. British cult favorite Topshop, which has only a handful of US stores, is a master at pumping out of-the-minute-fashion at reasonable prices. It can be a madhouse, and items sell quickly, but it's worth fighting the crowds. Slinky dresses are around $130, and jeans and jumpsuits are about $90. Coats and shoes are also standouts. Male stylistas can browse through the ground-level Topman. ✉ *480 Broadway, at Broome St., SoHo* ☎ *212/966–9555* 🌐 *www.topshop.com* Ⓜ *6 to Spring St.; N, R to Prince St.*

Tucker. Shopping here feels as if you're browsing through a friend's closet, thanks to the homey touches like antique rugs and furniture. Designer Gaby Basora's designs are elegant and contemporary. Some of the best bets are silk blouses, high-waisted trousers, and feminine dresses. ✉ *355 W. Broadway, between Grand and Broome Sts., SoHo* ☎ *212/938–0811* 🌐 *www.tuckerbygabybasora.com* Ⓜ *1 to Canal St.*

Vera Wang. Not content designing just wedding dresses, Wang is also a star at evening wear and casual-but-chic daywear. Her entire ready-to-wear collection is showcased here in this gleaming, all-white store. Choose from clothes ranging from sexy one-shouldered satin gowns to cashmere sweaters and wool pencil skirts. ✉ *158 Mercer St., between Prince and W. Houston Sts., SoHo* ☎ *212/382–2184* 🌐 *www.verawang.com* Ⓜ *N, R to Prince St.*

Vivienne Tam. Tam is known for her playful "China chic" take on familiar Asian images. Cold-weather creations in jewel-color silk are embroidered; the warm-weather clothes are floaty and romantic. ✉ *40*

Mercer St., at Grand St., SoHo ☎ 212/966–2398 🌐 www.viviennetam.com Ⓜ N, R to Prince St.

Warm. If you want to feel the love, come to this little boutique, owned by lifelong surfer Winnie Beattie. Everything has a sunny, beachy vibe, from leather sandals, bikinis, and bleached sweaters to hand-blown glass vases. There's also a collection of children's books and homewares. ✉ *181 Mott St., between Kenmare and Broome Sts., SoHo* ☎ *212/925–1200* 🌐 *www.warmny.com* Ⓜ *6 to Spring St.*

Fodor's Choice ★ **What Goes Around Comes Around.** Professional stylists flock here to dig up vintage items like Levi's and Azzedine Alaïa dresses, as well as one-of-a-kind rock-concert T-shirts. WGACA also sells its own line of vintage-inspired clothing, from dresses to coats and tops. The vintage rock tees (think Black Sabbath, Mötley Crüe) are great finds but can set you back an eye-watering $300–$600. ✉ *351 W. Broadway, between Grand and Broome Sts., SoHo* ☎ *212/343–1225* 🌐 *www.whatgoesaroundnyc.com* Ⓜ *J, N, Q, R, Z, 6 to Canal St.*

FOOD AND TREATS

Harney & Sons. Fancy a cuppa? Harney & Sons is famous for producing more than 250 varieties of loose tea, which can be sampled at its store and tea salon in SoHo. The design is sleek and dramatic, with a 24-foot-long tasting bar and floor-to-ceiling shelves stocked with tea. Shoppers will find classic brews like English Breakfast and Oolong, along with interesting herbals (ginger and liquorice, or mint verbena). And no cup of tea would be complete without a scone or two, available at the tea salon. ✉ *433 Broome St., between Broadway and Crosby St., SoHo* ☎ *212/933–4853* 🌐 *www.harney.com* Ⓜ *6 to Spring St.*

18

Fodor's Choice ★ **Jacques Torres Chocolates.** Visit the café and shop here and you'll literally be surrounded by chocolate. The glass-walled downtown space also houses Torres's chocolate factory, so you can watch the goodies being made while you sip a richly spiced cocoa or nibble on a Java Junkie bar. **TIP→ Signature taste: the "wicked" chocolate, laced with cinnamon and chili pepper.** ✉ *350 Hudson St., at King St., SoHo* ☎ *212/414–2462* 🌐 *www.mrchocolate.com* Ⓜ *1 to Houston St.*

Kee's Chocolates. Owner Kee Ling Tong whips up delicious truffles and macaroons with unusual, Asian-inspired flavors. Try the ginger peach and rosewater lychee macaroons, or truffles flavored with lemongrass mint and tamarind. ✉ *80 Thompson St., between Spring and Broome Sts., SoHo* ☎ *212/334–3284* 🌐 *www.keeschocolates.com* Ⓜ *C, E to Spring St.*

MarieBelle. The handmade chocolates here are nothing less than works of art. Square truffles and bonbons—which come in such flavors as Earl Grey, cappuccino, passion fruit, and saffron—are painted with edible dyes (cocoa butter dyed with natural coloring) so each resembles a miniature painting. Relax in the Cacao Bar and Tea Salon while sipping an Aztec hot chocolate, which is made from rich cacao, rather than cocoa powder. ✉ *484 Broome St., between W. Broadway and Wooster St., SoHo* ☎ *212/925–6999* 🌐 *www.mariebelle.com* Ⓜ *N, R to Prince St.*

Fodor's Choice ★ **Vosges Haut Chocolat.** This chandeliered salon lined with apothecary shelves takes a global approach to chocolate. Many of the creations are travel-inspired: the Budapest bonbons combine dark chocolate and

Hungarian paprika, and the Black Pearls contain wasabi, don't miss the best-selling chocolate bacon bars. ✉ *132 Spring St., SoHo* ☎ *212/625–2929* 🌐 *www.vosgeschocolate.com* Ⓜ *N, R to Prince St.*

HOME DECOR

de Vera. Owner Federico de Vera crisscrosses the globe searching for unique decorative products, so shoppers will never know what they might find here. Venetian glass vases, Thai Buddhas, and antique rose-cut diamond rings are typical finds. ✉ *1 Crosby St., at Howard St., SoHo* ☎ *212/625–0838* 🌐 *www.deveraobjects.com* Ⓜ *J, N, Q, R, Z, 6 to Canal St.*

Kiosk. Is it a gallery or a boutique? Duck under the neon arrow sign, head up the stairway, and you'll come upon this novelty-shop-cum-art-installation. The owners travel the globe in search of locally unique, interestingly designed or packaged items, then sell their gleanings at this outpost. A new destination is highlighted every few months. You might find pipe tobacco from Massachusetts or a sled from Sweden. ✉ *95 Spring St., 2nd Floor, SoHo* ☎ *212/226–8601* 🌐 *www.kioskkiosk.com* Ⓜ *N, R to Prince St.*

Fodor's Choice ★ **Matter.** This beautifully curated store will appeal to fans of sleek, modern furniture—if money is no object. How about the iconic Tank armchair by Alvar Aalto for a cool $5,000? Or a smoked glass coffee table by Established & Sons for $1,400? Even if your budget is limited, Matter is worth a drool for inspiration. ✉ *405 Broome St., between Centre and Lafayette Sts., SoHo* ☎ *212/343–2600* 🌐 *www.mattermatters.com* Ⓜ *6 to Spring St.*

FAMILY **Pylones.** It's hard to beat Pylones for crazily cheerful products. Utilitarian products like toasters and thermoses have been given makeovers of stripes or flowers, hairbrushes have pictures of frogs or ladybugs on their backs, and pepper mills are turned into pirates. **TIP→** There are plenty of fun gifts for less than $20, such as old-fashioned robot toys and candy-color boxes. ✉ *69 Spring St., between Crosby and Lafayette Sts., SoHo* ☎ *212/431-3244* 🌐 *www.pylones-usa.com* Ⓜ *6 to Spring St.*

Room & Board. Fans of streamlined, mid-century modern furniture will be in heaven here. This location is stocked with sleek sofas, beds, and children's furniture as well as accessories like rugs and lamps. Design afficionados can choose from iconic pieces like seating cubes from Frank Gehry and Eames molded plywood chairs, or items from up and coming designers. ✉ *105 Wooster St., between Spring and Prince Sts., SoHo* ☎ *212/334–4343* 🌐 *www.roomandboard.com* Ⓜ *N, R to Prince St.*

JEWELRY AND ACCESSORIES

Fodor's Choice ★ **Alexis Bittar.** Bittar began selling his first jewelry line, made from Depression-era glass, on a corner in SoHo. Now the Brooklyn-born designer counts A-list celebs and fashion editors among his fans. He makes clean-line, big-statement jewelry from vermeil, colored Lucite, pearls, and vintage glass. The store mirrors this aesthetic with a mix of old and new, like antique-white Victorian-era lion's-claw tables and Plexiglas walls. ✉ *465 Broome St., between Mercer and Greene Sts., SoHo* ☎ *212/625–8340* 🌐 *www.alexisbittar.com* Ⓜ *N, R to Prince St.*

Fragments. This spot glitters with pieces by emerging designers as well as established ones. Both fine jewelry and lower-priced "fashion" jewelry is available, so there's something for every budget. Try on a chunky blue topaz cocktail ring, or break the bank with a sapphire and diamond collar. ✉ *116 Prince St., between Greene and Wooster Sts., SoHo* ☎ *212/334–9588* 🌐 *www.fragments.com* Ⓜ *N, R to Prince St.*

Ivanka Trump. The Donald's daughter would like to see you dripping with her diamonds. Her Soho location has an art deco look, with black-and-white furniture and plenty of glittering chandeliers. But the real bling is the jewelry—drop earrings, tassel lariats, and bold cocktail rings. Don't miss the elegant Bridal Bar for wedding jewelry. ✉ *109 Mercer St., between Prince and Spring Sts., SoHo* ☎ *212/756–9912* 🌐 *www.ivankatrumpcollection.com* Ⓜ *N, R to Prince St.*

Robert Lee Morris. If you buy into the mantra that bigger is better, make a stop here. Morris designs big, chunky jewelry that is anything but understated. Gold and silver cuffs have a serious weight to them, and necklaces and earrings have dangling hammered disks for a "wind chime" effect. Some pieces incorporate diamonds; others have semiprecious stones like turquoise or citrine. ✉ *400 W. Broadway, between Broome and Spring Sts., SoHo* ☎ *212/431–9405* 🌐 *www.robertleemorris.com* Ⓜ *C, E to Spring St.*

Stuart Moore. Everything about this boutique is minimalist, from the architecture to the jewelry. Most of the designs (from Heinrich + Denzel to Beatrice Mueller) have a streamlined, almost industrial look: diamonds are set in brushed platinum, and gold bangles are impossibly delicate. ✉ *411 W. Broadway, at Spring St., SoHo* ☎ *212/941–1023* 🌐 *www.stuartmoore.com* Ⓜ *C, E to Spring St.*

18

Swarovski Crystallized. A shrine to all things sparkly, this crystal superstore is a combination boutique and café, and allows shoppers to customize their purchases. Shoppers mix and match pieces from the striking "library of light" to create designs. If you're lacking ideas, there's always ready-made jewelry. Look out for pieces created by top designers like Kenneth Jay Lane and Karen Millen. ✉ *499 Broadway, between Spring and Broome Sts., SoHo* ☎ *212/966–3322* Ⓜ *N, R to Prince St.; 6 to Spring St.*

Versani. Most of the jewelry here is big, bold, and unisex—and more than a little quirky. Silver teams up with all kinds of materials: leather, denim, and snakeskin, as well as semiprecious stones. There's a good selection of silver rings and pendants under $50. ✉ *152 Mercer St., between Prince and W. Houston Sts., SoHo* ☎ *212/941–7770* 🌐 *www.versani.com* Ⓜ *N, R to Prince St.*

SHOES, HANDBAGS, AND LEATHER GOODS

Camper. Urbanites love this Spanish footwear company for its funky but comfortable shoes. The new flagship features an unusual pagoda-style roof made from tubes and inside, there's a vertical garden. All the slip-ons and lace-ups here have generously rounded toes and a springy feel. ✉ *110 Prince St., Between Wooster and Green Sts., SoHo* ☎ *212/343–4220* 🌐 *www.camper.com* Ⓜ *N, R to Prince St.*

Frye Boots. This 6,000-square-foot mecca to boots has a Western feel, thanks to the exposed brick walls and reclaimed barn doors. Boots can be tattooed—or hot stamped—with your initials while you wait in the lounge. In addition to Frye's famed boots, shoppers can also pick from flats, oxfords, clogs, and mules. ✉ *113 Spring St., between Mercer and Greene Sts., SoHo* ☎ *212/226–3793* 🌐 *www.thefryecompany.com* Ⓜ *N, R to Prince St.*

WORD OF MOUTH

"For SoHo, I recommend a walk down Broadway south of Houston Street. There are many stores in this area, including the Prada Museum (that's what I call the shop), Bloomingdale's, Sephora, Pearl River Mart, etc. You can also wander along Spring and Prince toward West Broadway." —Proenza_Preschooler

Kate Spade. Spade's runaway success with classic kicky, retro-style tote bags has blossomed into a full-fledged lifestyle company. The flagship looks—and feels—like an elegant living room. The totes are still for sale, along with leather handbags, kitten heels, and accessories like eyeglasses and paper. Even the diaper bags are ridiculously stylish. Around the corner you'll find **Jack Spade,** filled with bags, dopp kits, and other men's accessories in a nostalgic setting. ✉ *454 Broome St., between Mercer and Greene Sts., SoHo* ☎ *212/274–1991* 🌐 *www.katespade.com* Ⓜ *C, E to Spring St.*

Longchamp. Its Le Pliage foldable nylon bags have become an Upper East Side and Hamptons staple, but don't think this label is stuffy - or all about nylon. There's a wide selection of leather handbags as well as wallets, belts, and shoes. Kate Moss also designs a line for Longchamp. ✉ *132 Spring St., at Elizabeth St., SoHo* ☎ *212/343–7444* 🌐 *www.longchamp.com* Ⓜ *N, R to Prince St.*

TOYS

FAMILY Fodor's Choice ★ **Kidrobot.** This shop will appeal to kids, nerds, and the young at heart, who all flock here to stock up on the latest toys from Asian designers. This is a far cry from Mattel—the shelves are stocked with Dunny bunnies, Tokidokis, and Devilrobots. There's also a selection of cool silk-screened T-shirts and hoodies. ✉ *118 Prince St., between Greene and Wooster Sts., SoHo* ☎ *212/966–6688* 🌐 *www.kidrobot.com* Ⓜ *N, R to Prince St.*

NOLITA

NoLIta, short for "North of Little Italy" has become a mecca for shopping, thanks to the abundance of independent boutiques that range from quirky to elegant. Like SoHo, NoLIta has gone from a locals-only, understated area to a crowded weekend magnet, as much about people watching as it is about shopping. Still, unlike those of its SoHo neighbor, these stores remain largely one-of-a-kind. Running along the parallel north–south spines of Elizabeth, Mott, and Mulberry Streets, between East Houston and Kenmare Streets, NoLIta's boutiques tend to be small and, as real estate dictates, somewhat pricey.

BEAUTY

Lafco New York. A heavy, iron-barred door leads to a hushed, scented inner sanctum of beauty products. This location is the official retailer of the 600-year-old Santa Maria Novella products from Italy, which include intriguingly archaic colognes, creams, and soaps such as Tooth Cleansing Water and pomegranate soap. Everything is packaged in bottles and jars with antique-style apothecary labels. ✉ *285 Lafayette St., between E. Houston and Prince Sts., NoLIta* ☎ *212/925–0001* 🌐 *www.lafcony.com* Ⓜ *N, R to Prince St.*

WORD OF MOUTH

"We are blessed with the original McNally [Jackson] bookstores. I would have to say these are the best, most fun bookstores I have ever been in." —ita

Le Labo. If you're bored with department store perfume offerings, come to this tiny boutique that features a rustic industrial vibe and a resident mixologist who will help you create your ideal perfume. After choosing your favorite scents, the perfume is mixed and a personalized label is created for your bottle. ✉ *233 Elizabeth St., between Prince and E. Houston Sts., NoLIta* ☎ *212/219–2230* 🌐 *www.lelabofragrances.com* Ⓜ *B, D, F, M to Broadway–Lafayette St.*

BOOKS AND STATIONERY

Fodor's Choice ★ **McNally Jackson.** This cozy, independent bookstore is a bibliophile's dream. The bright two-story space has hardwood floors, a delicious cafe, and plenty of chairs for lounging and curling up with a book. More than 50,000 books are stocked and the literary section is organized geographically. Budding authors can self-print their tomes on a device called the Espresso Machine. ✉ *52 Prince St., between Lafayette and Mulberry Sts., NoLIta* ☎ *212/274–1160* 🌐 *www.mcnallyjackson.com* Ⓜ *N, R to Prince St.*

18

CLOTHING

Creatures of Comfort. Owner Jade Lai has brought her popular LA outpost to New York. The open, airy boutique offers cool clothes from emerging designers alongside products sourced from around the world. Most of the colors are muted, and brands carried include Acne, MM6, and the house label, Creatures of Comfort. There's a small selection of shoes, plus you never know what you might find for sale on a side table, such as candy and lip gloss from Asia. ✉ *205 Mulberry St., between Spring and Kenmare Sts., NoLIta* ☎ *212/925–1005* 🌐 *www.creaturesofcomfort.us* Ⓜ *6 to Spring St.*

Dalaga. The turnover at this romantic little boutique is high—so come often, as you never know what you'll find. The prices are also affordable. The dresses, floaty tops, and skinny jeans are generally priced under $100. ✉ *85 Kenmare St., between Lafayette and Mulberry Sts., NoLIta* ☎ *646/449–8716* 🌐 *www.dalaganyc.com* Ⓜ *6 to Spring St.*

Fodor's Choice ★ **Duncan Quinn.** Shooting for nothing less than sartorial splendor, this designer provides everything from chalk-stripe suits to cuff links and croquet shirts, all in a shop not much bigger than its silk pocket squares. Off-the-rack shirts are handmade in England but if you want to splurge, get fitted for a bespoke shirt with mother-of-pearl buttons. ✉ *8 Spring*

St., between Elizabeth and Bowery Sts., NoLIta ☎ *212/226–7030* 🌐 *www.duncanquinn.com* Ⓜ *6 to Spring St.*

Frock. Models and stylists frequent this tiny shop for vintage women's wear from the 1960s through the early '90s. The store carries pieces from Oscar de la Renta, Galanos, and Givenchy, as well as Lanvin and Carolina Herrera. Sarah Jessica Parker is a big fan. ✉ *170 Elizabeth St., between Spring and Kenmare Sts., NoLIta* ☎ *212/594–5380* 🌐 *www.frocknyc.com* Ⓜ *B, D, F, M to Broadway–Lafayette St.*

INA. The clothing at this couture consignment store harks back only one or two seasons, and in some cases, the item has never been worn. Browse through the racks to spot gems from Lanvin, Chanel, and Alexander McQueen. Although there are multiple locations around the city, this flagship also carries menswear. ✉ *15 Bleecker St., at Elizabeth St., NoLIta* ☎ *212/228–8511* 🌐 *www.inanyc.com* Ⓜ *6 to Bleecker St.*

Jay Kos. There aren't too many boutiques where the owner sometimes whips up a snack for customers in the boutique's custom kitchen, but this designer—famous for dressing Diddy and Johnny Depp—wanted his new boutique to have a homey feel. The clothes veer toward the fabulous: suede shoes, linen suits, and cashmere sweaters, which are displayed in armoires. ✉ *293 Mott St., at E. Houston St., NoLIta* ☎ *212* 🌐 *www.jaykos.com* Ⓜ *B, D, F, M to Broadway–Lafayette St.*

Fodor's Choice ★ **Malia Mills.** Fit fanatics have met their match here—especially those gals who are different sizes on top and bottom (bikini tops go up to a size D). Bikini tops and bottoms are sold separately: halters, bandeaus, and triangle tops, plus boy-cut, side-tie, and low-ride bottoms. There's a collection of one-pieces as well, which are sold by bra size. ✉ *199 Mulberry St., between Spring and Kenmare Sts., NoLIta* ☎ *212/625–2311* 🌐 *www.maliamills.com* Ⓜ *6 to Spring St.*

Nanette Lepore. "Girly" may well be the description that comes to mind as you browse through this cheerful shop; skirts are pleated and adorned with bows, jackets are enhanced by embroidery and floral appliqués, fur shrugs have tiny sleeves. ✉ *423 Broome St., between Lafayette and Crosby Sts., NoLIta* ☎ *212/219–8265* 🌐 *www.nanettelepore.com* Ⓜ *6 to Spring St.*

Oak. This boutique looks like an art gallery, thanks to the huge sculpture winding its way though the middle of the store. Most of the clothing is in black and the store carries high-end designers as well as its own line. Come here for skinny jeans, capes, and draped jersey dresses. ✉ *28 Bond St., Between Lafayette St. and Bowery, NoLIta* ☎ *212/677–1293* 🌐 *www.oaknyc.com* Ⓜ *6 to Bleecker St.*

Paul Frank. The store's mascot, the cheeky Julius monkey, is plastered everywhere here—on flannel PJs, skateboards, and, of course, T-shirts. Also look for tees evoking such formative elements of '80s youth as corn dogs and breakdancing. A selection of monkey-free accessories, including perfect weekender bags, is more stylish than sassy. ✉ *195 Mulberry St., at Kenmare St., NoLIta* ☎ *212/965–5079* 🌐 *www.paulfrank.com* Ⓜ *6 to Spring St.*

Resurrection. If you're serious about vintage—and have deep pockets—Resurrection offers a treasure trove of pristine pieces from Chanel, Gucci, Halston, Alaia, and YSL among others. Kate Moss is a fan, and designers like Marc Jacobs and Anna Sui have sought inspiration among the racks. ✉ *217 Mott St., between Prince and Spring Sts., NoLIta* ☎ *212/625–1374* 🌐 *www.resurrectionvintage.com* Ⓜ *6 to Spring St.*

JEWELRY AND ACCESSORIES

Condor. Owner Loriann Smoak is the consummate world traveler, and she has stocked her serene, white-marbled clothing boutique with plenty of international designers, as well as local ones. Everything from coffee table books to dangly earrings and scarves is available here. ✉ *259 Elizabeth St., between E. Houston and Prince Sts., NoLIta* ☎ *212/966–4280* 🌐 *www.shopcondor.com* Ⓜ *6 to Bleecker St.; B, D, F, M to Broadway–Lafayette Sts.; N, R to Prince St.*

Dinosaur Designs. Translucent and colorful, this antipodean work uses an untraditional medium: resin. Some resins look like semiprecious stone, such as onyx or jade. The rest delve into stronger colors like aqua or crimson. Cruise the stacks of chunky bangles and cuffs or rows of rings; prices start at $50. There's some striking tableware, too. ✉ *211 Elizabeth St., between Prince and E. Houston Sts., NoLIta* ☎ *212/680–3523* 🌐 *www.dinosaurdesigns.com.au* Ⓜ *N, R to Prince St.*

Erica Weiner. This eponymous designer specializes in vintage-inspired jewelry as well as antiques: delicate art deco earrings, vintage lockets, and necklaces fashioned from antique compasses. The boutique's tile floor and wooden display cabinets reflect Weiner's aesthetic. Prices are surprisingly reasonable. ✉ *173 Elizabeth St., between Kenmare and Spring Sts., NoLIta* ☎ *212/334–6383* 🌐 *www.ericaweiner.com* Ⓜ *6 to Spring St.*

Me&Ro. Minimalist, Eastern styling has gained these designers a cult following. The Indian-inspired, hand-finished gold bangles, earrings, and necklaces are covered with tiny dangling rubies, sapphires, or brown diamonds. Although the fine jewelry is expensive, small sterling silver earrings start at around $120. ✉ *241 Elizabeth St., between Prince and E. Houston Sts., NoLIta* ☎ *917/237–9215* 🌐 *www.meandrojewelry.com* Ⓜ *N, R to Prince St.*

SHOES, HANDBAGS, AND LEATHER GOODS

Dolce Vita. The clothes here are stylish and on-trend but the real showstoppers are the shoes. Although you won't find big name designers, shoppers can choose from a wide selection of ballet flats, ankle boots, and sexy stilettos, all at affordable prcies. ✉ *255 Elizabeth St., between E. Houston and Prince Sts., NoLIta* ☎ *212/226–0635* 🌐 *www.dolcevita.com* Ⓜ *6 to Bleecker St.*

High Way. The bags here marry form and function. Totes and messenger bags come in durable leather and nylon, and some handbags open to disclose a wealth of inner pockets. ✉ *238 Mott St., between Prince and Spring Sts., NoLIta* ☎ *212/966–4388* 🌐 *www.highwaybuzz.com* Ⓜ *6 to Bleecker St.*

John Fluevog Shoes. The inventor of the Angelic sole (protects against water, acid, "and Satan"), Fluevog designs chunky, funky shoes and boots for men and women. ✉ *250 Mulberry St., at Prince St., NoLIta* ☎ *212/431–4484* 🌐 *www.fluevog.com* Ⓜ *N, R to Prince St.*

Kathryn Amberleigh. This designer, an FIT grad, has perfected the sexy-but-edgy look in her hand-crafted shoes. There are simple flats and wedges along with peep-toe ankle boots and sky-high heels. Most designs hover around the $250 mark. ✉ *219 Mott St., between Prince and Spring Sts, NoLIta* ☎ *212/842–2134* 🌐 *www.kathrynamberleigh.com* Ⓜ *6 to Spring St.*

Token. Although messenger bags are now ubiquitous, pay homage to the store that started it all. Super-durable messenger bags come in waxed canvas as well as nylon, and the line has expanded to include totes, duffels, and travel bags, all in unadorned, simple styles. ✉ *258 Elizabeth St., between E. Houston and Prince Sts., NoLIta* ☎ *212/226–9655* 🌐 *www.tokenbags.com* Ⓜ *N, R to Prince St.*

EAST VILLAGE AND LOWER EAST SIDE

EAST VILLAGE

The East Village is a fabulous hunting ground for independent boutiques.

ANTIQUES AND COLLECTIBLES

Lost City Arts. This sprawling shop is one of the best places to shop for 20th-century-design furniture, lighting, and accessories. Lost City can help you relive the Machine Age with an in-house, retro-modern line of furniture. ✉ *18 Cooper Sq., at 5th St., East Village* ☎ *212/375–0500* 🌐 *www2.lostcityarts.com* Ⓜ *6 to Astor Pl.*

Partners & Spade. Owners Andy Spade and Anthony Perduti have lined this small space with all kinds of carefully curated knickknacks, ranging from the silly to the sublime. You might find a surfboard fin or custom-painted ties. The shop's own line of books is wonderfully quirky, covering everything from girls on bikes to the benefits of looking up in Manhattan. The shop is open by appointment only midweek but is open to the public on weekends. ✉ *40 Great Jones St., between Lafayette St. and Bowery, East Village* ☎ *646/861–2827* 🌐 *www.partnersandspade.com* Ⓜ *6 to Bleecker St.*

BEAUTY

Bond No. 9. Created by the same fragrance team as Creed, this line of scents is intended to evoke the New York City experience, with a scent for every neighborhood: Central Park, a men's fragrance, is woodsy and "green," and Park Avenue is discreet but not too sweet. This flagship also carries candles and body creams. ✉ *9 Bond St., between Lafayette St. and Broadway, East Village* ☎ *212/228–1732* 🌐 *www.bondno9.com* Ⓜ *6 to Bleecker St.*

Fodor's Choice ★ **Kiehl's Since 1851.** At this favored haunt of top models and stylists, white-smocked assistants can help you choose between the lotions and potions, all of which are packaged in simple-looking bottles and jars. Some of the products, such as the Ultra Facial Cream, Creme with Silk Groom hairstyling aid, and superrich Creme de Corps, have attained near-cult status among fans. **TIP→ Kiehl's is known for being generous with samples, so be sure to ask for your own bag of take-home testers.**

✉ *109 3rd Ave., at 13th St., East Village* ☎ *212/677–3171* 🌐 *www.kiehls.com* Ⓜ *4, 5, 6, L, N, Q, R to 14th St.–Union Sq.*

BOOKS AND STATIONERY

St. Mark's Bookshop. Downtown residents, NYU students, and intellectuals in general love this store, spending hours poking through popular and oddball fiction and nonfiction. You'll find a truly eclectic, attitudinal collection of books here, not unlike the salespeople. On the main floor, books on critical theory are right up front, across from new fiction titles—this is perhaps the only place where you can find Jacques Derrida facing off against T. C. Boyle. Cultural and art books are up front as well; literature and literary journals fill the back of the store. **TIP→ It's open daily until midnight.** ✉ *31 3rd Ave., between 8th and 9th Sts., East Village* ☎ *212/260–7853* 🌐 *www.stmarksbookshop.com* Ⓜ *6 to Astor Pl.*

CLOTHING

Cloak & Dagger. Come here if you like refined but on-trend looks. The racks are lined with tulip skirts, belted dresses, and trenches. ✉ *441 E 9th St., between Ave. A and 1st Ave., East Village* 🌐 *www.cloakanddaggernyc.com* Ⓜ *6 to Astor Place.*

Fodor's Choice ★ **John Varvatos.** Varvatos has long been inspired by rock and roll. His ad campaigns have starred Franz Ferdinand and Green Day, so it is only fitting that he transformed the former CBGB club into his New York flagship. The space is dotted with vintage pianos and guitars, as well as old vinyl records. And the clothes? The jeans, leather pants, and suede shoes will give you rock star cred, but there are also classic, understated styles for the corporate set. ✉ *315 Bowery, between 1st and 2nd Sts., East Village* ☎ *212/358–0315* 🌐 *www.johnvarvatos.com* Ⓜ *6 to Bleecker St.*

Pas de Deux. Fashion editors love this little boutique—which looks like it was imported straight from Paris—thanks to the marble checkerboard floor, chandeliers, and fine woodwork. The well-edited selection includes dresses, trench coats, and denim from Isabel Marant, Thakoon, and Alexander Wang. There are also lots of lovely little accessories, like eyeglasses, cardholders, and delicate necklaces. ✉ *328 E. 11th St., between 1st and 2nd Aves., East Village* ☎ *212/475–0075* 🌐 *www.pasdedeuxny.com* Ⓜ *6 to Astor Pl.*

Patricia Field. If you loved Carrie Bradshaw's wild outfits on *Sex and the City*, this is the place for you. As well as designing costumes for the show, Field has been a longtime purveyor of flamboyant and campy club-kid gear. Her 4,000-square-foot East Village emporium is chockablock with teeny kilts, lamé, marabou, pleather, and vinyl, as well as wigs in every color and stiletto heels in some very large sizes. ✉ *306 Bowery, between Bleecker and E. Houston Sts., East Village* ☎ *212/966–4066* 🌐 *www.patriciafield.com* Ⓜ *6 to Bleecker St.*

Screaming Mimi's. Browse through racks bulging with vintage finds from the 1950s through '80s. Retro wear includes everything from dresses to soccer shirts and prom dresses. Although most of the non-designer finds are affordable, Screaming Mimi's also carries vintage designer duds from Valentino, Chloe, and Gaultier. ✉ *382 Lafayette*

The Lower East Side is a great area to shop for funky home furnishings.

St., between 4th and Great Jones Sts., East Village ☎ *212/677–6464* 🌐 *www.screamingmimis.com* Ⓜ *B, D, F, M to Broadway–Lafayette St.*

Tokio 7. Even fashion designers like Alexander Wang have been known to pop into this high-end consignment store to browse. Racks are loaded with goodies from A-list designers such as Gucci, Stella McCartney, DVF, and Philip Lim and the inventory changes almost daily. ✉ *83 E. 7th St., between 1st and 2nd Aves., East Village* ☎ *212/353–8443* 🌐 *www.tokio7.net* Ⓜ *6 to Astor Pl.*

Trash and Vaudeville. This punk mecca is famous for dressing stars like Debbie Harry and the Ramones back in the '70s, and its rock-and-roll vibe lives on. Goths, punks, and pro wrestlers shop here for bondage-inspired pants and skirts, as well as vinyl corsets and mini-kilts. ✉ *4 St. Marks Pl., between 2nd and 3rd Aves., East Village* ☎ *212/982–3590* 🌐 *www.trashandvaudeville.com* Ⓜ *6 to Astor Pl.*

FOOD AND TREATS

Fodor's Choice ★ **Max Brenner: Chocolate by the Bald Man.** This Aussie arrival is all about a Wonka-ish sense of entertainment. The café encourages the messy enjoyment of gooey creations like chocolate fondues and chocolate burgers for kids. Take-away treats include caramelized pralines and tins of hot-chocolate powder. ✉ *841 Broadway, between 13th and 14th Sts., East Village* ☎ *646/467–8803* 🌐 *www.maxbrenner.com* Ⓜ *4, 5, 6, L, N, Q, R to 14th St.–Union Sq.*

HOME DECOR

White Trash. Looking for a midcentury modern Danish desk? This is your place. Owner Stuart Zamsky crams his store with surprisingly affordable pieces that are mostly from the '40s through '70s, including tables, lamps, and chairs. Some pieces you might find include paper mobiles from the '70s, old fondue sets, and antique medical-office cabinets. ✉ *304 E. 5th St., between 1st and 2nd Aves., East Village* ☎ *212/598–5956* 🌐 *www.whitetrashnyc.com* Ⓜ *6 to Astor Pl.*

WORD OF MOUTH

"I used to shop at Other Music a lot when I [worked] around the corner. They always have these little gems in the nooks and the crannies; it's true!" —bellastarr

JEWELRY AND ACCESSORIES

Verameat. All the jewelry here is handmade in New York City and none of it is typical. Design motifs include pretzels, dinosaurs, and vampire teeth. Tilda Swinton is a fan. ✉ *315 East 9th St., between 1st and 2nd Aves., East Village* ☎ *212/388–9045* 🌐 *www.verameat.com* Ⓜ *6 to Astor Place.*

MUSIC STORES

Other Music. DJs and musicians flock here for hard-to-find genres on CD and vinyl, from Japanese electronica and Krautrock to acid folk and Americana. You can buy concert tickets at the in-house box office. **TIP→** There's also a great selection of used CDs, including seminal punk classics from the Clash and the Stooges. ✉ *15 E. 4th St., between Lafayette St. and Broadway, East Village* ☎ *212/477–8150* 🌐 *www.othermusic.com* Ⓜ *6 to Astor Pl.*

TOYS

Dinosaur Hill. Forget about Elmo and Barbie. This little shop stocks quirky gifts for kids like hand puppets and marionettes from Asia, mini-bongos, and wooden rattles. Don't miss the medieval themed toys, such as Camelot finger puppets. ✉ *306 E. 9th St., between 1st and 2nd Aves., East Village* ☎ *212/473–5850* 🌐 *www.dinosaurhill.com* Ⓜ *R to 8th St.–NYU; 6 to Astor Pl.*

18

WINE

Astor Wines & Spirits. Stock up on wine, spirits, and sake at this beautiful shop. For unwinding, and learning more about food and wine, there's also a wine library and kitchen for cooking classes. ✉ *399 Lafayette St., at 4th St., East Village* ☎ *212/674–7500* 🌐 *www.astorwines.com* Ⓜ *6 to Astor Pl.*

Fodor's Choice ★ **Union Square Wine & Spirits.** Tastings are easy at this well-stocked store, thanks to Enomatic machines. These card-operated contraptions let you sample dozens of wines. If machines don't do it for you, generous tastings are held most Fridays and Saturdays. ✉ *140 4th Ave., at 13th St., East Village* ☎ *212/675–8100* 🌐 *www.unionsquarewines.com* Ⓜ *L, N, Q, R, 4, 5, 6 to 14th St.–Union Sq.*

LOWER EAST SIDE

Head to the Lower East Side for excellent vintage finds. Once home to multitudes of Jewish immigrants from Russia and Eastern Europe, the Lower East Side has traditionally been New York's bargain beat. Today, tiny, no-nonsense clothing stores and scrappy stalls hang on to the past while funky local designers gradually claim more turf. A few cool vintage clothing and furniture spots bridge the two camps. Ludlow Street, one block east of Orchard, has become the main drag for twentysomethings with attitude, its boutiques wedged in between bars and low-key restaurants. Anything too polished is looked on with suspicion—and that goes for you, too. For the full scope of this area, prowl from Allen to Essex streets, south of East Houston Street down to Broome Street.

ANTIQUES AND COLLECTIBLES

Las Venus. Step into this kitsch palace and you may feel as though a time machine has zapped you back to the '50s, '60s, or groovy '70s. Look for bubble lamps, lots of brocade, and Knoll knockoffs. Midcentury modern Danish credenzas are also big here. ✉ *163 Ludlow St., between E. Houston and Stanton Sts., Lower East Side* ☎ *212/982–0608* 🌐 *www.lasvenus.com* Ⓜ *F to 2nd Ave.*

CLOTHING

Gargyle. This boutique serves up country club attire with a nudge and a wink. The floor is covered in astroturf, and the clothes reference classically preppy sports such as golf and tennis, but always in a fashionable way. Choose from argyle sweaters and miniskirts from top labels including Karen Walker, Lover, Shipley & Halmos, and Opening Ceremony. ✉ *16 Orchard St., between Canal and Hester Sts., Lower East Side* ☎ *917/470–9367* 🌐 *www.gargyle.com* Ⓜ *F to E. Broadway.*

SHOES, HANDBAGS, AND LEATHER GOODS

Altman Luggage. Having trouble bringing all your purchases home? Altman sells top-of-the-line luggage from Samsonite, Delsey, and Tumi at discount prices. A wide selection of pens is also for sale. ✉ *135 Orchard St., between Delancey and Rivington Sts., Lower East Side* ☎ *212/254–7275* 🌐 *www.altmanluggage.com* Ⓜ *F, J, M, Z to Delancey St.–Essex St.*

GREENWICH VILLAGE AND WEST VILLAGE

GREENWICH VILLAGE

The area around Washington Square and New York University has more than its fair share of touristy souvenir shops, cheap shoe boutiques along 8th Street, and chain stores, but there are also some gems to be found. For a more charming part of the village, head west, to the more residential West Village.

BEAUTY

C. O. Bigelow. Founded in 1838, this is the oldest apothecary-pharmacy in the United States; Mark Twain used to fill prescriptions here. They still fill prescriptions, but the real reason to come is for the hard-to-find-brands like Klorane shampoo and Elgydium toothpaste. Bigelow also has its own line of products, including green-tea lip balm and quince hand lotion. ✉ *414 6th Ave., between 9th and 10th, Greenwich Village* ☎ *212/473–7324* 🌐 *www.bigelowchemists.com* Ⓜ *B, D, F, M to W. 4th St.–Washington Sq.*

CLOTHING

Fodor's Choice ★ **La Petite Coquette.** Everything at this lingerie store is unabashedly sexy, and the helpful staff can find the perfect fit. The store's own line of silk slips, camisoles, and other underpinnings comes in a range of colors. ✉ *51 University Pl., between 9th and 10th Sts., Greenwich Village* ☎ *212/473–2478* 🌐 *www.thelittleflirt.com* Ⓜ *N, R to 8th St.–NYU.*

The tree-lined streets of the West Village have pretty, upscale boutiques.

WEST VILLAGE

It's easy to feel like a local, not a tourist, while shopping in the West Village. Unlike 5th Avenue or SoHo, the pace is slower, the streets are quiet, and the scale is small. This is the place to come for unusual finds rather than global brands (if you don't count Marc Jacobs).

Bleecker Street is a particularly good place to indulge all sorts of shopping appetites. Foodies love the blocks between 6th and 7th avenues for the specialty purveyors like Murray's Cheese (254 Bleecker Street). Fashion foragers prowl the stretch between West 10th Street and 8th Avenue. Hudson Street and Greenwich Avenue are also prime boutique-browsing territory. Christopher Street, true to its connection with the lesbian and gay community, has a handful of rainbow-flag stops. High rents mean there are fewer student-oriented shops around NYU than you might expect.

ANTIQUES AND COLLECTIBLES

Kaas Glassworks. From the outside, this shop is cuter than cute, with its old-fashioned sign and ivy-covered brick façade. The specialty here is decoupage that has been turned into quirky coasters and trays. Owner Carol Kaas uses vintage postcards, maps, and botanical prints in her works. ✉ *117 Perry St., between Greenwich and Hudson Sts., Greenwich Village* ☎ *212/366–0322* 🌐 *www.kaas.com* Ⓜ *1 to Christopher St.–Sheridan Sq.*

BEAUTY

Aedes De Venustas. Arguably the best place to buy fragrance in town, this boutique's super-knowledgeable staff will help shoppers find the perfect scent. High-end brands like L'Artisan Parfumeur and Anick

Goutal are stocked, along with luxurious skincare products and pricey candles and room diffusers. Their signature gift wrap is as beautiful as what's inside the box. ✉ *9 Christopher St., between 6th and 7th Aves., Greenwich Village* ☎ *212/206–8674* 🌐 *www.aedes.com* Ⓜ *1 to Christopher St.–Sheridan Sq.*

Jo Malone. This crisp black-and-white boutique offers a serene backdrop to sample tangy scents such as lime blossom and mandarin, or white jasmine and mint. Fragrances can be worn alone or layered. The flagship offers complimentary hand massages and a sampling bar to create a bespoke scent. ✉ *330 Bleecker St., between W. 10th and Christopher Sts., West Village* ☎ *212/242–1454* Ⓜ *1 to Christopher St.–Sheridan Sq.*

BOOKS AND STATIONERY

bookbook. This small, independent bookstore is crammed with the latest new releases as well as a thoughtful assortment of general nonfiction, guidebooks, and children's books. But the real focus here is the carefully selected sales tables that spill out onto the sidewalk—they have deals on everything from Graham Greene to Chuck Palahniuk. ✉ *266 Bleecker St., between 6th and 7th Aves., Greenwich Village* ☎ *212/807–8655* 🌐 *www.bookbooknyc.com* Ⓜ *1 to Christopher St.–Sheridan Sq.*

Three Lives & Company. Three Lives has one of the city's best book selections. The display tables and counters highlight the latest literary fiction and serious nonfiction, classics, quirky gift books, and gorgeously illustrated tomes. The staff members' literary knowledge is formidable, so don't be afraid to ask them for their own picks. ✉ *154 W. 10th St., at Waverly Pl., Greenwich Village* ☎ *212/741–2069* 🌐 *www.threelives.com* Ⓜ *1 to Christopher St.–Sheridan Sq.*

CLOTHING

Castor & Pollux. The store's interior signals a finely tuned balance of high taste (vintage Bergdorf Goodman display cases) and quirkiness (grasscloth wall coverings and small horse sculptures). Hard-to-find brands like Hache are mixed with better-known names like Acne and 3.1 Philip Lim. There's also an eye-catching in-house line of jewelry, clutches, and sweaters that are casual but classic. ✉ *238 W. 10th St., at Hudson St., West Village* ☎ *212/645–6572* 🌐 *www.castorandpolluxstore.com* Ⓜ *1 to Christopher St.–Sheridan Sq.*

Cynthia Rowley. Rowley delivers flirty, whimsical dresses that are perfect for cocktail parties. To complete the look, throw on some of her colorful pumps and sharply tailored coats. ✉ *376 Bleecker St., between Charles and Perry Sts., West Village* ☎ *212/242–3803* 🌐 *cynthiarowley.com* Ⓜ *1 to Christopher St.–Sheridan Sq.*

Fisch for the Hip. This high-end consignment store sells carefully edited men's and women's clothing and accessories, from top designers including Tom Ford, Balenciaga, and Lanvin. Hermès bags are a specialty. ✉ *33 Greenwich Ave., between W. 10th and Charles Sts., West Village* ☎ *212/633–9053* Ⓜ *1 to Christopher St.–Sheridan Sq.*

Hotoveli. This unprepossessing nook stocks some of the most elegant (and expensive) designers in the world, ranging from Alexander McQueen to Vivienne Westwood. If you have to ask how much an item costs, don't try it on. ✉ *378 Bleecker St., between Charles and Perry Sts., Greenwich Village* ☎ *212/206–7475* 🌐 *www.hotoveli.com* Ⓜ *1 to Christopher St.–Sheridan Sq.*

Khirma Eliazov. This former Vogue editor now designs an elegant line of handbags, clutches, and accessories. She uses luxury materials such as python, alligator, crocodile, and stingray skins. ✉ *102 Charles Street, between Hudson and Bleecker Sts., West Village* ☎ *646/998–5240* 🌐 *www.khirmaeliazov.com* Ⓜ *1 to Christopher St.–Sheridan Square.*

FOOD AND TREATS

Chocolate Bar. What sets this chocolate emporium apart is its midcentury modern design, which is also evident in the groovy packaging. Scoop up some retro chocolate bars, whose flavors include salty pretzel, coconut cream pie, and key lime. Or try a salted caramel bonbon and a steaming cup of spicy hot chocolate. ✉ *19 8th Ave., between Jane and W. 12th Sts., West Village* ☎ *212/366–1541* 🌐 *www.chocolatebarnyc.com* Ⓜ *A, C, E, to 14th St.; L to 8th Ave.*

Li-Lac Chocolates. They've been feeding the Village's sweet tooth since 1923. Indulge with almond bark and coconut clusters as well as such specialty items as chocolate-molded Statues of Liberty. ✉ *40 8th Ave., at Jane St., Greenwich Village* ☎ *212/924–2280* 🌐 *www.li-lacchocolates.com* Ⓜ *A, C, E to 14th St.; L to 8th Ave.*

Sockerbit. Who knew Scandinavians were obsessed with candy? There's much more than Swedish fish at this gleaming white candy emporium that stocks hard candies, gummies, licorice, and chocolate. Have fun pronouncing the names of the treats, such as Bumlingar Jordgubb and Zoo Klubba. ✉ *89 Christopher St., between Bleecker and W. 4th Sts., West Village* ☎ *212/206–8170* 🌐 *www.sockerbit.com* Ⓜ *1 to Christopher St.–Sheridan Sq.*

18

HOME DECOR

Olatz. Olatz Schnabel modeled her linen shop on a historic Havana pharmacy after a visit to Cuba. The black-and-white checkerboard floors and mint-green walls breathe a sort of lazy, faded elegance, a spot-on backdrop to her collection of luxurious sheets, blankets, and pajama sets, all of which have sky-high thread counts and are bordered with bold stripes or intricate damask embroidery. ✉ *43 Clarkson St., between Hudson and Greenwich Sts., Greenwich Village* ☎ *212/255–8627* 🌐 *www.olatz.com* Ⓜ *1 to Houston St.*

SHOES, HANDBAGS, AND LEATHER GOODS

Fodor's Choice ★ **Flight 001.** Frequent flyers can one-stop shop at this travel-themed store that puts a creative spin on everyday accessories. Shop for bright luggage tags, passport holders, satin sleep masks, and even paper soap. ✉ *96 Greenwich Ave., between W. 12th and Jane Sts., Greenwich Village* ☎ *212/989–0001* 🌐 *www.flight001.com* Ⓜ *A, C, E to 14th St.; L to 8th Ave.*

Fodor's Choice ★ **Leffot.** This simple, understated store focuses on one thing: selling top-quality men's shoes. Owner Steven Taffel, who previously worked at Prada, has stocked his shop with selections from Church's, Basil Racuk, and Artioli. These shoes are meant to last a lifetime, and many have a price tag to match. Bespoke footware is also available. ✉ *10*

Christopher St., at Gay St., West Village ☎ *212/989–4577* 🌐 *www.leffot.com* Ⓜ *1 to Christopher St.–Sheridan Sq.*

Lulu Guinness. Hit this black-and-white-stripe salon for cheerfully eccentric accessories such as handbags printed with images of lips, dolls, and cameos. The accessories, including umbrellas and luggage, are equally fun. ✉ *394 Bleecker St., between W. 11th and Perry Sts., Greenwich Village* ☎ *212/367–2120* 🌐 *www.luluguinness.com* Ⓜ *1 to Christopher St.–Sheridan Sq.*

CHELSEA AND THE MEATPACKING DISTRICT

CHELSEA

Chelsea offers one-stop shopping for some of the biggest retail brands.

BARGAIN SHOPPING

Loehmann's. This discount store doesn't attract hordes of tourists like Century 21, but you'll still have to dig through crammed racks to unearth bargains. Label searchers can turn up DVF wrap dresses for $100 and Betsey Johnson coats for around $200. For men, finds might include Juicy Couture T-shirts and Versace ties. The "back room" has the best women's designers. ✉ *101 7th Ave., at 16th St., Chelsea* ☎ *212/352–0856* 🌐 *www.loehmanns.com* Ⓜ *1, 2, 3 to 14th St.*

BOOKS AND STATIONERY

Books of Wonder. Readers young and old will delight in Manhattan's oldest and largest independent children's bookstore. The friendly, knowledgeable staff can help select gifts for all reading levels. Don't miss the extensive Oz section as well as the collection of old, rare, and collectible children's books and original children's book art. ✉ *18 W. 18th St., between 5th and 6th Aves., Chelsea* ☎ *212/989–3270* 🌐 *www.booksofwonder.com* Ⓜ *F, M to 14th St.; L to 6th Ave.*

Rob Warren Bookseller. Come to this plant-filled shop for out-of-print books in all categories, a large Beat Generation selection, literary first editions, and books on photography and art. ✉ *51 W. 28th St., between Broadway and 6th Ave., Chelsea* ☎ *212/759–5463* 🌐 *www.robwarrenbookseller.com* Ⓜ *N, R to 28th St.*

CLOTHING

Balenciaga. In this cavelike, Zen boutique, you might luck onto a reissue from the (Cristobal) Balenciaga archives, made up in modern fabrics. Don't miss the luxurious handbags and leather shoes. ✉ *542 W. 22nd St., between 10th and 11th Aves., Chelsea* ☎ *212/206–0872* 🌐 *www.balenciaga.com* Ⓜ *C, E to 23rd St.*

Comme des Garçons. The designs in this stark, white, swoopy space consistently push the fashion envelope with brash patterns, unlikely juxtapositions (tulle and neoprene), and cuts that are meant to be thought-provoking, not flattering. Architecture students come just for the interior design. ✉ *520 W. 22nd St., between 10th and 11th Aves., Chelsea* ☎ *212/604–9200* 🌐 *www.comme-des-garcons.com* Ⓜ *C, E to 23rd St.*

New York Vintage. Stylists to the stars, TV costumers, and the odd princess descend upon this boutique to browse racks of prime vintage clothing. Everything is high-end, so don't expect any bargains. If money is no object, take your pick from Yves Saint Laurent, Madame Grès, and Thierry Mugler pieces. There's a good selection of handbags and pumps, too. ✉ *117 W. 25th St., between 6th and 7th Aves., Chelsea* ☎ *212/647–1107* 🌐 *www.newyorkvintage.com* Ⓜ *1 to 28th St.*

GIFTS AND SOUVENIRS

Eleni's. Take a bite out of the Big Apple—in cookie form—with these perfectly decorated treats, shaped like yellow cabs, the Wall Street sign, and the Statue of Liberty. It's not just New York depicted here; the iced cookies come in every design imagineable, from iPhones to shoes and pirates. Cupcakes are also available. ✉ *Chelsea Market, 75 9th Ave., between 15th and 16th Sts., Chelsea* ☎ *212/255–6804* 🌐 *www.elenis.com* Ⓜ *A, C, E to 14th St.; L to 8th Ave.*

MUSIC STORES AND MEDIA

Jazz Record Center. If you're seeking rare or out-of-print jazz recordings, this is your one-stop shop. Long-lost Ellingtons and other rare pressings come to light here; the jazz-record specialist also stocks collectibles, DVDs, videos, posters, CDs, and LPs. ✉ *236 W. 26th St., between 7th and 8th Aves., 8th fl., Chelsea* ☎ *212/675–4480* 🌐 *www.jazzrecordcenter.com* Ⓜ *1 to 28th St.*

WINE

Bottlerocket Wine & Spirit. Fun and approachable, this shop puts a new spin on wine shopping. Vintages are organized by quirky factors like their compatibility with Chinese takeout and whom they'd best suit as gifts (ranging from "Someone You Barely Know" to "The Boss"). A reference library, kids' play nook, and doggie area make the space extra welcoming. ✉ *5 W. 19th St., between 5th and 6th Aves., Chelsea* ☎ *212/929–2323* 🌐 *www.bottlerocketwine.com* Ⓜ *L, N, Q, R, 4, 5, 6 to 14th St.–Union Sq.*

MEATPACKING DISTRICT

For nearly a century, this industrial western edge of downtown Manhattan was defined by slaughterhouses and meatpacking plants, blood-splattered cobblestone streets, and men lugging carcasses into warehouses way before dawn.

But in the late 1990s the area bounded by West 14th Street, Gansevoort Street, Hudson Street, and 11th Avenue speedily transformed into another kind of meat market. Many of the old warehouses now house ultrachic shops, nightclubs, and restaurants packed with angular fashionistas. Jeffrey, a pint-size department store, was an early arrival, followed by edgy but established brands like Alexander McQueen and a few lofty furniture stores. Despite the influx of a few chains—albeit stylish ones like Scoop—eclectic boutiques keep popping up. The one thing it's hard to find here is a bargain.

CAMERAS AND ELECTRONICS

Apple Store. Branch location at 401 West 14th Street. *See Midtown East for full review.*

Some shops in the Meatpacking District are definitely design-forward.

CLOTHING

Fodor's Choice ★ **Alexander McQueen.** The late designer's New York flagship is a futuristic, podlike space—an ideal setting for the avant-garde, luxurious clothing. Now under the helm of Sarah Burton, the designs are still theatrical with exquisite tailoring and a touch of softness. ✉ *417 W. 14th St., between 9th and 10th Aves., Meatpacking District* ☎ *212/645–1797* Ⓜ *A, C, E to 14th St.; L to 8th Ave.*

Catherine Malandrino. Celebs like Halle Berry love this French-born designer for her sexy-without-trying-too-hard looks. Shop for silk V-neck gowns or one-shouldered ruched wool dresses. ✉ *652 Hudson St., at 13th St., Meatpacking District* ☎ *212/929–8710* 🌐 *www.catherinemalandrino.com* Ⓜ *A, C, E to 14th St.; L to 8th Ave.*

Fodor's Choice ★ **Diane von Furstenberg.** At this light-filled New York flagship, try on the iconic DVF wrap dress in a myriad of patterns. The blouses, shorts, and skirts are equally feminine. ✉ *874 Washington St., at 14th St., Meatpacking District* ☎ *646/486–4800* 🌐 *www.dvf.com* Ⓜ *A, C, E to 14th St.; L to 8th Ave.*

Iris. As the Italian shoe manufacturers for stylish brands like John Galliano, Marc Jacobs, Veronique Branquinho, and Chloé, Iris's sole U.S. store is able to carry every style from those lines, including pieces not previously available on our shores. ✉ *827 Washington St., at Little W. 12th St., Meatpacking District* ☎ *212/645–0950* 🌐 *www.irisnyc.com* Ⓜ *A, C, E to 14th St.; L to 8th Ave.*

Jeffrey. The Meatpacking District really arrived when this Atlanta-based mini-Barneys opened its doors. You can find an incredible array of designer shoes—Valentino, Lanvin, and red-soled Christian Louboutin are some of the best sellers—plus top labels such as L'Wren Scott, Pucci, and Alaia. ✉ *449 W. 14th St., between 9th and 10th Aves., Meatpacking District* ☎ *212/206–1272* 🌐 *www.jeffreynewyork.com* Ⓜ *A, C, E to 14th St.; L to 8th Ave.*

Owen. FIT grad Phillip Salem transformed this space into a whimsical place to shop, thanks to the 25,000 paper bags that line the arched ceiling. This upscale boutique offers men's and womenswear from 70 established and independent designers. Come here for skinny jeans, luxurious sweaters, and dresses from J. Brand, Garter + Derringer, and Roksanda Ilincic. ✉ *809 Washington St., between Gansevoort and Horatio Sts., Meatpacking District* ☎ *212/524–9770* 🌐 *www.owennyc.com* Ⓜ *A, C, E to 14th St.; L to 8th Ave.*

Rebecca Taylor. Taylor is known for her soft, feminine designs, which run the gamut from sexy to understated, all with a slightly vintage flair. Her flagship is a serene, spacious environment for browsing racks of silky shirtdresses, embroidered tunics, and ruffled overcoats. Taylor's shoes, handbags, and jewelry are equally romantic. ✉ *34 Gansevoort St., between Greenwich and Hudson Sts., Meatpacking District* ☎ *212/243–2600* 🌐 *www.rebeccataylor.com* Ⓜ *A, C, E to 14 St.; L to 8th Ave.*

Tracy Reese. Unabashedly girly but wearable garb is Reese's specialty, as she plays with lush fabrics (silk chiffon is a favorite), quirky color combos, and glamorous touches such as ruffles. The cuts flatter all sorts of figures, often emphasizing the waist. This flagship carries both the ladylike Tracy Reese line and lower-price Plenty label, as well as home accessories. ✉ *641 Hudson St., between Horatio and Gansevoort Sts., Meatpacking District* ☎ *212/807–0505* 🌐 *www.tracyreese.com* Ⓜ *A, C, E to 14th St.; L to 8th Ave.*

JEWELRY AND ACCESSORIES

Ten Thousand Things. You might find yourself wishing for 10,000 things from the showcases in this elegant boutique. Designs run from delicate gold and silver chains to long Peruvian opal earrings. Many shapes are abstract reflections of natural forms, like twigs or seedpods. Prices start around $100. ✉ *423 W. 14th St., between 9th and 10th Aves., Meatpacking District* ☎ *212/352–1333* 🌐 *www.tenthousandthingsnyc.com* Ⓜ *A, C, E to 14th St.; L to 8th Ave.*

UNION SQUARE AND THE FLATIRON DISTRICT

FLATIRON DISTRICT

This neighborhood is one of the buzziest in New York, brimming with both large and small stores as well as excellent restaurants and the city's best greenmarket. Come here if you want to shop the big chains minus the midtown tourist crowds.

BOOKS AND STATIONERY

Idlewild Books. Named for the pre-1960s JFK Airport, this travel-inspired bookstore groups its goods by destination. It has much more than guidebooks, though; novels, histories, cookbooks, and children's books share each segment, giving you a fascinating look at any given locale. If those chairs look familiar, it may be because you spent a layover in one of them once upon a time in the American Airlines terminal. ✉ *12 W. 19th St., 2nd fl., at 5th Ave., Flatiron District* ☎ *212/414–8888* 🌐 *www.idlewildbooks.com* Ⓜ *4, 5, 6, L, N, Q, R to 14th St.–Union Sq.*

CHILDREN'S CLOTHING

Space Kiddets. The funky (Elvis-print rompers, CBGB onesies) mixes with the old-school (retro cowboy-print pants, brightly colored clogs, Bruce Lee T-shirts) and the high-end (Lilli Gaufrette, Kenzo, Boo Foo Woo from Japan) at this casual, trendsetting store that is a favorite of Julianne Moore. ✉ *26 E. 22nd St., between Broadway and Park Ave., Flatiron District* ☎ *212/420–9878* 🌐 *www.spacekiddets.com* Ⓜ *6 to 23rd St.*

CLOTHING

Anthropologie. Bohemian-chic is the aesthetic of this popular women's clothing and home accessories chain. ✉ *85 Fifth Ave.* ☎ *212/627–5885* 🌐 *www.anthropologie.com* Ⓜ *L, N, Q, R, 4, 5, 6 to 14th St.–Union Sq.* ✉ *Chelsea Market, 75 9th Ave., Chelsea* ☎ *212/620–3116* ✉ *375 W. Broadway, SoHo* ☎ *212/343–7070* ✉ *50 Rockefeller Center, Midtown West* ☎ *212/246–0386* .

Beacon's Closet. Brooklyn favorite Beacon's Closet has finally opened a Big Apple outpost. This simple space, which is lit by multiple chandeliers, offers a wide selection of gently used modern and vintage clothes. Comb through the racks and you might find pieces from Christian Dior, Marc Jacobs, or AllSaints. ✉ *10 W 13th St., between 5th and 6th Aves., Union Square* ☎ *917/261-4863* 🌐 *www.beaconscloset.com* Ⓜ *L, N, Q, R, 4, 5, 6 to 14th St.–Union Sq..*

Madewell. This J. Crew spinoff is ideal for casual women's staples like jeans, T-shirts, and sweaters with a vintage look. The two-story Manhattan flagship has a quirky, homespun design; merchandise is displayed on everything from old mill tables to meat hooks. Don't miss the shoe shop and home goods collection. ✉ *115 Fifth Ave., between 18th and 19th Sts., Flatiron District* ☎ *212/228–5172* 🌐 *www.madewell.com* Ⓜ *L, N, Q, R, 4, 5, 6 to 14th St.–Union Sq.*

Fodor's Choice ★ **Maison Kitsuné.** This decades-old French fashion and music label recently made its stateside debut. Come to this airy, sunwashed boutique for men's and womenswear classics with a stylish Gallic twist, ranging from cardigans and loafers to blazers and dresses. ✉ *NoMad Hotel, 1170 Broadway, at 28th St., Flatiron District* ☎ *212/481-6010* 🌐 *www.kitsune.fr* Ⓜ *N, R to 28th St.*

HOME DECOR

Fodor's Choice ★ **ABC Carpet & Home.** If you love eclectic goods from around the world, then this is your place. Spread over 10 floors is a superb selection of rugs, antiques, textiles, furniture, and bedding. Shoppers can find sleek sofas or Balinese daybeds. The ground floor is a wonderland of silk pillows and jewelry. To refuel, there's an in-house restaurant from Jean-Georges Vongerichten. More rugs and carpets are unrolled across the street at 881 Broadway. ✉ *888 Broadway, at 19th St., Flatiron District* ☎ *212/473–3000* 🌐 *www.abchome.com* Ⓜ *L, N, Q, R, 4, 5, 6 to 14th St.–Union Sq.*

CLOSE UP

Holiday Markets

Between Thanksgiving and Christmas, holiday markets—rows of wooden stalls, many with red-and-white-stripe awnings—spring up around town. The gifts and goods vary from year to year, but there are some perennial offerings: colorful handmade knitwear and jewelry; sweet-smelling soaps, candles, and lotions with hand-lettered labels; glittery Christmas ornaments of every stripe; and New York–theme gift items (a group called Gritty City offers T-shirts, coin purses, and undies printed with pictures of taxicabs and manhole covers).

While the holiday market in **Grand Central Terminal's Vanderbilt Hall** is indoors, most vendors set up outside. There's one every year at **Columbus Circle,** near the southwest entrance to Central Park, and another at **Bryant Park,** behind the New York City Public Library. The largest and most popular, however, is at the south end of **Union Square,** where you can go from the greenmarket to the stalls like the downtowners who meet in the afternoon or after work to look for unique or last-minute gifts.

Fodor's Choice ★ **Fishs Eddy.** The dishes, china, and glassware for resale come from all walks of crockery life, from corporate dining rooms to failed restaurants and ocean liners. Fishs Eddy also sells its own line of dishes, which have a classic look, and is a great place to pick up New York–themed gifts, such as mugs and trays. ✉ *889 Broadway, at 19th St., Flatiron District* ☎ *212/420–9020* 🌐 *www.fishseddy.com* Ⓜ *L, N, Q, R, 4, 5, 6 to 14th St.–Union Sq.*

Marimekko. If you love bright, cheerful patterns, make a beeline to the new Marimekko flagship. This 4,000-square-foot store is designed primarily in white, so the colorful merchandise pops. Everything from potholders and shower curtains to coats and dresses is available here in the signtaure Marimekko bold prints. If you're feeling crafty, pick up a few yards of fabric to whip up your own creations. ✉ *200 5th Ave., between 23rd and 24th Sts., Flatiron District* ☎ *212/843–9121* 🌐 *www.marimekko.com* Ⓜ *F, M to 23rd St.*

JEWELRY AND ACCESSORIES

Beads of Paradise. Not your ordinary bead store, the baubles here are sourced from around the world. Shoppers can choose silver from Bali and Mexico and ancient glass beads from China, along with semiprecious stones. Sign up for a class to learn how to put it all together. ✉ *16 E. 17th St., between 5th Ave. and Broadway, Flatiron District* ☎ *212/620–0642* 🌐 *www.beadsofparadisenyc.com* Ⓜ *L, N, Q, R, 4, 5, 6 to 14th St.–Union Sq.*

TOYS

Kidding Around. This independent shop is piled high with old-fashioned wooden toys, sturdy musical instruments, and plenty of arts-and-crafts materials. The costume racks are rich with dress-up potential. ✉ *60 W. 15th St., between 5th and 6th Aves., Flatiron District* ☎ *212/645–6337* 🌐 *www.kiddingaroundtoys.com* Ⓜ *L, N, Q, R, 4, 5, 6 to 14th St.–Union Sq.*

UNION SQUARE

If you want to browse the big retail chains such as J. Crew, Banana Republic, and Anthropologie without hordes of tourists, come here.

BEAUTY

Fresh. Long a beauty favorite, with ingredients that are good enough to eat (think brown sugar, soy, and black tea), Fresh recently revamped its New York flagship. The boutique has an apothecary-inspired look, with beautifully packaged soaps displayed like pastries in a glass case, and a Sensorial Bar, featuring discontinued perfumes on tap. Pull up at a seat at the communal Kitchen Table to try out a new product. ✉ *872 Broadway, between 18th and 19th Sts., Union Square* ☎ *212/477–1100* 🌐 *www.fresh.com* Ⓜ *L, N, Q, R, 4, 5, 6 to 14th St.–Union Sq.*

BOOKS AND STATIONERY

Fodor's Choice ★ **The Strand.** Opened in 1927, and still run by the same family, this monstrous book emporium—home to 2 million volumes and "18 Miles of Books"—is a symbol of a bygone era, a mecca for serious bibliophiles, and a local institution. The store has survived the Great Depression, World War II, competition from Barnes & Noble, and the tremendous shift in how readers are consuming literature. The stock includes both new and secondhand books, plus thousands of collector's items. A separate rare-book room is on the third floor and closes at 6:20 daily. The basement has discounted, barely touched reviewers' copies of new books, organized by author. **TIP→ If you're looking for souvenirs, visit the New York section of the bookstore; you'll find New York–centric literature, poetry, history, photography, and cookbooks, as well as T-shirts, gadgets, and totes.** ✉ *828 Broadway, at 12th St., Union Square* ☎ *212/473–1452* 🌐 *www.strandbooks.com* ⏲ *Mon.–Sat. 9:30 am–10:30 pm, Sun. 11–10:30* Ⓜ *L, N, Q, R, 4, 5, 6 to Union Sq.–14th St.*

CLOTHING

Forever 21. Branch location at 40 East 14th Street. *See Midtown West for full review.*

J. Crew. The preppy-chic brand that is a staple in so many people's closets continues to push the envelope. Yes, you can still get cardigans, cords, and tees in every pastel color of the rainbow, but some of the separates are downright sexy. The leather jackets and sequined skirts are also perfect for that casual, thrown-together look. This flagship carries women's, men's, and Crewcuts for children as well as a wedding gown collection. ✉ *91 5th Avenue, between 15th and 16th Sts, Union Square* ☎ *212/255–4848* 🌐 *www.jcrew.com* Ⓜ *L, N, Q, R, 4, 5, 6 to 14th St.–Union Square.*

MIDTOWN EAST

If money is no object, put on your shopping shoes and head to Midtown East. Some of the world's most luxurious brands—from Gucci to Christian Dior—have their flagship stores along Fifth Avenue.

ANTIQUES AND COLLECTIBLES

The Chinese Porcelain Company. Though the name of this prestigious shop indicates one of its specialties, its stock covers more ground, ranging from lacquerware to Khmer sculpture as well as European decorative arts. ✉ *475 Park Ave., at E. 58th St., Midtown East* ☎ *212/838–7744* 🌐 *www.chineseporcelainco.com* Ⓜ *N, Q, R to 5th Ave./59th St.*

Flying Cranes Antiques. At this world leader in Japanese antiques, shoppers will find a collection of rare, museum-quality pieces from the Meiji period, the time known as Japan's Golden Age. Items include ceramics, cloisonné, metalwork, baskets, and samurai swords and fittings. ✉ *Manhattan Art and Antiques Center, 1050 2nd Ave., between 55th and 56th Sts., Midtown East* ☎ *212/223–4600* 🌐 *www.flyingcranesantiques.com* Ⓜ *N, Q, R to Lexington Ave.; 4, 5, 6 to 59th St.*

Leo Kaplan Ltd. The impeccable items here include Art Nouveau glass and pottery, porcelain from 18th-century England, antique and modern paperweights, and Russian artwork. ✉ *114 E. 57th St., between Park and Lexington Aves., Midtown East* ☎ *212/355–7212* 🌐 *www.leokaplan.com* Ⓜ *N, Q, R to Lexington Ave.; 4, 5, 6 to 59th St.*

Newel Art Galleries. Housed in a six-story building, this huge collection spans the Renaissance through the 20th century. The nonfurniture finds, from figureheads to bell jars, make for prime conversation pieces. Newel is also a major supplier of antiques for Broadway shows, television, and film. ✉ *425 E. 53rd St., between 1st Ave. and Sutton Pl., Midtown East* ☎ *212/758–1970* 🌐 *www.newel.com* Ⓜ *6 to 51st St.; E, M to Lexington Ave./53rd St.*

BOOKS AND STATIONERY

Fodor's Choice ★ **Argosy Bookstore.** Family owned since 1925, Argosy keeps a scholarly stock of rare books and autographs. It's also a great place to look for low-price maps and prints that make ideal gifts. ✉ *116 E. 59th St., between Park and Lexington Aves., Midtown East* ☎ *212/753–4455* 🌐 *www.argosybooks.com* Ⓜ *N, Q, R to Lexington Ave.; 4, 5, 6 to 59th St.*

The Complete Traveller Antiquarian Bookstore. Founded in the '80s by two former travel writers, this store specializes in rare and antique voyage-related books, and holds the largest selection of out-of-print Baedeker travel guides. They stock surprisingly affordable vintage maps, unusual tomes with New York City themes, and a full spectrum of books—from history and geography to poetry and fiction—that emphasize travel. ✉ *199 Madison Ave., at 35th St., Midtown East* ☎ *212/685–9007* 🌐 *www.ctrarebooks.com* Ⓜ *6 to 33rd St.*

Posman Books. One of the last independent book stores in New York City, Posman Books has an outstanding selection of contemporary and classic books across genres. Don't miss the cheeky and serious high-quality greeting cards. ✉ *9 Grand Central Terminal, at Vanderbilt Ave. and 42nd St., Midtown East* ☎ *212/983–1111* 🌐 *www.posmanbooks.com* ✉ *30 Rockefeller Plaza, Concourse Level, Midtown West* ☎ *212/489–9100* Ⓜ *4, 5, 6, 7 to 42nd St.–Grand Central* ✉ *75 9th Ave., Chelsea Market, Chelsea* ☎ *212/627–0304.*

CAMERAS AND ELECTRONICS

Fodor's Choice ★ **Apple Store.** New York's flagship Apple Store features a 32-foot-high glass cube that appears to float over its subterranean entrance. The Apple obsessed will be happy to know this location is open 24/7 every day of the year, and stocks all the latest Apple products. Make an

18

appointment at the Genius Bar if you need tech help. ✉ *767 5th Ave., between 58th and 59th Sts., Midtown East* ☎ *212/336–1440* 🌐 *www.apple.com* Ⓜ *N, Q, R to 5th Ave./59th St.*

SONY Style. Located on the ground floor of the Sony Building, this sunny space is a wonderland of electronics. You'll find all the latest stereo and entertainment systems, digital cameras, high-def TVs, and MP3 players on the shelves. ✉ *550 Madison Ave., at 55th St., Midtown East* ☎ *212/833–8800* 🌐 *www.store.sony.com* Ⓜ *6 to 51st St.; E, M to Lexington Ave./53rd St.*

CLOTHING

Brooks Brothers. The clothes at this classic American haberdasher are, as ever, traditional, comfortable, and fairly priced. Summer seersucker, navy-blue blazers, and the peerless oxford shirts have been staples for generations. The women's and boys' selection have variations thereof. **TIP→ Get scanned by a digital tailor for precisely measured custom shirts or suits; appointments are recommended.** ✉ *346 Madison Ave., at 44th St., Midtown East* ☎ *212/682–8800* 🌐 *www.brooksbrothers.com* Ⓜ *4, 5, 6, 7, S to 42nd St.–Grand Central.*

Burberry. This six-story glass-and-stone flagship is a temple to all things plaid and British. The iconic trench coat can be made-to-measure here, and the signature plaid can be found on bikinis, scarves, and wallets. For children, there are mini-versions of quilted jackets and cozy sweaters. ✉ *9 E. 57th St., between 5th and Madison Aves., Midtown East* ☎ *212/407–7100* 🌐 *www.burberry.com* Ⓜ *N, Q, R to 5th Ave./59th St.*

Chanel. The Midtown flagship has often been compared to a Chanel suit—slim, elegant, and timeless, and decorated in the signature black-and-white colors. Inside, the famed suits themselves await, along with other pillars of Chanel style: chic little black dresses and evening gowns, chain-handled bags, and yards of pearls. There's also a small cosmetics area where you can stock up on the famed scents and nail polish. ✉ *15 E. 57th St., between 5th and Madison Aves., Midtown East* ☎ *212/355–5050* 🌐 *www.chanel.com* Ⓜ *N, Q, R to 5th Ave./59th St.*

Christian Dior. This very white, very glossy space offers a serene background to showcase the luxe, ready-to-wear collection along with handbags and accessories. If you're not in the market for an investment gown or fine jewelry, peruse the latest status bag. The Dior menswear boutique is next door; the rocking cigarette-thin suits are often pilfered by women. ✉ *21 E. 57th St., at Madison Ave., Midtown East* ☎ *212/931–2950* 🌐 *www.dior.com* Ⓜ *E, M to 5th Ave./53rd St.*

Fodor'sChoice ★ **Dunhill.** If you're stumped on what to buy the man in your life, head to Dunhill. The menswear is exquisitely tailored; the accessories like wallets and cuff links are slightly more affordable. The walk-in humidor stores top-quality tobacco and cigars. ✉ *545 Madison Ave., at 55th St., Midtown East* ☎ *212/753–9292* 🌐 *www.dunhill.com* Ⓜ *F to 57th St.*

Gucci. Located in the Trump Building, this 46,000-square-foot flagship with floor-to-ceiling glass windows is the largest Gucci store in the world. Shoppers will find a special "heritage" department, plus goods exclusive to the store. The clothing is edgy and sexy. Skintight pants might be paired with a luxe leather jacket; silk tops leave a little more to the imagination. The accessories, like wraparound shades or snakeskin shoes, many with signature horsebit detailing, continue to spark consumer frenzies. ✉ *725 5th Ave., at 56th St., Midtown East* ☎ *212/826–2600* 🌐 *www.gucci.com* Ⓜ *N, Q, R to 5th Ave./59th St.*

Massimo Dutti. Owned by Zara, think of this brand as its older, more sophisticated sibling. The three-story space specializes in sleek basics that are perfect for work or the weekends, such as blazers, trench coats, and denim. ✉ *689 5th Ave., between 54th and 55th Sts., Midtown East* ☎ *212/371–2555* 🌐 *www.massimodutti.com* Ⓜ *E, M to 5th Ave./53rd St.*

Tommy Hilfiger. The global flagship oozes old-school Americana, with its dark-wood paneling, shirts displayed on bookshelves, and scattering of antiques. It's filled with tailored suits for men, smart sweater sets and pencil skirts for women, and evening wear along with sportswear, plus a whole floor devoted to denim. ✉ *681 5th Ave., at 54th St., Midtown East* ☎ *212/223–1824* Ⓜ *E, M to 5th Ave./53rd St.*

Yves Saint Laurent. Tom Ford's successor, Stephano Pilati, is lightening up the fabled French house. Think seduction instead of sexpot, with white trench coats, Grecian column dresses, and ruffled silk blouses. ✉ *3 E. 57th St., between 5th and Madison Aves., Midtown East* ☎ *212/980–2970* 🌐 *www.ysl.com* Ⓜ *N, Q, R to 5th Ave./59th St.*

DEPARTMENT STORES

Fodor's Choice ★ **Bloomingdale's.** Only a few stores in New York occupy an entire city block; the uptown branch of this New York institution is one of them. The main floor is a crazy, glittery maze of mirrored cosmetic counters and perfume-spraying salespeople. Once you get past this dizzying scene, you can find good buys on designer clothes, bedding, and housewares. ✉ *1000 3rd Ave., at E. 59th St. and Lexington Ave., Midtown East* ☎ *212/705–2000* 🌐 *bloomingdales.com* Ⓜ *N, Q, R to Lexington Ave.; 4, 5, 6 to 59th St.*

18

Saks Fifth Avenue. Saks sells an astonishing array of clothing. The choice of American and European designers is impressive without being esoteric—the women's selection includes Gucci, Narciso Rodriguez, and Marc Jacobs, plus devastating ball gowns galore. The footwear collections are gratifyingly broad, from Ferragamo to Juicy. In the men's department, sportswear stars such as John Varvatos counterbalance formal wear and current trends. The ground-floor beauty department stocks everything from the classic (Sisley, Lancôme, La Prairie) to the fun and edgy (Nars, M.A.C.). ✉ *611 5th Ave., between 49th and 50th Sts., Midtown East* ☎ *212/753–4000* 🌐 *www.saksfifthavenue.com* Ⓜ *E, M to 5th Ave./53rd St.*

GIFTS AND SOUVENIRS

New York City Transit Museum Gift Shop. Located in the symbolic heart of New York City's transit system, the store features a wacky array of merchandise all linked to the MTA (Metropolitan Transportation Authority), from straphanger ties to earrings made from old subway tokens. ✉ *Grand Central Terminal, Vanderbilt Pl. and E. 42nd St., Midtown East* ☎ *212/878–0106* 🌐 *www.transitmuseumstore.com* Ⓜ *4, 5, 6, 7, S to 42nd St.–Grand Central.*

HOME DECOR

Armani Casa. In keeping with the Armani aesthetic, the minimalist furniture and homewares have a subdued color scheme (gold, grays, cream, and black). Big-ticket items include luxuriously upholstered sofas and sleek coffee tables. The desk accessories and throw pillows are equally understated. ✉ *Decoration & Design Building, 979 3rd Ave., Ste. 1424, between 58th and 59th Sts., Midtown East* ☎ *212/334–1271* 🌐 *www.armanicasa.com* Ⓜ *N, Q, R to Lexington Ave.; 4, 5, 6 to 59th St.*

JEWELRY AND ACCESSORIES

A La Vieille Russie. Antiques dealers since 1851, this shop specializes in European and Russian decorative arts, jewelry, and paintings. Behold bibelots by Fabergé and others, enameled or encrusted with jewels. If money is no object, there are also antique diamond necklaces and pieces of china once owned by Russian nobility. ✉ *781 5th Ave., at 59th St., Midtown East* ☎ *212/752–1727* 🌐 *www.alvr.com* Ⓜ *N, Q, R to 5th Ave./59th St.*

Cartier. Pierre Cartier allegedly won the 5th Avenue mansion location by trading two strands of perfectly matched natural pearls with Mrs. Morton Plant. The jewelry is still incredibly persuasive, from such established favorites as the Trinity ring and Tank watches to exquisite cuff links for men. ✉ *653 5th Ave., at 52nd St., Midtown East* ☎ *212/753–0111* 🌐 *www.cartier.com* Ⓜ *E, M to 5th Ave./53rd St.*

H. Stern. Sleek designs pose in an equally modern 5th Avenue setting; smooth cabochon-cut stones, most from South America, glow in pale wooden display cases. The designers make notable use of semiprecious stones such as citrine, tourmaline, and topaz. ✉ *645 5th Ave., between 51st and 52nd Sts., Midtown East* ☎ *212/655–3910* 🌐 *www.hstern.net* Ⓜ *E, M to 5th Ave./53rd St.*

Fodor'sChoice ★ **Tiffany & Co.** The display windows can be soigné, funny, or just plain breathtaking. Alongside the $80,000 platinum-and-diamond bracelets, much here is affordable on a whim (check out the sterling silver floor)—and everything comes wrapped in that unmistakable Tiffany blue box. ✉ *727 5th Ave., at 57th St., Midtown East* ☎ *212/755–8000* 🌐 *www.tiffany.com* Ⓜ *N, Q, R to 5th Ave./59th St.*

Van Cleef & Arpels. This French jewelry company is considerably more low-key than many of its blingy neighbors, in both the designs and marketing ethos (you won't see them opening a store in your average mall). Their best-known design is the cloverleaf Alhambra, which can be found on rings, necklaces, and earrings. Other designs are just as understated. ✉ *744 5th Ave., between E. 57th St. and E. 58th Sts., Midtown East* ☎ *212/644–9500* 🌐 *www.vancleef-arpels.com* Ⓜ *N, Q, R to 5th Ave./59th St.*

SHOES, HANDBAGS, AND LEATHER GOODS

Bally. If you want to channel your inner princess, you can't go wrong with the lady-like pumps and high-heeled boots here. The accessories and clothing are equally understated. ✉ *628 Madison Ave., at E. 59th St., Midtown East* ☎ *212/751–9082* 🌐 *www.bally.com* Ⓜ *N, Q, R to Lexington Ave.; 4, 5, 6 to 59th St.*

CLOSE UP

Department Store Discounts

If you don't have one of these stores in the state where you live, take advantage of special discounts available by showing a state ID card.

Bloomingdale's: Go to the visitor center on the balcony level between the ground and second floors for a 10% discount on all purchases bought that day.

Lord & Taylor: Hit the ground-floor information desk to pick up a coupon for 15% off that day's purchases.

Macy's: Stop by the visitor center on the balcony level between the ground and second floors for a 10% discount voucher. The coupon is valid for five days for US visitors and one month for international visitors.

Bottega Veneta. The signature crosshatch weave graces leather handbags, slouchy satchels, and shoes; the especially satisfying brown shades extend from fawn to deep chocolate. The stylish men's and women's ready-to-wear collection is also sold here. ✉ *699 5th Ave., between 54th and 55th Sts., Midtown East* ☎ *212/371–5511* 🌐 *www.bottegaveneta.com* Ⓜ *N, Q, R to Lexington Ave.; 4, 5, 6 to 59th St.*

Fendi. Once known for its furs, Fendi is now synonymous with decadent handbags. The purses are beaded, embroidered, and fantastically embellished within an inch of their lives, resulting in prices well over $1,000. Fancy leathers, ladylike evening dresses, coats, and other accessories are also available. ✉ *677 5th Ave., between 53rd and 54th Sts., Midtown East* ☎ *212/759–4646* 🌐 *www.fendi.com* Ⓜ *E, F to 5th Ave./53rd St.*

18

Fratelli Rossetti. Don't come here expecting sexy, skyscraper stilettos. This Italian leather goods company excels at beautiful, classic shoes. Their riding boots are among the most popular items, but there are also pumps, loafers, and slouchy ankle boots. Men can choose from oxfords and boots. There's also a line of leather handbags. ✉ *625 Madison Ave., between 58th and 59th Sts., Midtown East* ☎ *212/888–5107* 🌐 *www.fratellirossetti.com* Ⓜ *N, Q, R to Lexington Ave.; 4, 5, 6 to 59th St.*

Furla. Shoulder bags, oblong clutches, and roomy totes can be quite proper or attention-getting, from a cocoa-brown, croc-embossed zipper-top to a patent leather, cherry-red purse. ✉ *598 Madison Ave., at 57th St., Midtown East* ☎ *212/980–3208* 🌐 *www.furla.com* Ⓜ *N, Q, R to Lexington Ave.; 4, 5, 6 to 59th St.*

Fodor's Choice ★ **Louis Vuitton.** In the mammoth 57th Street store vintage examples of Vuitton's famous monogrammed trunks float above the fray on the ground floor, where shoppers angle for the latest accessories. Joining the initials are the Damier check pattern and colorful striated leathers, plus devastatingly chic clothes and shoes designed by Marc Jacobs. ✉ *1 E. 57th St., at 5th Ave., Midtown East* ☎ *212/758–8877* 🌐 *www.louisvuitton.com* Ⓜ *E, M to 5th Ave./53rd St.*

Salvatore Ferragamo. Elegance and restraint typify these designs, from black-tie patent to weekender ankle boots. The company reworks some of their women's styles from previous decades, like the girlish Audrey (as in Hepburn) ballet flat, released seasonally for limited runs. Don't miss the silk ties for men. ✉ *655 5th Ave., at 52nd St., Midtown East* ☎ *212/759–3822* 🌐 *www.ferragamo.com* Ⓜ *E, M to 5th Ave./53rd St.*

Stuart Weitzman. The broad range of styles, from wing tips to strappy sandals, is enhanced by an even wider range of sizes and widths. Bridal shoes are hugely popular, if pricey. ✉ *625 Madison Ave., between 58th and 59th Sts., Midtown East* ☎ *212/750–2555* 🌐 *www.stuartweitzman.com* Ⓜ *N, Q, R to Lexington Ave.; 4, 5, 6 to 59th St.*

TOYS

American Girl Place. No pink toy convertibles here; instead, the namesake dolls are historically themed, from Felicity of colonial Virginia to Kit of Depression-era Cincinnati. Each character has her own affiliated books, furniture, clothes, and accessories. There's a doll hairdressing station, a café, and a Dress Like Your Doll shop. ✉ *609 5th Ave., at 49th St., Midtown East* ☎ *877/247–5223* 🌐 *www.americangirl.com* Ⓜ *B, D, F, M to 47th–50th Sts./Rockefeller Center.*

Fodor's Choice ★ **FAO Schwarz Fifth Avenue.** A New York classic that's better than ever, this children's paradise more than lives up to the hype. The ground floor is a zoo of extraordinary stuffed animals, from cuddly $20 teddies to towering, life-size elephants and giraffes (with larger-than-life prices to match). FAO Schwartz stocks M&Ms in every color of the rainbow. Upstairs, you can dance on the giant musical floor keyboard, browse through Barbies wearing Armani and Juicy Couture, and take a tour with a Toy Soldier. ✉ *767 5th Ave., at 58th St., Midtown East* ☎ *212/644–9400* Ⓜ *4, 5, 6 to 59th St.*

MIDTOWN WEST

Whether you're window-shopping or have money to burn, Midtown West includes some of the best (and priciest) department stores, including Bergdorf Goodman and Henri Bendel.

CAMERAS AND ELECTRONICS

B&H Photo Video and Pro Audio. As baskets of purchases trundle along on tracks overhead, you can plunge into the excellent selection of imaging, audio, video, and lighting equipment. The staff is generous with advice, and will happily compare merchandise. Low prices, good customer service, and a liberal returns policy make this a favorite with pros and amateurs alike. **TIP→** Be sure to leave a few extra minutes for the checkout procedure; also, keep in mind that the store is closed Saturday. ✉ *420 9th Ave., between 33rd and 34th Sts., Midtown West* ☎ *212/444–6615* 🌐 *www.bhphotovideo.com* Ⓜ *A, C, E to 34th St.–Penn Station.*

CLOTHING

Banana Republic. Although there are nearly a dozen Banana Republic stores around the city, come to the flagship for the biggest selection of clothing. Don't miss the Heritage collection, or the big clearance racks. ✉ *Rockefeller Center, 626 5th Ave., at 51st St., Midtown West* ☎ *212/974–2350* 🌐 *www.bananarepublic.gap.com* Ⓜ *B, D, F, M at 47th–50th Sts./Rockefeller Center.*

FAO Schwarz is a true experience.

Cheap Jack's. Jack's two-floor space may be 12,000 square feet, but it's still jammed with interesting duds—although they are not as cheap as the name would suggest. There's almost everything you could wish for: track suits, bomber jackets, early 1980s madras shirts, old prom dresses, and vintage concert T-shirts with the eau-de-mothball stamp of authenticity. ✉ *303 5th Ave., at 31st St., Midtown West* ☎ *212/777–9564* 🌐 *www.cheapjacks.com* Ⓜ *B, D, F, M, N, Q, R to 34th St.–Herald Sq.*

Club Monaco. Think of this brand as a hipper Banana Republic. Now owned by Ralph Lauren, Club Monaco offers stylish cuts that stand out from the mass-market pack. ✉ *6 West 57th St., Midtown West* ☎ *212/459–9863* 🌐 *www.clubmonaco.com* Ⓜ *F to 57th St.; N, Q, R to 5th Ave.–59th St..*

Forever 21. The pounding music, plethora of jeggings, and graffiti-covered NYC taxicab parked inside will appeal to tween shoppers. But even if you are older than 21, you'll still find a reason to shop here. This location, clocking in at a whopping 90,000 square feet, is the biggest Forever 21 on the East Coast. Come for supertrendy clothes that won't break the bank, such as slouchy sweaters, shirtdresses, and pouffy skirts. Menswear and children's clothes are also sold here, and the jewelry is surprisingly well done. There are several other locations in Manhattan, including Union Square. ✉ *1540 Broadway, between 45th and 46th Sts, Midtown West* ☎ *212/302–0594* 🌐 *www.forever21.com* Ⓜ *B, D, F, M to 47th–50th St./Rockefeller Center.*

Gap. Gap may be as ubiquitous as Starbucks, but it is still a go-to place for classics such as denim, khakis, and sweaters in a rainbow of colors as well as on-trend capsule collections from top designers. This flagship also carries GapBody, GapMaternity, GapKids, and babyGap. ✉ *60 West 34th St., at Broadway, Midtown West* ☎ *212/760–1268* 🌐 *www.gap.com* Ⓜ *B, D, F, M, N, Q, R to 34th St.–Herald Square.*

H&M. Of-the-moment trends are captured for the mass market at this affordable European clothing chain, which has numerous stores in the city. ✉ *640 5th Ave., between 51st and 52nd Sts., Midtown West* ☎ *212/489–0390* 🌐 *www.hm.com* Ⓜ *E, M to 5th Ave./53rd St.* ✉ *435 7th Ave., at 34th St., Chelsea* ☎ *212/643–6955* 🌐 *www.hm.com*

Joe Fresh. Think of this brand as the Canadian version of H&M crossed with the Gap, offering stylish but classic clothes for men and women at affordable prices. The New York flagship offers everything from sweaters and denim to button-down shirts and shoes in a rainbow of colors. Just about all items are priced under $100. ✉ *510 5th Ave., between 42nd and 43rd Sts., Midtown West* ☎ *212/764–1730* 🌐 *www.joefresh.com* Ⓜ *7 to 5th Ave.*

Norma Kamali. A fashion fixture from the 1980s has a newly modern, though still '80s-influenced, line. Her luminously white store carries graphic bathing suits, Grecian-style draped dresses, and her signature poofy "sleeping-bag coats." The in-house Wellness Café sells olive oil–based beauty products and healthful snacks like kale chips. ✉ *11 W. 56th St., between 5th and 6th Aves., Midtown West* ☎ *212/957–9797* Ⓜ *N, Q, R 5th Ave./59th St.*

UNIQLO. At 89,000 square feet, this location is the biggest Uniqlo in the world (but there are also branches in SoHo and near Macy's). Shoppers can scoop up staples such as sweaters, skinny jeans, and button-down shirts in a rainbow of colors. Don't miss the limited edition collaborations with big name designers and stylists. The Heattech clothing range is always a big hit. **TIP→ Weekday mornings are the best time to avoid long lines for the dressing rooms.** ✉ *666 5th Ave., between 52nd and 53rd Sts., Midtown West* ☎ *877/486–4756* 🌐 *www.uniqlo.com* Ⓜ *E, M to 5th Ave./53rd St.*

Zara. This massive flagship, the biggest Zara store in the US, is a haven for cheap and chic fashion. New merchandise arrives twice a week and clothing is arranged throughout the store by color (neutrals on one side, neon on the other). There are also two lounge areas, in case you need a shopping break. ✉ *666 5th Ave., between 52nd and 53rd Sts., Midtown West* ☎ *212/765–0477* 🌐 *www.zara.com* Ⓜ *E, M to 5th Ave./53rd St.*

DEPARTMENT STORES

Bergdorf Goodman. This luxury department store is the ultimate shopping destination, offering ladies (and men) who lunch designer clothes, a stellar shoe department, and top notch service. The fifth floor is where to go for mid-priced lines. The range of products offered in the beauty department is unparalled—and shoppers can complete their look with highlights at the in-house John Barrett salon. If you need to refuel, grab a bite at the seventh-floor BG Restaurant, with Central Park views. ✉ *754 5th Ave., between 57th and 58th Sts., Midtown West* ☎ *212/753–7300* 🌐 *www.bergdorfgoodman.com* Ⓜ *N, Q, R to 5th Ave.*

Henri Bendel. Behind the graceful Lalique windows you'll discover a mecca of niche boutiques stocking beauty products, accessories, and gifts (but no clothing). Bendel's dedication to the unusual begins in the ground-floor cosmetics area and percolates through the floors of women's lingerie and jewelry, scarves, and sunglasses. If you really want to pamper yourself, the fourth floor is home to Frédéric Fekkai's hair salon. ✉ *712 5th Ave., between 55th and 56th Sts., Midtown West* ☎ *212/247–1100* 🌐 *www.henribendel.com* Ⓜ *E, M to 5th Ave./53rd St.*

Lord & Taylor. This is not your mother's Lord & Taylor. The department store has been working hard to attract a younger, hipper crowd. Thanks to a recent makeover, the clothing departments are easier to navigate and shoppers will find classic brands like Coach, Donna Karan, and Ralph Lauren. Don't miss the lovely ground floor beauty department. Best of all, it isn't nearly as crowded as competitor Macy's. ✉ *424 5th Ave., between W. 38th and W. 39th Sts., Midtown West* ☎ *212/391–3344* 🌐 *www.lordandtaylor.com* Ⓜ *B, D, F, M, N, Q, R to 34th St.–Herald Sq.*

Macy's. Macy's headquarters has more than 1 million square feet of retail space, so expect to lose your bearings at least once. Fashion-wise, there's a concentration on the mainstream rather than on the luxe. One strong suit is denim, with everything from Hilfiger and Calvin Klein to Earl Jeans and Paper Denim & Cloth. There's also a reliably good selection of American designs from Ralph Lauren, DKNY, and Sean John. ✉ *Herald Sq., 151 W. 34th St., between 6th and 7th Aves., Midtown West* ☎ *212/695–4400* 🌐 *www.macys.com* Ⓜ *B, D, F, M, N, Q, R to 34th St.–Herald Sq.*

HOME DECOR

Muji. If you're into simple, chic, cheap style, Muji will be your trifecta. The name of this Japanese import translates to "no brand," and indeed, you won't find a logo plastered on the housewares or clothes. Instead, their hallmark is streamlined, often monochromatic design. The whole range of goods, from milky porcelain teapots to wooden toys, is invariably user-friendly. At this branch, you can glimpse the lobby of the *New York Times*. ✉ *620 8th Ave., at 40th St., Midtown West* ☎ *212/382–2300* 🌐 *www.muji.us* Ⓜ *A, C, E to 42nd St.–Port Authority* ✉ *455 Broadway, SoHo* ☎ *212/334–2002* 🌐 *www.muji.us* ✉ *MoMa Design Store, 81 Spring St., SoHo* ☎ *646/613–1367* 🌐 *www.muji.us* ✉ *MoMa Design Store, 11 W. 53rd St., Midtown West* ☎ *212/414–9024* 🌐 *www.muji.us* ✉ *16 W. 19th St., Chelsea* ☎ *212/414–9024* 🌐 *www.muji.us.*

JEWELRY AND ACCESSORIES

Bulgari. This Italian company is certainly not shy about its name, which appears on watch faces, and an ever-growing accessories line. There are beautiful, weighty rings, pieces mixing gold with stainless steel or porcelain, and the brand's signature cabochon multicolored sapphires. Wedding and engagement rings are slightly more subdued. ✉ *730 5th Ave., at 57th St., Midtown West* ☎ *212/315–9000* 🌐 *www.bulgari.com* Ⓜ *N,Q, R to 5th Ave./59th St.*

Harry Winston. These jewels regularly adorn celebs at the Oscars, and you'll need an A-list bank account to shop here. The ice-clear diamonds are of impeccable quality, and are set in everything from emerald-cut solitaire rings to wreath necklaces resembling strings of flowers. No wonder the jeweler was immortalized in the song "Diamonds Are a Girl's Best Friend." ✉ *718 5th Ave., at 56th St., Midtown West* ☎ *212/399-1000* 🌐 *www.harrywinston.com* Ⓜ *F to 57th St.*

Mikimoto. The Japanese originator of the cultured pearl, Mikimoto presents a glowing display of high-luster pearls. Besides the creamy strands from their own pearl farms, check out diamond-and-pearl earrings, bracelets, and rings. ✉ *730 5th Ave., between 56th and 57th Sts., Midtown West* ☎ *212/457–4600* 🌐 *www.mikimotoamerica.com* Ⓜ *F to 57th St.*

MUSEUM STORES

Museum of Arts and Design. This well-curated gift shop stocks crafts such as beautiful handmade tableware, unusual jewelry, and rugs, often tied in to ongoing exhibits. It's a great place to stock up on gifts. ✉ *2 Columbus Circle, at 8th Ave., Midtown West* ☎ *212/299–7700* 🌐 *www.madmuseum.org* Ⓜ *1, A, B, C, D to 59th St.–Columbus Circle.*

Museum of Modern Art Design and Book Store. The redesigned MoMA expanded its in-house shop with a huge selection of art posters and a gorgeous selection of coffee-table books on painting, sculpture, film, and photography. Across the street is the **MoMA Design Store,** where you can find Charles and Ray Eames furniture reproductions, vases designed by Alvar Aalto, and lots of clever trinkets. ✉ *11 W. 53rd St., between 5th and 6th Aves., Midtown West* ☎ *212/708–9700* 🌐 *www.moma.org/visit/plan/stores* Ⓜ *E, M to 5th Ave./53rd St.*

PERFORMING ARTS MEMORABILIA

Drama Book Shop. If you're looking for a script, be it a lesser-known Russian translation or a Broadway hit, chances are you can find it here. The range of books spans film, music, dance, TV, and biographies. The shop also hosts Q&As with leading playwrights. ✉ *250 W. 40th St., between 7th and 8th Aves., Midtown West* ☎ *212/944–0595* 🌐 *www.dramabookshop.com* Ⓜ *A, C, E to 42nd St.–Port Authority.*

One Shubert Alley. This was the first store to sell Broadway merchandise outside of a theater. Today souvenir posters, tees, and other knickknacks memorializing past and present Broadway hits still reign at this Theater District shop. ✉ *1 Shubert Alley, between 44th and 45th Sts., Midtown West* ☎ *212/944–4133* Ⓜ *N, Q, R, S, 1, 2, 3, 7 to Times Sq.–42nd St.*

Triton Gallery. Theatrical posters large and small are available, and the selection is democratic, with everything from Marlene Dietrich's *Blue Angel* to recent Broadway shows represented. ✉ *630 9th Ave., Ste 808, between 44th and 45th Sts., Midtown West* ☎ *212/765–2472* 🌐 *www.tritongallery.com* Ⓜ *A, C, E to 42nd St.–Port Authority.*

SHOES, HANDBAGS, AND LEATHER GOODS

Cole Haan. This brand is known for its comfortable but hip footwear—many shoes have Nike Air cushioning in the heels. Everything from sandals to boots and pumps is available. ✉ *620 5th Ave., at Rockefeller Center, Midtown West* ☎ *212/765–9747* 🌐 *www.colehaan.com* Ⓜ *E, M to 5th Ave./53rd St.*

Manolo Blahnik. These sexy status shoes are some of the most expensive on the market. The signature look is a pointy toe with a high, delicate heel, but there are also ballet flats, gladiator sandals, and over-the-knee dominatrix boots that cost nearly $2,000. Pray for a sale. ✉ *31 W. 54th St., between 5th and 6th Aves., Midtown West* ☎ *212/582–3007* 🌐 *www.manoloblahnik.com* Ⓜ *E, M to 5th Ave./53rd St.*

Fodor'sChoice ★ **Smythson of Bond Street.** Although Smythson still sells stationery fit for a queen—check out the royal warrant from England's HRH—it is also a place to scoop up on-trend handbags, iPad cases, and wallets. The hues range from sedate brown and black to eye-popping tangerine. The softbound leather diaries, address books, and travel accessories make ideal gifts. ✉ *4 W. 57th St., between 5th and 6th Aves., Midtown West* ☎ *212/265–4573* 🌐 *www.smythson.com* Ⓜ *F to 57th St.*

TOYS

Toys "R" Us. The Times Square megastore is so big that a three-story Ferris wheel—complete with 14 individually themed cars—revolves inside. There's also a life-sized T-Rex that roars and a 4,000-square-foot Barbie dollhouse.With all the movie tie-in merchandise, video games, yo-yos, stuffed animals, and what seems to be the entire Mattel oeuvre, good luck extracting your kids from here. ✉ *1514 Broadway, at W. 44th St., Midtown West* ☎ *646/366-8800* 🌐 *www.toysrus.com* Ⓜ *1, 2, 3, 7, N, Q, R, S to Times Sq.–42nd St.*

THE UPPER EAST SIDE

This neighborhood is known for its antiques shops and high-end designers, such as Carolina Herrera, Oscar de la Renta, and Tom Ford. They are primarily sprinkled along Madison Avenue.

ANTIQUES AND COLLECTIBLES

Florian Papp. Established in 1900, this store has an unassailed reputation among knowledgeable collectors. Expect to find American and European antiques and paintings from the 18th to 20th century. Gilt mirrors and mahogany tables abound. ✉ *962 Madison Ave., between 75th and 76th Sts., Upper East Side* ☎ *212/288–6770* 🌐 *www.florianpapp.com* Ⓜ *6 to 77th St.*

Keno Auctions. Leigh Keno of *Antiques Roadshow* fame presides over this auction house, which specializes in Americana. As expected, he has a good eye and an interesting inventory; he's sold silver sauceboats from Paul Revere, paintings, and Chippendale furniture. ✉ *127 E. 69th St., between Park and Lexington Aves., Upper East Side* ☎ *212/734–2381* 🌐 *www.kenoauctions.com* Ⓜ *6 to 68th St.–Hunter College.*

BOOKS AND STATIONERY

Crawford Doyle Booksellers. You're as likely to see an old edition of Wodehouse as a best seller in the window of this shop. Bibliophiles will find a high-quality selection of fiction, nonfiction, and biographies, plus some rare books on the balcony. Salespeople offer their opinions *and* ask for yours. ✉ *1082 Madison Ave., between 81st and 82nd Sts., Upper East Side* ☎ *212/288–6300* Ⓜ *4, 5, 6 to 86th St.*

Shakespeare & Co. Booksellers. The stock here represents what's happening in just about every field of publishing today: students can grab a last-minute Gertrude Stein for class, then rummage through the homages

Shops on the Upper East Side are très sophisticated.

to cult pop-culture figures. ✉ *939 Lexington Ave., between 68th and 69th Sts., Upper East Side* ☎ *212/570–0201* 🌐 *shop.shakeandco.com* Ⓜ *6 to 68th St.–Hunter College.*

CHILDREN'S CLOTHING

Bonpoint. Celebrities love this French children's boutique for the beautiful designs and fine workmanship—think pony-hair booties and hand-embroidered jumpers and blouses. Older kids can rock Liberty print dresses and peacoats. ✉ *1269 Madison Ave., at 91st St., Upper East Side* ☎ *212/722–7720* 🌐 *www.bonpoint.com* Ⓜ *4, 5, 6 to 86th St.*

Infinity. Prep-school girls and their mothers giggle and gossip over the tween clothes (with more than a few moms picking up T-shirts and jeans for themselves) with Les Tout Petits dresses, Juicy Couture jeans, and tees emblazoned with Justin Beiber. ✉ *1116 Madison Ave., at s83rd St., Upper East Side* ☎ *212/734–0077* Ⓜ *4, 5, 6 to 86th St.*

CLOTHING

Barbour. The signature look here is the company's waxed cotton jacket, available for men and women. The quilted jackets, tweeds, moleskin pants, lamb's-wool sweaters, and tattersall shirts invariably call up images of country rambles. ✉ *1047 Madison Ave., at 80th St., Upper East Side* ☎ *212/570–2600* 🌐 *www.barbour.com* Ⓜ *6 to 77th St.*

BCBG Max Azria. If flirtation's your sport, you'll find your sportswear here: fluttering skirts, beaded camisoles, chiffon dresses, and leather pants fill the racks. ✉ *770 Madison Ave., at 66th St., Upper East Side* ☎ *212/717–4225* 🌐 *www.bcbg.com* Ⓜ *6 to 68th St.–Hunter College.*

Belstaff. Nearly a century old, this British brand specializes in motorcycle gear that has quite the pedigree—both Che Guevara and Steve McQueen have worn Belstaff. The relaunched company has expanded its collection to include luxury basics for men and women, including peacoats, waxed jackets, and body hugging dresses with luxury touches like python and crocodile. ✉ *814 Madison Ave., between 68th and 69th Sts., Upper East Side* ☎ *212/897–1880* 🌐 *www.belstaff.com* Ⓜ *6 to 68th St.–Hunter College.*

Bra Smyth. Chic and sweetly sexy French and Canadian underthings in soft cottons and silks line the shelves of this Uptown staple. In addition to the selection of bridal-ready white bustiers and custom-fit swimsuits (made, cleverly, in bra-cup sizes), the store is best known for its knowledgeable staff, many of whom can offer tips on proper fit and size you up on sight. Cup sizes run from AA to J. ✉ *905 Madison Ave., at 73rd St., Upper East Side* ☎ *212/772–9400* 🌐 *www.brasmyth.com* Ⓜ *6 to 68th St.–Hunter College.*

Calvin Klein. Though the namesake designer has bowed out, the label keeps channeling his particular style. This stark flagship store emphasizes the luxe end of the clothing line. Men's suits tend to be soft around the edges; women's evening gowns are often a fluid pouring of silk. There are also shoes, accessories, housewares, and makeup. ✉ *654 Madison Ave., at 60th St., Upper East Side* ☎ *212/292–9000* 🌐 *www.calvinklein.com* Ⓜ *4, 5, 6 to 59th St.; N, Q, R to Lexington Ave./59th St.*

Fodor's Choice ★ **Calypso St. Barth.** Catch an instant island-vacation vibe from Calypso's colorful silk women's wear, dangly jewelry, and boho housewares at the brand's New York flagship, which has a suitably beachy vibe (check out the shell chandeliers). There are multiple branches throughout the city with different themes, including an outlet on Broome Street. ✉ *900 Madison Ave., between 72nd and 73rd Sts., Upper East Side* ☎ *212/535–4100* Ⓜ *6 to 68th St.–Hunter College.*

Carolina Herrera. A favorite of the society set (and A-list celebs), Herrera's designs are ladylike and elegant. Her suits, gowns, and cocktail dresses offer luxurious fabrics in timeless silhouettes. ✉ *954 Madison Ave., at 75th St., Upper East Side* ☎ *212/249–6552* Ⓜ *6 to 77th St.*

DKNY. The signature style here is casual sophistication—in other words, a very New York look. Slinky wrap dresses, chunky-knit sweaters, and dark denim are some of the best bets. ✉ *655 Madison Ave., at E. 60th St., Upper East Side* ☎ *212/223–3569* 🌐 *www.dkny.com* Ⓜ *4, 5, 6 to 59th St.; N, Q, R to Lexington Ave./59th St.* ✉ *420 W. Broadway, SoHo* ☎ *646/613–1100 .*

Dolce & Gabbana. It's easy to feel like an Italian movie star amid these exuberant (in every sense) clothes. Corseted dresses are a favorite; the fabric could be sheer, furred, or leopard-print. Men's suits are slim and sharp. ✉ *825 Madison Ave., between 68th and 69th Sts., Upper East Side* ☎ *212/249–4100* 🌐 *www.dolcegabbana.com* Ⓜ *6 to 68th St.–Hunter College.*

Juliette Longuet. French-born designer Juliette Longuet recently opened her first boutique inside an elegant townhouse. Although the fabrics are produced in Europe, all of the clothing is made in New York.

Her designs combine the best of New York and Parisian chic; think leather leggings, chiffon blouses, and little black dresses. ✉ *153 E. 70th St., at Lexington Ave., Upper East Side* ☎ *646/360–3300* 🌐 *www.juliettelonguet.com* Ⓜ *6 to 68th St.–Hunter College.*

Fodor'sChoice ★ **Lanvin.** This French label has been around since 1889, and is the oldest French fashion house still in existence. With Alber Elbaz at the helm, the signature look is fluid and sexy; think one-shouldered cocktail dresses, cigarette pants, and ruffled blouses. This elegant town house is the first U.S. outpost. The interior design itself is a showstopper: the three-story space oozes old money and glamour with its art deco chandeliers and soothing gray walls. And the clothes? Just as slinky. ✉ *815 Madison Ave., between 68th and 69th Sts., Upper East Side* ☎ *646/439–0381* 🌐 *www.lanvin.com* Ⓜ *6 to 68th St.–Hunter College.*

La Perla. If money is no object, shop here for some of the sexiest underthings around. The collection includes lace sets, corsets, and exquisite bridal lingerie. ✉ *803 Madison Ave., between 67th and 68th Sts., Upper East Side* ☎ *212/570–0050* 🌐 *www.laperla.com* Ⓜ *6 to 68th St.–Hunter College.*

Lisa Perry. Perry takes an artist's approach to her clothing designs in this gleaming white space. She has created dresses printed with famous Andy Warhol photographs, such as the image of him drowning in a Campbell's Soup can. Pop art aside, her store is filled with a mix of '60s and '70s vintage clothes as well as her own designs. ✉ *988 Madison Ave., between 76th and 77th Sts., Upper East Side* ☎ *212/431–7467* 🌐 *www.lisaperrystyle.com* Ⓜ *6 to 77th St.*

Fodor'sChoice ★ **Ludivine.** Ignore the tacky surroundings and make a beeline for this store if you love French designers. Owner Ludivine Grégoire showcases of-the-moment Gallic (and a few Italian) designers like Vanessa Bruno, Jerome Dreyfuss, and Carvin. ✉ *1216 Lexington Ave., between 82nd and 83rd Sts., Upper East Side* ☎ *212/249–4053* 🌐 *www.boutiqueludivine.com* Ⓜ *4, 5, 6 to 86th St.*

Marina Rinaldi. If you are a curvy size 10–22 and want to celebrate your figure rather than hide it, shop here. Marina Rinaldi sells form-flattering knit dresses, wool trousers, and coats that are tasteful and luxurious. ✉ *13 E. 69th St., between Madison and 5th Aves., Upper East Side* ☎ *212/734–4333* 🌐 *www.marinarinaldi.com* Ⓜ *6 to 68th St.–Hunter College.*

Max Mara. Think subtle colors and plush fabrics—straight skirts in cashmere or heathered wool, tuxedo-style evening jackets, and several choices of wool and cashmere camel overcoats. The suits are exquisitely tailored. ✉ *813 Madison Ave., at 68th St., Upper East Side* ☎ *212/879–6100* 🌐 *www.maxmara.com* Ⓜ *6 to 68th St.–Hunter College.*

Michael Kors. Michael Kors keeps rolling out boutiques in the city. His newest flagship, spread over two levels, showcases his clean-cut, American classic clothing and accessories. If you need fashion inspiration, images from his runway shows are screened on an 18-foot high television. ✉ *667 Madison Ave., between 60th and 61st Sts., Upper East Side* ☎ *212/980–1550* 🌐 *www.michaelkors.com* Ⓜ *N, Q, R to 59th St./5th Ave.*

Milly. These bright, cheerfully patterned clothes look as at home on the Upper East Side as they would in Palm Beach or Marrakech. At designer Michelle Smith's first U.S. flagship, you'll find bold maxi dresses, 1970s-inspired tunics, and slouchy shoulder bags. There is also a small selection of wedding gowns. ✉ *900 Madison Ave., between 72nd and 73rd Sts., Upper East Side* ☎ *212/395–9100* 🌐 *www.millyny.com* Ⓜ *6 to 77th St.*

Morgane Le Fay. The clothes here have a dreamy, ethereal quality that is decidedly feminine. Silk gowns are fluid and soft; fitted velvet jackets have covered buttons. Her dresses are also popular with brides who want a minimalist look. ✉ *980 Madison Ave., between 76th and 77th Sts., Upper East Side* ☎ *212/879–9700* 🌐 *www.morganelefay.com* Ⓜ *6 to 68th St.–Hunter College.*

Oscar de la Renta. Come here for the ladylike yet lighthearted runway designs of this upper-crust favorite. Skirts swing, ruffles billow, embroidery brightens up tweed, and even a tennis dress looks like something you could go dancing in. ✉ *772 Madison Ave., at 66th St., Upper East Side* ☎ *212/288–5810* 🌐 *www.oscardelarenta.com* Ⓜ *6 to 68th St.–Hunter College.*

Fodor's Choice ★ **Polo Ralph Lauren.** Even if you can't afford the clothes, come just to soak up the luxe RL lifestyle. This women's flagship is housed in a 22,000-square-foot building built to look like a historic Beaux-Arts mansion (or small palace), complete with a curving marble staircase and stone floors. In addition to the complete women's collection, the brand's lingerie, home wares, and its first fine-jewelry and watch salon are here. The men's collection is just across the street in the Rhinelander Mansion. ✉ *888 Madison Ave., at 72nd St., Upper East Side* ☎ *212/434–8000* 🌐 *www.ralphlauren.com* Ⓜ *6 to 68th St.–Hunter College.*

18

Reed Krakoff. Coach's president and creative director has branched out to launch his own luxury lifestyle store. The clothing has an edgy look, with little black dresses in heavy wool and massive cuff bracelets. The handbags and shoes, however, lean more toward ladylike. ✉ *831 Madison Ave., between 69th and 70th Sts., Upper East Side* ☎ *212/988–0560* 🌐 *www.reedkrakoff.com* Ⓜ *6 to 68th St.–Hunter College.*

Roberto Cavalli. Rock-star style (at rock-star prices) delivers clothing decked out with fur, feathers, and lots of sparkle. Animal prints are big in this temple to the over-the-top. ✉ *711 Madison Ave., at 63rd St., Upper East Side* ☎ *212/755–7722* 🌐 *www.robertocavalli.com* Ⓜ *N, Q, R to 5th Ave./59th St.*

Tom Ford. Ford is famous for making Gucci supersexy, but the menswear here veers toward the traditional—albeit impeccably made. Shirts come in more than 300 hues, and off-the-rack suits start around $3,000. Glide up the ebony staircase for the made-to-measure services, which will customize anything from suits to pajamas. Don't miss the fragrance chamber either. ✉ *845 Madison Ave., at 70th St., Upper East Side* ☎ *212/359–0300* 🌐 *www.tomford.com* Ⓜ *6 to 68th St.–Hunter College.*

Tory Burch. The global flagship of this preppy boho label is housed in an elegantly restored townhouse, so it feels as if you're shopping in a very well-appointed home. The five-story space features Tory Burch's signature orange lacquer walls, purple curtains, and gold hardware. If you already own her iconic ballet flats, browse through the ready-to-wear collection, handbags, shoes, and jewelry. ✉ *797 Madison Ave., between 67th and 68th Sts., Upper East Side* ☎ *212/510–8371* 🌐 *www.toryburch.com* Ⓜ *6 to 68th St.–Hunter College.*

Valentino. The mix here is at once audacious and beautifully cut; the fur or feather trimmings, low necklines, and opulent fabrics are about as close as you can get to celluloid glamour. No one does a better red. ✉ *747 Madison Ave., at 65th St., Upper East Side* ☎ *212/772–6969* 🌐 *www.valentino.com* Ⓜ *6 to 68th St.–Hunter College.*

Vera Wang. This star wedding-dress designer churns out dreamy dresses that are sophisticated without being over-the-top. Choose from A-line and princess styles, and slinky sheaths. If money is no object, bespoke wedding dresses are available. Appointments are essential. ✉ *991 Madison Ave., at 77th St., Upper East Side* ☎ *212/628–3400* 🌐 *www.verawang.com* Ⓜ *6 to 77th St.*

Vilebrequin. Allow St-Tropez to influence your swimsuit; these striped, floral, and solid-color French-made trunks come in sunny hues. Waterproof pocket inserts keep your essentials safe from beachcombers. Many styles come in boys' sizes, too. ✉ *1007 Madison Ave., between 77th and 78th Sts., Upper East Side* ☎ *212/650–0353* 🌐 *www.vilebrequinonlinestore.com* Ⓜ *6 to 77th St.*

DEPARTMENT STORES

Barneys New York. Barneys continues to provide fashion-conscious and big-budget shoppers with irresistible, must-have items at its uptown flagship store. The extensive menswear selection has a handful of edgier designers, though made-to-measure is always available. The women's department showcases posh designers of all stripes, from the subdued lines of Armani and Nina Ricci to the irrepressible Alaïa and Zac Posen. The shoe selection trots out Prada boots and strappy Blahniks; the cosmetics department will keep you in Kiehl's, Sue Devitt, and Chantecaille; jewelry runs from the whimsical (Jennifer Meyer) to the classic (Ileana Makri). ✉ *660 Madison Ave., between E. 60th and E. 61st Sts., Upper East Side* ☎ *212/826–8900* 🌐 *www.barneys.com* Ⓜ *4, 5, 6 to 59th St.; N, Q, R to Lexington Ave./59th St.*

Fodor's Choice ★ **Fivestory.** This luxurious mini–department store, located inside a town house, carries clothing, accessories, shoes, and home decor for men, women, and children in an elegant setting (think marble floors and lots of velvet and silk). It specializes in independent designers but also showcases designs from heavy hitters such as Alexander McQueen and Lanvin. ✉ *18 East 69th St., between 5th and Madison Aves., Upper East Side* ☎ *212/288–1338* 🌐 *www.fivestoryny.com* Ⓜ *6 to 68th St.–Hunter College.*

FOOD AND TREATS

FP Patisserie. Famed French pâtissier François Payard has multiple boutiques around the city but this location is the flagship. Chocolates, pastries, and macarons are displayed like jewels in glass cases. If you need to calm the sugar rush, there's a small dining area offering dishes like croque-monsieur. ✉ *1293 3rd Ave., between 74th and 75th Sts., Upper East* ☎ *212/717–5252* 🌐 *www.payard.com* Ⓜ *6 to 77th St.*

La Maison du Chocolat. Stop in at this chocolatier's small tea salon to dive into a cup of thick, heavenly hot chocolate. The Paris-based outfit sells handmade truffles, chocolates, and pastries that could lull you into a chocolate stupor. ✉ *1018 Madison Ave., between 78th and 79th Sts., Upper East Side* ☎ *212/744–7117* 🌐 *www.lamaisonduchocolat.com* Ⓜ *6 to 77th St.*

HOME DECOR

Ankasa. Owners Sachin and Babi Ahluwalia used to source textiles for luxury designers like Oscar de la Renta. Now they are using that same design sensibility to produce a gorgeous line of housewares and accessories, which are globally inspired. The embroidery is exquisite. ✉ *1200 Madison Ave., between 87th and 88th Sts., Upper East Side* ☎ *212/996–5200* 🌐 *www.ankasa.com* Ⓜ *4, 5, 6 to 86th St.*

Jonathan Adler. Everything at this flagship is fun, groovy, and happy. Adler funks up midcentury modern designs with his striped, striated, or curvy handmade pottery (ranging from a $30 vase to a chunky $400 lamp) as well as the hand-loomed wool pillow covers, rugs, and throws with blunt graphics (stripes, crosses, circles). There's also a new children's line. ✉ *1097 Madison Ave., at 83rd St., Upper East Side* ☎ *212/772–2410* 🌐 *www.jonathanadler.com* Ⓜ *4, 5, 6 to 86th St.*

JEWELRY AND ACCESSORIES

Asprey. Asprey's claim to fame is jewelry; its own eponymous diamond cut has A-shape facets but this British brand caters to all kinds of luxury tastes. Everything from leather goods and rare books to polo equipment and cashmere sweaters is available. ✉ *853 Madison Ave., between 70th and 71st Sts., Upper East Side* ☎ *212/688–1811* 🌐 *www.asprey.com* Ⓜ *6 to 68th St.–Hunter College.*

Fred Leighton. If you're in the market for vintage diamonds, this is the place, whether your taste is for tiaras, art-deco settings, or sparklers once worn by a Vanderbilt. The skinny, stackable diamond eternity bands are hugely popular. ✉ *773 Madison Ave., at 66th St., Upper East Side* ☎ *212/288–1872* 🌐 *www.fredleighton.com* Ⓜ *6 to 68th St.–Hunter College.*

MUSEUM STORES

Fodor's Choice ★ **Cooper-Hewitt, National Design Museum.** Prowl the shelves here for intriguing urban oddments and ornaments, like sculptural tableware, Alexander Girard dolls, housewares by Alessi and Japanese notebooks by Postalco. ✉ *2 E. 91st St., at 5th Ave., Upper East Side* ☎ *212/849–8355* 🌐 *www.cooperhewitt.org* Ⓜ *4, 5, 6 to 86th St.*

Metropolitan Museum of Art Shop. This sprawling shop offers a phenomenal book selection, as well as posters, art videos, and computer programs. Reproductions of statuettes and other *objets* fill the gleaming cases in every branch. Don't miss the jewelry selection, with its Byzantine- and Egyptian-inspired baubles. ✉ *1000 5th Ave., at 82nd St., Upper East Side* ☎ *212/570–3894* 🌐 *store.metmuseum.org* Ⓜ *4, 5, 6 to 86th St.*

Museum of the City of New York. Satisfy your curiosity about New York City's past, present, or future with the terrific selection of books, cards, toys, and photography posters. ✉ *1220 5th Ave., at 103rd St., Upper East Side* ☎ *212/534–1672* 🌐 *www.mcny.org* Ⓜ *6 to 103rd St.*

Neue Galerie. Like the museum, this bookshop focuses on German, Austrian, and Central European art. The solid selection includes catalogs, literature, and decorative items, including lovely wrapping papers. Many designs found in the collection have been reproduced as part of the museum's own Neue Haus line. ✉ *1048 5th Ave., between 85th and 86th Sts., Upper East Side* ☎ *212/628–6200* 🌐 *www.neuegalerie.org* Ⓜ *4, 5, 6 to 86th St.*

SHOES, HANDBAGS, AND LEATHER GOODS

Charlotte Olympia. This luxury British shoe brand finally has a store in New York. The art deco-inspired space showcases the very sexy and very expensive stilettos, pumps, and flats. Accessories such as shoulder bags and clutches are also available. ✉ *22 E. 65th St., at Madison Ave., Upper East Side* ☎ *212/744–1842* 🌐 *www.charlotteolympia.com* Ⓜ *6 to 68th St.–Hunter College.*

Christian Louboutin. Lipstick-red soles are the signature of Louboutin's delicately sexy couture slippers and stilettos, and his latest, larger downtown store has carpeting to match. The pointy-toe creations come trimmed with brocade, tassels, buttons, or satin ribbons. ✉ *965 Madison Ave., between 75th and 76th Sts., Upper East Side* ☎ *212/396–1884* 🌐 *www.christianlouboutin.com* Ⓜ *6 to 77th St.*

Church's English Shoes. Beloved by bankers and lawyers, these shoes are indisputably of quality. You could choose something highly polished for an embassy dinner, a loafer or crepe-sole suede ankle boot for a weekend, or even a black-and-white spectator style worthy of Fred Astaire. ✉ *689 Madison Ave., at 62nd St., Upper East Side* ☎ *212/758–5200* 🌐 *www.church-footwear.com* Ⓜ *4, 5, 6 to 59th St.; N, Q, R to Lexington Ave./59th St.*

Devi Kroell. You may have spotted her snakeskin hobo on celebs such as Halle Berry and Ashley Olsen. This serene space is a perfect backdrop for the designer's luxury handbags and shoes, which are crafted from premium leather. Roomy shoulder bags come in python and calf leather, and evening bags have a touch of sparkle. There's also a selection of jewelry and scarves. ✉ *717 Madison Ave., between 63rd and 64th Sts., Upper East Side* ☎ *212/644–4499* 🌐 *www.devikroell.com* Ⓜ *4, 5, 6 to 59th St.; N, Q, R to Lexington Ave./59th St.*

Hermès. This legendary French retailer is best known for its iconic handbags, the Kelly and the Birkin, named for Grace Kelly and Jane Birkin, as well as its silk scarves and neckties. True to its roots, Hermès still stocks saddles and other equestrian items in addition to a line of beautifully simple separates. ✉ *691 Madison Ave., at 62nd St., Upper East Side* ☎ *212/751–3181* 🌐 *www.hermes.com* Ⓜ *4, 5, 6 to 59th St.; N, Q, R to Lexington Ave./59th St.*

Jimmy Choo. Pointy toes, low vamps, narrow heels, ankle-wrapping straps—these British-made shoes are undeniably vampy, and sometimes more comfortable than they look. ✉ *716 Madison Ave., between 63rd*

and 64th Sts., Upper East Side ☎ *212/759–7078* 🌐 *www.jimmychoo.com* Ⓜ *6 to 68th St.–Hunter College.*

Fodor's Choice ★ **Jack Rogers.** This brand, beloved by prepsters everywhere, is most famous for its Navajo sandal, which was worn by Jackie Onassis. You can still buy the Navajo at the Jack Rogers flagship store, as well as other footwear like ballet pumps, boots, and wedges. ✉ *1198 Madison Ave., between 87th and 88th Sts., Upper East Side* ☎ *212/259–0588* Ⓜ *4, 5, 6 to 86th St.*

John Lobb. If you truly want to be well heeled, pick up a pair of these luxury shoes, whose prices start at around $1,100. Owned by Hermès, John Lobb offers classic styles such as oxfords, loafers, and boots. ✉ *800 Madison Ave., between 67th and 68th Sts., Upper East Side* ☎ *212/888–9797* 🌐 *www.johnlobb.com* Ⓜ *6 to 68th St.–Hunter College.*

Robert Clergerie. Although best known for its chunky, comfy wedges, this French brand is not without its sense of fun. The sandal selection includes beaded starfish shapes, and for winter the ankle boots have killer heels but the soles are padded. ✉ *19 E. 62nd St., between 5th and Madison Aves., Upper East Side* ☎ *212/207–8600* 🌐 *www.robertclergerie.com/en/* Ⓜ *N, Q, R to 5th Ave./59th St.*

Tod's. Diego Della Valle's coveted driving moccasins, casual loafers, and boots are the top choice for jetsetters who prefer low-key, logo-free luxury goods. Though most of the women's selection is made up of low-heel or flat styles, an increasing number of high heels are bent on driving sales, rather than cars. The handbags and satchels have the same fine craftsmanship. ✉ *650 Madison Ave., near 60th St., Upper East Side* ☎ *212/644–5945* 🌐 *www.tods.com* Ⓜ *N, Q, R to 5th Ave./59th St.*

18

THE UPPER WEST SIDE

Although largely a residential neighborhood, the Upper West Side has some excellent food (Zabar's) as well as smaller boutiques.

BOOKS AND STATIONERY

Westsider Books & Westsider Records. This wonderfully crammed space is a lifesaver on the otherwise sparse Upper West Side. Squeeze in among the stacks of art books and fiction; clamber up the steep stairway and you'll find all sorts of rare books. ✉ *2246 Broadway, between 80th and 81st Sts., Upper West Side* ☎ *212/362–0706* 🌐 *www.westsiderbooks.com* Ⓜ *1 to 79th St.*

CAMERAS AND ELECTRONICS

Apple Store. Branch location at 1981 Broadway. *See Midtown East for full review.*

CHILDREN'S CLOTHING

A Time for Children. When you shop at this funky boutique, you'll also be doing some good, as 100% of the profits go to the Children's Aid Society. Choose from toys, books, and clothing, which include classics such as Petit Bateau as well as cool vintage-inspired onesies. ✉ *506 Amsterdam Ave., between 84th and 85th Sts., Upper West Side* ☎ *212/580–8202* 🌐 *www.atimeforchildren.org* Ⓜ *1 to 86th St.*

CLOTHING

BOC. Who needs to go downtown for cutting-edge designers? This sleek store is lit by a row of dainty chandeliers and the clothing in stock is just as pretty. Separates from Rebecca Taylor, Vivienne Westwood, and Alexander Wang line the shelves. ✉ *2191 Broadway, between 77th and 78th Sts., Upper West Side* ☎ *212/362–5405* Ⓜ *1 to 86th St.*

Fodor's Choice ★ **Intermix.** Whether you're looking for the perfect daytime dress, pair of J Brand jeans, or a puffer coat that won't make you look like the Michelin man, Intermix offers a well-edited mix of emerging and established designers. Expect to see designs from DVF, Chloe, and Missoni. ✉ *210 Columbus Ave., between 69th and 70th Sts., Upper West Side* ☎ *212/769–9116* 🌐 *www.intermixonline.com* Ⓜ *1, 2, 3 to 72nd St.*

Mint. Trendy dresses that won't break the bank are what Mint is all about. The collection includes Alice & Olivia, Susana Monaco, and Joe's Jeans. The walls are painted, of course, in mint. ✉ *448 Columbus Ave., between 81st and 82nd Sts., Upper West Side* ☎ *212/362–6250* 🌐 *www.shopmint.com* Ⓜ *1 to 79th St.*

FOOD AND TREATS

Le Palais des Thés. This French-owned tea boutique has varieties of black and green teas as well as rarer leaves and globally inspired blends, such as a Turkish hammam flavor that references roses and dates. The box sets and canisters make excellent gifts. ✉ *194 Columbus Ave., at 69th St., Upper West Side* ☎ *646/664–1902* 🌐 *www.palaisdesthes.com* Ⓜ *1 to 66th St.–Lincoln Center.*

Zabar's. When it comes to authentic New York food, it's hard to beat rugelach, bagels, or lox from this favorite specialty food emporium. ✉ *2245 Broadway, at 80th St., Upper West Side* ☎ *212/787–2000* 🌐 *www.zabars.com.*

SHOES, HANDBAGS, AND LEATHER GOODS

Fodor's Choice ★ **Tani.** Fashionable Upper West Side ladies love this shoe store for its huge selection and patient staff. Tani's selection is classic-with-a-twist, and shoppers will find off-the-radar brands such as Bensimon, Mugumi Ochi, and Butter. ✉ *2020 Broadway, between 69th and 70th Sts., Upper West Side* ☎ *212/873–4361* 🌐 *www.taninyc.com* Ⓜ *1, 2, 3 to 72nd St.*

WINE

Acker Merrall & Condit. Founded in 1820 and billing itself as America's oldest wine shop, Acker Merrall & Condit carries a superb selection of red burgundies. There's also a wide range of rare and fine wines. ✉ *160 W. 72nd St., between Amsterdam and Columbus Aves., Upper West Side* ☎ *212/787–1700* 🌐 *www.ackerwines.com* Ⓜ *1, 2, 3 to 72nd St.*

NIGHTLIFE

Updated by Jessica Colley

New Yorkers are fond of the "work hard, play hard" maxim, but the truth is, Gothamites don't need much of an excuse to hit the town. Monday is the new Thursday, which replaced Friday and Saturday, but it doesn't matter: the bottom line is that there's always plenty to do in this 24-hour city. Whether it's raising a glass in a divey 1930s saloon, a gay sports bar, the latest speakeasy-style cocktail den, or a swanky rooftop lounge, it isn't hard for visitors to get a piece of the action.

The nightlife scene still resides largely downtown—in dives in the East Village and Lower East Side, classic jazz joints in the West Village, and the Meatpacking District and Chelsea's see-and-be-seen clubs. Midtown, especially around Hell's Kitchen, has developed a vibrant scene, too, and plenty of preppy hangouts dot the Upper East and Upper West sides. Brooklyn, especially Williamsburg, is the destination for hipsters.

Keep in mind that *when* you go is just as important as *where* you go. A club that is packed at 11 might empty out by midnight, and a bar that raged last night may be completely empty tonight. *Paper* magazine has a good list of roving parties. You can check their online nightlife guide, *PM* (NYC), via their website 🌐 *www.papermag.com.* Another streetwise mag, the *L Magazine* (🌐 *www.thelmagazine.com*), lists what's happening at many of the city's lounges and clubs, as well as dance and comedy performances. Scour industry-centric websites, too, like *Eater* and *Grub Street,* which catalog the comings and goings of many a nightlife impresario. The *New York Times* has listings of cabaret and jazz shows, most comprehensively in their Friday and Sunday Arts sections. Bear in mind that a venue's life span is often measured in months, not years. Phone ahead or check online to make sure your target hasn't closed or turned into a polka hall (although you never know—that could be fun, too).

LOWER MANHATTAN

FINANCIAL DISTRICT

The Dead Rabbit. For exquisite cocktails without the dress code or pretentious door policy typical of some New York cocktail dens, venture to the tip of Manhattan for a night of Irish hospitality in a 19th-century-inspired saloon. The ground-floor taproom serves up craft beers and whiskeys of the world while the upstairs parlor specializes in 72 cocktails revived from history books—along with ragtime music played live on the piano. ✉ *30 Water St., Financial District* ☎ *646/422–7906* 🌐 *www.deadrabbitnyc.com* Ⓜ *R to Whitehall St.*

TRIBECA

BARS

B-flat. The decor is red-on-red here, and the Asian-style cocktails are particularly groovy (literally—one, with citrusy Japanese yuzu juice and vodka, is dubbed the Groovy) at this Japan-meets-'50s-America lounge. Get some fine Japanese treats and check out the upstairs area with amazing wall and ceiling murals of the Tokyo Bar. ✉ *277 Church St., between Franklin and White Sts., TriBeCa* ☎ *212/219–2970* 🌐 *www.bflat.info* Ⓜ *1 to Franklin St.*

Brandy Library. Alas, the only book in this exquisite, wood-paneled room is the leather-bound menu listing hundreds of brandies and single-malt scotches. The bottles are on gorgeous backlighted "bookshelves," though, and you can learn what makes each of them special by chatting with the spirit sommelier—or by attending the twice-weekly Spirit School tastings. ✉ *25 N. Moore St., between Varick and Hudson Sts., TriBeCa* ☎ *212/226–5545* 🌐 *www.brandylibrary.com* Ⓜ *1 to Franklin St.*

Canal Room. Polished wood floors, potted palms, and stylish chairs give this intimate club an air of glamour. Musicians perform here several times a month, but they also come just to enjoy themselves. The owners' record-business connections, a spectacular sound system, celeb sightings, and DJs with reputations as big as their turntables (size does matter) keep the crowds moving. ✉ *285 W. Broadway, at Canal St., TriBeCa* ☎ *212/941–8100* 🌐 *www.canalroom.com* Ⓜ *A, C, E to Canal St.*

M1-5. For the more bohemian of TriBeCa pub goers, this lipstick-red, high-ceiling spot is a vast playground (as in pool and darts). A reggae jukebox helps keep it real, as do discounts for local artists on the diverse cocktail menu. Extra points, too, for the bar's name, which cites TriBeCa's warehouse zoning law. ✉ *52 Walker St., between Broadway and Church St., TriBeCa* ☎ *212/965–1701* 🌐 *www.m1-5.com* Ⓜ *J, N, Q, R, Z, 6 to Canal St.*

Smith and Mills. Attractive scenesters frolic giddily at this tiny gem of a gin mill, where mixologists who resemble Daniel Day-Lewis dispense elixirs (and caviar) from a bar hung with pots and pans. There are cozy table-nooks for couples, and an elevator-toilet (yes, you read that correctly) for anyone who feels "nature's call" while heeding "the call of the wild." ✉ *71 N. Moore St., between Hudson and Green-*

wich Sts., TriBeCa ☎ *212/219–8568* 🌐 *www.smithandmills.com* Ⓜ *1 to Franklin St.*

Terroir Wine Bar. If the tag line—the Elitist Wine Bar for Everyone—isn't enough to get you in the door, the extensive wine list, including options by the glass, bottle, or adorable 3-ounce "taste" should do the trick. This low-lit neighborhood wine bar is easy to walk right by on charming Harrison Street, but once inside you'll find seats at the bar for wine-centric conversations with the sharp staff, or more private nooks for a romantic evening of wine and cheese. ✉ *24 Harrison St., TriBeCa* ☎ *212/625–9463* 🌐 *www.restauranthearth.com/terrior/Terroir.html* Ⓜ *1 to Franklin St.*

Ward III. You can get a solid Negroni or Manhattan at the exposed-brick lined watering hole Ward III, but where this bar really shines is with its bespoke cocktails. Fight for a seat at the bar if possible to watch the sharply clad mixologists whip up the house specialties, or simply give them a few descriptive words ("spirit-forward," "something with bourbon," "light and refreshing") and let them create a cocktail on the spot to match your thirst. ✉ *111 Reade St., between W. Broadway and Church St., TriBeCa* ☎ *212/240–9194* 🌐 *www.ward3tribeca.com* Ⓜ *1, 2, 3 to Chambers St.*

DANCE CLUBS AND DJ VENUES

Santos Party House. "Now *this* is what I call a dance club," says Arthur Baker, the legendary DJ (and legendary record producer), about this glorious downtown dance club, where the velvet ropes part for everyone. Co-owned by the rocker Andrew W. K., the bi-level Santos ain't fancy, but that's the point, and the customers are as eclectic (everybody from punks to Upper East Siders) as the DJs, including Mr. Baker, who flies in regularly from London. Hence the musical vibe—underground dance, mostly—is simply kaleidoscopic. ✉ *96 Lafayette St., between White and Walker Sts., TriBeCa* ☎ *212/584–5492* 🌐 *www.santospartyhouse.com* Ⓜ *J, N, Q, R, Z, 6 to Canal St.*

SOHO AND NOLITA

NOLITA

BARS

Sweet and Vicious. The name of this unpretentious butterfly-logo'ed lounge doesn't signify the looks (sweet) and attitude (vicious) of certain downtown pretty things that frequent the bars on this stretch. So what makes this bar in particular so sweet? A lovely back garden that's more private than the sceney bars they might otherwise hit in SoHo and NoLIta. ✉ *5 Spring St., between the Bowery and Elizabeth St., NoLIta* ☎ *212/334–7915* 🌐 *www.sweetandviciousnyc.com* Ⓜ *6 to Spring St.; J, Z to Bowery.*

SOHO

BARS

Broome Street Bar. A local hangout since 1972, the casual yet essential Broome Street Bar still feels like the old SoHo, before trendy boutiques replaced artists' lofts. There's an impressive selection of draft beers and a full menu of hefty burgers and other sturdy pub fare. ✉ *363 West Broadway, at Broome St., SoHo* ☎ *212/925–2086* 🌐 *broomestreetbar.ypguides.net* Ⓜ *C, E to Spring St.*

Don Hill's. An attempt by nightlife impresarios Paul Sevigny and Nur Khan (Beatrice Inn) to bring a punk ethos to downtown nightlife, the reborn Don Hill's is a downtown hotspot. Near the river in the sleepy area of Hudson Square, the nondescript building hides a raunchy interior stuffed with graffiti, explicit photographs, and oodles of boldface names, from Iggy Pop to the Olsen twins. Skip the cocktails in favor of a visit to the Jaegermeister machine. ✉ *511 Greenwich St., at Spring St., SoHo* ☎ *212/219–2850* 🌐 *www.donhills.com* Ⓜ *C, E to Spring St.*

Fanelli's. Linger over the *New York Times* at this terrific neighborhood bar and restaurant, which is pretty down-to-earth for a SoHo landmark that's been serving drinks (and solid cuisine—dig those burgers!) since 1847. Check out the hilarious old-timey photos on the walls, too. ✉ *94 Prince St., at Mercer St., SoHo* ☎ *212/226–9412* Ⓜ *N, R to Prince St.*

Jimmy. Way up on the top floor of the trendy James Hotel, Jimmy is the second project from the team behind the West Village's Hotel Griffou. Here their take on the rooftop hotel bar is better than it has to be, given the stellar views. Sit in a corner nook to gaze at the Empire State Building, or head toward the outdoor pool area to survey the bridges over the East River. Cocktails are a highlight, featuring seasonal ingredients and innovations like ice cubes made from cinnamon water. ✉ *15 Thompson St., at Grand St., SoHo* ☎ *212/465–2000* 🌐 *www.jameshotels.com* Ⓜ *C, E to Spring St.*

MercBar. This neighborhood staple keeps packing in the crowds. Eleven different martinis, 9 bourbons, and 13 single-malt scotches are just the beginning of the extensive drink menu. ✉ *151 Mercer St., between Prince and W. Houston Sts., SoHo* ☎ *212/966–2727* 🌐 *www.mercbar.com* Ⓜ *B, D, F, M to Broadway–Lafayette St.; N, R to Prince St.*

19

Pegu Club. Modeled after an officers' club in what's now Myanmar, the Pegu manages to feel expansive and calm even when packed. The well dressed and flirtatious come here partly for the exotically lovely surroundings, but primarily for the cocktails, which are innovative, prepared with superlative ingredients, and predictably pricey. ✉ *77 W. Houston St., 2nd fl., between W. Broadway and Wooster St., SoHo* ☎ *212/473–7348* 🌐 *www.peguclub.com* Ⓜ *B, D, F, M to Broadway–Lafayette St.; 6 to Bleecker St.*

Fodor's Choice ★ **Pravda.** This Russian retreat has more than 70 brands of vodka, including 10 house-infused flavored vodkas, which means your choice of martinis is nearly endless. The speak-easy feel of this underground spot is comfortable enough to spend the entire night, and Russian-inspired nibbles including caviar with blini will provide longevity to try yet another vodka variation, from cucumber-dill to ginger infused flavors. ✉ *281 Lafayette St., between Prince and W. Houston Sts., SoHo* ☎ *212/226–4944* 🌐 *www.pravdany.com* Ⓜ *B, D, F, M to Broadway–Lafayette St.*

CLOSE UP

Kickin' Karaoke

If you're looking for a venue other than your shower to bust out a rendition of Queen's "Somebody to Love," you're in good company. Otherwise jaded New Yorkers have become hooked on the goofy, addictive pleasure of karaoke. The K-word means "empty orchestra" in Japanese, and seems to tickle both downtown hipsters (who dig the irony of kitsch) and uptown financiers (who need a good rebel yell at the end of a workday), and everybody in between who loves to flex the golden pipes after a few drinks.

There are three ways of getting your lead-vocalist groove on: doing it in public at a barwide Karaoke Night; reserving a private space at a bar ("karaoke boxes," they're called), where only your friends can hear you scream—er, sing; and bounding up onstage in front of a live band.

The hardcore karaoke places tend to be either grungy or glitzy, with as many as 15 available boxes for rent by the hour or full night (each box includes a music machine, microphones, and bar service), as well as up to 80,000 songs on tap for you to warble. (Don't worry, that figure includes stuff by Journey, REO Speedwagon, Britney Spears, and other grotesquely catchy Top 20 music.) The most popular of this lot include Chinatown's scruffy **Winnie's** (✉ *104 Bayard St., at Baxter St.* ☎ *212/732–2384*), the East Village's **Sing-Sing** (✉ *9 St. Marks Place* ☎ *212/387–7800*), the triple-serving-of-cheesiness at Midtown's **Pulse** (✉ *135 W. 41st St., between Broadway and 6th Ave.* ☎ *646/461–7717*), and just about anywhere else in the unofficial Koreatown that sprawls around Herald Square. Try **Karaoke Duet 35** (✉ *53 W. 35th St., 2nd fl., between 5th and 6th Aves.* ☎ *646/233–2685*).

For live-band karaoke, head to the Lower East Side's hottest sing-fest: Monday-night rock-and-roll karaoke at **Arlene's Grocery** (✉ *95 Stanton St.* ☎ *212/995–1652*).

LIVE MUSIC VENUES

SOB's. The initials stand for "Sounds Of Brazil" (no, not what you—and everybody else—might think), and this is *the* place for reggae, African, and Latin music, with some jazz gigs like Marcus Miller sprinkled in. The late, great Cuban sensation Cachao used to hold court here, as does calypso's Mighty Sparrow when he's up north. Don't miss the monthly Southeast Asian party Basement Bhangra, the Haitian dance parties, or the bossa nova brunches. Dinner is served as well. ✉ *200 Varick St., SoHo* ☎ *212/243–4940* 🌐 *www.sobs.com* Ⓜ *1 to Houston St.*

EAST VILLAGE AND LOWER EAST SIDE

EAST VILLAGE

BARS

Beauty Bar. Grab a seat in a barber chair or under a dryer at this made-over hair salon where, during happy hour, the manicurist will do your nails for a fee that includes a drink. (How's that for multitasking?) The DJ spins everything from Britpop to rock—a great soundtrack for primping. ✉ *231 E. 14th St., between 2nd and 3rd Aves., East Village* ☎ *212/539–1389* 🌐 *www.thebeautybar.com* Ⓜ *4, 5, 6, L, N, Q, R to 14th St.–Union Sq.*

Fodor's Choice ★ **The Bourgeois Pig.** What do you get when you serve all kinds of different fondue concoctions as well as all kinds of inventively delicious cocktails in a velvety yet chilled-out French bordello setting that's smack dab in the middle of the East Village? This keeper of a lounge. ✉ *111 E. 7th St., between 1st Ave. and Ave. A, East Village* ☎ *212/475–2246* 🌐 *www.bourgeoispigny.com* Ⓜ *F to 2nd Ave.; 6 to Astor Pl.*

The Bowery Hotel. Combining old-world hunting-lodge elegance with the height of comfort, the Bowery sets a standard for what all hotel lobbies should feature: sofas you can get lost in, a grand fireplace, a beautiful garden, an unusually friendly staff, and enough good vibes to compensate for the loss of CBGB down the block. ✉ *335 Bowery, between 2nd and 3rd Aves., East Village* ☎ *212/505–9100* 🌐 *www.theboweryhotel.com* Ⓜ *F to 2nd Ave.; 6 to Astor Pl.*

Death + Company. It's all about "speakeasy chic" at this sister lounge to the equally imaginative and classy nearby bars Mayahuel and Bourgeois Pig. A hilarious wall mural toward the rear sets the tone for the tongue-in-cheek satanic vibe here, but in the end, it's all about the outlandishly delicious cocktails and accompanying bar bites. ✉ *433 E. 6th St., between 1st Ave. and Ave. A, East Village* ☎ *212/388–0882* 🌐 *www.deathandcompany.com* Ⓜ *F to 2nd Ave.; 6 to Astor Pl.*

Mayahuel. The Agave goddess is behind the name of this cocktail den, where all manner of Aztec spirits (raspberry tea–infused tequilas! pineapple-infused mescal!) make for the fiendishly rococo concoctions, courtesy of master mixologist Philip Ward. Equally good are snacks such as popcorn with lime, cheese, and chili. The bilevel setting conjures a sort of demonic south-of-the-border bordello. ✉ *304 E. 6th St., between 1st and 2nd Aves., East Village* ☎ *212/253–5888* 🌐 *www.mayahuelny.com* Ⓜ *F to 2nd Ave.; 6 to Astor Pl.; N, R to 8th St.–NYU.*

McSorley's Old Ale House. One of New York's oldest saloons (it claims to have opened in 1854) and immortalized by *New Yorker* writer Joseph Mitchell, McSorley's is a must-visit for beer lovers, even if only two kinds of brew are served: McSorley's Light and McSorley's Dark. It's also essential for blarney lovers, and much friendlier to women than it was before the '80s. (The motto here once was "Good ale, raw onions, and no ladies.") Go early to avoid the lines on Friday and Saturday night. ✉ *15 E. 7th St., between 2nd and 3rd Aves., East Village* ☎ *212/473–9148* 🌐 *www.mcsorleysnewyork.com* Ⓜ *6 to Astor Pl.*

Otto's Shrunken Head Tiki Bar & Lounge. Who says NYC doesn't appeal to all tastes? Should you get a sudden urge to visit a tiki bar while in the East Village—and who doesn't sometimes?—the ultra-popular Otto's is your ticket. You'll find more than just a bamboo bar here: namely fish lamps, a tattooed, punk-rock crowd, cute little banquettes, drinking mugs in the form of shrunken heads, beef jerky for sale, and DJs prone to spinning anything from '50s rock to "Soul Gidget" surf music. ✉ *538 E. 14th St., between Aves. A and B, East Village* ☎ *212/228–2240* 🌐 *www.ottosshrunkenhead.com* Ⓜ *L to 1st Ave.*

PDT. Those who crave their cocktails with a little mystery will flip over PDT (which stands for "Please Don't Tell"). Housed beside the hot-dog joint Crif Dogs, this pseudo-speakeasy can be reached only through a phone booth on the main floor. Patrons with phoned-in reservations are escorted through the phone booth's false back into the cocktail bar, which is decorated with warm wooden beams and tongue-in-cheek taxidermy. ✉ *113 St. Marks Pl., between 1st Ave. and Ave. A, East Village* ☎ *212/614–0386* 🌐 *www.pdtnyc.com* Ⓜ *6 to Astor Pl.*

Summit Bar. Manhattan's easternmost cocktail bar, Summit Bar serves up high-end sips in a low-key environment. Still, much thought and care is put into the drinks, right down to the herbs that come from the Summit's rooftop garden. The menu aims to please, and splits between "classic" and more ambitious "alchemist" sections, the latter boasting drinks with caraway-infused agave and shiso leaf. There's a snug outdoor patio as well, ideal for sampling the Summit's surprising take on a margarita come summer. ✉ *133 Ave. C, between 8th and 9th Sts., East Village* 🌐 *www.thesummitbar.net* Ⓜ *L to 1st Ave.*

Temple Bar. Unmarked and famous for its classic cocktails and romantic atmosphere, the Temple is prime first-date territory, especially once you drift past the sleekly wonderful bar to the back, where, swathed in almost complete darkness, you can lounge on a comfy banquette, order an Old Fashioned, and do what people on first dates do. ✉ *332 Lafayette St., East Village* ☎ *212/925–4242* 🌐 *www.templebarnyc.com* Ⓜ *B, D, F, M to Broadway–Lafayette St.; 6 to Bleecker St.*

CABARET AND PIANO BARS

Joe's Pub. Wood paneling, red-velvet walls, and comfy sofas make a lush setting for top-notch performers and the A-list celebrities who love them, or pretend to. Named for the Public Theater's near-mythic impresario Joe Papp, and located inside the Public, Joe's doesn't have a bad seat—but if you want to occupy one, buy tickets beforehand and/or arrive at least half an hour early for the Italian-inspired dinner menu. ✉ *425 Lafayette St., between E. 4th St. and Astor Pl., East Village* ☎ *212/539–8778* 🌐 *www.joespub.com* Ⓜ *6 to Astor Pl.*

ROCK CLUB

Fodor's Choice ★ **Lit Lounge.** With a rock roster that's included musical forces as diverse as Devendra Banhart and the Hold Steady, Lit is a wonderfully grungy East Village classic. The raucous arty crowd hits not only shows but its charming art gallery Fuse and its theme parties, which cater to fans of specific bands (the White Stripes, Devo, and the Buzzcocks, to name just three). ✉ *93 2nd Ave. #A, East Village* ☎ *212/777–7987* 🌐 *www.litloungenyc.com* Ⓜ *F to 2nd Ave., 6 to Astor Pl.*

LOWER EAST SIDE

BARS

Fodor's Choice ★ **Back Room.** The Prohibition-era touches here include tin ceilings, chandeliers, velvet wallpaper, mirrored bars, a fireplace, and a "hidden" outdoor entrance (which you'll find easily enough, though the back-alley walk to the second, indoor entrance puts you in the speakeasy spirit). The music consists of rock CDs rather than a live DJ, and the drinks come in old-fashioned teacups or wrapped in paper bags. These,

The crowd at SOB's can get pretty lively.

and other prize quirks, attract a slightly older clientele than many of its rowdy "boho" (aka bohemian) neighbors do. ✉ *102 Norfolk St., between Delancey and Rivington Sts., Lower East Side* ☎ *212/228–5098* Ⓜ *F, J, M, Z to Delancey St.–Essex St.*

Max Fish. One of the Lower East Side's most iconic bars, Max Fish has been the scene of many a shenanigan since it opened back in 1989. It has one of the most eclectic jukeboxes in town, a pool table in back, and a constant stream of rock-and-rollers and those who rock (and sometimes roll) with them. It's open till 4 am daily. ✉ *178 Ludlow St., between E. Houston and Stanton Sts., Lower East Side* ☎ *212/529–3959* 🌐 *www.maxfish.com* Ⓜ *F to 2nd Ave.*

Spitzer's Corner. No, you won't rub shoulders with disgraced ex-governor Eliot Spitzer here, but you will find 40 types of beer on tap plus a selection of the bottled variety, good food, floor-to-ceiling windows that pop open in fine weather, and wooden walls supposedly taken from pickle barrels. (Fortunately, the air is free of any scents from the barrel's former contents.) ✉ *101 Rivington St., at Ludlow St., Lower East Side* ☎ *212/228–0027* 🌐 *www.spitzerscorner.com* Ⓜ *F, J, M, Z to Delancey St.–Essex St.*

LIVE MUSIC VENUES

Arlene's Grocery. On Monday nights, crowds pack into this former Puerto Rican bodega for Rock and Roll Karaoke, where they live out their rock-star dreams by singing favorite punk anthems onstage with a live band. The other six nights of the week are for local bands, and are accordingly hit-or-miss. ✉ *95 Stanton St., between Ludlow and*

Orchard Sts., Lower East Side ☎ *212/358–1633* 🌐 *www.arlenesgrocery.net* Ⓜ *F to 2nd Ave.*

Fodor's Choice ★ **Bowery Ballroom.** This theater with art-deco accents is probably the city's top midsize concert venue. Packing in the crowds here is a rite of passage for musicians on the cusp of stardom, including the Gossip, Manic Street Preachers, and the exuberant Go! Team. Grab one of the tables on the balcony (if you can), stand (and thus get sandwiched) on the main floor, or retreat to the comfortable bar in the basement, which really fills up after each show. ✉ *6 Delancey St., between Bowery and Chrystie St., Lower East Side* ☎ *212/533–2111* 🌐 *www.boweryballroom.com* Ⓜ *J, Z to Bowery.*

Mercury Lounge. You'll have to squeeze past all the sardine-packed hipsters in the front bar to reach the stage, but it's worth it. Not only does this top-quality venue, a "little sister to the Bowery Ballrom," specialize in cool bands on the indie scene (Holly Golightly, Echo and the Bunnymen, and the Apostle of Hustle, anyone?), but it was where the late great Jeff Buckley used to stop by to do spontaneous solo shows. ✉ *217 E. Houston St., at Ave. A, Lower East Side* ☎ *212/260–4700* 🌐 *mercuryloungenyc.com* Ⓜ *F to 2nd Ave.*

Piano's. With two venues for live music and DJs—the Showroom downstairs and Lounge upstairs—as well as a full bar that serves food downstairs, there's something for everyone at this Lower East Side staple. It's a blast late nights. ✉ *158 Ludlow St., at Stanton St., Lower East Side* ☎ *212/505–3733* 🌐 *www.pianosnyc.com* Ⓜ *F, J, M, Z to Delancey St.–Essex St.*

GREENWICH VILLAGE AND WEST VILLAGE

GREENWICH VILLAGE

BARS

The Dove Parlour. On a colorful block that evokes the Greenwich Village of yore—cigar store, vegetarian cafés, a bootleg music shop, and not one but two stores specializing in chess—is this wonderful bar whose elegant atmosphere (red-velvet wallpaper, white-wood paneling) is belied by the revelry of the very sexy young customers. ✉ *228 Thompson St., between 3rd and Bleecker Sts., Greenwich Village* ☎ *212/254–1435* 🌐 *www.thedoveparlour.com* Ⓜ *A, B, C, D, E, F, M to W. 4th St.*

Vol de Nuit. Tucked away from the street, the "Belgian Beer Bar" (as everybody calls it) features a European-style, enclosed outdoor courtyard and a cozy interior, all red light and shadows. NYU grad-student types come for the mammoth selection of beers on tap as well as for the fries, which are served with a Belgian flair, in a paper cone with an array of sauces on the side. ✉ *148 W. 4th St., at 6th Ave., Greenwich Village* ☎ *212/982–3388* 🌐 *www.voldenuitbar.com* Ⓜ *A, B, C, D, E, F, M to W. 4th St.–Washington Sq.*

JAZZ VENUES

Fodor's Choice ★ **Blue Note.** Considered by many (not least its current owners) to be "the jazz capital of the world," the Blue Note was once the stomping ground for such legends as Dizzy Gillespie, and still hosts a varied repertoire from Chris Botti to the Count Basie Orchestra to Boz Scaggs. Expect a steep cover charge except for late shows on weekends, when the music goes from less jazzy to more funky. ✉ *131 W. 3rd St., near 6th Ave., Greenwich Village* ☎ *212/475–8592* 🌐 *www.bluenotejazz.com* Ⓜ *A, B, C, D, E, F, M to W. 4th St.–Washington Sq.*

Knickerbocker Bar and Grill. Jazz acts are on the menu on Friday and Saturday nights at this old-fashioned steak house, a longtime staple of the city's more intimate music scene. ✉ *33 University Pl., at E. 9th St., Greenwich Village* ☎ *212/228–8490* 🌐 *www.knickerbockerbarandgrill.com* Ⓜ *N, R to 8th St.–NYU.*

LIVE MUSIC VENUES

(Le) Poisson Rouge. Underneath the site of the late, lamented Village Gate jazz emporium is this cutting-edge jewel of a place, whose name means "the Red Fish" and whose parentheses around Le remain a mystery. Blending just the right mix of posh notes (the lush decor, the fine dining) and brave music programming (jazz, classical, electronic, cabaret, rock, folk—even, with the splendiferous Ralph's World, children's music), the Poisson is an essential NYC fixture. ✉ *158 Bleecker St., at Thompson St., Greenwich Village* ☎ *212/505–3474* 🌐 *www.lepoissonrouge.com* Ⓜ *A, B, C, D, E, F, M to W. 4th St.–Washington Sq.*

WEST VILLAGE

BARS

Corner Bistro. Opened in 1961, this charming neighborhood saloon serves what many think are the best (and most affordable) hamburgers in town. Once you actually get a seat, the space feels nice and cozy, but until then, be prepared to drink a beer amid loud and hungry patrons. ✉ *331 W. 4th St., at 8th Ave., West Village* ☎ *212/242–9502* 🌐 *www.cornerbistrony.com* Ⓜ *A, C, E to 14th St.; L to 8th Ave.*

19

Employees Only. The dapper, white-coated bartenders (many of them impressively mustachio'd) at this Prohibition era–style bar mix delicious, well-thought-out cocktails with debonair aplomb and freshly squeezed mixers. Sip one in the dimly lit, unpretentious bar area and you just might feel like you've stepped back in time—if it weren't for the crush of trendy West Village locals and visitors in the know at your back. Look for the green awning that says EO and the neon "Psychic" sign out front. Dinner is served in the restaurant at the back: it's quality, but pricey. ✉ *510 Hudson St., West Village* ☎ *212/242–3021* 🌐 *www.employeesonlynyc.com* Ⓜ *1 to Christopher St.–Sheridan Sq.; A, B, C, D, E, F, M to W. 4th St.–Washington Sq..*

Hudson Bar and Books. Along with its sister branches—Beekman Bar and Books on Beekman Place and Lexington Bar and Books on, yep, Lexington—the Hudson reflects a literary bent on its cocktails with names like the Dewey Decimal, the Cervantes Spritzer, and Alphabet Absinthe (topped off with floating letter-shape sugar cubes). Despite that, it's hardly a hushed library where well-read butlers serve you; no—the atmosphere here is more about book decor than serious literature. It's seriously clubby, with wood paneling and leather banquettes. And it's one of the few places you can still smoke. ✉ *636 Hudson St., at Horatio*

St., West Village ☎ *212/229–2642* 🌐 *www.barandbooks.cz* Ⓜ *A, C, E to 14th St.; L to 8th Ave.*

Fodor's Choice ★ **Little Branch.** The owners of the secretive, hard-to-access lounge Milk & Honey created this open-to-everyone cousin with the same high-quality cocktails. The dim lighting and snug booths make it the ideal spot for a conversation with friends (that you can actually hear) or an intimate date. ✉ *20 7th Ave., at Leroy St., West Village* ☎ *212/929–4360* Ⓜ *1 to Houston St.*

Otheroom. Ever wish that the bar you're drinking in had something more interesting on its walls than Budweiser signs? Head to the far west Otheroom, art gallery by day, upscale drinking spot by night. The menu is pretty creative, too, with dozens of microbeers as well as American wines available by the glass. ✉ *143 Perry St., between Greenwich and Washington Sts., West Village* ☎ *212/645–9758* 🌐 *www.theotheroom.com* Ⓜ *1 toChristopher St.–Sheridan Sq.*

White Horse Tavern. According to New York legend, Dylan Thomas drank himself to death in this historic and quintessential West Village tavern founded in 1880. The Horse remains perpetually popular with literary types, but thankfully it's lacking more death-by-alcohol-poisoning cases of late. When the weather's nice, try to snag a seat at one of the sidewalk tables for prime—and, given the neighborhood, we do mean prime—people-watching. ✉ *567 Hudson St., at W. 11th St., West Village* ☎ *212/989–3956* Ⓜ *1 to Christopher St.–Sheridan Sq.*

Wilfie & Nell. Combine the beloved cozy atmosphere and frothy pints standard at Irish pubs with a well-heeled West Village crowd and you get Wilfie & Nell, a candlelit bar full of communal tables for making new friends. This perpetually crowded neighborhood favorite, with its low ceilings and locally sourced food, is a popular singles spot as well as a good match for night owls: food and brews are served into the wee hours. ✉ *228 W. 4th St., between W. 10th St. and 7th Ave. S, West Village* ☎ *212/242–2990* 🌐 *www.wilfieandnell.com* Ⓜ *1 to Christopher St.–Sheridan Sq.*

CABARET AND PIANO BARS

The Duplex. No matter who's performing, the largely gay audience hoots and hollers in support of the often kitschy performers at this music-scene staple on busy Sheridan Square since 1951. Singers and comedians hold court in the cabaret theater, while those itching to take a shot at open mike head downstairs to the lively piano bar. ✉ *61 Christopher St., at 7th Ave. S, West Village* ☎ *212/255–5438* 🌐 *www.theduplex.com* Ⓜ *1 to Christopher St.–Sheridan Sq.*

GAY NIGHTLIFE

Cubbyhole. Early in the evening the crowd is mixed at this neighborhood institution, where the DJs, the unpretentious decor, and the inexpensive margaritas are popular. Later on, the women take charge. ✉ *281 W. 12th St., at W. 4th St., West Village* ☎ *212/243–9041* 🌐 *www.cubbyholebar.com* Ⓜ *A, C, E to 14th St.; L to 8th Ave.*

Fodor's Choice ★ **Henrietta Hudson.** The nightly parties at this laid-back West Village HQ for the Sapphic set attract young professional women, out-of-towners, and longtime regulars. Because the DJ and the pool table quickly create a crowd, though, stake your claim to a spot early, especially on—yup, you guessed it—weekends. ✉ *438 Hudson St., at Morton St., West Village* ☎ *212/924–3347* 🌐 *www.henriettahudson.com* Ⓜ *1 to Christopher St.–Sheridan Sq.*

JAZZ VENUES

Garage Restaurant & Café. Good news for you budget-minded jazzers: there's no cover *and* no minimum at this West Village hot spot, where two jazz groups jam seven nights a week and a fireplace sets the mood upstairs. ✉ *99 7th Ave. S, between Bleecker and Christopher Sts., West Village* ☎ *212/645–0600* 🌐 *www.garagerest.com* Ⓜ *1 to Christopher St.–Sheridan Sq.*

Fodor's Choice ★ **Village Vanguard.** This prototypical jazz club, tucked into a cellar in Greenwich Village since the 1940s, has been the haunt of legends like Thelonious Monk and Barbra Streisand (who recently came back for a one-night-only gig). Today you can hear jams from the jazz-star likes of Bill Charlap and Ravi Coltrane, and on Monday night the sizable resident Vanguard Jazz Orchestra blows its collective heart out. ✉ *178 7th Ave. S, between W. 11th and Perry Sts., West Village* ☎ *212/255–4037* 🌐 *www.villagevanguard.com* Ⓜ *1, 2, 3 to 14th St.*

CHELSEA AND THE MEATPACKING DISTRICT

CHELSEA

BARS

Half King. Writer Sebastian Junger (*The Perfect Storm*) is one of the owners of this would-be literary mecca. We say "would-be" because the ambience can be more pub-like than writerly—but that's fine, since the King draws such a friendly crowd (media types, mostly). We like it best for its frequent readings, gallery exhibits, and Irish-American menu. ✉ *505 W. 23rd St., between 10th and 11th Aves., Chelsea* ☎ *212/462–4300* 🌐 *www.thehalfking.com* Ⓜ *C, E to 23rd St.*

19

Fodor's Choice ★ **Tillman's.** Nothing in Chelsea is quite like this glorious "Old Harlem" lounge, resplendent as it is with a fireplace, banquettes, good eats, even better cocktails, inventive decor, jazz and blues sounds on the soundtrack, and tastefully uniformed servers complete with a cigarette girl. ✉ *165 W. 26th St., between 6th and 7th Aves., Chelsea* ☎ *212/627–8320* 🌐 *www.tillmansnyc.com* Ⓜ *F, M to 23rd St.; 1 to 28th St.*

COMEDY CLUBS

Fodor's Choice ★ **Upright Citizens Brigade Theatre.** Raucous sketch comedy, audience-initiated improv, and classic stand-up take turns onstage here at the city's absolute capital for alternative comedy. There are even classes available; the Upright Citizens bill their program as the world's largest improv school, where you can catch indie comic darlings like *SNL*'s Amy Poehler or *Human Giant*'s Rob Huebel. ✉ *307 W. 26th St., between 8th and 9th Aves., Chelsea* ☎ *212/366–9176* 🌐 *www.ucbtheatre.com* Ⓜ *C, E to 23rd St.*

Indie band Beirut blows away the Bowery Ballroom.

GAY NIGHTLIFE

Big Apple Ranch. Taking *Brokeback Mountain* style to the dance floor, the Ranch lets you unleash your inner "cowboy dancer" every Saturday night, with half-hour two-step lessons at 8 pm, line dancing at 8:30 pm, and then a down-home country-and-western dance party kicking off at 9 pm. ✉ *Dance Manhattan, 39 W. 19th St., 5th fl., Chelsea* ☎ *212/358–5752* 🌐 *www.bigappleranch.com* Ⓜ *F, M to 23rd St.; N, R to 23rd St.; 1 to 18th St.*

Gym Sports Bar. At New York's first gay sports bar, the plentiful flat-screen TVs and cheap Budweisers draw athletic enthusiasts of every stripe, from athlete to armchair. Nobly enough, the bar sponsors—and frequently hosts parties for—a number of local gay sports teams. ✉ *167 8th Ave., at 18th St., Chelsea* ☎ *212/337–2439* 🌐 *www.gymsportsbar.com* Ⓜ *A, C, E to 14th St.; L to 8th Ave.*

Fodor's Choice ★ **Splash.** At this large, perennially crowded Chelsea bar-club, beefy go-go boys vie for attention with equally buff bartenders who don't have on much more than underwear. The daily happy hour, with campy music videos on three huge screens, is a hit. Our only caveat: late-night covers can be high. ✉ *50 W. 17th St., between 5th and 6th Aves., Chelsea* ☎ *212/691–0073* 🌐 *www.splashbar.com* Ⓜ *F, M to 14th St.; L to 6th Ave.*

THE MEATPACKING DISTRICT

BARS

675 Bar. How can you not love a spot where the bouncer greets you with a grin instead of a scowl, board games abound, a giant black-lacquered horse stands guard next to the pool table, the drinks get amply poured, and each small room along the subterranean stone corridor is decorated in a different creative way? As an ideal spot for both dates (plenty of dark corners) and raucous merriment (bright, big central space), the 675 scores highest for having less attitude than the rest of the neighborhood. ✉ *675 Hudson St., between Hudson St. and 9th Ave. (enter on 13th St.), Meatpacking District* ☎ *212/699–2410* 🌐 *www.675bar.com* Ⓜ *A, C, E to 14th St.; L to 8th Ave.*

Hogs & Heifers. This raucous place is all about the saucy barkeeps using megaphones to berate male customers and bait the females to get up on the bar and dance (and add their bras to the collection on the wall). Celebrities of the *Us Weekly* variety still drop in from time to time to get their names in the gossip columns. ✉ *859 Washington St., at 13th St., Meatpacking District* ☎ *212/929–0655* 🌐 *www.hogsandheifers.com* Ⓜ *A, C, E to 14th St.; L to 8th Ave.*

Plunge. The Gansevoort Hotel's slick rooftop bar would be worth visiting even without its mouthwatering views. The adjectives sleek and glossy could easily be illustrated by Plunge, where the lighting is soft, the furnishings are cool and comfy (at least to a degree), the music isn't too loud, servers of both sexes are sexy, and there is ample space—indoors as well as out. ✉ *18 9th Ave., at 13th St., Meatpacking District* ☎ *212/660–6766* 🌐 *www.hotelgansevoort.com* Ⓜ *A, C, E to 14th St.; L to 8th Ave.*

Spice Market. The posh come here to gorge on Asian street fare served with upscale twists, along with equally exotic cocktails. Ginger margaritas, anyone? Or a kumquat mojito (when in season)? If you're looking for tranquility, the multilevel open space has slowly rotating fans, intricately carved woodwork, and flowing curtains that create an aura of calm. ✉ *403 W. 13th St., at 9th Ave., Meatpacking District* ☎ *212/675–2322* 🌐 *www.spicemarketnewyork.com* Ⓜ *A, C, E to 14th St.; L to 8th Ave.*

The Standard Hotel Biergarten, Grill, and Living Room. Practically the official bar of the High Line park, the Standard Biergarten is a sprawling and riotous space complete with ping pong tables and big steins of beer. There's also a grill bar and very cool indoor Living Room lounge. As for the chic hot spot on the top floor, unofficially called the Boom Boom Room, it's currently the hardest "door" in town ("hardest," that is, to get through), but given the quality of the accessible fun down below, we'll forgive their snobbery. ✉ *848 Washington St., at W. 13th St., Meatpacking District* ☎ *212/645–4646* 🌐 *www.standardhotels.com* Ⓜ *A, C, E to 14th St.; L to 8th Ave.*

DANCE CLUBS AND DJ VENUES

Cielo. Relatively mature dance club goers (if the word mature can ever be applied to such a crowd) gravitate to this small but sturdy Meatpacking District "music-head" mecca to toss back cocktails, dig the high-quality sound system, groove to top-flight DJs spinning soulful Latin beats and techno, boogie on the sunken dance floor, and smoke in the no-frills garden outside. Monday nights are home to the award-winning Deep Space parties, where resident DJs (as well as guest spinmeisters like Dmitri from Paris) rev up the faithful with everything from dubstep to Stravinsky. ✉ *18 Little W. 12th St., between 9th Ave. and Washington*

St., Meatpacking District ☎ *212/645–5700* 🌐 *www.cieloclub.com* Ⓜ *A, C, E to 14th St.; L to 8th Ave.*

Fodor's Choice ★ **Kiss & Fly.** One of New York's most discerning nightlife experts, the dance-music artist Sir Ivan, swears by Kiss & Fly, and it's obvious why: this modest-size dance club has sensational music (pumped as loud as can be, of course), a beautiful interior design (dig all the butterfly motifs), and creative lighting that actually lets you see who you're dancing/speaking/kissing/sipping with. It's pricey, tough to get into, and a bit snooty, but now that you've been duly warned, have a ball. ✉ *409 W. 13th St., between 9th Ave. and Washington St., Meatpacking District* ☎ *212/255–1933* 🌐 *www.kissandflyclub.com* Ⓜ *A, C, E to 14th St.; L to 8th Ave.*

UNION SQUARE, GRAMERCY, AND THE FLATIRON DISTRICT

GRAMERCY

BARS

Old Town Bar. The proudly unpretentious bilevel Old Town is redolent of old New York, and why not—it's been around since 1892. Tavern-style grub, mahogany everywhere, and atmosphere, atmosphere, atmosphere make this a fun stop on any pub crawl. Men, don't miss the giant, person-size urinals. ✉ *45 E. 18th St., between Broadway and Park Ave. S, Gramercy* ☎ *212/529–6732* 🌐 *www.oldtownbar.com* Ⓜ *4, 5, 6, L, N, Q, R to 14th St.–Union Sq.*

Pete's Tavern. This historic landmark (where O. Henry was a loyal customer) is one of the bars that claims to be the oldest continuously operating watering hole in the city. Pete's has charm to spare, with its long wooden bar and cozy booths, where locals crowd in for a beer or a fantastic burger. When weather warms up, sidewalk tables with red-checkered cloths on scenic Irving Place are a neighborhood favorite. ✉ *129 E. 18th St., at Irving Pl., Gramercy* ☎ *212/473–7676* 🌐 *www.petestavern.com* Ⓜ *4, 5, 6, L, N, Q, R to 14th St.–Union Sq.*

JAZZ VENUES

Fodor's Choice ★ **Jazz Standard.** The Standard's sizable underground room draws top names in the business. As a part of Danny Meyer's southern-food restaurant Blue Smoke, it's one of the few spots where you can get dry-rubbed ribs to go with your bebop. Bring the kids for the Jazz Standard Youth Orchestra concerts every Sunday afternoon. ✉ *116 E. 27th St., between Park and Lexington Aves., Gramercy* ☎ *212/576–2232* 🌐 *www.jazzstandard.net* Ⓜ *6 to 28th St.*

LIVE MUSIC VENUES

Fodor's Choice ★ **Irving Plaza.** This two-story venue is known for its solid rock performances, both indie (DJ Shadow and Sleater-Kinney) and more mainstream (Lenny Kravitz, Blues Traveler)—even if they can get a little pricey. Red walls and chandeliers add a Gothic touch. And if the main floor gets too cramped, seek sanctuary in the form of the chill bar upstairs. ✉ *17 Irving Pl., at E. 15th St., Gramercy* ☎ *212/777–6800* 🌐 *www.irvingplaza.com* Ⓜ *4, 5, 6, L, N, Q, R to 14th St.–Union Sq.*

FLATIRON DISTRICT

BARS

The Ace Hotel. A hot spot for the digital set, this hotel's lobby and adjoining restaurant spaces—the Breslin and the John Dory—have been packed since they opened at this Pacific Northwest import. If your bearded hipster friend came into some cash, his place would look like the lobby here, with reclaimed wood tables, beer signs, and beautiful folks in oversize eyeglasses drinking coffee by day or a craft brew by night (while a DJ spins in the background). ✉ *20 W. 29th St., between Broadway and 5th Ave., Gramercy* ☎ *212/679–2222* 🌐 *www.acehotel.com* Ⓜ *N, R to 28th St.*

Flatiron Lounge. Here, resident mixologists rely on the freshest (and sometimes most exotic) ingredients available. The cocktail menu changes often, but if you're stumped, tell the bartenders what you like and they'll happily invent a new concoction on the spot. ✉ *37 W. 19th St., between 5th and 6th Aves., Flatiron* ☎ *212/727–7741* 🌐 *www.flatironlounge.com* Ⓜ *F, M, N, R to 23rd St.*

UNION SQUARE

BARS

Rye House. A welcoming bar with slick cocktails and clever takes on comfort food, the Rye House beckons just steps from the chain store overload of Union Square. From boiled peanuts and fried pickles to their own take on a Sazerac, the space is a welcome respite from the hustle and bustle outside. ✉ *11 W. 17th St., between Broadway and 5th Ave., Union Square* ☎ *212/255–7260* 🌐 *www.ryehousenyc.com* Ⓜ *4, 5, 6, L, N, Q, R to 14th St.–Union Sq.*

MIDTOWN EAST

BARS

The Bar Downstairs. The bar without a name in the basement of the Andaz Fifth Avenue may lack a moniker, but it certainly has a pedigree. Alchemy Consulting, a joint venture from Chicago's Violet Hour and New York's Death and Co., designed the cocktails here; look for spins on the Negroni and Manhattan in the sleek subterranean space. The food menu is similarly up-market, with a variety of nebulously Spanish small plates on offer. ✉ *485 5th Ave., at 41st St., Midtown East* ☎ *212/601–1234* Ⓜ *4, 5, 6, 7, S to 42nd St.–Grand Central.*

Fodor's Choice ★ **Campbell Apartment.** Commuting professionals pack into this Grand Central Terminal bar on their way to catch trains home during the evening rush, but don't let the crush of humanity scare you away—you can have a deeply romantic time here in one of Manhattan's more beautiful rooms. The restored space dates to the 1920s, when it was the private office of an executive named John W. Campbell, and as the exquisite decor suggests, old JWC knew how to live. Sample the good life as you knock back a well-built cocktail from an overstuffed chair. Just try to avoid that weekday evening rush. ✉ *15 Vanderbilt Ave. entrance, Grand Central Terminal, Midtown East* ☎ *212/953–0409* 🌐 *www.grandcentralterminal.com* Ⓜ *4, 5, 6, 7, S to 42nd St.–Grand Central.*

Fodor's Choice ★ **Galway Pub.** This welcoming spot is sought out as one of midtown's most authentic, and best, Irish pubs. Even on a block with a high number of fine drinking establishments, this one stands out thanks to its gorgeous circular bar, intriguing orange lighting, spirited after-work crowd, and bartenders, some of whom might just actually hail from the Emerald Isle. Snag one of their business cards, too—on the back are words of wisdom from the best Irish writers. ✉ *7 E. 36th St., between 5th and Madison Aves., Murray Hill* ☎ *212/725–2353* 🌐 *www.galwayhookernyc.com* Ⓜ *6 to 33rd St.*

King Cole Bar. A justly beloved Maxfield Parrish mural of "Old King Cole" himself, as well as his psychedelic court, adds to the already considerable elegance at this romantic and essential midtown meeting place. Try a Bloody Mary—this is where the drink was introduced to Americans. Be warned: prices for a single cocktail are steep. ✉ *St. Regis Hotel, 2 E. 55th St., between 5th and Madison Aves., Midtown East* ☎ *212/339–6721* 🌐 *www.kingcolebar.com* Ⓜ *E, M to 5th Ave./53rd St.*

Middle Branch. Sasha Petraske's speakeasy-style cocktail bars have expanded into Murray Hill with Middle Branch, a two-story space and former antiques store with no sign outside to announce its presence. Cocktail lovers find the brick townhouse anyway, and inside, linger over small plates, live jazz, and a long list of sophisticated drink options. ✉ *154 E. 33rd St., Murray Hill* ☎ *212/213–1350* Ⓜ *6 to 33rd St.*

Pine Tree Lodge. Who says that the zaniest places are below 14th Street? This insane theme bar offers serious competition. Think "summer camp on psychedelics"—we're talking mounted wildlife, rafts, and other outdoorsy-kitsch decor. Don't overlook the spacious backyard or the racy raccoon picture in the comfy side room—you'll never view those critters the same way again. ✉ *591 1st Ave., at 34th St., Midtown East* ☎ *212/213–0990* 🌐 *www.pinetreelodgeny.com* Ⓜ *6 to 33rd St.*

P. J. Clarke's. Mirrors and polished wood and other old-time flair adorn New York's most famous Irish bar, a redbrick brawler of a joint. Steeped in Hollywood lore—Steve McQueen was once a regular, and scenes from the 1945 movie *Lost Weekend* were shot here—Clarke's draws in the after-work crowd that appreciates drinking beer and eating exceptionally juicy burgers around a sense of history. ✉ *915 Third Ave., 55th St., Midtown East* ☎ *212/317–1616* 🌐 *www.pjclarkes.com* Ⓜ *4, 5, 6 to 59th St.; N, Q, R to Lexington Ave./59th St.*

Rodeo Bar. If the honky-tonk music, the bison over the front bar, and peanut shells littering the floor at this neighborhood institution don't clue you in, the rockin' vibe and friendly service will: this is the go-to spot for good times and free live music every night of the week. The Tex-Mex food is good (try the Cowboy kisses: shrimp and jalapeños wrapped in bacon) but the real draw is the music. Local bands and touring pros play blues, bluegrass, country, alt-country, rockabilly, and rock 'n' roll. The margaritas are legendary, and the selection of beer includes hard-to-find quaffs like Shiner Bock from Texas. ✉ *375 3rd Ave., at 27th St., Midtown East* ☎ *212/683–6500* 🌐 *www.rodeobar.com* Ⓜ *6 to 28th St.*

Top of the Tower. There are lounges at higher altitudes, but this one on the 26th floor wins wide acclaim for its atmosphere of subdued elegance and East Side location, within spitting distance of the United Nations. There's live piano music Wednesday–Sunday nights. ✉ *Beekman Tower Hotel, 3 Mitchell Pl., near 1st Ave. at 49th St., Midtown East* ☎ *212/980–4796* 🌐 *www.thebeekmanhotel.com* Ⓜ *6 to 51st St.; E, M to Lexington Ave./53rd St.*

Fodor's Choice ★ **The Volstead.** Named for the Volstead Act, which instituted Prohibition back in the '20s, this subterranean bastion of cool is simply indispensable. In a tasteful setting that features just the right mix of mirrors, chandeliers, polished wood, and velvet wallpaper, a friendly staff and an ace barkeep serve up specialties like jalapeno margaritas and strawberry caipiroskas. ✉ *125 E. 54th St., between Park and Lexington Aves., Midtown East* ☎ *212/583–0411* 🌐 *www.thevolstead.com* Ⓜ *E, M to Lexington Ave./53rd St.*

GAY NIGHTLIFE

Evolve Bar and Lounge. Rising from the ashes of a popular gay club on the same site, this glossy, raucous Chelsea-style bar-club gets Midtown East rocking, with its sexy-yet-genial staff and theme nights like Pop-off Thursday, Bulge Friday, and Disco Balls Sunday. ✉ *221 E. 58th St., between 2nd and 3rd Aves., Midtown East* ☎ *212/355–3395* 🌐 *www.evolvebarandloungenyc.com* Ⓜ *4, 5, 6 to 59th St.; N, !, R to Lexington Ave./59th St.*

Townhouse Bar. It's the elegant yin to the rowdy yang of **Evolve**, across the block at East 58th Street. Distinguished mature men from the Upper East Side meet younger would-be versions of themselves at this "gentlemen's club," which looks like the home of a blueblood with superb taste. The attire is "uptown casual," if not fancier. ✉ *236 E. 58th St., between 2nd and 3rd Aves., Midtown East* ☎ *212/754–4649* 🌐 *www.townhouseny.com* Ⓜ *4, 5, 6 to 59th St.; N, !, R to Lexington Ave./59th St.*

MIDTOWN WEST

BARS

Cellar Bar. Underneath the Bryant Park Hotel is one of the more spectacular spaces in midtown. As a DJ with a taste for classic R&B spins the night away, a fashion-industry crowd gets up to dance—and spills its collective drink. ✉ *40 W. 40th St., between 5th and 6th Aves., Midtown West* ☎ *212/642–2211* 🌐 *www.cellarbarbryantparkhotel.com* Ⓜ *B, D, F, M to 42nd St.–Bryant Park; 7 to 5th Ave.*

Fodor's Choice ★ **Joe Allen.** Everybody's en route either to or from a show at this "old reliable" on the boisterous Restaurant Row, celebrated in the musical version of *All About Eve*. Chances are you'll even spot a Broadway star at the bar or in the dining room. Still, our favorite thing about Joe's is not the fun show crowd but the hilarious "flop wall," adorned with posters from musicals that bombed, sometimes spectacularly. (Check out the ones for *Paradox Lust, Got To Go Disco,* and *Dude,* which was the unfortunate sequel to *Hair.*) ✉ *326 W. 46th St., between 8th and 9th Aves., Midtown West* ☎ *212/581–6464* 🌐 *www.joeallenrestaurant.com* Ⓜ *A, C, E to 42nd St.–Port Authority.*

Russian Vodka Room. Forget **Russian Samovar** across the block—here's where the serious vodka drinking goes down. The Vodka Room features a sophisticated front room with nightly piano music, a more sumptuous back room, a generous Attitude Adjustment Hour (that's Russki for "Happy Hour"), and exotically infused vodkas with flavors like horseradish, ginger, and pepper. For those who crave variety, a vodka tasting menu is available, as are culinary standards like borscht. ✉ *265 W. 52nd St., between Broadway and 8th Ave., Midtown West* ☎ *212/307–5835* 🌐 *www.russianvodkaroom.com* Ⓜ *C, E to 50th St.; 1 to 50th St.*

Salon de Ning. Take a break from 5th Avenue shopping at this glass-lined penthouse bar on the 23rd floor of the über-ritzy Peninsula Hotel. Drinks are pricey, of course, but what isn't in this neighborhood? The views are worth it, especially from the rooftop terraces. ✉ *Peninsula Hotel, 700 5th Ave., at 55th St., Midtown West* ☎ *212/956–2888* 🌐 *www.salondening.com* Ⓜ *E, M to 5th Ave./53rd St.*

COMEDY CLUBS

Caroline's on Broadway. This high-gloss club presents established names as well as comedians on the edge of stardom. Janeane Garofalo, David Alan Grier, Colin Quinn, and Gilbert Gottfried have all headlined. ✉ *1626 Broadway, between 49th and 50th Sts., Midtown West* ☎ *212/757–4100* 🌐 *www.carolines.com* Ⓜ *N, Q, R to 49th St.; 1 to 50th St.*

Chicago City Limits. This crew touts itself as performing in the longest-running improv show in the city. Heavy on audience participation, the improv shows take place Friday and Saturday (with stand-up comics taking the stage the rest of the week) and seldom fail to whip visitors into what the comics might call a "phun phrenzy." ✉ *318 W. 53rd St., between 8th and 9th Aves., Midtown West* ☎ *212/888–5233* 🌐 *www.chicagocitylimits.com* Ⓜ *C, E to 50th St.*

DANCE CLUBS AND DJ VENUES

Pacha. Maybe you've been to the exclusive Pacha clubs in Buenos Aires, Ibiza, and London. But the jewel in the crown of the Pacha empire may well be here. Assuming you pass muster to enter, you'll find four stories' worth of high-tech fittings (blinding lights, go-go girls, humungous sound), plus celeb DJs and celeb customers. ✉ *618 W. 46th St., between 11th and 12th Aves., Midtown West* ☎ *212/209–7500* 🌐 *www.pachanyc.com* Ⓜ *C, E to 50th St.*

GAY NIGHTLIFE

Posh. Lest you think that Hell's Kitchen has no fine gay lounges, Posh has walls covered in fine canvases by local artists, trophies over the bar, ample room for kibitzing and dancing, plenty of neon decor, and hours that are "4 pm to 4 am GUARANTEED." Who says nothing is certain anymore? ✉ *405 W. 51st St., at 9th Ave., Midtown West* ☎ *212/957–2222* 🌐 *www.poshbarnyc.com* Ⓜ *C, E to 50th St.*

JAZZ VENUES

Birdland. This place gets its name from bebop saxophone great Charlie "Yardbird" (or just "Bird") Parker, so expect serious musicians such as John Pizzarelli, the Dave Holland Sextet, and Chico O'Farrill's Afro-Cuban Jazz Orchestra (on Sunday night). The dining room serves moderately priced American fare with a Cajun accent. ✉ *315 W. 44th St., between 8th and 9th Aves., Midtown West* ☎ *212/581–3080* 🌐 *www.birdlandjazz.com* Ⓜ *A, C, E to 42nd St.–Port Authority.*

Iridium. This cozy, top-drawer club is a sure bet for big-name talent like the David Murray Black Saint Quartet and Michael Wolff. The sight lines are good, and the sound system was designed with the help of Les Paul, the inventor of the solid-body electric guitar, who used to play here every Monday night. The rest of the week sees a mix of artists like Chuck Mangione and the Eddie Daniels Band. ✉ *1650 Broadway, at 51st St., Midtown West* ☎ *212/582–2121* 🌐 *www.theiridium.com* Ⓜ *1 to 50th St.; N, Q, R to 49th St.*

LIVE MUSIC VENUES

B. B. King Blues Club & Grill. This lavish Times Square club is vast and shiny and host to a range of musicians, from the Harlem Gospel Choir to George Clinton and the P-Funk All-Stars. It's also where surviving rock legends like Little Richard, Chuck Berry, and, yes, the still-relentlessly-touring owner play as well. (If you happen to meet Mr. King here, give our regards to Lucille, his guitar.) ✉ *237 W. 42nd St., between 7th and 8th Aves., Midtown West* ☎ *212/997–4144* 🌐 *www.bbkingblues.com* Ⓜ *A, C, E to 42nd St.–Port Authority; 1, 2, 3, 7, N, Q, R, S to Times Sq.–42nd St.*

UPPER EAST SIDE

BARS

American Trash. You might tell from the name that this isn't exactly your granddad's UES drinking establishment. Bicycle tires, golf clubs, and other castoffs cover the walls and ceiling, ensuring that the 20-year-old Trash, a sanctum of sleaze, merits its descriptive name. Eight plasma TVs, three video games, a defiantly rock-and-roll jukebox, and a pool table keep the neighborhood crowd (as well as stray bikers who hate them) busy. Some nights local bands play classic rock. ✉ *1471 1st Ave., between 76th and 77th Sts., Upper East Side* ☎ *212/988–9008* 🌐 *www.americantrashnyc.com* Ⓜ *6 to 77th St.*

Fodor's Choice ★ **Auction House.** This Victorian lounge brings a touch of downtown chic to the sometimes suburban-feeling Upper East Side with candlelit tables, high tin ceilings, and velvet couches. Rap and hip-hop fans should look elsewhere (the only tunes coming out of this joint are alternative and rock), and baseball caps and sneakers are strictly forbidden, as are—at the other end of the spectrum—fur coats. ✉ *300 E. 89th St., between 1st and 2nd Aves., Upper East Side* ☎ *212/427–4458* 🌐 *www.auctionhousenyc.com* Ⓜ *4, 5, 6 to 86th St.*

Bar Pleiades. The cocktail bar companion to Café Boulud, also in the Surrey Hotel, Bar Pleiades is a livelier alternative to the more staid atmosphere at the Carlyle's Bemelmans Bar. The decor is classic to a fault, employing a black-and-white theme that's positively Audrey Hepburn–esque. Drinks rotate seasonally, and there are nibbles from the café kitchen to create a base layer. Though it doesn't have the same drink menu, the rooftop bar is a cozy aerie good for people- (and sky-scraper-) watching. ✉ *Surrey Hotel, 20 E. 76th St., between 5th and*

Madison Aves., Upper East Side ☎ *212/772–2600* 🌐 *danielnyc.com/BarPleiades.html* Ⓜ *6 to 77th St.*

Opia. The motto for this upscale-yet-unpretentious bar-restaurant—"If you like us, tell your friends, and if you don't, tell your enemies!"—isn't necessary, given its manifold charms: a drop-dead-gorgeous design, plenty of space for canoodling and cavorting, a romantic balcony (though 57th Street isn't exactly a scenic beach), plus live jazz on Tuesday and Saturday nights. Opia is ideal for couples in full-on infatuation or spouses hoping to remember the wine-and-roses days before the kids. ✉ *130 E. 57th St., between Lexington and 3rd Aves., Upper East Side* ☎ *212/688–3939* 🌐 *www.opiarestaurant.com* Ⓜ *N, Q, R to Lexington Ave./59th St.; 4, 5, 6, to 59th St.*

CABARET AND PIANO BARS

Fodor's Choice ★ **The Carlyle.** The hotel's sophisticated Café Carlyle hosts such top cabaret and jazz performers as Christine Ebersole, John Pizzarelli, and Steve Tyrell. Stop by on a Monday night and take in Woody Allen, who swings on the clarinet with the Eddy Davis New Orleans Jazz Band. The less fancy (though still pricey) **Bemelmans Bar,** with a mural by the author of the *Madeline* books, features a rotating cast of pianist-singers. ✉ *35 E. 76th St., between Madison and Park Aves., Upper East Side* ☎ *212/744–1600* 🌐 *www.thecarlyle.com* Ⓜ *6 to 77th St.*

Feinstein's at Loews Regency. That the world-touring Michael Feinstein performs a residency here only once a year (usually in winter) and still gets the venue named after him speaks volumes about the charismatic cabaret star. This tastefully appointed space in Loews Regency Hotel presents Broadway babe and *30 Rock* regular Jane Krakowski and other top names in the business—plus, when we're lucky, Tony Danza. ✉ *540 Park Ave., at E. 61st St., Upper East Side* ☎ *212/339–4095* 🌐 *feinsteinsattheregency.com* Ⓜ *N, Q, R to Lexington Ave./59th St.; 4, 5, 6, to 59th St.*

GAY NIGHTLIFE

Fodor's Choice ★ **Brandy's Piano Bar.** A singing waitstaff warms up the mixed crowd at this delightful and intimate Upper East Side lounge, getting everyone in the mood to belt out their favorite tunes. In fact, the Brandy's scene is so cheerful that some patrons have used this as a musical Prozac, keeping depression at bay. ✉ *235 E. 84th St., between 2nd and 3rd Aves., Upper East Side* ☎ *212/744–4949* 🌐 *www.brandyspianobar.com* Ⓜ *4, 5, 6 to 86th St.*

UPPER WEST SIDE

BARS

Ding Dong Lounge. "Gabba gabba hey," kids—the CBGB's punk ethos is most alive and well not downtown but way up near Columbia University, at this out-and-out rock-and-roll bar. All manner of music posters (along with punk chanteuse Patti Smith's actual birth certificate) adorn the walls; the bathrooms are wallpapered entirely with do-it-yourself concert fliers. An exuberant young student crowd swills the many beers on tap, and candles at every table do little to dispel the near-total darkness. Just wear night-vision goggles—and maybe a crash helmet, given how often the DJs really shake up the joint. ✉ *929 Columbus Ave., between 105th and 106th Sts., Upper West Side* ☎ *212/663–2600* 🌐 *www.dingdonglounge.com* Ⓜ *B, C to 103rd St.*

The Empire Hotel Rooftop Bar. The only thing better than hanging out in Lincoln Center on a lovely night is hanging out a dozen stories above Lincoln Center on a lovely night. Thanks to the radically refurbished Empire Hotel's sprawling new rooftop bar, you can enjoy that pleasure even on nights that are less than lovely. We're talking thousands of square feet here, most of it outdoors, and heated in winter. ✉ *44 W. 63rd St., between Broadway and Columbus Ave., Upper West Side* ☎ *212/265–7400* 🌐 *www.empirehotelnyc.com* Ⓜ *1 to 66th St.–Lincoln Center.*

JAZZ VENUES

Smoke. If you can't wait until sunset to get your riffs on, head uptown to this lounge near Columbia University, where the music starts as early as 6 pm. Performers include some of the top names in the business, including turban-wearing organist Dr. Lonnie Smith and the drummer Jimmy Cobb (who laid down the beat on Miles Davis's seminal album *Kind of Blue*). ✉ *2751 Broadway, between 105th and 106th Sts., Upper West Side* ☎ *212/864–6662* 🌐 *www.smokejazz.com* Ⓜ *1 to 103rd St.*

HARLEM

BARS

Corner Social. With nearly 20 beers on tap, sports on big screens, and bar food that's anything but boring, it's no surprise that this neighborhood favorite is packed on weekends. In warm weather an outdoor patio gives a front-row seat to the scene on Lenox Avenue. ✉ *321 Lenox Ave., at 126th St.* ☎ *212/510–8552* 🌐 *www.cornersocialnyc.com* Ⓜ *2, 3 to 125th St.*

Ginny's Supperclub. Head downstairs from Marcus Samuelsson's renowned Red Rooster restaurant and you'll find yourself in what amounts to a glamorous lounge that seems right out of the 1920s. The cocktails are classic with a modern flair and there is live music and/or DJs most Saturday evenings and some weeknights, as well as a gospel brunch. ✉ *310 Lenox Ave., at 125th St.* ☎ *212/421–3821* 🌐 *www.ginnyssupperclub.com* Ⓜ *2, 3 to 125th St.*

BROOKLYN

DUMBO

BARS

reBar. Occupying several rooms inside a former factory, this cavernous industrial space does multiple duty as bar, lounge, indie movie theater, gastropub, and supper club. Sample one of the many beers and enjoy the dungeony vibe under terra-cotta ceilings and antique chandeliers. ✉ *147 Front St., DUMBO* ☎ *718/766–9110* 🌐 *www.rebarnyc.com* Ⓜ *F to York St.; A, C to High St.*

Superfine. The huge orange pool table is a focal point (it's free) at the front of this sprawling restaurant and bar at the base of the Manhattan

Bridge. Rotating artwork, exposed-brick walls lined with tall windows, sunken secondhand chairs, and mellow music (including a bluegrass brunch on Sunday) make this a fun, neighborhoody place to hang out. ✉ *126 Front St., between Jay and Pearl Sts., DUMBO* ☎ *718/243–9005* ⊙ *Closed Mon.* Ⓜ *F to York St.*

PERFORMANCE SPACE

Galapagos Art Space. Performances here almost take a back seat to the unique decor of red banquettes floating above a huge lagoon of water (hold on to your purse!). Thankfully, the theater, music, and performance art is dynamic enough to keep your attention. ✉ *16 Main St., DUMBO* ☎ *718/222–8500* ⊕ *www.galapagosartspace.com* 🎫 *Ticket prices vary* ⊙ *Opening times vary* Ⓜ *F to York St.; A, C to High St.*

WILLIAMSBURG

BARS

Barcade. Like Chuck E. Cheese for grown-up hipsters, Barcade invites you to stop reminiscing about your arcade-loving youth and start playing the more than 30 vintage arcade games. You'll find everything from familiar favorites like Ms. Pacman to rarities like Rampage. And it's not just about the games; there's also a full menu of small-label beers to choose from. ✉ *388 Union Ave., near Ainslie St., Williamsburg* ☎ *718/302–6464* ⊕ *www.barcadebrooklyn.com* Ⓜ *L to Lorimer St.*

Bembe. This steamy bilevel lounge is Williamsburg's answer to Miami clubbing, except it's constructed of found items from all over New York, including the old redwood front door from a winery. The crowd is as eclectic as the DJ-spun beats, from reggae to Brazilian, often accompanied by live drumming. The tropical bar menu gives it proper Latin cred. ✉ *81 South 6th St., at Berry St., Williamsburg* ☎ *718/387–5389* ⊕ *www.bembe.us* ⊙ *Mon.–Thurs. 7:30 pm–4 am, Fri.–Sun. 7 pm–4 am.* Ⓜ *J, M to Marcy Ave.*

Brooklyn Bowl. This former ironworks foundry packs in 16 bowling lanes, a cocktail bar, a music stage, and a restaurant—the food is conjured up by the team behind Blue Ribbon and includes Louisiana-style southern specialties like po' boy sandwiches, Cajun catfish, and excellent signature fried chicken. Hipster crowds congregate over local brews on tap. Weekends means crowds so it can take a while to get a bowling lane but you'll have a blast while you wait. ✉ *61 Wythe Ave., at N. 11th St., Williamsburg* ☎ *718/963–3369* ⊕ *www.brooklynbowl.com* 🎫 *$20 per lane for 30 min* ⊙ *Weekdays 6 pm–2 am; weekends noon–2 am* Ⓜ *L to Bedford Ave.*

Brooklyn Brewery. Brooklyn was once America's brewing capital: at the turn of the 20th century Williamsburg alone was home to nearly 60 breweries. The originals are mostly gone, but this relative newcomer has been bringing hops back to the 'hood since 1996. Friday-evening happy hour means $4 beers—the Brooklyn Lager is popular, as is the Belgian-inspired Local 1, and there are usually seasonal brews, too. Beer buffs can join a free tour on Saturday or Sunday afternoon; other tours are by reservation only. ✉ *79 N. 11th St., between Berry St. and Wythe Ave., Williamsburg* ☎ *718/486–7422* ⊕ *www.brooklynbrewery.com* ⊙ *Fri. 6–11, Sat. and Sun. noon–6* Ⓜ *L to Bedford Ave.*

Pete's Candy Store. A retro feel, friendly crowd, and cheerful bartenders make this a perennial favorite, slightly off the Willamsburg beaten path. The back room, smaller than a subway car, hosts music performances nightly. Hipsters come out for spelling bees, bingo, and the infamous quiz-off contest every Wednesday night. There's a short menu of sandwiches and cocktails but no actual candy. Pete's is also home to one of Brooklyn's preeminent reading series, held on alternate Thursday evenings. ✉ *709 Lorimer St., between Frost and Richardson Sts., Williamsburg* ☎ *718/302–3770* 🌐 *www.petescandystore.com* Ⓜ *L to Lorimer St.*

Radegast Hall & Biergarten. The perfect alternative if you don't want to trek out to Queens for al fresco Slavic beers, Radegast Hall & Biergarten serves Central European suds and hearty eats under a retractable roof. Schnitzel, goulash, and pretzels are authentic complements to the beer, along with live music on some nights. ✉ *113 N. 3rd St., Williamsburg* ☎ *718/963–3973* 🌐 *www.radegasthall.com* Ⓜ *L to Bedford Ave.*

Spuyten Duyvil. Only the geekiest of beer geeks will recognize the obscure names of the more than 100 imported microbrews available here. Fortunately for the rest of us, the friendly connoisseurs behind the bar are more than happy to offer detailed descriptions and make recommendations. ✉ *359 Metropolitan Ave., near Havermeyer St., Williamsburg* ☎ *718/963–4140* 🌐 *www.spuytenduyvilnyc.com* Ⓜ *L to Lorimer St.*

Union Pool. This former pool-supply store is a funky warehouse-like venue complete with a corrugated-tin-backed bar, a photo booth, a small stage for live music, and cheap PBR. The back patio has a taco truck and a fire pit, all part of the hipster-paradise package. ✉ *484 Union Ave., near Meeker Ave., Williamsburg* ☎ *718/609–0484* 🌐 *www.union-pool.com* ⏲ *Weekdays 5 pm–4 am; weekends 1 pm–4 am* Ⓜ *L to Lorimer St.*

LIVE MUSIC VENUES

Knitting Factory. This concert venue for rock, indie, and underground hip hop does double duty as a neighborhood watering hole, with a dimly lit bar up front and a small stage behind a glass wall. There's a happy hour daily (5–7 pm) and 10 beers on tap, including Brooklyn Brewery's Pennant Ale. ✉ *361 Metropolitan Ave., at Havemeyer St., Williamsburg* ☎ *347/529–6696* 🌐 *bk.knittingfactory.com* 🎟 *Admission $8–$35* ⏲ *Bar daily 5 pm–4 am* Ⓜ *L to Lorimer St.*

Music Hall of Williamsburg. This former mayonnaise factory is Brooklyn's answer to the Bowery Ballroom and, indeed, it's run by the bookers for Bowery Presents. The three-level venue with balcony seating has rounded ceilings and walls, which makes for excellent acoustics; no surprise that it draws die-hard live-music hawks. ✉ *66 N. 6th St., near Wythe Ave., Williamsburg* ☎ *718/486–5400* 🌐 *www.musichallofwilliamsburg.com* 🎟 *$10–$20* Ⓜ *L to Bedford Ave.*

PARK SLOPE

BARS

Barbès. It's not *quite* like stepping into the funky Parisian neighborhood of the same name, but this cozy bar does have French-accented bartenders, pressed-tin ceilings, and a red-tinted back room. Diverse events range from the energetic Slavic Soul Party performance on Tuesday to classical music concerts. ✉ *376 9th St., at 6th Ave., Park Slope* ☎ *347/422–0248* 🌐 *www.barbesbrooklyn.com* Ⓜ *F, G to 7th Ave.*

The Bell House. A 1920's Brooklyn warehouse has found new life as The Bell House, a live music venue and events space with vintage details, a dozen beers on draft, and a reasonable $10 cocktail list. Expect everything from live bands or DJs to comedy acts to take the stage on any given night; check the online events calendar for details on upcoming shows. ✉ *149 7th St., Park Slope* ☎ *718/643–6510* 🌐 *www.thebellhouseny.com* Ⓜ *F to 4th Ave.; R to 9th St.*

Union Hall. Comfortably hip is the name of the game at this Brooklyn hangout. Grab a beer in the "library" area up front, cozy up around the fireplace in winter, or if you're up for a little sport, join the friendly locals in a game of bocce. In the basement, check out some rising indie rock stars on stage. ✉ *702 Union St., at 5th Ave., Park Slope* ☎ *718/638–4400* 🌐 *www.unionhallny.com* Ⓜ *R to Union St.*

QUEENS

ASTORIA

Bohemian Hall & Beer Garden. Warm summer nights and cold beers have been savored by locals for over 100 years at the Bohemian Hall & Beer Garden. With pitchers of beer, picnic tables, live music, and Czech dishes from the kitchen, this sunny garden is an ideal spot for getting together with old friends—or making new ones over big mugs of Staropramen and Pilsner Urquell. ✉ *29-19 24th Ave., Astoria* ☎ *718/274–4925* 🌐 *www.bohemianhall.com* Ⓜ *N, Q to Astoria Blvd.*

LONG ISLAND CITY

Dutch Kills. The dark bar and cozy wooden booths at Dutch Kills—a cocktail den with a nod to the neighborhood's historic roots—serves up finely crafted drinks at a few dollars cheaper than similar Manhattan watering holes. Expect precisely chiseled chunks of ice and skilled bartenders that, with a few queries into your preferences and curiosities, can create a concoction just to your taste. ✉ *27-24 Jackson Ave., Long Island City* ☎ *718/383–2724* 🌐 *www.dutchkillsbar.com* Ⓜ *E, M, R to Queens Plaza.*

THE PERFORMING ARTS

20

Updated by Jess Moss

"Where do you wait tables?" is the not-so-ironic question New York performers get when they say they're in the arts. But even more telling is that most of these toughened artists won't miss a beat when they respond with the restaurant's name. Fact is, if you're an aspiring performer here, you'd better be tough and competitive. There is a constant influx of artists from around the globe, and all these actors, singers, dancers, and musicians striving for their big break infuse the city with a crackling creative energy.

Just as tough are the audiences—many out-of-towners, many discerning local patrons—who help drive the arts scene as they thrive on keeping up with the latest: flocking to a concert hall to hear a world-class soprano deliver a flawless performance, then crowding into a cramped café to support young writers floundering through their own prose.

New York has somewhere between 200 and 250 legitimate theaters (meaning those with theatrical performances, not movies or strip shows), and many more ad hoc venues—parks, churches, lofts, galleries, rooftops, even parking lots. The city is also a revolving door of special events: summer jazz, one-act-play marathons, film festivals, and music and dance celebrations from the classical to the avant-garde, to name just a few. It's this unrivaled wealth of culture and art that many New Yorkers cite as the reason they're here, and the reason why many millions more say they're visiting here.

PLANNING

DANCE, OPERA, THEATER . . .

In addition to theater, New York is one of the premier cities in the world for seeing dance, opera, and classical music. In addition to our performing arts venue listings, take into consideration that there several New York–based companies that are in residence at various times of the year. These include the American Ballet Theater (🌐 *www.abt.com*), the New York City Ballet (🌐 *www.nycballet.com*), the Metropolitan Opera (🌐 *www.metoperafamily.org*), and the New York City Opera (🌐 *www.nycopera.com*). There are also visiting arts companies from around the world. For more about these companies, see the Lincoln Center listing.

WHAT'S ON?

To find the most up-to-date information about what's going on when you're in town, New York is rich with easily accessible and comprehensive listings resources in both print and online formats. The *New York Times* (🌐 *www.nytimes.com*) listings are concentrated in its Thursday, Friday, and Sunday papers, as well as online. The *New Yorker* (🌐 *www.newyorker.com*) is highly selective, but calls attention to performances with its succinct reviews. It hits the stands on Monday. In *New York* magazine (🌐 *www.nymag.com*), also on newsstands on Monday, see The Week section for hot-ticket events. The free tabloid *Village Voice* (🌐 *www.villagevoice.com*) comes out on Wednesday; it has extensive listings—especially for theater, music, and dance—as well.

Online-only venues 🌐 *www.nytheatre.com* (especially for Broadway) and 🌐 *indietheater.org*, and 🌐 *offoffonline.com* (for Off- and Off-Off-Broadway) provide synopses, schedules when theaters are dark, accessibility info, run times, seating charts, and links to ticket purchases. The best general source online for dance and smaller opera and classical music companies is 🌐 *www.smarttix.com*.

BUYING TICKETS AT FULL PRICE

What do tickets sell for, anyway? Not counting the limited "premium seat" category (or discount deals), the top ticket price for Broadway musicals is now hovering at $136; the low end for musicals is in the $50–$75 range. Nonmusical comedies and dramas start at about $70 and top out at about $120. Off-Broadway show tickets average $50–$90, and Off-Off-Broadway shows can run as low as $15–$25. Tickets to an opera start at about $25 for nosebleed seats and can soar over $400 for prime locations. Classical music concerts go for $25 to $100 or more, depending on the venue. Dance performances are usually in the $15 to $60 range, but expect seats for the ballet in choice spots to cost more.

Scoring tickets is fairly easy, especially if you have some flexibility. But if timing or cost is critical, the only way to ensure you'll get the seats you want is to make your purchase in advance—and that might be months ahead for a hit show. In general, tickets for Saturday evening and for weekend matinees are the toughest to secure, and the priciest.

For smaller performing-arts companies, and especially for Off-Broadway shows, try **Ticket Central**, which is right in the center of Theatre Row; service charges are nominal here. **SmartTix** is a reliable resource for (usually) smaller performing-arts companies, including dance and music; their service charges are nominal as well.

Sure bets for Broadway (and some other big-hall events) are the box office or either **Telecharge** or **Ticketmaster**. Virtually all larger shows are listed with one service or the other, but never both; specifying "premium" will help you get elusive—and expensive (sometimes topping

$500)—seats. A broker or your hotel concierge should be able to procure last-minute tickets, but prices may even exceed "premium" rates. Be prepared to pay steep add-on fees (per ticket *and* per order) for all ticketing services.

TIP→ Although most online ticket services provide seating maps to help you choose, the advantage of going to the box office is twofold: there are no add-on service fees, and a ticket seller can personally advise you about sight lines—and knee room—for the seat location you are considering. Broadway box offices do not usually have direct phone lines; their walk-in hours are generally 10 am until curtain.

BUYING DISCOUNT TICKETS

The cheapest—though chanciest—ticket opportunities are found at participating theater box offices on the day of the performance. These rush tickets, usually about $25–$40, may be distributed by lottery and are usually for front-row (possibly neck-craning) seats, though it can vary by theater. Check the comprehensive planner on *www.nytix.com* or go to the box office of the show you are interested in to discover whether they have such an offer and how to pursue it. Obstructed-view seats or those in the very rear balcony are sometimes available for advance purchase; the price point on these is usually in the $35–$40 range.

But for advanced discount purchases, the best seating is likely available by using a discount code. Procure these codes, good for 20% to 50% off, online. (You will need to register on each website.) The excellent no-subscription-required *www.broadwaybox.com* is comprehensive and posts all discount codes currently available for Broadway shows. As with all discount codes offered through online subscriber services—**TheaterMania, Playbill,** and **Best of Off Broadway** among them—to avoid service charges, you must bring a printout of the offer to the box office, and make your purchase there.

For seats at 25% to 50% off the usual price, go to one of the **TKTS booths:** there's one in Times Square and one in Downtown Brooklyn. A third location at South Street Seaport was closed indefinitely at this writing; check online for updates. Although they do tack on a $4-per-ticket service charge, and not all shows are predictably available, the broad choices and ease of selection—and of course, the solid discount—make TKTS the go-to source for the flexible theatergoer. You can browse available shows for that day online, or check the electronic listings board near the ticket windows to mull over your options while you're in line. At the spiffed-up Times Square location (look for the red glass staircase), there is a separate *"Play Express"* window (for nonmusical events) to further simplify—and speed—things. Times Square hours are: Monday and Wednesday–Sunday 3–8, and Tuesday 2–8 for evening performances; for Wednesday and Saturday matinees 10–2; for Sunday matinees 11–3; and for Sunday evening shows, from 3 until a half hour before curtain. Brooklyn hours are Monday–Saturday 11–3 and 3:30–6. With the exception of matinee tickets at the Brooklyn location, which sells these for next-day performances only, all shows offered are for that same day. Credit cards, cash, or traveler's checks are accepted at all locations. **TIP→** Ticket-booth hours may vary over holiday periods.

CONTACTS

Best of Off Broadway *www.bestofoffbroadway.com.*

Playbill *www.playbill.com.*

SmartTix *212/868–4444 www.smarttix.com.*

Telecharge *212/239–6200, 800/432–7250 outside NYC wwww.telecharge.com.*

TheaterMania *www.theatermania.com.*

Ticket Central *416 W. 42nd St., between 9th and 10th Aves., Midtown West 212/279–4200 www.ticketcentral.com Daily noon–8 M A, C, E to 42nd St.–Port Authority.*

Ticketmaster *212/307–4100, 866/448–7849 automated service, 212/220–0500 premium tickets www.ticketmaster.com.*

TKTS *Duffy Sq., W. 47th St. and BroadwayMidtown West www.tdf.org M 1, 2, 3, 7, N, Q, R, S, to Times Sq.–42nd St.; N, Q, R, to 49th St.; 1 to 50th St. 1 Metrotech Center, between Myrtle St. Promenade and Jay St., Downtown Brooklyn M A, C, F to Jay St.–MetroTech; 2, 3, 4, 5, to Borough Hall; R to Court St.*

THE PERFORMING ARTS IN NEW YORK CITY

Listings are alphabetical by neighborhood.

LOWER MANHATTAN

FINANCIAL DISTRICT

MUSIC

WFC Winter Garden. Count on the WFC Winter Garden for an inspired array of musical events from gospel to site-specific sonic installations—and a little theater, dance, and film as well—all presented within its spectacular crystal-encased atrium or on its outdoor plaza. It's all free, and all befitting the incomparable setting overlooking the Hudson. *World Financial Center, West St. between Vesey and Liberty Sts., Financial District 212/945–0505 www.artsworldfinancialcenter.com M E to World Trade Center; 1 to Rector St.*

20

READINGS AND LECTURES

Poets House. Situated in a bright and airy building near the Hudson River, Poets House has a setting that rises to its theme: it is an open resource for all ages, one that offers a 50,000-volume library and readings and events that exalt the art of poetry. *10 River Terr., at Murray St., Battery Park City, Financial District 212/431–7920 www.poetshouse.org M E to World Trade Center; 1, 2, 3 to Chambers St.; A, C to Chambers St.*

TRIBECA

MUSIC

FAMILY **Tribeca Performing Arts Center.** This center celebrates theater (with a clever children's series) and dance, but more so, jazz in all its forms. Highlights in Jazz and Lost Jazz Shrines are two of its special series. *199 Chambers St., at Greenwich St., TriBeCa 212/220–1459 www.tribecapac.org M 1, 2, 3 to Chambers St.*

CLOSE UP

Best Tips for Broadway

Whether you're handing over hundreds of dollars for a top seat or shoestringing it in with a standing-room ticket, seeing one show or seven, you'll have better Broadway experiences to brag about if you take our advice.

Do your homework. Remember—your friend's "must-see" may not be yours. Subscribe to online services ahead of your trip; you'll get access to show synopses, special ticket offers, and more. If it's a classic play, like Shakespeare, you might enjoy it more if you read it before you go.

Reserve ahead. The TKTS booth is great if you're up for what the fates make available, but for must-sees, book early. While you're at it, ask whether the regular cast is expected. (An in-person stop at the box office is the most reliable way to score this information, but don't hold them to it unless it's the day of performance. If there is a change then—and the replacement cast is not acceptable to you—you may get a refund.) For musicals, live music will always add a special zing; confirm when ticketing to avoid surprises on the rare occasion when recorded music is used.

Check theater seating charts. Front mezzanine is a great option; with seats that overhang the stage, they can be better (though not always less expensive) than many orchestra locations. Book with a seating chart at hand (available online and at the box office); it can be worth splurging for the best sight lines. Check accessibility, especially at older theaters with multiple flights of stairs and scarce elevators.

Know when to go. Surprisingly, Friday evening is a good option; Saturday night and weekday matinees are the most difficult. Or do as the locals do and go on weeknights. Tuesday is especially promising, and typically an earlier curtain—7 or 7:30 instead of the usual 8 pm—helps ensure that you'll get a good night's sleep for your next day of touring.

Dress right. You can easily throw on jeans to go to the theater these days, but personally we feel shorts and sneakers have no place on Broadway. Bring binoculars if your seats are up high, leave behind the heavy coat (coat checks are *not* the norm), and drop bags and packages off at your hotel room in advance.

Travel smart. Trying to get to the show on time? Unless you don't mind watching the meter run up while you're stuck in traffic, avoid cabs into or out of Times Square. Walk, especially if you're within 10 blocks of the theater. Otherwise, take the subway.

Dine off Broadway. Dining well on a budget and doing Broadway right are not mutually exclusive notions. The key is avoiding the temptation to eat in Times Square proper—even the national chains are overpriced. Consider instead supping in whatever neighborhood you're touring that day. Or, if you're already in midtown, head west of the district to 9th Avenue. That's where many actors and other theater folk actually live, and you never know who you'll see on the street or at the next table. Prix-fixe deals and ethnic eateries are plentiful.

The Tribeca Film Festival brings celebrities out to the red carpet, but plenty of "regular" people get tickets too.

PERFORMANCE CENTER

92YTribeca. Programs at 92YTribeca include films, talks, and a variety of music; many are intended to appeal to a twenty- to thirty-ish set, but visitors of all ages will find something to their liking in the extensive daytime and evening lineups. Film series emphasize participation, with directors often on hand for post-film Q&A, and strive for fresh concepts, with the likes of Closely Watched Films (classics revisited) and a late-night sing-along series. Readings and talks can be equally eclectic, ranging from history and politics to chefs and restaurateurs or technology. ✉ *200 Hudson St., at Canal St., TriBeCa* ☎ *212/601–1000* 🌐 *www.92y.org/92yTribeca* Ⓜ *1, A, C, E to Canal St.*

SOHO

READINGS AND LECTURES

Housing Works Bookstore Cafe. Amid its collection of 20,000 titles for sale, Housing Works hosts a wide range of literary and cultural events, from quirky readings and Tumblr parties to book launches and storytelling or music nights. This cozy nonprofit is staffed largely by volunteers, and all profits go toward fighting homelessness and HIV/AIDS. ✉ *126 Crosby St., between E. Houston and Prince Sts., SoHo* ☎ *212/334–3324* 🌐 *www.housingworksbookstore.com* Ⓜ *N, R to Prince St.; B, D, F, M to Broadway–Lafayette St.; 6 to Bleecker St.*

The Jerome L. Greene Performance Space (The Greene Space). Local favorite WNYC Radio invites the public into its intimate (125 seats), technologically forward-thinking digs where live shows—music, audio theater, interviews—match its renowned, and equally forward-thinking, on-air programming. ✉ *44 Charlton St., at Varick St., SoHo* ☎ *646/829–4000* 🌐 *www.thegreenespace.org* Ⓜ *C, E to Spring St.; 1 to Houston St. or Canal St.*

THEATER

HERE. Celebrating all manner of contemporary, genre-bending productions, the original home of Eve Ensler's 1997 Obie winner *The Vagina Monologues* also has art exhibitions and a café. ✉ *145 6th Ave., between Spring and Broome Sts., SoHo* ☎ *212/352–3101 for tickets* 🌐 *www.here.org* Ⓜ *C, E to Spring St.*

EAST VILLAGE AND LOWER EAST SIDE

EAST VILLAGE

FILM

Anthology Film Archives. Dedicated to preserving and exhibiting independent and avant-garde film, Anthology Film Archives comprises a film repository and two gemlike screening rooms in a renovated redbrick courthouse. Committed cinephiles make their way here for hard-to-find films and videos. The Essential Cinema series delves into the works of filmmakers from Stan Brakhage and Maya Deren to Robert Bresson and Jean Cocteau. **TIP→** This is an experience for film lovers, not casual moviegoers—screening rooms can be very hot or cold depending on the outside temperature, and there are no standard movie theater amenities. ✉ *32 2nd Ave., at 2nd St., East Village* ☎ *212/505–5181* 🌐 *www.anthologyfilmarchives.org* Ⓜ *F to 2nd Ave.*

Village East Cinema. With programming more on the indie side than that of its SoHo sister the Angelika, this cinema is housed in a former Yiddish theater that was restored and converted to a six-screen multiplex. Most screening rooms are small and unimpressive, but the Grand Theater is a real treat, with its Moorish Revival–style decor, domed ceiling, and grand chandelier. Call ahead to find out what's playing on this screen. ✉ *181–189 2nd Ave., at 12th St., East Village* ☎ *212/529–6799* 🌐 *www.villageeastcinema.com* Ⓜ *6 to Astor Pl.; L to 1st Ave.*

READINGS AND LECTURES

Nuyorican Poets Cafe. The reigning arbiter of poetry slams, the Nuyorican Poets Cafe schedules open-mic events and hosts the influential granddaddy (b. 1989) of the current spoken-word scene, the Friday Night Poetry Slam. Other performances, from hip hop open mic nights to jazz acts, round out the weekly schedule. **TIP→** Line up early for the Friday Night Poetry Slam; the small venue gets packed quickly. ✉ *236 E. 3rd St., between Aves. B and C, East Village* ☎ *212/780–9386* 🌐 *www.nuyorican.org* Ⓜ *F to 2nd Ave.*

The Poetry Project. Launched in 1966, the Poetry Project has been a source of sustenance for poets (and their audiences) ever since. This is where Allen Ginsberg, Amiri Baraka, and Sam Shepard first found their voices, and where you're likely to find folks of the same caliber today. Prime times: Monday, Wednesday, and Friday. ✉ *St. Mark's Church in-the-Bowery, 131 E. 10th St., at 2nd Ave., East Village* ☎ *212/674–0910* 🌐 *www.poetryproject.org* Ⓜ *6 to Astor Pl.*

THEATER

Classic Stage Company. At the cozy 178-seat theater belonging to the Classic Stage Company you can see excellent literary revivals—such as Chekhov's *Three Sisters* or Shakespeare's *The Tempest*—perhaps with a modern spin, and often with reigning theatrical stars. ✉ *136 E. 13th St., between 3rd and 4th Aves., East Village* ☎ *212/677–4210, 212/352–3101, 866/811–4111 for tickets* 🌐 *www.classicstage.org* Ⓜ *4, 5, 6, L, N, Q, R to 14th St.–Union Sq.*

La MaMa E.T.C. Ellen Stewart, also known as La Mama, founded La MaMa E.T.C. in a small basement space in 1961. It's grown now, and her influential Experimental Theater Club continues to support new works that cross cultures and performance disciplines. ✉ *74A E. 4th St., between Bowery and 2nd Ave., East Village* ☎ *212/475–7710 tickets* 🌐 *lamama.org* Ⓜ *F to 2nd Ave.; B, D, F, M to Broadway–Lafayette St.; 6 to Bleecker St.*

New York Theatre Workshop (NYTW). Works by new and established playwrights anchor this theater's repertoire. Jonathan Larson's *Rent* got its pre-Broadway start here, and current works by Tony Kushner (*Homebody/Kabul)*, Caryl Churchill, Amy Herzog, and Paul Rudnick are staged. Hit the box office for Sunday night CheapTix; those seats are $20—in cash—as available (advance purchase is recommended). ✉ *79 E. 4th St., between Bowery and 2nd Ave., East Village* ☎ *212/460–5475, 212/279–4200 for tickets* 🌐 *www.nytw.org* Ⓜ *F to 2nd Ave.; B, D, F, M to Broadway–Lafayette St.; 6 to Astor Place.*

Performance Space 122 (PS122). While the East Village venue that typically hosts PS122's productions remains closed for renovations, you can still catch the contemporary performances and artists they produce at various locations around the city. Performance Space 122 became a launching pad for now well-recognized talent like the Blue Man Group, John Leguizamo, and Eric Bogosian, and it continues to offer an impressive selection of acts from the fringe. ✉ *150 1st Ave., at 9th St., East Village* ☎ *212/477–5829 for tickets* 🌐 *www.ps122.org* Ⓜ *6 to Astor Pl.*

The Public Theater. Fresh theater, such as the musical production of *Giant,* has a refreshed home at the Public Theater, which unveiled new renovations to its historic building in late 2012. Many noted productions that began here (*Hair, A Chorus Line)* went on to Broadway. Some shows offer limited-availability $20 rush standby tickets at the box office one hour before curtain (two tickets max; cash only). Check online for available performances.

In summer you won't want to miss their incomparable—and free—**Shakespeare in the Park** performances, which are held at the Delacorte Theatre in Central Park. Although you can stand in line for hours—and still not get a ticket voucher—the easiest way to score these scarce tickets is to register online with their "virtual line" after midnight on the night before the performance you would like to attend; an e-mail response confirms (or denies) success. ✉ *425 Lafayette St., south of Astor Pl., East Village* ☎ *212/539–8500, 212/967–7555 for tickets* 🌐 *www.publictheater.org* Ⓜ *6 to Astor Pl.; N, R to 8th St.–NYU.*

Theater for the New City. This four-theater cultural complex stages short runs of shows by new and emerging American playwrights. Favorite longtime troupers and presenters of seriously giant puppets (upward of 12 feet is typical), the 1960s NYC-rooted, and still seriously political, Bread & Puppet Theater puts in an annual appearance as well. ✉ *155 1st Ave., between 9th and 10th Sts., East Village* ☎ *212/254–1109* 🌐 *www.theaterforthenewcity.net* Ⓜ *6 to Astor Pl.; L to 1st Ave.*

LOWER EAST SIDE

FILM

Sunshine Cinema. With vestiges of its life as a vaudeville theater all but gone, the Sunshine Cinema, with its five decent-size screens, is the neighborhood go-to for a mix of art-house and smaller-release mainstream independent films. ✉ *143 E. Houston St., between 1st and 2nd Aves., Lower East Side* ☎ *212/260–7289* 🌐 *www.landmarktheatres.com* Ⓜ *F to 2nd Ave.*

GREENWICH VILLAGE AND WEST VILLAGE

GREENWICH VILLAGE

FILM

Angelika Film Center. Foreign, independent, and, some mainstream films are screened at the Angelika Film Center. Despite its (six) tunnel-like theaters, small screens, and the occasionally audible subway rumble below, it's usually packed; get a snack at the café while you wait for your movie to be called. ✉ *18 W. Houston St., at Mercer St., Greenwich Village* ☎ *212/995–2570* 🌐 *www.angelikafilmcenter.com* Ⓜ *B, D, F, M to Broadway–Lafayette St.; 6 to Bleecker St.*

Cinema Village. The three tiny screening rooms at this theater have surprisingly good sight lines and show a smart selection of hard-to-find (some might say obscure) first-run domestic and foreign films. ✉ *22 E. 12th St., between University Pl. and 5th Ave., Greenwich Village* ☎ *212/924–3363* 🌐 *www.cinemavillage.com* Ⓜ *4, 5, 6, L, N, Q, R to 14th St.–Union Sq.*

Quad Cinema. Movie lovers are quite attached to the Quad Cinema despite the patina of its early 1970s vintage—probably because the four teacup-size theaters feel so much like their own private screening rooms. A finely balanced selection of first-run art documentaries and foreign films is the fare here. ✉ *34 W. 13th St., between 5th and 6th Aves., Greenwich Village* ☎ *212/255–2243* 🌐 *www.quadcinema.com* Ⓜ *1, 2, 3 to 14th St.; F, M to 14th St.; L to 6th Ave.*

READINGS AND LECTURES

Center for Architecture. This contemporary glass-faced gallery hosts lively discussions (which may be accompanied by films or other visuals) on topics like radical architecture in Mexico City or what to expect when you renovate an apartment. ✉ *536 LaGuardia Pl., between 3rd and Bleecker Sts., Greenwich Village* ☎ *212/683–0023* 🌐 *www.aiany.org* Ⓜ *A, B, C, D, E, F, M to W. 4th St.–Washington Sq.*

The New School. At The New School topical panels (typically free–$5) predominate ("Women Writers of the Diaspora"), but are complemented with poetry ("An Evening with John Ashbery") and film; expect incisive and thought-provoking results, whether the subject is philosophy, economics, or design. Jazz and chamber music performances are also part of New School's low-priced lineup (free–$20). ✉ *66 W. 12th St., between 5th and 6th Aves., Greenwich Village* ☎ *212/229–5600* 🌐 *www.newschool.edu/events* Ⓜ *1, 2, 3 to 14th St.; F, M to 14th St.; L to 6th Ave.*

New York Studio School. The venerable New York Studio School hosts two—always free, almost always on Tuesday and Wednesday—evening lecture series on contemporary issues in art. Hear from both emerging and established artists, and from some of the biggest names in art history and criticism. ✉ *8 W. 8th St., between 5th and 6th Aves., Greenwich Village* ☎ *212/673–6466* 🌐 *www.nyss.org* Ⓜ *A, B, C, D, E, F, M to W. 4th St.–Washington Sq.*

THEATER

Skirball Center for the Performing Arts. A pristine wood-lined theater, the 866-seat Skirball supports emerging artists, with a growing repertoire of interesting dance, music, and theater events, often in collaboration with other esteemed companies—including its Village neighbor, the Public. This contemporary Kevin Roche–designed venue on the New York University campus provides a rare larger-scale anchor for the arts in this part of town. ✉ *566 LaGuardia Pl., at Washington Sq. S, Greenwich Village* ☎ *212/998–4941, 212/352–3101 for tickets* 🌐 *www.nyuskirball.org* Ⓜ *A, B, C, D, E, F, M to W. 4th St.–Washington Sq.*

WEST VILLAGE

FILM

Fodor's Choice ★ **Film Forum.** In addition to premiering new releases, this very special nonprofit theater with three small screening rooms, hosts movies by directors from Hitchcock to Bertolucci, genre series with themes from pre-Code to Fritz Lang's Hollywood, and newly restored prints of classic works. The café in their sleek little Euro-style lobby serves tasty cakes and fresh-popped popcorn. **TIP→** This is not your state-of-the-art megaplex; be prepared for small seats and a cash-only box office (though credit cards can be used to purchase tickets online in advance). ✉ *209 W. Houston St., between 6th Ave. and Varick St., West Village* ☎ *212/727–8110* 🌐 *www.filmforum.org* Ⓜ *1 to Houston St.*

20

READINGS AND LECTURES

Cornelia Street Café. Founded by three artists in 1977, the Cornelia Street Café is a good bet for original poetry, fiction and nonfiction readings, live jazz, and the superb monthly Entertaining Science evenings hosted by the Nobel laureate chemist Roald Hoffmann. Upstairs, you can tuck into a good meal of steak frites or black sesame–crusted salmon, or simply share a bottle of merlot at a street-side table on this quiet West Village lane. ✉ *29 Cornelia St., between 4th and Bleecker Sts., West Village* ☎ *212/989–9319* 🌐 *www.corneliastreetcafe.com* Ⓜ *A, B, C, D, E, F, M to W. 4th St.–Washington Sq.*

Lesbian, Gay, Bisexual & Transgender Community Center. Come here for engaging and topical talks (and occasional films, dance, or theatrical events), with themes ranging from out lawyers to Elaine Stritch. Popular events include the long-running Second Tuesdays lecture series and Center Voices, which emphasizes artistic expression and innovation from community members. ✉ *208 W. 13th St., between 7th and 8th Aves., West Village* ☎ *212/620–7310* 🌐 *www.gaycenter.org* Ⓜ *1, 2, 3 to 14th St.; A, C, E to 14th St.; F, M to 14th St.; L to 8th Ave.*

THEATER

Lucille Lortel Theatre. A venerable neighborhood survivor, the Lucille Lortel Theatre has its roots in the 1950s Brechtian traditions championed by its namesake owner of the time—it first became known for its influential interpretations of works by Brecht and Dos Passos. Previously known as the Theatre De Lys, this 299-seater has forged on to become the home to 21st-century productions of the MCC Theater company (known for Neil LaBute's challenging plays in the century's first decade) and free summer shows that appeal to both children and adults by Theatreworks/USA. ✉ *121 Christopher St., between Hudson and Bleecker Sts., West Village* ☎ *212/924–2817 for tickets* 🌐 *www.lortel.org* Ⓜ *1 to Christopher St.–Sheridan Sq.*

CHELSEA

DANCE

New York Live Arts. Formerly the Dance Theater Workshop, this Chelsea space teamed up with the Bill T. Jones/Arnie Zane Dance Company in 2011 and now serves as the home stage for the innovative dance troupe. New York Live Arts also continues to act as a laboratory for new choreographers and artists in residence, and hosts non-choreographed events such as panel discussions. ✉ *219 W. 19th St., between 7th and 8th Aves., Chelsea* ☎ *212/691–6500* 🌐 *www.newyorklivearts.org* Ⓜ *1 to 18th St.; A, C, E to 14th St.; L to 8th Ave.*

Fodor's Choice ★ **Joyce Theater.** In a former art-deco movie house in Chelsea, the 472-seat Joyce Theater has superb sight lines and presents a full spectrum of contemporary dance. **Garth Fagan Dance** (🌐 *garthfagandance.org*), **Ballet Hispanico** (🌐 *www.ballethispanico.org*), and taut and athletic **Parsons Dance** (🌐 *www.parsonsdance.org*) are regulars on the Joyce's always rewarding lineup. ✉ *175 8th Ave., at W. 19th St., Chelsea* ☎ *212/691–9740, 212/242–0800 for tickets* 🌐 *www.joyce.org* Ⓜ *A, C, E to 14th St.; L to 8th Ave.*

THEATER

The Kitchen. This is *the* place for interdisciplinary performance art, and has been a crucible for artists on the experimental edge—think Charles Atlas, Kiki Smith, Philip Glass, Elizabeth Streb—since 1971. Music, visual arts, and dance are represented as well as theater. Literary events are often free; most others can be seen for as little as $10–$15. ✉ *512 W. 19th St., between 10th and 11th Aves., Chelsea* ☎ *212/255–5793* 🌐 *www.thekitchen.org* Ⓜ *A, C, E to 14th St.; L to 8th Ave.*

MIDTOWN WEST

DANCE

Baryshnikov Arts Center (BAC). Famed dancer, actor, and choreographer Mikhail Baryshnikov's longtime vision has come to fruition in this modern venue for contemporary performance. Works here are dedicated to movement, which can be as much about theater as it is about dance. The center hosts a range of resident artists, from dancers to musical groups, as well as productions by of a roster of boundary-breaking international choreographers (George Stamos, Donna Uchizono, and Emmanuèle Phuon). The vibrant—and very well-priced—programming is presented in the center's 238-seat Jerome Robbins Theater and the 136-seat Howard Gilman Performance Space. ✉ *450 W. 37 St., between 9th and 10th Aves., Midtown* ☎ *646/731–3200* 🌐 *www.bacnyc.org* Ⓜ *A, C, E, to 34th St.–Penn Station.*

FILM

Museum of Modern Art (MoMA). You'll find some of the most engaging international film repertory around at MoMA's state-of-the-art Roy and Niuta Titus Theaters 1 and 2. Movie tickets are available at the museum for same-day screenings (a limited number are released up to one week in advance for an extra fee); they're free if you have purchased museum admission ($25), otherwise cost $12 for the film entry alone. ✉ *11 W. 53rd St., between 5th and 6th Aves., Midtown West* ☎ *212/708–9400* 🌐 *www.moma.org* Ⓜ *E, M to 5th Ave./53rd St.; B, D, F, M to 47th–50th Sts./Rockefeller Center.*

The Paris. Across from the Plaza Hotel sits the The Paris—a rare stately remnant of the single-screen era. Opened in 1948, it retains its wide screen (and its balcony) and is a fine showcase for new movies, often foreign and with a limited release. ✉ *4 W. 58th St., between 5th and 6th Aves., Midtown West* ☎ *212/688–3800* 🌐 *www.theparistheatre.com* Ⓜ *N, Q, R to 5th Ave./59th St.; F to 57th St.*

Ziegfeld Theatre. Its vintage is late 1960s, but the Ziegfeld Theatre is as close as you'll come to a movie-palace experience in New York today. Its chandeliers and crimson decor, raised balcony, wide screen, some 1,100 seats, good sight lines, and solid sound system make the Ziegfeld a special place to view anything it serves up. Grand-opening red-carpet galas often take place here as well. ✉ *141 W. 54th St., between 6th and 7th Aves., Midtown West* ☎ *212/307–1862* 🌐 *www.clearviewcinemas.com* Ⓜ *F to 57th St.; N, Q, R to 57th St.–7th Ave.; B, D, E to 7th Ave.*

MUSIC

The Town Hall. Garrison Keillor's *A Prairie Home Companion* radio show sometimes broadcasts from this historic venue, which was built more than 90 years ago as a meeting spot for suffragists. The Town Hall grew as a center for discourse and the arts, and now hosts programs of jazz, cabaret, and rock; the Peoples Symphony Concert series; and a variety of international music, theater, and dance events. ✉ *123 W. 43rd St., between 6th and 7th Aves., Midtown West* ☎ *212/840–2824* 🌐 *www.the-townhall-nyc.org* Ⓜ *1, 2, 3, 7, N, Q, R, S to Times Sq.–42nd St.*

DID YOU KNOW?

The term Great White Way refers to Broadway along the Theater District. Stories vary, but some attribute this nickname to the showy display of lamps that lighted the theater marquees there in the early days of incandescent lighting.

FAMILY Fodor's Choice ★ **Carnegie Hall.** Carnegie Hall is, of course, one of the world's most famous concert halls. Its incomparable acoustics make it one of the best venues—anywhere—to hear classical music, but its presentations of jazz, pop, cabaret, and folk music are superlative as well. Since Tchaikovsky conducted the opening-night concert on May 5, 1891, virtually every important musician the world has known has performed in this Italian Renaissance–style building, often at the peak of his or her creative powers. Leonard Bernstein had his debut here; Vladimir Horowitz made his historic return to the concert stage here. The world's top orchestras perform in the grand and fabulously steep 2,804-seat **Isaac Stern Auditorium,** the 268-seat **Weill Recital Hall** often features young talents making their New York debuts, and the subterranean 599-seat **Judy and Arthur Zankel Hall** attracts big-name artists such as the Kronos Quartet and Milton Nascimento to its modern and stylish space. A noted roster of family concerts is also part of Carnegie's programming. **TIP→** The Carnegie box office offers $10 rush tickets for some shows on the day of performance, or you may buy partial-view seating in advance at 50% off the full ticket price. ✉ *881 7th Ave., at W. 57th St., Midtown West* ☎ *212/247–7800* 🌐 *www.carnegiehall.org* Ⓜ *N, Q, R to 57th St.–7th Ave.; B, D, E to 7th Ave.*

OPERA

Gotham Chamber Opera. This opera company presents less-known chamber works from the baroque era to the present in inspired productions. Catching a broader audience's attention, shows include Moisés Kaufman's acclaimed rendition of the 1947 *El Gato Con Botas* by Xavier Montsalvatge (staged at the New Victory Theater); Handel's *Arianna in Creta*; a collaboration with choreographer Karole Armitage, *Ariadne Unhinged*; and Mozart's *Il sogno di Scipione* (1772), a revival of the opera's first production. ✉ *410 W. 42nd St., between 9th and 10th Aves., Midtown West* ☎ *212/868–4460* 🌐 *www.gothamchamberopera.org* Ⓜ *A, C, E to 42nd St.–Port Authority.*

PERFORMANCE CENTERS

New York City Center. Pause as you enter this neo-Moorish building, built in 1923 for the Ancient and Accepted Order of the Mystic Shrine, and admire the beautifully ornate tile work that plasters the lobby. City Center's 2,200-seat main stage is perfectly suited for its role as a showplace for dance and special theatrical events.

Many distinguished companies are based here, including City Center's Principal Dance Company, Alvin Ailey American Dance Theater, as well as New York City Opera and Manhattan Theatre Club. The calendar is rounded out by a roster of productions by the center itself and by renowned visiting artists, including the popular Encores! musicals-in-concert series. Tickets for City Center's annual Fall for Dance festival cost $15 and sell out quickly. ✉ *131 W. 55th St., between 6th and 7th Aves., Midtown West* ☎ *212/581–1212 CityTix* 🌐 *www.nycitycenter.org* Ⓜ *N, Q, R to 57th St.–7th Ave.; F to 57th St.*

Radio City Music Hall. This icon of New York City was built to enchant everyone who stepped inside its doors. Shortly after the stock market crash of 1929, John D. Rockefeller wanted to create a symbol of hope in what was a sad, broke city. Targeting a piece of real estate in an area of Manhattan then known as "the speakeasy belt," he partnered with the Radio Corporation of America to build a grand theater, a place where everyday people could see the finest entertainment at sensible prices.

Every inch of the interior was designed to be extraordinary. When it opened, some said Radio City Music Hall was so grand that there was no need for performances, because people would get more than their money's worth simply by sitting there and enjoying the space. Despite being the largest indoor theater in the world with its city-block-long marquee, it feels warm and intimate. One-hour "Stage Door" walking tours run year-round, but avoid taking the tour during show times, as access is limited. Day-of tour tickets are sold at the Radio City Avenue Store on a first-come, first-served basis; advanced tickets are available by phone or through the website (*$19.95* *Tours daily 11–3*).

Although there are performances and media events here year-round, more than a million visitors every year come to see the *Radio City Christmas Spectacular,* starring the iconic Rockettes. Make reservations as early as possible. The shows tend to sell out, but you can usually find tickets until mid-October. Happily there are no bad seats at Radio City Music Hall, so if you are booking late, grab what you can get. Tickets—$35–$299 per person for the 90-minute show—can be purchased at the Radio City Music Hall box office; on the Web (*www.radiocitychristmas.com*); by phone on the Christmas Spectacular hot line (*866/858–0007*); or through Ticketmaster. *1260 6th Ave., between 50th and 51st Sts., Midtown West* *212/247–4777* *www.radiocity.com* M *B, D, F to 47th–50th/Rockefeller Center; N, Q, R to 49th St.*

READINGS AND LECTURES

New York Public Library. LIVE from the NYPL features a rich program of lectures and reading events from the biggest names in books. Programs are held at the famous main library and its branches elsewhere in the city. *Stephen A. Schwarzman Building, W. 42nd St. at 5th Ave., Midtown West* *212/930–0855* *www.nypl.org* M *B, D, F, M to 42nd St.–Bryant Park.*

THEATER

American Airlines Theatre. The onetime Selwyn—the venerable home to the works of Coward, Kaufman, and Porter in their heyday—is now known as the American Airlines Theatre. After rumored incarnations as a burlesque hall and pornographic movie house, this splendidly restored 1918 Venetian-style playhouse is now home to the not-for-profit **Roundabout Theatre Company**, which is acclaimed for its revivals of classic musicals and plays, such as a production of Oscar Wilde's *The Importance of Being Earnest* with Brian Bedford. *227 W. 42nd St., between 7th and 8th Aves., Midtown West* *212/719–1300 for tickets* *www.roundabouttheatre.org* M *1, 2, 3, 7, N, Q, R, S to Times Sq.–42nd St.; A, C, E to 42nd St.–Port Authority.*

New Amsterdam Theater. In 1997 Disney refurbished the elaborate 1903 Art Nouveau New Amsterdam Theater, where Bob Hope, Jack Benny, Fred Astaire, and the Ziegfeld Follies once drew crowds. *The Lion King* ruled here for the first nine years of its run; followed by *Mary Poppins*. Call ahead for current productions. ✉ *214 W. 42nd St., between 7th and 8th Aves., Midtown West* ☎ *212/282–2907* Ⓜ *1, 2, 3, 7, N, Q, R, S to Times Sq.–42nd St.; A, C, E to 42nd St.–Port Authority.*

FAMILY Fodor's Choice ★ **The New Victory Theater.** In a magnificently restored century-old performance space, The New Victory Theater presents an international roster of supremely kid-pleasing plays, music, and dance performances. The little ones and their parents can also learn more about the theater process, from set design to Shakespeare, through the organization's workshops and exhibits. Count on reasonable ticket prices ($14 and up), high-energy and high-class productions, and the opportunity for kids to chat with the artists after many performances. ✉ *209 W. 42nd St., between 7th and 8th Aves., Midtown West* ☎ *646/223–3010* 🌐 *www.newvictory.org* Ⓜ *1, 2, 3, 7, N, Q, R, S to Times Sq.–42nd St.; A, C, E to 42nd St.–Port Authority.*

Playwrights Horizons. Known for its support of new work by American playwrights, Playwrights Horizons was the first home for eventual Broadway hits such as *Grey Gardens* and Wendy Wasserstein's *Heidi Chronicles*. This is where you will find the latest work from Annie Baker, Amy Herzog, and Edward Albee. ✉ *416 W. 42nd St., between 9th and 10th Aves., Midtown West* ☎ *212/564–1235, 212/279–4200 for tickets* 🌐 *www.phnyc.org* Ⓜ *A, C, E to 42nd St.–Port Authority.*

Signature Theatre Company. The new Frank Gehry–designed Pershing Square Signature Center houses three theater spaces—all the better to present their roster of past and present playwrights-in-residence (Amy Baker, Edward Albee, Horton Foote, Sam Shepard, and Tony Kushner among them). The new space makes it possible to explore the work of several playwrights at once, and all tickets are $25 for a show's initially announced run. A central space with a café and bookstore connects the theaters, so come early, or stay late for a bite to eat; the café is open until midnight Tuesday through Sunday. ✉ *Pershing Square Signature Center, 480 W. 42nd St., between 9th and 10th Aves., Midtown West* ☎ *212/244–7529* 🌐 *www.signaturetheatre.org* Ⓜ *A, C, E to 42nd St.–Port Authority.*

St. James. Home of Mel Brooks's juggernaut *The Producers* in its heyday, and where a Tony-laden revival of *Gypsy* held sway late in the first decade of the 21st century, the St. James is where Lauren Bacall was an usherette in the '40s, and where a little show called *Oklahoma!* premiered, with a rousing score and choreography to match, and changed the musical forever. Today the stage is operated by Jujamcyn Theaters, which has produced a long list of Broadway hits. ✉ *246 W. 44th St., between Broadway and 8th Ave., Midtown West* ☎ *212/239–6200 for tickets* 🌐 *www.jujamcyn.com* Ⓜ *1, 2, 3, 7, N, Q, R, S to Times Sq.–42nd St.; A, C, E to 42nd St.–Port Authority.*

UPPER EAST SIDE

PERFORMANCE CENTER

FAMILY **92nd Street Y.** Well-known soloists, jazz musicians, show-tune stylists, and chamber music groups perform in the 92Y's 905-seat **Kaufmann Concert Hall.** But the programming is hardly limited to music—purchase tickets early for their popular lectures-and-readings series featuring big-name authors, poets, playwrights, political pundits, and media bigwigs. Also worth the Upper East Side trek here are the Harkness Dance Festival, film programs, and all manner of family-friendly events. ✉ *1395 Lexington Ave., at 92nd St., Upper East Side* ☎ *212/415–5500 for tickets* ⊕ *www.92y.org* Ⓜ *6 to 96th St.*

READINGS AND LECTURES

Works & Process. Insight into the creative process is what the superb Works & Process program is all about. Often drawing on dance and theater works-in-progress, live performances are complemented with illuminating discussions with their (always top-notch) choreographers, playwrights, and directors. ✉ *Guggenheim Museum, 1071 5th Ave., at 89th St., Upper East Side* ☎ *212/423–3587* ⊕ *www.worksandprocess.org* Ⓜ *4, 5, 6 to 86th St.*

UPPER WEST SIDE

MUSIC

The Cathedral Church of St. John the Divine. Great Music in a Great Space, the church's organ and choral program, is aptly named given the great choir where performances are held. Any music you come to hear at St. John the Divine will likely be an unforgettable experience, but the seasonal programming of the **Early Music New York** (☎ *212/749–6600, 212/280–0330 for tickets* ⊕ *www.earlymusicny.org*) ensemble is essential. ✉ *1047 Amsterdam Ave., at 112th St., Upper West Side* ☎ *212/316–7490* ⊕ *www.stjohndivine.org* Ⓜ *1 to Cathedral Pkwy.–110th St.; B, C to Cathedral Pkwy.–110th St.*

Jazz at Lincoln Center. This Columbus Circle jazz mecca a few blocks south of Lincoln Center's main campus is dedicated entirely to the musical genre. Stages in Rafael Viñoly's crisply modern **Frederick P. Rose Hall** feature the 1,200-seat **Rose Theater** (where a worthy Jazz for Young People series joins the buoyant adult programming a few times each year). Also here is the **Allen Room,** an elegant and intimate 310–460-seater, and the even-more-intimate 140-seat **Dizzy's Club Coca-Cola,** known for its late-night After Hours concerts. ✉ *Time Warner Center, Broadway at 60th St., 5th fl., Upper West Side* ☎ *212/258–9800* ⊕ *www.jalc.org* Ⓜ *1, A, B, C, D to 59th St.–Columbus Circle.*

Miller Theatre. Adventurous programming of jazz, classical, early and modern music, and dance continues at the Miller Theatre. A well-designed 688-seater, this is a hall that rewards serious listeners. ✉ *Columbia University, 2960 Broadway, at 116th St., Morningside Heights* ☎ *212/854–1633, 212/854–7799 box office* ⊕ *www.millertheatre.com* Ⓜ *1 to 116th St.–Columbia University.*

The fountain in front of Lincoln Center is particularly lovely in the evening.

PERFORMANCE CENTERS

Fodor's Choice ★ **Lincoln Center for the Performing Arts.** This massive white travertine-clad complex contains 23 theaters, as well as the Juilliard School, the New York City Ballet, and the Film Center of Lincoln Center, making it one of the most concentrated places for the performing arts in the nation. Its 16-acre campus was built over the course of several years from 1962 to 1969, on the once gritty urban ground that set the scene for the muscial *West Side Story*. In August, Lincoln Center's longest-running classical series, the Mostly Mozart Festival (🌐 *mostlymozart.org*), captures the crowds. You can purchase tickets to performances online, by phone, or at the various box offices.

TIP→ Discounted day-of-show tickets for many Lincoln Center venues may be purchased in person at the David Rubenstein Atrium on Broadway between West 62nd and West 63rd streets; there is a limit of four tickets per customer, and the amount of discount depends on the performance. The box office is closed Monday, but available tickets for Monday performances are sold on Sunday. Box office hours: Tues.–Sat. noon–7:45, Sun. noon–5:45.

Alice Tully Hall (✉ *1941 Broadway, at 65th St.* ☎ *212/671–4050*) is considered to be as acoustically perfect as a concert hall can get; the hall's primary resident is the Chamber Music Society of Lincoln Center (☎ *212/875–5788* 🌐 *www.chambermusicsociety.org*). **Avery Fisher Hall** (✉ *10 Lincoln Center Plaza, at 64th St.* ☎ *212/875–5030*) is home to the New York Philharmonic (☎ *212/875–5656* 🌐 *nyphil.org*); the season is late September to late June. Orchestra rehearsals at 10 am are open to the public on selected weekday mornings (usually Wednesday or Thursday). A popular Young People's Concerts series is offered on Saturday afternoon, four times throughout the season.

The largest hall, the **Metropolitan Opera House** (✉ *30 Lincoln Center Plaza, Columbus Ave. between 62nd and 65th Sts.* ☎ *212/362–6000*), is notable for its dramatic arched entrance as well as its lobby's immense Swarovski crystal chandeliers and Marc Chagall paintings, both of which can be seen from outside later in the day. The titan of American opera companies and an institution since its founding in 1883, the **Metropolitan Opera** (☎ *212/362–6000* 🌐 *www.metfamilyopera.org*) brings the world's leading singers to the vast stage here from September to May. An extra perk is that all performances, including those sung in English, are unobtrusively subtitled on small screens on the back of the seat in front of you. Also resident at the Met is the **American Ballet Theatre** (ABT) (☎ *212/477–3030* 🌐 *www.abt.org*), renowned for its gorgeous full-program renditions of the 19th-century classics (*Swan Lake, Giselle, The Sleeping Beauty*) with choreography reenvisioned by 20th-century masters. ABT has two New York seasons: eight weeks of performances begin in May here at the Met, and during the holiday season their *Nutcracker* is staged at the Brooklyn Academy of Music (BAM) *(⇨ see full listing)*.

The **David H. Koch Theater** (✉ *20 Lincoln Center Plaza, at 62nd St.* ☎ *212/870–5570*), may not be as famous as the Met next door, but the **New York City Opera** (🌐 *www.nycopera.com*) has its own vibrant personality. Founded in 1943, the company is known for its diverse repertory and its soft spot for American composers. City Opera performs October to November and March to April. Supertitles—the opera's libretto, line-by-line—are displayed above the stage. Sharing the Koch is the formidable **New York City Ballet** (NYCB) (🌐 *www.nycballet.com*), with its unmatched repertoire of 20th-century works, predominantly by George Balanchine, Jerome Robbins, and Peter Martins. The company particularly excels at short-form programs. Its fall season starts in September and early October, then returns in late November through December for their beloved annual production of Balanchine's *The Nutcracker*. Its winter repertory program runs in January and February, and a spring season runs from April into May.

The **Lincoln Center Theater** complex, home to a rich tradition of plays and musicals, houses the **Vivian Beaumont Theater,** the intimate **Mitzi E. Newhouse Theater**, and, as of 2012, the new rooftop **Claire Tow Theater**, which has 131 seats and a small outdoor terrace for attendees.

The auditorium of the **Walter Reade Theater** (✉ *165 W. 65th St., between Broadway and Amsterdam Ave.* ☎ *212/875–5600* 🌐 *www.filmlinc.com*) shows film series devoted to "the best in world cinema" that run the gamut from silents and documentaries to retrospectives and recent releases, often on the same theme or from the same country. There are also showings, on periodic Saturdays, of *The Met: Live in HD* screenings.

The **Elinor Bunin-Munroe Film Center** (✉ *W. 65th St., between Broadway and Amsterdam Ave.* 🌐 *www.filmlinc.com*) has two small screening rooms, a café, and an ampitheater that hosts lectures and panel discussions.

TIP→ The David Rubinstein Atrium, on Broadway between 62nd and 63rd streets, is open weekdays 8 am–10 pm and weekends 9 am–10 pm and has free Wi-Fi, tables and lounge nooks, a branch of Tom Colicchio's 'wichcraft café, and that rarest of NYC commodities, a public restroom. ✉ *62nd to 66th Sts. from Broadway/Columbus Ave. to Amsterdam Ave., Upper West Side* ☎ *212/875–5000, 212/721–6500 CenterCharge, 212/875–5456 for accessibility information* 🌐 *www.lincolncenter.org* Ⓜ *1 to 66th St.–Lincoln Center.*

FAMILY **Symphony Space.** Presenting an energetic roster of music (including the famed Wall to Wall day-long thematic programs), from world to classical, Symphony Space excels in non-musical productions as well. On the literary front, its two halls—the **Peter Jay Sharpe Theatre** and the **Leonard Nimoy Thalia** (formerly the Thalia, but renamed to honor Mr. Spock)—host a celebrated roster of literary events, including Bloomsday on Broadway and the famed Selected Shorts series of stories read by prominent actors and broadcast live on National Public Radio. Opera in Cinema and Thalia Docs on Sunday (usually a true-to-its-roots art-house screening) round out the adult programming. For the family, turn to their hugely popular **Just Kidding** lineup for a nonstop parade of zany plays, sing-alongs, midday Saturday (and sometimes Sunday) movies, and animations. ✉ *2537 Broadway, at 95th Street, Upper West Side* ☎ *212/864–5400* 🌐 *www.symphonyspace.org* Ⓜ *1, 2, 3 to 96th St.*

THEATER

Shakespeare in the Park at the Delacorte Theater. Some of the best things in New York are, indeed, free—including summer Shakespeare in the Park performances at this open-air stage. Casts are often studded with Hollywood stars. Meryl Streep, Michelle Pfeiffer, Christopher Walken, Helen Hunt, Morgan Freeman, and Kevin Kline are just a few of the big names that have performed here. Tickets are free and are given out starting at 1 pm on the day of each show—and always sell out. Lines are *long*, and what you save in money, you make up for in time and tedium. Plan to line up by midmorning or earlier if there have been good reviews. It's not unheard of for theatergoers to show up at 7 am with a breakfast picnic to weather the wait. Each person in line is allowed two tickets for that evening's performance. Tickets are also available online; making a donation to the Public is one way to avoid the lines and be sure you get a ticket. ✉ *Central Park, midpark near 81st St., Upper West Side* ☎ *212/539–8500* 🌐 *www.publictheater.org* Ⓜ *6 to 77th St.; B, C to 81st St.–Museum of Natural History.*

HARLEM

MUSIC

Apollo Theater. If the Apollo's famed Amateur Night doesn't get you off the couch, consider its more intimate Apollo Music Cafe events on Friday and Saturday nights, featuring a variety of underground artists across a range of genres, from jazz to pop and rock. In May the Apollo teams up with Harlem Stage and JazzMobile to present the notable weeklong Harlem Jazz Shrines festival, with performances in venerable nearby venues Lenox Lounge, Minton's Playhouse, and Showman's

Cafe. ✉ *253 W. 125th St., at 8th Ave./Frederick Douglass Blvd., Harlem* ☎ *212/531–5300, 800/745–3000 tickets (Ticketmaster)* 🌐 *www.apollotheater.org* Ⓜ *A, B, C, D to 125th St.; 2, 3 to 125th St.; 4, 5, 6 to 125th St.*

BROOKLYN

BROOKLYN HEIGHTS

MUSIC

Bargemusic. In Brooklyn, Bargemusic keeps chamber music groups busy year-round on a re-outfitted harbor barge with a fabulous view of the Manhattan skyline. Some concertgoers report feeling seasick on the floating performance space. ✉ *Fulton Ferry Landing, Old Fulton and Furman Sts., Brooklyn Heights* ☎ *718/624–2083* 🌐 *www.bargemusic.org* Ⓜ *A, C to High St.; 2, 3 to Clark St.*

DOWNTOWN BROOKLYN

PERFORMANCE CENTERS

Fodor's Choice ★ **Brooklyn Academy of Music (BAM).** America's oldest performing arts center, BAM presented its first show in 1861. Today it has a much-deserved reputation for the unusual and the unexpected, presented in grand-scale stagings. Contemporary dance, music, opera, and cross-media productions mingle here with an array of classics. BAM has three primary performance spaces: the 2,090-seat **Howard Gilman Opera House,** a restored Renaissance Revival palace built in 1908; the 865-seat **Harvey Theater,** an updated 1904 theater a block away at 651 Fulton Street; and the newest addition, the BAM Fisher at 321 Ashland Place, which includes the 250-seat-maximum Fishman Space and the Hillman Studio. Every fall the Next Wave Festival fills the house with crackling energy and events that highlight a global mix of remarkable artists. The holidays bring a run of American Ballet Theatre's *Nutcracker,* and with springtime comes a top-notch roster of international theater companies (such as England's renowned Royal Shakespeare Company) in repertory. Year-round you can catch a movie at the four-screen **BAM Rose Cinemas,** which offers BAMcinématek, an eclectic repertory series (A Pryor Engagement to Rendez-Vous with French Cinema), as well as first-run indies, documentaries, and foreign-language films. Or, hit the industrial-glam **BAMcafé** (☎ *718/623–7811 reservations*) for the Eat, Drink & Be Literary series on select Wednesday nights, and free music on Friday and Saturday nights. **TIP→ BAM gets kudos for its down-to-earth range of ticket prices; $20 to $60 is typical.** ✉ *Peter Jay Sharp Bldg., 30 Lafayette Ave., between Ashland Pl. and St. Felix St., Fort Greene* ☎ *718/636–4100* 🌐 *www.bam.org* Ⓜ *2, 3, 4, 5, B, D, N, Q, R to Atlantic Ave.–Barclays Ctr.; G to Fulton St.; C to Lafayette Ave. (2, 3, 4, 5 to Nevins St. for Harvey Theater).*

THEATER

FAMILY **Puppetworks.** Finely detailed wooden marionettes and hand puppets are on the bill at Puppetworks. Kid-friendly performances like *The Prince and the Magic Flute* come to life on weekends in this 75-seat neighborhood theater. Reservations are required; credit cards are not

CLOSE UP

New York's Film Festivals

New York's extreme diversity is what makes it a cinephile's heaven: you'll find dozens of festivals for niche interests and for those just wanting to be at the front end of what's out there. New releases and premieres dominate the festival scene, but the city has its share of retrospective events, especially in summer.

The city's preeminent film event is the annual **New York Film Festival** (🌐 *www.filmlinc.com*), sponsored by the **Film Society of Lincoln Center**, from late September into October. Screenings are announced more than a month in advance and often sell out quickly. Film venues are usually Lincoln Center's Alice Tully Hall and Walter Reade Theater. In January, the Film Society joins forces with the Jewish Museum to produce the **New York Jewish Film Festival**; in March it joins with MoMA to present **New Directors/New Films**, and June brings its collaboration with the **Human Rights Watch Film Festival**.

The **Tribeca Film Festival** (🌐 *www.tribecafilm.com/festival*) takes place in mostly downtown venues for about two weeks starting in mid-April, and features mainstream premieres along with indie treasures, as well as a **Family Festival**, which attracts big crowds for its street fair and movies for all ages.

Fans also flock to other noteworthy annuals like the **New York Korean Film Festival** (🌐 *koreanfilmfestival.org*) in February at BAM; the **Asian American International Film Festival** (🌐 *www.asiancinevision.org*) from late July to early August (usually at the Clearview Chelsea Cinemas); the **New York International Latino Film Festival** (🌐 *www.nylatinofilm.com*) later in August and also screening at the Clearview Chelsea Cinemas; the Paley Center for Media's **DocFest** (🌐 *paleycenter.org*) in October; and in November at the American Museum of Natural History, the **Margaret Mead Film Festival** (🌐 *www.amnh.org/explore/margaret-mead-film-festival*), which presents a rich roster of international documentaries.

And for kids, the year-round programs of the **New York International Children's Film Festival (NYICFF)** (🌐 *www.gkids.com*) peak in March with an extravaganza of about 100 new films and videos for ages 3–18.

Summer in New York sees a bonanza of alfresco film; screenings are usually free (but arrive early to secure a space; screenings begin at dusk). The **HBO Bryant Park Summer Film Festival** (☎ *212/512–5700* 🌐 *www.bryantpark.org*) has classic films at sundown on Monday nights, June–August. The Hudson River Park (🌐 *www.hudsonriverpark.org*) **River-Flicks** series in July and August has movies for grown-ups on Wednesday evening on Pier 63; RiverFlicks for kids are at Pier 46 on Fridays. The Upper West Side has Summer on the Hudson (🌐 *www.nycgovparks.org*) with Wednesday night screenings on Pier 1. **Rooftop Films'** (🌐 *www.rooftopfilms.com*) Underground Movies Outdoors is NYC's most eclectic film series, with shows outdoors in summer on rooftops in all five boroughs. Check their schedule for off-season screenings as well. Summer Thursday nights, check out **Movies with a View** in Brooklyn Bridge Park (🌐 *www.brooklynbridgepark.org*).

FILM SERIES AND REVIVALS

Although many of the screens listed here also show first-run releases, old favorites and rarities are the heart of their programming. These gems—which include every film genre from noir to the most au courant experimental work—frequently screen at museums, cultural societies, and other public spaces, such as the **French Institute** (☎ *212/355–6100* 🌐 *www.fiaf.org*), **Scandinavia House** (☎ *212/879–9779* 🌐 *www.scandinaviahouse.org*), **Instituto Cervantes** (☎ *212/308–7720* 🌐 *www.cervantes.org*), and even branches of the **New York Public Library** (🌐 *www.nypl.org*). Harlem's **Maysles Cinema** (🌐 *www.mayslesinstitute.org*), under the aegis of legendary documentary filmmaker Albert Maysles, is, no surprise, the place for doc screenings, old and new. A reliably creative range of repertory screenings can always be found at **Anthology Film Archives** (☎ *212/505–5181* 🌐 *www.anthologyfilmarchives.org*), **Film Forum** (☎ *212/727–8110* 🌐 *www.filmforum.org*), the **Museum of Modern Art (MoMA)** (☎ *212/708–9400* 🌐 *www.moma.org*), the **Museum of the Moving Image** (☎ *718/784–0077* 🌐 *www.movingimage.us*), **BAM Rose Cinemas/BAMcinématek** (☎ *718/636–4100* 🌐 *www.bam.org*), and **Walter Reade Theater** (☎ *212/875–5600* 🌐 *www.filmlinc.com*).

accepted. ✉ *338 6th Ave., at 4th St., Park Slope* ☎ *718/965–3391* 🌐 *www.puppetworks.org* Ⓜ *F to 7th Ave.*

DUMBO

THEATER

Fodor's Choice ★ **St. Ann's Warehouse.** Set in a former warehouse, St. Ann's has hosted everything from the boundary-stretching *La Didone* opera to award-winning performances from the famous Edinburgh Fringe Festival. ✉ *29 Jay St., at Plymouth St., DUMBO* ☎ *718/254–8779* 🌐 *www.stannswarehouse.org* Ⓜ *A, C to High St.; F to York St.*

QUEENS

FILM

FAMILY **Museum of the Moving Image: film programs.** Special film programming complements the museum's radical face-lift and relaunch in 2011, featuring video art, digital screenings, live musical collaborations, and in-person appearances by moviemaker luminaries. You'll also find the sort of retrospectives and themed repertory the museum programmed previously, like an Alain Resnais series, Recovered Treasures (from world archives), or Avant-Garde Masters. Daily short films are screened in Tut's Fever Movie Palace, the fab Red Grooms and Lysiane Luong–designed installation that's a holdover from this 1920 Astoria Studio building's first incarnation as a museum in the late 1980s. Weekend Family Film matinees make this museum a great choice for kids. ✉ *36-01 35th Ave., at 37th St., Astoria* ☎ *718/777–6888* 🌐 *www.movingimage.us* Ⓜ *M, R to Steinway St.; N, Q to 36th Ave.*

TRAVEL SMART NEW YORK CITY

GETTING HERE AND AROUND

New York City packs a staggering range of sights and activities into the 322 square miles of its five boroughs. You'll probably want to focus most of your visit in Manhattan, but with more time, taking a trip to Brooklyn or one of the other "outer" boroughs (Queens, the Bronx, or Staten Island) is worthwhile.

If you're flying into one of the three major airports that service New York—John F. Kennedy (JFK), LaGuardia, or Newark, which is in New Jersey—pick your mode of transportation for getting to Manhattan before your plane lands. The route tourists typically take is to hire a car or wait in the taxi line, but those aren't necessarily the best choices, especially if arriving during rush hour. Public transportation is inexpensive and should be considered, especially if you are traveling light and without young children. Keep in mind that it's particularly expensive to take a cab from Newark, making the AirTrain or another form of public transportation a better deal.

Once you're in Manhattan, getting around can be a breeze when you get the hang of the subway system. When not in a rush, just walk—it's the best way to discover the true New York. Not quite sure where you are or how to get where you're headed? Ask a local. You may be surprised at how friendly the city's inhabitants are, debunking their reputation for rudeness. In the same getting-there-is-half-the-fun spirit, find water, land, and air journeys to see the city from a whole new perspective.

AIR TRAVEL

Generally, international flights go in and out of John F. Kennedy or Newark airport, while domestic flights go in and out of both of these, as well as LaGuardia Airport.

Airlines and Airports Airline and Airport Links.com (🌐 *www.airlineandairportlinks.com*) has links to many of the world's airlines and airports.

Airline Security Issues The Transportation Security Administration (🌐 *www.tsa.gov*) has answers for almost every question that might come up.

AIRPORTS

The major air gateways to New York City are LaGuardia Airport (LGA) and JFK International Airport (JFK) in the borough of Queens, and Newark Liberty International Airport (EWR) in New Jersey.

TIP→ Long layovers don't have to be only about sitting around or shopping. These days they can be about burning off vacation calories. Check out 🌐 www.airportgyms.com for lists of health clubs that are in or near many US and Canadian airports.

Airport Information JFK International Airport (*JFK*). ☎ *718/244–4444* 🌐 *www.jfkairport.com*. **LaGuardia Airport** (*LGA*). ☎ *718/533–3400* 🌐 *www.laguardiaairport.com*. **Newark Liberty International Airport** (*EWR*). ☎ *973/961–6000, 888/397–4636* 🌐 *www.newarkairport.com*.

TRANSFERS—CAR SERVICES

Car services can be a great convenience because the driver will often meet you in the baggage-claim area and help you with your luggage. The flat rates and tolls are often comparable to taxi fares, but some car services will charge for parking and waiting time at the airport. To eliminate these expenses, other car services require that you telephone their dispatcher when you land so they can send the next available car to pick you up. New York City Taxi and Limousine Commission rules require that all car services be licensed and pick up riders only by prior arrangement; if possible, call 24 hours in advance for reservations, or at least a half day before your flight's departure. Drivers of nonlicensed vehicles (gypsy cabs) often solicit fares outside the terminal in baggage-claim areas. Don't take them: you run the risk of an unsafe ride, and you'll definitely pay more than the going rate.

⇨ *For phone numbers, see Taxi Travel.*

TRANSFERS—TAXIS AND SHUTTLES

Outside the baggage-claim area at each of New York's major airports are taxi stands where a uniformed dispatcher helps passengers find taxis (⇨ *Taxi Travel*). Cabs are not permitted to pick up fares anywhere else in the arrivals area, so if you want a taxi, take your place in line. Shuttle services generally pick up passengers from a designated spot along the curb.

New York Airport Service runs buses from JFK and LaGuardia airports to Grand Central Terminal, the Port Authority Bus Terminal, and Penn Station. Fares cost between $12 and $15 one-way and $21 to $25 round-trip.

SuperShuttle vans travel between Manhattan and JFK, LaGuardia, and Newark. These blue vans will stop at offices, hotels, or residential addresses in most parts of Manhattan. There are courtesy phones at the airports. For travel to the airport, the company recommends that you make your request 24 hours in advance. Fares range from $15 to $23 per person. **TIP→ A shuttle is less expensive than a cab, but factor in extra time for the shuttle's other pick-ups/drop-offs along the way.**

Shuttle Service New York Airport Service ☎ *718/875–8200* 🌐 *www.nyairportservice.com.* **SuperShuttle** ☎ *800/258–3826* 🌐 *www.supershuttle.com.*

TRANSFERS FROM JFK INTERNATIONAL AIRPORT

Taxis charge a flat fee of $52 plus tolls (which may be as much as $6.50) to Manhattan only, and take 35–60 minutes. Prices are roughly $20–$55 for trips to most other locations in New York City. You should also tip the driver.

JFK's clean and fast AirTrain ($5) connects JFK Airport to the New York City Subway (A, E, J trains) and the Long Island Railroad (LIRR)—both of which will take you to Manhattan. The monorail system runs 24 hours. **TIP→ Not sure which train to take? Check Hopstop.com for the best route to your destination.** Subway travel between JFK and Manhattan takes less than an hour and costs $2.75 in subway fare plus $5 for the AirTrain. The LIRR travels between Penn Station and JFK in around 30 minutes, for a total cost of about $13. When traveling from Manhattan to the Howard Beach station, be sure to take the A train marked "Far Rockaway" or "Rockaway Park," not "Lefferts Boulevard."

JFK Transfer Information AirTrain JFK ☎ *718/244–4444* 🌐 *www.airtrainjfk.com.* **Long Island Railroad** ☎ *718/217–5477* 🌐 *www.mta.info/lirr.*

TRANSFERS FROM LAGUARDIA AIRPORT

Taxis cost $30–$50 plus tip and tolls (which may be as high as $6.50) to most destinations in New York City, and take at least 20–40 minutes.

For $2.25 (pay with a MetroCard or exact change only) you can ride the M60 public bus to 106th Street and Broadway on Manhattan's Upper West Side, with connections en route to the Q48 bus (which will take you to the Main Street subway station in Queens, where you can transfer to the 7 train) and several New York City Subway lines (N, Q, 2, 3, 4, 5, 6, A, B, C, D trains). Allow at least 90 minutes for the entire trip to Midtown.

TRANSFERS FROM NEWARK AIRPORT

Taxis to Manhattan cost $50–$70 plus tolls and tip and take 20–45 minutes. "Share and Save" group rates are available for up to four passengers between 8 am and midnight—make arrangements with the airport's taxi dispatcher. If you're heading to the airport from Manhattan, there's a $17.50 surcharge on top of the normal taxi rate.

AirTrain Newark, an elevated light rail system, can take you from the airline terminal to the Newark Liberty International

Airport Station. From here you can take New Jersey Transit (or, for a much higher price, Amtrak) trains heading to New York City's Penn Station. It's an efficient and low-cost way to get to New York City, particularly if you don't have many in your group and aren't carrying massive amounts of luggage. Total travel time to New York Penn Station in Manhattan via a New Jersey Transit train is approximately 30 minutes and costs $12.50. In contrast, a similar, slightly faster trip on an Amtrak train costs roughly $35. The AirTrain runs every 3 minutes from 5 am to midnight and every 15 minutes from midnight to 5 am. Note that New Jersey Transit trains first make a stop at the confusingly named Newark Penn Station before they reach New York City's Penn Station. If you're not sure when to get off the train, ask a conductor or a fellow passenger.

Coach USA with Olympia Trails buses leave for Grand Central Terminal and Penn Station in Manhattan about every 15 to 30 minutes until midnight. The trip takes roughly 45 minutes, and the fare is $16. Headed from the Port Authority or Grand Central Terminal to Newark, buses run every 20 to 30 minutes. The trip takes 55 to 65 minutes.

Newark Airport Information AirTrain Newark ☎ *888/397-4636* 🌐 *www.airtrainnewark.com.* **Coach USA** ☎ *877/863-9275* 🌐 *www.coachusa.com.* **PATH Trains** ☎ *800/234-7284* 🌐 *www.panynj.gov/path.*

TRANSFERS BETWEEN AIRPORTS

There are several transportation options for connecting to and from area airports, including shuttles, AirTrain and mass transportation, and car service or taxi. New York Airport Service runs buses between JFK and LaGuardia airports. AirTrain provides detailed, up-to-the-minute recorded information on how to reach your destination from any of New York's airports. Note that if you arrive after midnight at any airport, you may wait a long time for a taxi. Consider calling a car service, as there is no shuttle service at that time.

Contacts AirTrain ☎ *800/247-7433* 🌐 *www.panynj.gov/airtrain.*

BOAT TRAVEL

The Staten Island Ferry runs across New York Harbor between Whitehall Street next to Battery Park in Lower Manhattan and St. George terminal in Staten Island. The free 25-minute ride gives you a view of the Financial District skyscrapers, the Statue of Liberty, and Ellis Island.

New York Water Taxi, in addition to serving commuters, shuttles tourists to the city's many waterfront attractions between the West and East sides and Lower Manhattan (including the 9/11 Memorial), the South Street Seaport, and Brooklyn's waterfront parks.

The Hop-On/Hop-Off one-day pass ticket is $26; the Hop-On/Hop-Off +9/11 Memorial pass (which allows passengers to visit the 9/11 Memorial as part of their sightseeing package) is also $26.

Information New York Water Taxi (*NYWT*). ☎ *212/742-1969* 🌐 *www.nywatertaxi.com.* **Staten Island Ferry** 🌐 *www.siferry.com.*

BUS TRAVEL

Most city buses in Manhattan follow easy-to-understand routes along the island's street grid. Routes go up or down the north–south avenues, or east and west on the major two-way crosstown streets: 96th, 86th, 79th, 72nd, 66th, 57th, 42nd, 34th, 23rd, and 14th. Usually bus routes operate 24 hours, but service is infrequent late at night. Traffic jams can make rides maddeningly slow, especially along 5th Avenue in Midtown and the Upper East Side. Certain bus routes provide "limited-stop service" during weekday rush hours, which saves travel time by stopping only at major cross streets and transfer points. A sign posted at the front of the bus indicates that it has limited service; ask the driver whether the bus stops near where you want to go before boarding.

To find a bus stop, look for a light-blue sign (green for a limited bus) on a green pole; bus numbers and routes are listed, with the stop's name underneath.

Bus fare is the same as subway fare: $2.25. Pay fare when you board, with exact change in coins (no pennies, and no change is given) or with a MetroCard. MetroCards (⇨ *Public Transportation Travel*) allow you one free transfer between buses or from bus to subway; when using coins on the bus, you can ask the driver for a free transfer coupon, good for one change to an intersecting route. Legal transfer points are listed on the back of the slip. Transfers generally have time limits of two hours.

Since 2008, the city has introduced so-called Select Bus Service (SBS) on several routes, including along 1st and 2nd Avenues and 34th Street in Manhattan. The buses, which are distinguished from normal city buses by flashing blue lights on their front, make fewer stops. In addition, riders must pay for their rides before boarding with either a MetroCard or coins at a machine mounted on the street. The machine prints out a receipt. This receipt is the only proof that you have paid, so be sure to hold onto it for your entire SBS trip or risk a ticket for fare evasion.

Route maps and schedules are posted at many bus stops in Manhattan, at major stops throughout the other boroughs, and at 🌐 *MTA.info*. Each of the five boroughs of New York has a separate bus map; they're available from some station booths, but rarely on buses. The best places to obtain them are the MTA booth in the Times Square Information Center, the information kiosks in Grand Central Terminal and Penn Station, and the MTA's website.

Most buses that travel outside the city depart from the Port Authority Bus Terminal, on 8th Avenue between West 40th and 42nd streets. You must purchase your ticket at a ticket counter, not from the bus driver, so give yourself enough time to wait in a line. Several bus lines serving northern New Jersey and Rockland County, New York, make daily stops at the George Washington Bridge Bus Station from 5 am to 1 am. The station is connected to the 175th Street Station on the A line of the subway, which travels down the West Side of Manhattan.

A variety of discount bus services, including BoltBus and Vamoose Bus, offer direct routes from cities such as Philadelphia, Boston, and Washington, D.C., with the majority of destinations lying along the East Coast. These budget options, priced from about $20 one-way, depart from locations throughout the city.

Buses in New York **Metropolitan Transportation Authority (MTA) Travel Information Line** ☎ *511* 🌐 *www.mta.info.*

Buses to New York **Academy Bus Lines** ☎ *732/291–1300, 800/442–7272* 🌐 *www.academybus.com.* **Adirondack, Pine Hill & New York Trailways** ☎ *800/225–6815* 🌐 *www.trailways.com.* **BoltBus** ☎ *877/265–8287* 🌐 *www.boltbus.com.* **Coach** ☎ *800/631–8405* 🌐 *www.coachusa.com.* **Greyhound Lines Inc.** ☎ *800/231–2222* 🌐 *www.greyhound.com.* **New Jersey Transit** ✉ *New Jersey* ☎ *973/275–5555* 🌐 *www.njtransit.com.* **Vamoose Bus** ☎ *877/393–2828* 🌐 *www.vamoosebus.com.*

Bus Stations **George Washington Bridge Bus Station** ✉ *4211 Broadway, between 178th and 179th Sts., Washington Heights* ☎ *800/221–9903* 🌐 *www.panynj.gov.* **The Port Authority of New York and New Jersey** ✉ *625 8th Ave., at 42nd St., Midtown West* ☎ *212/564–8484* 🌐 *www.panynj.gov.*

CAR TRAVEL

If you plan to drive into Manhattan, try to avoid the morning and evening rush hours and lunch hour. The deterioration of the bridges to Manhattan, especially those spanning the East River, means that repairs will be ongoing for the next few years. Tune in to traffic reports on the radio (i.e., WCBS 880 or 1010 WINS on the AM radio dial) before you set off, and don't be surprised if a bridge is partially closed or entirely blocked with traffic.

Driving within Manhattan can be a nightmare of gridlocked streets, obnoxious drivers and bicyclists, and seemingly suicidal jaywalkers. Narrow and one-way streets are common, particularly downtown, and can make driving even more difficult. The most congested streets of the city lie between 14th and 59th streets and 3rd and 8th avenues.

GASOLINE

Gas stations are few and far between in Manhattan. If you can, fill up at stations outside the city, where prices are 10¢ to 50¢ cheaper per gallon. In Manhattan, you can refuel at stations along the West Side Highway and 11th Avenue south of West 57th Street and along East Houston Street. Some gas stations in New York require you to pump your own gas; others provide attendants.

PARKING

Free parking is difficult to find in Midtown, and on weekday evenings and weekends in other neighborhoods. If you find a spot on the street, check parking signs carefully, and scour the curb for a faded yellow line, the bane of every driver's existence. Violators may be towed away or ticketed literally within minutes. If you do drive, use your car sparingly in Manhattan. Instead, park it in a guarded parking garage for at least several hours; hourly rates (which can be as much as $23 for two hours) decrease somewhat if a car is left for a significant amount of time. **TIP→** Best Parking (*nyc.bestparking.com*) will help you find the cheapest parking-lot options for your visit; search by neighborhood, address, or attraction.

CAR RENTALS

When you reserve a car, ask about cancellation penalties, taxes, drop-off charges (if you're planning to pick up the car in one city and leave it in another), and surcharges (for being under or over a certain age, for additional drivers, or for driving across state or country borders or beyond a specific distance from your point of rental). All these things can add substantially to your costs. Request car seats and extras such as GPS when you book.

Rates are sometimes—but not always—better if you book in advance or reserve through a rental agency's website. There are other reasons to book ahead, though: for popular destinations, during busy times of the year, or to ensure that you get certain types of cars (vans, SUVs, exotic sports cars).

TIP→ Make sure that a confirmed reservation guarantees you a car. Agencies sometimes overbook, particularly for busy weekends and holiday periods.

Rates in New York City are around $50–$110 a day and $250–$425 a week for an economy car with air-conditioning, automatic transmission, and unlimited mileage. This includes the state tax on car rentals, which is 19.87%. Rental costs are lower just outside New York City, specifically in such places as Hoboken, New Jersey, and Yonkers, New York.

CAR-RENTAL INSURANCE

If you own a car and carry comprehensive car insurance for both collision and liability, your personal auto insurance will probably cover a rental, but read your policy's fine print to be sure. If you don't have auto insurance, then you should probably buy the collision- or loss-damage waiver (CDW or LDW) from the rental company. This eliminates your liability for damage to the car. Some credit cards offer CDW coverage, but it's usually supplemental to your own insurance and rarely covers SUVs, minivans, luxury models, and the like. If your coverage is secondary, you may still be liable for loss-of-use costs from the car-rental company (again, read the fine print). But no credit-card insurance is valid unless you use that card for *all* transactions, from reserving to paying the final bill.

■ TIP→ Diners Club offers primary CDW coverage on all rentals reserved and paid for with the card. This means that Diners Club's company—not your own car insurance—pays in case of an accident. It doesn't mean that your car-insurance company won't raise your rates once it discovers you had an accident.

You may also be offered supplemental liability coverage. The car-rental company is required to carry a minimal level of liability coverage insuring all renters, but it's rarely enough to cover claims in a really serious accident if you're at fault. Your own auto-insurance policy will protect you if you own a car; if you don't, you have to decide whether you are willing to take the risk.

US rental companies sell CDWs and LDWs for about $20 to $40 a day; supplemental liability is usually more than $10 a day. The car-rental company may offer you all sorts of other policies, but they're rarely worth the cost. Personal accident insurance, which is basic hospitalization coverage, is an especially egregious rip-off if you already have health insurance.

■ TIP→ You can decline the insurance from the rental company and purchase it through a third-party provider such as Travel Guard (*www.travelguard.com*)—$9 per day for $35,000 of coverage. That's sometimes just under half the price of the CDW offered by some car-rental companies.

PUBLIC TRANSPORTATION

When it comes to getting around New York, you have your pick of transportation in almost every neighborhood. The subway and bus networks are extensive, especially in Manhattan, although getting across town can take some extra maneuvering. If you're not pressed for time, take a public bus (⇨ *Bus Travel*); they generally are slower than subways, but you can also see the city as you travel. Yellow cabs (⇨ *Taxi Travel*) are abundant, except during the evening rush hour, when many drivers' shifts change. Like a taxi ride, the subway (⇨ *Subway Travel*) is a true New York City experience; it's also often the quickest way to get around. But New York (especially Manhattan) is really a walking town, and depending on the time of day, the weather, and your destination, hoofing it could be the easiest and most enjoyable option.

During weekday rush hours (from 7:30 am to 9:30 am and 5 pm to 7 pm) avoid the Midtown area if you can—subways and streets will be jammed, and travel time on buses and taxis can easily double.

Subway and bus fares are $2.50 for a single ride ticket, or $2.25 per ride if you buy a MetroCard for two or more rides or pay with coins on the bus. Reduced fares are available for senior citizens and people with disabilities during nonrush hours.

You pay for mass transit with a MetroCard, a plastic card with a magnetic strip. As you swipe the card through a subway turnstile or insert it in a bus's card reader, the cost of the fare is automatically deducted. With the MetroCard, you can transfer free from bus to subway, subway to bus, or bus to bus, within a two-hour period.

MetroCards are sold at all subway stations and at some stores—look for an "Authorized Sales Agent" sign. The MTA sells two kinds of MetroCards: unlimited-ride and pay-per-ride. Seven-day unlimited-ride MetroCards ($29) allow bus and subway travel for a week. If you will ride more than 13 times, this is the card to get.

Unlike unlimited-ride cards, pay-per-ride MetroCards can be shared between riders. (Unlimited-ride MetroCards can be used only once at the same station or bus route in an 18-minute period.)

You can buy or add money to an existing MetroCard at a MetroCard vending machine, available at most subway station entrances (usually near the station booth). The machines accept major credit cards and ATM or debit cards. Many also accept cash, but note that the maximum amount of change they will return is $6, which will be doled out in dollar coins.

Schedule and Route Information Metropolitan Transportation Authority (MTA) Travel Information Line ☎ *511* 🌐 *www.mta.info.*

SUBWAY TRAVEL

The subway system operates on more than 840 miles of track 24 hours a day and serves nearly all the places you're likely to visit. It's cheaper than a cab, and during the workweek it's often faster than either taxis or buses. The trains are well lighted and air-conditioned. Still, the New York subway is hardly problem-free. Many trains are crowded, the older ones are noisy, the air-conditioning can break, and platforms can be dingy and damp. Homeless people sometimes take refuge from the elements by riding the trains, and panhandlers head there for a captive audience. Although trains usually run frequently, especially during rush hours, you never know when some incident somewhere on the line may stall traffic. In addition, subway construction sometimes causes delays or limitation of service, especially on weekends.

Most subway entrances are at street corners and are marked by lampposts with an illuminated Metropolitan Transportation Authority (MTA) logo or globe-shape green or red lights—green means the station is open 24 hours and red means the station closes at night (though the colors don't always correspond to reality). Subway lines are designated by numbers and letters, such as the 3 line or the A line. Some lines run "express" and skip stops, and others are "local" and make all stops. Each station entrance has a sign indicating the lines that run through the station. Some entrances are also marked "uptown only" or "downtown only." Before entering subway stations, read the signs carefully. One of the most frequent mistakes visitors make is taking the train in the wrong direction. Maps of the full subway system are posted in every train car and usually on the subway platform (though these are sometimes out of date). You can usually pick up free maps at station booths.

For the most up-to-date information on subway lines, call the MTA's Travel Information Center or visit its website. The website Hopstop is a good source for figuring out the best line to take to reach your destination. Alternatively, ask a station agent.

You can transfer between subway lines an unlimited number of times at any of the numerous stations where lines intersect. If you use a MetroCard (⇨ *Public Transportation*) to pay your fare, you can also transfer to intersecting MTA bus routes for free. Such transfers generally have time limits of two hours.

Pay your subway fare at the turnstile, using a MetroCard bought from a vending machine.

Subway Information HopStop. A related app is available for iOS and Android phones. 🌐 *www.hopstop.com.* **Metropolitan Transportation Authority (MTA) Travel Information Line** ☎ *511* 🌐 *www.mta.info.*

TAXI TRAVEL

Yellow cabs are in abundance almost everywhere in Manhattan, cruising the streets looking for fares. They are usually easy to hail on the street or from a cabstand in front of major hotels, though finding one at rush hour or in the rain can take some time. Even if you're stuck in a downpour or at the airport, do not accept a ride from a gypsy cab. If a cab is not yellow and does not have a numbered aqua-color plastic medallion riveted to the hood, you could be putting yourself (or at least your wallet) in danger by getting into the car.

You can see whether a taxi is available by checking its rooftop light. If the center panel is lighted and the side panels are dark, the driver is ready to take passengers. Once the meter is engaged (and if it isn't, alert your driver; you'll seldom benefit from negotiating an off-the-record ride), the fare is $2.50 just for entering the vehicle and 50¢ for each unit thereafter. A unit is defined as either ⅕ mile when the cab's cruising at 6 mph or faster or as 60 seconds when the cab is either not moving or moving at less than 6 mph. New York State adds 50¢ to each cab ride. There's also a 50¢ night surcharge added between 8 pm and 6 am, and a much-maligned $1 weekday surcharge is tacked on between 4 pm and 8 pm.

One taxi can hold a maximum of four passengers (an additional passenger under the age of seven is allowed if the child sits on someone's lap). There is no charge for extra passengers. You must pay any bridge or tunnel tolls incurred during your trip (a driver will usually pay the toll himself to keep moving quickly, but that amount will be added to the fare when the ride is over). Taxi drivers expect a 15% to 20% tip.

To avoid unhappy taxi experiences, try to know where you want to go and how to get there before you hail a cab. **TIP→ Know the specific cross streets of your destination (for instance, "5th Avenue and 42nd Street") before you enter a cab; a quick call to your destination will give you cross-street information, as will a glance at a map.** Also, speak simply and clearly to make sure the driver has heard you correctly—few are native English speakers, so it never hurts to make sure you've been understood. When you leave the cab, remember to take your receipt. It includes the cab's medallion number, which can help you track the cabbie down in the event that you lose your possessions in the cab or if, after the fact, you want to report an unpleasant ride.

Taxis can be extremely difficult (if not impossible) to find in many parts of Brooklyn, Queens, the Bronx, and Staten Island, and you may have no choice but to call a car service. Locals and staff at restaurants and other public places can often recommend a reliable local company. Always determine the fee beforehand when using a car service sedan; a 10%–15% tip is customary above that.

Car-Service Companies **Carmel Car Service** ☎ *212/666-6666, 866/666-6666* 🌐 *www.carmelcarservice.com.* **Dial 7 Car Service** ☎ *212/777-7777* 🌐 *www.dial7.com.* **London Towncars** ✉ *Long Island City* ☎ *212/988-9700, 800/221-4009* 🌐 *www.londontowncars.com.*

TRAIN TRAVEL

⇨ *For information about traveling by subway within New York City, see Subway Travel.*

Metro-North Railroad trains take passengers from Grand Central Terminal to points north of New York City, both in New York State and Connecticut. Amtrak trains from across the United States arrive at Penn Station. For trains from New York City to Long Island and New Jersey, take the Long Island Railroad and New Jersey Transit, respectively; both operate from Penn Station. The PATH trains offer service to Newark, Jersey City, and Hoboken. All of these trains generally run on schedule, although occasional delays occur.

Information **Amtrak** ☎ *800/872-7245* 🌐 *www.amtrak.com.* **Long Island Rail Road** ☎ *511* 🌐 *www.mta.info/lirr.* **Metro-North Railroad** ☎ *212/532-4900, 511* 🌐 *www.mta.info/mnr.* **New Jersey Transit** ☎ *973/275-5555* 🌐 *www.njtransit.com.* **PATH** ☎ *800/234-7284* 🌐 *www.pathrail.com.*

Train Stations **Grand Central Terminal** ✉ *87 E. 42nd St., at Park Ave., Midtown East* ☎ *212/532-4900 Metro-North* 🌐 *www.grandcentralterminal.com.* **Penn Station** ✉ *W. 31st to W. 33rd Sts., between 7th and 8th Aves., Midtown West.*

ESSENTIALS

COMMUNICATIONS

INTERNET

You can check your email or surf the Internet at cafés, copy centers, libraries, many public parks, and most hotels. By far the best equipped and probably most convenient is Cyber Café in Times Square, which has dozens of computers plus scanners, color printers, and camera chip readers; it's open from 8 am to 11 pm on weekdays and 11 am to 11 pm on weekends. The organization NYCwireless keeps track of free Wi-Fi hot spots in the New York area, while the JiWire website and apps can help you find Wi-Fi hot spots in cafés, hotels, libraries, parks, and other locations throughout the city.

Contacts **JiWire** 🌐 *v4.jiwire.com/search-hotspot-locations.htm.* **NYCwireless** 🌐 *www.nycwireless.net.*

Internet Cafés **Cybercafe** ✉ *250 W. 49th St., between 8th Ave. and Broadway, Midtown West* ☎ *212/333–4109* 🌐 *www.cyber-cafe.com.*

Other Internet Locations **New York Public Library–Mid-Manhattan Library** ✉ *455 5th Ave., at E. 40th St., Midtown East* ☎ *212/340–0863* 🌐 *www.nypl.org.*

DISABILITIES AND ACCESSIBILITY

New York has come a long way in making life easier for people with disabilities. At most street corners, curb cuts allow wheelchairs to roll along unimpeded. Many restaurants, shops, and movie theaters with step-up entrances have wheelchair ramps. And though some New Yorkers may rush past those in need of assistance, you'll find plenty of people who are more than happy to help you get around.

NYC & Company's website (🌐 *nycgo.com*) has information on the accessibility of many landmarks and attractions, as well as a downloadable guide. Big Apple Greeter's Access Program offers tours of New York City tailored to visitors' personal preferences. If you need to rent a wheelchair or a scooter, while you are in New York, Scootaround will deliver to your hotel or another location, and reservations can be made up to a year in advance.

Local Resources **Big Apple Greeter** ☎ *212/669–8159* 🌐 *www.bigapplegreeter.org.* **NYC & Company** 🌐 *www.nycgo.com/accessibility.* **Scootaround** ☎ *888/441–7575* 🌐 *www.scootaround.com/rentals/n/newyork.*

LODGING

Despite the Americans with Disabilities Act, the definition of accessibility seems to differ from hotel to hotel. Some properties may be accessible by ADA standards for people with mobility problems but not for people with hearing or vision impairments, for example.

If you have mobility problems, ask for the lowest floor on which accessible services are offered. If you have a hearing impairment, check whether the hotel has devices to alert you visually to the ring of the telephone, a knock at the door, and a fire/emergency alarm. Some hotels provide these devices without charge. Discuss your needs with hotel personnel if this equipment isn't available, so that a staff member can personally alert you in the event of an emergency.

If you're bringing a guide dog, get authorization ahead of time and write down the name of the person with whom you spoke.

RESERVATIONS

When discussing accessibility with an operator or reservations agent, ask hard questions. Are there any stairs, inside *or* out? Are there grab bars next to the toilet *and* in the shower/tub? How wide is the doorway to the room? To the bathroom? For the most extensive facilities meeting the latest legal specifications, opt for newer accommodations. If you reserve through a toll-free number, consider also calling the hotel's local number to confirm the information from the central reservations office. Get confirmation in writing when you can.

SIGHTS AND ATTRACTIONS

Most public facilities in New York City, whether museums, parks, or theaters, are wheelchair-accessible. Some attractions have tours or programs for people with mobility, sight, or hearing impairments.

TRANSPORTATION

Although the city is working to retrofit stations to comply with the ADA, not all stations are accessible and they are unlikely to be in the near future. Accessible stations are clearly marked on subway and rail maps. Visitors in wheelchairs will have better success with public buses, all of which have wheelchair lifts and "kneelers" at the front to facilitate getting on and off. Bus drivers will provide assistance.

Reduced fares are available to disabled passengers; if you're paying with cash, you will need to present a Medicare card or Paratransit card. You may also apply for a Temporary Reduced Fare MetroCard in advance of your visit. Visitors to the city are also eligible for the same Access-a-Ride program benefits as New York City residents. Drivers with disabilities may use windshield cards from their own state or Canadian province to park in designated handicapped spaces.

The U.S. Department of Transportation Aviation Consumer Protection Division's online publication *New Horizons: Information for the Air Traveler with a Disability* offers advice for travelers with a disability, and outlines basic rights. Visit 🌐 *disability.gov* for general information.

Information and Complaints **MTA Reduced Fare MetroCard** ☎ *511* 🌐 *www.mta.info/accessibility/transit.htm.* **U.S. Department of Transportation Aviation Consumer Protection Division** 🌐 *airconsumer.dot.gov/publications/horizons.htm.*

GAY AND LESBIAN TRAVEL

Attitudes toward same-sex couples are very tolerant in Manhattan and many other parts of the city. Hell's Kitchen, Chelsea, and (to a lesser degree) Greenwich Village are the most prominently gay neighborhoods, but gay men and lesbians feel right at home almost everywhere. The world's oldest gay-pride parade takes place on 5th Avenue the last Sunday in June.

PUBLICATIONS

For listings of gay events and places, check out *Next,* which is online and also distributed on some streets and in many gay bars throughout Manhattan. The magazines *New York, Paper,* and *Time Out New York* have a gay-friendly take on what's happening in the city, as do most other local publications.

Local Information **Lesbian, Gay, Bisexual & Transgender Community Center** (*The Center*). ✉ *208 W. 13th St., between 7th and 8th Aves., Greenwich Village* ☎ *212/620–7310* 🌐 *www.gaycenter.org.*

Gay Publications ***Gay City News*** 🌐 *www.gaycitynews.com.* ***Next*** 🌐 *www.nextmagazine.com.*

KIDS IN NEW YORK

For listings of children's events, consult *New York* magazine and other local media. The Friday *New York Times* Arts section also includes children's activities. Other good sources on happenings for youngsters are the websites NYMetroParents and New York Family (and their respective magazines). If you have access to cable television, check the local all-news channel New York 1, where you'll find a spot aired several times daily that covers current and noteworthy children's events. *Fodor's Around New York City with Kids* (available in bookstores everywhere) can help you plan your days together.

LODGING

Before you consider using a cot or fold-out couch for your child, ask just how large your hotel room is—New York City rooms are usually small. Most hotels in New York allow children under a certain age to stay in their parents' room at no extra charge, but others charge for them as extra adults; be sure to find out the cutoff age for children's discounts.

PUBLIC TRANSPORTATION

Children shorter than 44 inches (about 1.1 meters) ride for free on MTA buses and subways. If you're pushing a stroller, don't struggle through a subway turnstile; ask the station agent to buzz you through the gate (the attendant will ask you to swipe your MetroCard through the turnstile nearest the gate). Keep a sharp eye on young ones while in the subway; at some stations there is a gap between the train doors and the platform.

MONEY

In New York, it's easy to get swept up in a debt-inducing cyclone of $60-per-person dinners, $100 theater tickets, $20 nightclub covers, and $300 hotel rooms. But one of the good things about the city is that you can spend in some areas and save in others. Within Manhattan, a cup of coffee can cost from 75¢ to $4, a pint of beer from $5 to $8, and a sandwich from $7 to $10. Generally, prices in the outer boroughs are lower than those in Manhattan.

The most generously bequeathed treasure of the city is the arts. The stated admission fee at the Metropolitan Museum of Art is a suggestion; you can donate a lesser amount and not be snubbed. Many other museums in town have special times during which admission is free. The Museum of Modern Art, for instance, is free on Friday from 4 to 8. In summer a handful of free music, theater, and dance performances, as well as films (usually screened outdoors), fill the calendar each day.

Prices throughout this guide are given for adults. Substantially reduced fees are typically available for children, students, and senior citizens.

CREDIT CARDS

The following abbreviations are used: AE, American Express; D, Discover; DC, Diners Club; MC, MasterCard; and V, Visa.

Record all your credit-card numbers—as well as the phone numbers to call if your cards are lost or stolen—in a safe place, so you're prepared should something go wrong. Both MasterCard and Visa have general numbers you can call if your card is lost, but you're better off calling the number of your issuing bank, since MasterCard and Visa usually just transfer you anyway. Your bank's number is usually printed on your card.

Reporting Lost Cards **American Express** ☎ *800/528–4800 in U.S.* 🌐 *www.americanexpress.com.* **Diners Club** ☎ *800/234–6377* 🌐 *www.dinersclub.com.* **Discover** ☎ *800/347–2683 in U.S.* 🌐 *www.discovercard.com.* **MasterCard** ☎ *800/627–8372* 🌐 *www.mastercard.com.* **Visa** ☎ *800/847–2911* 🌐 *www.visa.com.*

RESTROOMS

Seinfeld fans might recall George Costanza's claim that if you named any given coordinates in New York City, he could instantly name the closest and most worthy public restroom in the vicinity. Regrettably, unless you're traveling with your own George, public restrooms in New York are few and far between.

If you find yourself in need of a restroom, head for Midtown department stores, museums, or the lobbies of large hotels to find the cleanest bathrooms. Public atriums, such as those at the Citicorp Center and Trump Tower, also provide good public facilities, as do Bryant Park and the many Starbucks coffee shops in the city. If you're in the area, the Times Square Information Center, on Broadway between 46th and 47th streets, can be a godsend.

Restaurants usually allow only patrons to use their restrooms, but if you're dressed well and look as if you belong, you can often just sail right in. And if you're too self-conscious for this brand of nonchalance, just ask the host or hostess nicely. Be aware that cinemas, Broadway theaters, and concert halls have limited amenities, and there are often long lines before performances and during intermissions.

Find a Loo The Bathroom Diaries. This website is flush with unsanitized info on restrooms the world over—each one located, reviewed, and rated. *www.thebathroomdiaries.com.*

SAFETY

New York City is one of the safest large cities in the country. However, do not let yourself be lulled into a false sense of security. As in any large city, travelers in New York remain particularly easy marks for pickpockets and hustlers.

After the September 11, 2001, terrorist attacks security was heightened throughout the city. Never leave any bags unattended, and expect to have yourself and your possessions inspected thoroughly in such places as airports, sports stadiums, museums, city buildings, and sometimes even subway stations.

Ignore the panhandlers on the streets and subways, people who offer to hail you a cab (they often appear at Penn Station, the Port Authority, and Grand Central), and limousine and gypsy-cab drivers who (illegally) offer you a ride.

Keep jewelry out of sight on the street; better yet, leave valuables at home. Don't carry wallets, smartphones, or other gadgets in your back pockets, and make sure bags and purses stay closed.

Avoid deserted blocks in unfamiliar neighborhoods. A brisk, purposeful pace helps deter trouble wherever you go.

The subway runs around the clock and is generally well trafficked until midnight (and until at least 2 am on Friday and Saturday nights), and overall it is very safe. If you do take the subway late at night, ride in the center car, with the conductor. Watch out for unsavory characters lurking around the inside or outside of stations.

When waiting for a train, head to the center of the platform, and stand far away from its edge, especially when trains are entering or leaving the station. Once the train pulls into the station, avoid empty cars. While on the train, don't engage in verbal exchanges with aggressive riders. If a fellow passenger makes you nervous while on the train, trust your instincts and change cars. When disembarking, stick with the crowd until you reach the street.

Travelers Aid International helps crime victims, stranded travelers, and wayward children, and works closely with the police.

TIP→ Distribute your cash, credit cards, IDs, and other valuables between a deep front pocket, an inside jacket or vest pocket, and a hidden money pouch. Don't reach for the money pouch once you're in public.

Information Travelers Aid International *JFK International Airport, Terminal 4, Queens 718/656–4870 jfk.travelersaid.org* *Newark International Airport, Terminal B, Newark, New Jersey 973/623–5052 www.travelersaid.org.*

SENIOR-CITIZEN TRAVEL

The Metropolitan Transportation Authority (MTA) offers lower fares for passengers 65 and over.

To qualify for age-related discounts, mention your senior-citizen status up front when booking hotel reservations (not when checking out). Be sure to have identification on hand. When renting a car, ask about promotional car-rental discounts, which can be cheaper than senior-citizen rates.

Educational Programs Road Scholar *800/454–5768, 978/323–4141 international* *callers, 877/426–2167 TTY* 🌐 *www.roadscholar.org.*

Information **MTA Reduced Fare info** ☎ *511* 🌐 *www.mta.info/nyct/fare/rfindex.htm.*

SPORTS AND THE OUTDOORS

The City of New York's Parks & Recreation division lists all of the recreational facilities and activities available through New York's Parks Department. *The New York Times*'s sports section lists upcoming events, times, dates, and ticket information.

Contact Information **Department of Parks & Recreation** ☎ *311 in New York City, 212/639–9675* 🌐 *www.nycgovparks.org.*

BASEBALL

The subway will get you directly to the stadiums of both New York–area major-league teams: the New York Mets play at Citi Field, at the next-to-last stop on the 7 train in Queens, while the Yankees defend their turf at Yankee Stadium in the Bronx, accessible via the B, D, or 4 trains. Affiliated with the Mets since 2001, the minor-league Brooklyn Cyclones are named for Coney Island's famous wooden roller coaster. They play 38 home games at KeySpan Park, next to the boardwalk, with views of the Atlantic over the right-field wall and views of historic Astroland over the left-field wall. Most people make a day of it, with time at the beach and amusement rides before an evening game. Take the D, F, or Q subway to the end of the line, and walk one block to the right of the original Nathan's Famous hot dog stand.

For another fun, family-oriented experience, check out the Staten Island Yankees, one of New York's minor-league teams, which warms up many future New York Yankees players. The stadium, a five-minute walk from the Staten Island Ferry terminal, has magnificent panoramic views of Lower Manhattan and the Statue of Liberty.

Contact Information **Brooklyn Cyclones** ✉ *MCU Park, 1904 Surf Ave., at 19th St., Coney Island, Brooklyn* ☎ *718/449–8497* 🌐 *www.brooklyncyclones.com* Ⓜ *D, F, N, Q to Stillwell Ave..* **New York Mets** ✉ *Roosevelt Ave. off Grand Central Pkwy., Flushing, Queens* ☎ *718/507–8499* 🌐 *www.mets.com* Ⓜ *7 to Mets/Willets Pt..* **New York Yankees** ✉ *Yankee Stadium, 161st St. at River Ave., Bronx* ☎ *718/293–6000* 🌐 *www.yankees.com* Ⓜ *B, D, 4 to 161st St.–Yankee Stadium, or some Metro-North Hudson Line trains.* **Staten Island Yankees** ✉ *Richmond County Bank Ballpark, 75 Richmond Terr., St. George, Staten Island* ☎ *718/720–9265* 🌐 *www.siyanks.com.*

BASKETBALL

The New York Knicks arouse intense hometown passions, which means tickets for home games at Madison Square Garden are hard to come by. Try StubHub to score tickets. In late 2012, the New Jersey Nets were rechristened the Brooklyn Nets and moved to their new home at the swanky Barclays Center, in Prospect Heights, Brooklyn. The men's basketball season runs from late October through April. The New York Liberty, a member of the Women's NBA, had its first season in 1997; some of the team's players are already legendary. The season runs from mid-May through August, with home games played at Madison Square Garden.

If the professional games are sold out, try to attend a college game where New York stalwarts Fordham, Hofstra, and St. John's compete against national top 25 teams during invitational tournaments

Contact Information **Brooklyn Nets** ✉ *Barclays Center, 620 Atlantic Ave., at Flatbush Ave., Prospect Heights, Brooklyn* ☎ *201/935–3900 box office, 800/765–6387* 🌐 *www.nba.com/nets* Ⓜ *2, 3, 4, 5, B, D, N, Q, R to Atlantic Avenue–Barclays Center.* **Madison Square Garden** ✉ *4 Pennsylvania Plaza, near W. 32nd St. and 6th Ave.* ☎ *212/465–6741* 🌐 *www.msg.com* Ⓜ *1, 2, 3 to 34th St.–Penn Station.* **New York Knicks** ☎ *212/465–5867* 🌐 *www.nba.com/knicks.* **New York Liberty** ☎ *212/465–*

6766 tickets, 212/564-9622 fan hotline 🌐 *www.wnba.com/liberty.*

BICYCLING

Although bicycling around Manhattan and elsewhere in New York is probably still not for casual cyclists, in recent years city government and biking organizations have made it safer than it had been for decades. Check the Department of Transportation's website for a cycling map that maps the best routes, including roads with designated bike lanes.

For biking under more controlled conditions, head to New York's major parks. Central Park has a 6-mile circular drive with a couple of decent climbs. It's closed to car traffic from 10 am to 3 pm (except the southeast portion between 6th Avenue and East 72nd Street) and 7 pm to 7 am on weekdays, and from 7 pm Friday to 7 am Monday. On holidays it's closed to car traffic from 7 pm the night before until 7 am the day after.

The bike lane along the Hudson River Park's esplanade parallels the waterfront from West 59th Street south to the esplanade of Battery Park City. The lane also heads north, connecting with the bike path in Riverside Park and the promenade between West 72nd and West 110th streets, and continuing all the way to the George Washington Bridge. A two-way bike lane runs along the park's Terrace Drive, a popular route across the park at 72nd Street. From Battery Park it's a quick ride to the Wall Street area, which is deserted on weekends, and over to South Street and a bike lane along the East River.

The 3.3-mile circular drive in Brooklyn's Prospect Park is closed to cars year-round except from 7 am to 9 am and 5 pm to 7 pm on weekdays. It has a long, gradual hill that tops off near the Grand Army Plaza entrance.

Bike Rentals Bicycle Rentals at Loeb Boathouse ✉ *Midpark near E. 74th St., East 72nd St. & Park Dr. North, Central Park* ☎ *212/517-2233* 🌐 *www.centralparknyc.org* ⏲ *Apr.–Nov., weekdays 10–6, weekends 9–6* Ⓜ *6 to 68th St./Hunter College.* **Bicycles NYC** ✉ *1400 3rd Ave., between E. 79th and E. 80th Sts., Upper East Side* ☎ *212/794-2929* 🌐 *www.bicyclesnyc.com* Ⓜ *4, 5, 6 to 86th St.* **Pedal Pusher Bike Shop** ✉ *1306 2nd Ave., at E. 69th St., Upper East Side* ☎ *212/288-5592* 🌐 *www.pedalpusherbikeshop.com* Ⓜ *6 to 68th St./Hunter College.* **Toga Bike Shop** ✉ *110 West End Ave., at W. 64th St., Upper West Side* ☎ *212/799-9625* 🌐 *togabikes.wix.com/toga* Ⓜ *1 to 66th St.*

CITI BIKE BICYCLING SHARE

New York's bike sharing program, similar to the ones in Paris and other major cities, is set to be up and running in the spring of 2014. There will hundreds of stations around Manhattan and the boroughs, with bikes for short-term rental. You can unlock a bike at one station and then lock it back up at another station. Passes will be available in 24-hour ($9.95) and 7-day ($25) increments; annual membership is $95. Check the 🌐 *www.citibikenyc.com* for more information.

GROUP BIKE RIDES

For organized rides with other cyclists, call or email before you come to New York. Bike New York runs a 40-mile, five-borough bike ride the first Sunday in May. The Five Borough Bicycle Club organizes day and weekend rides. The New York Cycle Club sponsors weekend rides for every level of ability. Time's Up!, a nonprofit advocacy group, leads free recreational rides at least twice a month for cyclists as well as skaters; the Central Park Moonlight Ride, departing from Columbus Circle at 10 pm the first Friday of every month, is a favorite.

Contact Information Bike New York ☎ *212/870-2080* 🌐 *www.bikenewyork.org.* **Five Borough Bike Club** ☎ *347/688-2925* 🌐 *www.5bbc.org.* **New York Cycle Club** 🌐 *www.nycc.org.* **Time's Up!** ☎ *212/802-8222* 🌐 *times-up.org.*

BOATING AND KAYAKING

Central Park has rowboats (plus one Venetian gondola for glides in the moonlight) on the 22-acre Central Park Lake.

Rent your rowboat at Loeb Boathouse, near East 74th Street, from April through November ($12 an hour); gondola rides are available only in summer and can be reserved ($30 per half hour). In summer at the Pier 96 Boathouse in Midtown West, you can take a sturdy kayak out for a paddle for free on weekends and weekday evenings from mid-May through mid-October. Pier 40, in the West Village, and the pier at West 72nd Street have similar schedules. Beginners learn to paddle in the calmer embayment area closest to shore until they feel ready to venture farther out into open water. More experienced kayakers can partake in the three-hour trips conducted every weekend and on holiday mornings. Because of high demand, there is a lottery to determine who gets to go out each morning; to be entered, you must be at the pier to sign up before 8 am. No reservations are taken in advance. Manhattan Kayak Company gives lessons for all levels and runs trips on the Hudson River between May and late September, including a fun New York After Dark tour for $80.

Contact Information Loeb Boathouse ✉ *Midpark near E. 74th St., Central Park* ☎ *212/517–2233* 🌐 *www.thecentralparkboathouse.com/boats.php* Ⓜ *6 to 68th St./Hunter College.* **Manhattan Kayak Company** ✉ *The Boathouse, Pier 66, W. 26th St. at 12th Ave., Chelsea* ☎ *212/924–1788* 🌐 *www.manhattankayak.com* Ⓜ *C, E to 23rd St.* **Pier 96 Boathouse** ✉ *56th St. at the Hudson River, Midtown West* 🌐 *www.downtownboathouse.org* Ⓜ *1, A, C, E to 59th St.*

FOOTBALL

The football season runs from September through December. The enormously popular New York Giants play at MetLife Stadium in East Rutherford, New Jersey. Most seats for Giants games are sold on a season-ticket basis—and there's a long waiting list for those. However, single tickets are occasionally available at the stadium box office or on ticket resale sites like StubHub. The New York Jets also play at MetLife Stadium. Although Jets tickets are not as scarce as those for the Giants, most are snapped up by fans before the season opener.

Contact Information New York Giants ☎ *201/935–8222 for tickets* 🌐 *www.giants.com.* **New York Jets** ☎ *800/469–5387 for tickets* 🌐 *www.newyorkjets.com.*

ICE-SKATING

The outdoor rink in Rockefeller Center, open from October through early April, is much smaller in real life than it appears on TV and in movies—though it *is* as beautiful, especially when Rock Center's enormous Christmas tree towers above it. Tickets are first come, first served, so be prepared to wait—especially around the holidays. And be prepared to pay, too: skating rates are $20 for adults, which doesn't include skate rental ($10). The city's outdoor rinks, open from roughly November through March, all have their own character. Central Park's beautifully situated Wollman Rink offers skating until long after dark beneath the lights of the city. Be prepared for daytime crowds on weekends. The Lasker Rink, at the north end of Central Park, is smaller and usually less crowded than Wollman. Chelsea Piers' Sky Rink has two year-round indoor rinks overlooking the Hudson. Skate rentals are available at all rinks. Citi Pond at Bryant Park offers "free" skating, although this doesn't include skate rental ($14) or the likely fee you'll pay to either buy a lock for a locker or have bags checked ($7–$10). Citi Pond is open from late October through early March, from 8 am to 10 pm Sunday through Thursday and from 8 am to midnight Friday and Saturday. A $20 Citi Pond FastPass (available online, includes skate rental and bag check) allows you to skip the line.

TIP→ Head to the Standard Hotel's teeny ice rink in the Meatpacking District in winter. The scene is cool and the cocktails are hot! Skate tickets are $12 and skate rental is $3; the rink, at 848 Washington Street at West 13th Street, is open from noon to midnight on weekdays and 9 am to 1 am on weekends.

Contact Information **Bryant Park** ✉ *1065 6th Ave., between 40th and 42nd Sts., Midtown West* ☎ *212/661–6640* 🌐 *www.citipondatbryantpark.com* Ⓜ *B, D, F to 42nd St.* **Lasker Rink** ✉ *Midpark near E. 106th St., 2 Lenox Ave., Central Park* ☎ *917/492–3856* 🌐 *www.laskerrink.com* Ⓜ *B, C to Cathedral Parkway (110th St.)–Central Park West; 2, 3 to Central Park North (110th St.).* **Rockefeller Center** ✉ *50th St. at 5th Ave., lower plaza, Midtown West* ☎ *212/332–7654* 🌐 *www.therinkatrockcenter.com* Ⓜ *B, D, F to 47th–50th Sts./Rockefeller Center; E, M to 5th Ave.–53rd St.* **Sky Rink** ✉ *Pier 61, W. 23rd St. & the Hudson River, Chelsea* ☎ *212/336–6100* 🌐 *www.chelseapiers.com/sr* Ⓜ *C, E to 23rd St.* **Trump Wollman Skating Rink** ✉ *North of 6th Ave. and Central Park South entrance, between 62nd and 63rd Sts.* ☎ *212/439–6900* 🌐 *www.wollmanskatingrink.com* Ⓜ *A, B, C, D, 1 to 59th St./Columbus Circle.*

JOGGING

All kinds of New Yorkers jog, some with dogs or babies in tow, so you'll always have company on the regular jogging routes. What's not recommended is setting out on a lonely park path at dusk. Go running when and where everybody else does. On Manhattan streets, roughly 20 north–south blocks make a mile.

In Manhattan, Central Park is the busiest spot, specifically along the 1.6-mile path circling the Jacqueline Kennedy Onassis Reservoir, where you jog in a counterclockwise direction. A runners' lane has been designated along the park roads; the entire loop road is a hilly 6 miles. A good 1.75-mile route starts at the Tavern on the Green along the West Drive, heads south around the bottom of the park to the East Drive, and circles back west on the 72nd Street park road to your starting point. Riverside Park, along the Hudson River bank in Manhattan, is glorious at sunset. You can cover 4.5 miles by running from West 72nd to 116th Street and back, and the Greenbelt trail extends 4 more miles north to the George Washington Bridge at 181st Street. Other favorite Manhattan circuits are the Battery Park City esplanade (about 2 miles), which connects to the Hudson River Park (about 1.5 miles), and the East River Esplanade (just over 3 miles from East 63rd to East 125th streets).

STUDENTS IN NEW YORK

New York is home to such major schools as Columbia University, New York University, Fordham University, and the City College of New York. With other colleges scattered throughout the five boroughs, as well as a huge population of public and private high-schoolers, it's no wonder the city is rife with student discounts. Wherever you go, especially museums, sightseeing attractions, and performances, identify yourself as a student up front and ask if a discount is available. However, be prepared to show your ID as proof of enrollment and/or age.

A great program made available to children between the ages of 13 and 18 (or anyone in middle or high school) is High 5 for the Arts. Tickets to a wide variety of performances (though only rarely Broadway shows) are sold for $5 online or by phone. Check the website to find out about upcoming events.

IDs and Services **High 5 for the Arts** ✉ *520 8th Ave., at 36th St., Midtown* ☎ *212/750–0555* 🌐 *www.highfivetix.org.* **STA Travel** ✉ *722 Broadway, between Washington Pl. and Waverly Pl.* ☎ *212/627–3111, 800/781–4040 24-hr service center* 🌐 *www.sta.com.*

TAXES

A sales tax of 8.875% applies to almost everything you can buy retail, including restaurant meals. However, prescription drugs and non-prepared food bought in grocery stores are exempt. Clothing and footwear costing less than $110 are also exempt.

TIPPING

The customary tipping rate for taxi drivers is 15%–20%, with a minimum of $2; bellhops are usually given $2 per bag in luxury hotels, $1 per bag elsewhere. Hotel maids should be tipped $2 per day of your stay. A doorman who hails or helps you into a cab can be tipped $1–$2. You should also tip your hotel concierge for services rendered; the size of the tip depends on the difficulty of your request, as well as the quality of the concierge's work. Waiters should be tipped 15%–20%, though at higher-end restaurants, a solid 20% is more the norm. Tip $1 or $2 per drink you order at the bar.

VISITOR INFORMATION

The Grand Central Partnership (a business-improvement district) has installed a number of information booths in and around Grand Central Terminal (there's one near Vanderbilt Avenue and East 43rd Street). They're loaded with maps and helpful brochures on attractions throughout the city and staffed by friendly, knowledgeable, multilingual New Yorkers.

NYC & Company's Times Square Visitors Center (at 7th Avenue and West 46th Street) is decked out with lots of fun and helpful tools like multilingual kiosks. The bureau also has a Midtown visitor center on 7th Avenue (near West 52nd Street) and runs kiosks in Lower Manhattan at City Hall Park; in Chinatown at the triangle where Canal, Walker, and Baxter Streets meet; and in Harlem at the Apollo Theater at 253 West 125th Street.

The Downtown Alliance has information on the area encompassing City Hall south to Battery Park, and from the East River to West Street. For a free booklet listing New York City attractions and tour packages, contact the New York State Division of Tourism.

THE FODORS.COM CONNECTION

Before your trip, be sure to check out what fellow travelers are saying in Talk on www.fodors.com.

CONTACTS

City Information Downtown Alliance ☎ *212/566–6700* 🌐 *www.downtownny.com.* **Grand Central Partnership** ☎ *212/883–2420* 🌐 *www.grandcentralpartnership.org.* **NYC & Company Convention & Visitors Bureau** ✉ *Midtown Information Center, 810 7th Ave., between W. 52nd and W. 53rd Sts., Midtown West* ☎ *212/484–1222* 🌐 *www.nycgo.com.* **Times Square Information Center** ✉ *1560 Broadway, between 46th and 47th Sts., Midtown West* ☎ *212/730–7555* 🌐 *www.timessquarenyc.org* Ⓜ *N, Q, R, S, 1, 2, 3, 7 to 42nd St./Times Square.*

Statewide Information New York State Division of Tourism ☎ *800/225–5697* 🌐 *www.iloveny.com.*

INDEX

D

E

F

Q

R

PHOTO CREDITS

Cover: Cameron Davidson/Corbis. 1, Songquan Deng/Shutterstock. 2, Kord.com/age fotostock. 5, Liberty Helicopters, Inc. Chapter 1: Experience New York City: 8-9, Rudy Sulgan/age fotostock. 10, Luc Novovitch/age Fotostock. 11 (left), LHB Photo/Alamy. 11(right), Oote Boe Photography/Alamy. 14, Ace Stock Limited/Alamy. 16, Alija/iStockphoto. 18, (left), Rome and Greece gallery by Xuan Che http://www.flickr.com/photos/rosemania/2157661526/Attribution License. 18 (top center), Kord.com/age fotostock. 18 (top right), New York. MoMA by Tomas Fano http://www.flickr.com/photos/tomasfano/2713778452/Attribution-ShareAlike License. 18 (bottom), Doug Scott/age fotostock.19 (top left), SuperStock/age fotostock. 19 (bottom left), Craig Chesek/AMNH. 19 (right), Picture-Quest. 20, Black Star/Alamy. 21 (left), David H. Wells/age fotostock. 21 (right), Richard Levine/Alamy. 23, 110613-N-TT977-235 by http://www.flickr.com/photos/thejointstaff/ 5830275495/Attribution License. 24, Brooklyn Bridge Park Etienne Frossard/www.brooklynbridgeparknyc.org. 25 (left), Frances M. Roberts/Alamy. 25 (right), Union Square by adactio http://www.flickr.com/photos/adactio/3817931108/Attribution-License. 29 (left), David Berkowitz/Flickr. 29 (right), emilydickinsonridesabmx/Flickr. 31, Jeff Greenberg/Alamy. 32, Corbis. 33, Photodisc. 35 (top), Liberty Helicopters, Inc. 35 (bottom), Joshua Haviv/shutterstock. 37 (top), Library of Congress Prints and Photographs Division. 37 (bottom), Library of Congress Prints and Photographs Division. Chapter 2: Lower Manhattan: 39, Bill Grove/iStockphoto. 41, Heeb Christian. 42, Chuck Pefley/Alamy. 46, Silverstein Properties. 47 (top), White House Photo/Alamy. 47 (bottom), Sondra Paulson/iStockphoto. 48 (top left), Fireball erupting in the South Tower by Robert http://www.flickr.com/photos/themachinestops/88181088/Attribution-ShareAlike License. 48 (top right), Jim Watson/CHINFO, Navy Visual News Service (Public Domain), via Wikimedia Commons. 48 (bottom), RodneyRamsey/Flickr. 49 (left), Jim Watson/CHINFO, Navy Visual News Service (Public Domain), via Wikimedia Commons. 49 (center), Peter Comitini/Flickr. 49 (right), Denise Gould (Public Domain), via Wikimedia Commons. 50-51 (top), Silverstein Properties. 50 (bottom), Silverstein Properties. 51 (bottom left and bottom right), Joe Woolhead/Silverstein Properties. 52 (top left), Luca Cepparo/iStockphoto. 52 (top right), FaceMePLS/Flickr. 52 (bottom left), p_c_w/Flickr. 52 (bottom right), cytech/Flickr. 56-57, kropic1/Shutterstock. 59, Estormiz/Wikimedia Commons. Chapter 3: SoHo, NoLIta, Little Italy, and Chinatown: 61, Art Kowalsky/Alamy. 63, Ambient Images Inc./Alamy. 64, Yadid Levy/Alamy. 66-67, Renault Philippe/age fotostock. 69, OK Harris Works of Art. 71, Philip Lange/Shutterstock.Chapter 4: The East Village and the Lower East Side: 73, Jeff Greenberg/Alamy. 75, peyri/Flickr. 76, New York. East Village. Stop the Violence. E 12TH St by http://www.flickr.com/photos/tomasfano/2710315445/Attribution-ShareAlike License. Chapter 5: Greenwich Village and the West Village: 83, wdstock/iStockphoto.85, Tenement Houses Overlooking Washington Square Park, New York City by http://www.flickr. com/photos/43533334@N07/5139725894/Attribution License. 86, wdstock/iStockphoto. 87, Ambient Images Inc./Alamy. 90, PCL/Alamy. Chapter 6: Chelsea and the Meatpacking District: 93, David Berkowitz/Flickr. 95, Black Star/Alamy. 96, By Gryffindor [CC-BY-SA-3.0 (www.creativecommons.org/licenses/by-sa/3.0)], via Wikimedia Commons. 98-99, Kord.com/age fotostock. 103, Kokyat Choong/Alamy. Chapter 7: Union Square, the Flatiron District, and Gramercy Park: 105, David Shankbone/Wikipedia.org. 107, Kord.com/age fotostock. 108, Yadid Levy/Alamy. 109, Russell Kord/Alamy. 111, naphtalina/iStockphoto.112, IMG_0776 by Jan-Erik Finnberg http://www.flickr.com/photos/wheany/2233336954/Attribution-NonCommercial License. Chapter 8: Midtown East: 115, Kord.com. 117, Jaap Hart/iStockphoto. 118, svlumagraphica/iStockphoto. 120, Rudy Sulgan/age fotostock. 123, Stuart Monk/iStockphoto/Thinkstock.124, Sylvain Grandadam/age fotostock. 127, Empire State Sunset by Eric E Yang http://www.flickr.com/photos/midweekpost/142493669/Attribution License. Chapter 9: Midtown West: 129, Times Square - New York by C.line http://www.flickr.com/photos/pepsiline/4247882387/Attribution-ShareAlike License. 131, Bruno Perousse/age fotostock. 132, (c) Mirceani | Dreamstime.com. 135, New York. Radio City Music Hall by Tomas Fano http://www.flickr.com/photos/tomasfano/2738549430/Attribution-ShareAlike License. 136, oversnap/iStockphoto. 141, New York. MoMA by Tomas Fano http://www. flickr.com/photos/tomasfano/2713778452/Attribution-ShareAlike License. Chapter 10: The Upper East Side: 143, Nicholas Pitt/Alamy. 145, JayLazarin/iStockphoto. 146, Janine Wiedel Photolibrary/Alamy. 149, Doug Scott/age fotostock. 150, Geoffrey Clements. 152, Brooks Walker. 153, Renaud Visage/age fotostock. 154 (top), Renaud Visage/age fotostock. 154 (center), Metropolitan Museum of Art. 154 (bottom), An East Greek Late Archaic Alabastron in the Form of a Kore by http://www.flickr.com/photos/antiquitiesproject/5515795335/Attribution License. 156 (top), the new American wing by Kristen Bonardi Rapp http://www.flickr.com/photos/gezellig girl/3835837758/Attribution-ShareAlike License. 156 (bottom), Metropolitan Museum of Art. 157, Wild Bill Studio/Metropolitan Museum of Art. 158 (top and bottom), Metropolitan Museum of Art. Chapter 11: Central Park: 161 and 162 (top), Piero Ribelli. 162 (center), Rudy Sulgan/age fotostock. 162 (bottom), Library of Congress Prints & Photographs Division.163 (left), Chase Guttman. 163 (right), Sandra Baker/Alamy. 164, Worldscapes/age fotostock. 165 (left), Chris Lee. 165 (right), Michal Daniel. 166, Peter Arnold, Inc./Alamy. 167 (left), Craig Hale/iStockphoto.167 (right), Agency Jon Arnold Images/age fotostock. 168 (top left), Walter Bibikow/age fotostock. 168 (top right), Terraxplorer/iStockphoto. 168 (bottom), Sandra Baker/Alamy. 169 (top left), Darren Green Photography/Alamy. 169 (top right), Chuck Pefley/Alamy. 169 (bottom), Chase Guttman. 170, Piero Ribelli. 171 (left), Sandra Baker/Alamy. 171 (right), Piero Ribelli. 172-173 (bottom), gary718/Shutterstock. 172 (top left), Peter Arnold, Inc./Alamy. 172 (top right), TNT Magazine/Alamy. 173 (top left), Chuck Pefley/Alamy. 173 (top right), LMR Group/Alamy. 174 (left), Piero Ribelli. 174 (right), Jon Arnold/Agency Jon Arnold Images. 175, by Christian http://www.flickr.com/photos/ottosv/3757952801/Attribution-ShareAlike License. 176, Mario Savoia/iStockphoto. Chapter 12: The Upper West Side: 177, Kord.com/age fotostock. 179, Momos/Wikimedia Commons. 180, Kord.com/age fotostock. 182, Ken Ross/viestiphoto. 183, Ken Ross/viestiphoto. 184 (top left), (c) Sepavo | Dreamstime.com. 184 (top right), Craig Chesek/AMNH. 184 (bottom), Dennis Finnin/AMNH. 186, American Museum of Natural History. 187 and 188, Denis Finnin/AMNH. 189 (top), C. Chesek/AMNH. 189 (bottom), D. Finnin/C. Chesek/AMNH. Chapter 13: Harlem: 193, Cristian Baitg/iStockphoto. 195, Joe Malone/Agency Jon Arnold Images/age fotostock. 196, SuperStock/age fotostock. 199, Rieger /age footstock. Chapter 14: Brooklyn: 203, Jeff Greenberg/age fotostock. 205, SuperStock/age fotostock. 206, Ace Stock Limited/Alamy. 207, Brooklyn Bridge Park Julienne Schaer/www.brooklynbridgeparknyc.org. 210-211, Lucas Vallecillos / age fotostock. 221, Colin D. Young/Shutterstock. 224, michele lugaresi/iStockphoto. Chapter 15: Queens, the Bronx, and Staten Island: 227, Sylvain Grandadam. 229, Michel Friang/Alamy. 230, Siobhan O'Hare. 237, Doug Milner. 241, Johnny Stockshooter. Chapter 16: Where to Eat: 243, Mimi Giboin. 244, Ace Stock Limited/Alamy. 248, The Spotted Pig. 249 (top), stocksolutions/Shutterstock. 249 (bottom), rakratchada/Shutterstock. 256, Dina Litovsky/Stregoica Photography. 260, Dina Litovsky/Stregoica Photography. 275, Dina Litovsky/Stregoica Photography. 290, Dina Litovsky/Stregoica Photography. 298, Frances M. Roberts/Alamy. 300, The Modern. 320, Per Se. Chapter 17: Where to Stay: 351, Arcaid/Alamy. 352, On The Ave Hotel. 360 (top), Simon Brown/Firmdale Hotels. 360 (bottom left), Courtesy of The Chatwal / Photographer Phillip Ennis. 360 (bottom right), Courtesy of The Standard. 368 (top), Courtesy Of Mandarin Oriental. 368 (bottom left), Photographed by Todd Eberle Courtesy of The Mark Hotel. 368 (bottom right), Courtesy of The Ritz-Carlton New York, Central Park. 373, (all) Roy Wright. 380 (top), Courtesy of Ace Hotel/Eric Laignel. 380 (bottom left), Courtesy Of Library Hotel. 380 (bottom right), Claudia Hehr Photography. Chapter 18: Shopping: 389, Bruno Perousse/age fotostock. 390, Richard Levine/Alamy. 399, Piero Ribelli. 414 (top), Las Venus. 417, Frances Roberts/Alamy. 422, Piero Ribelli. 433, Piero Ribelli. 438, Piero Ribelli. Chapter 19: Nightlife: 447, Michael Belardo/Alamy. 448, Louis Armstrong Centennial Band At Birdland, New York City By Jazz Guy Http://Www.Flickr.Com/Photos/Flickr4jazz/3668870123/Attribution-Noncommercial License. 455, Francisco Rosario. 460, Beirut @ Bowery Ballroom by Tammy Lohttp://www.flickr.com/photos/tammylo/489390788/Attribution-License. Chapter 20: The Performing Arts: 473, Jazz at Lincoln Center. 474, JPEG Manhattan, New York City by Jazz Guy http://www.flickr.com/photos/flickr4jazz/4027850338/Attribution License. 479, Brian Palmer. 486, Ted Pink / Alamy. 491, Brian Stanton.

NOTES

NOTES

NOTES

NOTES

NOTES

NOTES

NOTES

ABOUT OUR WRITERS

Sarah Amandolare is a freelance journalist who has lived in Brooklyn for the past five years. Previously, she worked on *Fodor's Prague* guidebook. Her travel writing has also appeared in *The New York Times* "Globespotters" blog, *New York* magazine, and *Budget Travel*. She updated our Brooklyn chapter.

Jessica Colley is a travel and food writer working from the desk (and sometimes fire escape) of her apartment in TriBeCa. She adores New York for its bubbling pizza pies, storied cobbled streets, and picnics on the bank of the Hudson River. Jessica blogs regularly for Fodor's and shares her travels and New York tips on Twitter @jessicacolley.

David Farley is the author of the award-winning travel memoir *An Irreverent Curiousity* and writes about food and travel for *AFAR* magazine, *The New York Times*, and *National Geographic Traveler*. He teaches writing at New York University. He updated the Where to Eat chapter of this edition of *Fodor's New York*.

From sailing the Nile in a *felucca* to dancing on rooftops in Essaouira, **Anuja Madar's** best memories are from her travels. She's been a travel writer and editor for more than six years, and has spent nearly nine years calling NYC home. She updated the Harlem section of this edition of *Fodor's New York*.

Megan Eileen McDonough is a New York City–based travel writer and Founder of *Bohemian Trails*, an online magazine covering global art, culture, and off-the-beaten path destinations. She moved to New York in 2009 and has since written for *USA Today* and *The Huffington Post*, among other publications. She updated the Queens, Bronx, and Staten Island chapter of this edition of *Fodor's New York*.

Jess Moss, a former Fodor's editor, has lived in New York City for six years and wonders at what point she should start calling herself a "New Yorker." For this edition she dove into the city's arts and culture scene to update the Performing Arts chapter.

Irish-born writer **Jacinta O'Halloran**, a former in-house editor at Fodor's, has been calling New York City home for more than 15 years. She can walk the part (i.e., fast) and talk the part (i.e., when she's mad at cabdrivers, ordering bagels, or giving directions) of a local, but she still sees and feels the city like a visitor (i.e., she still looks up!).

John Rambow, a former in-house editor at Fodor's, has written for *Travel + Leisure*, *Fast Company*, *Budget Travel*, and *New York* magazines, as well as several blogs and guidebooks. From a base in Queens, he aims to stay on top of all the amazing things happening throughout the whole city. His website is *www.johnrambow.com*.

Christina Valhouli edits the award-winning website *iTraveliShop.com*, which covers luxury travel and shopping around the world. She is the former staff travel writer at *Forbes.com* and has contributed to several Fodor's guidebooks, including *Fodor's London* and *Fodor's New England*. Her travels have taken her to more than 30 countries, but she now calls the New York City area home.

Manhattan Subway Lines
Central Park
Hudson River
East River
NEW JERSEY
ROOSEVELT ISLAND
86 ST
79 ST
72 ST
66 ST/ LINCOLN CENTER
59 ST/ COLUMBUS CIRCLE
7 AVE
50 ST
49 ST
42 ST/ 8 AVE
TIMES SQ
34 ST/ PENN STN
28 ST
23 ST
18 ST
14 ST/8 AVE
14 ST
CHRISTOPHER ST/ SHERIDAN SQ
W 4 ST/ WASHINGTON SQ
HOUSTON ST
CANAL ST
FRANKLIN ST
CHAMBERS ST
PARK PLACE
WORLD TRADE CENTER
(Temporarily Closed)
CORTLANDT ST
WALL ST
RECTOR ST
BROAD ST
BOWLING GREEN
WHITEHALL/SOUTH FERRY
SOUTH FERRY
81 ST
72 ST
57 ST
5 AVE
47-50 ST/ ROCKEFELLER CENTER
42 ST/ 6th AVE
34 ST/ HERALD SQ
23 ST
14 ST/ 6 AVE
8 ST
PRINCE ST
SPRING ST
CANAL ST
77 ST
68 ST
63 ST
59 ST
LEXINGTON AVE
51 ST
42 ST/ GRAND CENTRAL
33 ST
28 ST
23 ST
14 ST/UNION SQ
1 AVE
3 AVE
ASTOR PL
BLEECKER ST
BROADWAY/LAFAYETTE
2 AVE
SPRING ST
DELANCEY ST
ESSEX ST
GRAND ST
BOWERY
E BROADWAY
CANAL ST
BROOKLYN BR/ CITY HALL
CHAMBERS ST
CITY HALL
BROADWAY/ NASSAU
FULTON ST
WALL ST
0 1500 feet
0 500 meters
KEY
Subway line
Terminal
Express stop
Local stop
Express and local stop
Free transfer (express & local)
Free transfer (local)